CHOSNEK

NETWORK ARCHITECTURE AND
DEVELOPMENT SERIES

Switched, Fast, and

Gigabit Ethernet,

Third Edition

Robert Breyer
Sean Riley

Trademark Acknowledgments

Warning and Disclaimer

Feedback Information

At New Riders Publishing, our goal is to create in-depth technical books of the highest quality and value. Each book is crafted with care and precision, undergoing rigorous development that involves the unique expertise of members from the professional technical community.

Readers' feedback is a natural continuation of this process. If you have any comments regarding how we could improve the quality of this book, or otherwise alter it to better suit your needs, you can contact us at nrfeedback@newriders.com. Please make sure to include the book title and ISBN in your message.

We greatly appreciate your assistance.

Publisher
David Dwyer

Executive Editor
Al Valvano

Marketing Manager
Stephanie Layton

Publicity Manager
Susan Nixon

Managing Editor
Caroline Roop

Acquisitions Editor
Brett Bartow

Development Editor
Kitty Wilson Jarrett

Project Editor
Theresa Mathias

Copy Editors
Hugh Vandivier
Keith Cline

Indexer
Tina Trettin

Acquisitions Coordinator
Amy Lewis

Manufacturing Coordinator
Jim Conway

Book Designer
Anne Jones

Cover Designer
Karen Ruggles

Proofreader
Megan Wade

Production
Steve Balle-Gifford
Darin L. Crone

About the Authors

Robert Breyer joined the networking industry in 1990, when he joined Intel in Folsom, California, as a product marketing engineer. His work there involved the sales and marketing of Ethernet 10BASE-T transceiver and controller chips. One of Robert's projects was the LAN on Motherboard program, which integrated Ethernet directly into PCs.

In 1993, Robert moved to Intel's network adapter group in Portland, Oregon, to develop the concept of value-added software for Intel's new line of network adapters. Subsequently, Robert was part of the team that launched the first 10/100 PCI adapter, as well as the first 10/100 intelligent server adapter.

Robert moved back to Johannesburg, South Africa, in 1995, where he became Intel's South African representative. During this time, Robert received the Intel Achievement Award, Intel's highest award. Robert was part of a team that set up an International Telecommunications Union (ITU) video-conferencing telemedicine demonstration featuring Dr. Andrew Grove, president and CEO of Intel, and Nelson Mandela, president of South Africa. From 1996 to 1998, Robert established and subsequently managed the official Intel sales subsidiary in South Africa.

Robert is currently a director of dot-com investments, a South African Internet venture capital firm. He also serves on the board of cybercellar, an online wine merchant, as well as AXiZ, a computer components distributor.

Robert has a bachelor's degree in electrical engineering from the University of the Witwatersrand in Johannesburg, South Africa. In addition, Robert holds a master's of science in electrical engineering and a master's of business administration from the University of California at Davis. He has written a number of white papers and application notes on local area networking technologies.

Sean Riley, began work in the networking industry in 1992. Beginning in Intel's Folsom, California, factory as a technical marketing engineer, Sean worked on several early versions of Ethernet silicon products. In 1993, Sean moved to Portland, Oregon, to develop and champion a new technology called Fast Ethernet.

During the next four years, Sean was involved early on in the High-Speed Working Group of the Institute of Electrical and Electronic Engineers (IEEE). This resulted in Sean becoming a founding member of the Fast Ethernet Alliance and a signing member of the IEEE 802.3u subcommittee, which standardized 100BASE-T Fast Ethernet.

Concurrently, Sean was a key member of Intel's Fast Ethernet product development team. For work in developing early Fast Ethernet products and technology, Sean won the Intel Achievement Award in 1995. In 1996, Sean led Intel into the Fast Ethernet hub and switch business.

From 1997 to 1998, Sean was director of marketing for Intel's networking products in Europe, the Middle East, and Africa.

Sean is currently the business unit manager of Intel's network systems division in Portland, Oregon.

Sean Riley has a bachelor's and master's of science in electrical engineering from Arizona State University. He has written a multitude of white papers and application notes on various networking technologies, including a chapter in the *Gigabit Ethernet Handbook*.

About the Technical Reviewer

This book's technical reviewer, Matt Birkner, contributed his considerable practical, hands-on expertise to the development process for *Switched, Fast, and Gigabit Ethernet*. As the book was being written, he reviewed all the material for technical content, organization, and flow. His feedback was critical to ensuring that *Switched, Fast, and Gigabit Ethernet* fits our readers' need for the highest quality technical information.

Matthew H. Birkner has been working in the networking industry for seven years. He has been a network design engineer, network operations center engineer, and technical support engineer. Formerly senior networking engineer in MCI's outsourcing unit, he was responsible for the resolution of complex customer networking issues. He is currently employed as a network consulting engineer at Cisco Systems, where he works on enterprise network designs and performance/analysis. Matt holds a bachelor's of science from Tufts University, where he majored in electrical engineering, and he is a Cisco Certified Internetwork Expert (CCIE).

Acknowledgments

When we got together to co-author the first edition of this book, back in 1994, we were breaking new ground. At that time, Ethernet switching and Fast Ethernet were both new technologies. There were a few books around that covered switching in general; and one or two that discussed the emerging 100Mbps version of Ethernet. Yet no single book really approached both subjects together. Many of the network professionals we knew were struggling with how to put both technologies into their networks simultaneously; hence the inspiration for the first edition of this book, which was published in 1995.

In 1996, ATM started getting a lot more press coverage, so we agreed to a second edition that included a chapter on ATM integration. It had been just over a year since the publication of the first edition, yet we were surprised by how many new Ethernet developments there had been in such a relatively short time period. The phenomenal success of Switched and Fast Ethernet meant that both technologies became mainstream virtually overnight, finding their way into large and small networks everywhere. Soon after the publication of the second edition, we noticed that the "all roads lead to ATM" hype was starting to subside. Instead, the debate shifted to the merits of Gigabit Ethernet and Layer 3 switching. We saw the same promise in them as we originally saw in Switched and Fast Ethernet. It also became clear to us that Gigabit Ethernet and Layer 3 switching went hand-in-hand.

This brings us to the third edition of this book. In June 1998, the IEEE ratified 802.3z, the Gigabit Ethernet standard, as well as the new 802.1p priority switching standard. The networking industry was off on yet another high-bandwidth race. Yet Gigabit Ethernet and Layer 3 switching are, in fact, just two out of about a dozen recent Ethernet innovations.

When we first spoke to New Riders Publishing about the third edition, we vastly underestimated the number of new Ethernet developments. Our original goal was to have this book in print at around the same time as the Gigabit Ethernet standard would be approved. That didn't happen because it took us a lot longer than anticipated to research all the new topics and to separate the facts from the hype. Finally, you have the finished product in your hands: A practical guide to deploying a Switched, Fast, and Gigabit Ethernet LAN, complete with an in-depth discussion of Layer 3 switching. Along the way, we were able to incorporate all the latest IEEE Ethernet, VLAN, trunking, priority switching, and 1000BASE-T standards. We were also able to include the latest hot-off-the-press EIA/TIA cabling and associated tester developments.

Numerous individuals have helped make this new and improved third edition a reality. We would like to thank John Chambers, Doug Wills, and Maureen Kasper from Cisco Systems for contributing the Foreword to this book. We are also grateful to Kevin Tolly and Charlie Bruno from the Tolly Group for their interesting perspectives on Ethernet's future, covered in the Epilogue. Many thanks go to our technical reviewer, Matt Birkner, who taught us a thing or two about the IETF, bridging, and routing. We also want to thank Tony Beam from AMP, who provided some valuable input for Chapter 6, "Cabling and More on Physical Layers," and Sven Iversen from Intel, who lent us his considerable knowledge of network management.

We would also like to thank Kitty Jarrett and Amy Lewis from Macmillan Technical Publishing, who literally made the third edition happen. Finally, we would like to thank Brett Bartow at New Riders for backing this project 100% (even though his authors resembled slugs at times).

We wish you luck with your new Switched, Fast, and Gigabit Ethernet networks. We hope you learn as much from reading this book as we did from writing it. Feel free to email us with comments, especially fourth edition suggestions!

—Sean Riley (Sean.Riley@intel.com)
 Robert Breyer (Robert_A_Breyer@yahoo.com)
 July 1999

Contents at a Glance

Table of Contents

Foreword

More than 200 years ago, the Industrial Revolution forever changed the fortunes of people, companies, and countries. Similarly, the Internet Revolution of today is driving economic growth and reshaping businesses and governments world-wide. What we are witnessing is the emergence of a new economy in which computer networking is changing the way people work, live, play, and learn.

Over the past year, we have seen a key shift in how networking technology is being used to define competitive advantage and create new jobs and market opportunities worldwide. Combined with electronic commerce applications, decision support systems, and enterprise resource planning systems, networking technology is used strategically by business, government, and individuals for a wide range of applications, most of which are run on Ethernet-based networks.

The networking industry moves at an Internet pace—new products and stan-dards are developed and become obsolete much more rapidly than in other industries. However, Ethernet is one of the few technologies that has withstood the test of time. Over the past 25 years, Ethernet has steadily increased its domi-nance as a LAN technology and is now a dominant data networking standard.

Ethernet's remarkable success can be attributed to two factors. First, Ethernet has continuously reinvented itself to keep up with rapidly changing market requirements, evidenced by such recent innovations as Gigabit Ethernet, Layer 3 switching, virtual LANs, and priority switching. Second, new Ethernet technolo-gies have evolved the price/performance curve without making obsolete past iterations. As a result, Ethernet has changed to meet the newer challenges of the networking world.

Now, the biggest challenge for Ethernet still lies ahead, with the convergence of data, voice, and video communications. The consolidation of the traditional data, voice, and video telecommunications services will result in the growth of packet-switch-based networks, and Ethernet is very well positioned to carry the IP traffic of the integrated data/voice/video networks of the future.

Cisco is dedicated to the furthering of Ethernet. This is evident in our long-standing pioneering of new Ethernet technologies and leadership in the standardization process established by such bodies as the IEEE, giving customers a wider choice of Ethernet solutions best suited for their individual network environments.

We are working on future Ethernet technologies to address the challenges of scalability, reliability, accelerating performance, and changing traffic patterns across enterprise networks. Based on established standards, Ethernet technology appears to have a bright and promising future as a mechanism for transferring data and voice around the globe well into the future.

—John Chambers, President and Chief Executive Officer, Cisco Systems, Inc.

Introduction

1998 marks the 25-year anniversary of Ethernet. Today Ethernet is more than just another type of LAN; it is the de facto worldwide standard for local area networking hardware, with almost 200 million nodes installed worldwide. Over the past four years, Switching and Fast Ethernet have become increasingly popular, and today these technologies are about to eclipse the proven 10Mbps shared version of Ethernet. Gigabit Ethernet and Layer 3 switching, the most recent Ethernet innovations, will ensure that Ethernet remains the top-selling LAN technology for another decade. That's because Gigabit Ethernet and Layer 3 Switching are evolutionary, standards-based, affordable, and supported by almost every networking vendor in the business.

This is not an academic book that will inundate you with theory and specifications. Many good books are available that cover the theory of Gigabit Ethernet, Switching, Layer 3 routing, and VLANs. This book is very different. We took a hands-on approach in this book, focusing on how to use Switched, Fast, and Gigabit Ethernet products. Our objective is to teach you the practical aspects of upgrading to, building, managing, and troubleshooting a high-speed, multilayer Ethernet network.

We combined the topics of Gigabit Ethernet and Layer 3 switching in one book because they represent the latest Ethernet innovations and are often implemented together. Gigabit Ethernet gives Ethernet technology the ultimate scalability it has traditionally lacked, while Layer 3 switching provides cost-effective performance improvements for Ethernet backbones. We think you'll often be considering a new Gigabit switch with Layer 3 capabilities, so the two technologies go hand in hand. We have also covered other Ethernet innovations in this book. VLANs, link aggregation, and (in 802.1p) "traffic class expediting" are features found on most of today's Ethernet switches; we will explain how they work and what benefits they provide.

Is This Book for You?

This book is designed for Ethernet users. We have made various assumptions about you, the reader. We assume that you already have some experience with LANs in general and Ethernet in particular; that you believe network infrastructure is a fundamental, necessary, long-term investment to ensure your company's competitiveness; and that you are or will be experiencing performance bottlenecks in your existing LAN.

If you can identify with one of the following descriptions, then this book is for you!

- You are the chief information officer of a large company putting together a strategic plan for your high-speed LAN to be rolled out over the next five years.

- You are a LAN administrator who has to upgrade a severely overloaded network segment next weekend. You have two days to decide what equipment to purchase.

- You are a network manager who has made a strategic decision to move the network to ATM, but are now rethinking that decision.

- You are a network manager who needs to devise an upgrade plan for moving from your company's shared 10BASE-T LAN to a high-speed LAN.

- You are a management information systems director who is evaluating different consultant and vendor proposals for upgrading your existing overloaded network. You need to decide which consultant's recommendations to follow.

- You are trying to cope with the added traffic the Internet and intranet are putting on your network.

- You are experiencing performance-related problems as more and more of your traffic is forwarded to the backbone.

- You have "future-proofed" your network with 10/100Mbps LAN adapters and want to know the next step.

- You are interested in what is happening in Gigabit Ethernet, Full-Duplex Ethernet, or other advancements in frame switching.

- You have a routed network and are trying to determine how a Layer 3 switch will fit. Or you might just be wondering whether LAN routers are in fact becoming obsolete.

- You are interested in high-speed networking technology and know a fair amount about networking.

Overview

Since the first and second editions of this book were published, we have received numerous letters, phone calls, and email messages about how readers have used the contents of our book to help upgrade networks to Switched and Fast Ethernet. Finally, we have been getting an increasing amount of email regarding Gigabit Ethernet and Layer 3 switching. With this, the third edition of the book, we hope to bring you up to speed on these two technologies.

Gigabit Ethernet addresses one of the chief complaints of Ethernet users: scalability. One of the main reasons why so many people considered ATM was that it provided scalable bandwidth. With the explosion of Web servers and Intranets, scalable bandwidth has become a good thing to have. Gigabit Ethernet now makes Ethernet a serious alternative to ATM in the scalability department. Layer 3 switching addresses one of the other historical weaknesses of Ethernet networking—its dependence on routing. Routers of the past were big, slow, and expensive. With Layer 3 switching etched into silicon chips, you'll soon see a profusion of low-cost switches with Layer 3 capabilities. This means Ethernet can now be routed quickly and inexpensively. The challenge is how to combine these two technologies into one upgrade, thereby limiting the cost and downtime of your network.

The first seven chapters serve primarily as educational background. Chapter 1, which is also Part I, is called "The History of Ethernet." Part I discusses how Ethernet has evolved over the last 25 years from a wireless 4800-bps radio transmission network into today's 1000-Mbps LAN. Part II, "Repeating, Bridging, Switching, and Layer 3 Switching," serves as an educational background on the different Ethernet standards and technologies. Chapter 2 contrasts Ethernet with ATM, as well as some of the other earlier high-speed LAN opponents. We will discuss why Ethernet has emerged as the undisputed winner, and why ATM has clearly failed in the LAN department. Chapter 3 delves into the topic of Fast and Gigabit Ethernet standards and how these high-speed variants differ from the proven 10Mbps shared-media version. Chapter 4 discusses the basics of bridging and switching; and then analyzes some important related Layer 2 standards, such as 802.1D spanning tree, 802.3x full-duplex/flow-control, and 802.3ad link aggregation standards. Chapter 5 discusses some basics of routing, as well as the standards behind Layer 3 switching, including a comprehensive look at virtual LANs.

Part III, "Determining Your Ethernet Needs," consists of three chapters. Chapter 6 highlights recent changes in cabling, a subject often overlooked by LAN managers. Specific attention is paid to UTP (unshielded twisted pair) and fiber cabling requirements, test equipment, and certification. Chapter 7 discusses bandwidth. Bandwidth is what this book is really all about, and this chapter will describe how to measure it and how to determine the amount of traffic (bandwidth) your network is actually capable of handling. We will also talk about some of the applications that are using up more and more precious bandwidth. Chapter 8 introduces the various network building blocks and the features to look for when buying network adapters, repeaters, workgroup switches, backbone switches, Layer 3 switches, and routers.

Part IV is the hands-on part of this book, and is called "Deploying, Managing, and Troubleshooting." Part IV focuses on the installation, usage, management, and troubleshooting of Switched, Fast, and Gigabit Ethernet networks. Chapter 9 describes a step-by-step approach to upgrading an existing 10Mbps shared-media Ethernet network to a new high-speed Ethernet network. It includes discussions about the use of Layer 3 switches in the place of routers and how best to integrate VLANs into your network architecture. Chapter 10 discusses six real-world case studies designed to illustrate the step-by-step upgrade method discussed in Chapter 9. Network management in a switched environment is somewhat different than management in today's shared network, and Chapter 11 contrasts some of these differences. Chapter 12 provides some tips and insights into troubleshooting a high-speed Ethernet LAN. Special attention is paid to troubleshooting a Gigabit Ethernet LAN where the tools we all know and love aren't necessarily available yet.

This is followed by Part V, which consists of three appendixes. Most LAN hardware vendors today sell Ethernet and Fast Ethernet products. Gigabit Ethernet, being relatively new, is not yet as widely supported as Fast Ethernet. Appendix A lists companies that sell Gigabit Ethernet equipment. Appendix B contains additional references that we found useful during the course of writing this book. In Appendix C, we list some interesting and useful Web sites.

Please note that you do not need to read this book cover to cover. Each chapter has been written to stand alone, so you can easily use this book as a reference guide. If you are using Ethernet today and want to learn about next-generation high-speed Ethernet options, then this book belongs on your bookshelf.

PART I

The History of Ethernet

CHAPTER 1

The History of Ethernet

Over the course of 25 years, Ethernet has evolved from a 4800bps contention-based radio channel transmission system to the most popular local area networking standard, capable of transmitting 1 billion bps over unshielded twisted-pair telephone cable. The development history of Ethernet is fascinating from a personal as well as a technical perspective: Companies were started, fortunes were made, and entire industries were created based on the concept of connecting different computing devices.

This chapter shares some of the history of the past 25 years with you. This is the third edition of this book. In the first edition, we remarked that Fast Ethernet, today's state-of-the-art Ethernet version, wasn't going to be the last chapter. We weren't wrong. We've completely revised this third edition to include a Gigabit version of Ethernet, as well as an in-depth discussion of Layer 3 switching.

The Origins of Ethernet: The ALOHA Radio System (1968–1972)

The key concept of Ethernet is the use of a shared transmission channel. The idea of a shared data transmission channel began at the University of Hawaii in the late 1960s when Norman Abramson and his colleagues from the University of Hawaii developed a radio network called the ALOHA system. This ground-based radio broadcasting system was developed to connect the university's IBM 360 mainframe, located on the main campus on the island of Oahu, with card readers and terminals dispersed among different islands and ships at sea.

The original speed of this system was 4800bps, and it was later upgraded to 9600bps. The system used separate inbound and outbound radio channels for two-way data transmission. The outbound channel (that is, mainframe to remote island) was straightforward: The data originating from the mainframe was transmitted out to all remote islands and ships simultaneously. The destination address was put in the header of the transmission and decoded by the appropriate receiving station, which knew what address to seek. The inbound channel (that is, remote island or ship to mainframe) was more interesting because it used a method of randomized retransmission to prevent loss of data in the event of simultaneous transmission by more than one remote station. Here is how the inbound data transmission worked. A remote island station would send off its message or packets after the operator pressed the Enter key.

This station would then wait for the base station to send a message acknowledging receipt. If this acknowledgment was not returned on the outbound channel within a certain period of time (200 to 1500 nanoseconds), the remote station would assume that another station had attempted to transmit simultaneously and that a collision had occurred, which corrupted the transmitted data. At that point, both stations would choose a random backoff time, after which each station would attempt to retransmit its packet, with a very high probability of success. This kind of network is called a *contention-based network* because the different stations are competing or contending for the same channel.

Figure 1.1 shows a diagram of the original ALOHA network.

Two of the implications of this contention-based network were as follows:

- This scheme allowed multiple nodes to communicate over the exact same frequency channel in a simple and elegant manner.

- The more stations that utilized the channel, the more collisions were likely to occur, resulting in transmission delays and reduced data throughput.

Norman Abramson published a series of papers on the theory and applications of the ALOHA system, including one in 1970 detailing a mathematical model for calculating the theoretical capacity of the ALOHA system. This model estimated the efficiency of the ALOHA system to be 17% of the theoretical capacity. In 1972, ALOHA was improved to become slotted ALOHA, a change that more than doubled its efficiency.

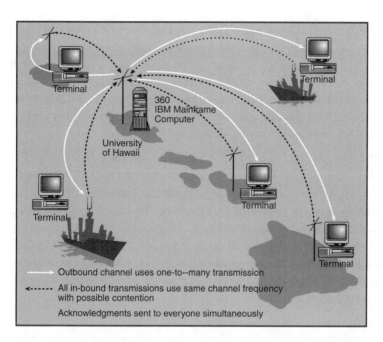

FIGURE 1.1   *The ALOHA network, developed by the University of Hawaii in the 1960s, was the first contention-based network and the foundation for Ethernet.*

The work that Abramson and his colleagues did has become the foundation for most packet broadcast systems in use today, including Ethernet and various satellite transmission systems. In March 1995, Abramson received the IEEE's Kobayashi award for his pioneering work in contention-based communication systems.

Note

Norman Abramson left the University of Hawaii to form ALOHA Networks in 1995. He is chief technical officer at the company, a San Francisco–based startup that will provide satellite-based Internet access called SkyDSL.

Building the First Ethernet at Xerox PARC (1972–1977)

Ethernet as we know it today started in July 1972, when Bob Metcalfe went to work at the Computer Science Laboratory of the Xerox Palo Alto Research Center (PARC), Xerox's world-famous research facility. In 1972, PARC researchers had already invented the world's first laser printer, called EARS, and the first PC with a graphical user interface, the ALTO (as in Palo Alto). Xerox hired Metcalfe as PARC's networking specialist, and his first job was to connect the Xerox ALTO computer to the Arpanet (the predecessor of the Internet). In the fall of 1972, Metcalfe stumbled across Abramson's earlier work on the ALOHA system. While reading Abramson's famous 1970 paper on the ALOHA model, Metcalfe realized that Abramson had made some questionable assumptions, and that through optimization, the efficiency of the ALOHA system could be increased by almost 100%. (Metcalfe later received his Ph.D. from Harvard for his work on packet-based transmission theory.)

In late 1972, Metcalfe and his colleague David Boggs designed a network to connect the various ALTO (and later NOVA) computers to the EARS laser printer. During the development cycle, Metcalfe referred to his work as the ALTO ALOHA network because it was based on the ALOHA system and connected numerous ALTO computers. The ALTO ALOHA Network, the world's first local area network for personal computers, first ran on May 22, 1973. That day Metcalfe wrote a memo announcing that he was changing the name to *Ethernet*, after the "ether through which electromagnetic radiation was once thought to propagate."

Note

For many years ether *was thought to be a passive, omnipresent, homogeneous medium or substance that was capable of carrying electromagnetic waves. In the late 19th century, scientists Albert Michelson and Edward Morley disproved the existence of such a material.*

The original experimental PARC Ethernet ran at 2.94Mbps.

Ethernet was a big improvement over the original ALOHA network. It featured *carrier-sense*, meaning that a station would listen first before transmitting its own data stream, and an improved retransmission scheme, allowing a network utilization of almost 100%.

By 1976, the experimental Ethernet had grown to connect 100 nodes at PARC, running over a 1000-meter thick coaxial cable. Xerox, which was busy trying to turn Ethernet into a product, changed the name to Xerox wire. (In 1979, when DEC, Intel, and Xerox came together to standardize it, the name reverted to Ethernet.) In July of that year, Metcalfe and Boggs published the now famous paper "Ethernet: Distributed Packet Switching for Local Area Networks" in the *Communications of the ACM*.

Note

Both Norman Abramson's and Bob Metcalfe's papers were written before the Internet became popular. If you are interested, they are both reprinted in a book Norman Abramson wrote called Multiple Access Communications: Foundations for Emerging Technologies. *The book is available from the IEEE at* www.ieee.org/ieeestore/commbk.html#pc2873.

In late 1977, Metcalfe and three colleagues received a patent for their "Multipoint Data Communication System with Collision Detection." This multipoint transmission system has since become known as Carrier-Sense Multiple Access with Collision Detection, or CSMA/CD. And so Ethernet was born.

DEC, Intel, and Xerox Standardize Ethernet (1979–1983)

By the late 1970s, dozens of different local area network technologies had emerged, and Ethernet was only one of them. Besides Ethernet, the most prominent ones were Data General's MCA, Network Systems Corporation's Hyperchannel, Datapoint's ARCnet, and Corvus's Omninet. What made Ethernet the ultimate victor was not technical superiority or speed but Metcalfe's vision to turn Ethernet into an industry standard and not keep it a vendor-specific proprietary technology.

In early 1979, Metcalfe received a phone call from Gordon Bell at Digital Equipment Corporation. Bell wanted to talk about how DEC and Xerox could work together on building Ethernet LANs. At this point, working together with different vendors to promote Ethernet seemed like a good idea, but Metcalfe's hands were tied because Xerox, notoriously protective of its patents, restricted him from working with DEC. Metcalfe suggested that DEC directly approach Xerox management about turning Ethernet into an industry standard. Xerox decided this was a good idea.

One of the obstacles to getting DEC and Xerox to work together on an industry standard was antitrust legislation. Howard Charney, an attorney and a friend of Metcalfe's, recommended that Metcalfe turn over the actual Ethernet technology to a standards organization. (Later that year, Charney would become co-founder of 3Com.)

On a trip to the National Bureau of Standards (NBS) in Washington, D.C., Metcalfe met with engineers from Intel Corporation who were visiting the NBS to find new applications for their state-of-the-art 25MHz VLSI NMOS integrated circuit process technology. The fit was obvious: Xerox would provide the technology, DEC would add systems engineering capability and become a supplier of Ethernet hardware, and Intel would provide Ethernet silicon building blocks. Soon afterward, Metcalfe left Xerox to become a full-time corporate marriage broker and entrepreneur.

Note

VLSI NMOS stands for Very Large Scale Integration Negative Doping Metal Oxide Silicon. VLSI has the capability to squeeze—at the time many thousands of transistors—into a single piece of silicon, known as a chip. NMOS was Intel's latest process technology, NMOS describing the type of material being used.

By June 1979, DEC, Intel, and Xerox were contemplating trilateral meetings. In the fall of 1979, the first meetings actually took place. A year later, DEC, Intel, and Xerox published the Ethernet Blue Book, or DIX (for DEC, Intel, Xerox) Ethernet V1.0 specification. The experimental Ethernet originally ran at 2.94Mbps, and then DIX specified 20Mbps, but subsequently the speed was reduced to 10Mbps. Over the next two years DIX refined the standard, culminating with the Ethernet Version 2.0 specification, which was published in 1982.

Note

2.94Mbps is a rather odd number. This speed was chosen because the first Ethernet interfaces were clocked using the ALTO computer's system clock. This meant sending a pulse every 340 nanoseconds, which translates to 2.94Mbps.

While DIX was starting to work on Ethernet, the Institute of Electrical and Electronic Engineers (IEEE), a worldwide professional organization, was forming a committee to define and promote industry LAN standards with a focus on office environments. This committee was called Project 802. The DIX consortium had produced the Ethernet specifications but not an internationally accepted standard.

In June 1981, the IEEE Project 802 decided to form the 802.3 subcommittee to produce an internationally accepted standard based on the DIX work. A year and a half later, 19 companies announced the new IEEE 802.3 draft standard. In 1983, this draft was finalized as the IEEE 10BASE5 standard. (The acronym 10BASE5 was chosen because the standard specified a 10Mbps transmission speed using baseband signaling and allowing for 500 meter node-to-node distances. 802.3 is technically different from DIX Ethernet 2.0, but the differences are minor.)

Today Ethernet and 802.3 are considered synonymous. As part of the standardization process, Xerox turned over its four Ethernet patents to the IEEE, and today anyone can license Ethernet from the IEEE for a fixed fee of $1000. International recognition for the IEEE standard 802.3 came in 1989 when the International Organization for Standards (ISO) adopted Ethernet as standard number ISO 88023, ensuring worldwide presence.

3Com Productizes Ethernet (1980–1982)

While DEC, Intel, and Xerox engineers were still finalizing the Ethernet specifications, Metcalfe was already pursuing other entrepreneurial interests. Metcalfe even turned down Steven Jobs's offer to join Apple Computer to develop networks. In June 1979, Bob Metcalfe, Howard Charney, Ron Crane, Greg Shaw, and Bill Kraus founded the Computer, Communication, and Compatibility Corporation, better known today as 3Com Corporation.

In August 1980, 3Com announced its first product, a commercial version of TCP/IP for UNIX, which shipped in December 1980. By March 1981, 18 months before the official IEEE 802.3 standard was published, 3Com was already shipping its first hardware product, the Ethernet 3C100 transceiver. Later on in 1981, the company started selling transceivers and cards for DEC PDP/11s and VAXes, as well as Intel Multibus and Sun Microsystems machines.

3Com's original business plan was based on the concept of developing Ethernet adapters for the new personal computers that were sprouting up all over the world. By 1981, Metcalfe was talking to all the major PC companies, including IBM and Apple, about building Ethernet adapters. Steven Jobs at Apple was quick to say yes, and 3Com's first Ethernet product for Apple shipped a year later. The Apple Ethernet devices were officially called "Apple boxes," were unwieldy boxes connected to the Apple II's parallel port, and were a market failure. IBM, which had made history that year by announcing the original IBM PC, said no to 3Com because the company was busy inventing its own Token Ring network.

3Com, however, decided to proceed without IBM's cooperation and started developing the EtherLink ISA adapter. Eighteen months later, the first EtherLink shipped, along with the appropriate DOS driver software. The first EtherLink was a technical breakthrough for many reasons:

- Advances in semiconductor technology made possible the EtherLink network interface card. In 1981, 3Com had entered into a silicon partnership with a start-up called Seeq Technologies. Seeq had promised that with its VLSI semiconductor technology, most of the discrete controller functions could be contained on a single chip, reducing the number and cost of the components on the board. In mid-1982, the EtherLink became the first network interface card (NIC) to incorporate an Ethernet VLSI controller chip: the Seeq 8001.

- More importantly, the EtherLink became the first ISA bus Ethernet adapter for the IBM PC. This represents a milestone in the history of Ethernet itself.

- The Seeq chip meant lower cost, so 3Com could set the price the EtherLink at $950, which at the time was far less than any other card and transceiver combination.

- Before the EtherLink adapter arrived, all Ethernet devices featured an external medium attachment units (MAU) transceiver that was connected to the thick coaxial Ethernet cable. The use of the VLSI controller chip freed up sufficient space so that the transceiver could be integrated on the card itself. Because the classic thick coaxial cable had numerous disadvantages, 3Com introduced a new, thinner cabling method.

This radical thinner cabling innovation, called Thin Ethernet, was invented by the EtherLink design engineer Ron Crane and became a de facto standard soon afterward. It had numerous benefits: It eliminated the need for an external transceiver and transceiver cable, was cheaper, and made networking much more user-friendly because thin coaxial cable was easier to install and use. Figure 1.2 shows a photo of the original 3Com EtherLink. Figure 1.3 contrasts a 10BASE5 connection and the 10BASE2/Thin Ethernet card.

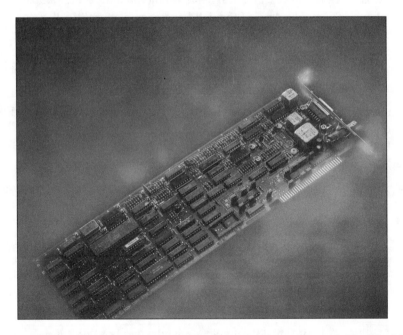

FIGURE 1.2 *The original 3Com EtherLink network interface card. The EtherLink pioneered the concept of thin Ethernet and was the world's first ISA Ethernet adapter.*

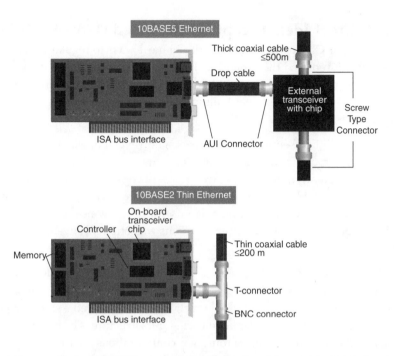

FIGURE 1.3 *10BASE5 connections use an external transceiver to interface to the cable. Thin Ethernet network adapters incorporate the transceiver on the NIC itself and use the thinner coaxial cable.*

Metcalfe's decision to focus on the IBM PC paid off handsomely for 3Com. Although IBM had designed its PC to be primarily a home computer, companies rather than home users were the main buyers. Demand for the PC exceeded all expectations. By 1982, the IBM PC was shipping 200,000 units a month (three times the company's original forecasts), and it took IBM's factories over 2 and a half years to catch up with demand. By early 1983, the IBM XT shipped and IBM captured 75% of the business market for PCs. IBM failed to realize early on that companies would want to link their personal computers to a network. By 1983, EtherLink sales were booming, and, in 1984, 3Com was able to file for its first public offering of stock.

3Com, ICL (International Computers Limited), and Hewlett-Packard later submitted the concept of thin Ethernet to the IEEE, which adopted it as an official standard in 1984. Because the node-to-node distance had been reduced to 200 meters, the standard was known as 10BASE2, or, due to its cheaper and thinner coaxial cable, as Cheapernet.

StarLAN: A Great Idea, Except for Its Speed (1984–1987)

Thin Ethernet, or Cheapernet, was superior in most ways to regular Ethernet. For one thing, it replaced the expensive thick yellow coaxial cable with a cheaper, thinner, and more manageable coaxial cable. In addition, most thin Ethernet NICs had the transceiver built in, translating into easier installation and lower costs.

Thin Ethernet still had some major drawbacks, however. For example, if a user accidentally severed or otherwise disconnected the coaxial cable (something that occurred regularly), the entire network would come to a halt. In addition, proper termination at both ends of the network was required. Network reconfiguration in particular was a problem: If a user physically moved, the network cable had to be rerouted to follow the user. This was often inconvenient and disruptive to other users.

In late 1983, Bob Galin from Intel started working with AT&T and NCR to run Ethernet over unshielded twisted-pair (UTP) telephone cable. NCR proposed a bus topology similar to that of thin Ethernet, but AT&T favored a star configuration similar to the existing telephone wiring infrastructure. The benefits of a UTP star configuration were numerous: Star configurations are easier and cheaper to install, configure, manage, and troubleshoot. The star configuration was a breakthrough in its own right because it allowed for a structured wiring system, where a single wire connects each node to the central hub. This has obvious advantages in terms of installation, troubleshooting, and reconfiguration, reducing the cost of installation and ownership for the entire network. A bus and star configuration is shown in Figure 1.4.

In early 1984, 14 other companies started participating in the UTP Ethernet initiative. Several discussions followed, mainly centered on how fast Ethernet would be able to run over UTP wire. It was proven that a slower version of Ethernet, around 1 to 2Mbps, could be run over Category 3 wiring and still meet EMI (electromagnetic interference) regulations and crosstalk limitations. Some vendors strongly opposed this radical reduction in speed and quickly lost interest. 3Com and DEC, two leaders in Ethernet, were among them. Other participants argued that 1Mbps was fast enough for PC networks featuring IBM PC and XT machines. After many heated technical discussions, the group voted to scale Ethernet back to 1Mbps.

Ten companies decided to proceed with 1Mbps Ethernet and approached the IEEE. The IEEE 802 group chartered the StarLAN task force, chaired by Galin. By the middle of 1986, 1BASE5 was approved as a new IEEE 802.3 standard.

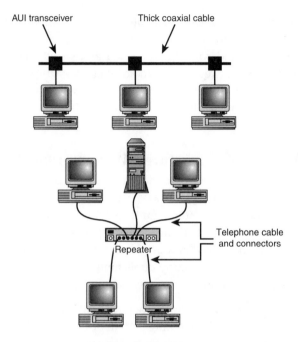

FIGURE 1.4   *A structured cabling system with nodes arranged in a star configuration around a central hub has many advantages.*

Note

StarLAN ran at 1Mbps, hence the number 1. StarLAN could support distances of up to 250 meters from hub to node, or 500 meters from node to node, hence the number 5 in 1BASE5.

The Demise of StarLAN

In 1984, IBM announced the PC AT, based on Intel's 80286 microprocessor. Two years later, in 1986—the year that the StarLAN/1BASE5 standard was approved—Intel had already introduced the 80386 microprocessor, a 32-bit CPU that was many times more powerful than the previous-generation 80286. By 1986, numerous vendors, led by Hewlett-Packard and AT&T, were shipping StarLAN hubs and NICs.

Although StarLAN shipped several million connections in the 1980s, many vendors, including 3Com and DEC, had decided early on that 1Mbps was too slow. In an industry that was getting used to doubling performance every two years, some customers and vendors perceived 1Mbps Ethernet as a step backward. As a result, StarLAN was never able to gain enough industry or market momentum to get off the ground properly.

The demise of StarLAN came in 1987, when SynOptics introduced LATTISNET and delivered full-speed 10Mbps Ethernet performance over regular telephone wire. Soon afterward, the IEEE standardized LATTISNET as Twisted-Pair Ethernet, also known as 10BASE-T. Credit needs to be given to StarLAN and Galin for pioneering the concept of Ethernet over unshielded twisted-pair and a star-shaped wiring topology, but once 10BASE-T arrived on the scene, StarLAN's days were numbered.

The History of 10BASE-T and Structured Wiring (1986–1990)

By the mid-1980s, the PC revolution really had picked up steam. By 1986, personal computer sales were booming as applications began to drive demand. Lotus 1-2-3 had become *the* "killer application" for the IBM PC AT. Every business had to have it. Apple's Macintosh, launched in 1986, was starting to sell briskly because it offered an unparalleled graphical user interface. People wanted to print their spreadsheets and desktop publishing creations on expensive shared laser printers, so networking sales were booming as well.

Two events occurred that gave Ethernet another boost. In 1985, Novell started shipping NetWare, a high-performance operating system designed exclusively for networking IBM-compatible personal computers. The other event was, of course, 10BASE-T: full-speed 10Mbps Ethernet running over UTP telephone wire.

Fiber Ethernet and UTP Ethernet

The first Ethernet network utilized a thick coaxial cable. A few years later, Metcalfe and Eric Rawson proved that a CSMA-type signal could run over fiber-optic cable as well. In the early 1980s, with fiber optic cabling experiencing a surge in popularity, Xerox decided to investigate running Ethernet over fiber optic cable. Rawson was appointed as the project leader for Fiber Ethernet and was joined by Ron Schmidt soon afterward. Rawson and Schmidt discovered that Ethernet could indeed run over fiber, but only in a star configuration, not the typical Ethernet bus topology.

In 1985, Schmidt modified the Fiber Ethernet hardware to run over shielded twisted pair (STP) wire as well. Because STP cable was expensive and bulky compared to regular UTP wiring, Schmidt also did some experiments later that year to show that Ethernet could run over regular UTP cable.

Structured Wiring: StarLAN and Token Ring

In 1985, IBM finally started shipping its 4Mbps Token Ring LAN six years after Metcalfe had originally approached IBM about building Ethernet network adapters for the IBM PC and almost three years after the first 3Com ISA

EtherLink network adapter was sold. Although Token Ring was less than half the speed of 10Mbps Ethernet, it had one major advantage over Ethernet. It was based on a structured cabling system approach, which incorporates a central concentrator or hub and shielded twisted-pair wire to connect to the nodes.

At about the same time, the Ethernet camp finished its work on StarLAN, which also utilized a structured cabling system. Unfortunately, StarLAN ran at only 1Mbps, 10% of the original Ethernet speed, and hence was not a viable replacement for regular 10Mbps Ethernet or 4Mbps Token Ring. The appearance of Token Ring and StarLAN, however, made it clear that the future was in twisted-pair wiring and centralized wiring hubs.

SynOptics Communications Is Founded

In 1983, Schmidt started searching for a business unit within Xerox to market the Fiber Ethernet technology he invented at Xerox PARC, but his search was unsuccessful. Schmidt's search for a product group was successful in another respect,though: he found his future partner in a business planner at Xerox by the name of Andy Ludwig. By the summer of 1985, Schmidt and Ludwig had come to an agreement with Xerox whereby the two of them could start their own company, with Xerox being a minority shareholder. Venture capital was secured, and in November 1985 eight Xerox employees, led by Schmidt and Ludwig, left the company to start ASTRA Communications. The new company would sell structured wiring fiber and STP Ethernet hubs.

> **Note**
>
> The name ASTRA *didn't last very long, as NEC had already trademarked the name and was threatening to sue the new company for trademark violations. The new name, SynOptics Communications, was proposed by one of the board's directors after browsing through a dictionary and coming across the word* synopsis.

10BASE-T Is Approved as an IEEE Standard

In 1986, SynOptics started working on 10Mbps Ethernet over UTP telephone cable. The first SynOptics product, called LATTISNET, shipped on August 17, 1987. On the same day, the IEEE 802.3 working group met to discuss the best way to implement 10Mbps Ethernet over UTP, later to be called 10BASE-T.

In addition to the SynOptics LATTISNET scheme, many competing proposals were submitted, the most notable being from 3Com/DEC and Hewlett-Packard. For over three years, engineers from around the world met regularly under the IEEE 802.3 umbrella to find the best implementation of 10Mbps Ethernet running over UTP. In the end, the IEEE agreed to a standard that was based on Hewlett-Packard's multiport repeater proposal and an improved version of the SynOptics LATTISNET technology. In the fall of 1990, the new 802.3i/10BASE-T standard was officially adopted. The next year, Ethernet sales nearly doubled, fueled largely by new 10BASE-T repeaters, twisted-pair MAUs, and NICs.

Note

The original IEEE 802.3 standard has undergone several additions and revisions over the last 20 years. Each addition or revision to the original standard gets a new suffix letter.

The advent of the star wiring configuration was a significant milestone for Ethernet. First, from this point on Ethernet started looking more and more like a telephone system, with a central switch located in the wiring closet and dedicated wires running to each node. Second, IBM's Token Ring lost its two biggest advantages: the structured cabling approach and the use of twisted-pair wiring.

Novell NetWare: The Networked "Killer Application"

In the early 1980s, a small software company in Provo, Utah, called Novell developed a network operating system called NetWare. Before being able to run the NetWare operating system, however, companies needed to buy the associated networking hardware. Novell seized this opportunity and started selling NICs, which all just happened to be Ethernet. Almost overnight NetWare became *the* killer app for offices, allowing PCs to access shared printers, send email, exchange files, and access central databases. The huge success of NetWare in turn fueled the demand for Ethernet adapters in general, making Ethernet the clear market leader. Later on NetWare was modified to run on ARCnet and Token Ring as well, but by then Ethernet was outshipping all other LAN technologies combined.

In 1989, Novell sold its NIC business and began licensing its Novell Engineering (NE) Ethernet adapter card designs to anybody who wanted them, thereby enabling a huge NE2000 clone business to emerge, similar to the IBM PC clone industry. All of a sudden, companies operating out of someone's garage could go into the NIC business by buying the chips from National Semiconductor and licensing the name, the design, and the appropriate software from Novell. Some companies didn't even bother licensing the design. They just bought the 8390 chips from National Semiconductor and shipped the cards without software, labeling them "NE2000-compatible."

Fierce competition between the NE2000 clones on the one hand and 3Com on the other drove prices down radically. By 1988, literally dozens of NE2000 card manufacturers were in business, and Ethernet NICs could be purchased for as little as $200, whereas IBM's Token Ring cards cost more than $1000. By 1990, some NE2000 vendors, such as Western Digital (later SMC), and a consortium of Taiwanese companies even started cloning the National 8390 Ethernet chip itself. The result was that Ethernet sales just kept on growing, fueled by lower prices, broader vendor availability, and innovation resulting from the pressure of competition.

The Demise of Token Ring

Until as late as 1992, many industry and market research analysts predicted that Token Ring would one day outship Ethernet. The truth is that Token Ring's future was dealt a fatal blow in December 1987, when SynOptics shipped its first Ethernet hubs to Texas Instruments and the Boeing Aircraft Company. By the late 1980s, not even IBM could ignore Ethernet anymore. The company started selling Microchannel Ethernet adapters for its personal computers and AS/400 minicomputers, providing customers with connectivity options they had been requesting for almost 10 years.

Another example of how IBM had to adapt to the changing world was in its RS/6000 engineering workstation line. While Sun Microsystems, the workstation leader, had long ago adopted Ethernet as the standard, building it into every machine, it was not until 1991 that IBM's workstation division did the unthinkable and adopted Ethernet as its standard. Finally, the RS/6000 machine came equipped with an Intel 32-bit Ethernet coprocessor built in.

Only in the 1990s did IBM's networking division come to the realization that Token Ring would not replace Ethernet and that its strategy had failed. At this point, Ethernet was outshipping Token Ring by a ratio of 3 to 1, and the trend was accelerating. In a last-minute attempt to shore up its market share, IBM tried copying the Novell Engineering clone strategy. In 1992, the company decided to license its Token Ring chipset to National Semiconductor, hoping to generate a broad-based, cheap clone industry. But by 1992 it was all over for Token Ring: Ethernet had become the de facto standard for local area networks in small and large companies around the world. In four years, Ethernet sales had grown tenfold, from 1 million units in 1988 to 10 million units in 1992.

Ethernet Switching and Full-Duplex Emerge (1990–1994)

Numerous market forces were driving the need for faster network infrastructure in the late 1980s:

- Standalone PCs and new servers were added to existing networks, resulting in higher traffic levels.

- More new PCs were sold, also resulting in more traffic.

- More powerful PCs using graphical user interfaces started generating more graphics-based network load.

- Multiple Ethernet LANs were being connected together. Shared Ethernet depends on a single shared-media connection for all users, where only one station can transmit at any point in time. Joining these different LANs increased traffic significantly, as more users were now competing for the same limited bandwidth.

Two-port bridges (connecting only two LANs) that are almost as old as Ethernet itself became popular during this time to connect LANs while keeping traffic levels manageable. By the late 1980s, a new type of bridge was emerging: the intelligent multiport bridge, sold by companies such as Alantec, Synernetics, Racal-Milgo, Clearpoint, and others. But in 1990, a radically different bridge appeared: the Kalpana EtherSwitch EPS-700.

The EtherSwitch was very different from most other bridges at the time for several reasons:

- The switch consisted of an architecture that allowed for multiple simultaneous data transmission paths, just like a telephone switch. This meant users were no longer sharing the bandwidth with each other, improving overall throughput significantly.

- The EtherSwitch used a new bridging technology called *cut-through* rather than the store-and-forward technology used by conventional bridges. This improved delay times through the switch by an order of magnitude.

- What ultimately made Kalpana famous was that the company founders Vinod Bhardwaj and Larry Blair took a very different approach to marketing their product. The EtherSwitch was sold as a networking switch to boost a particular LAN's performance, rather than as a bridge to interconnect different LANs. The differences were subtle, but almost overnight the EtherSwitch created a new market category: the network switch.

- Apart from being positioned differently than bridges, switches also looked different inside. Instead of using a microprocessor to analyze every packet individually, switches started utilizing smarter fixed-logic Ethernet chips to perform the bridging function in hardware rather than in software.

Full-Duplex Ethernet

In 1993, Kalpana fostered another breakthrough: full-duplex Ethernet. Regular shared-media Ethernet works only in half-duplex mode. A station is either transmitting or receiving, but not doing both at once. Shared Ethernet depends on a single shared-media connection for all users, and simultaneous transmitting and receiving is technically not possible. A switched or point-to-point 10BASE-T connection, on the other hand, can be operated in such a way as to make simultaneous transmitting and receiving possible. The benefits of full-duplex were obvious: Transmitting and receiving simultaneously can theoretically double the data transmission rate. Kalpana was the first company to add this feature to its switches, and other vendors soon followed.

In 1995, the IEEE started work on an industry-standard full-duplex implementation. By 1997 this work was complete when the 802.3x full-duplex/flow-control standard was ratified.

Fast Ethernet Emerges (1992–1995)

Network switches were excellent devices for reducing network congestion, but each Ethernet switch could only deliver a maximum of 10Mbps throughput per port. The only serious contender for applications requiring more than 10Mbps throughput was Fiber Distributed Data Interface (FDDI), an expensive 100Mbps, fiber-based LAN. Administrators of larger networks were starting to implement FDDI network backbones and FDDI server connections. In some instances, they were even connecting clients or workstations to an FDDI ring. In the 1980s, companies such as DEC, Advanced Micro Devices (AMD), National Semiconductor, and IBM poured millions of dollars into FDDI semiconductor and product development. In 1991, Sun Microsystems even considered adding an FDDI connection to every SPARCstation machine (all Sun SPARCstations already had a 10Mbps Ethernet connection built in). Unfortunately, FDDI never became a mainstream technology due to its high price and complexity.

Meanwhile, Ethernet prices continued to plummet, driven by phenomenal growth. Some networking companies started building switching hubs that contained both high-speed FDDI and Ethernet ports. Crescendo Communications was one of these. It built a workgroup switch that featured both FDDI and switched 10BASE-T ports. Yet many customers were growing concerned about the long-term prospects of Ethernet, because the technology was now 10 years old, an eternity in the computer industry.

In August 1991, Ethernet old-timers Howard Charney, David Boggs, Ron Crane, and Larry Birenbaum were brainstorming the idea of founding a new company. The idea was to start selling networking test equipment, but during the conversation, Birenbaum asked if Ethernet could be run at 10 times its original speed. Crane and Boggs affirmed that it could.

The rest is history. On February 28, 1992, Charney, Birenbaum, and others founded Grand Junction Networks to design, build, and market high-speed Ethernet equipment. Grand Junction immediately began work on 100Mbps Ethernet.

By late 1992, word was starting to spread that a start-up company in California was working on 100Mbps Fast Ethernet technology. Grand Junction hence decided to confirm the rumors and make public its work on 100Mbps Ethernet in September 1992.

The IEEE 802.3 100Mbps Standards Wars

One item on the agenda of the 1992 plenary meeting of the IEEE project 802 was higher speed networks. Two technical proposals were presented. One was from Grand Junction Networks, which proposed retaining the existing Ethernet protocol. This approach was endorsed by 3Com Corporation, Sun Microsystems, and SynOptics. The second proposal came from Hewlett-Packard and detailed a completely new MAC (Media Access Control) method for 100Mbps transmission. This marked the start of the "Fast Ethernet wars."

During 1993, the IEEE's high-speed study group continued its work on 100Mbps. Various proposals were made, but the main issue was still to be resolved: Would the 802.3 group adopt a new MAC as proposed by Hewlett-Packard, or would the existing Ethernet CSMA/CD MAC be retained? Most members of the group were in favor of retaining Ethernet, but the required majority of 75% could not be garnered, so the debate continued. Grand Junction, Intel, LAN Media, SynOptics, Cabletron, National Semiconductor, Standard Micro Systems (SMC), Sun Microsystems, and 3Com soon grew tired of the endless debates and political gridlock in the IEEE standards and met to pick up the pace. The Fast Ethernet Alliance was founded with the stated objective "to advance 100Mbps Ethernet solutions based on the original Ethernet standard." This pitted the entire industry against a handful of companies led by Hewlett-Packard and AT&T.

Unfortunately, Hewlett-Packard and AT&T refused to retain the CSMA/CD Ethernet protocol for 100Mbps transmission, insisting that its demand-priority protocol was so superior that it outweighed the issue of backward compatibility. The Fast Ethernet camp naturally did not agree, and to clear the impasse the IEEE finally allocated a new group called 802.12 for the demand-priority access method camp. The following events occurred:

- In October 1993, the Fast Ethernet Alliance published its 100BASE-X interoperability specification, today known as 100BASE-TX. That same month, Grand Junction shipped the world's first Fast Ethernet hubs and NICs: the FastSwitch 10/100 and FastNIC100.

- In May 1994, Intel and SynOptics announced and demonstrated Fast Ethernet equipment.

- For most of 1994, the IEEE 802.3 group was busy working on other parts of the 100Mbps Ethernet standard, such as 100BASE-T4, MII, repeater, and full-duplex.

- During the same year, the Fast Ethernet Alliance grew to more than 60 members. Numerous initial supporters of the new 802.12 technology also abandoned the demand-priority camp altogether or publicly endorsed both technologies.

- By late 1994, Intel, Sun Microsystems, and Networth started shipping 100BASE-TX–compliant products. In the first quarter of 1995, Cogent, 3Com, Digital Equipment Corporation, SMC, Accton, SynOptics/Bay Networks, and others followed.

- In March 1995, IEEE members and the Executive committee approved the IEEE 802.3u specification.

A few months later, the Fast Ethernet Alliance disbanded, its job accomplished. The standard was done, and it was time to get back to the business of selling Ethernet products. By late 1995, vendors were announcing new Fast Ethernet products on a daily basis. Fast Ethernet had arrived in full force.

Taking Ethernet into the Next Century: VLANs and Layer 3 Switching (1996–1998)

Fast Ethernet was a big technology performance boost for Ethernet, but it also marked a significant symbolic turning point for Ethernet overall. Until 1995, the mindset in the industry and the marketplace had been that Ethernet, almost 25 years old, was going to be replaced by ATM sooner or later, and that Fast Ethernet would only delay that inevitable transition by a year or two.

Something very interesting happened with the advent of Fast Ethernet in 1995. The phenomenal success of a faster version of Ethernet confounded most critics. Even the authors, having been Ethernet bigots for years, were surprised at the market response to Fast Ethernet. Fast Ethernet apparently reinvigorated the entire Ethernet industry with enthusiasm and, more importantly, key ideas on how Ethernet could be further enhanced to make it live another quarter of a century. The perceived threat of ATM in particular and its key benefits—such as more raw bandwidth and Quality of Service (QoS) scalability—triggered a broader discussion on the other technical issues surrounding Ethernet. One could almost say that the perceived threat of ATM was a wake-up call to the Ethernet industry overall.

The IEEE has been at the forefront of many different efforts to take Ethernet into the next century. Following the adoption of the IEEE 802.3u standard in 1995, several different Ethernet innovations were launched. Among these is of course Gigabit Ethernet (802.3z), the new IEEE 802.3x full-duplex/flow control standard, the 802.1p standard for prioritizing packet flow, and the 802.1Q standard for virtual LAN (VLAN) tagging. Layer 3 switching, which is not a new standard in itself, but rather a combination made possible by hardware innovation, can also be added to this list. Let's look at some of these areas of innovation in a bit more detail.

What Is a VLAN?

A typical LAN comprises an electrical connection of different devices (PCs, servers, printers, and so on). These devices share the same broadcast domains, even if connected via a switch. Broadcast traffic is data sent from one station to all other ones, even if not all other stations need to listen. Excessive broadcast traffic can bog down a LAN significantly. Layer 3 Routers can subdivide a large LAN with a lot of broadcast traffic into smaller sub-LANs. This reduces the amount of broadcast traffic present.

A virtual LAN, or VLAN, on the other hand, uses the concept of grouping different nodes into a broadcast domain and thereby restricting broadcasts. A VLAN is a creation of the network administrator that manages a particular physical LAN. Conceptually, one VLAN is separated by another VLAN through a router. Therefore, many switches offering VLANs often contain routing or Layer 3 functionality as well.

VLANs allow for great performance management on a LAN because power users or servers can be assigned to a particular high-performance virtual LAN with fewer users, whereas normal users will reside on a more heavily loaded LAN where performance is less of an issue. VLANs make network management and changes much easier. For example, VLAN technology will allow LAN administrators to improve performance for selected nodes such as power users and servers where required without upgrading any hardware.

Two topics that we will cover in more depth in this book are VLANs and Layer 3 switching. Chapter 4, "Layer 2 Ethernet Switching," covers Layer 2 switching and VLANs, followed by Chapter 5, "VLANs and Layer 3 Switching," which discusses Layer 3 switching. VLANs and Layer 3 switching are technologies that are hardware-independent: They don't care if the underlying bits and bytes are transferred via Ethernet, Token Ring, or FDDI frames. VLANs and Layer 3 switching do present significant evolutionary milestones in the evolution of Ethernet as a networking technology, and that's why we would like to cover them here in our history section.

VLANs

In 1994, Bay Networks brought out its first Fast Ethernet switch, called the 28115. This was a 10/100 Ethernet backbone switch: the first one of its kind. The Grand Junction switches shipping at the time were either 10 or 100 Mbs, not selectable 10/100, and were workgroup switches that allow for a limited number of port addresses (we'll have more on the technical details later). The 28115 also set another milestone: for the first time an Ethernet switch offered VLAN capability. Thus, the 28115 really combined three industry firsts: first 10 or 100 switch, first backbone capability and first VLANs. But Bay's engineers bit off more than they could chew: The product was so complex that it was over a year late. At the same time, customers were lining up to buy this breakthrough product. When the switch finally shipped, it took Bay months to catch up with demand.

Sometimes a LAN administrator will want to set up a VLAN that comprises nodes connected to different switches. Unfortunately, all of today's VLAN-capable switches are still proprietary. This means that you can only extend a VLAN to *more than one single switch* if you buy all your switches from the same vendor, which is not a good idea.

The IEEE is currently developing an open VLAN standard, based primarily on Cisco's Inter-Switch Link (ISL) work. The IEEE 802.1Q VLAN standard will use the concept of frame tagging, which means adding certain bits to each frame to identify which VLAN group the packet actually belongs. This standard should be complete in 1998. This VLAN standard will provide leading-edge twenty-first-century network management benefits to Ethernet.

Layer 3 Switching

Layer 3 switching is really the combination of two technologies. Technically speaking, a Layer 3 switch is really a limited-purpose hardware-based router. The term *Layer 3 switch* is derived in the following way: In the OSI, routing is known as Layer 3 function. Inside, however, a Layer 3 switch looks more like a regular (Layer 2, for example) switch than a router. Therefore, the hybrid term *Layer 3 switch* was created: it acts like a router, but inside it looks and works like a switch.

Note

OSI *stands for open systems interconnect, and refers to a layererd communications model. It is covered in detail in Chapters 3, "Ethernet, Fast Ethernet, and Gigabit Ethernet Standards," and 4, "Layer 2 Ethernet Switching."*

Let's briefly look at the history of routing to see how we arrived at these Layer 3 switches.

The first Cisco routers were proprietary devices, originally used for remote (WAN) connections or to connect different protocol-based LANs that were running different protocols. The first Cisco routers were rather slow and proprietary, and used early routing technologies, such as Border Gateway Protocol (BGP) and Internet Group Management Protocol (IGMP), which were the first router protocols developed.

In the late 1980s, as technologies such as RIP and OSPF appeared, routing became more standardized and interoperable. (RIP and OSPF and newer Router protocols are covered in Chapter 5, "VLANS and Layer 3 Switching.") Routers, however, remained slow and expensive.

The role of the router has evolved over the past few years to take on a much broader role within the larger LAN environment. Routers now segment a single physical LAN into a number of smaller sub-LANs or connect different LANs via a backbone. The problem with using routers in these newer places is that they are still very expensive, slow, and somewhat of an overkill for the application. That's because a router is an intelligent device: It examines each and every individual packet. The heart of a router is a fast microprocessor, plus lots of memory to run the complicated routing software. Routers trying to cope with Fast or Gigabit Ethernet data rates require very fast CPUs plus large amounts of memory, which drives up the cost.

Contrast this with switches. Switches have no intelligence (that means no CPU, no program memory, and no software). The switching function is performed in hardware or silicon. Each port has a smart chip connected to it, which has sufficient intelligence to examine each packet superficially and decide to which port to send it. These chips are not programmable, though; they can only switch Ethernet frames. These chips are powerful enough to perform switching at wire speed rates, though, which is something unheard of in the router world.

Recent technological advances in the semiconductor field have enabled a new kind of router: one where the routing function happens in hardware, as opposed to in software. This breakthrough has enabled the Layer 3 switch, which is a new category of network product. About 25 years ago, Gordon Moore, co-founder of Intel, observed that semiconductor technology would allow for more and more transistors to be crammed into a chip, about twice as many transistors every two years. This observation, today known as Moore's Law, of course means that microprocessors and memory chips advance rapidly. It also means that other lesser known chips, such as specialized Ethernet switching chips, would become more powerful. Today we are at a point where chips are becoming capable of performing routing in hardware at wire speeds.

A few years ago, vendors such as 3Com, Ipsilon, and Cabletron started developing technologies to implement routing in hardware. Unfortunately, these first hardware-based Layer 3 switches were not using common routing standards, such as RIP and OSPF, but rather proprietary technologies, such as "route first, switch rest."

These days we are witnessing the emergence of a new generation of Layer 3 switch. Today's Layer 3 switch combines the best of both worlds: It is standards-based (meaning that it uses standards like RIP or OSPF) but also performs the routing function in hardware, as opposed to in software.

Layer 3 switches don't exist as standalone devices. A Layer 2 switch is always sold with the built-in extra feature of Layer 3 switching. As such, you can use a Layer 3 switch as a regular switch or as a backbone or VLAN switch. The Bay Networks 28115 switch could be considered part of the first generation of Layer 3 switches.

Its Layer 3 throughput was comparable to that of a router: 100,000 packets per second. Newer, second-generation Layer 3 switches are capable of throughput rates exceeding a million packets per second because the routing is done entirely in hardware. Today, Cisco, 3Com, Cabletron, Intel, and other vendors offer Layer 3 capabilities in their switch product lines.

The emergence of Layer 3 switches has significantly blurred the line between routers and switches. Layer 3 switches are certainly becoming an alternative to routers in certain places. Table 1.1 provides a comparison of the new Layer 3 switches with classic routers.

TABLE 1.1 COMPARISON OF A CLASSICAL ROUTER AND A NEWER LAYER 3 SWITCH

Feature	Classical Router	Layer 3 Switch
OSI layer function performed	Mostly Layer 3, some Layer 2	Mostly Layer 2, some Layer 3
Routing performed via	Software	Hardware
Performance	Slow to medium	Fast
Price/port	High	Low
Programmability	Extremely high	Little to none
Protocols supported	All	IP, maybe IPX
Application	WAN connection Connection of dissimilar WANs	Collapsed backbone VLAN segmentation

Industry Merger and Acquisition Trends (1993–1999)

1993 started a year of industry consolidation in the data communications industry. Prior to 1993, the industry was pretty fragmented, with each major player being synonymous with just one technology or product line. For example, Cisco and Wellfleet focused on routers; SynOptics and Cabletron were known primarily as chassis hub companies; Hewlett-Packard and 3Com were known for their stackable hubs; and 3Com, SMC, and Intel were battling it out in the NIC market. The mergers and acquisitions of the past six years have changed the face of the networking industry substantially. Let's look at some of the more important mergers and acquisitions of the past few years, and how they have shaped the Ethernet industry lately.

In the early 1990s, networking vendors realized that they had to offer one-stop shopping, not just individual products, in order to remain competitive.

Despite the consolidation among the larger players, today's networking industry is still very much technology-driven, with new companies being founded daily on the premise of a new breakthrough technology. The classic Silicon Valley start-up has one underlying premise: It needs to develop better products and bring them to market faster than the big established players in order to be a viable business. Ultimately, most networking start-ups are also founded with an exit strategy in mind: Develop a technology first, then bring it to market, and ultimately be bought by one of the major players, or go public first, and then be bought out.

Today's one-stop shopping networking giants, on the other hand, have become less innovative, and at times are having a tough time competing with the smaller, nimble Silicon Valley start-ups. Cisco in particular chose a technology acquisition-based strategy, instead of developing the technology in-house. The advantage of this approach is that a major networking vendor can take a wait-and-see approach to a new technology, instead of wasting precious internal research and development resources on developing a potentially risky technology. The downside, of course, is that each vendor will pay a lot more for a proven company and its associated technology than if it had funded the research and development internally.

In the last few, years the number of mergers and acquisitions has increased significantly. In the early1990s "data" companies trying to acquire new technologies, or broadening their product line drove mergers. In the last few years, the convergence of voice and data has led to a new round of mergers and acquisitions.

Let's take a look at how technology acquisitions in particular have affected the major players in today's networking market.

3Com

3Com has always been a big believer in Ethernet and has therefore always focused heavily on internal research and development in Ethernet technology. In 1995, 3Com decided it required some high-end chassis-hub technology to compete better with Cisco, Cabletron, and Bay. The result was that 3Com purchased chassis-hub manufacturer Chipcom for $775 million. At the time, this marked the biggest high-tech acquisition ever. In 1997, the biggest high-tech deal ever was struck when 3Com merged with modem manufacturer US Robotics, the value of the deal being $7.5 billion. Today, the new 3Com provides WAN and LAN technology, from NICs and modems to chassis hubs to routers.

Nortel Networks

Canadian company Nortel, previously known as Northern Telecom, is a major supplier of telephone switching equipment. Nortel bought California-based Bay Networks for $9.1 billion in 1998. The Nortel/Bay Networks acquisitions illustrates the shape of things to come: One-stop shopping for LAN and WAN equipment for both voice and data communication. Nortel explicitly cited Bay Network's Switching and Gigabit Ethernet capabilities as a driving force for the acquisitions.

In 1995 Bay Networks had itself purchased Gigabit Ethernet pioneer Rapid City Communications. Prior to that, Bay Networks itself was created through the merger of Wellfleet and SynOptics, which offered customers both hubs and routers from the same supplier.

Cisco Systems

Cisco has maintained a technology-acquisition approach for several years. Five years ago, Cisco was very skeptical about the long-term future of Ethernet, hedging its bets with a lot of ATM development. Over the last five years, Cisco's Ethernet-related acquisitions have made it a very serious player in the Switched, Fast, and Gigabit Ethernet market:

- In September 1993, Cisco purchased Crescendo, one of the early pioneers of switching and high-speed UTP technology (Crescendo pioneered CDDI, or FDDI over copper).

- In October 1994, Cisco purchased Ethernet switching inventor Kalpana for $203 million.

- In September 1995, Cisco Systems purchased Grand Junction Networks for $348 million. Grand Junction was, of course, the Fast Ethernet company. Among the company's firsts were the first 10Mbps workgroup switch, as well as the first Fast Ethernet NICs, repeaters, and switches.

- In 1996, Cisco acquired Gigabit Ethernet pioneer Granite Systems for $220 million. Granite Systems was founded in 1995 by Andy Bechtolsheim, who previously developed the engineering workstation at Stanford University and then went on to found Sun Microsystems. The interesting part about this acquisition was that Cisco paid $220 million for a pure technology acquisition because Granite had no products shipping at the time!

Cabletron

Cabletron, at one point the same size as archenemy SynOptics, missed the Fast and Switched Ethernet boat altogether, starting a steady drop in the company's market share. In 1995, Cabletron acquired SMC's Ethernet switching division, which finally gave Cabletron an entry into this key market segment. Two years later, Digital Equipment Corporation, trying to focus on its core business of servers and systems, sold its entire networking division to Cabletron. (This was really the beginning of the end for Digital Equipment Corporation. The semiconductor operation went to Intel, and in 1998 Compaq Computer Corporation acquired all of what remained of Digital.) In early 1998, Cabletron acquired Yago Systems, a privately held Gigabit Ethernet and Layer 3 switching start-up.

The Giants of the Networking Industry

Five years ago, Cisco, 3Com, and Bay were considered the three heavyweights of the networking industry, with Cabletron trailing slightly. This picture has changed rapidly over the last few years. Cisco's revenue growth, based on its core router business and its very shrewd technology acquisitions, have made it the dominant force in networking today.

Yet we are seeing the dawn of a new era in the communications world: the arrival of the "500-pound gorillas." Nortel's acquisition of Bay Networks makes the company a formidable competitor in the new world of voice and data. Then there is of course Lucent, with revenues that are three times that of rival Cisco. Lastly, Intel's success depends largely on how much of the company's microprocessor profits the company chooses to invest in networking. Table 1.2 compares the revenue and profits of the four largest networking companies.

TABLE 1.2 ANNUAL REVENUE AND MARKET CAPITALIZATION OF THE LARGEST NETWORKING COMPANIES

	Cabletron	Cisco	Intel	Lucent	Nortel	3Com
Annual Revenue (US $B)[1]	1.4	11	28.2	34.8	18.5	5.8
Market Capitalization (US $B)[2]	2.25	202.9	213	204.3	57.6	9.0

[1] *Trailing twelve months.*
[2] *Data as of July 24, 1999.*

Gigabit Ethernet (1995–1999)

After the concept of a faster version of Ethernet had been developed, a super-fast version of Ethernet was almost a no-brainer. If the frequency of Ethernet could be increased from 10Mbps to 100Mbps, why not 1000Mbps as well?

The ink had barely dried on the IEEE's 802.3u Fast Ethernet standard when a new IEEE task force started looking at an even faster version of Ethernet: Gigabit Ethernet. In November 1995 the IEEE 802.3 standards committee formed a new high-speed study group to investigate running Ethernet at speeds of around one gigabit per second. In January 1996, this group set some objectives. In March 1996, the IEEE formed the new 802.3z working group to investigate and standardize Gigabit Ethernet.

In May 1996, the original proponents of Fast Ethernet, as well as some new start-ups, formed the Gigabit Ethernet Alliance (GEA). The 11 companies were 3Com Corp, Bay Networks, Inc., Cisco Systems, Inc., Compaq Computer Company, Granite Systems, Inc., Intel Corporation, LSI Logic, Packet Engines Inc., Sun Microsystems Computer Company, UB Networks, and VLSI Technology. A month later, another 28 companies, including Hewlett-Packard, joined the alliance. (This was, of course, a radical departure for Hewlett-Packard, who had for over three years insisted that the CSMA/CD protocol was obsolete and that it needed to be replaced by a new protocol called Demand Priority, also known as 100VGAnyLAN.) By September 18, 1996, the first Gigabit Ethernet technology demonstrations were being held at the annual NetWorld+Interop tradeshow in Atlanta.

At this point, we're not quite sure who the inventors of Gigabit Ethernet were. Packet Engines, led by Bernard Daines, one of the founders of Grand Junction Networks, made the first public announcements in September 1995 and hosted the first industry meeting in October 1995. We are sure, however, that numerous people and companies must have been working on the same thing at the same time. Fast Ethernet had set the precedent; it was just a question of who would talk about it first.

During 1997, the IEEE worked on refining the standard. The focus of Gigabit Ethernet was initially switched full-duplex operation over fiber-optic cabling, as opposed to shared-media copper. The reasoning was that Gigabit Ethernet would be used primarily for connecting different backbones or superservers and workstations. Some IEEE members felt, however, that both a copper-based implementation and a shared-media version needed to be included in the new standard. As a result, the IEEE adopted a compromise. The 802.z task force itself would focus on full-duplex switched operation, with fiber as the primary cabling standard. A higher quality copper-based cabling (not UTP, for example) would also be investigated. The Gigabit development focused around Category 5 to the desktop would be spun off as a separate task force, known as 802.3ab. This would ensure that the more complex and time-consuming Category 5 cabling development would not delay the high-speed backbone focus.

Note

The 802.3 committee had to go to 2-letter designations, as it had used up all single letters up to and including the letter z.

Like the IEEE 802.3u Fast Ethernet working group, the 802.3z engineers chose not to reinvent the wheel but borrowed proven technology elsewhere. Fast Ethernet borrowed fiber physical-layer technology from FDDI, the Gigabit cabling standard was derived from a proven technology called Fiber Channel, and Gigabit Ethernet includes a buffered repeater section, which allows for affordable, shared media repeaters to be built.

By late 1997, the 802.3z standard looked pretty complete, with the official ratification date expected to be early 1998. At the last minute, a fiber-optic–based transmission glitch was caught, delaying final ratification by a quarter. In the end, the 802.3z Gigabit Ethernet standard was officially signed off in June 1998, three months later than originally planned. The final specification includes a Gigabit Ethernet CSMA/CD MAC engine, as well as three cabling standards. These are 1000BASE-SX and LX for fiber, as well as 1000BASE-CX for high-quality copper cabling, known as twinax. The 802.3ab task force completed its work on Category 5-based cabling standard June 1999. This is known as 1000BASE-T and utilizes four pairs of Category 5 cabling.

Table 1.3 summarizes the evolution of Ethernet over the past few years.

TABLE 1.3 THE EVOLUTION OF THE ETHERNET STANDARD

Colloquial Ethernet Standard Name	Official Ethernet Standard or abbreviation	IEEE Spec Supplement	Speed (Mbps)
Thick Ethernet (Original Ethernet Specification)	10BASE5	802.3	10
Thin Ethernet or Cheapernet	10BASE2	802.3a	10
Broadband Ethernet	10BROAD36	802.3b	10
10Mbps Repeaters	Repeaters	802.3c	10
Fiberoptic Inter-Repeater Link	FOIRL	802.3d	10
StarLAN	1BASE5	802.3e	1
StarLAN Multipoint Extension	1BASE5	802.3f	1
Layer Management		802.3h	10
Twisted Pair Ethernet	10BASE-T	802.3i	10
Fiber Ethernet	10BASE-F	802.3j	10
Layer Management for 10Mbps Repeaters		802.3k	10
10BASE-T Protocol Implementation Conformance Statement (PICS)	10BASE-T PICS	802.3l	10
2nd Maintenance Ballot		802.3m	10
3rd Maintenance Ballot		802.3n	10
Layer Management for Medium Attachment Units		802.3p	10
Guidelines for the Development of Managed Objects (GDMO)		802.3q	N/A
10BASE5 PICS	10BASE5 PICS	802.3r	10
4th Maintenance Ballot		802.3s	10
120 Ohm cables for 10BASE-T		802.3t	10
Fast Ethernet	100BASE-TX	802.3u	100
	100BASE-T4		
	100BASE-FX		

IEEE Spec Supplement	Year Approved	Topology	Segment Length	Medium Support
802.3	1983	Bus	500	50 Ohm coaxial (thick)
802.3a	1988	Bus	185 or 300	50 Ohm coaxial (thin)
802.3b	1985	Bus	1800	75 Ohm coaxial
802.3c	1987	Bus	N/A	50 Ohm coaxial (thick or thin)
802.3d	1987	Star	1000	optical fiber
802.3e	1987	Star	250	100 Ohm 2-pair Category 3 UTP
802.3f	Disbanded	Star	250	100 Ohm 2-pair Category 3 UTP
802.3h	1990	N/A	N/A	N/A
802.3i	1990	Star	100	100 Ohm 2-pair Category 3
802.3j	1993	Bus or Star	up to 2000	optical fiber
802.3k	1992	N/A	N/A	N/A
802.3l	1992	Star	2000	multimode or singlemode fiber
802.3m	1995	N/A	N/A	N/A
802.3n	1995	N/A	N/A	N/A
802.3p	1993	N/A	N/A	N/A
802.3q	N/A	N/A	N/A	N/A
802.3r	1996	N/A	N/A	N/A
802.3s	1995	N/A	N/A	N/A
802.3t	1995	N/A	100	120 Ohm 2-pair Category 3 UTP
802.3u	1995	Star	100	100 Ohm 2-pair Category 5 UTP
			100	100 Ohm 4-pair Category 3 UTP
			2000	Optical fiber

TABLE 1.3 CONTINUED

Colloquial Ethernet Standard Name	Official Ethernet Standard or abbreviation	IEEE Spec Supplement	Speed (Mbps)
150 Ohm cables for 10BASE-T		802.3v	10
Enhanced MAC or Binary Logarithmic Arbitration Method	BLAM	802.3w	N/A
Full-duplex/Flow-control	FDX	802.3x	100
Fast Ethernet over 2-pair Category 3	100BASE-T2	802.3y	100
Gigabit Ethernet	1000BASE-SX 1000BASE-LX 1000BASE-CX	802.3z	1000
5th Maintenance Ballot	100BASE-T	802.3aa	100
Gigabit Ethernet for Cat5 UTP	1000BASE-T	802.3ab	1000
VLAN frame extension	VLAN	802.3ac	N/A
Trunking	Link Aggregation	802.3ad	N/A
VLAN Tagging	VLAN Tagging	802.1Q	N/A
Traffic Expediting	Priority Switching	802.1p	N/A
MAC Bridges, includes Spanning Tree Algorithm	MAC Bridges	802.1D	N/A

IEEE Spec Supplement	Year Approved	Topology	Segment Length	Medium Support
802.3v	1995	N/A	100	150 Ohm 2-pair Category 3 UTP
802.3w	Disbanded	N/A	N/A	N/A
802.3x	1997	N/A	N/A	N/A
802.3y	1997	N/A	100	100 Ohm 2-pair Category 3 UTP
802.3z	1998	Star	300 550 3000 25	multimode fiber multimode fiber singlemode fiber twinax 150 Ohm copper cable
802.3aa	In progress	Star	N/A	N/A
802.3ab	1999	N/A	100	100 Ohm 4-pair Category 5 or better UTP
802.3ac	1998	N/A	N/A	N/A
802.3ad	1998	N/A	N/A	N/A
802.1Q	1998	N/A	N/A	N/A
802.1p	1998	N/A	N/A	N/A
802.1D	revised in 1998	N/A	N/A	N/A

Figure 1.5 is a graphical timeline illustrating the major milestones in the first 25 years of Ethernet.

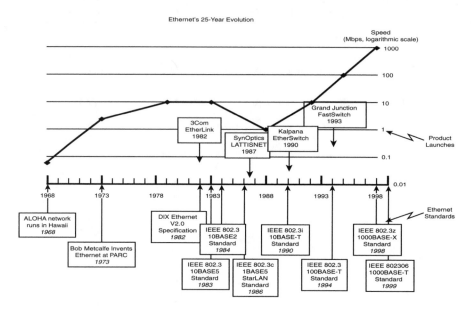

FIGURE 1.5 *Ethernet is 25 years old.*

Summary

Ethernet is 25 years old and more popular than ever. Proven, backward-compatible Ethernet frames, combined with Ethernet Switching technology seem to offer the best of both worlds. Ethernet Switching and Gigabit Ethernet have already built up significant market momentum. It is clear that Ethernet will continue to reinvent itself and remain the data communications standard for at least another decade.

PART II

Repeating, Bridging, Switching, and Layer 3 Switching

CHAPTER 2

An Overview of High-Speed
LAN Technologies

As we write this book—and in particular this chapter—we are making certain assumptions about you, the reader. We assume you are using 10Mbps Ethernet as a LAN technology. Because Ethernet is approaching 90% market share today, we think that's a safe assumption. If you aren't using Ethernet today, you are probably considering it; otherwise, you wouldn't have bought this book. We also assume you want to migrate to a higher-speed LAN technology at some point because whatever you are using today is running out or has run out of bandwidth. Obviously, one of the higher-speed Ethernet derivatives is on your shopping list, which may be why you bought this book. Therefore, the big question is this: Which LAN technology is the right choice? As a LAN manager today, you essentially face two choices for high-speed technologies and standards: Ethernet or Asynchronous Transfer Mode (ATM). That hasn't always been the case. As recently as three years ago, about half a dozen different high-speed contenders were vying for a share of the high-speed networking hardware market.

This chapter provides a broad overview of high-speed LAN technologies, past and present. The discussion focuses primarily on a comparison between ATM and Ethernet. In the end, we hope to convince you that Ethernet is the only choice.

This chapter is divided into three sections. Because choosing the right high-speed technology to migrate to is a strategic decision that requires careful consideration, the first section of this chapter discusses the different selection criteria an Ethernet LAN manager needs to think about when selecting his or her next-generation high-speed LAN standard.

The second section discusses the different high-speed technologies that have at one point or another attempted to compete with Ethernet: FDDI, TCNS, Iso-Ethernet, 100VG-AnyLAN, Fibre Channel, and HIPPI. Although you might consider some of this material redundant, proponents of some of these technologies positioned them as being viable alternatives to Ethernet as recently as three years ago. We can learn some valuable lessons by considering why none of these technologies have been commercially successful.

The third section of this chapter contrasts Ethernet with ATM (the only two viable contenders today). In this section, we also discuss why we think Ethernet is the smart choice for local area networking hardware.

We wrote this book from the perspective of an Ethernet user. Because we do realize that about 10% of all networks still use Token Ring, we have included a short section for Token Ring LAN managers at the end of this chapter, including some discussion of Switched and High-Speed Token Ring.

A Historical and Somewhat-Biased Perspective

This chapter briefly contrasts several high-speed technologies. Some of these technologies, such as Iso-Ethernet, never even made it off the drawing board, some did and have since disappeared, and some are still shipping but are in a state of decline. The notable exception is, of course, ATM. This chapter covers ATM in detail.

A review of the three editions of this book helps illustrate how the high-speed networking landscape has changed over the past five years. You will find a strong element of "we told you so" in this chapter—only because we have been advocating the superiority of Ethernet for many years, and will continue to do so. This third edition is no exception. Now we have the benefit of hindsight, having seen various competitors come and go. We also aren't going to pretend that we are offering you an unbiased view of technology. Some authors or journalists may pretend to offer you "just the facts," but even facts often contain a huge element of bias you may not recognize as such. We would never reprint the results of a reputable market research firm that concluded that ATM would outship Ethernet in 1999, for example. These might be considered facts, but we choose to find "our own set of facts" instead: a market research report that concluded the opposite. You would be impressed with our data, of course, and would never know that some study out there had concluded the exact opposite!

When we wrote the first edition of this book in 1995, Fast Ethernet was just being introduced. In that edition, we extensively debated the pros and cons of 100BASE-T versus 100VG-AnyLAN, the competing proposal from Hewlett-Packard. Well, 100VG-AnyLAN has come and gone. At the time, most people used the term *coexistence*, with 100BASE-T taking a slightly larger market share. We didn't buy into the coexistence theory because people migrate to a single standard. Our favorite article on 100VG-AnyLAN was one titled "100VG-NowhereLAN," which was written by Kevin Tolly and printed in the November 1994 issue of *Data Communications*.

For our second edition, published in 1996, our publisher asked us to include a chapter on ATM. Readers of our first edition told us likewise. That's because in 1996, ATM was being hyped as the be-all and end-all of networking technologies. We didn't quite see it that way, but in the interest of constant improvement, we agreed, albeit reluctantly, to include a chapter on ATM integration.

For this third edition, we have become Ethernet purists again. The ATM integration chapter has been cut. Instead, we have included two new chapters on Ethernet Layer 2 and 3 switching, as well as Gigabit Ethernet. Looking back, this microcosm trend within the context of our book also represents what has happened out there in the real world. For a few years, ATM was on the rise, but with the advent of Gigabit Ethernet and numerous other Ethernet innovations, ATM seems to be very much on the defensive. Just to put things in absolute numbers: The installed base of Ethernet nodes is now around 200 million, whereas the installed base of ATM is less than a million. That's a 200:1 ratio.

Migration Issues

Imagine that you are the network manager for a LAN that is running out of bandwidth and want to migrate or move your users, servers, and peripherals to a higher-speed network. Unfortunately, the number of competing high-speed technologies has created a lot of confusion in the marketplace. Some of these technologies are complementary, whereas others clearly compete with each other. This section outlines the most important issues you should consider before deciding on a particular high-speed technology. We assume in this chapter that you are running an Ethernet LAN, probably shared. That's a safe assumption, considering that well over 80% of all installations are Ethernet-based. (The balance includes Token Ring, FDDI, and ATM, with Token Ring accounting for the lion's share.)

When making your migration decision, you should consider several factors, including connection cost, performance, quality of service, ease of migration, your understanding of the technology, scalability, multivendor support, and standards. The following sections discuss these factors one at a time. After that, the discussion focuses on the capabilities of Ethernet and ATM with respect to these factors.

Connection Costs

The cost of a new LAN technology should be measured in terms of *connection costs*, which include the cost of the client or server NIC as well as the workgroup hub or switch port on the other end of the wire. You also need to factor into this calculation the cost of new network management software or any other additional hardware, such as backbone switches or routers, that need to be purchased.

Performance Considerations

Because you are reading a book about high-speed Ethernet options, performance is probably your number-one concern. Different vendors measure and promote their products' performance in various ways. Here are a few thoughts on what to look for in the small print:

- *Wire speed and data throughput rate*—You can measure performance in data networks in different ways. The *wire speed* is the maximum theoretical bit transmission rate for the network, inclusive of any overhead. For shared Ethernet, the wire speed is 10Mbps only after a node gets access to the network. The term *wire speed* is used because it implies the number of bits on the wire, regardless of the kind of bits, data, or overhead. The data throughput rate is always much lower, depending on such things as access method and protocol efficiency, whether it's a shared or switched connection, and whether it's half-duplex or full-duplex transmission.

- *Shared bandwidth*—Most of today's Ethernet networks share the total available bandwidth among many users, and the average data throughput rate available to each user is significantly less than the wire speed. One way to calculate average data throughput would be to take the wire speed number and divide it by the number of stations that share the network. A fully loaded Ethernet segment that has 200 users contending for the same 10Mbps channel delivers only 10Mbps/200 = 0.05Mbps of average throughput per station. This of course assumes that all stations generate the same amount of traffic all the time. The reality is that most of today's data traffic is very uneven or bursty at all times.

- *Dedicated bandwidth*—Some LAN technologies do not use a shared-media approach, and in such cases the available bandwidth can actually approach the wire speed. Switched Ethernet provides for a dedicated connection without sharing the bandwidth with other users, so the available bandwidth is close to the wire speed.

- *Utilization*—Utilization is defined as how much of the theoretical available bandwidth is being used up. Shared Ethernet uses the carrier sense media access with collision detection (CSMA/CD) access method. CSMA/CD works extremely well with smaller numbers of users, large frames, and light traffic; with an increasing number of users and heavy traffic, however, collisions become a limitation. As a result, the utilization rate of a large shared Ethernet network has to be significantly less than 100%. Only in a point-to-point or Switched Ethernet environment does the actual throughput rate come close to the wire speed because a switched network in essence contains only two nodes and minimizes collisions.

- *Inherent frame or cell inefficiencies*—All networking transport methods require some kind of overhead, reducing efficiency to less than 100%. That's because such things as the address and error checking are sent over the wire but don't represent actual data. Ethernet efficiency varies widely, for example, depending on the frame size, from 40% for small frames to as high as 98% for maximum frame size. ATM efficiency is 90% at all times. Note that this efficiency refers to the data within the packet or frame and does not include efficiency calculations that result from different access methods.

- *Full-duplex (FDX) throughput*—*Full-duplex* means that data can be simultaneously transmitted and received, effectively doubling the nominal wire speed. Full-duplex is a relatively new phenomenon for data networks, having been made possible by twisted pair or fiber cabling, where one media pair can send while the second pair is receiving data. Coaxial cable, on the other hand, uses one single wire for either transmitting or receiving, and hence cannot accommodate full-duplex traffic. Note that full-duplex works only in a switched or point-to-point environment where both stations can support this capability.

Many Ethernet vendors now advertise FDX as a feature and claim 20 or 200Mbps throughput. Switch-to-switch connections operating in full-duplex mode can yield this 100% improvement, but a full-duplex server or desktop connection will show hardly any improvement at all. The reason full-duplex shows marginal gains over half-duplex in these environments is that today's data flow is very lopsided. Applications such as Internet access are typically 90% downloads and 10% uploads, for example. For these applications, full-duplex merely adds a performance improvement of a few percent. Many networking protocols also cannot take full advantage of bidirectional simultaneous traffic flows.

The bottom line is that wire speed does not tell the entire performance story. The type of access method used and its efficiency are equally important considerations. A switched 100Mbps full-duplex Ethernet connection using 1.5KB frames, for example, will have a data throughput rate of 100Mbps $\times$ 2 $\times$ 98%, or 196Mbps. We cover this topic in more detail in Chapter 7, "Bandwidth: How Much Is Enough?"

Quality of Service

Quality of service (*QoS*) is a relatively new buzzword in the LAN industry, but has been in existence in the telecommunications industry for quite some time. QoS means that the recipient of the data gets the data *when* and *where* he or she needs it. Telephone companies measure QoS in terms of delay time or latency, signal-to-noise ratio, echo, wrong numbers dialed, and so on. QoS never used to be important for data networks, and with today's networked applications it is mostly not an issue. Take a very busy Ethernet network as an example, where a user is trying to send email over the network. The sender attempts to transmit his or her data stream right away but cannot because the LAN is busy. At some point, a time slot becomes available on the wire, and the transmission occurs. This process is transparent to the receiver, who doesn't care or know that the email message arrived a fraction of a second later.

QoS is becoming more important because today's data networks are increasingly utilized for time-critical applications, such as real-time voice and video transmissions. Latencies are acceptable for time-critical applications as long as they are relatively small and constant. A voice transmission with a constant delay of 0.1 second from sender to receiver will not be noticed, for example. Longer latencies could become an issue. Variable delays are a real problem for multimedia data transmissions. A changing latency is not acceptable because it will make audio transmissions sound like a tape recorder whose speed is varying, which is a sign of bad quality. Video transmissions are also particularly sensitive to variable latencies because jumpy picture quality, known as *jitter*, will result.

Another important part of QoS is congestion control. What happens if the network is very busy or overloaded? Is the data still guaranteed to arrive, will the sender be told to wait until bandwidth becomes available, or will the message be discarded? Guaranteed availability of a minimum amount of bandwidth is a key ingredient of QoS.

In general, dedicated connections provide the best QoS, allowing for guaranteed bandwidth at all times and constant latency. All shared-media technologies inherently exhibit variable delay times because the transmission channel is shared with other users.

Ease of Migration

Ease of migration is probably the most important consideration in determining the best technology for upgrade. If you are building a new network from scratch, this section doesn't apply to you. If you already have a network that you are growing or that needs a performance boost, however, this section is probably the most important point to consider.

You need to leverage your existing investment as much as possible. This investment includes the hardware itself, but also the tools, and your knowledge of the technology itself.

To ensure an easy migration, ask yourself these five questions:

- *Can my cabling plant support the higher-speed networking technology?*

  Before you decide to purchase high-speed networking hardware, make sure you understand the capabilities of your existing cabling plant. Your investment in cable, conduits, wiring closets, and patch panels can exceed the cost of the networking hardware itself! You need to make sure your new high-speed networking gear can run on your existing wiring wherever possible. If that's not the case, factor in potentially huge additional costs for upgrading your cabling plant to accommodate the new LAN standard.

- *How do I boost performance of my existing clients and servers with minimum cost and disruption to my users?*

  Most LAN managers will want to keep as much of their existing equipment as possible because it's working, proven, and already paid for. Replacing equipment is always disruptive and time-consuming and should be avoided wherever possible. Replacing network adapters should be avoided at all cost, for example; whereas the price of a new NIC alone may not seem that high, the cost of installation, configuration, and associated user disruption often exceeds the cost of the NIC itself. If redesigning your network and replacing a single strategic hub instead can increase the performance of the network, choose that way.

  You should avoid replacing equipment prematurely. Networking gear is part of a company's capital budget, meaning that the equipment needs to last for a period of five years before it is, in effect, paid for. Your accountants will tell you that replacing equipment before the five-year depreciation period is over can be prohibitively expensive because the equipment needs to be depreciated in one go for those purposes, which is a costly undertaking.

- *How do I connect new users or servers to the new network infrastructure?*

When you add new users to your network, choose the best equipment available at the time. These new users will likely have faster machines, requiring a higher-speed network connection. Make sure the new technology scales to accommodate faster user and server connections.

- *How do I join a new section of my network with an older part?*

New sections of your network will need to be seamlessly connected to your existing network. Think about how you are going to integrate the old and new sections. If you need to purchase additional hardware or software equipment, this will affect your overall cost. User disruption or server downtime should be minimized, if possible. Don't forget network management: Make sure your new networking gear can blend seamlessly into your existing network management map.

- *What happens to the replaced equipment? Can I use it somewhere else in my LAN?*

Another point to consider when upgrading to a new high-speed LAN is what to do with the old equipment. Often, new high-speed equipment is added one step at a time, replacing at least some existing equipment. Your cost analysis needs to reflect whether the replaced equipment can be used somewhere else or whether it becomes obsolete.

Understanding the Technology

Your technical understanding of a new technology needs to be a key part of deciding which hardware technology to migrate. If you buy something completely new, you and your network/IT staff will need to learn about the new technology before you can deploy it. A steep learning curve will accompany a new technology, and years of familiarity will have to be relearned.

Maintaining a new technology presents its own set of challenges, too. You will need to buy and learn new network management and troubleshooting tricks and tools. Some people say that today's investment in IT is 20% hardware and software and 80% worker knowledge on how to use this hardware. Therefore, although it may sometimes seem to pay to buy something completely new, make sure the benefits outweigh the hidden costs.

Scalability

Your technology should grow as your network continues to grow. Can you upgrade one more step or are you buying a technology that has reached its limits? Does your network design lend itself to further upgrades? Scalability, for example, can mean that the technology can support a higher speed, that you can upgrade from a shared-media environment to a faster point-to-point or switched environment, or that you can add different hubs somewhere on your network to improve the overall throughput capability.

Multivendor Support

Make sure as many vendors as possible support whatever you buy. The following are some reasons why you should buy products manufactured by multiple vendors:

- *Lower prices*—Multivendor support means you have choices, and the more choices you have, the better. Multiple vendors are likely to compete more aggressively, ensuring lower prices for you. An early lead in terms of market share can turn into a formidable lead for a particular technology. Lower prices early on will drive up the volume of goods sold. This in turn will lead to economies of scale for a technology. Economies of scale occur in the high-tech manufacturing industry when the volume of goods consumed causes significant reductions in the associated cost. In this case, the cost of manufacturing hubs, switches, routers, and NICs will decrease significantly as the volume of product manufactured increases. That's why first-to-market products and standards often become so firmly entrenched in the market: They develop an early market share lead, prices decline, sales then skyrocket, and the lead widens even more. Sometimes nothing but a technological breakthrough can ever compete again.

- *Innovation*—Choice means that your particular supplier needs to work harder to earn your dollars. Innovation is just as important as lower prices because it ensures that future products will provide more features, higher performance, and other improvements that will benefit you in the long run. The more vendors that support a technology, the more innovation there will be, as competitors need to innovate to differentiate their products.

- *Availability of the necessary building blocks*—Today's network consists of many building blocks—chassis or stackable hubs and switches, bridges, routers, desktop, server and notebook NICs, MAUs, management software, and so on. No single vendor can supply all the building blocks, no matter what they tell you. Choosing technologies with broad vendor support means that you can buy all the building blocks you need for your network, not just some or most of them.

Standards

Most LAN hardware sold adheres to some industry standard, yet the quality standards vary. A *good* standard means that hardware vendors can build equipment that is truly interoperable. *Interoperable* means you can buy two pieces of hardware from two different vendors, you can connect the two devices together, and they will work without fine-tuning or detailed configuration work. To accomplish that, the standards documents must be clear, unambiguous, and, above all, leave little open to interpretation. A standard, however, needs to be open enough to enable vendors to add their own features to differentiate their products. In addition, a good standard needs to be respected, or *authoritative*. This means that vendors building products will actually go to the trouble of obtaining and understanding the standards documents and specifications before building products. Overall, writing good standards takes experience and requires a good sense of balance.

An Ethernet Primer

We need to recap Ethernet for you briefly to compare Ethernet to the other high-speed LAN choices discussed in this chapter. Let's take a look at the inner workings of Ethernet, as well as its current market position:

- *Frame-based*—Ethernet is a frame-based LAN standard that was designed as a data transmission technology 25 years ago. With the exception of ATM, all LAN technologies use frames. Frames are per definition of variable length. In the case of Ethernet, the frame size varies from 64 to 1522 bytes.

- *Speed*—Ethernet was conceived as a 10Mbps shared media LAN technology, but has been modified over the past five years to run at 100Mbps and 1Gbps as well. A 10Gbps version seems inevitable.

- *Market share*—Ethernet is the most widely used LAN standard, with an installed base that now exceeds more than 80% of the installed base. New Ethernet shipments are approaching 90% market share, meaning that the dominance of Ethernet is still increasing. The market share growth of Ethernet is coming at the expense of such technologies as Token Ring,

FDDI, 100VG-AnyLAN, and older technologies, such as TCNS and ArcNET. To put things in perspective: Ethernet has an installed base of almost 200 million nodes. FDDI, ATM, and 100VG-AnyLAN each have an installed base of just several hundred thousand nodes, or about 0.1% of that of Ethernet. The only other LAN standard with a significant market share is Token Ring, which accounts for about 1 in 10 nodes.

Ethernet has reached a stage where it is becoming ubiquitous. Many new PCs now ship with a 10/100Mbps Ethernet built in. In 1997, 13 million PCs, or about 20%, included the familiar 10/100Mbps RJ-45 connector next to the serial and parallel port.

Figures 2.1 and 2.2 show 1997 data for both Ethernet switch port and NIC sales. Shared-media hubs still account for about 50% of all port shipments, although this number is declining rapidly as switch prices decline. Because ATM is only a switching technology, shared media hub sales are not shown.

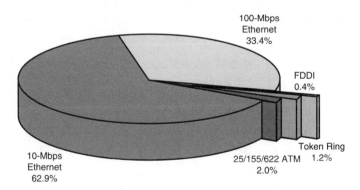

1997 Switch Port Shipments
Total 23 Million Ports
Source: IDC, June 1998

FIGURE 2.1   *Actual 1997 switch port shipments, according to International Data Corporation (IDC). Ethernet switch ports accounted for 96.3%, whereas ATM accounted for only 2%. Total port shipments were 23 million units, which excludes another 20 million or so shared-media port shipments.*

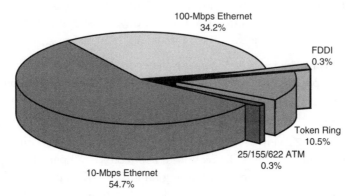

1997 NIC Shipments
Total 44 Million Units
Source: IDC, June 1998

100-Mbps Ethernet
34.2%

FDDI
0.3%

Token Ring
10.5%

25/155/622 ATM
0.3%

10-Mbps Ethernet
54.7%

FIGURE 2.2   *According to IDC, 44 million NICs were sold in 1997. Note that ATM accounted for a mere 0.3% of all NIC shipments, whereas 10Mbps and 10Mbps/100Mbps Ethernet NICs made up almost 90%.*

- *Standard*—Since 1980, the IEEE 802.3 committee has been setting Ethernet standards. In the past few years in particular, the IEEE has been very active with improving Ethernet. As a result, six major addenda have been published in the past five years.

- *Pricing*—Today, a single 10Mbps shared Ethernet connection costs as little as $50 (for a NIC and a hub). Compare that to the cost of the original 3Com EtherLink NIC 15 years ago: It cost $1,000 back then! A move to 100Mbps or a switched 10Mbps connection costs about twice as much. Gigabit Ethernet connection cost is still relatively high, around $2,000 per node. In terms of cost per Mbps, Ethernet is by far the cheapest LAN standard out there.

- *Vendor support*—Every local area networking vendor in the business supports Ethernet. That means lower prices, choices, and the availability of all the necessary building blocks.

- *Shared, Switched, and Full-Duplex Ethernet*—Ethernet was originally designed as a shared-media technology in which multiple nodes share the same bandwidth. In this configuration, the CSMA/CD MAC is operative and controls all data transmissions. Over the past few years, Ethernet switching has emerged whereby only two nodes reside on one single Ethernet. All three Ethernet speed versions can be switched—that is, operated in a point-to-point method. In addition, multiple switched Ethernet connections can now be connected in parallel to increase the overall throughput (called Link Aggregation). Ethernet is relatively simple and, because of its huge installed base, is well understood and documented.

- *Works with IP*—All data transmissions use the OSI Reference Model, which is covered in more detail in Chapter 3, "Ethernet, Fast Ethernet, and Gigabit Ethernet Standards." Ethernet operates at Layer 2 and works extremely well with all Layer 3 software, including the Internet Protocol (IP).

Ethernet does have some disadvantages as well. Ethernet has been designed as a data transmission technology, as opposed to real-time voice technology. This means that Ethernet does not have any built-in quality-of- or class-of-service guarantees. Recent efforts, such as the IEEE 802.1p and IETF RSVP standards, will improve Ethernet's capabilities in this respect, but true QoS will remain elusive.

Note

In this chapter only, we refer to the different 10Mbps, 100Mbps, 1000Mbps Shared and Switched Ethernet options collectively as Ethernet.

Pricing in this chapter refers to late 1998 data.

Revolutionary Versus Evolutionary Technologies

Today, the computer and communications industry experiences essentially two types of technological innovations. *Evolutionary* innovations build on the installed base and provide some migration path. The innovation typically occurs in smaller steps. The PC industry as we know it is built on evolutionary progress. Windows was designed to run on top of DOS, not in its place, so that people could still run their existing DOS applications. Likewise, Windows NT/95/98 all run the huge collection of existing DOS and Windows applications. All Intel microprocessors are backward compatible (the "X86 family"), yet each new generation adds some additional features.

Revolutionary technology, on the other hand, implies a really radical breakthrough of some kind. This typically requires the forklift upgrade, which means scrapping the installed base of product. With revolutionary technologies, the benefit of moving to the technology must clearly outweigh the costs of making obsolete the existing technology. A fairly recent example of a revolutionary technology is the compact disc, which made the vinyl record obsolete.

As our society has become more technologically oriented, revolutionary technologies have become few and far between. That's because the installed base has become so large that the cost of obsolescence for a large installed base has become insurmountable.

> **Note**
>
> *In the networking industry, the term* forklift upgrade *often describes the concept of wholesale replacement of one technology by another. The term is derived from the concept of ripping or lifting out all the existing equipment, carting it away, and then bringing in truckloads of new equipment.*

An example of a failed revolutionary product is the video laser disc. The laser disc used a completely new size disc, which meant purchasing a new player as well as new media. There was no backward-compatibility with anything. Whereas laser discs offered superb video and audio quality, that wasn't enough to cause everyone to throw away their VHS players and cassette collections and buy an expensive laser disc player instead. The inventors of DVD players chose a different path: DVD offers laser disc-type quality, yet is backward compatible with today's audio and data CD formats. The success of DVD as the replacement of today's audio CD players, laser discs, VHS players, and CD-ROMs is almost guaranteed.

The Most Common High-Speed Technologies Compared

This section compares yesterday's and today's high-speed technologies and discusses their strengths and weaknesses and current market positions. We use the previously discussed migration issues to guide us through this analysis. We look at FDDI, 100VG-AnyLAN, TCNS, Fibre Channel, HIPPI, and Iso-Ethernet. Many of these technologies have tried to compete head-on with Ethernet and have fallen by the wayside. Other technologies focused on specialized niche areas, however, and are still in production but with negligible overall market share.

We have dedicated an entire separate section to ATM, which is the only viable alternative to Ethernet at this point.

FDDI

Mainframe companies, such as Sperry, Burroughs, and Control Data Corporation, first developed Fiber Distributed Data Interface (FDDI) more than 10 years ago. Standardized by the ANSI X3T9.5 committee in 1990, FDDI incorporates many features of IBM's Token Ring technology, such as the Token Ring frame format and shared-media ring architecture. FDDI also has sophisticated management, control, and reliability features not found in classic Ethernet or

Token Ring. An optional second counter-rotating network ring improves overall reliability, for example. FDDI supports cable lengths of up to 2km for multimode fiber. FDDI products first appeared in 1988. For many years, it was the only viable high-speed backbone technology available.

FDDI was created at a time when scientists and engineers were still predicting that fiber cabling would reach every office and home by the year 2000. One of the inventors of FDDI claims that he chose a 100Mbps data rate to make FDDI so fast that no copper-based LAN technology would ever be able to match its speed.

> **Note**
>
> *The choice of making FDDI run at 100Mbps so that no copper-based LAN would ever be able to match its speed seems pretty ironic these days. A few years after FDDI was introduced, the UTP-based CDDI technology was introduced. More ironic still is the fact that we are now talking about Gigabit Ethernet over UTP.*
>
> *Historically, ANSI was always the standards authority for high-speed data transmission technologies, high-speed being 100Mbps. The IEEE, on the other hand, focused on the slower LAN standards, such as Ethernet and Token Ring. Of course, this has changed with Fast and Gigabit Ethernet.*

Over the past 10 years, twisted-pair wiring and structured cabling systems rapidly replaced coaxial cable as the most popular LAN media, preventing fiber cabling from becoming widely accepted. In addition, engineers figured out a way to run FDDI over twisted-pair wiring. This technology is called *TP-PMD*, short for *twisted-pair physical media dependent*. The ANSI TP-PMD standard uses a transmission scheme called *MLT-3*, short for *Multilevel Transmission 3*. The standard requires two pairs of Category 5 data-grade wire and supports a maximum distance of 100 meters. Crescendo Communications, now part of Cisco, pioneered this technology and called it *CDDI*, short for *Copper Distributed Data Interface*.

Strengths of FDDI/CDDI are as follows:

- FDDI delivers 100Mbps throughput capability with little overhead. It is a shared-media technology; unlike Ethernet, FDDI does not use a collision-based access method, so there is no performance degradation at high usage rates. This allows utilization rates of 80 to 90%, translating to close to 80 to 90Mbps data throughput.

- The FDDI standard was in the making for almost 10 years. Products have been shipping for more than about 10 years as well. The technology is proven, mature, and well understood.

- At its peak, FDDI had broad multivendor support. All the major networking suppliers, including Cisco, Bay Networks, 3Com, and Cabletron, offer FDDI products. FDDI chipsets from Motorola, AMD, and National Semiconductor provide a source of semiconductor building blocks to the networking industry.

- The second counter rotating network ring provides an element of redundancy to FDDI networks. Should one ring go down, dual attached stations (DAS) can continue communicating over the second ring.

The weaknesses of FDDI/CDDI are the following:

- FDDI is too expensive to compete effectively with Ethernet or even Fast Ethernet. To this day, FDDI and CDDI prices are many times higher than Fast Ethernet's prices.

- Upgrading from Ethernet to FDDI is difficult and expensive because FDDI uses a different frame format—meaning that complex and expensive routers are required.

- Many people view FDDI as a high-performance technology that is expensive and only suitable for backbones. This perception always makes customers leery of buying FDDI for anything other than a backbone technology.

FDDI-II, an improved version of the proven FDDI standard, was supposed to offer improved support for multimedia data transmissions. It offered isochronous data transmission, which means predictable and guaranteed access time. In addition, the FDDI-II proposal included a prioritization scheme to ensure low latency, which is important for video transmission in particular. The ANSI X3 committee set some FDDI-II standards from 1994 to 1997. The vendor community decided to focus on Fast Ethernet, however, and no FDDI II-compatible products ever made it to market (as far as we know).

> **Note**
>
> *What exactly is isochronous data? Isochronous data technologies can accept data at specified and guaranteed intervals. Isochronous data transmission provides what ATM calls a constant bit rate (CBR) service. This capability is important for voice and video transmission, where no interruptions or delays in the traffic flow can be tolerated without degrading the quality of service.*
>
> *Integrated Services Digital Network (ISDN), Iso-Ethernet, FDDI-II, Fibre Channel, and ATM all contain isochronous data-carrying capabilities. Ethernet, on the other hand, does not. Ethernet provides for asynchronous data transfer, which means the data is transferred in a best-effort manner.*

When working on a Fast Ethernet standard, the IEEE Fast Ethernet engineers chose to use the existing and proven FDDI and CDDI physical layer technologies. The Fast Ethernet equivalents became the 100BASE-FX and 100BASE-TX standards.

Until Fast Ethernet and ATM appeared on the market in the mid-1990s, FDDI was the only high-speed LAN standard to deliver true 100Mbps performance. As a result, many users, resellers, and manufacturers used FDDI as a backbone technology. FDDI sales grew steadily from 1988 until about 1996, at which point Fast Ethernet and ATM became the de facto standards for new backbone installations. Many manufacturers continue to support FDDI, but the technology is clearly in a state of decline, with no new products being designed. Current sales support existing installations only.

TCNS and 100VG-AnyLAN

TCNS and 100VG-AnyLAN were both market failures, despite the fact that they both delivered true 100Mbps performance at reasonable prices. We mention TCNS and 100VG here because they provide two examples that failed the upgrade test.

TCNS was a proprietary 100Mbps solution developed by Thomas-Conrad in Austin, Texas in the early 1990s. (Compaq Computer purchased Thomas-Conrad in 1995). TCNS stands for Thomas-Conrad Networking System and is based on the ANSI ArcNET 878.1 specification. The technology uses a token-passing bus access method and operates in a shared-media mode. It supports fiber cable of 900 meters, coaxial cable of 150 meters, and STP or UTP of 100 meters. Thomas-Conrad started shipping TCNS NICs and hubs in 1990, and in 1993 more than 20,000 TCNS NICs were sold, representing a significant share of the high-speed NIC market at the time. No other vendor ever built TCNS-compatible equipment.

100VG-AnyLAN is a 100Mbps shared-media technology jointly developed by Hewlett-Packard and AT&T's Microelectronics (now Lucent) from 1991 to 1994. 100VG incorporates an access method protocol called *demand priority*, which allows time-critical applications to transmit ahead of other noncritical packets. The IEEE standardized 100VG-AnyLAN is the new 802.12 standard. But Hewlett-Packard unsuccessfully positioned 100VG as its own version of Fast Ethernet. 100VG products first appeared in 1994.

TCNS and 100VG failed for two reasons:

- *Multivendor support is critical to the survival of any technology*—TCNS was a proprietary technology from the beginning, and Thomas-Conrad was the only vendor selling TCNS equipment. Whereas 100VG is nominally an industry standard, all major industry players backed the competing 802.3u Fast Ethernet proposal, leaving Hewlett-Packard as the only major vendor promoting 100VG. This effectively made both technologies proprietary, which had numerous drawbacks. Customers buying single-vendor products put themselves at significant risk because no single vendor can or wants to provide all possible building blocks of a complete network.

- *Customers want evolutionary technologies; they don't want to replace everything they own today*—TCNS and 100VG also failed in this area because there was no easy upgrade path from shared Ethernet to either 100Mbps technology. TCNS deployment requires that both NICs and hubs be replaced altogether. This was expensive and time consuming. Whereas Hewlett-Packard is still selling 10/100VG NICs, the lack of 10/100Mbps hubs or switches made seamless migration very difficult.

Technically, nothing is wrong with either TCNS or 100VG. But faced with stiff and growing competition from both Fast and Switched Ethernet offered by literally hundreds of networking vendors both small and large, both TCNS and 100VG were doomed to fail. TCNS is no longer in production. 100VG is still in production to serve a niche market consisting of the Hewlett-Packard installed base.

Note

In some ways, 100VG was designed to provide the best of both worlds. It was supposed to provide backward compatibility with both Ethernet and Token Ring. 100VG can use either Ethernet or Token Ring frame formats, supposedly allowing for easy migration from either technology. In addition, Hewlett-Packard engineers changed the Ethernet MAC to improve the utilization and multimedia capabilities. As recently as two years ago, people still thought that 100VG might become a viable alternative to 100BASE-T. Why then did 100VG fail? There were several reasons:

- Hewlett-Packard lost the first round when the IEEE decided that 100VG was not Ethernet and that a newly formed IEEE 802.12 committee would be put in charge of standardizing 100VG. This made it clear to the industry and customers that 100VG was not Ethernet. The demand priority MAC from Hewlett-Packard was technically more elegant than the Ethernet CSMA/CD MAC. Over the years, however, dozens of attempts have been made to improve the Ethernet MAC algorithm. People lost interest in 100VG because it was called something other than Ethernet.

- Hewlett-Packard ignored the fact that one medium-size networking vendor cannot change the world on its own. While Hewlett-Packard was promoting 100VG, the networking giants (Cisco, 3Com, and Bay, as well as dozens of other medium and small vendors) were backing Fast Ethernet.

continues

- *The standard Ethernet MAC is already on its way out. Ethernet switching effectively replaces the CSMA/CD algorithm with simultaneous transmission and reception of frames.*

- *The Ethernet camp reused many different building blocks, including the proven 10Mbps MAC and the FDDI physical layer. This meant that semiconductor and passive components were readily available and cheap. Hewlett-Packard chose to reinvent practically everything from the ground up. 100VG, on the other hand, had little support from the semiconductor community, and therefore VG was more expensive to produce.*

In early 1996, Hewlett-Packard's networking division announced plans to support 100BASE-T as well. The company went to great lengths to explain that these developments were not diminishing Hewlett-Packard's commitment to 100VG, but most savvy analysts saw that this marked the beginning of the end for 100VG. The 100VG debacle cost Hewlett-Packard millions of dollars in research, development, and marketing. Worse still, it isolated Hewlett-Packard from the mainstream networking business for a number of years. At one time, Hewlett-Packard was a major networking player, including the number-one vendor of stackable hubs. These days, Hewlett-Packard is a mere shadow of its former self in the networking industry.

Iso-Ethernet

Conventional wisdom has it that Ethernet, today's standard for data communications, is unsuitable for time-critical multimedia applications. At the same time, ISDN was supposed to become a pervasive standard for high-speed digital dialup WAN connectivity. In the early 1990s, National Semiconductor developed a technology called *isochronous Ethernet* or *Iso-Ethernet*, which combines the best of Ethernet and ISDN. This technology, which was adopted as the IEEE 802.9a standard in 1995, features a regular 10Mbps Ethernet channel for non-critical data transmission, and additional support for up to 96 ISDN B channels (for data) and one ISDN D channel (for signaling and control). The total capacity of Iso-Ethernet is 97×64Kbps + 10Mbps, or 16.16Mbps total.

The concept was powerful, yet elegant and simple. An internal (data) LAN utilized Iso-Ethernet's Ethernet channel to transfer bursty data. Time-critical data was transferred by making an ISDN call within a LAN or to the outside world via an external BRI connection located in the hub. The hub contains more than one BRI ISDN connection to the outside world to allow multiple LAN users to make external ISDN calls simultaneously.

Iso-Ethernet essentially suffered from the same fate that beset TCNS and 100VG:

- Iso-Ethernet required both new hubs and NICs—the notorious forklift upgrade.

- Iso-Ethernet did deliver on its promise of isochronous data transmission capability for time-critical voice and video transmission. Unfortunately, the technology provides no substantive increase in overall data throughput, which is what most LAN managers were seeking. Iso-Ethernet provides for only 96 64Kbps data channels, a total of 6.16Mbps of isochronous data capacity for an entire network. Therefore, the total data capacity was 16.16Mbps. While this technology was being proposed, the Fast Ethernet people were promoting 100Mbps capacity, at price points similar to Iso-Ethernet.

- ISDN never took off as forecasted.

The rest of the industry chose to ignore Iso-Ethernet, and backed such alternatives as Fast Ethernet or ATM instead.

Fibre Channel and HIPPI

Fibre Channel and HIPPI were developed in the late 1980s and are computer-to-computer or high-speed peripheral connection technologies. Both are used primarily to link different mainframes, supercomputers, and their peripherals together. Fibre Channel, as the name implies, is based primarily on fiber-optic media, but it supports shielded twisted-pair (STP) as well.   It runs at speeds ranging from 100Mbps to 800Mbps. *HIPPI* stands for high-performance parallel interface and runs on a 50-pair parallel cable at speeds of either 800Mbps or 1.6Gbps. HIPPI uses a parallel transmission method (a bus of either 32 or 64 bits), but Fibre Channel uses serial data transmission. (Just to confuse things, a serial version of HIPPI was developed later on, which actually makes the two technologies competitors.) Both Fibre Channel and HIPPI are ANSI X3T11 standards.

Both technologies are flexible enough to be used as high-speed LANs as well. Fibre Channel in particular incorporates features that could have made it a very successful high-speed LAN. Neither Fibre Channel nor HIPPI ever achieved any significant volumes, however, and they never really expanded beyond their mainframe, supercomputer, or high-speed peripheral connectivity niche areas.

Fibre Channel uses an 8B/10B encoding scheme that increases the baud rate (bits on the wire) to 1.062Gbaud. Therefore Fibre Channel and HIPPI were actually the first LAN technologies to pioneer Gigabit data rates.

Instead of developing something from scratch, IEEE engineers chose to use the proven Fibre Channel physical layer and encoding standard for the Gigabit Ethernet standard. Therefore, although Fibre Channel was never successful as a LAN technology, parts of it live on under the Gigabit Ethernet name. Table 2.1 compares Fibre Channel and HIPPI.

Both Fibre Channel and HIPPI are still being supported by vendors, such as Sun, Hewlett-Packard, and IBM, for their large computing platforms.

TABLE 2.1 A COMPARISON OF FIBRE CHANNEL AND HIPPI

Variable	Fibre Channel	HIPPI
Data rate	100, 200, 400 or 800Mbps	800 or 1600Mbps
Transmission method	Serial	32- or 64-bit parallel bus
Frame type	0-byte to 2048-byte payload	1K or 2K packets[1]
Standard	ANSI X3T11	ANSI X3T11
Cable options	25m of 2-pair STP (Type 1)	25m of 50-pair STP (1 or 2 cables)
	Two strands of 2km multimode fiber (MMF)	Four strands of 1km MMF[2]
	Two strands of 10km singlemode fiber (SMF)	Four strands of 10km SMF[2]

[1] *HIPPI transmits 256 words of 32 or 64 bits each (1KB or 2KB packets). It transmitted in a half-duplex way with flow control.*

[2] *Serial HIPPI.*

ATM

ATM has emerged as the only serious and viable long-term alternative to Ethernet. This section discusses ATM as a technology, as well as the pros and cons of migrating to ATM or staying with Ethernet as a LAN solution. This section does not pretend to be a complete and thorough examination of ATM: We cover the basics only. We also focus on the local area networking aspects of ATM rather than the much-touted wide area networking properties of the technology.

A Brief History of ATM

In 1994, when we wrote this book's first edition, the high-speed networking market was filled with numerous contenders. Slowly, one-by-one, they all disappeared. By 1996, when we published this book's second edition, it was becoming increasingly clear that the high-speed LAN race was becoming a two-horse event: Ethernet and ATM. At the time, our publisher convinced us that we needed to include a chapter on ATM integration. We did, although reluctantly. Two years ago, ATM offered some clear benefits over Ethernet. Gigabit Ethernet and 802.1p QoS in particular have eroded this advantage. Therefore, we decided to cut the ATM chapter for this third edition. Overall, we think that ATM is clearly on the defensive, and that there is no place for ATM in the local area network.

This section doesn't pretend to be a complete and unbiased comparison of Ethernet and ATM. You can find literally hundreds of different textbooks on ATM out there, many more than on Ethernet. That fact alone tells us a lot about the complexity of the technology. We want to highlight the changing sentiment that has surrounded Ethernet and ATM, give you an overview of ATM, and then present our opinion as to why Ethernet is the only choice.

In 1994, ATM was considered to be the answer to a worldwide seamless voice and data network. *All Roads Lead to ATM* and *When ATM to the Desktop?* were the headlines du jour. As people began to get first-hand experience with ATM products, however, the press and vendor hype subsided and reality set in. Over the past four years, the tide has turned on ATM from hype to skepticism to downright pessimism. The following is a collection of ATM articles from our "ATM press clippings" archives.

"ATM Growing Pains," wrote *LAN Times*, saying "Standards progressed in 1995, but the hype machine hit a wall." People started joking that *ATM* stood for "after the millennium," sarcastically referring to the number of unfinished ATM standards proposals under way as well as the general lack of maturity and interoperability of the technology and the slower-than-forecasted rate of adoption. Yet "after the millennium" implied that ATM was still going to be the next-generation LAN and that it had only been delayed until after the year 2000.

The 25Mbps version of ATM was being touted as delivering ATM all the way to the desktop, which never happened. By 1996, "ATM was under the Gun" (*Network World*), referring to cheap and effective 10Mbps and 10/100Mbps Ethernet workgroup switches that were a far more cost-effective workgroup upgrade than ATM. Most analysts at this point started scaling back their "All Roads Lead to ATM" theory, and it became clear that ATM to the desktop was not going to be a viable choice anytime soon.

ATM vendors, having invested heavily in the technology, kept pushing ATM as a backbone and WAN technology, hoping that ATM would migrate down to the desktop at some later point. That same year, literally thousands of articles and numerous books appeared on how to convert existing Ethernet or Token Ring LAN traffic to ATM, as LAN managers struggled to even understand subjects such as LAN Emulation, IP over ATM, MPOA, Cells in Frames, and so on. The sheer number of articles written is an indication of the complexity of ATM as a technology and the migration challenges one faces if trying to migrate from a frame-based Ethernet network to ATM. Some headlines started becoming downright pessimistic about the technology. "ATM: Dangerous at Any

Speed?" was the title of a paper presented at an IEEE Gigabit Ethernet conference that year.

By 1997, ATM was under attack in one of its last two strongholds: the high-speed LAN backbone. ATM, capable of running 622Mbps as opposed to Fast Ethernet's 100Mbps speed, clearly had the bandwidth edge for high-speed backbones. With the imminent introduction of 1000Mbps Ethernet, that advantage would disappear. In July 1996, CRN already wrote that "Gigabit Ethernet to Threaten ATM," referring to market research that indicated customers were going to wait for Gigabit Ethernet instead of implementing ATM backbones. An excellent article on the current state of mind appears in the September 1998 issue of *Network Magazine*. In "Frames Reaffirmed at ATM's Expense," Kevin Tolly examines the diminishing role of ATM (www.networkmagazine.com/magazine/current/9809tech1.htm). Today, ATM even faces stiff competition in its two last holdouts: the wide area network and LAN applications requiring QoS. In the WAN, ATM is under attack by such technologies as Frame Relay and IP packets over WAN links such as SONET. In late 1997, *byte* Magazine called it "ATM's Shrinking Role…Once the unsinkable Titanic of high-speed networking, ATM looks like it might have a hole in its hull."

For many years, analysts were forecasting that voice and video applications requiring QoS would bog down best-effort Ethernet LANs. This hasn't happened. In addition, Ethernet and IP have narrowed the QoS gap with ATM substantially over the past two years. For the few LAN applications that do require QoS, the new IEEE 802.1p and IETF RSVP standards go a long way to providing QoS.

Note

Over the past few years, many high-speed WAN services have become available. Two noteworthy ones are Frame Relay, and Packets over SONET, sometimes abbreviated as POS. Both have become very popular and are now viable alternatives to ATM as a WAN technology. Both Frame Relay and POS use variable-length frames or packets, as opposed to ATM cells.

Frame Relay has been around for a while. The well-known T1/E1 and T3/E3 leased lines utilize Frame Relay technology. Frame Relay has become widely available at lower costs. Some vendors are also working on faster versions of Frame Relay.

Packets over SONET is a way of transporting IP packets over the Synchronous Optical Network (SONET) physical layer, an ANSI standard for long-haul, high-quality fiber. The SONET fiber standard is widely used by the telephone companies and is used by ATM as a physical layer.

Overall, the telecommunications carriers' decisions will more likely dictate the successful future of a WAN technology than the decisions that data network managers make.

So what does the future hold for ATM? Some people still think that ATM and Ethernet will coexist within the local area network, but we don't believe that. Why mix and match when one homogeneous environment can do it all for you? People advocating mixing and matching typically tend to be found in the following camps:

- Vendors that sell both ATM and Ethernet that need to recover their ATM investments

- Analysts, LAN managers, or journalists who previously advocated ATM and are too scared to admit their past mistakes

- Die-hard technologists, also known as propeller-heads, who pretend a forklift upgrade is a realistic upgrade option

- Telecommunications industry members who don't understand the LAN market

The telecommunications industry originally developed ATM to transport voice and data. The telecommunications industry works very slowly, much slower than the data communications and computer industries. Witness how digital exchanges are more than 20 years old now, yet analog exchanges were still built in parts of the world five years ago. Telephone company ATM plans have been in the works for many years: New ATM equipment is being purchased and will be deployed for voice switching. Corporate LANs can act and react much more quickly, however, and ATM seems relegated to play only a minor role in the WAN.

The Origins of ATM

To understand ATM and its origins properly, you need to understand the "bigger picture." Today, the communications industry is essentially split into four different sectors. Data communication consists of two distinctly separate sectors, namely local and wide area networking. Technologies such as Ethernet are firmly rooted in the local-area, data communications world. For transporting data across extended distances, other technologies are used. You have literally dozens of WAN technologies from which to choose. The most popular ones are X.25, PPP, leased lines (T1/E1), Basic and Primary Rate ISDN, and Frame Relay. When data travels from a LAN across a WAN, a data conversion of some kind always needs to take place: This is known as *routing*. Private corporations own the LAN hardware and typically rent capacity from a telecommunications company for their WAN needs. LAN bandwidth has always been extremely cheap, essentially free after the hardware has been purchased, and is measured in Mbps. WAN bandwidth, on the other hand, has historically been very expensive, rented on a per-month basis, and is typically measured in Kbps.

Voice communication also has two separate areas. In the local area, companies purchase private branch exchanges (PBXs) to communicate within an office. (Rolm, now part of Siemens, is often credited as being the inventor of the PBX.) For wide-area voice communications, digital circuit switching from a local or long-distance telecommunications carrier is used. (The term *WAN* is not used in the voice world.) ANSI and the ITU (previously the CCITT) govern standards for voice communications.

Like the name says, ISDN was designed to *integrate* voice and data into one digital WAN switching technology. Basic Rate ISDN was designed for individual telecommunications subscribers using existing copper wiring. Primary Rate ISDN is an aggregation of a number of BRI ISDN channels to deliver a much faster link. Broadband ISDN uses different media to deliver even higher-speed capability. ISDN was invented almost 20 years ago, is available in many countries, and works well. Early advocates of ISDN hoped that every business and residential telephone line would ultimately be converted to ISDN, but the actual market adoption rate has been disappointing. Germany and France lead ISDN deployment with about 5% of telephone lines offering ISDN capability. In the United States, it's less than 1%. (Offering this capability doesn't mean the user has chosen to subscribe to the typically higher-priced service.) To this date, some countries don't offer ISDN and probably never will—newer technologies, such as cable TV networks and copper-based and satellite-based DSL, are becoming available.

Note

One of ATM's key benefits has been seamless LAN/WAN integration. The premise is a seamless, integrated worldwide ATM LAN/WAN infrastructure or, simply put, 53-byte voice and data cells circling the globe. Ethernet now matches ATM in terms of scalability and performance and has caught up substantially in the QoS department. Therefore, the seamless LAN/WAN story remains one of ATM's clear advantages.

Yet the reality looks very different here, too. LAN managers don't seem to want seamless LAN/WAN integration. The reasons primarily lie in the areas of network control and cost. LAN managers pay dearly for WAN access and therefore want to control the amount of data that travels across the WAN. In addition, security aspects have become a key issue. The firewall industry is growing faster than just about any other part of the networking industry. Special devices that connect LANs and WANs, such as routers, often provide the control features that LAN managers are looking for to maintain separate LANs and WANs.

ATM is based on Broadband ISDN (B-ISDN) work done by the different telecommunications companies in the late 1970s and early 1980s. Like B-ISDN, ATM was designed to carry both voice and data. ATM was designed as both a local and wide area network technology. That's in contrast to B-ISDN and Ethernet, which were designed respectively for WAN or LAN access only. ATM's vision is elegant and admirable: one worldwide, homogeneous network for integrated voice and data (see Figure 2.3).

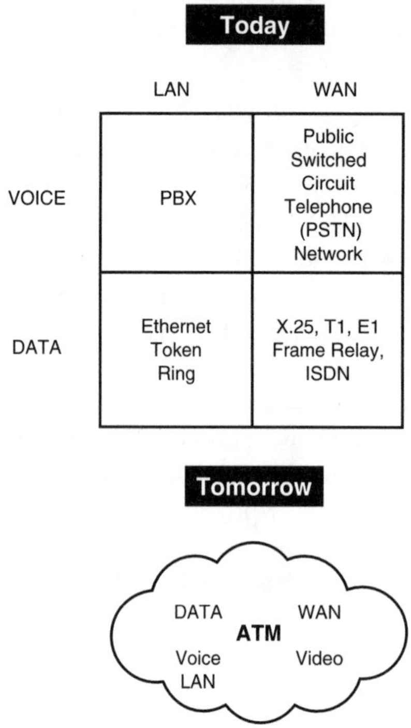

Today

	LAN	WAN
VOICE	PBX	Public Switched Circuit Telephone (PSTN) Network
DATA	Ethernet Token Ring	X.25, T1, E1 Frame Relay, ISDN

Tomorrow

DATA   WAN
ATM
Voice   Video
LAN

FIGURE 2.3   *ATM promises voice and data over one seamless network.*

A Closer Look at ATM

Let's take a closer look at how ATM works:

- *Cells versus frames*—Ethernet, Token Ring, TCNS, and FDDI use variable-length frames to transmit data from source to destination. ATM, on the other hand, uses fixed-length 53-byte cells to transmit data, voice, and video over both LANs and WANs. Figure 2.4 shows an ATM fixed-length frame, which consists of a 5-byte header and the 48-byte payload. The 5-byte header is the addressing mechanism.

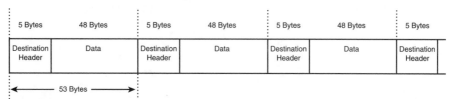

FIGURE 2.4 *ATM uses 53-byte fixed-length cells, whereas Ethernet transports data in variable-length frames.*

- *Switching only and connection-oriented*—Unlike Ethernet, ATM does not offer a shared-media, best-effort transmission method. Like B-ISDN and all digital voice switching technologies, ATM is a true switching-based technology. When information needs to be communicated between two nodes, a connection is first established between source and destination. When setting up this connection, the sender specifies the type, speed, and other attributes of the connection. After the call has been established, the voice or data transfer can start. The connection can be permanent, called a *permanent virtual circuit*, or temporary, called a *switched virtual circuit*. A permanent virtual circuit is analogous to a leased line within a larger pipe—a certain part of the connection is permanently reserved. One problem with this approach is that the sender needs to know what the circuit requirements have to be before initiating a transmission. Today's data applications don't work that way. Data applications just send data, such as email, without caring too much about what priority the connection should have, how fast the connection needs to be, or for how long the connection should be set up.

- *Based on the OSI Reference Model*—Like Ethernet, ATM is based on a modular architecture. ATM provides a choice of different data rates. For LAN transmission multiples of 25Mbps data rates are offered: Currently offered are 25Mbps, 100Mbps, 155Mbps, 622Mbps, and 2.4Gbps versions. ATM also offers different physical layers, borrowing at times existing physical layer designs from other technologies. The Token Ring 16Mbps physical layer combined with 8B/10B encoding is used for the 25Mbps version, for example. UTP, STP, multimode, single-mode fiber, and multiplexed fiber are all supported. For public carrier (WAN) transmission, ATM offers standardized data rates similar to those of existing T1/E1 and T3/E3 WAN technologies.

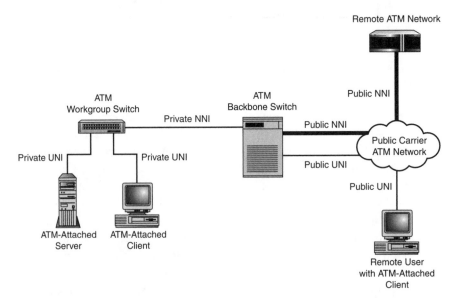

Figure 2.5 shows a typical ATM network.

Figure 2.5 *A typical ATM network. Note the seamless LAN/WAN infrastructure. Individual nodes are connected to the network with user-to-network interfaces (UNIs), whereas different networks are linked using network-to-network interfaces (NNIs).*

Standards and Specifications

ATM spans a much broader range of communications than does Ethernet. ATM's WAN capabilities in particular mean that huge telecommunications companies as well as regulatory entities are involved in the setting of standards. Therefore numerous companies, organizations, and even countries are involved with ATM specifications. The IEEE, on the other hand, has always been a small, tight-knit group of engineers from a handful of data networking companies and consulting firms. The following are some of the most common standards and specifications:

- *ATM Forum Technical Committee (TC)*—The ATM Forum was formed a few years ago by a handful of companies, and today membership exceeds several hundred. The ATM Forum can be compared to the Fast or Gigabit Ethernet Alliances. It is not a formal standards body, but often will develop new technical specifications. The technical committee includes data networking vendors, public carriers, and equipment companies. This has resulted in two different sets of activities: specifications for private, LAN-type data networks; and public carrier specifications. The latter thrust overlaps significantly with the ITU-T, discussed next.

- *International Telecommunications Union-Telecommunications Standards Sector (ITU-T)*—The ITU-T is the successor to the CCITT. The ITU-T is a world-wide standards authority. Many countries have their own national standards bodies, such as ANSI in the United States. Key contributors to ITU standards are ANSI, the ATM Forum TC, and many private enterprises such as AT&T, Lucent, and other telecommunications companies.

- *Internet Engineering Task Force (IETF)*—The IETF works on standards for running the TCP/IP protocol over ATM. The ATM Forum TC and the IETF have nicely divided the areas of responsibility. Sometimes, technologies or standards developed by these two bodies do end up competing against each other in the marketplace.

A Comparison of Ethernet and ATM

A detailed analysis of ATM is beyond the scope of one chapter. Instead we contrast ATM and Ethernet based on the factors listed in the "Migration Issues" section earlier in the chapter. We compare the two technologies and provide a score.

We briefly discuss each migration topic and contrast Ethernet and ATM. Then we assign a score to the technology that we think has the upper hand at this point in time. The scores can range from Ethernet having a significant advantage today to ATM having a significant advantage today.

> **Note**
>
> *Both technologies are of course evolving. This comparison represents a snapshot in time, taken in late 1998. This kind of comparison will date very quickly. Before the advent of Gigabit Ethernet, for example, ATM had a clear advantage in both the performance and scalability departments. This, as we know, all changed in 1997/1998. Therefore note that this is late-1998 data. Prices are bound to change rapidly, for Gigabit Ethernet in particular. Note also that we use the Full-Duplex Switched version of Ethernet for this comparison.*

Raw Performance and Scaling

Before the advent of Gigabit Ethernet, 100Mbps was the maximum data rate for Ethernet. Therefore if you wanted to build an Ethernet backbone that exceeded 100Mbps, multiple proprietary Fast Ethernet links needed to be connected in parallel (for example, Cisco Fast EtherChannel trunking). In that situation, ATM had an edge with its 622Mbps version. With the advent of Gigabit Ethernet and the proposed 802.3ad Link Aggregation/trunking standard, Ethernet backbones of several gigabits per second can be built. This gives Ethernet a definite edge when competing with ATM.

Ethernet now scales from 10 to 100 to 1000Mbps and beyond. ATM speeds range from 25 to 622Mbps. The Ethernet Link Aggregation proposal will work for both switches and servers, whereas ATM does not allow server Link Aggregation.

The 53-byte ATM cell structure is less efficient than Ethernet's frame structure. If 1KB Ethernet frames are chosen (Ethernet frames can range from 64 bytes to 1522 bytes), Ethernet protocol efficiency is 98%, compared to ATM's 90%.

Ethernet has a great advantage in the performance area. It's a draw in the scaling arena.

Connection Cost

ATM is an inherently more complex technology than Ethernet. In addition, Ethernet production run rates are two or three orders of magnitude larger than ATM production rates. That means ATM prices will always be significantly higher than comparable Ethernet equipment. In 1998, 100Mbps Ethernet connection cost has dropped to less than $200 (street price) for a switched Layer 2 port and NIC combination. Similar 155Mbps ATM equipment still costs around

$2000, which means Ethernet costs about one-seventh the price of ATM if we take the different speeds into consideration. Gigabit Ethernet is still relatively new, and therefore price competition is not as intense yet. But comparing 622Mbps ATM equipment with Gigabit Ethernet shows that Ethernet is already half the price of ATM, with price declines of 40% forecasted for Gigabit Ethernet for the next few years. Because Gigabit Ethernet is 50% faster than ATM, the current price delta is more like 3 to 1.

In the cost realm, Ethernet boasts a great advantage.

Multivendor Support

Both ATM and Ethernet are widely supported by *all* major networking vendors. In terms of absolute numbers, however, many more vendors support Ethernet than ATM. The Ethernet hardware market has attracted many more suppliers than the ATM market because of the following reasons:

- Ethernet is a simpler technology to build and support.

- The market for Ethernet products is a hundred times larger than that for ATM devices.

- Ethernet chips are available from dozens of different semiconductor suppliers.

- Ethernet, being widely understood by both manufacturers and customers, has lower product support costs. On the downside, margins for Ethernet suppliers are razor thin.

Over the past few years, some Ethernet product categories, such as NICs, hubs, entry-level switches, and branch office routers, have become pure commodity items, being sold at your local PC supermarket or even across the Internet. These days 10/100Mbps Ethernet NICs and hubs are available at most personal computer retailers, for example. Trying to find a single retailer or Internet Web merchant to sell you an ATM NIC or switch will be a challenge.

In this area, Ethernet has the advantage.

Ease of Migration

The migration path from Ethernet to ATM is littered with what we consider almost insurmountable obstacles. ATM will run for the most part on the same cabling that Fast or Gigabit Ethernet runs on (Category 5 and multimode or single-mode fiber). Therefore, you can reuse your existing cabling infrastructure. That's about it in terms of migration. Everything else really requires wholesale replacement.

Let's examine this issue in a bit more detail. In terms of networking hardware, two possible migration paths to ATM emerge: the slow step-by-step migration or the wholesale forklift upgrade. The forklift upgrade might be possible for someone building a network from scratch, but for LAN managers living within real-world financial constraints, this is just not a realistic alternative.

Therefore, the only economically feasible option is a slow migration. The ATM Forum has created LAN Emulation (LANE) and a slew of other technologies that supposedly enable a smooth migration from legacy LANs to a true ATM environment. No simple or elegant migration path exists from Ethernet to ATM. ATM's attractiveness lies in its radically different approach of integrated LAN/WAN and voice/data traffic, and this also becomes its biggest drawback. The two technologies are just too different to enable a smooth migration. "Migration enablers," such as LANE, are (in our opinion) just technologies that allow an ATM network section to talk to an existing Ethernet network. They don't do much in terms of an easy migration itself. Moving to ATM still requires a step-by-step replacement in certain sections of your network and then joining up the existing Ethernet section to the new ATM section using LANE.

If ATM is used only as a backbone technology (that is, no ATM-attached clients or servers), LANE is not required. In this case, the addition of an ATM backbone is relatively painless. The addition of a Gigabit Ethernet backbone is a no-brainer by comparison. Migrating from Ethernet to Fast or Gigabit Ethernet is relatively easy, and the second half of this book covers this in detail.

Ethernet has a huge advantage in the migration department.

Quality of Service

In the telecommunications industry, bandwidth is scarce. QoS is key in voice communications, where users will switch to a different long-distance company if they hear the slightest echo or noise. QoS means significant revenue dollars and profits for the telephone companies. Therefore, it's no surprise that ATM, having been designed by the telco industry, offers state-of-the art QoS. The analogy is first-class airline seats, which reap high profits and get the passenger there in style.

ATM offers different QoS classes. ATM connections specify the bit rate, or bandwidth, for a given connection. The four different bit rates allow a LAN manager to match up infrastructure capabilities with application and end-station requirements. Certain data traffic may be able to tolerate long and variable latencies, for example, but other traffic (such as voice or video) may need to be prioritized to avoid jitter. The bad news is that ATM's QoS benefits work only in true ATM environments: The end stations need to be running ATM. ATM QoS sets the bandwidth requirements in terms of bit rates (BRs). There are four different bit rate priorities. Constant bit rate (CBR) specifies a fixed, predetermined constant bit rate for a permanent virtual circuit. Variable bit rate (VBR) is next on the priority list and is used for high-priority traffic. Unspecified and available bit rates (UBR and ABR) basically work like Ethernet where the transmission bandwidth depends on the network availability. Figure 2.6 shows the different ATM QoS options.

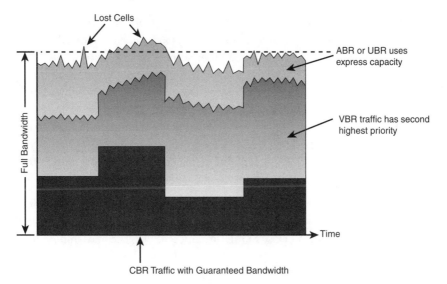

FIGURE 2.6 *ATM traffic can be categorized as CBR, VBR, UBR, or ABR. Only CBR and VBR offer QoS guarantees.*

The data communications industry, on the other hand, had never been concerned with QoS until ATM came along. Let's be honest here. Shared Ethernet offers zero QoS. These are economy seats all the way, as long as we get there! Switched Ethernet was a step forward, and recent Ethernet innovations have closed the QoS gap even more. A gap remains nonetheless. On paper, therefore, ATM offers superior QoS. That's so much for the theory. Let's look at reality for a second:

- *New packet-based technologies have narrowed the gap*—Over the past two years, many Ethernet innovations have narrowed the QoS gap between Ethernet and ATM significantly. Ethernet equipment incorporating the new full-duplex/802.3x and priority switching/802.1p technologies is now available. These switches, combined with Layer 3 QoS standards such as RSVP, mean that you can now build Ethernet LANs with QoS. Chapter 5, "VLANs and Layer 3 Switching," discusses the new IEEE 802.1p standard in more detail.

- *ATM's QoS benefits are overhyped*—With LANE, ATM does not offer any QoS. Therefore, if you want first-class QoS, you need to install ATM top-to-bottom.

- *Raw bandwidth is a pretty good substitute for QoS*—QoS is necessary if a network is overloaded, and sporadic delays are a normal part of the operation of the network. If your shared Ethernet network has a utilization of less than 20%, for example, it will exhibit almost negligibly small and relatively constant delays, so QoS becomes a mute point. Only if a network becomes busy does QoS matter at all. Most Ethernet LANs are mostly what we call over-engineered: They offer significantly more bandwidth than actually required. Ethernet has always been much more affordable than any other LAN technology. Many network managers have therefore chosen the "bigger pipe" approach to accommodate QoS-sensitive applications.

Over-engineering WAN links, on the other hand, do not make economic sense, because WAN links are charged for in units of time. As a result, WAN links always run at close to full capacity, and QoS becomes important.

- *Are we really running QoS-sensitive applications on our network?*—What applications are really driving the need for more bandwidth? We examine this question in more detail in Chapter 7, "Bandwidth: How Much Is Enough?" In a nutshell, however, the bandwidth crunch is not a result of running voice and data on your LAN. It's the result of the explosion of the Internet and running more of today's existing applications. The key point is that QoS-sensitive video or voice applications are not running on many of today's LANs and don't look likely to migrate to your LAN in full force tomorrow either. That has profound implications for the Ethernet versus ATM debate.

  The bigger question is whether voice and data networks really are combining. So far, this hasn't happened. Some say this is a chicken-and-egg situation—that voice and video aren't running on existing networks together because today's networks don't provide the right QoS to support voice and video, so we need to move to ATM. We disagree with that. Even the most heavily loaded Ethernet networks could support the additional demands of hundreds of audio calls or dozens of video streams. The PC must overcome far bigger issues before it replaces the telephone. These issues include usability, reliability, familiarity, interoperability, WAN bandwidth, and cost. It makes little sense to boot up your PC and load a telephone software application if it all takes five minutes just to establish the call. Your regular telephone can take you there in a few seconds. Why then do we need to apply voice traffic QoS requirements to data traffic? We think most people will prefer economy- or business-class travel rather than first-class.

  On paper, ATM is superior to Ethernet in this department. ATM can specify QoS requirements for both permanent virtual circuits and switched virtual circuits.

In this area, ATM has a great advantage, but we must add the proviso that the availability of 802.1p-capable equipment will narrow the gap so that ATM will have much less of an advantage.

Understanding of the Technology

Ethernet is well understood by everyone because it is so widely deployed, 25 years old, and very simple. ATM, on the other hand, is relatively new, very complex, and still occupies a market niche in the LAN.

The technology is incredibly complex in our opinion, especially if one wants to migrate from Ethernet to ATM. In the past eight years, the ATM industry has created so many new acronyms that even we don't understand them all. Deploying ATM means going back to school for you and everyone in your department.

In this area, Ethernet has a great advantage.

Standards

Ethernet standards are mature and proven, and allow vendors to build truly interoperable products. Over the years, the IEEE has regularly published standards revisions to remove ambiguities, eliminate mistakes, or further clarify items. The current 802.3aa working group, for example, will be publishing a Fast Ethernet maintenance release.

Ethernet truly does provide plug-and-play interoperability, *out of the box*, which is the result of 25 years of experience. Although ATM standards have evolved significantly over the past five years, ATM still has a long way to go. First, there is the sheer number of ATM standards. The ATM standards are also not nearly as specific or authoritative as Ethernet standards. As a result, ATM interoperability still leaves much to be desired. We haven't heard of a single large multivendor ATM network that didn't require the help of the manufacturers' field-support engineers to get it working properly, for example.

About 10 years ago, the University of New Hampshire set up an InterOperability Lab (www.iol.unh.edu), that tests new products (and standards) on behalf of different vendor communities. This lab has tested Fast and Gigabit Ethernet as well as ATM products. At a Gigabit Ethernet conference in London in July 1998, lab manager Barry Reinhold called Gigabit Ethernet "the most mature and well-documented standard" he had ever seen. He also remarked that it was "pretty solid, better than Fast Ethernet, and much better than ATM."

Ethernet has a great advantage in this area.

Why Ethernet Is a Better Choice Than ATM

Table 2.2 summarizes the comparison of Ethernet and ATM. We think the table speaks for itself. Overall, Ethernet is the winner in six out of eight categories. The only area where ATM has a definite edge today is in the QoS department. We firmly believe that for the next few years existing Ethernet customers will be best served by one of the higher-speed versions of Ethernet.

TABLE 2.2 COMPARISON OF ETHERNET AND ATM

Criterion	Great Ethernet Advantage	Ethernet Advantage	Draw	ATM Advantage	Great ATM Advantage
Connection cost	✓				
Performance		✓			
Scalability			✓		
Migration	✓				
QoS					✓
Multivendor support		✓			
Understanding the technology	✓				
Clear and usable standards		✓			

High-Speed Token Ring Options

If this is a book about Ethernet, why are we talking about Token Ring? Token Ring still comprises about 10% of all network installations. This is not an insignificant share, although this number is steadily decreasing. Also, many enterprise networks contain a mixture of Ethernet and Token Ring. Therefore, we thought you might have a need for information about the Token Ring upgrade options available.

Many Token Ring users are rightly concerned about the future of Token Ring as a technology. Although many new options are available to Ethernet users, today's Token Ring customers have far fewer choices. For many years, IBM, the inventor and principal proponent of Token Ring, seemed to have abandoned

Token Ring altogether as a technology, focusing its research and development on ATM instead. According to IBM, ATM was supposed to be the natural successor to all shared-media LANs, including Token Ring. As the ATM hype subsided, however, it also became very clear that the future for Token Ring wasn't going to be ATM. What was it going to be? While Ethernet users were flocking to Switched and Fast Ethernet, Token Ring users were wondering what to do. Some decided to switch to Ethernet, others decided to take the ATM plunge, but most took a wait-and-see attitude.

The good news is that some options have emerged recently for improving the speed of your Token Ring network. After years of stagnation, the Token Ring industry seems to be showing some life. The three upgrade choices available today are Switched Token Ring, Full-Duplex Token Ring (also known as Dedicated Token Ring, or DTR), and High-Speed Token Ring (HSTR). If this sounds familiar, it is. All three technologies have effectively copied the familiar and successful concepts of Switched, Full-Duplex, and Fast Ethernet.

Token Ring LANs are not quite as overloaded as Ethernet LANs for two reasons. First, Token Ring uses a more efficient media access method. The utilization of a large Token Ring LAN can reach up to over 90%, compared to about 50 to 60% for Ethernet. Second, Token Ring uses a faster wire speed, 16Mbps versus Ethernet's 10Mbps. That means Token Ring can actually deliver well over 10Mbps throughput, versus about 5 to 6Mbps for Ethernet. Nonetheless, Token Ring LANs are experiencing congestion in many places, too. Just like Ethernet, Token Ring is a shared-media technology. Just like Ethernet, Token Ring can be bridged or segmented into smaller domains.

New Token Ring Developments

Let's look at Switched, Full-Duplex, and 100Mbps Token Ring in a bit more detail:

- *Switched Token Ring*—A few years ago, the first Token Ring switches appeared. Therefore, your first and probably best option for upgrading an overloaded Token Ring network is to add Token Ring switches. Token Ring switches work just like their Ethernet equivalents, providing a dedicated 16Mbps connection on every port. Replacing a Token Ring repeater (called a concentrator) with a switch provides an immediate bandwidth increase. Backbones can be built with Token Ring switches.

Another benefit of Token Ring switches is speed matching. Some older rings out there still operate at 4Mbps. To get the entire ring to operate at 16Mbps, all users need to have a NIC capable of operating at the faster rate. Most Token Ring switches allow you to intermix 4Mbps-only and 16Mbps users because the switches are capable of running at dual speeds on each port. This is often a more cost-effective way of getting your users to 16Mbps without having to upgrade all remaining 4Mbps NICs out there.

- *Dedicated Token Ring (DTR)*—DTR is also known as Full-Duplex Token Ring and effectively creates 32Mbps of bandwidth with simultaneous transmission in both directions. Most shipping Token Ring switches and NICs can operate in the DTR mode. The IEEE 802.5r standard defines DTR.

- *High-Speed Token Ring (HSTR)*—Token Ring is about to get its own Fast Token Ring, called *HSTR*. Conceptually, HSTR uses the Token Ring MAC running at 100Mbps, coupled to the existing and proven Fast Ethernet PHYs. Some people had advocated running Token Ring at 155 or 160Mbps, which would be either 10 times the speed, or the same speed as ATM-155. The choice of 100Mbps was made because Fast Ethernet PHY components could be used, and this meant lower component cost and getting to market relatively quickly. 100Mbps also was considered fast enough. The 802.5t committee is standardizing HSTR.

- *Other developments*—Other Token Ring developments planned include a Gigabit version of Token Ring (802.5v), as well as VLAN and Link Aggregation proposals. IBM already ships a technology called TokenPipes, which is a proprietary Link Aggregation technology similar to Cisco's EtherChannel.

Analyzing the New Token Ring Options

With the arrival of a 100Mbps version, Token Ring does have some life left in it after all. We need to make you aware of some "small print" issues, however.

First, multivendor support is a big issue. Only three vendors are keeping Token Ring alive at this point: IBM, Madge, and Olicom. Bay Networks is part of the high-speed Token Ring alliance, but we don't see Bay investing heavily in Token Ring. Early on, Cisco pledged its support for HSTR, but then withdrew (much to the disgust of the other participants). Cisco's official line was that Cisco's Inter-Switch Link (ISL) technology would do the same as HSTR, but that was a thinly disguised polite way of saying that Cisco saw no long-term future in Token Ring. Can you imagine building a network without Cisco routers? Or 3Com network adapters? Without support from vendors like Cisco and 3Com, HSTR could mean just that.

The second issue is that Token Ring connection costs will continue to be very high. Token Ring prices have always been significantly higher than Ethernet's prices. The price delta seems to have increased as numerous vendors have abandoned Token Ring and competition in the Ethernet field has intensified. These days, a 16Mbps shared Token Ring connection costs more than a 100Mbps Ethernet connection. That's about a 6-to-1 price-performance ratio! 16Mbps Token Ring switches are now costing just less than $500 per port, which will buy you an entire 10-port, 10Mbps Ethernet switch. The reason that Token Ring pricing is so high is twofold. The market is essentially a captive market; many customers are reluctant to move to Ethernet. The other reason is that only three serious players are competing for your business; therefore there is little chance of significant price competition.

The real question is whether you want to stay with Token Ring in the long run or whether you should consider migrating to Ethernet now. You could, for example, keep existing users on a Token Ring LAN but start connecting new users in that department with 10/100Mbps Ethernet NICs. You could run a new backbone on Fast Ethernet. You would have to add a router to link the Fast Ethernet backbone and new Ethernet workgroup to the existing Token Ring network, but routing from Token Ring to Ethernet has become very easy and cost effective, especially through larger chassis hubs. You may already be routing from Ethernet to Token Ring somewhere if you are currently managing a heterogeneous environment.

You could, of course, go all the way and just rip out your entire Token Ring setup and replace it with Fast Ethernet gear everywhere. This wholesale replacement is a radical upgrade, but we have heard of more than one customer actually doing this, citing huge cost savings for Fast Ethernet equipment compared to Token Ring switches. We think you know what our recommendation is.

Summary

As recently as five years ago, half a dozen technologies competed with Ethernet. Some such as Iso-Ethernet and FDDI-II never got off the drawing board. Other technologies, such as TCNS or 100VG, put up a good fight for a year or two before surrendering. Fibre Channel and HIPPI live on, serving niche markets, such as high-speed storage. Token Ring and FDDI are still alive, but barely, with sales steadily declining as the installed base continues converting to Ethernet.

Over these past five years, Ethernet has totally reinvented itself, changing to meet tomorrow's market requirements. Five years ago, Ethernet was a shared-media, 10Mbps-only LAN technology. Today, Ethernet can run at 1Gbps—in Switched or Full-Duplex mode and with traffic prioritization—and can utilize multiple parallel links, running over just about any kind of physical layer out there. Yet today's Ethernet has maintained backward compatibility with the Ethernets of 20 years ago, which has proven a powerful and unbeatable combination.

ATM is the only viable alternative to Ethernet. Although this may still be the subject of much debate, ATM is clearly on the defensive. Gigabit Ethernet, in particular, has leapfrogged ATM in terms of raw bandwidth capabilities, threatening ATM in its last LAN stronghold, the backbone. Some market researchers are now forecasting that Gigabit Ethernet alone will outship all ATM by the year 2000. Ethernet has truly become the universal LAN dial tone.

To end this chapter, Table 2.3 summarizes the different high-speed options discussed earlier.

TABLE 2.3 MAKING SENSE OF HIGH-SPEED COMMUNICATION TECHNOLOGIES

Feature	FDDI/CDDI	Fibre Channel	TCNS[1]	100VG-AnyLAN
Standard	ANSI X3T9.5	ANSI X3T11	Proprietary	IEEE 802.12
Major vendors promoting	All	Sun, HP, IBM	Thomas-Conrad 10	HP
Ease of migration from 10BASE-T	New NICs, new hubs	New NICs, new hubs	New NICs, new hubs	New NICs, new hubs
Quality of service	Poor	Good	Poor	Okay[3]
Wire Speed	100Mbps	100 to 1000Mbps	100Mbps	100Mbps
Future Plans	None (FDDI II plans shelved)	2 Gbps, 4 Gbps	None	None
Connection Cost (Shared)	$2000	$2000	N/A	$200
Connection Cost (Layer 2 Switched)	$3000	$3000	N/A	N/A
Switched Cost/Mbps[6]	$30	$30	N/A	$5.50
Type of technology	Frame, shared media	Frame, shared media, or switched	Frame, shared media	Frame, shared media
Shipping since	1988	?	1990	1994
More info from	Many books and links on the Web	www.fibrechannel.com	www.compaq.com	www.hp.com

1   *TCNS was developed by Thomas-Conrad and is based on the ArcNET standard. It is no longer in production. Thomas-Conrad is now part of Compaq.*

2   *Iso-Ethernet is no longer in production.*

3   *In theory, 100VG offered good QoS, but this required software modifications, which were always unlikely to happen, given 100VG's small market share.*

HSTR	ATM	Iso-Ethernet[2]	100BASE-T	1000BASE-X
IEEE 802.5t	Evolving - ITU-T, ATM Forum	IEEE 802.9a	IEEE 802.3u	IEEE 802.3z/ab
IBM, Madge, Olicom	Many, including Cisco, Bay, 3Com	National Semiconductor		Everyone
New NICs, new hubs	New NICs, new hubs	New NICs, new hubs	Very easy	Very easy
Poor	Excellent	Very good	Shared: Poor[4] Switched: Good 802.1p: Very good	
100Mbps	25 to 622 Mbps	10Mbps/6Mbps isochronous	100Mbps	1Gbps
1000 Mbps TR	2.4Gbps ATM	None	GbE	10Gbps Ethernet
TBD, estimated $2000	N/A	$500	$100	$500
TBD, estimated $3000	$2000[5]	N/A5	$200	$1000
	$20	N/A	$2	$1
Frame, shared media, or switched	Cell switching, connect-ionless	Shared-media/ point-to point hybrid	Frame, shared media, or switched	Frame, shared media, or switched
1998	1993	1995	1994	1997
www.hstra.org	www.atmforum.com	www.nsc.com members.aol. com/dhawley/ isonet.html	This book	

4 *Shared/switched/802.1p section applies to both 100BASE-T and 1000BASE-X.*
5 *For 155-Mbps connection.*
6 *Shared cost used if available.*

CHAPTER 3

Ethernet, Fast Ethernet, and Gigabit Ethernet Standards

This chapter discusses the theory and standards of the three versions of Ethernet around today: regular 10Mbps Ethernet, 100Mbps Fast Ethernet, and 1000Mbps Gigabit Ethernet. The goal of this chapter is to educate you as a LAN manager or IT professional about essential differences between shared 10Mbps Ethernet and these newer technologies. This chapter focuses on aspects of Fast Ethernet and Gigabit Ethernet that are relevant to you and doesn't get into too much technical detail.

Read this chapter and the following two (Chapter 4, "Layer 2 Ethernet Switching," and Chapter 5, "VLANs and Layer 3 Switching") together. This chapter focuses on the different Ethernet MAC and PHY standards, as well as repeaters, also known as *hubs*. Chapter 4 examines Ethernet bridging, also known as Layer 2 switching. Chapter 5 discusses VLANs, some basics of routing, and Layer 3 switching. These three chapters serve as a precursor to the second half of this book, namely the hands-on implementation in Chapters 8 through 12. After you understand the key differences between yesterday's shared Ethernet and today's Switched, Fast, and Gigabit Ethernet, evaluating products and building a network with these products should be relatively straightforward.

The chapter is split into seven sections:

- "Ethernet and the OSI Reference Model" discusses the OSI Reference Model and how Ethernet relates to the physical (PHY) and Media Access Control (MAC) layers of the OSI model.

- The second section, "10Mbps Ethernet MAC and PHY Standards," delves into the 10Mbps Ethernet MAC in more detail and discusses the various Ethernet physical layer implementations available today: Thick, Thin, Twisted-Pair, and Fiber Ethernet. You can skip this section if you are very familiar with Ethernet. We included it as a refresher to set the stage for our discussion of the new Fast Ethernet standard and switching technology.

- Ethernet was designed to be a shared-media, half-duplex technology. The third section of this chapter, "Half- and Full-Duplex Ethernet," discusses the transition from half-duplex to full-duplex transmission.

- The fourth section of this chapter, "100BASE-T/Fast Ethernet," introduces the IEEE 802.3u Fast Ethernet standard and discusses how it differs from the regular 10Mbps Ethernet standard. This section explains the Fast Ethernet MAC and the four different PHY standards in more detail.

- In the section "Gigabit Ethernet," you learn about the new Gigabit Ethernet MAC and PHY standard, as well as the new 1000BASE-T PHY for Category 5 or better UTP cable.

- Next, we discuss the auto-negotiation standard. Auto-negotiation was first introduced as part of the Fast Ethernet standard. It is an automatic speed-selection method, connecting different devices together.

- In the final section, "Ethernet Repeaters," we start explaining deployment by means of repeaters. In particular, this section discusses Ethernet and Fast Ethernet repeater standards, as well as the Gigabit Ethernet buffered distributor/repeater design specification. We also cover repeater design rules.

Chapter 6, "Cabling and More on Physical Layers," covers the Fast and Gigabit Ethernet physical layers and the corresponding encoding and cabling specifications in much more detail.

Ethernet and the OSI Reference Model

Most data communications protocols in use today are defined in terms of a layered model called the Open Systems Interconnection (OSI) Reference Model. Table 3.1 describes the layers of this model.

TABLE 3.1 NOVELL'S NETWARE OPERATING SYSTEM ADHERES TO THE ISO/OSI REFERENCE MODEL MORE CLOSELY THAN MOST OTHER OPERATING SYSTEMS

Layer Name	Layer Number	Examples	Comment
Application	7	NetWare NLMs	Provides access to the network.
Presentation	6		Formats data for workstation-based interpretation/display.
Session	5	NetWare Core Protocol (NCP)	Layers 5–7 are often not clearly defined and vary by operating system. Some applications span all three layers.
Transport	4	SPX (Sequenced Packet Exchange)	Provides end-to-end management, including acknowledgment, error correction.
Network	3	IPX (Internetwork Packet Exchange), IPX RIP (IPX Routing Information Protocol)	Routes packets. Dissimilar LANs communicate through Layer 3 routing.
Data link	2	LLC: IEEE 802.2 LLC standard	Bridges are Layer 2 devices. Generates source and destination addresses. AUI interfaces between Layers 1 and 2.
		MAC: IEEE 802.3 Ethernet, Fast Ethernet, Gigabit Ethernet	
Physical	1	UTP, coax, fiber	Specifies the electrical and signal/coding characteristics on the cable. Repeaters operate at this level.

Both ANSI and the IEEE have used this seven-layer model in the past for good reason. Breaking down a technology into different layers allows a given layer to be changed without impacting the remainder of the model. The IEEE was able to add unshielded twisted-pair support to Ethernet while still keeping Ethernet's core intact—just as different software protocols, such as IPX, TCP/IP, and NetBEUI, can be used with the same hardware because each component forms an independent layer. In this way, interoperability between network applications is greatly improved. Next, we discuss Layers 1 through 4 in more detail. (Layers 5 through 7 are not relevant to this book, so we do not cover them here.)

Layer 1: The Physical Layer

The physical layer, or PHY, protocol defines the electrical signaling, symbols, line states, clocking requirements, encoding of data, and connectors for data transmission. An example of a PHY layer is 10BASE-T, which uses Manchester encoding to transmit data. Repeaters are Layer 1 devices in that they only retransmit signals without decoding them. That means a repeater has no MAC, and the data is only handled by a PHY on the receiving and transmitting ports.

All higher layers talk to the physical layer through a predefined interface. For 10Mbps Ethernet, this is the attachment unit interface (AUI). You can use a DB-15 connector to connect Layer 1 to Layer 2. 100Mbps Ethernet calls this interface the media-independent interface (MII), whereas Gigabit Ethernet calls it the Gigabit media-independent interface (GMII).

Layer 1 interfaces to the actual cable by means of the media-dependent interface (MDI). The MDI for 10BASE-T is the RJ-45 connector, for example.

Layer 2: The Data Link Layer

The data link layer actually consists of two separate pieces: MAC and the Logical Link Control (LLC). The LLC is a standardized interface between a hardware-specific MAC and Layer 3.

The IEEE has published a rather complex LLC specification, called 802.2. All IEEE-approved MACs, such as Ethernet and Token Ring, use this LLC interface to talk to Layer 3. Even some non-IEEE defined MACs, such as FDDI, chose to use this LLC as a standardized, independent interface. The LLC function happens primarily in software.

The MAC layer is of particular interest in this book. The MAC describes how a station schedules, transmits, and receives data in a shared-media environment. All Layer 2 MACs send and receive frames. The MAC generates the physical source and destination addresses for a particular frame, ensures reliable transfer of information across the link, synchronizes data transmission, recognizes errors, and controls the flow of data. The IEEE has defined a number of MAC/Layer 2 specifications over the years, with Ethernet being the most common one. Other IEEE-defined MACs are Token Ring/802.5, Token-Bus/802.4, and 100VG-AnyLAN/802.11. In general, MACs are very important in shared-media environments where multiple nodes can connect to the same transmission medium. The MAC sends and receives data via Layer 1, the media or physical layer.

You can link two different LAN segments via a bridge. You can connect a Thinnet segment (10BASE2) to a 10BASE-T segment by means of a bridge, for example. Bridging is often called a Layer 2 function these days. A bridge contains a MAC and PHY for every port. We discuss fast multiport bridges, better known as Layer 2 switches, in more detail in Chapter 4.

Layer 3: The Network Layer

Ethernet, the focus of this book, operates at Layer 2. With Layer 3 switches, however, you can now buy a Layer 2 and Layer 3 device in one box, so we have added a chapter to cover this topic.

Layer 2 uses frames, and Layer 3 uses packets. A packet comprises one or more frames: It might take more than one frame to transfer a complete packet. The network layer is responsible for setting up the actual connection between source and destination. Often, different paths exist between two endpoints, and Layer 3 needs to determine the best *routes* for getting the packet to the final destination. Therefore, Layer 3 is synonymous with routing.

Sometimes, dissimilar networks consisting of different types of MAC standards need to be connected together. A company may have an FDDI backbone, for example, but workgroups are connected using Ethernet. In this case, the network layer is required to convert between the dissimilar frames present in the Ethernet and FDDI networks. You can do this by taking the individual frames, reassembling the original packet, and then sending out frames in the new framing format again. Layer 3, and routing in particular, is a very complex subject; there are many books that cover this topic.

Figure 3.1 illustrates the workings of repeaters, bridges, and routers with respect to the OSI model.

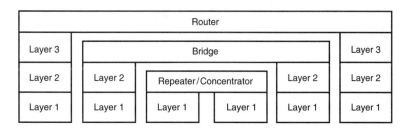

FIGURE 3.1 *Repeaters operate at Layer 1 of the OSI model, bridges at Layer 2, and routers at Layer 3.*

10Mbps Ethernet MAC and PHY Standards

Ethernet is strictly based on a layered OSI model. As a result, you can easily combine the Ethernet MAC with different PHYs. This section discusses the 10Mbps Ethernet MAC standards, and the four major baseband PHY specifications.

The Ethernet CSMA/CD MAC

The Ethernet MAC technology is called *carrier-sense multiple access with collision detection* (CSMA/CD). Figure 3.2 illustrates the CSMA/CD flow.

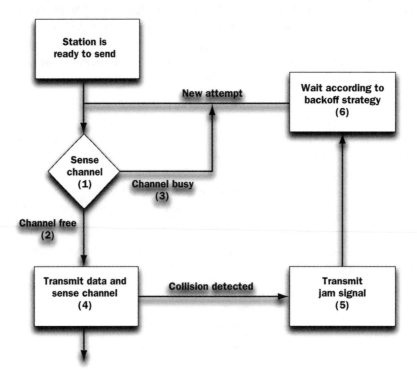

FIGURE 3.2 *A flow diagram illustrating the CSMA/CD MAC.*

CSMA/CD is the shorthand version for about seven different steps that make up an Ethernet transmission. Notice the analogy to human speech among multiple individuals:

1. A station wanting to transmit a frame of information has to ensure that no other nodes or stations are currently using the shared media, so the station listens to the channel first. (This is the *carrier sense* part, also known as "listen before talking.")

2. If the channel is quiet for a certain minimum period of time, called the interframe gap (IFG), the station may initiate a transmission ("talk if quiet").

3. If the channel is busy, it is monitored continuously until it becomes free for the minimum IFG time period. At this point, transmission begins (known as *multiple access*, or "wait for quiet before talking").

4. A collision (two stations transmitting on the cable at the same time) may occur when two or more stations listen while waiting to transmit, simultaneously determine that the channel is free, and begin transmitting at almost the same time. This event would lead to a collision and destroy both data frames. Ethernet continuously monitors the channel during transmission to detect collisions (*collision detection*, or "listen while talking").

5. If a station detects a collision during transmission, that transmission immediately stops. A jam signal is sent to the channel to guarantee that all other stations detect the collision and reject any corrupted data frame they may have been receiving (also part of the collision detection, or "one talker at a time").

6. After a waiting period (called a *backoff*) the stations that wish to transmit attempt to make a new transmission. A special random backoff algorithm (called binary exponential backoff, or BEB) determines a delay time that the different stations will have to wait before attempting to send their data again. Of course, another collision could occur after the first one, especially when many nodes are trying to obtain access at the same time. After 16 consecutive collisions for a given transmission attempt, the packet will be dropped. This can and does happen if the Ethernet channel is overutilized. This is also part of the multiple access method.

7. The sequence returns to step 1.

Ethernet uses frames of data to transmit the actual information, also known as *payload*, from source to destination. Like most other LANs in existence today, Ethernet transmits a frame of variable length. The length of the frame changes because the payload or data field can vary.

The original Ethernet frame specified by Digital, Intel, and Xerox is known as the DEC-Intel-Xerox Ethernet V2.0 frame, or just DIX or Ethernet II frame. The official IEEE Ethernet frame subsequently replaced it. The only difference is in the 2-byte frame type/length field. Figure 3.3 shows both frame types.

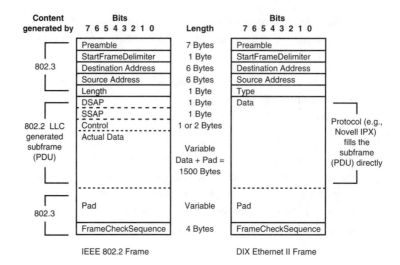

FIGURE 3.3   *The official IEEE and the older DIX Ethernet II frame differ in some respects.*

Let's look at the individual fields that comprise the Ethernet frame:

- The preamble is sent to allow the receiver to synchronize with the incoming transmission and locate the start of the frame. The preamble is a sequence of 01010101..., 7 bytes long.

- The start of frame delimiter (SFD) indicates that the MAC frame is about to commence. The SFD octet or byte is specified as 10101011.

- The source address denotes the sender. Each node has a unique address. The first three bytes of the address are called the block ID or organizationally unique identifier (OUI) and identify the manufacturer of the equipment. The IEEE assigns them. Intel, for example, is identified by the 00-AA-00 (hex) address, 3Com uses the 00-20-AF address, and Cisco uses 00-00-0C. The other three bytes are called the device ID and are assigned by each manufacturer. These are always unique. Three bytes of device ID allows for 16 million different and unique addresses: $2^{24}-1$ or 16,777,215 to be exact. Some of the major Ethernet vendors have shipped more than 16 million Ethernet MAC devices and have started using new OUIs. Some of the references given in Appendix C, "Useful Web Links," show the complete list of vendor OUIs.

- The destination address specifies where the frame will be sent.

- The protocol type is a field in the original DIX V2.0 frame type. It specified which kind of Layer 3 protocol the data contained. A hexadecimal value of 08 00 indicates a TCP/IP packet, for example, and 81 37 indicates a Novell NetWare packet.

- The newer IEEE frame differs from the Ethernet II or DIX frame type in one key area. The IEEE frame is much more popular these days and no longer uses the protocol type field, where it has been replaced with the length field. This specifies the total length of the data that will be transmitted, which can vary from 0 to 1500 bytes. If the contents of this field are 0 to 1500 bytes, you can be sure that it is the length we are discussing. If the contents of the type length/type field are greater than 1500 bytes (for example, 81 37), we are talking about the old DIX frame type.

- The data field can vary from 0 to 1500 bytes in length. The data field is also known as the protocol data unit (PDU). We discuss the contents of the data field in more detail later.

- If the actual data is less than a minimum length required, the MAC will add a variable pad to maintain a minimum total frame size of 64 bytes. If the data is longer than the maximum frame allows, Layer 3 will typically split the packet into more than one frame.

- Finally, a frame check sequence (FCS) ensures accurate transmission. The cyclical redundancy check method (CRC) checks for invalid frames. This value is calculated from the rest of the packet's data and sent along in the FCS frame. The receiving station performs the same calculations and compares its results with the FCS transmitted with the packet. If the results are different, the packet is rejected.

- The maximum total frame size is 1518 bytes. (The frame officially starts with the source address.)

There are a total of four different frame types. The DIX Ethernet II frame discussed previously, plus three different versions of the IEEE frame type: the Ethernet 802.3 frame (also known as Novell Raw LLC), the 802.2 frame, and the 802.2 with SNAP frame. All look slightly different. Figure 3.4 shows the contents of the 1500-byte data field for the four different frame types. The following list details the three different versions of the IEEE frame type:

- The Novell Raw frame format is used only by Novell's NetWare operating system, and uses the 802.3 frame shell type without adding an IEEE 802.2 LLC header within the data field. In this case, NetWare adds its own IPX information. This type of frame is called "Novell Raw" because it encapsulates the IPX data in raw form without any 802.2 LLC information. Because the frame doesn't use the IEEE 802.2 LLC information, this frame type is actually Novell-proprietary and not 802.3 compliant.

- For the 802.2 frame type, the data field contains the 802.2 LLC-embedded information. The IEEE frame contains the protocol type information within the LLC subframe. Three fields are located at the beginning of the data field. The DSAP field, a 1-byte SSAP field, and a 1-byte Control field. The IEEE frame assigns Service Access Point numbers; among those currently defined are E0 for Novell, F0 for NetBIOS, 06 for TCP/IP, and AA for the Subnetwork Access Protocol (SNAP).

- The 802.2 with SNAP frame is almost identical to the 802.2 frame, except it supports more than 256 protocol types by adding a 5-byte Protocol Identification field. On any SNAP packet, both the DSAP and SSAP fields are set to AA, and the Control field is set to 03. The 5-byte protocol field then follows.

Table 3.2 lists all the relevant Ethernet MAC frame parameters. Most 10Mbps Ethernet/802.3 MAC parameters are listed in bit times. The Ethernet MAC is inherently scalable. All the parameters can be measured in terms of the time taken to transmit 1 bit of data, referred to as *bit times*. Note that the actual speed of Ethernet (10Mbps) is not mentioned in the MAC specification at all. This makes it very easy to run Ethernet at different speeds.

TABLE 3.2 KEY 10MBPS ETHERNET MAC AND FRAME PARAMETERS, SPECIFIED IN BIT TIMES

Parameter	Value (Bit Times)
Time	512 bit times
MinInterFrameGap	96 bit times (or 9.6 µs)
AttemptLimit	16 (tries)
BackoffLimit	10 (exponent)
JamSize	32 bits
MaxFrameSize	12144 bits (1518 bytes)
MinFrameSize	512 bits (64 bytes)
AddressSize	48 bits

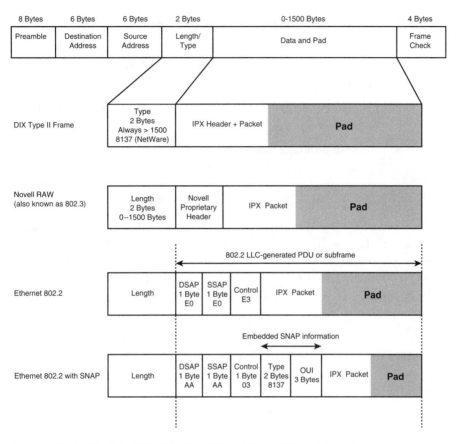

FIGURE 3.4 *The data field of the four different frame Ethernet types in use.*

Calculating the time to transmit 1 bit for 10Mbps Ethernet transmission becomes very easy:

$$1\ \text{bit-time} = \frac{1\ \text{bit}}{10\text{Mhz}} = 0.1\mu s\ \text{or}\ 100ns$$

For 1Mbps Ethernet/StarLAN, the frame looks exactly the same. The only thing that changes is the bit time. For StarLAN, the bit time is 1/1MHz = 1µs, or 1000ns. Fast Ethernet works exactly the same way: The frame is identical again, but the bit time is reduced to 1/10, or 10ns.

Ethernet PHYs

This section looks at the different PHY implementations for 10Mbps Ethernet (see Figure 3.5). There are officially five ways to transmit 10Mbps Ethernet:

- 10BASE5 is the original thick Ethernet coaxial cable standard, dating back to the early 1970s.

- 10BASE2, also known as thin Ethernet, was added in the early 1980s and uses a thinner coaxial cable.

- In 1990, Ethernet over unshielded twisted-pair, known as 10BASE-T, was standardized.

- 10BASE-F, although less well known, is very important because it utilizes fiber cabling to carry Ethernet over extended distances. The physical layers mentioned so far all use baseband transmission methods, which means the entire frequency spectrum transmits the data.

- 10BROAD36 is different from all the other Ethernet PHY standards in that it uses broadband transmission technology to transmit. This allows different channels to communicate simultaneously on the same cable. 10BROAD36 is far less popular and no similar 100Mbps broadband PHY exists, so we will not discuss 10BROAD36 in this book.

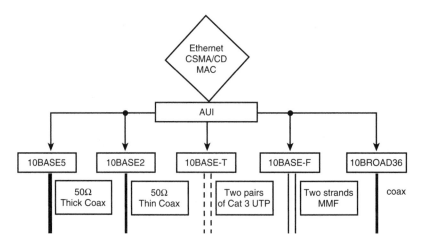

FIGURE 3.5   *The different Ethernet/802.3 PHYs.*

10BASE5: Thicknet

10BASE5 is the original Ethernet 802.3 standard. 10BASE5 utilizes a thick, often yellow, coaxial cable that has a physical diameter of 10mm. The cable has to be terminated with a 50Ohm/1W resistor. Up to 100 stations per segment are allowed.

10BASE5 utilizes a bus topology, as all stations are connected via one single continuous coax cable. The maximum length of one coax segment is 500 meters, a function of the quality of coaxial cable.

Stations using a network interface card (NIC) are attached with a DB-15 connector to the short AUI cable. The AUI cable in turn connects to a media attachment unit (MAU) that is bolted to the coax cable by means of a device commonly called the vampire connector. The MAU contains the actual transceiver that connects to the coaxial cable.

For proper CSMA/CD operation, one end node needs to sense that a collision has occurred at the other end of the wire. The maximum network diameter of an Ethernet network is limited by the time it takes for a signal to travel from one end to the other, called the *propagation delay*. The network diameter for 10BASE5 is limited to 2500 meters, consisting of five 500-meter segments with four repeaters.

10BASE5 derives its name from the MAC 10Mbps signaling rate (*10*), baseband transmission (10*BASE*), and the maximum 500-meter distance between stations on one segment (10BASE*5*).

Note

The IEEE Ethernet naming convention works as follows. The 10 indicates the transmission speed in Mbps. The term BASE indicates baseband transmission, as opposed to BROAD for broadband transmission. Originally, the last variable contained a number to indicate segment length. The 5, for example, means 500-meter segment length, synonymous with the original thick Ethernet standard. One would think that the 2 in 10BASE2 indicates 200-meter segment length. Yet 10BASE2 is specified to be only 185 meters, or 300 meters in a point-to-point configuration without repeaters. Maybe the 2 is an arithmetic mean, or 185 meters rounded up? With newer Ethernet standards, the IEEE chose letters to describe the physical layer rather than numbers. The T in 10BASE-T, for example, indicates unshielded twisted-pair cabling. The T4 in 100BASE-T4 indicates four pairs of unshielded twisted-pair cabling.

The different Ethernet standards have several spelling versions. Many people use lowercase to write the word BASE, but in IEEE terminology BASE is always capitalized. Often we see a hyphen inserted between the word BASE and the next designator. The hyphen is only inserted for readability purposes (for example, 10BASE-F). If the standard can be read clearly otherwise, no hyphen is used (for example, 10BASE5).

10BASE5 uses Manchester encoding to transmit data. This encoding scheme translates a logical 1 to a fall in voltage, also known as a 1-0 bit pattern, a vise in voltage or 0-1 bit pattern.

10BASE2: Thin Ethernet

10BASE2 is similar to 10BASE5 and was invented primarily to reduce the cost and complexity of installation of 10BASE5. The differences between 10BASE5 and 10BASE2 are as follows:

- This standard uses an RG-58 50Ohm coaxial cable that is cheaper and thinner than that used for 10BASE5, hence the name Cheapernet or Thinnet, which is short for "Thin Ethernet."

- 10BASE2 integrates the functions of the MAU and the transceiver/AUI cable onto the NIC itself. A BNC barrel connector replaces the AUI or DB-15 connector on the NIC.

- The inferior cable quality means reduced distance limits. The maximum length of a 10BASE2 segment has been reduced to 185 meters, as opposed to 500 meters for 10BASE5.

- 10BASE2 allows only 30 nodes per segment, versus 100 nodes for 10BASE5.

- 10BASE2 retains the four repeater/five segment rule from 10BASE5, allowing a maximum network diameter of $5 \times 185m = 925m$. If no repeaters are used, you can extend the maximum length of the single segment to 300 meters.

Compared with Thick Ethernet, Thin Ethernet is much easier to install, stations are easier to add, and most importantly, Thinnet costs significantly less. As a result, Thinnet became very popular, effectively replacing Thick Ethernet as a workgroup cabling solution.

10BASE-T: Twisted-Pair Ethernet

In 1990, the IEEE adopted the 802.3i 10BASE-T standard, a completely new physical layer standard for Ethernet. 10BASE-T is very different from coaxial Thick and Thin Ethernet in many respects:

- 10BASE-T utilizes two pairs of unshielded twisted-pair telephone-type cable: one pair of wiring to transmit data, and a second pair to receive data. Eight-pin modular plugs, type RJ-45, are used as connectors.

- Just like the other Ethernet PHY standards, 10BASE-T uses Manchester encoding, but with predistortion of the electrical signal to allow transmission over UTP. (*Predistortion* means the electrical signal uses an offset voltage and doesn't always return to 0V when idle.) The signaling frequency is 20MHz, and UTP cable (Category 3 or better) must be used.

- 10BASE-T was the first Ethernet PHY to incorporate the Link Integrity feature that makes installation and troubleshooting cabling problems a lot easier. The two devices at each end of the wire send out a heartbeat pulse every 16 meters. Both hub and NIC look for this signal when connected to each other, for example. Receiving the heartbeat signal means that a physical connection has been established. Most 10BASE-T equipment features an LED indicating that the link is good. LAN managers typically start troubleshooting wiring problems by looking at the state of the link LED on both ends of the wire.

- The maximum segment length is 100 meters, which is in accordance with the EIA/TIA 568-A wiring standard. Repeater-repeater links are also limited to a maximum of 100 meters. (We discuss 10BASE-T wiring in greater detail in Chapter 4.)

- The topology is changed to a star, and only two nodes per segment are allowed (the station and the repeater, or repeater-repeater, or station-station with a crossover cable).

- 10BASE-T retains the four repeater/five segment rule from 10BASE5. This means a 10BASE-T LAN can have a maximum diameter of 500 meters.

- External MAUs are allowed, but most 10BASE-T equipment integrates the functions of the MAU in the data terminal equipment (abbreviated as DTE, also called node) or the hub itself. (A *DTE* is defined as an Ethernet node that has a Layer 2 function—that is, a NIC or a bridge or switch. A repeater is a Layer 1 device and is not a DTE.)

From a pure cabling perspective, 10BASE-T, or Twisted-Pair Ethernet as it is also known, actually represented a step backward. That's because coax cabling is far superior to UTP in terms of bandwidth. Yet 10BASE-T was a major step forward for Ethernet overall. 10BASE-T became popular overnight because it adopted the prevalent structured cabling system developed by the telecommunications industry. This structured cabling system mandated central repeaters and a star-shaped, planned, and structured wiring topology. This was very different and far superior to the point-point, no-structure, single failure point coax cable method that had previously been used by both 10BASE5 and 10BASE2.

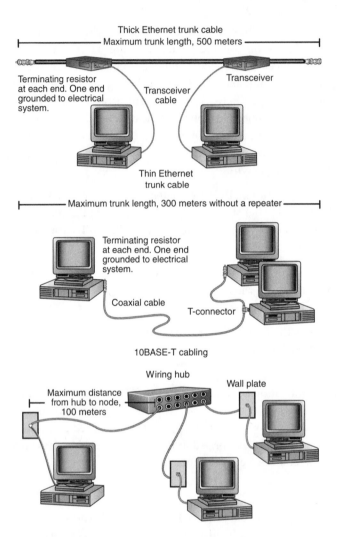

FIGURE 3.6   *The three classic Ethernet standards are 10BASE5, 10BASE2, and 10BASE-T.*

10BASE-F: Fiber Ethernet

10BASE-F became an official IEEE standard in 1993, although Fiber Ethernet equipment had been available for a number of years before that. 10BASE-F is based on the Fiber Optic Inter-Repeater Link (FOIRL) specification of 1987, which was created to interconnect repeaters using an extended distance fiber-optic cable link.

10BASE-F utilizes duplex fiber (two strands of multimode or single-mode glass fiber), transmitting on one strand and receiving on the other. Multimode fiber (MMF) of 62.5/125 µm diameter is most often used with 10BASE-F to carry infrared light from LEDs. The IEC BFOC/2.5 miniature bayonet connectors have become the de facto standard. This device is also known as the ST connector, which was popularized by AT&T.

The umbrella term *10BASE-F* actually refers to three different sets of fiber-optic specifications, namely 10BASE-FL, 10BASE-FP, and 10BASE-FB. The 10BASE-FL (*L*, as in link) standard replaces the older FOIRL specifications and is backward compatible with existing FOIRL-based equipment. 10BASE-FL is the most universal 10Mbps fiber standard and can be used to connect DTEs, repeaters, or switches. 10BASE-FL is the most widely used portion of the 10BASE-F fiber-optic specifications, and equipment is available from a large number of vendors. The 10BASE-F standard also incorporates the 10BASE-FB (*B* as in backbone), and 10BASE-FP (*P* as in passive) standards. These are extremely rare, however. Table 3.3 provides a comparison of the different 10BASE-F choices. Table 3.4 summarizes the specific 10BASE-FL distance limitations.

TABLE 3.3 THE FOUR 10BASE-F OPTIONS

10BASE-F Version	Application	Number of Repeaters	Distance Limitation
FOIRL	Prestandard, repeaters only	2	1000 meters
10BASE-FL	New standard, universal, including repeaters, switches, nodes	4	400–2000 meters
10BASE-FB	Backbone repeaters with embedded AUI		2000 meters
10BASE-FP	Central repeater without AC power	1 passive STAR	500 meters or 300 meters

TABLE 3.4 10BASE-FL DISTANCE LIMITATIONS FOR DIFFERENT CONNECTIONS

Connection Type	Distance
Any repeater-to-DTE fiber segment	400 meters
With four repeaters and five segments	500 meters
Any inter-repeater fiber segment	1000 meters
Without a repeater (DTE-DTE or switch-switch)	2000 meters

Table 3.5 provides a summary of the 10Mbps Ethernet/802.3 PHY standards.

TABLE 3.5 SUMMARY OF DIFFERENT 10MBPS ETHERNET/802.3 PHY STANDARDS

Parameter	10BASE5	10BASE2	10BASE-F	10BASE-T
Maximum segment length	500m	185m	Varies from 400m to 2000m	100m
Topology	Bus	Bus	Star	Star
Medium	50-Ω thick coax	50-Ω thin coax	Multimode fiber (a few vendors provide for single-mode equipment, too)	100-Ω UTP
Connector	NICDB15	BNC	ST[1]	RJ-45
Medium attachment	MAU bolted to coax	External or on NIC	External or on NIC	External or on NIC
Stations/cable segment	100	30	N/A	2 (NIC and repeater)
Maximum segments	5	5	5	5

[1] ST is the official connector, but SC and MIC are actually more popular.

Half- and Full-Duplex Ethernet

Regular Ethernet is a shared-media access method. All networks that utilize a MAC are based on a shared-media operation (hence the term *media access*, which implies that the transmission media are shared and access is negotiated and not always given).

By definition, a shared-media LAN transmission method also implies half-duplex operation. *Half-duplex* means that a station is either transmitting or receiving, but not both, at the same time. That's because in CSMA/CD, a station has to listen to see whether the channel is available, and only if it is can a station start transmitting. When one station is transmitting data, all others have to listen. Therefore, it is an either-or situation for all stations on the LAN. This method of operation was very efficient for the coaxial cable on which Ethernet grew up. Running a single coaxial cable throughout an entire office and providing everyone an access opportunity to the cable every few milliseconds was very efficient. Sharing the transmission media also brought with it collisions, something that has given Ethernet a bit of a bad name. The truth is that collisions are a very effective and efficient method of preventing overload.

Full-duplex, on the other hand, means that a station is simultaneously transmitting *and* receiving. In the early 1990s, many events occurred that have made Full-Duplex Ethernet a reality:

- The introduction of 10BASE-T wiring offered the capability for separate transmit and receive data paths. Before the arrival of 10BASE-T, coaxial cable didn't offer this capability; only one electrical (coax) wire made simultaneous transmission and reception impossible.

Note

Technically speaking, a single cable can carry separate transmit and receive data streams in two directions. This is known as dual-duplex and requires a specially designed physical layer. The electronic circuitry required to do this is very complex, and typically requires a sophisticated DSP. Until recently, the cost and complexity associated with DSP technology was considered prohibitive. 1000BASE-T, however, will utilize simultaneous transmit and receive on four pairs of UTP. With 10BASE-T, the existing physical layer could be kept for full-duplex transmission.

- The emergence of multiport Ethernet bridges or switches meant that the physical media were no longer being shared by multiple users but were increasingly being used to connect two switches or a switch and a NIC together in a point-to-point manner.

In 1992, Kalpana seized on this opportunity so that it could effectively double the speed of Ethernet through full-duplex transmission. Kalpana started working with several other industry vendors to establish a de facto industry standard for full-duplex Ethernet over UTP wire. Kalpana proposed the following scheme:

- One pair of UTP wire (or one fiber strand) would be used exclusively for transmission and one for reception of data.

- A new kind of multiport bridge or switch would be required at both ends of the wire.

The Ethernet MAC algorithm would be modified as follows:

- No carrier-sense (CRS) would be required, because a cable pair would now be dedicated for both transmission and reception.

- Similarly, no collision-detection (CDT) jam or exponential backoff are required because collisions are no longer present: They happen in a multiple-user segment only.

Essentially, *full-duplex* Ethernet means running Ethernet without the CSMA/CD MAC in operation (refer to Figure 3.2, without steps 1, 2, 3, 5, and 6). Ethernet frames are transmitted and received simultaneously on two pairs of UTP or fiber at any time. The only possible problem is one of data overflow. We can deal with this issue through flow control. Kalpana proposed that artificial collisions be generated by the receiving station if an overload condition exists.

Figure 3.7 illustrates the evolution of Ethernet from a shared-media coaxial-cable LAN with collisions to a dedicated media full-duplex technology.

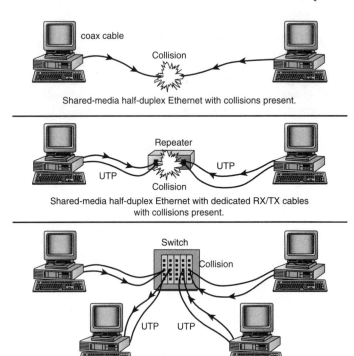

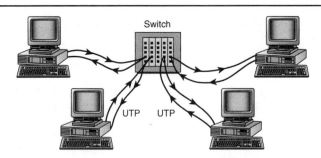

FIGURE 3.7 *The evolution of Ethernet from shared-media, half-duplex to dedicated media full-duplex.*

Note

A two-user switched connection is a prerequisite to Full-Duplex Ethernet because full-duplex requires a point-to-point connection with only two stations present. Note that Switched Ethernet does not automatically imply full-duplex operation.

Full-duplex has played an increasingly important role with the introduction of Fast and Gigabit Ethernet. In 1997, the 802.3X full–duplex/flow control standard was approved. (Chapter 4 covers this in more detail.) Some people in the IEEE even advocated making Gigabit Ethernet a full-duplex–only technology, which means dropping the all-too-familiar CSMA/CD MAC concept altogether. In the end, the half-duplex followers prevailed, and CSMA/CD operation was included in the standard. It is doubtful whether we will ever see any half-duplex shared Gigabit Ethernet equipment in the marketplace, however.

A trend is currently in place to move from repeated half-duplex to Switched full-duplex Ethernet. With the advent of Gigabit Ethernet in particular, it looks like CSMA/CD and collisions are heading for extinction. What will live on is the language of Ethernet, namely the 802.3 frame format. Our well-known Ethernet frames will be zooming along at 1, 10, 100, 1000, and someday 10000Mbps.

100BASE-T/Fast Ethernet

100BASE-T is the 100Mbps version of the classic Ethernet standard. The IEEE officially adopted the new IEEE 802.3u Fast Ethernet/100BASE-T specification in May 1995. The salient features of 100BASE-T are as follows:

- The 100BASE-T MAC uses the original Ethernet MAC operating at 10 times the speed.

- The 100BASE-T standard is designed to include multiple physical layers. Three different 100BASE-T physical layers are part of the 802.3u standard: two for UTP and one for multimode fiber. An additional UTP PHY was added later as the 802.3y specification.

- Like 10BASE-T and 10BASE-F, 100BASE-T requires a star-wired configuration with a central hub.

- 100BASE-T also includes a specification for an MII, a 100Mbps version of today's AUI. The MII layer is a digital interface connecting MAC and PHY and allows for external transceivers.

The differences between 10BASE-T and 100BASE-T are in the PHY standards and network design areas. That's because the new IEEE 802.3u 100BASE-T specification contains many new rules for repeaters and network topology. Figure 3.8 provides an overview of the new IEEE 802.3u standard.

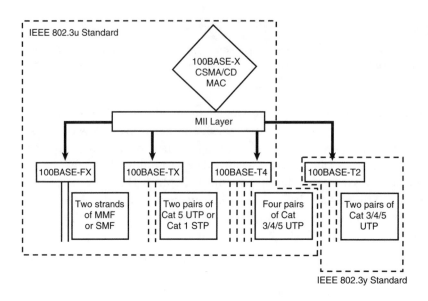

FIGURE 3.8 *An overview of the 100BASE-T 802.3u standard showing MAC, MII, and the three original PHYs. (100BASE-T2 was added as 802.3y a year later.)*

The Fast Ethernet CSMA/CD MAC

The 100BASE-T MAC is almost identical to the 10Mbps "classic" Ethernet MAC. As mentioned earlier, the 802.3 CSMA/CD MAC is inherently scalable, which means that it can run at different speeds and be interfaced to different physical layers. StarLAN/1BASE5 took advantage of this scalability to run Ethernet at 1Mbps. Table 3.6 compares 10Mbps and the new 100Mbps Ethernet MAC standards. Note that the 100Mbps Ethernet MAC retains all the 10Mbps Ethernet MAC parameters except for InterFrameGap, which has been decreased to one-tenth its original value, from 9.6µs to 0.96µs. A Fast Ethernet frame has the same framing format as a 10Mbps Ethernet frame, except that it is transmitted across the wire at 10 times the speed.

TABLE 3.6 10MBPS COMPARED TO 100MBPS ETHERNET MAC PARAMETERS (MOST VALUES ARE IDENTICAL WHEN MEASURED IN BIT TIMES, BUT ONE-TENTH THE VALUE WHEN MEASURED IN REAL TIME)

Parameter	Ethernet/802.3	Fast Ethernet/802.3u
slotTime	512 bit times	Same[1]
Minimum InterFrameGap	96 bit times (9.6µs)	Same (=0.96µs)
attemptLimit	16 (tries)	Same
backoffLimit	10 (exponential number)	Same
jamSize	32 bits	Same

Parameter	Ethernet/802.3	Fast Ethernet/802.3u
maxFrameSize	1518 bytes	Same
MinFrameSize	64 bytes (512 bits)	Same
AddressSize	48 bits	Same

1 *Same means same value in bit times as 10 Ethernet (for example, the value in the column to the left).*

You can calculate the 100BASE-T bit time as follows:

$$1 \text{ bit-time} = \frac{1 \text{ bit}}{100 \text{Mhz}} = 10\text{ns}$$

Fast Ethernet PHYs

As with 10BASE-T, 100BASE-T combines the CSMA/CD MAC with different physical layer specifications. The IEEE 802.3u specification contains three new physical layers for 100Mbps Ethernet:

- 100BASE-TX, which requires two pairs of Category 5 UTP or Type 1 STP cabling
- 100BASE-FX, which uses two strands of multimode fiber
- 100BASE-T4, which requires four pairs of Category 3 or better cabling

Then there is the IEEE 802.3y 100BASE-T2 PHY standard, which was completed about a year after the original Fast Ethernet standard. 100BASE-T2 utilizes only two pairs of Category 3 cable, but is virtually unheard of. 100BASE-TX and 100BASE-FX are the most popular 100BASE-T physical layers. They were based on the FDDI/CDDI physical layer, utilizing the 4B/5B encoding method. (Chapter 6, "Cabling and More Physical Layer Details," gives more information on the 4B/5B encoding method.) 100BASE-TX is the de facto standard for high-speed horizontal connections; 100BASE-FX is becoming increasingly popular for vertical/backbone connections. 100BASE-T4 is rarely used, whereas we know of no 100BASE-T2 products that are shipping.

Like 10BASE-T and 10BASE-F, all 100BASE-T PHY specifications require a star configuration with a central hub. All 100BASE-T UTP PHYs use the RJ-45 connector and specify a maximum 100-meter cable distance.

This section provides an overview of the different 100BASE-T physical layers.

100BASE-FX: Fast Ethernet for Fiber-Optic Cabling

100BASE-FX (like 100BASE-TX) borrows its physical layer from the ANSI X3T9.5 FDDI physical layer media-dependent (fiber PMD) standard. 100BASE-FX utilizes two strands of the multimode (62.5/125μm) fiber cabling made popular by FDDI. The maximum segment length for fiber-optic connections varies.

For two switches or a switch-adapter connection using multimode fiber, 412 meters is allowed. You can increase this number to 2000 meters if the link is full duplex. (The IEEE did not specify SMF as part of the 802.3u standard, but numerous vendors are selling SMF-based equipment with distances ranging from 10km to 20km.) 100BASE-FX repeater diameters can be up to 320 meters.

100BASE-TX: Fast Ethernet for Category 5 UTP

100BASE-TX is based on the ANSI-developed copper FDDI twisted-pair physical layer-dependent sublayer technology (TP-PMD), also known as CDDI. 100BASE-TX has numerous similarities to 10BASE-T. It utilizes the same two pairs of unshielded twisted-pair cable, the same RJ-45 connector, and the same maximum segment length of 100 meters. As in 10BASE-T, one pair of wiring transmits data, and the second receives data.

100BASE-T4: Fast Ethernet for Four-Pair Category 3 UTP

100BASE-T4 was the only new PHY developed for 100BASE-T. It was designed to cater to the huge installed base of Category 3 voice-grade wiring. 100BASE-T4 utilizes four pairs of voice or data grade unshielded twisted-pair Category 3 or better cable. Unlike 10BASE-T and 100BASE-TX, no separate dedicated transmit and receive pairs are present, so full-duplex operation is not possible. Note that all four pairs need to be terminated for 100BASE-T4 operation.

Why Did T4 Flop?

Both 100BASE-TX and 100BASE-FX were based on the FDDI/CDDI physical layer technology. Originally, the 100Mbps MAC and these two original PHYs were collectively known as 100BASE-X. (The X was chosen because Fast Ethernet was based on the 100Mbs Ethernet MAC coupled to the FDDI PHY technology.) 100BASE-X is also synonymous with prestandard products. When the IEEE standard was approved, however, everyone quickly adopted the official designation terminology.

Borrowing from the existing ANSI FDDI technology meant that the IEEE 802.3u standard could be finished relatively quickly. More importantly, however, 100BASE-X products were able to get

to market very quickly. FX and TX products could be built and sold *before* the actual 802.3u standard was officially ratified because existing FDDI/CDDI semiconductor and magnetics components were available to build TX or FX NICs, hubs, and switches.

T4 was also part of the original 802.3u specification and was supposed to cater to the huge installed base of Category 3 voice-grade wiring. Unfortunately, T4 has been a market flop because T4 products only started shipping a year after the standard was approved. This two-year delta gave TX products a head start. As a result, 100BASE-TX is by far the most widely used physical layer specification for

continues

continued

100BASE-T today, accounting for more than 95% of all Fast Ethernet shipments.

T4 required four pairs, whereas both 10BASE-T and 100BASE-TX only utilized two pairs. This issue caused a lot of confusion. The original EIA/TIA 568 cabling rules specify four pairs to be installed, which meant using two pairs for 10BASE-T and two spare pairs. Yet some people chose to use the two spare pairs for voice or only installed two pairs in the first place,

making the cabling plant unsuitable for T4.

In some ways, T4 was also a defensive marketing effort in the controversy with 100VG-AnyLAN, covered in Chapters 1 and 2. At the time, the 100VG advocates made a big deal of the fact that 100BASE-TX required Category 5 cable, whereas 100VG ran on four pairs of Category 3. The adoption of the IEEE T4 standard effectively neutralized the 100VG argument. Later on, the 100VG people adopted a two-pair Category 5 version as well, but 100VG had already lost the battle by that time.

100BASE-T2: Fast Ethernet for Two-Pair Category 3 UTP

100BASE-T2 is virtually unknown. It is an IEEE standard, but no products ever made it to market. We wanted to cover it mainly for completeness and because 100BASE-T2 technology will reappear soon with the 1000BASE-T PHY. IEEE engineers came up with 100BASE-T2 because they thought 100BASE-T4 had two shortcomings they could improve. First, T4 requires four pairs of Category 3 wire, but some installations only have two pairs present or usable. The other issue with T4 is that it cannot do full-duplex. When 100BASE-T4 was designed, it was thought that four pairs would be required to transfer 100Mbps. Due to advances in digital signal processing (DSP) and integrated circuit chip technology, it has become possible to transfer 100Mbps over only two pairs of Category 3 UTP. The IEEE worked for about two years on the 100BASE-T2 standard. By the time the standard was complete, however, 100BASE-TX already dominated the market to such an extent that no T2 products were ever built. The following are the main features of 100BASE-T2:

- Utilizes two pairs of voice or data grade unshielded twisted-pair Category 3, 4, or 5 cable.

- Uses both pairs for simultaneous transmitting and receiving on both pairs, also known as dual-duplex.

- Uses a more complicated five-level encoding scheme called PAM5x5. (*PAM* stands for pulse amplitude modulation.)

TABLE 3.7 A SUMMARY OF THE DIFFERENT 100BASE-T PHYSICAL LAYERS

PHY Parameter	10BASE-T	100BASE-TX
Origin of Technology		CDDI TP PMD (ANSI X3T9.5)
IEEE standard	802.3i-1990	802.3u-1995
Encoding	Manchester	4B/5B
Cabling required	UTP Category 3/4/5	UTP Category 5 or STP Type 1
Signal frequency	20MHz	125MHz
Number of pairs required	2	2
Number of transmit pairs	1	1
Distance	100m	100m
Full-duplex capable?	Yes	Yes

1 150m for repeater-DTE, 412m for DTE-DTE, 2000m for full-duplex DTE-DTE, and 10km for single-mode full-duplex DTE-DTE.

Table 3.7 compares 10BASE-T with the four 100BASE-T physical layer specifications. We discuss the different physical layers and their cabling requirements in more detail in Chapter 6.

Fast Ethernet MII

MII is similar to AUI for 10Mbps Ethernet. The MII layer defines a standard electrical and mechanical interface between the 100BASE-T MAC and the various PHY layers. This standard interface works like AUI in the classic Ethernet world in that it allows manufacturers to build media- or wiring-independent products, with external MAUs being used to connect to the actual physical cabling.

The electrical signals differ between MII and AUI. AUI has a stronger signal, capable of driving 50-meter cable lengths; the MII signals are digital logic-type signals, capable of driving 0.5 meters of cable. MII uses a 40-pin connector, similar to the SCSI connector, although it is smaller. Figure 3.9 shows an external MII 100BASE-FX transceiver. We don't think you will see too many of these because most Fast Ethernet hubs and NICs already include the transceiver.

MII never became as popular as AUI. AUI became a de facto standard because Thick Ethernet hardware wasn't available with an onboard transceiver. That only came later, with 10BASE2 or 10BASE-T. Yet with 10BASE2 and 10BASE-T, the AUI connector provided the capability for backward compatibility through an external transceiver. With 100BASE-T, most hardware manufacturers decided to skip MII and offer different products that integrate the physical layer transceiver already. NIC manufacturers, for example, often sell the same basic design in a 100BASE-TX and in a 100BASE-T4 version. You have to choose up front which media type you need. Think of it as a choice between Thinnet-only or 10BASE-T–only products, as opposed to combo or AUI-only cards using

100BASE-T4	100BASE-FX	100BASE-T2
New; developed from 1995 to 1996	FDDI PMD (ANSI X3T9.5)	New; developed from 1994 to 1995
802.3u-1995	802.3u-1995	802.3y-1996
8B/6T	4B/5B	PAM5x5
UTP Category 3/4/5	Multimode or single-mode fiber	UTP Category 3/4/5
25MHz	125MHz	25MHz
4	2	2
3	1	2
100m	150/412/2000m[1]	100m
No	Yes	Yes

external transceivers. An example of a device with an MII connector is the Intel Pro/100 Server adapter, which uses an MII connector to provide you with the flexibility of either attaching an external fiber or a UTP PHY transceiver.

FIGURE 3.9 *Fast Ethernet MII transceivers are similar to the old Ethernet AUI transceivers, but are very rare because most Fast Ethernet hardware includes an onboard transceiver. MII uses a 40-pin connector very similar to SCSI-2.*

Gigabit Ethernet

In 1995, Fast Ethernet seemed like such an ingenious, yet simple, idea. 100BASE-T became an overnight success, and it was only a matter of time before the frequency would be increased another order of magnitude. Work started on Gigabit shortly after the Fast Ethernet standard had been ratified. Three years later, on June 25, 1998, the IEEE 802.3z standard was officially adopted.

If you have read this chapter's information on Fast Ethernet, we should just ask you to go back and read everything with an extra zero added everywhere. Gigabit Ethernet is that simple. Some differences arise in the physical layers, network design, and minimum frame size that we cover here and in Chapter 6. For the most part, however, Gigabit Ethernet is just supercharged Fast Ethernet.

The IEEE 802.3z standard includes the Gigabit Ethernet MAC, as well as three physical layers that use the 8B/10B encoding originally developed as part of the ANSI Fibre Channel technology.

Essentially, the IEEE engineers bolted the existing Fibre Channel PHY to the Ethernet MAC running at 10 times the speed of the Fast Ethernet MAC. The 802.3z standard encompasses two fiber physical layer standards, 1000BASE-LX and 1000BASE-SX as well as one copper PHY, 1000BASE-CX. The copper-based PHY was also inherited from the Fibre Channel standard and was included to enable cost-effective and quick cross-connects. A fourth PHY, called 1000BASE-T, is still under development.

Note

The ANSI X3T11 committee is responsible for the Fibre Channel technology. ANSI decided to spell Fibre with an re rather than an er to differentiate it from the fiber-optic cable on which it runs.

The IEEE has also defined a Gigabit MII (GMII), which is similar to the Fast Ethernet MII and connects Gigabit MAC and PHY. The GMII is only an electrical interface specification, and unlike the Fast Ethernet MII, the specification does not include a connector. The biggest benefit of the GMII is that it allows circuit designers to use existing Fibre Channel PHY chips and will allow for easy redesign of existing 1000BASE-LX equipment to accommodate future PHY transceivers.

Some people in the IEEE wanted to make Gigabit Ethernet a full-duplex–only technology; others wanted to preserve the classic CSMA/CD algorithm and the half-duplex shared operation. The reason for preserving the CSMA/CD part of

Ethernet was twofold. First, many vendors didn't want to redesign their Ethernet MAC chips completely. (Running it at 10 times the clock frequency didn't take a complete redesign.) Second, some IEEE members just wanted to preserve the 25-year heritage of CSMA/CD itself.

Figure 3.10 shows all the different Gigabit Ethernet components.

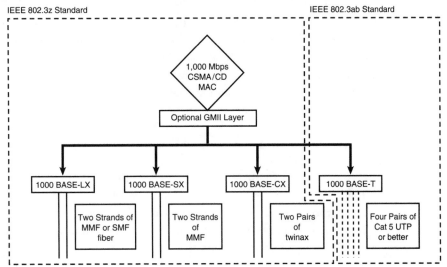

FIGURE 3.10 *A Gigabit Ethernet block diagram showing the MAC, GMII, and four different physical layers.*

100BASE-X refers to the original Fast Ethernet MAC and FX/TX PHYs. Similarly, 1000BASE-X refers to the 1000Mbps MAC and the LX/SX/CX transceiver technology.

The Gigabit Ethernet MAC

The main points of the Gigabit Ethernet MAC are the following:

- Gigabit Ethernet uses the official 802.3 frame format, identical to that of 10Mbps and 100Mbps Ethernet (refer to Figure 3.3).

- Like 10Mbps and 100Mbps Ethernet, Gigabit Ethernet can operate in both half- and full-duplex mode.

- The 1000Mbps MAC uses the original Ethernet MAC operating at 100 times the speed. Running the Ethernet MAC at Gigabit speeds has created some challenges in terms of the implementation of CSMA/CD. To make CSMA/CD work at 1GHz, a minor modification was required. The slot time has been increased to 512 bytes, as opposed to 64 bytes for 10 and 100Mbps Ethernet. The slot time, in essence, is the allocated time during which the complete frame needs to be transmitted. During the slot time, the transmitter retains control of the media. If the transmitted frame is smaller than 512 bytes, an extra carrier extension is added. The carrier extension concept is similar to the PAD that is added to the end of the data field within the frame. The carrier extension is added at the end of the completed frame to make it meet the new slot time of 512 bytes.

- IEEE 802.3z specification defines both half- and full-duplex operation. When very small frames are transmitted in a half-duplex environment, many carrier extension bits will be added. This makes Gigabit Ethernet very inefficient because large amounts of useless carrier extension bits are transmitted. Assume, for example, that we wanted to transmit only 64-byte minimum size frames. The carrier extension would add 438 bytes of carrier extension to meet the spec of a 512-byte slot time. To calculate the overall efficiency, we still need to add the interframe gap (IFG) overhead of 12 bytes: $64/(512+12) = 12\%$ efficiency, or 122Mbps. This is only marginally better than 100BASE-T! Small frames are quite common, so this inefficiency for small frame sizes needed to be addressed. The IEEE 802.3z Gigabit MAC includes a feature called *burst mode*. In this case, a station may continuously transmit multiple smaller frames, up to a maximum of 8192 bytes worth of data. The interframe intervals will also be filled with carrier extension so that the wire never appears free to any other stations during the burst cycle.

Table 3.8 compares the 10, 100, and 1000Mbps Ethernet MAC parameters.

TABLE 3.8 A COMPARISON OF 10, 100, AND 1000MBPS ETHERNET MAC PARAMETERS

Parameter	Ethernet/802.3	Fast Ethernet/ 802.3u	Gigabit Ethernet/802.3z
SlotTime	512 bit times	Same[1]	512-byte times (4096 bit times)
Minimum InterFrameGap	96 bit times	Same	Same
AttemptLimit	16 (tries)	Same	Same
BackoffLimit	10 (exponential number)	Same	Same
JamSize	32 bits	Same	Same
MaxFrameSize	1518 bytes	Same	Same
MinFrameSize	64 bytes (512 bits)	Same	Same
AddressSize	48 bits	Same	Same

[1] *Same means same value in bit times as 10 or 100Mbps Ethernet (for example, the value in the column to the left).*

Gigabit Ethernet PHYs

The 802.3z Gigabit Ethernet standard includes three PHYs: 1000BASE-SX and LX to support fiber-optic cable and 1000BASE-CX for shielded 150-Ohm copper cable. Gigabit Ethernet used the same proven concept that Fast Ethernet had already pioneered: It uses an off-the-shelf PHY standard. In this case, the ANSI X3T11 Fibre Channel PHY was chosen. Fibre Channel was a natural choice, as it was proven, and components were readily available. The only issue was speed. The Fibre Channel PMD runs at 1Gbaud and uses 8B/10B encoding. This translates to a data rate of only 800Mbps. The IEEE therefore increased the Fibre Channel PHY speed to 1.25Gbaud to obtain an actual data throughput of 1Gbps. This means the Fibre Channel components had to be retested or even redesigned for the 25% speed increase. See Figure 3.11 for an illustration.

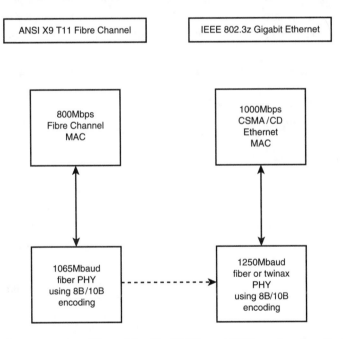

FIGURE 3.11 *Three of the Gigabit Ethernet PHYs are based on the ANSI Fiber Channel PHY running at 1.25Gbaud.*

Finally, the 802.3ab 1000BASE-T physical layer enables Gigabit Ethernet over Category 5 UTP. This standard was approved in June 1999.

1000BASE-SX: Gigabit Ethernet for Horizontal Fiber

1000BASE-SX is targeted at cost-sensitive, shorter backbone, or horizontal connections (*S* as in "short wavelength or shorter cable runs"). 1000BASE-SX uses the same physical layer as LX and uses affordable 850nm short-wavelength optical diodes. 1000BASE-SX uses only multimode fiber (MMF). The distance supported varies from 220 meters to 550 meters, depending on the type of fiber cable used.

1000BASE-LX: Ethernet for Vertical or Campus Backbones

1000BASE-LX is targeted at longer backbone and vertical connections (*L* as in "long wavelength or longer runs"). LX can use either SMF or MMF. LX requires expensive 1300nm lasers. The IEEE has specified *a* segment length of 5000m for LX using SMF. For LX using MMF, the distance is 550m (full-duplex connections). Table 3.9 summarizes the different 1000BASE-SX and LX distance combinations. The IEEE specifies the SC connector for both 1000BASE-SX and 1000BASE-LX.

TABLE 3.9 1000BASE-SX AND LX MAXIMUM LENGTH VARIES DEPENDING ON TYPE AND QUALITY OF FIBER CABLING USED

Wave-length	Fiber Type	Fiber Size (μm)	Bandwidth	Attenuation	Maximum Distance[1]
			1000BASE-SX		
850	MMF	50/125μm[2]	400MHz/km	3.25	500m
			500MHz/km	3.43	550m
		62.5/125μm[3]	160MHz/km	2.33	220m
			200MHz/km	2.53	275m
			1000BASE-LX		
1300	MMF	50/125μm	400/500MHz/km	2.32	550m
		62.5/125μm	500MHz/km	2.32	550m
	SMF	10/125μm	Huge/infinite[4]	4.5	5000m

[1] *All distances are for full-duplex. We don't know of a single vendor building half-duplex 1000BASE-X equipment. For the record, half-duplex distances are 316m for all 1000BASE-LX connections and between 220m to 316m for 1000BASE-SX.*

[2] *The maximum length depends on the type of 50μm or 62.5μm fiber used. The 400MHz/km stuff can only accommodate 500m, but the 500MHz/km fiber is specified at 550m.*

[3] *Again, the maximum length depends on the type of 62.5μm fiber used. The 160MHz/km stuff can only accommodate 220m, but the 200MHz/km fiber is specified at 275m. Most of the installed base of 62.5μm fiber has a bandwidth of 160MHz/km. The lower bandwidth 160 and 400MHz/km fiber is more prevalent in Europe than in the United States.*

[4] *SMF has a modal bandwidth that exceeds the capabilities of today's electronics components. For practical purposes, it cannot be measured and is therefore infinite.*

Going the Extra Mile?

The IEEE distance limitations for Gigabit Ethernet are extremely conservative. The Gigabit Ethernet Alliance boasts on its own Web page (www.gigabit-ethernet.org/) that it could demonstrate 1000BASE-SX running over 380 meters at a recent tradeshow (the specification says 220 meters). Mier Communications in New Jersey tested eight different 1000BASE-SX switches over a 1km 62.5μm MMF fiber run. All of them ran flawlessly.

The 5km-distance limitation was also a very conservative worst-case specification. Many 1000BASE-LX vendors guarantee their products for much longer distances: 10km seems to be the going distance. Cisco has given its product a different name, calling it 1000BASE-LH. The caveat is that a vendor will require its equipment to be present at both ends of the wire. Some vendors, such as Extreme and nBASE, have started shipping fiber extenders, allowing for distances of up to 80km! This makes Gigabit Ethernet a viable metropolitan and even wide area networking technology! Imagine a Gigabit Ethernet WAN connection!

1000BASE-CX: Gigabit Ethernet for Copper-Twinax Cabling

The third Fibre Channel-based physical layer, 1000BASE-CX (C as in "cross-connect," or "interconnect," or "copper"), was designed for short interconnects of hubs, switches, or routers in the wiring closet. Copper is the preferred media because it is easier and quicker to assemble copper jumper cables than fiber. 150-Ω twinax cabling, similar to IBM's original Token Ring cabling, was chosen as a cable. The maximum cable length is 25 meters (half- or full-duplex). Two connectors are specified for 1000BASE-CX. Because the 1000BASE-X physical layers were derived from the Fibre Channel standard, it made sense to use the same connector: the High-Speed Serial Data Connector (HSSDC), commonly known as Fibre Channel Style 2 connector. The IEEE also specified the nine-pin D-subminiature connector, which is also used for Token Ring and the STP version of 100BASE-TX.

1000BASE-T: Gigabit Ethernet for Four-Pair Category 5 UTP

The IEEE 802.3ab committee is completing a new standard that defines Gigabit Ethernet transmission over four-pair Category 5 or better cable. 1000BASE-T, as the standard is known, is an incredible engineering feat. When 100MHz Category 5 cabling was first conceived, the maximum data rate was considered to be around 100Mbps. The IEEE engineers have managed to squeeze *10 times that* out of Category 5 cabling. It is worth spending a few minutes on how they propose doing this. 1000BASE-T combines several tricks to achieve 1000Mbps over Category 5:

- 1000BASE-T uses all four pairs of Category 5 cabling. You can still use a regular Category 5 RJ-45 connector.

- 1000BASE-T uses simultaneous transmission and reception on all four pairs. All other physical layers in use today either transmit or receive, but never both. This simultaneous transmission from both ends is sometimes called *dual-duplex*.

- To make better use of the available bandwidth, 1000BASE-T uses the same encoding scheme that was developed for 100BASE-T2, namely PAM5. 1000BASE-T operates at 125MHz, the same frequency as 100BASE-TX, which is five times that of 100BASE-T2. Because 1000BASE-T is essentially a combination of 100BASE-TX and 100BASE-T2, this encoding scheme is also called *enhanced TX/T2*.

- 1000BASE-T combines many existing technological features, but the combination of four simultaneous transmission and reception on all four pairs, the complex PAM5 encoding, and the high symbol rate of 125MHz make it a state-of-the-art transmission technology. This requires a highly sophisticated DSP to make it actually work. The PHY transceiver chip at both ends of the cable will actually be a complex DSP engine that will contain more than 200,000 transistors, about the same as an Intel 486 microprocessor!

Note

DSP *is an abbreviation for digital signal processor, a specialized microprocessor designed to analyze and process analog signals.*

The 1000BASE-T standard was completed in June 1999, products are expected to start shipping before the end of 1999.

Table 3.10 summarizes the four different Gigabit Ethernet physical layers.

TABLE 3.10 A SUMMARY OF THE DIFFERENT GIGABIT ETHERNET PHYSICAL LAYER
IMPLEMENTATIONS

PHY Parameter	1000BASE-T	1000BASE-SX	1000BASE-LX	1000BASE-CX
IEEE Standard	802.3ab[1] June 1999		802.3z (July 1998)	
Number of pairs required	Four pairs	Two strands	Two strands	Two pairs
Cable Category required	Category 5 or better	50 or 62.5 um MMF	50 or 62.5 um MMF or 8–10μm SMF	150-Ω Twinax
Cable length	100m	220-550m	5000m (SMF) 550m (MMF)[2]	25m
Encoding	4D-PAM5	8B/10B	8B/10B	8B/10B
Connector specified	RJ-45	√	SC	HSSC or DB-9
Proven	Not yet	√	√	√
Full-duplex capable	Yes	√	√	√
Broad product support	None shipping yet[1]	√√	√	Probably not[3]

[1] 802.3ab approved in June 1999. Products are expected later in 1999.
[2] Requires special DMD patch cord. See Chapter 6 for more details.
[3] By September 1998, not a single Gigabit Ethernet vendor was shipping CX-based product.

The IEEE Auto-Negotiation Standard

When 100BASE-T was invented, it was no longer safe to assume that a typical Ethernet RJ-45 connector would be carrying 10BASE-T. Instead, a UTP cable could carry one of seven different Ethernet signals: 10BASE-T, 10BASE-T full-duplex, 100BASE-TX, 100BASE-TX full-duplex, 100BASE-T4, 100BASE-T2, or 100BASE-T2 full-duplex. The IEEE incorporated a very elegant scheme into the 802.3u standard that has simplified your life as a LAN manager tremendously. The IEEE's auto-
negotiation technology, originally developed by National Semiconductor and known as NWay, can tell what speed the other end of the wire can handle. The repeater, switch, or NIC will then automatically adjust its speed to the highest common denominator—the fastest speed that both can handle. This is how auto-negotiation works:

- Both devices need to contain the auto-negotiation logic. (All Fast Ethernet equipment shipping after mid-1996 includes this feature.)

- Auto-negotiation is an enhancement of the 10BASE-T link integrity sig-

- New equipment incorporating the auto-negotiation feature still allows you to select one of the possible modes manually. NICs typically do this via a command-line option; switches can be set via the management software.

This technology has several benefits. Assume that you are working in some-one's office, connecting his or her PC. You can tell that the PC has an older ISA 10BASE-T NIC installed. You want to connect the PC to the RJ-45 Ethernet outlet via a UTP patch cord, but you are not sure what hub the outlet is connected to in the wiring closet. It could be a newer 10/100BASE-TX hub, or an older 10BASE-T hub. Without auto-negotiation, you would have to walk back to the wiring closet to find out because connecting a 10BASE-T NIC to a 100BASE-TX hub could cause some serious problems, because the electrical signal levels are incompatible. Auto-negotiation will eliminate this possibility; it will not allow dissimilar technologies to connect or interfere with each other. If this outlet has a 10BASE-T hub connected to it, everything is okay. If you do indeed have a 10/100TX hub installed, it will auto-negotiate its speed down to 10Mbps.

Another scenario would be when you wanted to upgrade a user from a 10Mbps connection to 100Mbps. Let's say you had the foresight a few years ago to install 10/100TX NICs everywhere. Now you have bought some new 10/100 workgroup switches. All you need to do is swap out the old 10BASE-T hub for the new 10/100 switch, and the upgrade is done. All the NICs will sense that they are now connected to a 100Mbps switch; you do not need to visit each workstation.

Auto-negotiation uses a series of fast link pulses (FLPs), similar to the 10BASE-T link integrity (LI) pulses. Both hub and NIC send out this sequence of pulses, which allows the other end of the wire to identify the type of Ethernet connection the host is capable of (see Figure 3.12).

Because different Ethernet devices can support multiple Ethernet functions, a prioritization scheme exists to make sure the highest or fastest available option is chosen. This scheme will ensure that a 10/100 full-duplex device will always prioritize 100Mbps over 10Mbps operation, and full-duplex over half-duplex, and so on. Table 3.11 illustrates this prioritization.

100BASE-T2 is prioritized ahead of 100BASE-TX and 100BASE-T4 because 100BASE-T2 runs across a broader spectrum of copper cabling and can support a wider base of configurations. 100BASE-T4 is ahead of 100BASE-TX because 100BASE-T4 runs across a broader spectrum of copper cabling. Full-duplex is always ahead of half-duplex because if the capability exists you want to take advantage of it. 10BASE-T is last because it runs at the slowest speed.

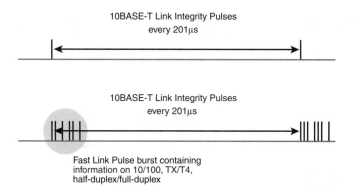

10BASE-T Link Integrity Pulses
every 201µs

10BASE-T Link Integrity Pulses
every 201µs

Fast Link Pulse burst containing
information on 10/100, TX/T4,
half-duplex/full-duplex

F I G U R E 3 . 1 2 *The auto-negotiation FLP is similar to the 10BASE-T link integrity pulse and encodes information to determine the highest possible speed.*

TABLE 3.11 AUTO-NEGOTIATION DEFINES A PRIORITY HIERARCHY FOR ENSURING THAT TWO CONNECTIONS COMMUNICATE AT THE HIGHEST COMMON SPEED

Priority	Comment
1	1000BASE-T full-duplex[1]
2	100BASE-T2 full-duplex
3	100BASE-T2
4	100BASE-TX full-duplex
5	100BASE-T4
6	100BASE-TX
7	10BASE-T full-duplex
8	10BASE-T

[1] *1000BASE-T also uses the same RJ-45 connector. We expect the auto-negotiation scheme to be modified to include 1000BASE-T full-duplex as the number one priority.*

Fiber-optic auto-negotiation also exists. Most fiber-optic devices only support one mode, however, and it is not possible at this point to build dual-speed devices. The only benefit of auto-negotiation for fiber devices is to arbitrate between half- and full-duplex.

Before the IEEE officially adopted auto-negotiation as the part of the 100BASE-T/802.3u standard, some vendors were shipping proprietary auto-sensing network adapters. A lot of 10/100 NICs installed out there are running at 10Mbps today, to be upgraded to 100Mbps at some point in the future. Table 3.12 illustrates how different hubs and NICs will interoperate with and without the auto-negotiation scheme.

TABLE 3.12 INTEROPERABILITY OF PRESTANDARD AUTO-SPEED AND AUTO-NEGOTIATION SWITCHES AND NICs

NIC-Only Hub	10BASE-T–Only Hub	100BASE-TX-10/100TX Hub
10BASE-T–only NIC	No choices can be made.	N/A (better buy a new NIC!)
Pre-standard auto-sensing 10/100TX NIC[2]	NIC automatically selects 10 mode.	NIC automatically selects 100 mode.
New auto-negotiation 10/100TX NIC[3]	NIC auto-negotiates to 10 mode.	NIC auto-negotiates to 100 mode.

[1] For example, the SynOptics 28115 hub will operate at either 10 or 100Mbps, but does not automatically adjust its speed. The speed adjustment has to happen manually via the switch management software.

[2] Examples are the Intel EtherExpress Pro/100, or the 3Com Fast EtherLink.

[3] The Intel EtherExpress Pro/100 Model B and the 3Com EtherLink XL include auto-negotiation.

Ethernet Repeaters

Repeaters extend the size of a network by joining multiple segments into a larger segment. A repeater works at the physical layer (Layer 1) of the OSI model. That means the repeater does not process the data at all. A repeater has no MAC, only PHYs, and merely receives the incoming signals and reconditions them for immediate retransmission on all ports. Repeaters are synonymous with shared media. A repeater is invisible to all nodes on a repeated LAN. It appears as though all nodes are connected via one cable.

Repeaters are almost as old as Ethernet itself. Fast and Gigabit Ethernet make provisions for repeaters, although the trend toward dedicated media and switching has been accelerating for the past five years. With Gigabit Ethernet in particular, repeaters might soon be outdated. Figure 3.13 shows the internal workings of a repeater.

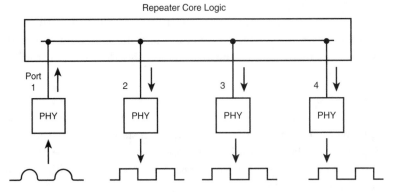

FIGURE 3.13 A repeater operates at Layer 1 of the OSI model: it only contains PHYs and some core logic, but no MACs. This figure shows a repeater receiving a degraded signal on port 1 and retransmitting a clean signal on ports 2–4.

1st -Generation 10/100 Hub (No Auto-Sensing)[1]	New Auto-Negotiation
Hub manually set to 10 mode (with management software).	Hub auto-negotiates to 10 mode.
Manually set hub to 100 mode, NIC will automatically adjust to 100 mode also.	Manually set hub and NIC to 100 mode.
Manually set hub and NIC to 100 mode.	Both hub and NIC auto-negotiate to 100 mode.

How Repeaters Work

All Ethernet repeaters work as follows:

1. An encoded data signal is received on a particular port, either from a node, a switch, or another repeater. This signal has been electrically degraded because it has traveled some distance from the source to the repeater over less-than-perfect cable. (This applies to both UTP and fiber; the degradation just takes longer over fiber.)

2. The incoming port, PHY, processes the data and re-creates the perfect digital data internally.

3. Finally, the digital signal is forwarded to all ports, where the PHY on each port converts the data into an encoded signal, to be transmitted over the wire again.

Note that no data is stored, no frames are re-created, and every received bit is sent on, irrespective. Figure 3.14 illustrates the flow diagram of a repeater.

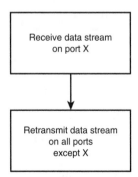

FIGURE 3.14 *Flow diagram of the repeater forwarding logic: There isn't much to it. Later on you will see the same diagram for a switch, which is much more complex.*

The Repeater Collision Domain

A *segment* is defined as a group of nodes connected to the same repeater. Multiple segments can be connected via repeaters. A repeater propagates all network traffic present on one segment to all other segments to which it is connected. All interconnected segments are in one *electrical collision domain*.

Electrical signals take a certain time to travel across a cable. In addition, all repeater hops introduce a small delay or latency. This is the delay between the time an incoming signal is received and the time that signal is transmitted again to all ports. These two forwarding delays and their impact on Ethernet collision detection is a key factor for determining 10, 100, and 1000Mbps Ethernet network design and diameter rules.

A collision occurs when two nodes simultaneously sense that the media is available and then attempt to transmit at the same time. Somewhere in the shared collision domain the two data patterns literally collide, causing a voltage surge on the cable. The voltage surge travels back along the cable to the two sources, where it is detected by the transmitters. A collision must be detected by the nodes causing the collision before they stop transmitting, including the one at the farthest end of the cable; otherwise, the nodes would never know that their transmission had been corrupted and would proceed as though nothing had happened. After the transmitting station recognizes that a collision has occurred, a JAM signal is generated, which is equivalent to canceling the last transmission. The worst case for collision detection is very short frames, because they leave very little time for the collision signal to travel back to the transmitter. Figure 3.15 shows the collision domain and minimum frame size.

Let's look at how the maximum network diameter depends on the minimum frame size. First, we need to define a variable called the transmission time. This is the amount of time that the transmission takes, from beginning to end. It is also equal to the time that any collision has to travel back to the transmitting station.

The minimum transmission time can be calculated from the minimum frame size. For 10Mbps Ethernet, the minimum transmission time is

```
Minimum transmission time = Minimum frame size (512 bits) x Bit-time (100ns) = 51.2µs
```

The signal needs to travel from the transmitter to the point where the collision occurs. Then the collision signal needs to travel back to the transmitter again. The minimum transmission time number in the preceding equation needs to be divided by 2 to account for round-trip delays. Therefore, the minimum transmission time is equal to 25.6µs (round-trip).

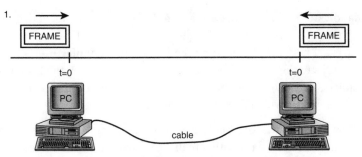

1.

Both stations sense an idle network and get ready
to transmit, albeit simultaneously.

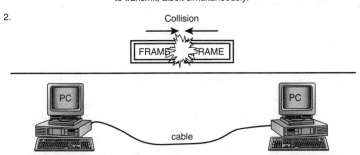

2.

The 2 frames have collided. Both transmitting stations have stopped
transmitting and are back at idle and therefore have no idea the collision has occurred.

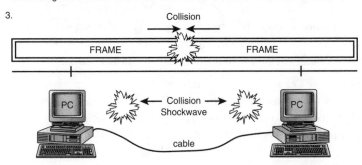

3.

In this example, the transmission is still in progress when the collision
occurs. In addition, there is sufficient part of the transmission that is incomplete
to allow the collision signal to travel back to the transmitters.

FIGURE 3.15 *Collisions occur when two nodes attempt to transmit simultaneously. The maximum network diameter is directly related to the minimum frame size.*

Copper and fiber cable have a delay of between 0.5 and 0.6μs/100m. To calculate the maximum network diameter, we merely need to divide the minimum transmission time of 25.6 μs by the cable delay.

$$\text{Network diameter} = \frac{25.6\mu s}{0.6\mu s/100m} > 4,000m$$

This calculation still excludes any delays introduced by repeaters, nodes, and so on. Many manufacturers specify the latency of their repeaters, so you could calculate the exact network diameter depending on the manufacturer's numbers. This is very cumbersome. To make our lives a little easier, the IEEE came up with a quick and easy-to-remember rule that limits the 10Mbps network size to 2500 meters. The rule is described in more detail later.

When 10Mbps Ethernet was originally designed, the minimum frame size of 512 bits was chosen to come up with a realistic network diameter. The problem with Fast Ethernet and Gigabit Ethernet is the bit time. The network diameter is directly related to the minimum frame size, as well as the bit time.

```
Network diameter = K x  Frame size
                        ─────────
                        Bit-time
```

As we move from 10 to 100 to 1000Mbps, the bit time decreases by an order of 10 every time. If we have a network diameter of 2500 meters for 10BASE-T, this shrinks to one-tenth, or approximately 250 meters for 100BASE-T, which is already marginal. For Gigabit Ethernet, the network diameter would shrink to 25 meters, which is clearly not a viable option. Therefore, the IEEE decided to increase the minimum frame size for Gigabit Ethernet to 512 bytes (or 4096bits), as opposed to 64 bytes for 10 and 100Mbps Ethernet. This, as you might notice, is only an eight-fold improvement. This yields a network diameter of around 200 meters for Gigabit Ethernet. Table 3.13 summarizes the different collision diameter variables for 10, 100, and 1000Mbps Ethernets.

You can calculate the exact maximum network diameter for any network using the delays for cable and manufacturers specifications for latencies, but nobody would really want to do that. (For you die-hards who insist, we have put down some guidelines. See the section "Calculating Your Own Collision Diameter," later in this chapter.)

The IEEE made things easy and developed a set of guidelines. We discuss these cheat sheet guidelines for 10, 100, and 1000Mbps repeater segments in the following section.

10Mbps Ethernet Repeater Rules

You can easily memorize the 10Mbps Ethernet golden rule as the *5-4-3-2-1* rule:

- *Five* segments are allowed (of 500-meter diameter each).

- This implies *four* repeater hops in the data path.

- *Three* of these segments may be populated with nodes.

- *Two* segments cannot be populated but are only inter-repeater links.

- All of this makes *one* large collision domain with a maximum of 1024 stations. Total network diameter can be up to 2500 meters.

TABLE 3.13 THE COLLISION DIAMETER FOR 10, 100, AND 1000MBPS ETHERNETS ARE A FUNCTION OF MINIMUM FRAME SIZE AND BIT TIME

Parameter	10Mbps	100Mbps	1000Mbps
Minimum frame size	512 bits (64 bytes)	512 bits (64 bytes)	4096 bits (512 bytes)[1]
Collision diameter (bit times)[2]	512 bit times	512 bit times	4096 bit times
Bit time (µs)[3]	0.1µs	0.01µs	0.001µs
Maximum round-trip delay (µs)[4]	51.2µs	5.12µs	4.096µs
Maximum network diameter, without repeaters [5]	Approximately 45710m	457m (1/10 of Ethernet)	3661 m (8/10 of Fast Ethernet)
Maximum IEEE-specified network diameter, with 100-meter UTP connections [6]	2500m	205m	200m
Maximum number of repeaters with specified network diameter[7]	~5	2 or 1	1

1 This number is eight times the regular or Fast Ethernet minimum frame size. This doesn't entirely make up for the one-tenth reduction in diameter due to the speed increase, but it comes close. To be totally correct, the actual Ethernet frame size has not increased. Instead, the minimum Gigabit Ethernet frame size is still 64 bytes, just like 10 and 100Mbps Ethernet frames. The 802.3z specification requires a carrier extension to be added to small frames to keep the wire busy for a minimum of 512 bytes. In this way, it looks like the minimum frame size is 512 bytes.
2 Collision diameter = minimum frame size. The IEEE specifies the minimum frame size.
3 Bit time = 1/data rate. Depends on the speed of Ethernet.
4 Round-trip delay = bit time * minimum frame size.
5 Absolute best case, calculated using a copper delay of 0.56µs/100m segment. Ignores 100m UTP limitation. Also assumes no repeater delays, so this is a theoretical number. Because fiber cabling has similar delays to copper, this number comes close to the half-duplex fiber network diameter specifications.
6 This is the real-world number that includes a budget for repeaters, too.
7 We discuss exact repeater rules later in the chapter.

Figure 3.16 illustrates this 5-4-3-2-1 design rule, which applies to 10Mbps Ethernet only. This 5-4-3-2-1 rule is only a rough guideline, but it works very well in most cases. Actual numbers vary by manufacturer. We have seen from four to seven repeater hops being specified. (In theory, as discussed previously, a 10Mbps Ethernet LAN could have a collision diameter of at least 4000 meters, if no repeaters were present. This is a number that can be attained only by using a point-to-point single fiber connection because all copper-based cabling will need to be repeated multiple times to go this far.)

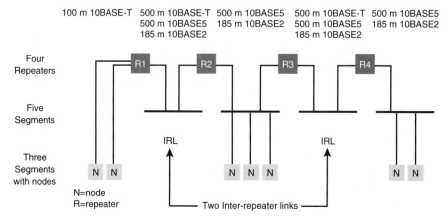

One Single Collsion
domain of maximum 1024 nodes

100 m 10BASE-T	500 m 10BASE-T	500 m 10BASE5	500 m 10BASE-T	500 m 10BASE5
	500 m 10BASE5	185 m 10BASE2	500 m 10BASE5	185 m 10BASE2
	185 m 10BASE2		185 m 10BASE2	

F IGURE 3.16 *The Ethernet 5-4-3-2-1 repeater rule stipulates a maximum of five segments, four reporters, three populated segments, and two repeater links, making up one collision domain.*

Figure 3.16 illustrates this 5-4-3-2-1 design rule, which applies to 10Mbps Ethernet only. This 5-4-3-2-1 rule is only a rough guideline, but it works very well in most cases. Actual numbers vary by manufacturer. We have seen from four to seven repeater hops being specified. (In theory, as discussed previously, a 10Mbps Ethernet LAN could have a collision diameter of at least 4000 meters, if no repeaters were present. This is a number that can be attained only by using a point-to-point single fiber connection because all copper-based cabling will need to be repeated multiple times to go this far.)

100BASE-T Repeater Rules

The IEEE repeater rules have hence been significantly changed for 100BASE-T. The IEEE 802.3u Fast Ethernet standard contains some specifications for Fast Ethernet repeaters. Due to the faster speed, the Fast Ethernet network diameter has been reduced from 2500 meters to approximately one-tenth that size.

The actual diameter depends on two things:

- *The type of cable used*—Fiber cable has a slightly smaller delay: about 0.5µs/ 100, as opposed to UTP, which has a delay of 0.56µs/100m. (Note that all UTP segments still need to be 100 meters, as this is an EIA/TIA spec.)

- *The type of repeater used*—With 10BASE-T, latency was not an issue, but with 100BASE-T, it becomes a major differentiating feature for a repeater. As the network diameter is rather limited for Fast Ethernet, the IEEE has defined two different classes of repeaters, called Class I and Class II:

  - A Class I repeater can have a relatively large port-port timing delay

- Class II repeaters have a lower latency of 0.46μs or less. Class II repeaters do not regenerate the digital signal like a Class I repeater does. A Class II repeater immediately repeats the incoming signal to all other ports without a complete translation process. Class II repeaters are preferred from a network design perspective because the lower latency allows for two repeater hops. The drawback of Class II repeaters is a single repeater cannot mix different media PHYs.

Class I and Class II differ with respect to their internal design and latency characteristics. This allows a more accurate network diameter calculation to get closer to the limit.

If two 100-meter UTP links are used, this configuration allows for an inter-repeater link of 5-meter UTP to yield a total network diameter of 205 meters. Alternatively, two fiber connections and an inter-repeater fiber link with a total length of 228 meters are permitted. Most Fast Ethernet repeaters shipping today are Class II.

The two cases just described both use only one media type for the entire network diameter. The IEEE has also laid down some guidelines for mixed copper-fiber installations, but these situations are rare. Table 3.14 illustrates the network diameter guidelines for these situations. Figure 3.17 graphically depicts Table 3.14.

TABLE 3.14 FAST ETHERNET COLLISION DIAMETER RULES

Connection	All UTP	Mixed-Media 100BASE-TX[1] and 100BASE-FX	All Fiber
Repeated Network Segment Diameter			
One Class II repeater	200m	309m	320m
One Class I repeater	200m	261m	272m
Two Class II repeaters	205m	216m	228m
Point-to-Point Connections[2]			
Node-node or switch-switch half-duplex	100m	N/A	412m
Node-node or switch-switch full-duplex	100m	N/A	2000m

[1] T4 allows for a few meters more.

[2] We have shown the point-to-point distance limitations for reference only. For single-mode fiber connections operating in full-duplex, even longer segments are possible, but the IEEE didn't specify SMF as part of the Fast Ethernet standard.

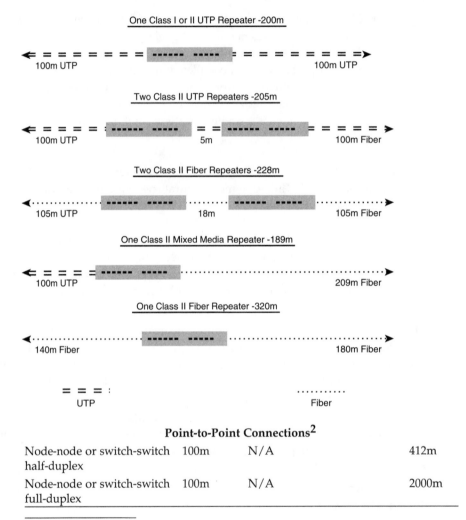

One Class I or II UTP Repeater -200m

100m UTP   100m UTP

Two Class II UTP Repeaters -205m

100m UTP   5m   100m Fiber

Two Class II Fiber Repeaters -228m

105m UTP   18m   105m Fiber

One Class II Mixed Media Repeater -189m

100m UTP   209m Fiber

One Class II Fiber Repeater -320m

140m Fiber   180m Fiber

= = = :   . . . .
UTP   Fiber

Point-to-Point Connections[2]

Node-node or switch-switch half-duplex	100m	N/A	412m
Node-node or switch-switch full-duplex	100m	N/A	2000m

[1] *T4 allows for a few meters more.*

[2] *We have shown the point-to-point distance limitations for reference only. For single-mode fiber connections operating in full-duplex, even longer segments are possible, but the IEEE didn't specify SMF as part of the Fast Ethernet standard.*

Figure 3.17   *The network diameter for a 100BASE-T network can range from 200 meters for UTP to 320 meters for fiber, assuming one repeater.*

Some people originally viewed the Fast Ethernet repeater specification (two repeater hops and a 205-meter UTP network diameter) as a big issue. Most people soon realized, however, that one could effectively work around both issues with the use of stackable repeaters and switching hubs to get to any network diameter and an infinite number of hops. Refer to the deployment chapis started at the switch, and 205 meters is sufficient to get to most nodes with one or two intermediate repeater hops. If the distance from switch to node is longer than 205 meters, another switch must be added to further extend the network diameter. Alternatively, 100BASE-FX could be run to repeaters or nodes that are longer than 205 meters away from the switch.

- Standalone, unmanaged 100BASE-T repeaters will be rare. Most 100BASE-T repeaters will be stackable, meaning that many repeaters can be physically placed on top of each other and connected via a fast back-plane bus. The fast backplane bus does not count as a repeater hop and makes the entire stack look like one larger repeater. In fact, most 100BASE-T stackables can be stacked four or more high. Electrically, the repeater stack appears as one larger repeater.

Calculating Your Own Collision or Network Diameter

You can calculate your own network diameter if you like. Use the following equation to make sure your repeated Ethernet network segment will function satisfactorily:

```
(repeater delays + cable delays + NIC delays) x 2 < Maximum round-trip delay
```

Note the following:

- You can obtain the maximum round-trip delay from Table 3.15. It is 51.6μs for 10Mbps Ethernet, 5.12μs for Fast Ethernet, and 4.096μs for Gigabit Ethernet.

- The factor 2 accounts for round-trip delays as the frame needs to travel from transmitter, to the collision point and back to the transmitter again.

- We can obtain repeater and NIC delays from the manufacturer. Ethernet repeaters typically have latencies of 2μs or less. Fast Ethernet Class I repeater delays are less than 0.7μs; Class II delays are less than 0.46μs. A 10Mbps NIC delay is about 1μs; Fast Ethernet NIC delay is 0.25μs. All networks are terminated on both ends: two NICs or a NIC and a switch port.

- We can obtain the cable delays from Table 3.15. Cable delays do not at all depend on the Ethernet speed. Cable delays typically are measured as a fraction of the speed of light and mostly depend on the insulation mater-ial used. A 100-meter UTP section still takes about 0.55μs one way.

- For 10Mbps networks, 51.2µs allows for quite a few repeaters, cable segments, and DTEs to exist without exceeding the collision domain restrictions. In most real-world 10BASE-T networks, you will find it very difficult to exceed this number.

TABLE 3.15 INDIVIDUAL NETWORK COMPONENT DELAYS FOR CALCULATION OF NETWORK DIAMETER

Component	Maximum Delay Times in µs
Two Fast Ethernet NICs or switch ports	0.5
Fast Ethernet MII	0.2
100m Category 5 cable segment	0.556
1m Category 5 cable	0.00556
100m Fiber optic cable segment	0.5
1m fiber cable	0.005
Fast Ethernet Class I repeater	0.7 max
Fast Ethernet Class II repeater	0.46 max
Two Gigabit Ethernet NICs	0.864 max
Gigabit Ethernet repeater	0.488 max

Figure 3.18 illustrates the different delay components in a shared-media network.

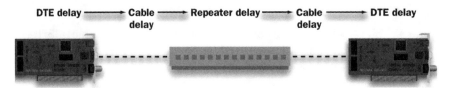

FIGURE 3.18 *If you want to calculate your own maximum network diameter, you need to add up the delays of the individual components and make sure they don't exceed half the minimum frame size.*

Some additional points to note:

- If you are using an MII cable, you need to add it to the cable segment length.

- Decide on an appropriate safety margin. (We recommend five bit times.)

- You will see that it is actually possible to build 100BASE-T networks with three or even four repeater hops if the individual cable segments are significantly less than 100 meters.

Gigabit Ethernet Repeater Rules

As mentioned previously, with CSMA/CD, the capability of a station to detect collisions directly relates to the round-trip propagation delay on the cable. This variable is in turn related to the original 64-byte minimum frame size for Ethernet, which yielded a practical network diameter of 2500 meters. With Fast Ethernet, the 64-byte minimum frame size was kept the same, but the network diameter was reduced from 2500 meters to 205 meters (Category 5 UTP).

Some people in the IEEE wanted to drop half-duplex and, therefore, CSMA/CD altogether from the Gigabit Ethernet specification. This didn't fly, and the IEEE decided that Gigabit Ethernet should still have a half-duplex repeater option. Therefore, the IEEE had two choices. First, the IEEE could keep the frame size the same and reduce the network diameter again by a factor of 10, which would have meant a network diameter of merely 20 meters. Alternatively, the IEEE could increase the frame size to increase the network diameter again. The IEEE opted for the latter and increased the minimum frame size to 512 bytes. This minimum frame size allows for a practical network diameter of between 200 and 220 meters, depending on the cable used. Table 3.16 summarizes the IEEE Gigabit Ethernet network diameter rules.

TABLE 3.16 GIGABIT ETHERNET NETWORK DIAMETER SPECIFICATIONS

Media	Maximum Collision Diameter
Point-to-Point, Half-Duplex	
1000BASE-CX node-node or switch-switch[1]	25m
1000BASE-T node-node or switch-switch[1]	100m
1000BASE-SX or LX node-node or switch-switch[1]	316m
One Repeater Segment	
1000BASE-CX	50m
1000BASE-T[2]	200m
1000BASE-SX or LX	220m

[1] *Remember these distances are half-duplex. For full-duplex operation, see Table 3.9.*
[2] *Mixed-media repeater limitations are 210 meters for UTP/fiber, 220 meters for twinax/fiber.*

The Gigabit Ethernet repeater rule is simple: 1 repeater, 2 UTP, or fiber segments of 100 meters each. It is very unlikely, however, that you will ever need to apply this 802.3z IEEE Gigabit Ethernet rule. That's because you probably won't ever see a true Gigabit Ethernet repeater for sale. At the time of this writing, no Gigabit Ethernet repeaters exist. Maybe the 1000BASE-T standard will change that, but we doubt it because the new 802.3X full-duplex flow/control standard, approved in March 1997, has effectively made half-duplex Ethernet redundant. Instead of CSMA/CD repeaters, vendors are building a hybrid device called a full-duplex repeater. This device looks like a repeater, but doesn't have some of the disadvantages of regular repeaters.

Gigabit Ethernet Full-Duplex Repeaters

Gigabit Ethernet vendors are building a new class of device, called the *full-duplex repeater*. This device is also known as a *buffered distributor*, nonfiltering switch, or CSMA/CD in a box. We like to use the term *full-duplex repeater* because the device acts like a repeater.

The full-duplex repeater combines the cost-effectiveness of a repeater with the performance characteristics of a switch. The device is a full-duplex, multiport, repeater-like device. Regular repeaters operate only in half-duplex mode; full-duplex repeaters and buffered distributors, on the other hand, feature full-duplex links on all ports and a MAC and a PHY on every port. We discuss these devices in more detail in the next chapter, after we examine switches in general and the 802.3x flow-control/full-duplex standard more closely.

Here are the key characteristics of a full-duplex repeater:

- Like a repeater, the full-duplex repeater forwards all incoming packets to all connected links except the originating port. That's the shared bandwidth repeater part.

- All the ports operate at the same speed, 1Gbps in this case. The full-duplex repeater concept, however, is not at all linked to wire speed.

- The full-duplex repeater has a very rudimentary MAC function on every port. The MAC will make sure a complete frame is received, perform the FCS to make sure the frame is valid, and then buffer it in internal memory. Full-duplex repeaters have enough memory capacity for a small number of frames to be buffered.

- The full-duplex repeater also looks a little bit like a switch. All connections use full-duplex links, so the full-duplex repeater can simultaneously transmit and receive on an individual port.

- The full-duplex repeater uses flow control to make sure that the internal buffers don't overflow. When memory begins to fill, the full-duplex repeater invokes 802.3x flow control to inform the transmitting node to stop sending while it empties its buffers.

The following are some important points that differentiate a full-duplex repeater from a switch:

- Switches forward only to the appropriate port, not to all ports like the full-duplex repeater.

- Switches typically have much larger internal memory capacity. Full-duplex repeaters have storage for just a few frames at most.

- Switches have backplanes that support bandwidths greater than the individual port rate to accommodate multiple data streams simultaneously. The backplane of a full-duplex repeater is exactly equal to the data rate.

- A full-duplex repeater will not work properly unless all transmitting nodes comply with 802.3x and operate at the same wire speed, which is Gigabit Ethernet in this case. A switch, on the other hand, can typically accommodate different data rates and half- or full-duplex nodes.

- A full-duplex repeater does not examine the contents of the frame beyond the FCS; no source or destination address analysis is done. The device blindly forwards all good frames to all ports (except the originating one).

Figure 3.19 shows an internal block diagram of a full-duplex repeater.

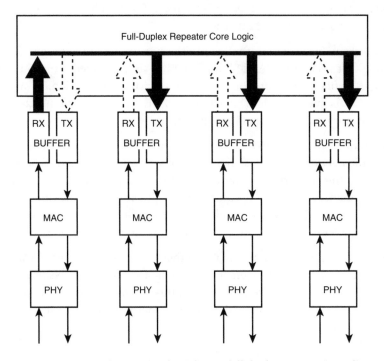

FIGURE 3.19 *The new Gigabit Ethernet full-duplex repeater is sending and receiving via its buffer memory on all ports. Internally, the round-robin logic is busy forwarding the data stored in port 1's receive buffer to the transmit buffers for ports 2–4.*

Summary

This chapter covered Layer 1 and Layer 2 aspects of the three different versions of Ethernet. The Ethernet MAC operates at the data link layer (Layer 2) of the OSI model. The Ethernet MAC utilizes a transmission algorithm called CSMA/CD.

The Ethernet MAC has scaled by a factor of 100 over the past 20 years, originally starting at 10Mbps, then speeding up to 100Mbps, and now 1000Mbps. A 10Gbps version is technically very feasible.

We looked at the different physical layers (OSI Layer 1) associated with each different Ethernet speed version. 10Mbps Ethernet typically utilizes UTP, known as 10BASE-T. 10Mbps Ethernet started off as a coax-based networking technology, known as 10BASE5 or 10BASE2. These days, 10Mbps Ethernet typically runs on UTP or fiber (10BASE-T or 10BASE-F).

The 100Mbps Ethernet standard encompasses four different physical layers, with the prevalent ones being 100BASE-TX and 100BASE-FX. 100Mbps Ethernet is also known as Fast Ethernet.

Gigabit Ethernet, the latest incarnation of Ethernet, can be run over four different cabling types. The 1000BASE-SX and LX fiber variants cater to many different qualities of fiber. The future of the shielded twisted-pair version, known as 1000BASE-CX, is questionable. The new 1000BASE-T standard will utilize existing Category 5 cabling for 1000Mbps transmission.

Ethernet started off as a shared-media technology. Repeaters are used in a shared media network to increase the network size. As the speed of Ethernet has increased, the network diameter has had to shrink proportionally. With 10Mbps Ethernet, at least five repeater hops are possible. With 100Mbps Fast Ethernet, this had to be reduced to one or two. Gigabit Ethernet employs a trick called carrier extension to even make one repeater hop possible.

We most likely will never see any Gigabit Ethernet shared-media hardware. Over time, technological enhancements have enabled Ethernet to become a full-duplex, switched technology. In essence, this means Ethernet is no longer using the CSMA/CD access method. Only the Ethernet framing format remains the same.

CHAPTER 4

Layer 2 Ethernet Switching

This chapter discusses the theory, standards, and practical uses of Ethernet Layer 2 switching. It assumes you have read Chapter 3, "Ethernet, Fast Ethernet, and Gigabit Ethernet Standards." This chapter focuses only on the Layer 2 aspects of Ethernet. Chapter 5, "VLANs and Layer 3 Switching," discusses routing, virtual LANs, and Layer 3 switching.

In this chapter, we first examine the concept of a Layer 2 switch and the fact that it is actually a bridge under a different name. We look at how a switch functions and examine the different methods of switching, namely cut-through, store and forward, and modified cut-through, or error-free. We also look at some of the architectural features of switches, such as backplane capacity and shared memory. You won't see too many Ethernet bridging standards out there. We do, however, cover the old but proven IEEE 802.1D spanning-tree algorithm (STA).

For many years, Ethernet bridges didn't receive much attention. Recently, however, two new standards have been approved. We look at the new 802.3x full-duplex/flow-control standard that has greatly enhanced Ethernet switches of all speeds. We also discuss the new 802.3ad Link Aggregation proposal.

Ethernet has been given a new face recently—two faces in fact. Both Fast and Gigabit Ethernet are less than five years old, which is quite young compared to Ethernet's 25-year history. These two new technologies have increased the wire-speed capabilities of Ethernet dramatically, but switching has been an even bigger breakthrough than faster wire speeds. Without switches, Fast Ethernet would be limited to a network diameter of 200 meters, which is basically useless, except for very small installations. In some areas, switching provides a higher-quality connection than just raw bandwidth via Fast Ethernet. That other great foe of Ethernet, ATM, has been synonymous with switching. Ethernet switching represents the best of both worlds: backward compatibility with today's existing Ethernet frames and state-of-the-art connection switching technology.

Ethernet Bridging and Switching

Ethernet switches first appeared in 1991 when Kalpana launched the original EtherSwitch. (Kalpana was acquired by Cisco in 1994.) From an Ethernet perspective, however, switches are really just multiport bridges that have been around for many years. Technically, bridging is an OSI Layer 2 function, and all of today's common networking standards—such as the three different Ethernet standards, Token Ring, FDDI, and so on—can all be bridged. What differentiate today's switches from yesterday's bridges are the features and uses of these modern multiport bridges.

A few years ago, two-port Ethernet bridges were used to connect two different LANs together. Then vendors started building intelligent multiport bridges, which are essentially a number of two-port bridges connected together. Today, these multiport bridges have been enhanced and are called switches. These switches are now used within an existing network to disconnect or segment a larger LAN into many smaller ones.

Because bridging or switching is an OSI Layer 2 function, today's Ethernet switching is not a new IEEE standard at all; it is just an application of existing standards. If you skipped Chapter 3 and are not familiar with the OSI Layer 1, 2, and 3 functions, go back to the preceding chapter and take a quick look at Table 3.1 and Figure 3.1. Because this book has *Switched* in its title, we would like to provide you with some insights into the technology behind Ethernet switching. First, let's look at how bridges function. Then we will discuss the IEEE 802.1D spanning-tree protocol, which is the only IEEE specification relevant to bridges and switches.

Repeaters

A *repeater* is a network device that indiscriminately regenerates and forwards a received Ethernet frame, whether it's good or bad. Repeaters are known as *passive*, or *shared*, components of the network because they do not logically act on incoming frames. Repeaters just regenerate incoming signals, thus extending the diameter of the network. In this way, repeaters are invisible to network events such as collisions or errors, merely propagating them along. Hence, a repeater cannot extend the collision domain of a network. Repeaters enlarge an existing network.

Bridges

Bridges and routers, on the other hand, connect different Ethernet LANs. Bridges perform basic frame filtering functions before retransmitting the incoming frame. Whereas repeaters forward all frames, a bridge forwards only those frames that are necessary. If a frame does not need to be forwarded, the bridge filters it out.

To connect an Ethernet LAN to an FDDI backbone, for example, would require either a bridge or a router. Because Ethernet and FDDI use different frame types, a translational bridge would be required.

Bridges also do speed matching: Regular 10Mbps Ethernet and 100Mbps Fast Ethernet can only be connected by means of a bridge.

Every Ethernet frame has two fields defined as the *destination* and *source* *address.* This tells a bridge where a frame originated and where it is ultimately destined. Figure 4.1 shows the structure of an Ethernet frame and the location of the destination and source addresses.

8 Bytes	6 Bytes	6 Bytes	2 Bytes	0-1500 Bytes	4 Bytes
Preamble + SFD	Destination Address	Source Address	Type/Length Field	Data and Pad	Frame Check

FIGURE 4.1 *Bridges examine both the destination and source address of a received frame. The bridge forwards a frame according to its destination address.*

Bridges look at an incoming Ethernet frame and analyze the destination address encapsulated in the frame's header. From this information, the bridge can check its internal memory of past frames and determine whether to forward the frame to another port or filter it out—that is, do nothing and discard the frame. In this way, bridges can isolate network traffic between network segments. Bridges also check for errors and don't forward damaged or incomplete frames.

A bridge works like a good postal mail delivery system. A bridge knows exactly where everyone resides. It delivers a piece of mail only to the intended recipient, looking at the address on every envelope and delivering the envelope to that particular address. If an envelope or frame is damaged or contains an error, a bridge mail system ignores the damaged mail.

A repeater works very differently. A repeater mail system uses the brute-force approach to mail delivery. A repeater makes a copy of every piece of mail it receives, and then delivers a copy to you and everyone in your neighborhood.

You get not only your mail but also copies of everyone else's mail. You must decide which mail is actually intended for you. Damaged mail is copied and distributed just like regular mail. Repeaters typically are cheaper to buy than bridges because they don't need to be able to read, sort, or return damaged mail.

See Table 4.1 for a comparison of Ethernet repeaters and bridges.

TABLE 4.1 COMPARING ETHERNET REPEATERS AND BRIDGES

Device Parameter	Repeater	Bridge
OSI layer	Layer 1/PHY	Layer 2/MAC
Number of hops	Four	Unlimited[1]
Looks at frames?	No, only regenerates entire frame	Yes, looks at individual address of every frame
Invisible device?	Yes	No
Port-port latency	< 1µs	50–1500 bit times[2]
Propagates errors?	Yes	No[3]
Network design implications?	Extends collision domain	Extends broadcast domain and divides collision domain
Principal use	Enlarges an existing network	Connects different networks[4]

[1] Theoretically, this number is unlimited. In reality, each bridge adds a delay. Too large of a delay can cause higher-level problems. The spanning-three algoritm also limits the number of hops to 7. See next section.

[2] The latency depends on two things: the frame size and the forwarding mechanism. See the "Switch Architectures and Performance" section.

[3] Bridges do not forward Layer 2 type errors, such as runt or CRC error frames. Higher-level, such as Layer 3, errors will be forwarded.

[4] Routers can also connect different networks. We examine routers and Layer 3 in more detail in the next chapter.

An In-Depth Look at How Bridges Work

Let's look at bridges in a bit more detail. A bridge contains a MAC and PHY on every port as well as some internal bridging logic. With bridges, this logic is in the form of a CPU and some memory. With switches, the logic is embedded in hardware in some specially designed chips. Figure 4.2 shows a block diagram of a bridge.

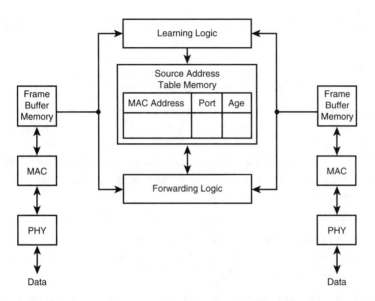

FIGURE 4.2 *Bridge internal block diagram. Bridges contain software-based learning and forwarding logic, whereas switches use hardware for this function.*

The major components of a bridge are as follows:

- *MAC/PHY*—A network interface card (NIC) consists of a MAC and a PHY. A bridge also contains a MAC and PHY on every port. This means that a bridge looks like multiple NICs coupled together. The bridge PHY will receive the incoming bit stream and pass it to the MAC, which reassembles the original frames.

- *Learning logic and source address table (SAT)*—The learning logic will look at the source address (SA) within a received frame and populate the source address table with three columns: MAC address, port number, and age. The MAC address is the same as the source address that a sender has embedded into the frame. The age item will be a date stamp to indicate when the last frame was received from a particular MAC SA. The port number in our case can be 1 or 2. The SAT is also known as the Bridge Forwarding Table (BFT).

- *Forwarding logic*—Forwarding logic is the essential component of a bridge. It looks at the destination address (DA) of a received frame. This now becomes the new MAC address, which is then compared with the entries in the SAT.

Four different forwarding options are possible and are illustrated in Figure 4.3. Figure 4.4 shows the internal workings of the bridge learning and forwarding logic.

Let's take a look at how the bridge learning and forwarding logic works:

- If the destination address is a specific address, known as a broadcast address, the frame is destined for all ports on the network. In this case, the bridge will forward the frame to all ports, except the one on which the frame was received. Figure 4.3 shows this case as destination address FFF. A broadcast address is six bytes with all ones, or FF.FF.FF.FF.FF.FF in hexadecimal notation.

- If the MAC address is found in the SAT and the corresponding port number is different from the received port, the frame is forwarded to that particular port number only. This would be MAC address U sending a frame to MAC address X in Figure 4.3.

- If the MAC address is found in the SAT and the port number is the same as the received port number, the frame is not forwarded; instead, it is discarded. This is known as *filtering*. The frame is discarded because the transmitting station and the receiving station are connected on the same shared LAN segment on that particular port and the receiver has already tuned into the frame. This would be MAC address V sending a frame to MAC address U in Figure 4.3.

- If the MAC address is not found in the table, the frame is forwarded to all ports. The reason a particular destination address is not present in the SAT table is that the receiving device could be new on the network, or the recipient has been very quiet (has not recently sent a frame). In both cases, the bridge SAT will not have a current entry. Flooding the frame on all ports is the brute way of ensuring that the frame definitely gets to its intended recipient. This would be MAC address X sending a frame to MAC address T, an unknown MAC address, in Figure 4.3.

- Bridges use the *age* entry in the SAT to determine whether that MAC address is still in use on the LAN. If the age has exceeded a certain preset value, the entry is removed. This conserves memory space and makes the bridge faster because fewer entries need to be scanned for address matching.

- Finally, the frame buffers will store frames on each port in case there is a backlog of frames to be forwarded.

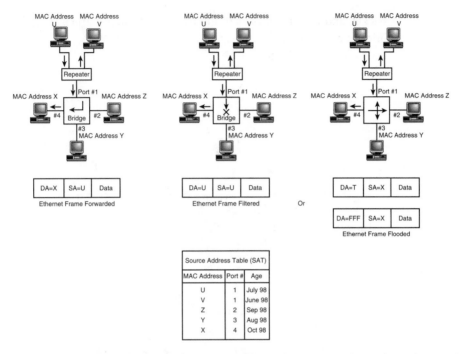

FIGURE 4.3 *Bridges have three alternative methods of processing a frame: forwarding to a known MAC address, filtering a frame, or flooding it on all ports.*

Routers

A router is an OSI Layer 3 device. Ethernet and bridges use frames, whereas routers work in packets. The Layer 3 software—for example, NetWare IPX or TCP/IP—generates the packet. Packet and frame sizes are not related. If a packet is larger than what a frame can carry, the packet needs to split into multiple frames. This is called *fragmentation*.

Bridges use MAC addresses in frames, whereas routers use the network address information in packets to make forwarding decisions.

Routers have traditionally been used for two purposes:

- Routers link networks over extended distances, also known as WANs. WAN traffic often can travel over multiple routes, and the different routers along the way choose the fastest or cheapest cost route (hence the term *router*).

- Routers are required to connect dissimilar LANs. For example, an Ethernet LAN is often connected to an FDDI backbone through a router, which analyzes each individual Ethernet frame, regenerates the original packet, and then reconverts it into new FDDI frames. Translational bridges can accomplish the same thing, but only if the same protocol is used on the two different LANs.

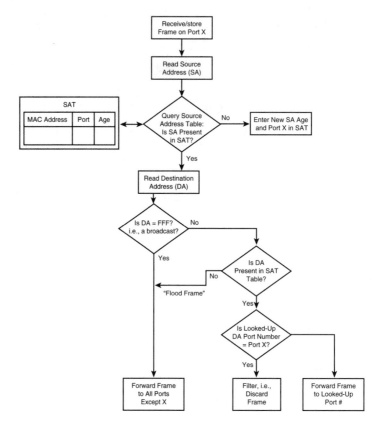

FIGURE 4.4 *The flow diagram of a bridge. Contrast this with the flow diagram of a repeater, shown in Figure 3.14 in Chapter 3.*

Over the past few years, high-performance routers have also become popular for linking homogeneous LANs, such as different smaller Ethernets within a larger company. In such situations, these routers effectively replace bridges and are sometimes called *segmentation routers*. Some people use routers in large networks because bridges have some drawbacks that do not affect routers.

Until recently, the term *switching* has been synonymous with a Layer 2 bridging function. These days, *switching* seems to be the latest buzzword in the networking industry, and numerous networking vendors have started talking about the concept of "Layer 3 switching." This is getting quite confusing because a Layer 3 switch is technically still a router, just as a Layer 2 switch is still a bridge. We examine Layer 3 routers and Layer 3 switches in more detail in Chapter 5.

The 802.1D Spanning-Tree Algorithm

Bridges were originally designed to connect different LANs together. Bridges do not allow for multiple active parallel paths between different LAN segments. Parallel paths create loops, which bridges cannot handle. If multiple paths exist, this would mean duplicate entries in different bridges, causing excess traffic flow and false entries in the SATs. Worse still, if a broadcast or flooded frame enters a parallel bridge network, the broadcasts start circulating and will grow on themselves. Ultimately, the single broadcast can turn into a broadcast storm, which will completely overload the network and bring it to its knees. The spanning-tree algorithm was invented many years ago by Radia Perlman of Digital Equipment Corporation to deal with this problem. The following are some important points about the spanning-tree algorithm (STA):

- Bridges build a logical tree-like structure by exchanging information about the topology of the overall network. All bridges send out specific frames, called bridge protocol data units (BPDUs), to build the tree.

- The STA is always active. During power-up time, the individual bridges communicate via BPDUs to build the initial tree, which takes about between 15 and 50 seconds. The base of the tree, or *root*, is determined in such a way as to provide only one possible data path between any two different bridges within the bridging fabric. At this time, the STA also eliminates circular paths by temporarily disconnecting all parallel links. These parallel links are in effect dormant, to be reactivated later if needed. By eliminating parallel links, the STA has, in effect, built a structure that looks like a tree, with the root or master bridge located at the base.

- The STA allows for redundant or parallel backup links. The dynamic nature of STA means that if an existing link (or branch) between two bridges is broken, the STA will reactivate a dormant link in less than a minute. This provides bridged networks with an element of resiliency.

- The STA became an IEEE standard in 1990 and is known as 802.1D. The STA used to be an optional feature with early bridges. These days, all bridges and switches incorporate this feature. The STA can be turned off with most bridges.

- Unlike bridges, routers *do* allow for multiple active paths. In fact, routers have enough intelligence to take advantage of multiple paths for both redundancy and cost optimization. Routers use algorithms similar to the STA to determine the optimum path between two stations connected via a WAN.

- The STA limits the number of bridge hops to 7.

Figure 4.5 shows a bridged network topology with multiple paths.

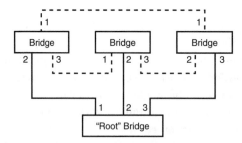

FIGURE 4.5   *A network with parallel bridged paths showing how STA has created a tree configuration. Dotted lines indicate parallel links disabled by the STA.*

Differences Between Bridges and Switches

A switch connects a sender and a receiver in real time. A telephone switch is the best example. Even the old, manual exchanges were true switches. The only thing that has changed is that the destination address can be dialed in automatically these days. A bridge, on the other hand, stores the data for a limited time period before forwarding it to the destination.

By definition, a switch relies on some sort of permanent or temporary electrical connection to exist between sender and receiver. If the data is temporarily stored, like in a bridge, one could argue that technically the device is no longer a switch. Because the data is often only stored for a fraction of a second, or fractions of a frame, however, we won't debate the nuances here of what constitutes a switch and what doesn't. Therefore, from an Ethernet perspective, switches are multiport bridges.

Some other architectural differences between bridges and switches include the following:

- The heart of a bridge (or router, for that matter) is a microprocessor and the associated program memory to run the bridging software. Switches, on the other hand, have no reprogrammable intelligence to bridge the data (for example, a CPU and associated program memory and software). The switching function is performed in hardware or silicon. In this case, the hardware has sufficient intelligence to examine each frame and decide to which port to send it. These chips are not programmable, however; all they can do is analyze and forward Ethernet frames. (Today's switches often contain a CPU for network management, configuration, STA, and so on. The key is that the CPU does not involve itself in the forwarding of every single frame.)

- Switches are much cheaper than bridges; their initial cost is lower, and they have achieved higher production volumes over time.

- Bridges can analyze and forward only one frame at a time. Switches, on the other hand, have multiple parallel data paths. Switches use tempo-rary, or *virtual*, connections to connect source and destination ports for the time it takes to forward a frame. After the frame has been sent from source to destination, the virtual connection is terminated. To accommo-date these multiple data paths, a switch needs to have a backplane that has enough capacity to carry all the data from multiple ports simultane-ously. Bridges typically are bandwidth-limited by the CPU and its I/O capabilities. The switched parallel approach means that switches are much faster than conventional bridges.

- Switches feature different forwarding mechanisms, such as cut-through or store-and-forward, whereas bridges use only the store-and-forward methodology.

- The biggest difference between switches and bridges is the positioning. Yesterday's bridges were relatively slow and expensive devices that were sold to connect different LANs together. Today's switches are fast and cheap, and they most often are used to improve the speed of an existing network.

Full-Duplex Ethernet

Many people think that switching and full-duplex are synonymous, but that is not correct. In essence, switching means multiple simultaneous bridged trans-missions. Full-duplex means simultaneous transmission and reception on sepa-rate pairs of cable or fiber. In a switched environment, individual transmissions can be either half- or full-duplex.

A full-duplex transmission requires a point-to-point connection with only two stations present on a segment; a station's transmitter is connected to the other side's receiver and vice versa. That wouldn't be possible if there were more than two nodes. Thus, switched Ethernet is a prerequisite to full-duplex, but does not automatically imply full-duplex.

Full-duplex Ethernet is not a part of any Ethernet PHY or MAC specifications. Instead, the separate 802.3x specification governs full-duplex devices with flow control. Refer to Chapter 3 for a discussion of the Full-Duplex Ethernet and the 802.3x standard.

The New IEEE 802.3x Full-Duplex/Flow-Control Standards

In 1997, the IEEE completed its work on an official full-duplex/flow-control Ethernet standard. The standard uses the full-duplex method first developed by Kalpana and detailed in Chapter 3, with two major additions. First, the standard will allow for automatic sensing of full-duplex capability via auto-negotiation (also discussed in Chapter 3). Second, the standard includes a new feature, called *flow control*, which prevents congestion and overloading. Whereas full-duplex and flow control are separate technologies, you will understand the rationale for this joint IEEE standard after reading the following section on flow control.

Here are some facts on the full-duplex standard:

- The physical transmission medium must be full-duplex capable. All Gigabit Ethernet media options, and most Fast Ethernet physical layers are full-duplex capable. On the other hand, 10BASE5, 10BASE2, 10BASE-FP, 10BASE-FB, and 100BASE-T4 are not full-duplex capable because these physical layers share the medium for both transmitting and receiving.

- There must be exactly two stations on the LAN in a point-to-point configuration. This could mean switch-switch, switch-NIC, NIC-NIC, or Gigabit Ethernet full-duplex repeater connections. The link between the two stations carries separate transmit and receive channels. Because there is no contention for the use of a shared channel any more, the CSMA/CD algorithm no longer applies.

- Both stations need to be full-duplex capable. The two stations will automatically adjust to full-duplex mode based on the auto-negotiation scheme discussed previously. Manual configuration is still possible for switches or NICs that predate the auto-negotiation standard, making this technology 100% backward compatible.

Flow Control

Flow control is an issue in all communications technologies where different nodes of varying speed communicate with each other. Consider what would happen if a 100Mbps server were to send data to a slower 10Mbps client. Classic shared Ethernet has several means of ensuring that the client can keep up with the flow of data coming to it from the server. First, because the client is typically capable of receiving 10Mbps of data, the shared channel is usually the bottleneck. Second, if the client has more data than it can handle and wants to stop the server from sending more data, it can prevent the server from overloading it with transmissions merely accessing the channel itself. The client can do this either by creating a collision or by pretending to be sending data, which will automatically prevent the server from transmitting further. This flow control method is called "back pressure." It violates the CSMA/CD specification, but many Ethernet vendors utilized prior to an official flow control standard being in place.

Also, consider a shared LAN with many users. If too many stations try to send data across a busy shared LAN, the network will become increasingly busy and start showing more and more collisions, which will prevent the network from overloading. (This state is called *saturation* and is covered in more detail in Chapter 7, "Bandwidth: How Much Is Enough?") In this way, the Ethernet network itself exhibits *congestion control*.

Half-Duplex Flow Control

Bridged or Switched Ethernet has a built-in method for dealing with transmissions between stations using different speeds. It involves a concept called *backpressure*. Consider the example of our fast 100Mbps server sending data to a 10Mbps client via a switch. The internal frame buffers of the switch store as many frames as possible. After the switch buffers are full, the switch needs to signal to the server to stop transmitting; otherwise, the buffers will overflow, and data will be lost. (The higher layers will make sure a retransmission occurs, so the data will still ultimately arrive.)

In a half-duplex environment, the switch can force collisions with the server (causing the server to back off), or the switch can keep the server port busy by pretending to be transmitting data. In this situation, the server will stop transmitting for a limited time, allowing the switch to work off the data accumulated in its buffers. Figure 4.6 illustrates this.

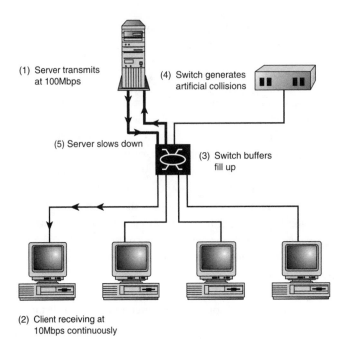

(1) Server transmits
    at 100Mbps

(4) Switch generates
    artificial collisions

(5) Server slows down

(3) Switch buffers
    fill up

(2) Client receiving at
    10Mbps continuously

FIGURE 4.6 *Half-duplex flow control uses artificial collisions or transmissions.*

In a full-duplex environment, the connection between server and switch is a dedicated send and receive channel, with CSMA/CD turned off. Therefore, the switch cannot generate a collision or access the shared channel to stop the server from transmitting. The server therefore carries on transmitting until the switch frame buffers overflow. Because of this, the IEEE needed to develop an effective flow-control method to go with the full-duplex standard.

Note

Flow control is not new to communications technologies. Consider the simple analog modem dialup connection. An analog telephone modem, operating as a point-to-point channel, utilizes the XON and XOFF methods for flow control. If data from the other side is overloading the receiver, it merely sends the XOFF signal that stops the transmission. XON means resume transmission, which is asserted when the receiver has time to process the data.

Full-Duplex Flow Control

The IEEE 802.3x standard defines a new way of accomplishing flow control in a full-duplex environment. The scheme is very simple yet elegant and uses the concept of a PAUSE frame and an associated PAUSE time to slow down the transmitter temporarily, similar to the XOFF function for analog modems.

This PAUSE frame uses a well-known multicast address, which is not forwarded by bridges and switches (in accordance with the IEEE 802.1D bridging standard). This means that the PAUSE frame does not generate additional traffic and does not interfere with flow control in different parts of the network.

If the 10Mbps client is receiving too much data from the switch, for example, the client can send a PAUSE frame to slow down the switch. The switch discards the PAUSE frame and the data is not forwarded to the server.

This is a very elegant and powerful technology, which has other future benefits. Priority frame transmission is possible with the new MAC control layer, for example.

The auto-negotiation scheme discussed in Chapter 3 will also be updated to include a bit that will signal that the station is flow-control capable.

Let's look at our example again and consider a situation where the server overloads the switch with too much data. The following series of events would occur:

1. When powering up, the server NIC and corresponding switch would sense that they were both 100Mbps full-duplex capable and adjust their transmission modes accordingly.

2. The client NIC is only capable of 10Mbps full-duplex operation. The switch port would also be set to 10Mbps full-duplex operation. Note that full-duplex automatically implies flow-control capable as well.

3. The server starts transmitting on its transmit channel (which is the switch's receive channel).

4. The switch receives frames and forwards them to the 10Mbps client, but at a much slower rate.

5. When the switch's internal buffers are close to full, the switch sends a PAUSE frame to the server NIC via its transmit channel (the server's receive channel). This stops server transmission for a limited time, depending on the PAUSE time specified in the PAUSE frame. As long as the switch is sending repeated PAUSE frames, the server pauses or interrupts its own transmission.

6. The switch transfers data out of its buffers to the slower client until its internal buffers are capable of receiving data again.

7. When the buffers are relatively empty, the switch stops sending the PAUSE signal to the server, which then restarts transmission.

Let's now look at a scenario where the switch overloads the client. This wouldn't normally happen, because the pipe from the switch to the client is only a 10Mbps connection. Therefore, let's assume that the client has temporarily stopped accepting data because the hard disk is full. Here is what happens in that situation:

1. The client starts sending PAUSE frames to the switch. These PAUSE frames stop transmissions from the switch.

2. The switch does not forward the PAUSE frames. Instead, the switch discards the PAUSE frames because the frame type was chosen to be a special multicast frame type that bridges do not forward.

3. As soon as the user has cleared space off the hard disk, the client stops sending PAUSE frames and resumes the download.

Figure 4.7 illustrates this procedure.

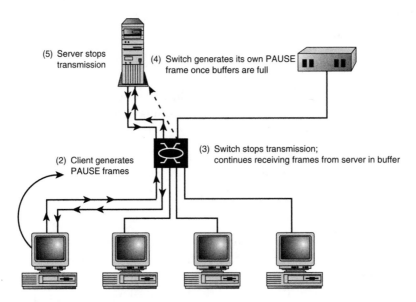

(5) Server stops
    transmission

(4) Switch generates its own PAUSE
    frame once buffers are full

(2) Client generates
    PAUSE frames

(3) Switch stops transmission;
    continues receiving frames from server in buffer

(1) Client hard disk full

(6) Client frees up space, PAUSE frames
    stop, transmission resumes

FIGURE 4.7 *Full-duplex flow control using PAUSE frames.*

Sometimes the frame buffers and the corresponding full and empty points are compared to a water storage tank. The full condition is also sometimes referred to as the "high water mark," and the "empty tank" analogy is the "low water mark." Figure 4.8 shows this analogy.

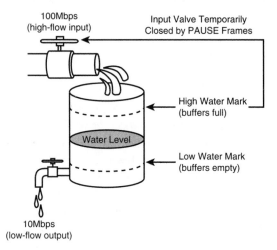

FIGURE 4.8 *Full-duplex input buffers are often compared with a water tank. The point where the PAUSE frames start to be transmitted is the high water mark. The low point is where the buffer is empty and is called the low water mark.*

Most Fast Ethernet equipment and all Gigabit Ethernet equipment shipping today are 802.3x-compliant. Older prestandard equipment will operate in full-duplex mode through manual configuration and will typically use one of the backpressure methods to prevent internal buffers from overflowing.

Switch Architectures and Performance

Let's briefly examine the four basic components that fundamentally affect a switch's performance. These are backplane capacity, forwarding mechanisms, port speed, and buffer size. We examine these features in more detail in Chapter 8, "Network Components."

Port Speed

Internally, a switch contains a MAC and PHY on every port. That means each switch port has an associated preprogrammed MAC address. In addition, a switch contains frame buffers. This architecture allows different ports on a switch to have different speeds. It also allows switches to be constructed as dual speed devices, where one port can change its speed from, say, 10 to 100 or 100 to 1000. A faster port on a switch is typically called an uplink port because it links up to a faster piece of the network.

Backplane Capacity

Switches allow for multiple simultaneous transmissions. Each transmission path consists of an input and an output port and occurs at wire speed. Most switches have multiple ports, and if more than one port pair is transferring data, throughput goes up accordingly. A switch's total bandwidth is determined by adding the bandwidth available for each connection. The aggregate bandwidth of a switch or bridge can be calculated as follows:

$$\text{Theoretical aggregate forwarding rate} = \frac{\text{Number of ports x Wire speed}}{2}$$

The 2 is required because a half-duplex transmission requires two ports. A 16-port 100BASE-T switch has an aggregate throughput of 800Mbps, for instance. By comparison, a 16-port 100BASE-T repeater still only gives 100Mbps of aggregate throughput. If 16 nodes are trying to contend for the available bandwidth, the average bandwidth per node becomes much smaller. Sometimes the maximum realizable forwarding rate of a switch is less than the theoretical aggregate forwarding rate because of internal design limitations. In that case, internal blocking exists.

Most switches use an internal backplane that interconnects all ports via the switch logic. The backplane capacity ultimately dictates the overall switch bandwidth and should be equal or close to the aggregate forwarding rate. If the backplane capacity is less than the aggregate forwarding rate, internal blocking could occur, maybe in the form of an internal overload. All 10Mbps and most 100Mbps switches are non-blocking these days, but not all Gigabit switches have the necessary backplane capacity yet; therefore, make sure to inquire about this when buying a new Gigabit switch.

Switch Forwarding Mechanisms

Switches use three kinds of frame-forwarding techniques. Frame forwarding may be *store-and-forward*, *cut-through*, or *modified cut-through*. Each one has its own advantages and disadvantages. Chapter 8 discusses the different features of switches in more detail, but here is a brief overview:

- *Store-and-forward*—All conventional bridges use the store-and-forward method of forwarding frames. Store-and-forward bridges and switches completely store the incoming frame in internal buffers before sending it out on another port. Under this method, the switch latency equals an entire frame. Store-and-forward is also known as error-free because the switch will receive the entire frame, including the FCS bits at the end to perform the CRC check. The switch discards frames with errors.

- *Cut-through*—Cut-through switches examine a frame only up to the destination address. This allows the frame to be forwarded almost immediately, resulting in very low switch latencies. Any frame arriving with a valid destination address will be forwarded. The drawback to cut-through switching is that bad frames will also be forwarded, because the CRC bits are received right at the end.

- *Modified cut-through*—Modified cut-through switches attempt to offer the best of both worlds by holding an incoming Ethernet frame until the first 64 bytes have been received. If the frame is bad, it can almost always be detected within the first 64 bytes of a frame, so a trade-off between switch latency and error-checking is achieved. In effect, modified cut-through switches act like a store-and-forward switch for short frames, which usually are acknowledge frames and are very latency-critical. For large frames, modified cut-through switches act like cut-through switches. Modified cut-through is also known as runt-free because this forwarding method discards runt frames. (Runt frames are partial frames that have been damaged by a collision, and are 64 bytes.)

Figure 4.9 illustrates these three frame-forwarding methods. The point at which a frame is forwarded is shown for each type of forwarding mechanism.

A debate has raged about which type of switching was best. The obvious trade-off used to be latency versus error-free switching. With 10Mbps Ethernet, the delay issue was still worth debating, because the delay for a 1500-byte frame could be 1.2 milliseconds. Cascading several switches could make this delay even longer. As the wire speed has increased by a factor of 10 for Fast Gigabit Ethernet and 100 for Gigabit Ethernet, the delay has been reduced by the same amount. This makes the debate a moot point: Fast Ethernet store-and-forward delays are 120µs, and Gigabit Ethernet delays are 12µs!

Also, moving frames from a slower receiving port (such as 10Mbps) to a faster transmitting port (such as 100Mbps) will require the store-and-forward method. The transmitting port would run out of bits to send as the receiving data rate is an order of magnitude slower. Therefore, an entire frame needs to be received before transmission can be started. Because most switches today feature either dual-speed 10/100 ports or 100 or 1000Mbps uplinks, the store-and-forward method has become the de facto standard.

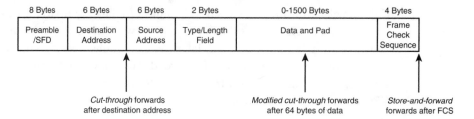

8 Bytes	6 Bytes	6 Bytes	2 Bytes	0-1500 Bytes	4 Bytes
Preamble /SFD	Destination Address	Source Address	Type/Length Field	Data and Pad	Frame Check Sequence

Cut-through forwards after destination address

Modified cut-through forwards after 64 bytes of data

Store-and-forward forwards after FCS

F IGURE 4.9 *Ethernet frame and the three different forwarding points for cut-through, modified cut-through, and store-and-forward switching.*

Memory Size

Switches contain two types of memory: the source address table and the frame buffer memory. Both are important for performance. If the SAT memory is too small and overflows at some point, a frame's previously known destination address could have disappeared. This will cause the switch to forward the frame to all ports, which generates excess traffic.

The frame buffer is more important because particularly dual-speed switches need to have plenty of memory. That's because an input port can be receiving at one speed, and an output port can potentially only transmit at one-tenth that speed. This will require significant internal buffering. Of course, flow control will take care of things, but small internal buffers only shift the memory problem to another component of the network.

Link Aggregation

The 802.1D spanning-tree algorithm allows parallel redundant links interconnecting two switches. STA will disable any parallel links, only reactivating them for backup purposes. If the active link goes down, STA will enable a backup link after a few seconds. Figure 4.10 shows this.

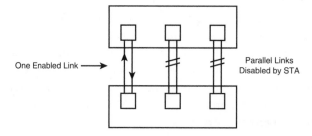

One Enabled Link ⟶

Parallel Links Disabled by STA

F IGURE 4.10 *The spanning-tree algorithm temporarily disables parallel bridged links.*

Sometimes you will want to connect different Ethernet switch ports in parallel to increase the bandwidth. Let's consider an example where you want to build a server farm using a Fast Ethernet switch as well as a workgroup switch, as shown in Figure 4.11. The switches are connected via their 100Mbps uplink port. In addition, each switch has 16 10Mbps ports, each capable of generating 20Mbps full-duplex traffic. If you add up the bandwidth requirements for each switch, you will see that each switch can generate 320Mbps of full-duplex data. If all the data needs to travel across the backbone, one 200Mbps FDX interconnection is not enough. This link is what is termed *oversubscribed*. This scenario assumes that all traffic needs to traverse the uplink, and that no traffic is local to a switch. This could be the case where all 16 connections at the bottom of the figure are clients trying to access three different servers connected to the top switch. The obvious answer would be to aggregate two 200Mbps links, but this is not possible due to STA.

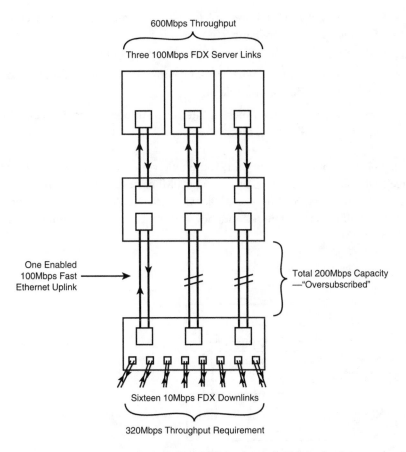

FIGURE 4.11 *The single 100Mbps FDX Interswitch Link is clearly oversubscribed; it is being asked to carry more than twice its rated capacity.*

Several switch vendors came up with their own proprietary link aggregation or port trunking scheme, the best known being Cisco's Fast EtherChannel that again dates back to the Kalpana days.

Here are some of the features and benefits of Cisco's EtherChannel technology:

- EtherChannel allows between two and four parallel links. This allows for scaling of bandwidth.

- EtherChannel is speed- and media-independent and will work for all media flavors of 10, 100, and Gigabit Ethernet.

- EtherChannel provides load balancing by dividing the data flow evenly over the different links.

- In the event of a link failure, STA takes up to a minute to reconnect or converge again. EtherChannel, on the other hand, reconverges in less than a second, avoiding network interruption altogether.

- EtherChannel used its own Cisco-developed Port Aggregation Protocol (PagP) to manage the multiple links.

- Some network adapters, such as Intel, also support EtherChannel, allowing for multiple parallel links to servers.

Let's go back to our example again. You would connect the two switches with three Fast EtherChannel links, providing 600Mbps of full-duplex bandwidth. You might only need 320Mbps of capacity, which equates to two links. The third link will provide some redundancy and future growth capability. Figure 4.12 shows this.

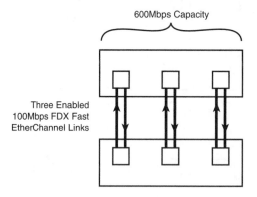

FIGURE 4.12   Cisco's Fast EtherChannel technology in operation.

802.3ad Link Aggregation

The 802.1D spanning-tree algorithm unfortunately doesn't allow for link aggregation because it was designed for single-port bridges more than a decade ago. Despite all its great benefits, EtherChannel remains a Cisco-proprietary technology. Other vendors have their own similar schemes, but the problem is that different vendors' switches cannot be aggregated together. The IEEE 802.3ad working group is currently working on an official link aggregation standard, which will be based on the EtherChannel technology (expected to be completed in 1999). Switch-to-switch, switch-to-server, switch-to-client, and switch-to-router link aggregation will be possible. Trunking will occur at Layer 2.

Summary

Layer 2 switches are incredibly useful devices for building fast, affordable Ethernets of all sizes. We will examine the usage of switches in more detail in the deployment half of this book, but we briefly want to summarize the major benefits of switches:

- Switches, the evolutionary successors to bridges, allow you to join different standalone networks.

- You can use switches to segment larger shared LANs with excessively high traffic levels into smaller LANs, thereby reducing the traffic level. This process is called *segmenting a LAN* and is one of the most effective ways of improving your network bandwidth.

- Switches are crucial for connecting Ethernet LANs of different speeds together. The internal buffering of switches makes this possible. Without switches, migration from 10Mbps Ethernet to the 100 or 1000Mbps versions would be very difficult and would involve that notorious "forklift upgrade" (throwing away all your existing equipment). Therefore, most switches offer ports of different speeds.

- Like most Fast Ethernet NICs, many switches offer 10/100 speed on the same port. This makes them ideal plug-and-play devices for easy upgrade and investment protection; you connect to a port and don't really need to care whether you have connected your node to the correctly set port.

- Regular shared Ethernet has a network diameter of 2500 meters, whereas Fast and Gigabit Ethernets are restricted to approximately one-tenth of that, which makes large shared Fast and Gigabit Ethernet LANs unrealistic. Switches come to the rescue; they can extend a Fast or Gigabit Ethernet network to any network diameter size.

- Like repeaters, Layer 2 switches require no (or little) configuration, because they are self-learning devices. This is in stark contrast to both routers and Layer 3 switches, covered in Chapter 5. The self-learning nature of this feature makes installation and usage of switches very easy. These days, switches do have a lot of features that require some configuration—for example STA, link aggregation, forwarding mode, full-duplex, and so on. These configuration options are relatively straight-forward, however. Many out-the-box switches will typically still work without any kind of configuration at all as a drop-in replacement for a repeater.

- Upgrading from repeaters to switches is a drop-in replacement. Disconnect the old shared-media repeater, install a switch in its place, and you have upgraded your network bandwidth by an order of magni-tude. Few things in your (networking) life are that simple.

- Today, switches offer superb price and performance. A few years ago, only a handful of vendors were selling Ethernet switches, meaning prices were high. Today, every single networking vendor sells an Ethernet switch of some kind, making them incredibly cheap. In terms of price and performance, they are hard to beat.

- Switches are fault-tolerant, yet foolproof. Through the spanning-tree algo-rithm, switches include an element of fault tolerance for multiple backup links. The spanning-tree standard also ensures that switches are plug-and-play in terms of installation, however.

- Link aggregation provides for scalable bandwidth. The connection band-width between switches or servers can be increased step-by-step, making switched connections scalable on demand. If your server is running at 100Mbps, for example, but you aren't quite ready to buy a Gigabit switch and NIC, Link Aggregation allows you to increase your performance to 200Mbps relatively easily. Link Aggregation also enhances the level of fault tolerance in a switched network.

In 1997, the IEEE finished its work on the 802.3x full-duplex/flow-control stan-dard. Full-duplex Ethernet is one of those Ethernet innovations that has gone relatively unnoticed. The obvious benefit of full-duplex Ethernet is that it enables simultaneous transmission and reception, effectively doubling the the-oretical throughput of Ethernet. Full-duplex Switched Ethernet, however, is significantly altering the future of Ethernet in general. Full-duplex Ethernet makes the 25-year old Ethernet CSMA/CD MAC effectively obsolete, replacing it with the best of both worlds. On the one hand, full-duplex Ethernet maintains backward compatibility by utilizing the existing Ethernet frame format. On the other hand, full-duplex Ethernet enables state-of-the art switching technology, allowing for dedicated, switched connections.

Does all this sound too good to be true? "Where is the catch?" you might be asking yourself. There is only one: Classic Ethernet repeaters are very easy to manage and troubleshoot, but switches are not. That's because a repeater shares the bandwidth across all ports, allowing you to connect to one port and essentially listen in to the entire network. Switches divide the network into many different segments, which requires sophisticated management and troubleshooting tools. Chapters 11, "Managing Switched and Fast Ethernet Networks," and 12, " Troubleshooting," discuss switch management and troubleshooting in more detail.

Very large enterprise networks can be built with only Layer 2 switches. The absolute limit to the size of a pure Layer 2 network is the subject of many debates. It is probably a lot larger than most people think. One limiting factor of a Layer 2 switch is that it indiscriminately forwards most multicast and broadcast traffic. When a very large network is built using only Layer 2 switches, the amount of multicast and broadcast traffic can become excessive.

In the past, this drawback was typically addressed by adding a router to the network, somewhere, to subdivide the large single broadcast traffic domain into smaller broadcast domains. (Switches are added to divide larger repeated collision domains into smaller ones.)

Lately, VLANs and Layer 3 switches have appeared. They perform the same kind of broadcast containment function as a router. VLANs essentially limit broadcasts to an artificially created broadcast domain, whereas Layer 3 switches can examine individual multicast or broadcast frames more closely before deciding whether to forward them. VLANs and Layer 3 switches are the topic of the next chapter. Chapter 6, "Cabling and More on Physical Layers," more closely examines the measurement of broadcasts.

CHAPTER 5

VLANs and Layer 3 Switching

This chapter covers the relatively new topics of virtual LANs (VLANs) and Layer 3 switching. The first part of this chapter discusses the concepts and benefits of VLANs and the different VLAN implementation methods, such as port, protocol, MAC address, and IP Subnet. We look at distributed VLANs, which require some kind of trunking. We look at the proprietary VLAN trunking method from Cisco called Interswitch Link (ISL), as well as the new IEEE 802.1Q VLAN tagging standard. We then look at the different methods of connecting VLANs.

We also examine the IEEE 802.1p priority switching technology that was designed to improve the delivery of time-critical data. Whereas 802.1p is not directly related to VLANs, the 802.1p standard utilizes the additional VLAN tagging field to provide for improved delivery of time-critical data. Therefore, this chapter is a good place to deal with it.

The second part of this chapter discusses Layer 3 switches. We first cover some of the basics of routing; then we attempt to explain the current hype surrounding Layer 3 switches, which are merely hardware-based IP or IPX LAN routers. We contrast the different types of Layer 3 switches, namely packet-to-packet, and a host of other methods that rely on cut-through methods. (For more information on cut-through methods, see Chapter 4, "Layer 2 Ethernet Switching.")

Next, we take an in-depth look at Layer 3 switches. Layer 3 switches are replacing classic IP LAN routers in certain places, because they offer more performance at significantly lower prices with easier configuration. Different VLANs need to be connected via a Layer 3 device, such as a classic router. The required use of routers has slowed the adoption rate of VLANs tremendously. The recent emergence of fast, easy to configure, and affordable Layer 3 hardware-based switches has made VLANs a popular mainstream tool for LAN managers everywhere.

Finally, we discuss Layer 4 switching, which is the latest hot concept. We also discuss why Layer 4 switching isn't really switching at all.

Before we begin, we need to point out a few things:

- We cover a lot of information in this chapter. To discuss both VLANs and Layer 3 switches in detail in one chapter is ambitious. Therefore, this chapter doesn't go into too much detail. Entire books have been written on just VLANs or Layer 3 switching. Many excellent white papers from the vendor community also are available on the Web. Please refer to Appendixes B and C for suggestions for further reading.

- VLANs are not specific to Ethernet but are based on the OSI Layer 2. As such, you can apply VLANs to any frame-based LAN technology that follows the OSI model. For example, VLANs are already a feature on some of today's FDDI or Token Ring switches. The standards we discuss in this chapter, such as 802.1Q/p, are not 802.3/Ethernet specific; they were designed to work for Token Ring and other frame-based LAN standards as well.

- We discuss Layer 3 aspects of the OSI model. Note that, like VLANs, Layer 3 switching technology could be built into any OSI-compliant LAN hardware standard. Networking vendors chose to focus their Layer 3 switching efforts on Ethernet, and Fast and Gigabit Ethernet in particular. For example, we quite possibly will see some Layer 3 Token Ring switches one day.

- TCP/IP is the most popular Layer 3 networking protocol today and is fast becoming the de facto standard. We assume you are somewhat familiar with the routing aspects of TCP/IP. We included a number of references for additional reading.

Before we delve into VLANs in more detail, let's take a small detour into the frame world.

Unicast, Multicast, and Broadcast Frames

This is a quick tutorial on the subject of unicast, multicast, and broadcast frames. These three frame transmissions differ in terms of their destination address.

Unicast Frames

Ethernet frames typically are sent from a particular source address (SA) to a specific destination address (DA), which is a one-to-one transmission. This is known as *unicast*, or *unique address broadcast*. The DA field in a unicast frame is the MAC address of the destination and is always a unique 6-byte number. An example of a unicast DA is 00-A0-EF-12-34-56 (hex). A switch directly forwards a unicast frame from source port to destination port. Most of today's LAN traffic consists of point-to-point transmissions.

Multicast Frames

Sometimes, the same source data needs to be sent to multiple receivers. This could be an email sent to everyone in a specific department within a company or a company-wide mailing list. Newer applications, such as server-based audio or video streaming (covered in Chapter 7, "Bandwidth: How Much Is Enough?"), also fall into this category of one-to-many communication. From a bandwidth-usage perspective, broadcasting to multiple users at once is much more efficient than generating multiple individual unicast transmissions for every individual user. The one-to-many transmission, broadcasting to multiple users at once, is called *multicasting*. One-to-many transmissions are becoming increasingly popular as new applications, such as server-based streaming, groupware, videoconferencing, and IP multicasting, become more mainstream. The receiver typically decides whether to join a specific multicast transmission. Multicasts are identified by means of a particular DA range of addresses. An example of a multicast DA is 01-80-C2-00-00-00 (which is a spanning tree multicast address).

> ### Note
>
> *Many recent one-to-many applications utilize IP multicasting, which is different from Ethernet multicasting. We discuss IP multicasts later in this chapter.*
>
> *When Layer 2 switches do not know the destination address of a particular frame, they flood or forward the frame to all ports. Although this is not a multicast, it is similar in nature because it creates a lot of extra traffic on all segments.*

Broadcast Frames

Broadcasts are one-to-all transmissions addressed to everyone on the network. A variety of sources can generate broadcast frames:

- The spanning tree Bridge Protocol Data Unit (BPDU) (discussed in Chapter 4) is a typical example of a multicast frame. This frame needs to be conveyed to all bridges and switches on the LAN to build one tree.

- Some network operating system (NOS) clients and servers, such as NetWare, use broadcasts to advertise their presence on the LAN. Most networking protocols, such as IPX, AppleTalk, and NetBIOS, make regular use of broadcasts to discover addresses, routers, and servers.

- IP routing protocols, such as RIP and DVMRP, use broadcasts extensively to discover routing paths, to exchange information about the optimal route, or to match IP and MAC addresses.

With broadcasts, the DA frame field is set to all *1s*. This indicates to all stations on the LAN that this particular frame is destined for everyone. All broadcast frames have the destination address field set to all *1s* (or FF-FF-FF-FF-FF-FF, in hexadecimal notation).

Broadcast Storms

Like Ethernet collisions, broadcasts have received a bad reputation over the years because they often do not represent an actual data transmission but more network Layer 2 or 3 overhead.

A unicast transmission will occupy only the direct path from source to destination, whereas a broadcast will permeate all corners of a network. Thus, many people view broadcasts as wasted bandwidth. The truth is that broadcast transmissions cannot be eliminated: They are part of the normal workings of any network. Only excessive broadcast rates are a problem, and they are typically the result of too large a network or faulty hardware. Excessive broadcast rates affect the net bandwidth available to users, causing the network to become very sluggish.

Faulty hardware or an incorrectly configured network can lead to the network being overwhelmed with broadcasts, also known as a *broadcast storm*. A broadcast storm describes a situation in which the entire network is used to transmit broadcasts, leaving no bandwidth for regular traffic. This will result in timeouts and network errors, which is the equivalent of freeway "gridlock."

Really, only two possible things can create a broadcast storm:

- Bridge loops (such as that shown in Figure 4.5 in Chapter 4) running without the spanning tree algorithm (STA) in operation. This is very rare, because most new bridges and all switches include STA. (Alternatively, STA could be disabled on a bridge or switch.)

- The other, more likely, source of broadcasts is faulty hardware (NICs or switches). The device in question is malfunctioning and possibly sending out broadcast frames permanently.

Both scenarios are very unlikely these days; NICs now have an MTBF (mean time between failure) rate of well over 10 years, and all bridge switches include the STA.

Broadcast Domains

In a shared or repeated Ethernet segment, all nodes are in the same collision domain. A repeater is invisible to all nodes in a shared-media segment. Nodes operating in a shared environment collide with each other if they attempt a transmission at the same time. When two nodes collide, all other nodes hear the collision: hence the term *collision domain*. Collisions do not traverse a bridge or a switch; therefore, these devices form the edges or borders of a collision domain.

The broadcast domain is the network area that a broadcast frame will fill. As discussed in Chapter 4, switches or bridges operate at Layer 2 and blindly forward all broadcast traffic received (as well as all unknown destination address frames), making switches invisible to broadcasts. Figure 5.1 illustrates this.

Problems with Very Large Broadcast Domains

Theoretically, you can build very large networks with hundreds or even thousands of nodes using only Layer 2 switches. The term *flat network* is used because, from a hierarchical perspective, all these switches are on the same level: no higher level Layer 3 routers are present. In practice, the size of a flat, switched Layer 2 network has a limit. The following factors limit the size of a Layer 2 network:

- *Broadcasts grow with network size*—As previously discussed, broadcasts tend to travel everywhere within a switched network. Many NOSs and their associated protocols, such as NetWare, AppleTalk, LAN Manager, and LANServer, are rather chatty: They create a fair amount of broadcast traffic. That's because these network operating systems' protocols were designed to operate on local area networks where bandwidth has traditionally not been a problem. When enlarging a Layer 2 switched network from say 100 to 1000 users, the broadcast rate will grow at least tenfold, too. If your broadcast rate in a 100-user network is 2%, the 1000-user network will have a broadcast rate of at least 20%, which is a rather significant number. Even 20% broadcast traffic is tolerable, because it leaves you with almost 80% usable bandwidth in a switched environment. The good news is that TCP/IP is a very quiet (or, non-chatty) protocol because it was designed to operate over WAN links, where bandwidth is scarce. Therefore, as more networks migrate from other protocols to TCP/IP, the broadcast rate will decrease.

- *Control*—The big issue with large networks is that a broadcast storm will crash the entire network. Although broadcast storms are extremely rare, the occurrence of one will bring your entire network to its knees, and 1000 angry users is nothing to sneeze at.

- *Lack of IP addresses*—Networks using IP must contend with another issue: lack of IP addresses. In an IP environment, every node receives an IP address that is either permanently (statically) assigned or dynamically assigned via the Dynamic Host Configuration Protocol (DHCP). The number of 254 IP addresses that can be assigned on a particular IP subnet is limited, imposing an artificial limit on the maximum number of users in a particular broadcast domain.

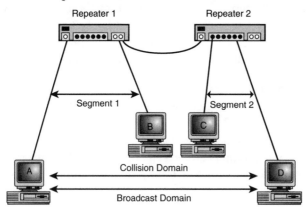

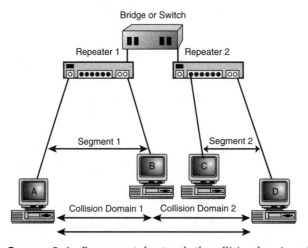

FIGURE 5.1   *For a repeated network, the collision domain and broadcast domain are the same. Introducing a bridge or switch creates two separate collision domains, yet all nodes still share the same broadcast domain.*

The Old Way of Dealing with Large Broadcast Domains: Routers

Historically, you connected LANs together over short distances with bridges. You used routers to connect LANs together over extended distances. You joined these different LANs via multiple routers, sometimes with different path choices. Routers set up an optimum routing path depending on various criteria, therefore the term *routers*. Routers operate at Layer 3 and don't forward broadcasts or multicasts automatically, so LAN managers started using routers to link similar LANs over shorter distances. As corporate networks became larger, routers started moving to the center of the network to segment larger, flat Layer 2 networks into smaller broadcast domains or subnets. Routers became the centerpieces for large enterprise networks, using architectures such as distributed or collapsed backbones (more on this in the second half of this book) to generate multiple smaller subnets.

This solves all of the issues of large flat Layer 2 networks: Every subnet can have its range of IP addresses, broadcasts are contained within a subnet, possible broadcast storms only affect one subnet, and protocol routing still occurs. (This assumes a particular type of IP address, namely a Class C address.) Figure 5.2 shows a switched network that has been subdivided by means of a router. The nodes A, B, C, and D (shown in Figure 5.2) physically reside in the same broadcast domain, and nodes E, F, and G reside in broadcast domain 2. The limits for broadcast domains 1 and 2 are the outer physical boundaries set by switch 1 and switch 2. If, for example, node D wanted to join broadcast domain 1, the node would have to be physically moved and connected to switch 1.

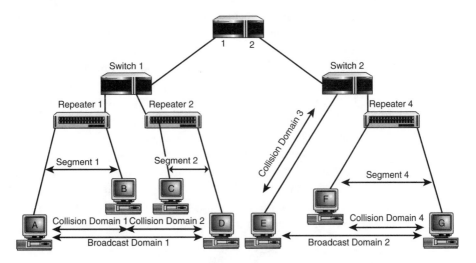

FIGURE 5.2 *Introducing a router into our previously shown network creates two different broadcast domains. Nodes A, B, C, and D are part of broadcast domain 1, whereas nodes E, F, and G are part of broadcast domain 2.*

> **Note**
>
> *Interestingly, the broadcast rate in most pure Layer 2 networks is not excessive. What LAN managers fear most is the entire network coming to a halt. Unfortunately, broadcast storms can cause that, extremely rare as they are. So it is often the fear of broadcast storms, not of existing broadcast rates, that causes network managers to look for ways of dividing up larger Layer 2 networks into smaller broadcast domains.*
>
> *So before you go out and buy more routers to segment your flat Layer 2 network to reduce broadcasts, we urge you to take a closer look at what exactly your broadcast traffic rate is. Chapter 7, "Bandwidth: How Much Is Enough?" discusses some tools that allow you to measure broadcasts. In our opinion, a 10% broadcast rate is quite acceptable.*

> **Note**
>
> *Routers often subdivide a larger flat network into multiple broadcast domains. The router is placed at the center of the network to accomplish this. There's another reason why routers often are found at the center of large networks. Historically, different operating systems have all used different networking protocols. Only recently has TCP/IP emerged as the clear leader. For many years, Novell NetWare ran on IPX, Digital used LAT, Microsoft favored NetBEUI or NetBIOS, and the UNIX world was synonymous with TCP/IP. Then, of course, Banyan, IBM, Apple, and the like all used different protocols again. So most corporate networks required a powerful protocol router somewhere so that everyone could communicate with everyone else. Putting this router at the edge of the network wasn't very efficient because it meant the routed traffic needed to traverse multiple switches twice. Thus, routers became the centerpieces of larger mixed-protocol environments.*

VLANs

No textbook definition or standard describes a VLAN perfectly, but over the past few years, a commonly accepted definition has emerged. A VLAN is a logical grouping of nodes, consisting of clients and servers that reside in a common broadcast domain, without any router hops. The word *virtual* means that the LAN manager has artificially created the broadcast domain within the switching fabric. Whereas a VLAN is a single broadcast domain, the different nodes within this VLAN need not be physically connected to the same switch or even be in the same physical area. Nodes that are members of the same VLAN appear as though they are connected to one Layer 2 bridge or switch, sharing broadcasts, but they may not actually be. These different nodes may, in fact, be connected to different switches in different buildings altogether and connected only via a VLAN. Alternatively, these VLAN members may be connected to the same switch but may not be able to see all the broadcast traffic originating from other ports on that very same switch.

Figure 5.3 shows the previous network example from Figure 5.2 with two different VLANs.

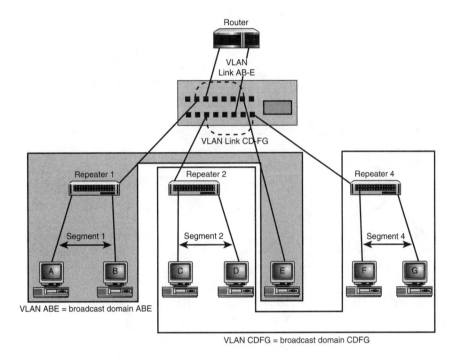

FIGURE 5.3 *Our two Layer 2 switches have been replaced with a single VLAN-capable switch. The VLAN-capable switch sets up the broadcast domains internally. Nodes A, B, and E now reside in VLAN ABE, and nodes C, D, F, and G share broadcast domain CDFG. A router will be required to communicate between VLANs ABE and CDFG.*

Benefits of VLANs

Let's look at some of the benefits of VLANs:

- *More bandwidth*—VLANs isolate broadcasts. Fewer broadcasts mean more bandwidth is available for regular unicast traffic.

- *Frees up your network from physical limitations*—A VLAN is a grouping of network nodes that share similar resources. Unlike a pure Layer 2–switched LAN, these resources do not have to be physically located next to each other in the network. For instance, a marketing department that is spread over Buildings HQ and SALES can all access the marketing department's shared servers, despite the fact that the server is located in the basement of the IT building. The benefit of a VLAN is obvious: shared resources don't need to be in the same physical area. Figure 5.4 shows this example.

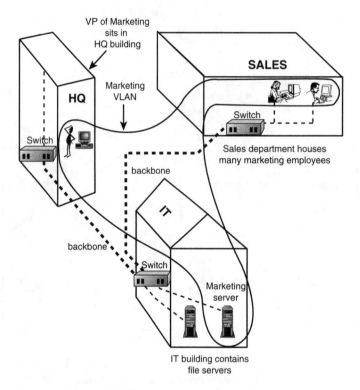

FIGURE 5.4 *A VLAN groups users and shared resources, often located in physically different areas. Shown is a marketing department spread out over two different buildings, accessing shared servers in a third building.*

- *Broadcast containment*—According to our definition, VLANs are synonymous with broadcast domains. Routers also contain broadcast traffic within a VLAN domain. Thus, VLAN-enabled switches can replace routers with the added benefit of being cheaper and easier to configure than routers, which saves you time and money.

- *Multicast containment*—Yes, VLANs will contain broadcasts. In addition, VLANs will also contain multicasts, reducing overall network traffic.

- *Easy changes*—Because VLANs enable the dynamic allocation of resources, VLANs also enable you to make changes easily. If a user wants to change office location from the HQ building to the IT building, this move can be easily accommodated by extending the VLAN to include the new office location in the IT building.

- *Easily shares resources*—A server or desktop can actually be part of multiple VLANs. This reduces the need to route traffic and provides greater flexibility and access to resources when and where they are needed.

- *Performance*—VLANs offer the capability of bandwidth on demand. If, for example, some users on a particular VLAN complain about the lack of bandwidth, you could create a new dedicated VLAN and move several users to this new VLAN, thereby improving performance. This new VLAN would involve less traffic, thereby improving performance.

- *Security*—In a flat switched environment, everyone shares broadcasts. If some of these broadcasts contain secure information, someone unauthorized could conceivably obtain access to confidential information. VLANs offer you the benefit of true broadcast security. If, for example, the HR department wants to keep all its traffic confidential, you could create a VLAN with just the HR staff as part of it. This benefit is questionable in our opinion, as very few broadcasts will contain confidential information. In general, higher level security measures are easier to set up and maintain.

VLAN Membership

So, how do you decide what nodes to group together in a particular VLAN? VLANs come in numerous different types, and choosing how to group nodes together is sometimes not easy. Going back to our definition of VLANs will give you some pointers on how to group nodes together: VLANs are broadcast domains set up to share resources. VLAN memberships are also sometimes referred to as *policies*.

How do these VLAN implementations help in the management of an enterprise network? We'll look at each briefly and give some pluses and minuses.

Port-Based VLANs

With port-based VLANs, you manually assign a switch port to a particular VLAN number. For example, you can assign switch port 8 to a VLAN called FINANCE. This typically means that another switch or repeater is attached to that port and all nodes on that port are in the same VLAN. This would make sense if all finance people work in close physical proximity to each other and all connect to the same repeater or switch hanging off port 8.

Alternatively, you can connect multiple VLAN switch ports to form a common VLAN. For example, switch port 1 could connect to the marketing people in building HQ, port 2 could connect to the marketing employees in the SALES building, and port 5 could connect to the servers in the IT building. Grouping these three ports into one VLAN sets up MARKETING VLAN. In this case, the switch will analyze each received broadcast frame and forward it only to the ports that have been assigned the same VLAN. Unicast frames, however, will be forwarded only to the required port.

Figure 5.5 shows an example of a port-based VLAN.

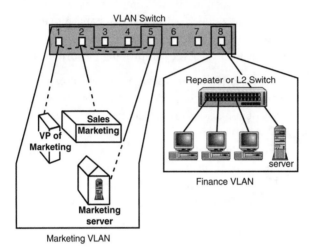

FIGURE 5.5 *Port-based VLANs are useful when the physical network resembles your logical layout.*

Advantages
Port-based VLAN setup is quick and easy to understand: There aren't that many ports on a switch.

Some first generation VLAN switches supported only this kind of configuration.

Disadvantages
You must manually keep track of all VLAN names, port numbers, and associated nodes connected.

A user physically connected to one port and moving to a different port will require reconfiguration.

MAC Address-Based VLANs
This method requires you to add individual MAC addresses manually to specific VLANs. This means that a given end-station, no matter where it is on a network, will be a member of that VLAN. The management of MAC-based VLANs is also manual: You need to track MAC Addresses and relevant VLAN

group numbers. For example, a VLAN called HR could consist of nodes with MAC addresses 00-A0-C9-12-3A-F3 and 00-60-06-44-35-D2.

Figure 5.6 shows an example of a MAC address-based VLAN.

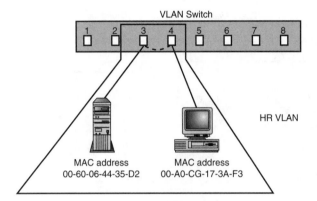

FIGURE 5.6 *VLANs are useful when the individual Ethernet MAC addresses are known and you have the time to enter them all manually.*

Advantages
Every NIC has a hardcoded MAC address. If you move the PC or notebook and the installed NIC, you automatically move the MAC address, too. The switch will retain the original VLAN membership, however, regardless of physical location. Therefore, you can use this VLAN management technique when your users connect laptops from anywhere in the building at any time.

Disadvantages
The biggest disadvantage is that every MAC address needs to be entered manually or added to a VLAN, which can be rather cumbersome.

While the idea of transparent moves sounds appealing, particularly for large notebook installations, there is a catch with docking stations, many of which have the NIC installed in them instead of in the notebooks. Thus, a user who moves to a different docking station will not be able to rejoin one's original VLAN group unless you account for this in the original VLAN setup.

If the NIC or the PC are faulty and is replaced, the switch VLAN configuration needs to be updated.

Layer 3 Protocol-Based VLANs
With Layer 3 protocol-based VLANs, you must be running more than one protocol. In this situation, you set up a VLAN based on what specific protocol is in

use. For example, VLAN 4 could be a grouping of all nodes using the IPX protocol, and VLAN 5 could comprise clients and servers using the IP protocol.

Figure 5.7 shows an example of a protocol-based VLAN.

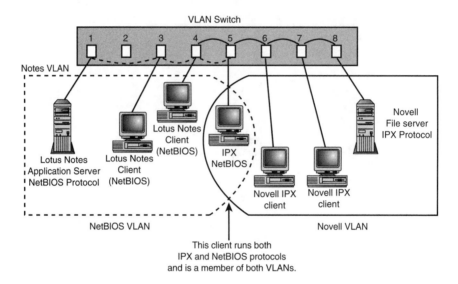

FIGURE 5.7 *Protocol-based VLANs are useful when different applications use different protocols.*

Advantage

Often, particular applications use a specific protocol. Segmenting traffic by protocol type allows you, in effect, to create an application-specific VLAN. Users can move to anywhere on the network and retain their VLAN membership so long as they keep using the same protocol.

Alternatively, you can segment by NOS server by choosing NetWare and NT as policies (via their respective protocols, such as IPX and IP). This is by far the most common use of this kind of VLAN.

Disadvantage

Analyzing the protocol type on every packet is very time-consuming. MAC- and port-based VLAN switching, on the other hand, involves almost no switch intervention at all and is very fast by comparison. Many networks are standardizing on IP everywhere, in effect creating one flat IP VLAN. That makes this VLAN method superfluous.

You can set up nonroutable protocol VLANs, but this doesn't make much sense because you cannot communicate outside of this VLAN. If you want to keep traffic local on a particular VLAN, though, this could work for you.

Layer 3/IP Network Address VLANs

IP is a protocol that assigns an individual address to every node: for example, 172.16.2.1 uniquely identifies a specific node. Different IP nodes can be grouped together to form one VLAN. This VLAN policy is similar to the MAC address scheme in that you need to know individual IP addresses. Whereas every node has a MAC address, not all nodes will run IP, and therefore, not all nodes will have an IP address. Because IP addresses often are assigned in ranges, setting up VLAN is preferred to coincide with an IP range of addresses, called a Subnet. Of course, this method of setting up VLANs won't work if you use DHCP because it assigns a different IP address every time a user connects to the network.

Layer 3/Network Subnet Address VLANs

Layer 3/network address VLAN assignment is similar to the protocol-based method in that it uses Layer 3 information to determine VLAN membership. This method works very well for IP LANs, where each individual node can have a unique IP subnet address. For example, a VLAN called Subnet 2 could comprise all nodes with the IP subnet address 172.16.2.0 and mask 255.255.254.0. This means that all 254 nodes within the IP address range 172.02.100.1–172.0.100.254 communicate within VLAN Subnet 2.

A VLAN switch might apparently act like a router when assigning VLAN membership according to Layer 3 information. This isn't the case. In fact, the VLAN switch acts as a grouper: It merely bundles a particular protocol or subnet traffic into a VLAN. In order to communicate among different protocols or subnets, a router is still required. That's why most, if not all, of today's VLAN switches are actually a combination of a VLAN switch and a Layer 3 switch.

Figure 5.8 shows an example of a subnet-based VLAN.

Advantages

This type of VLAN management works well if your VLAN grouping matches your physical IP subnet structure.

Subnet-based VLANs are probably the easiest to configure. In this case, a VLAN switch can often replace a classic router used for subnetting. This is the most backward-compatible version of VLANs with respect to replacing existing routers.

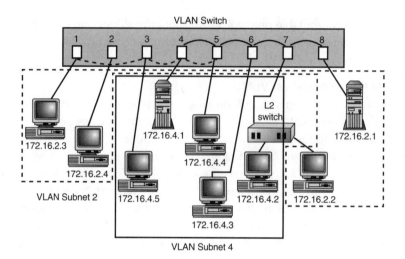

FIGURE 5.8   *Here is an example of a subnet-based VLAN. In this situation, a VLAN switch can often replace a classic router.*

Disadvantages

Network address-based VLANs only work for IP-based nodes.

Just as in MAC address-based VLANs, you need to keep track of individual IP addresses.

Multiple VLAN Membership

Some combinations of the previous VLAN policies are possible, too. Consider the following example: the HR VLAN is a MAC address-based VLAN (see Figure 5.6). Right now, switch ports 4 and 5 have only MAC node connected. You could add switch port 5 permanently to this VLAN. By assigning this port to the HR VLAN altogether, you can ensure that all nodes that are subsequently added to port 5 will also become part of the same VLAN. That way you don't have to worry about future configurations. If someone is connected to this port by accident, however, that person will have access to all the HR confidential data. This is basically a "mix-and-match" approach.

IP Multicast Address-Based VLANs

We can also identify a VLAN with an IP multicast address, which is a proxy address for a larger group of IP addresses. If a frame needs to go to this group of IP addresses, it is sent first to the proxy IP address and then forwarded to the entire group. Membership in the group is voluntary: Each desktop can determine if its IP address should be included in the group. This kind of VLAN identification is useful in networks where video or audio data is being broadcast on the network and only a select few users are allowed or want to view or listen to the information.

An IP multicast VLAN is set up at Layer 3 or higher and has nothing to do with the actual VLAN switching hardware involved. IP multicast VLANs are also temporary, as a node can leave the multicast domain at any time. IP multicast VLANs don't provide broadcast containment: they are merely a grouping of nodes. By definition, IP multicast VLANs can also span WANs. Table 5.1 summarizes the different VLAN membership options. Figure 5.9 shows the VLAN configuration software of an actual Layer 3 switch. The switch shown has been configured with many different VLANs.

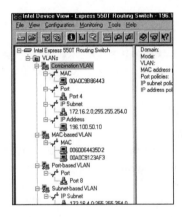

FIGURE 5.9 *VLAN configuration is made easy through good management software. For example, Intel's DeviceView switch management software contains an "Explorer" function that allows you to explore the switch by selecting individual VLANs. Double-clicking will reveal the different VLAN policies.*

TABLE 5.1 VLAN POLICY OR MEMBERSHIP OPTIONS

Type	Information Required	Example
Port-based	Switch port number	Port 8→Finance VLAN[1]
		Ports 1, 2, 5→Marketing VLAN
MAC-based	Client and server MAC	MAC addresses 00-A0-C9-12-3A-F3 addresses (from NIC) and 00-60-06-44-35-D2→HR VLAN
Layer 3/protocol[2]	Protocol Type	NetBIOS packets→Notes VLAN IPX packets→Novell VLAN

continues

TABLE 5.1 CONTINUED

Type	Information Required	Example
Layer 3/IP subnet	IP Subnet and Mask	IP Subnet nodes with address 172.16.2.X and Mask 255.255.255.0 are on VLAN SUBNET2; nodes with 172.16.4.X and Mask 255.255.254.0 are on VLAN SUB-NET4.
IP multicast-based	IP Multicast address	IP Multicast address X is and Mask associated with VLAN
Multiple VLAN membership	Combinations of above	Add port 5 to HR VLAN member ships (so far a MAC-based VLAN)

[1] The → symbol indicates "assigned to."

[2] Nonroutable protocols, such as NetBIOS, are rarely used to define VLANs because you cannot communicate outside of this VLAN. You would more typically use IP and IPX to define protocol-based VLANs.

The Evolution of VLANs and VLAN Membership

Let's take a look at the three generations of VLAN switches, from the first-generation, standalone switches to today's third-generation, distributed, standards-based VLAN switches.

First Generation: Standalone VLAN Switches

First-generation, VLAN-capable switches were limited to one switch only. An individual VLAN could encompass only a single switch, which severely limited VLAN deployment. For example, transparent user moves are one of the benefits of VLANs, but a user moving in a larger organization will unlikely be connected to the very same switch at the new location, which defeats the whole purpose of VLANs.

Second Generation: Distributed Proprietary VLANs

A VLAN spanning more than one switch is called a *distributed VLAN*. Second-generation VLAN switches could share VLAN membership information among different switches. In effect, a link or trunk between different switches or a server connection would contain traffic that was part of more than one VLAN. Cisco's Inter-Switch Link is probably the best-known distributed VLAN technology, having been licensed to many other vendors, such as Intel for its server NICs. ISL explicitly tags each frame with a particular VLAN group identifier. Other networking vendors have developed similar schemes. For example, 3Com switches use VLAN trunking (known as VLT), which is also a frame-tagging method like ISL. The issue with all these VLAN membership communication methods was that they were all proprietary: you could build a distributed VLAN only if using switches from a single vendor.

Figure 5.10 shows an example of a distributed VLAN.

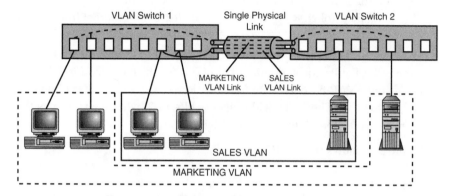

FIGURE 5.10 *The capability to distribute VLANs among different switches has really made VLANs a powerful concept for managing networks.*

Third Generation: Distributed, Standards-Based VLANs

The vendor community and the IEEE realized that a VLAN trunking standard was necessary because the proprietary nature of VLANs limited their acceptance. Two approaches were possible. First, different switches could exchange tables with relevant VLAN information, such as node MAC addresses, VLAN group membership, and so on. The spanning tree algorithm uses a similar table exchange method for broadcasting BPDU frames. This method's drawback is that it creates lots of extra LAN broadcast traffic, which VLANs are trying to limit. The other option seeks to identify each packet explicitly with a VLAN group membership number through a tagging approach.

In the end, the IEEE chose a standard that was based on Cisco's ISL frame-tagging developments. In the new 802.1Q standard, a special 4-byte tag is inserted into every Ethernet frame in between the source address and Length/Type field. This tag field contains two fields of information, the Tag Control Information (TIF) and Tag Protocol Identifier field (TPID):

- The Tag Control Information (TIF) field, which consists of the VLAN ID, the USER PRIORITY field, and a CFI bit.

- Twelve bits represent the VLAN ID, which determines the actual VLAN group. All switches in the network use this VLAN ID to communicate VLAN membership.

- The USER PRIORITY field is 3 bits long, and we will cover it in more detail in the next section.

- There is also the Canonical Format Indicator (CFI) bit, which is only used for Token Ring transmission. This bit indicates that the current frame is actually a Token Ring frame encapsulated in an Ethernet frame format.

The three fields of the TIF just mentioned add up to 16 bits, or 2 bytes. Then there is the Tag Protocol Identifier field (TPID), which is used for Token Ring, FDDI, and SNAP-encoded data transmissions. For Ethernet, it is of no concern and set to 81-00. The TPID field is also 16 bits, or 2 bytes, which brings the total for the total tag length to 32 bits, or 4 bytes.

Figure 5.11 shows the 802.1Q tag.

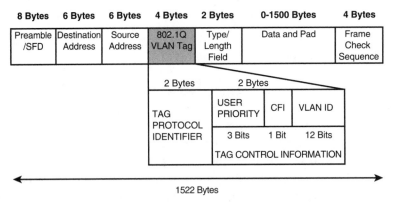

FIGURE 5.11 *The 801.Q VLAN standard uses a frame-tagging approach to identify VLAN membership. The four extra tagging bytes have forced the IEEE to increase the maximum Ethernet frame size to 1522 bytes. This is covered in the 802.3ac standard.*

The extra field has necessitated a maximum frame size increase. The new IEEE 802.3ac standard has increased the maximum Ethernet frame size from 1518 bytes to 1522 bytes.

We can communicate VLAN membership in two ways: explicit and implicit communication. Implicit VLAN membership communication means that the switch or switches know implicitly or indirectly to which particular VLAN a packet belongs. VLAN grouping by IP Subnet addresses is an example of implicit VLAN communication: every packet contains all the information required to identify the VLAN group to which a particular packet belongs.

Explicit membership communication means that the packet or frame needs to be explicitly marked as belonging to a particular VLAN. For example, traffic from a particular MAC address belonging to a specific VLAN would be marked with a specific VLAN identifier.

In general, MAC and port-based VLANs rely on explicit communication, whereas VLANs relying on a Layer 3-based attribute, such as protocol type or Subnet number, can use implicit tagging. Figure 5.12 shows this.

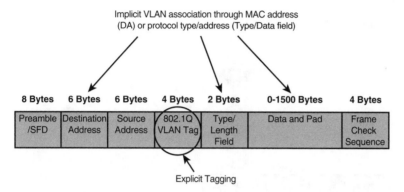

FIGURE 5.12 *VLAN membership can be communicated explicitly or implicitly. First-generation VLANs used only the implicit method: the membership was derived from some other frame variable. The new 802.1Q VLAN tagging standard uses explicit communication.*

VLAN ID numbers need to be centrally assigned and communicated among different switches and nodes on a network; otherwise, the same VLAN ID could exist multiple times. The Generic Attribute Registration Protocol (GARP) is one of the original 802.1P bridging protocol standards. GARP has been used as a foundation for VLAN membership communication among different switches. The GARP VLAN registration protocol (GVRP) assigns and distributes VLAN membership information.

Inter-VLAN Communication

A VLAN is a Layer 2 broadcast domain set up according to a specific grouping parameter. You need to route in order to communicate with another VLAN. There are essentially two ways that routing can occur: either centralized in the form of a classic router or on the edge of the network, for example within a client or server node. The centralized routing is far more popular.

Centralized VLAN Routing

Centralized VLAN routing involves a centralized router that connects the different VLANs at the center of the network, similar to a classic backbone enterprise router.

The so-called "one-armed router" or "router on a stick" attaches to a particular VLAN switch via only a single link. Normally, routers have at least two network links to route among different LANs or a LAN and a WAN link. In this case, the one-armed router receives the VLAN packet to be routed on its port and performs the address resolution and path calculation. It then sends the packet back with the appropriate routing information so it will reach the correct destination.

Figure 5.13 shows a one-armed router.

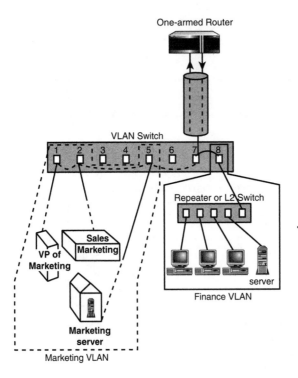

FIGURE 5.13   *A one-armed router can communicate among different VLANs. The term is derived from the fact that this kind of router has only one LAN interface, instead of the customary two.*

Edge Routing

In edge routing, the routing function resides at the perimeter, or edge, of the network and not at the core. For example, a server that is a member of multiple VLANs can perform the routing function. Both NetWare and NT servers can perform the routing function in software. The server could have a dedicated NIC for each VLAN or a single NIC for all VLANs, if the new VLAN tagging standard is supported. If the VLANs are protocol-based, one NIC will also do. Alternate methods will have the clients be part of multiple VLANs from the start, thereby effectively negating the need for routing. Alternatively, a router could be placed at the edge of the network. Figure 5.14 shows an edge routing example using a server.

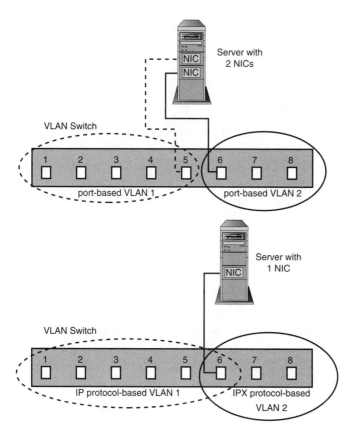

FIGURE 5.14 *Servers can be used as edge routers. Depending on the type of VLAN routing that needs to happen, one or more NICs need to be installed in the server. For example, if the NIC supports the 802.1Q VLAN standard, one NIC is sufficient.*

Layer 3 Switching

The natural evolution of the one-armed router is to integrate both the VLAN switching and routing function into one physical device. Most of the time, this has been accomplished by adding the VLAN function to a high-performance router. The newer method is to add the VLAN and Layer 3 functions to a Layer 2 switch.

802.1p Priority Switching

One of ATM's strengths is its capability to prioritize traffic into different classes. Ethernet, on the other hand, has been criticized for its inability to differentiate time-critical data from less important traffic. That's because Ethernet itself is a best-effort data transmission technology, which means there are no service guarantees. Over the last few years, many technologies like 100VG-AnyLAN, 802.3x/BLAM, and 3Com's PACE have tried to improve upon the CSMA/CD access method to improve digital voice and video transmission, but none have been successful to date. With the advent of Fast and Gigabit Ethernet, the overall bandwidth capabilities of Ethernet have vastly improved. Some people argue that full-duplex switched 10, 100, and 1000Mbps Ethernet provides some kind of QoS. This is not true. In effect, full-duplex and switching only increase the bandwidth capabilities of Ethernet. Thus, Ethernet still has no QoS guarantees and no capability to prioritize traffic. (Please refer to Chapter 7 for a general discussion of QoS.)

The new IEEE 802.1Q standard contains a field that allows prioritization of Ethernet traffic. The 3bit field allows you to set eight (that is, $2^3=8$) different user priorities for time-critical information.

> **Note**
>
> Sometimes the traffic prioritization standard 802.1p is referred to as 802.1Q/p. Whereas traffic prioritization and the associated protocols are part of the 802.1p spec, the 3bit priority field within an Ethernet frame has been defined within the 802.1Q standard, which also contains the 12-bit VLAN identifier. Thus, priority is really a combination of both 802.1Q and 802.1p, and subsequently, it is often written as the 802.1Q/p standard.

In the past, raw bandwidth was always the cure for delivering time-critical traffic on time. The 802.1Q/p standard now allows manufacturers to build switches and NICs with the inherent capability to prioritize time-critical traffic flows, such as voice or video.

Let's look at an example of how this traffic prioritization works. Figure 5.15 shows two servers that are connected through the same 802.1Q/p-capable switch. The Fileserver is used as a regular file server to deliver large amounts of raw data to a single client (shown as packet stream "FS" in the figure). The Videoserver delivers an IP multicast-based video stream to several nodes. (This is shown as the packet stream labeled "VS.") Switches typically process packets on a FIFO-basis (short for first-in-first-out: The first packet received is also the first one processed for delivery). A problem could arise if the smaller packets of latency-sensitive video traffic (VS) from the server are queued up behind a large file transfer taking place (FS) at the same time. The video data would be waiting to be sent while the file transfer was taking place. This would result in jitter, which is unacceptable for QoS-sensitive applications, such as video.

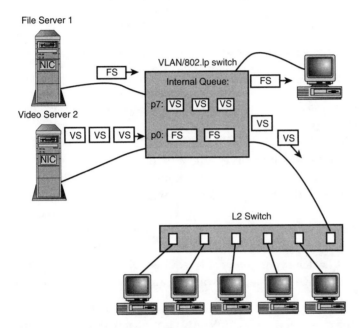

FIGURE 5.15   *The 802.1Q/p priority switching standard ensures on-time delivery of high-priority data and provides Ethernet with QoS capabilities.*

The combination of a server NIC and a switch using the 802.1Q/p priority classification would deliver the video traffic on time, ahead of the file transfer. You would just have to set the file transfer at a lower priority, say priority pO, and set the video stream to a higher priority setting, say priority p7. All switches use a queuing system to analyze and forward traffic. The switch would immediately place incoming frames with priority p7 ahead of the frames with priority pO, ensuring reliable video transmission. For an excellent real-world test of 802.1p-based hardware, take a look at the Tolly Group's test results. Download test report 8283 from www.tolly.com.

In our example, both servers communicate through the same VLAN-capable switch. VLANs don't dedicate bandwidth within a switch on their own, so both VLANs are treated equally in the switch.

> **Note**
>
> **Providing End-to-End QoS**
>
> *The IEEE802.1Q/p standard is a Layer 2 traffic classification. The frame priority is typically lost once it reaches a Layer 3 router (unless the router is redesigned or upgraded to understand 802.1p). To provide true end-to-end QoS, you need to use some kind of Layer 3 traffic classification. The Internet Engineering Task Force (IETF) has published an RFC called Resource Reservation Protocol (RSVP) that allows bandwidth to be reserved within a Layer 3 environment to deliver real-time video and audio data streams. The combination of Layer 2/802.1Q/p and RSVP operating at Layer 3 has enabled Ethernet with the capability to compete with ATM in terms of delivering QoS for time-critical applications. The big catch is that existing Ethernet and routing hardware, as well as operating systems and applications, need to be modified to take advantage of these standards. That's going to take a long time.*

So Why Haven't VLANs Taken Over the World?

VLANs seem to be very useful entities with numerous benefits. There are, however, many issues that have prevented the widespread adoption of VLANs. Let's look at some of these. In order to be implemented correctly, VLAN nodes require a switched connection. Yes, you can set up VLANs with repeaters "hanging off" switched ports, but in order to implement a VLAN properly, a 100% switched environment is required. This is very rare: Few of today's networks have implemented switching all the way to the desktop.

Technically, VLANs are a Layer 2 function, requiring a router to connect different VLANs. The most effective use of VLANs is probably protocol- or subnet-based VLAN membership. However, a multiport LAN router also can segment a large network into smaller, port-based Subnets, which in some ways accomplishes the same as a VLAN. The high cost and complexity of multiport LAN routers has slowed VLAN adoption. Of course, the new Layer 3 switches discussed in the next section will change all that.

Being a relatively new concept, it will take time for VLANs to be understood, deployed, and managed. You and your networking staff need to learn about these new concepts. Then, of course, come the practical questions, such as what VLAN equipment to buy, how to define membership policies, how to configure VLANs using the new management tools, and so on.

One of the biggest drawbacks to date has been the lack of a distributed VLAN standard. The good news is that the new IEEE 802.1Q VLAN trunking standard will be approved by the time this book is in print, and hardware based on this standard is already shipping.

VLANs group nodes according to specific traffic patterns. Historically, the 80/20 rule has applied to LAN traffic. This means that 80% of traffic is destined for a node in the local workgroup, whereas 20% is transmitted to a destination outside the workgroup. In a properly defined VLAN environment, this means that 80% of node traffic remains within a VLAN, whereas 20% of traffic is routed to other VLANs or nodes. With the advent of the Web, traffic patterns no longer seem to follow the 80/20 rule. Instead, traffic seems to have taken on more of a 20/80 rule, where 20% of traffic is local and 80% is destined for remote destinations. This is further discussed in Chapter 7 but the implications for VLANs are rather significant. If 80% of traffic leaves a VLAN, why bother at all with grouping nodes according to shared resources? The only benefit of VLANs then becomes broadcast containment. Figure 5.16 illustrates the changing nature of local area traffic flow patterns.

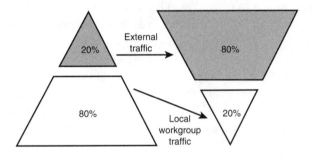

FIGURE 5.16 *Traditionally, 80% of traffic remained in the local workgroup, whereas 20% was external. Recent data shows that this trend is turning upside-down, which has significant implications for VLANs.*

Layer 3 Switching

Now let's discuss Layer 3 switches. We will first look at some of the basics of routing. Then we will look at the evolution of routers, leading up to today's Layer 3 switches. Finally, we will look more closely under the hood of a typical Layer 3 switch.

Simply put, a Layer 3 switch is a different name for a limited purpose, IP/IPX-only router. Depending on what vendor you talk to, Layer 3 switches are also known as routing switches, switch routers, switching routers, wire-speed routers, or hardware-based routers. Taken together, these different names actually describe a Layer 3 switch rather well. We define a Layer 3 switch as a limited-purpose, wire-speed LAN router that uses hardware instead of software to perform packet-to-packet IP routing.

Routing in hardware has two benefits. First, it gives Layer 3 switches the capability to perform routing at wire speeds: such as 10, 100, or even 1000Mbps, which is something that classic software-based routers couldn't do. Second, hardware-based routers cost significantly less than traditional software-based routers.

A lot of hype has surrounded Layer 3 switches. A word of caution is appropriate at this point. Have you noticed how every hardware manufacturer is hyping Layer 3 switches as though these devices were the answer to all your networking problems? Have you also noticed that Cisco has not been part of this hype frenzy? There's a good reason for this. We all know that Cisco dominates the router market and the high-end backbone LAN router market in particular. These high-end routers, such as the 12,000 and 7X00, are the most profitable pieces of networking hardware equipment sold today, and they provide huge revenues and profits to Cisco. Yet today Cisco's competitors (Bay, 3Com, Cabletron, and new players, such as Extreme, Packet Engines, and Intel) have few alternatives to offer. Therefore, Cisco's competitors have realized that they will never be able to challenge Cisco head-on in the router marketplace. The strategy is simple: If your name isn't Cisco Systems, the only way to get a piece of the backbone action is to change the rules of the game. You have to make believe that routers are obsolete and bet that you can beat Cisco in the new Layer 3 switching game. (Cisco isn't sitting still; it also has a line of Layer 3 switches.)

The analogy is the mainframe and client/server computing. Mainframes were pronounced dead at least a decade ago, yet IBM still derives a very large percentage of its revenues and profits from these heavy iron machines. Mainframes, of course, haven't died yet because they offer a lot of other features that even the best servers to date can't match.

Yes, Layer 3 switches are a technological breakthrough, but don't expect classic multiprotocol chassis routers to disappear overnight.

Layer 3 Background

This isn't a book about routing, so we can't venture too far into the Layer 3 world. The next section will provide some background on Layer 3 protocols. Packet-based Layer 3 routers use standard routing protocols to forward packets. Routing protocols define how routers communicate with each other. Different routers always exchange information that mainly contains route tables, which are similar to the bridge address tables discussed previously, yet they contain a lot more information such as route hops, age, and cost. Most, but not all, networking protocols are routable.

Networking Protocols

Many different Layer 3 networking protocols are in existence today. The most commonly used ones are IP, IPX, SNA, NetBIOS, NetBEUI, AppleTalk, and DECnet. To us, this sounds like *NIH* (not invented here). Historically, individual networking software or hardware vendors needed to invent their own protocols. Consequently, dozens of different protocols are in use to this date. For example, Novell decided the Internet Protocol wasn't good enough and invented Extended IP. Most protocols in use today are LAN focused. They aren't routable and make extensive use of broadcasts to advertise the existence of servers on the LAN. All protocols have their advantages and disadvantages, which in a way is a moot point, as IP is fast becoming the de facto standard.

Routable Protocols

Only IP, IPX, DECnet, and AppleTalk protocols are routable. Other nonroutable protocols can be routed through a technology called IP Tunneling, where the nonroutable packets are transported in IP packets. If a protocol cannot be routed, it must be bridged. Table 5.2 summarizes the most popular networking protocols today.

TABLE 5.2 SUMMARY OF COMMON NETWORKING PROTOCOLS

Protocol	Short for	Vendor	Products using	Routable?
IP	Internet Protocol	IETF Open Standard	All	Yes
IPX	Internetwork Protocol Exchange	Novell	NetWare	Yes
AppleTalk	Apples talking to each other	Apple	Macintosh PCs and Servers	Yes
NetBIOS	Network Basic Input/Output System	Microsoft, IBM	Microsoft Windows, Microsoft LAN Manager, IBM LANServer	No
NetBEUI	NetBIOS Extended User Interface	Microsoft, IBM	Same as NetBIOS	No
SNA	Systems Network Architecture	IBM	Legacy Mainframes	No
DECnet	DEC[1] Network	Compaq[1]	Legacy Alpha/VAX	Yes
LAT	Local area transport	Compaq	Legacy Alpha/VAX	No

[1] *Compaq Computer acquired Digital Equipment Corporation in 1998.*

> *Note*
>
> *The Internet Engineering Task Force (IETF) is the definitive standards authority for Layer 3 and 4 technologies. Essentially, the IETF is to Layer 3 and 4 what the IEEE is to Layer 2 and Ethernet. The IETF publishes Request For Comments (or RFC) standards documents. The term RFC is a little misleading. There are draft RFCs, and official standards RFCs. Drafts are documents circulated for discussion, and approved IETF RFCs become Internet routing standards.*

Routing Protocols

Different protocols require different routing protocols, too. The most common IP routing protocols are RIP, RIP2, and OSPF. IPX uses the RIP protocols too, but it's slightly different from the IP RIP protocol.

RIP (also known as RIP1 or RIPv1) stands for *routing information protocol* and was the first industry standard IP routing standard. It was initially developed for the BSD version of UNIX but became an industry standard over time. RIP2 is an improved version of the original RIP1 protocol in one sense because it uses fewer broadcasts.

OSPF stands for *open shortest path first* and is a newer IP development. OSPF has many advantages over RIP. Layer 2 allows for only one active path. The spanning tree algorithm shuts down parallel paths. Routed networks, on the other hand, encourage multiple redundant paths. OSPF allows routers to determine the lowest cost and shortest path from different choices more accurately. If the active path fails, OSPF will change the route much more quickly than RIP. OSPF also doesn't send out route tables like RIP does, reducing broadcast traffic rates. For LAN routing, the added benefit of OSPF does not always outweigh its added complexity.

Over the years, several multicast routing protocols have also been developed. Table 5.3 shows the most common routing protocols in use.

TABLE 5.3 Summary of common IP and IPX routing protocols

Protocol Supported	Routing Protocol	Short For	Standard
IP	RIP, RIP2	Routing Information Protocol, Routing Information Protocol 2	RFC 950/1058; RFC 173
IP	OSPF	Open Shortest Path First	RFC 1583, RFC1850
IP	DVMRP, IGMP	Distance Vector Multicast Routing Protocol, Internet Group Membership Protocol	IETF RFC 1162

Protocol Supported	Routing Protocol	Short For	Standard
IP	IGRP, EIGRP	Interior Gateway Routing Protocol, Enhanced IGRP	Cisco proprietary
IPX	RIP, SAP, NLSP	Routing Information Protocol, Service Advertising Protocol, NetWare Link Services Advertising Protocol	Novell proprietary

How Routers Work

Routers are used in various places in today's networks and form the core of many large networks today.

A detailed discussion of routers is really beyond the scope of this chapter and this book. Here is a quick overview of how routers work.

Figure 5.17 shows a router flow diagram. (Feel free to page back and contrast this diagram with the flow diagram for a Layer 2 bridge shown in Figure 4.4.)

A router performs the following functions:

- A received frame is stored and stripped of all its Layer 2 header information. The exposed *data* field then contains the actual Layer 3 packet. This means that the router needs to discard the Ethernet SA, DA, and so on.

- The protocol type is identified. With some Ethernet frame types, the header will contain this information, but in general, the actual protocol can only be identified by looking at the data field itself.

- The router determines whether the protocol is routable. If it is not, the packet is reassembled into its original Layer 2 frame and switched or bridged. (Refer to Chapter 4 for details.)

- If the protocol is routable (IP, IPX, AppleTalk, or DECnet), the router will perform some housekeeping items like check the hopcount number. A maximum of 15 router hops are typically allowed, after which a packet is discarded. This prevents packets from endlessly being routed in a loop should two routers think that the path to the destination is via the other. This is commonly known as a routing loop.

- The router will look up the destination IP address in its routing table and identify the relevant destination network. If the destination network is directly attached to the router, it will assemble a frame and forward it to the MAC address of the destination mode.

- If the destination network is not directly attached (another router hop needs to occur), the router will assemble a frame and forward it to the MAC address of the next hop router.

In general, a router functions similarly to a bridge in that it looks up the destination address in a table. The key differences between bridges and routers occur in how the address table, or the route, is communicated among different routers. Whereas switches and bridges act as standalone devices (they create their own address tables, based on SA and DA information learned from frames received), a router obtains its table information through both learning and exchanging routing tables with other routers. A router is, in essence, part of a larger routing fabric that knows the exact traffic route spanning multiple routers.

Historically, routers were used as remote access devices to link different LANs together over remote distances. The Internet, for example, is essentially a worldwide maze of different interconnected IP routers.

When customers implemented new technologies, such as FDDI, routing needed to take place in order to convert traffic from Ethernet to the new FDDI frame format.

As LANs began to grow in size and traffic volume, routers migrated to the center of the network to form a central backbone. This provides several benefits:

- The WAN access point is now centrally located.

- The protocol conversion happens at the most efficient point, namely in the center.

- Dividing up a large flat Layer 2 network into multiple Layer 3 broadcast domains reduces the network utilization, boosting performance.

- Multiple subnets made the network less susceptible to broadcast storms.

- Different VLANs needed to communicate via a router.

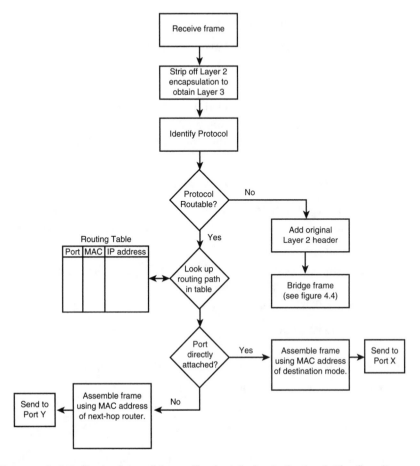

FIGURE 5.17 *Router internal forwarding logic looks similar to a bridge flow diagram shown in Figure 4.4. It does contain an added branch that performs the routing function.*

Ultimately, large backbone routers made a network more stable, reliable, and manageable.

Routers cannot translate from one protocol to another. If one LAN uses the Novell IPX protocol and a second network utilizes IP, a gateway is required to translate between the two.

What Exactly Is a Layer 3 Switch?

Layer 3 switches are limited-purpose, hardware-based IP routers. The term *Layer 3 switch* is a marketing creation, just like Ethernet Layer 2 switches are all really just multiport bridges. So, technically, IEEE Layer 2 bridging and IETF Layer 3 routing standards govern Layer 3 switches.

Layer 3 switches do the following:

- They operate primarily at Layer 3 of the OSI model but also perform frame forwarding at Layer 2.

- They only route IP or IPX protocols (see Table 5.4). Packet routing is done in accordance with established Layer 3 routing standards, for example through the exchange of routing tables based on industry standard routing protocols, such as RIP. (See the section "Router Protocols" earlier in this chapter.)

- They switch nonroutable traffic at Layer 2.

- They forward frames at wire speed rates, such as 10, 100, or 1000Mbps, with minimal latencies, typically a few microseconds. (See the section "So How Fast Is Wire Speed?" later in this chapter.)

- They support only LAN-based routing. Right now, only Ethernet Layer 3 switches are available. Someone might very likely build a Token Ring Layer or FDDI Layer 3 switch one day.

- They are substantially cheaper than similar performance routers.

Table 5.4 compares classical LAN routers with Layer 3 switches.

TABLE 5.4 A COMPARISON OF LAYER 3 SWITCHES AND ROUTERS

Feature	Classical LAN Router	Layer 3 Switch
OSI layer function performed	Layer 3	Layer 3
Routing performed	Software (CPU plus software)	Hardware (ASIC chips)
Layer 2 MAC supported	Ethernet, Token Ring, FDDI, ATM, WAN	Fast and Gigabit Ethernet only (so far)
Performance	Slow to medium, depending on CPU performance and cost	Fast, near wire speed
Price/port	High	Low
Latency	Approximately 200μs	<10μs (100Mbps)
Programmability and manageability	Extremely high	Little to none
Protocols supported	All	IP, sometimes IPX[1]
Routing protocols	All	RIP1, RIP2, sometimes OSPF and DVMRP[2]

Feature	Classical LAN Router	Layer 3 Switch
Application	Creating broadcast domains via a collapsed or distributed backbone	Most places where a Layer 2 switch is used today
	WAN connection	Collapsed backbone
	Multiprotocol routing	Inter-VLAN routing

[1] *Some vendors are talking about embedding additional protocols in hardware. The two that are being mentioned are AppleTalk and DECnet, both of which are routable but have relatively small and shrinking market share. Over time, more protocols will be added into hardware, and, after IPX, these two are next.*

[2] *Just like the number of protocols embedded in hardware is bound to increase, so is the number of routing protocols. Right now, most vendors support RIP and RIP 2. One or two switches feature OSPF and DVMPP. The list of protocols is bound to grow over time.*

So How Fast Is Wire Speed?

Wire speed can be measured in Megabits-per-second or packets-per-second. Layer 3 devices are measured in packets-per-second, not frames-per-second. That's because routers operate at Layer 3, where packets are the norm, as opposed to Layer 2, where frames are the norm. A Layer 3 packet is always encapsulated within a Layer 2 frame, so packet and frame rates are the same. The frame is a little larger than a packet, because it contains some additional bytes like SA, DA, and preamble. In this context, you can use frame and packet interchangeably. Sometimes, pps is even used for Layer 2 devices, although that is technically not correct. This might occur to avoid confusion with video transmission, where frames-per-second is the prevalent way of measuring video transfer rates.

When comparing the performance of Ethernet Layer 3 switches, you need to know what packet size was used to measure the speed. Most labs stress-test switches for different packet sizes, ranging from the minimum to the maximum packet sizes. The minimum packet size of 64 bytes will result in the maximum packet rate, which is 100Mbps Ethernet 148,810 packets per second (fps) to be exact. This will stress a switch to the limit, as the switch will have to perform an IP routing function for every packet forwarded. For the maximum packet size of 1518 bytes, the packet rate is 8127 fps for 100Mbps Ethernet. For 10Mbps Ethernet, these numbers are one-tenth; for Gigabit Ethernet, the maximum packet rate can be an astounding 1.48 million packets per second.

Table 5.5 shows the calculation of the maximum packet rates. Note that many tests show packets-per-second, which is confusing, as Ethernet operates at Layer 2, where the term *frames* is used. This can become very confusing, especially when testing Layer 3 devices, where both frame and packet rates are applicable.

TABLE 5.5 100MBPS ETHERNET WIRE SPEED FRAME RATES

Packet Size[1] (bytes)	Preamble + IFG[2] (bytes)	Packet + Preamble + IFG[3] (bytes)	Total Packet Size[4] (bits)	Packet Length[5] (μs)	Maximum Rate[6] (pps)
64	20	84	672	6.72	148,810
1518	20	1538	12,304	120	8127

[1] *Minimum and maximum packet size in bytes is shown.*
[2] *Every Ethernet frame has a Preamble, which is 8 bytes. IFG is the minimum Ethernet Interframe Gap that separates subsequent frame transmissions and is 12 bytes long.*
[3] *Packet size added to (Preamble + IFG).*
[4] *Packet size in bits is (frame + preamble + IFG)×8 bits.*
[5] *Bit-time in nanoseconds = 1/wire speed. For 100Mbps Ethernet, bit-time = 1/[100×10E+06] = 10ns. packet length = bit-time×packet size.*
[6] *Maximum packet rate in packets-per-second (pps) = wire speed/packet length.*

The latency of Layer 3 switches is typically a few microseconds. The relevant IP information needs to be decoded before the frame can be forwarded. Most Layer 3 switches allow you to select store-and-forward or cut-through. If the switch operates in store-and-forward mode, the entire frame needs to be received, in which case the latencies can be as large as the longest frames encountered. In cut-through mode, the latency can be as low as a few hundred bit-times. For 100Mbps switches, this translates to a few microseconds.

Market Trends

Let's look at some recent market trends that have enabled the emergence of Layer 3 switches:

- *Switching is the LAN buzzword of the 90s*—Over the past five years, Layer 2 Ethernet switch sales have exploded, driven by intense competition and declining prices. Workgroup switches connect users at 10Mbps, servers and uplinks connect to 100Mbps switches, and then Gigabit Ethernet backbone switches tie it all together. The vision is simple: Switching everywhere.

  Of course, the ATM hype helped fuel this one, too: Shared Ethernet, and to a lesser degree, routing, are no longer politically correct. We hear someone disagreeing in the background: "Houston, we have a problem." We can't really live without routers yet. So some clever marketing people read about the old Kalpana idea of calling a bridge a switch. Why not just call the new router a switch, too? In order to differentiate these switching routers from classic bridging switches, something else was needed: Add the word *Layer 3* and *BINGO*. We have a new product category: the Layer 3 switch.

- *ASIC capabilities have increased exponentially*—Gordon Moore, cofounder of Intel, observed about 20 years ago that the transistor density on an integrated circuit can double every 24 months. While this so-called Moore's law is well-known in the PC industry (see Chapter 7), this exponential increase in circuit complexity allows very sophisticated chips to be designed for other functions, too.

  Layer 3 switches often use a type of chip known as an *ASIC*, short for *application-specific integrated circuit*. ASICs are nothing new: They have been around for at least a decade (although some switch vendors pretend like they personally invented the ASIC only yesterday, specifically for their particular switch). ASICs are high-density integrated circuits designed for a specific task only, to be produced in a relatively short time and in smaller numbers, with limited complexity. Custom chips, on the other hand, take longer to design, are more complex, and require higher run rates in order to recover the more expensive and time-consuming upfront development. General-purpose integrated circuits, such as microprocessors, memory chips, Ethernet MAC, and PHYs, are all custom chips. ASICs have grown in complexity over the last few years, due to Moore's law and advances in ASIC design tools. As a result, both Layer 2 and Layer 3 routing function can now be hardwired into an integrated circuit chip, as opposed to being performed by a software program.

- *The undisputed winner of the protocol wars is IP*—A few years ago, numerous networking protocols existed side-by-side with IPX dominating in the PC world and SNA in the mainframe world. There were, of course, other protocols from Microsoft, DEC, Banyan, and IBM. Then there was the UNIX world and the Internet, where TCP/IP ruled. With the explosion of the Internet, IP has emerged as the de facto standard. Building a multiprotocol router in hardware would technically be possible, but the complexity of such a design would probably mean a development effort costing far too much money for anyone to attempt. This standardization on IP has made it possible to build IP and only IP routing into Layer 3 switches. (Every new protocol to be routed would increase the complexity of the hardware tremendously.)

- *IP is mature and stable*—One of the advantages of classic software-based routing is that routers are reprogrammable. If a bug emerges in the routing software or the protocol standard evolves, you can merely download a new version of the relevant routing software and upgrade the router software, which is typically stored in Flash memory. Putting the routing logic in hardware has tremendous speed advantages but locks you into the same logic for life! Imagine buying a few new chips and hauling out your soldering iron every time you want to upgrade your router software! The good news is that IP and associated IP routing standards, such as RIP or RIP2, have matured tremendously over the last few years. Today, IP is so stable and has proven that it lends itself to being embedded in hardware.

The bottom line is that semiconductor advances and the de facto standardization of IP have enabled the emergence of Layer 3 switches.

A History of Layer 3 Switches

Before answering this question, let's take a router tour for a few minutes. We have categorized routers into four different generations. We have had to simplify things a bit. Often, the transitions from one generation to the next aren't always that clear-cut, but we think this categorization will give you a better idea of how Layer 3 switches originated.

First-Generation Routing: Cisco Routers Linking LANs

Cisco was founded in 1984 with the purpose of linking the different LANs at Stanford University. The first routers sold by Cisco 12 years ago were small boxes designed to connect different LANs. These early routers all used Cisco-developed proprietary routing protocols. Each of these early routers connected to another Cisco router at the other end (not that there was anyone else building routers at that time), so the proprietary nature of the routing protocols didn't bother anyone. The architecture consisted of a microprocessor, an associated program, and packet-buffering memory. The routing was performed by individually analyzing each packet, determining the next relevant route, and then forwarding it. The speed was typically measured in tens of thousands of packets per second (pps).

Second-Generation Routers for the Internet

After a few years, routers became more popular, being used as Internet links. Other router manufacturers emerged, notably Wellfleet. The IETF and different vendors began standardizing routing protocols. RIP and RIP2 emerged during this time.

Looking inside a second-generation router, you'd find a significantly faster microprocessor, a lot more memory, and maybe a 100Mbps LAN connection instead of 10Mbps. Maybe a chassis-based version was now available to provide the capability to route among a wider choice of protocols, but essentially the router architecture was unchanged. The speed of one of these routers would be measured in hundreds of thousands of packets per second.

Third-Generation Proprietary Cut-Through Routers

The traditional way of building a faster router was the brute force approach. This typically meant more CPU MIPS, more memory, and faster LAN or WAN ports, but this approach also meant higher costs. A few years ago, engineers started looking for nontraditional ways of speeding up routers. Some routers started using hardware acceleration to speed up packet processing. For example, Cisco started using an accelerator chip called the Silicon Switching Engine (SSE) to perform certain routing tasks in hardware, as opposed to software. This was similar to a floating-point unit or math coprocessor in the PC world. Yet, the main CPU still performed the core routing function, which inevitably caused a bottleneck.

About five years ago, different vendors started working on the concept of performing the entire routing function in hardware. These switching routers started looking very different inside. Instead of a CPU analyzing each frame or packet, the routing function was performed mostly in hardware. Yet the hardware still wasn't fast enough to keep up with traffic flows of 150,000 pps per port, so engineers needed to come up with additional tricks to boost performance to acceptable levels. They wanted a shortcut for the time-consuming hardware routing function. 3Com used the terminology "route-once, switch thereafter," implying that the first packet needed to be completely analyzed in a regular routing fashion. Once the traffic route was established, the packets could be forwarded at Layer 2 for significant speed and throughput improvements.

Cisco used the concept of tagging packets once the traffic flow or route had been identified, saving subsequent packets from being analyzed again.

Basically, all networking vendors developed some proprietary hardware acceleration method. Numerous different terms described these different, proprietary, hardware-based routers. *Cut-through routing*, *flow-based-routing*, *tag-switching*, and *IP switching* are the better-known ones.

Third-generation routers started appearing in 1996 and did indeed speed up the routing function significantly. Packet rates were approaching a million pps, with prices declining. Yet, the proprietary nature of these hardware-based routers meant that you couldn't build a heterogeneous network and still get the needed performance improvement.

Table 5.6 summarizes the different shortcut routing methods developed by various vendors over the past several years.

TABLE 5.6 A COMPARISON OF THIRD-GENERATION CUT-THROUGH ROUTING METHODS

Manufacturer	Technology	Method	Info Available From
Ipsilon[1]	IP switching	Flow-based cut-through	`www.ipsilon.com/`
Cisco	NetFlow switching and Cisco Express Forwarding	Tag switching	Cisco white paper at `www.cisco.com/`
3Com	FastIP	Tag switching	`www.3com.com/ technology/tech_net/ white_papers/ 500646.html`
Cabletron	SecureFast	Tag switching	Cabletron white paper at `www.cabletron.com/`
IBM	Multiport switching services	Tag switching	`www.ibm.com/`
ATM Forum	Multiprotocol over ATM	Flow-based cut-through	`www.atmforum.com/`

[1] *Ipsilon is now owned by Nokia.*

Fourth-Generation Routers

It was only a matter of time before someone managed to perform the entire routing function in hardware at wire speeds. We are not sure who gets first prize, but Bay Networks and Extreme are definitely contenders. These fourth-generation routers are what we call true Layer 3 switches because they truly route every single packet: thus, the term *packet-by-packet routing*. Some Gigabit Ethernet fourth-generation routers are already shipping. These routers can process up to 1.48 million pps on every port. Some fourth-generation routers are now delivering aggregate throughputs of more than 10 million pps. The aggregate number is a bit misleading, as it indicates more of a backplane capacity and number of ports, as opposed to the actual port-based routing speed.

With current ASIC technology, only a limited number of protocols can be built into hardware. Therefore, most of today's fourth-generation routers feature only a limited number of routing protocols. This should change as designs improve over time. Table 5.7 shows many fourth-generation routers that are shipping at the time this book went to press. It's just a question of time, though, before every networking vendor will have one of these products in its lineup.

TABLE 5.7 A COMPARISON OF FOURTH-GENERATION PACKET-TO-PACKET ROUTERS

Manufacturer	Switch	Protocols Supported	Info Available From
Intel	500 Series routing switch	IP: RIP, RIP2 IPX: RIP/SAP	www.intel.com/network
Bay Networks	Accelar routing switch	RIP, RIP2, OSPF, DVMRP	www.baynetworks.com/
Extreme	Summit	RIP, RIP2, OSPF, IGMP, DVMRP	www.extremenetworks.com/
Cisco Systems	Catalyst 8500 routing switch	RIP, RIP2, OSPF	www.cisco.com/
PacketEngines[1]	PowerRail routing switch	RIP, RIP2, OSPF, IGMP, DVMRP	www.packetengines.com/

---

[1] *Packet Engines is now owned by Alcatel.*

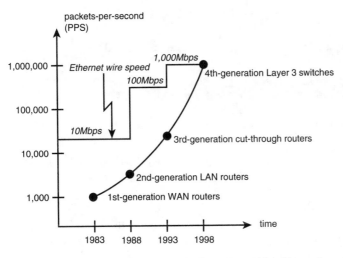

FIGURE 5.18 *Routing performance has improved by three orders of magnitude over the last 15 years. Today's Layer 3 switches can route at Gigabit wire speeds.*

Note

Some vendors call Layer 3 switches third-generation switches, instead of fourth-generation routers. Basically, it depends on whether you start counting from the switch end or the router end. If you start counting from the switch end, multiport Layer 2 bridges are the first-generation of switches. Second-generation switches are what we have categorized as proprietary hardware routers, and third-generation switches are our fourth-generation routers.

What Does a Layer 3 Switch Really Look Like?

Conceptually, Layer 3 switches are a combination of multiple Layer 2 VLAN domains, connected by means of a Layer 3 router. Figure 5.19 shows the internal workings of a Layer 3 switch. In the default mode, the entire Layer 3 switch is set to one VLAN, which means the switch acts like a regular Layer 2 switch. Multiple VLANs are then added to create new broadcast domains. Each port can become its own subnet-based VLAN, thereby creating multiple subnets. These different subnets are then interconnected via the Layer 3 router.

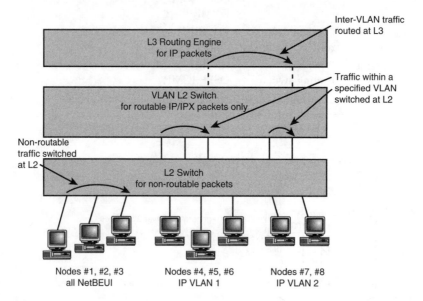

FIGURE 5.19 *A Layer 3 switch consisting of the routing engine plus multiple VLANs.*

Layer 4 Switching

Just when you thought you knew it all, along comes the latest buzzword in the networking industry: *Layer 4 switching*. So if Layer 2 switching is really bridging and Layer 3 switching is really routing, what is Layer 4 switching?

We need to start at the basics again. The OSI Layer 4 is known as the transport layer (refer to Chapter 2, "An Overview of High-Speed LAN Technologies"). Layer 4 takes care of delivery rules, flow control, acknowledgments, error detection and correction, and ultimately the delivery of the data to the next layer. There are three popular Layer 4 standards: Transmission Control Protocol (TCP/IP), User Data Protocol (the UDP part of UDP/IP), and Sequenced Packet Exchange (the SPX part of SPX/IPX). As you can see, all Layer 4 standards go hand-in-hand with the relevant Layer 3 technology and cannot be separated from Layer 3, although Layer 3 exists separately from Layer 2. That's only where the trouble *starts*.

The second problem with Layer 4 switching is that, according to our definition of *switching*, Layer 4 switching is an oxymoron because switching involves a point-point connection based on some sort of address (see Chapter 4 for our definition of switching). In the case of Layer 4, the addressing happens at Layer 2 or 3; Layer 4 just makes sure the data is conveyed correctly.

Today, many vendors offer Layer 3 switches with Layer 4 switching as a feature, so let's explore Layer 4 switching a bit further. (Because most Layer 3 and Layer 4 switches support only IP, we will only discuss TCP and UDP, not SPX.)

Port-Based Prioritization

TCP is used for connection-oriented traffic, such as file transfers, guaranteeing packet arrival. UDP, on the other hand, is a connectionless communication layer used for applications, such as multicasting or SNMP polling where dropped packets are tolerated.

TCP and UDP both include the concept of port numbers. A particular node normally has one TCP/IP address/stack combination running, but multiple higher level applications running at the same time. For example, a node may be both engaged in a file transfer (FTP), as well as browsing the Web (HTTP). Each particular application protocol is assigned a specific port number.

The port numbers are divided into three ranges: the well-known ports, the registered ports, and the dynamic and/or private ports. The "well-known" ports are those from 0 through 1023. The "registered" ports are those from 1024 through 49,151. The "dynamic and/or private" ports are those from 49,152 through 65,535. The IETF RFC1700 specifies individual port assignments. Table 5.8 shows a list of well-known port numbers.

TABLE 5.8 WELL-KNOWN TCP AND UDP PORT NUMBERS

Application	Short For	Application	Port Number
FTP	File Transfer Protocol	File transfer	20 (data) 21 (control)
Telnet		Remote control	23
SMTP	Simple Message Transfer Protocol	Email	25

continues

TABLE 5.8 CONTINUED

Application	Short For	Application	Port Number
HTTP	Hypertext Transfer Protocol	Web browsing	80
SNMP	Simple Network Management Protocol	Network management	161
SNMP	SNMP TRAPS	SNMP warnings and alarms	162

The combination of a particular device IP address and port number is called a *socket*.

Layer 4 information can and is used by today's network hardware. Firewall routers, for example, rely upon Layer 4 to keep traffic in or out of a network. Today's Layer 4 switching technology is again a hybrid term that has been created. We would say that *Layer 4 traffic filtering* or *application switching* are more appropriate terms, but we don't write the dictionary on networking.

Layer 4 switches are devices that can examine individual port numbers of IP packets and control traffic at Layer 4 according to some pre-specified criteria.

Layer 4 Applications

Layer 4 switching provides the capability to provide Class of Service. This means that you as the LAN administrator can determine the overall quality and priority of a particular application, given its Layer 4 port number. Let's look at some examples of Layer 4 switching.

Application Firewalls

You may not want to let an application like Telnet run outside of your LAN. In that case, your Layer 4 switch would filter out or discard all port 23 IP packets.

RSVP

RSVP is briefly discussed in Chapter 4. The bandwidth reservation protocol allows a user to dedicate certain bandwidth within a larger pipe. The combination of a Layer 3 QoS protocol and Layer 2 prioritization allow for true QoS in packet-based networks. To implement RSVP, switch designers will depend on technologies like Layer 4 port-based bandwidth reservation.

Prioritizing Mission-Critical Applications

You may decide that some applications on your LAN are more important than others. For example, SAP R/3 or Peoplesoft may receive a higher priority than a simple file transfer or an email. A switch on a Layer 4 port prioritizes some applications over others.

Layer 4 Switching Issues

The biggest issues are understanding and managing Layer 4 environments, accompanied by the bigger question of interoperability standards.

The first issue is one of understanding Layer 4 prioritization. What application corresponds to what port? Should port 20 be prioritized over port 80? If multiple FTP-based applications are running, which one receives highest priority?

Another issue with port prioritization is that some applications actually assign different ports at different times, making tracking and management tricky. For example, FTP uses port 20 for data and port 21 for control. If you are trying to set up an access list, port 21 is the source port from the FTP server when it tries to establish the data connection back to the client. The destination port is a high-numbered port greater than 1023. So which port number do you track?

Layer 4 switching is hot off the press. No standards exist yet for Layer 4 switching in heterogeneous environments. For example, if you have multiple switches in a given traffic path, how do all the switches know a particular port's priority?

There is also the issue with overlapping technologies. The IEEE 802.1p standard discussed previously allows for traffic prioritization as well, although at a different level. In this case, the end-station or the switch that inserts a specific priority tag sets the priority. Which one do you use when? If both Layer 4 port-based and Layer 2 tag-based prioritization are at work, which priority scheme has priority? The Layer 2-based IEEE 802.1p method or the Layer 4 port-based version? How do you get these different schemes to work together and not work against each other?

Layer 4 switching bears a lot of promise, particularly in the area of application-based traffic prioritization. For the time being, Layer 4 switching remains on our "developments to watch" list, but all the issues mentioned previously will inevitably be resolved, with the necessary standards being developed along the way. This will take a few years, though. Look for the answers in our fifth edition!

Summary

This chapter discussed some of the Ethernet technologies that have recently emerged. VLANs provide LAN managers with broadcast isolation techniques and, once properly set up, with much-improved network management capabilities. The IEEE 802.1p priority standard will enable on-time and constant-latency delivery of time-critical voice and data traffic over Ethernet networks. 802.1p, in combination with the Layer 3 RSVP standard, gives Ethernet the capability to match the much-touted QoS capabilities of ATM. The new 802.3Q standard now allows you to build distributed, multivendor VLANs.

Layer 3 switches are a new and powerful building block for interconnecting VLANs or subdividing larger LANs into smaller broadcast domains. Layer 3 switches are going to replace expensive LAN routers in the corporate backbone as IP continues to grow in popularity. Finally, we briefly discussed the emerging concept of Layer 4 switching.

PART III

Determining Your Ethernet Needs

CHAPTER 6

Cabling and More on Physical Layers

Did you know that cabling problems, result in the most network downtime, causing more disruptions than anything else? Cabling accounts for less than 10% of an IT budget, but cabling problems cause more than 50% of all problems. In this chapter, we discuss the importance of thinking strategically about networking hardware. Paying attention to network cabling issues up front will save you trouble in the future. Whereas personal computers and networking hardware have a useful life of between three and five years, your building's cabling plant should outlast the network infrastructure itself by many years. Most cabling companies now offer 15- to 20-year performance warranties for their installation work, so planning ahead makes a lot of sense! Taking shortcuts or trying to save money during the installation can have disastrous consequences; troubleshooting cabling problems can be very time-consuming, expensive, and disruptive.

Cabling is a topic that is worthy of an entire book in its own right. This chapter assumes that you already know a fair amount about data cabling and premises distribution systems. If you are not familiar with cabling, we strongly urge you to consult one of the books in Appendix B, "Further Reading." We also mention several vendors and their products in this chapter. Please refer to Appendix C, "Useful Web Links," to obtain further information on these vendors.

This chapter focuses on the cabling requirements for Fast and Gigabit Ethernet. We start by examining the TIA/EIATIA/EIA 568-A standard, the de facto worldwide standard for voice and data building distribution systems. We also examine the controversial subject of UTP Category 5, 6, and 7 cabling. Then we provide a recap of the different IEEE Fast and Gigabit Ethernet physical layers that have been developed to run on the TIA/EIATIA/EIA 568-A system. (We have already briefly discussed these in Chapter 3, "Ethernet, Fast Ethernet, and Gigabit Ethernet Standards.") We examine the cabling requirements for the new 1000BASE-T/802.3ab standard in detail, and we provide some practical tips on how to certify your cabling infrastructure and how to deal with cabling contractors. Finally, we provide some tips on what to pay special attention to when running Fast and Gigabit Ethernet over Category 5 UTP.

We also cover two related subjects: the pros and cons of running fiber to the desktop and encoding/compression techniques.

Encoding and Compression Techniques

Cabling equipment is rated in terms of megahertz (MHz).   For example, Category 3 cabling is rated up to a maximum frequency of 16MHz and is synonymous with 10BASE-T, which transmits 10Mbps. Yet the same cable can transmit 100Mbps using 100BASE-T4 technology. How can that be possible?

Sometimes people confuse the terms *MHz* and *Mbps*. In the old days, one could say that it took a hertz (which equals a clock cycle) to transmit a bit (or a million hertz to transmit a million bits). Cabling is rated in MHz, which is the maximum frequency that can be transmitted reliably. To attain higher transmission rates, engineers today typically use several tricks to reduce the frequency of the signal to meet the bandwidth requirements of cable. The important thing to remember is that the data rate and the bandwidth required can be very different. Let's look at encoding in a bit more detail.

Number of Pairs

The number of pairs is the most obvious way of increasing the transmission capability of cable. 10BASE-T uses only one dedicated transmission pair as well as one dedicated reception pair. Some faster versions of Ethernet use multiple transmission pairs. The data is split up over these multiple pairs, thereby reducing the bandwidth requirements for each individual pair.

For example, 100BASE-T4 utilizes a total of four pairs. Two pairs are dedicated as either transmit or receive, but the other two can act as either transmit or receive pairs. This means that a total of three transmission pairs are available at any one time. The downside of this *floating pair* scheme is that full-duplex transmission is not possible. 1000BASE-T goes one step further and uses four pairs for transmission.

Switched Ethernet Cabling Requirements

The switched versions of 10, 100, or 1000Mbps Ethernet can all operate on the same cable as their shared-media versions because their wire speed is the same. The only difference is the number of end stations on that segment, which is two for a fully switched connection. If the switched connection operates in full-duplex mode, the cabling distance can often be extended, as no collisions will be present in a full-duplex environment. Note that not all Ethernet physical layers are full-duplex capable. 10BASE-T, 10BASE-FL, 100BASE-TX, 100BASE-FX, 100BASE-T2, and all Gigabit Ethernet physical layers are full-duplex capable, but 10BASE5, 10BASE2, 10BASE-FP, 10BASE-FB, and 100BASE-T4 are not. Please refer to Chapter 3 for more details on full-duplex Ethernet.

Dual-Duplex Transmission

Recent advances in DSP technology allow for *simultaneous* transmission and reception on the *same* pair of cabling, also known as dual-duplex. The new 1000BASE-T physical layer uses both simultaneous transmission and reception on all four pairs. This means full-duplex transmission.

Bandwidth-Efficient Encoding

The earlier 10Mbps versions of Ethernet all used Manchester encoding, which is a simple, but not very efficient, encoding scheme. With the higher data rates of Fast and Gigabit Ethernet, engineers have been forced to use more sophisticated coding methods for transmitting data over limited-capacity UTP cabling. Let's look at the encoding technology in a bit more detail.

Ethernet transmission uses two different kinds of encoding schemes: block and line encoding. Block encoding takes several bits (four or eight, for example) and sends it out as one new code word. Line coding takes the parallel data stream and encodes it as a serial bit stream, ready to be transmitted across the wire in a serial fashion.

When calculating the overall bandwidth requirements (or efficiency) of a transmission scheme, you need to take into consideration the overall data rate, the block encoding efficiency, and the line encoding implications.

Block Encoding

Block encoding takes Ethernet raw parallel data (a series of bits) and encodes it according to a predetermined lookup table. 100BASE-TX, for example, uses a block-encoding scheme called 4B/5B. The 4B/5B encoding takes 4 bits of data (4B) and expands it to 5 coded bits (5B). Four of the coded bits contain the actual data in accordance with some table. The fifth, "spare," bit is added to transmit additional information. There are three reasons for adding this extra bit as part of the coding scheme:

- The receiving station needs to receive the clock signal in order to decode the data accurately. Sending the clock separately would not be a very efficient use of the cabling infrastructure. The 5-bit code word can be chosen so that a clock transition is present often enough for the receiving station to regenerate the clock.

- The extra bit also allows the coded words to be chosen carefully so that an equal number of logical 0s and 1s are transmitted, which means the digital signal has no DC component, allowing for an easier design of the hardware.

- The 4B/5B encoding allows some error correction capability to be incorporated into the data stream. The 4B/5B coding scheme was originally developed for use with FDDI.

All coding schemes are typically abbreviated xB/yB. This always means x data bits are encoded into y coded bits. Sometimes three-level encoding schemes are used, in which case the shorthand becomes xB/yT.

The most common block encoding schemes are, of course, 4B/5B used for 100BASE-TX/FX, and the newer 8B/10B used for 1000BASE-X, which was originally developed by IBM for Fibre Channel. The lesser known 8B/6T coding scheme is used for 100BASE-T4 and is a new development. The most complex coding scheme is the PAM 5x5, which uses five different amplitudes (that is, voltage levels) and five different phases to generate 25 different codes.

The downside of the xB/yB encoding schemes is that they create a higher transmission rate. For example, the extra bit transmitted with the 4B/5B encoding of 100BASE-TX increases the transmission rate to 125Mbaud. (You can calculate this by taking the five coded bits and dividing them by the four raw bits, multiplied by the original data rate.)

Symbols and Bauds

The speed or bit rate of a digital transmission is measured in bits per second (bps). Some transmission schemes, for example PAM5, don't just use 0's and 1's to transmit data, they use more complicated signals. PAM5 uses five different codes, not just two, to transmit the data. In this case, five different states or *symbols* are present. A particular voltage level actually contains two bits of information, or two *bits/symbol*.

The number of symbols transmitted per second is called the *baud rate*. The baud rate is only of interest to someone looking "under the hood" of a particular data transmission technology. That's because, ultimately, a certain baud rate will always be decoded into a bit rate again.

With simpler encoding schemes, such as Manchester, NRZ, and NRZI, the baud rate is typically twice the bit rate because a simple 0 to 1 transition represents an individual data bit. All the newer and more complex encoding schemes, such as PAM5, 4B/5B, 8B/10B, and 8B/6T, use more than two symbols, and therefore the bit and baud rate are quite different. For example, 100BASE-TX uses 4B/5B encoding that creates 5-bit words out of 4 bits of data via a lookup table. This kind of encoding contains 0.8 bits/symbol. That's because an extra bit is carried along for every four bits of data transmitted. This extra bit fulfills other purposes but does not actually constitute any useful data transfer. In this case, the bit rate is 100Mbps, but the baud rate is $5/4 \times 100$, or 125 Mbaud.

Line Encoding

Line encoding converts a digital word (or series of bits) into a serial bitstream that can be transmitted over the wire. The common types of line encoding in use today with Ethernet are Non-Return-to-Zero (used for all fiber optic based Ethernet versions), Manchester (10BASE-T), and Multilevel-Threshold-3 (100BASE-TX). Let's look at the different line or serial bit encoding schemes in a bit more detail:

- Non-Return-to-Zero (NRZ) is a very simple encoding scheme. Some would say it's not an encoding scheme at all because it is similar to the raw data. NRZ signal is high for a logical 1 and low for a logical 0. NRZ encoding has a bandwidth efficiency index of 1: the bandwidth requirement equals half the data transmission rate.

- Return-to-Zero (RZ) code stays low for 0s. For logical 1s, RZ goes high for half a bit period and low for the remaining half bit.

- Non-Return-to-Zero Invert on Ones (NRZI) is a scheme in which a logical 0 is represented by a change in level. A *1* means change no level, which means that the level will go from low to high or high to low if a 0 is transmitted (that is, the "invert on ones" part) but will stay the same for logical 1s. NRZI is used by 100BASE-FX. NRZI, like NRZ, has a bandwidth efficiency index of 1: the bandwidth requirement equals half the data transmission rate.

Note

The problem with NRZ, RZ, and NRZI encoding is that they have no logical transitions in the bitstream if a series or 0s or 1s are transmitted: the receiver cannot make out the clock. In all three cases, some block encoding guarantees bit transitions in order for the receiver to decode the clock.

- Manchester code has automatic transitions. It has a level transition in the middle of each bit. For a binary 1, the first half of the bit is high, and the second half is low. For a logical 0, the first half is low, and the second half is high. This encoding scheme guarantees easy clock decoding on the receiving end, but the drawback of this scheme is that it requires a lot of bandwidth. Manchester encoding has a bandwidth efficiency index of 2: the bandwidth requirement equals the data transmission rate. Because bandwidth was not a problem with the early versions of Ethernet (coaxial cable has a much higher bandwidth than UTP), all 10Mbps versions of Ethernet used this encoding scheme (including 10BASE-T).

- Multilevel-Threshold-3 (MLT-3) is unofficially named after its three inventors at Crescendo Communications: Mario Mazzola, Luca Cafiero, and Tazio De Nicolo. (Crescendo pioneered running FDDI over copper, which then became known as CDDI. Cisco acquired Crescendo in 1993.) MLT-3 is an encoding scheme that uses three different voltage levels (all previous ones discussed use two). The three levels are -1V, 0V, and +1V. For this reason, it can only be used with copper cabling because fiber uses either an on or off state. The level stays the same for consecutive logical 0s or 1s. A change in a bit means a change in the voltage level. The change occurs in a circular pattern of 0V, +1V, 0V, -1V, 0V, +1V. This circular, sinusoidal pattern change means that MLT-3 encoded data always resembles a smooth sine wave of a much lower frequency than the original bitstream, making it ideally suited for high-speed data transmission over UTP cabling. MLT-3 has a bandwidth efficiency of two-thirds, meaning the transmitted signal requires a bandwidth of only a quarter of the original transmission rate.

- PAM5 stands for pulse amplitude modulation—5. It is similar to MLT in that it uses more than two levels: five different voltage levels in this case.

Figure 6.1 shows the 100BASE-T physical layer, its 4B/5B block encoding/decoding, and the MLT-3 line encoding/decoding.

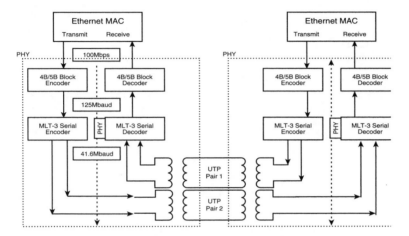

FIGURE 6.1 *The Ethernet physical layer architecture consists of block encoding/decoding and serial or line encoding/decoding. The figure shows 100BASE-TX as an example.*

Table 6.1 shows the most popular Ethernet PHYs in use (column 1). The table provides an overview of the different encoding and compression schemes that we just discussed. Columns 1 through 6 deal with the digital part of a physical layer. Columns 7 through 11 refer to the cabling and analog part of the physical layer. Let's discuss this table in a bit more detail:

- On the left, read the number of transmit pairs used for a particular PHY (column 2). The data rate per pair in column 3 is equal to the nominal data rate or wire speed divided by the number of transmit pairs.

- The PHY design engineers choose the block encoding scheme listed in column 4. Next, the coding efficiency is a function of the particular block encoding used (column 5).

- Next, go to column 6. This is the symbol rate in Mbaud for each cabling pair, which can be calculated by taking the data rate per pair (column 3) and dividing it by the coding efficiency (column 5).

TABLE 6.1 DIFFERENT ETHERNET STANDARDS AND THEIR ENCODING
METHODS PRODUCE DIFFERENT DATA RATES AND BANDWIDTH USAGE

1.	2.	3.	4.	5.	6.
Technology	# of Transmit (TMT) Pairs	Data Rate/ Pair (=Data Rate / # of TMT Pairs)	Block Encoding Used[3]	Coding Efficiency[2] (Bits/ Symbol on Each Pair)	TMT[1] Symbol Rate/Pair (=Data Rate / Coding Efficiency)
UTP PHYs					
10BASE-T	1[6]	10Mbps	Manchester[7]	0.5[8]	20 Mbaud
100BASE-TX	1[6]	100Mbps	4B/5B[9]	0.8[10]	125 Mbaud
100BASE-T4	3[11]	33Mbps	8B/6T[12]	1.33[13]	25Mbaud
100BASE-T2	2[15]	50Mbps	PAM5[16]	2[17]	25Mbaud
1000BASE-T	4[15]	250Mbps	PAM5[18]	2[17]	125Mbaud
Fiber PHYs					
10BASE-F	1 strand	10Mbps	NRZI[7]	0.5	20Mbaud
100BASE-FX	1 strand	100Mbps	4B/5B[9]	0.8[10]	125Mbaud
1000BASE-X	1 strand	1000Mbps	8B/10B or 8B/1Q4[14]	0.8[19]	1250Mbaud

[1]*The required symbol rate can be calculated by dividing the data rate by the coding efficiency.*

[2]*The encoding efficiency is an indication of how much data is transferred over the total cable within a given unit of time.*

[3]*Block encoding is a tried and tested digital transmission technology. Many different encoding schemes are in use today.*

[4]*This point refers to the frequency point at which there is no more signal (or power spectral density) present.*

[5]*Nyquist, a famous mathematician, came up with a theory that the minimum theoretical channel bandwidth needs to be half the symbol rate in order to recover the original data stream. Another famous mathematician, Shannon, came up with a theory to calculate exactly how much bandwidth was required, but we won't bore you with these mathematical details.*

[6]*Both 10BASE-T and 100BASE-TX use a dedicated transmit and receive pair.*

[7]*In the old days, cable bandwidth was plentiful. (Remember that coaxial cable had lots more bandwidth than today's UTP versions.)*

[8]*Manchester is terribly inefficient, only being able to transfer one bit in two clock cycles or 0.5 bits per symbol.*

[9]*The 4B/5B takes four bits and generates five code bits. 4B/5B was derived from the ANSI FDDI standard.*

[10]*100BASE-TX uses the available bandwidth more efficiently than Manchester. It can transfer 0.8 bits per symbol, calculated by taking four bits divided by five code-word bits. It requires 1.25 clock cycles to transfer a bit of data.*

[11]*T4 uses one dedicated pair for transmission or reception, alternating two pairs in either direction. The fourth pair required is primarily a control pair. T4 cannot do full-duplex.*

[12]*The 100BASE-T4 scheme converts 8 bits (8B) into three different levels (3T): 0, +1, and -1.*

7.	8.	9.	10.	11.
Signal conditioning/ Line Encoding	Zero of Frequency Spectrum (=Clock Frequency)4	Nyquist Minimum Channel Bandwidth Required	Cable Specified (= Half of Frequency Spectrum)5	Cable Bandwidth
		UTP PHYs		
	20MHz	10MHz	Category 3	16MHz
MLT-3[20]	125MHz	62.6MHz	Category 5	100MHz[20]
		12.5MHz	Category 3	16MHz
	25MHz	12.5MHz	Category 3	16MHz
Trellis forward error correction	125MHz	62.5MHz	Category 5	100MHz
		Fiber PHYs		
=10×2 =20Mbps	20MHz	10MHz	Fiber	16MHz
=100×2 =200Mbps	125MHz	62.5MHz	Fiber	>Giga hertz
=1000×2 =2000Mbps	1250MHz	625MHz	Fiber	>Giga hertz

[13] *100BASE-T4 is better still. Due to its 8B/6T encoding that uses three different voltage levels, its efficiency is 1.33 bits per symbol. The 8B/6T encoding scheme efficiency is calculated by dividing eight bits into six three-level voltages: 4/3=1.33.*

[14] *1000BASE-X uses the Fibre Channel 8B/10B encoding, which generates a 10bit code word from eight bits of data. The name of the encoding scheme is about to be changed from 8B/10B to 8B/1Q4.*

[15] *Both 100BASE-T2 and 1000BASE-T use simultaneous bidirectional transmission over same pairs, also known as dual-duplex technology.*

[16] *The 100BASE-T2 encoding is also known as PAM5x5 because it transmits PAM 5 simultaneously on two pairs of cable.*

[17] *The PAM5 encoding used by 100BASE-T2 and 1000BASE-T can transmit two bits per symbol (five different voltage levels). It requires only 0.5 clock cycles to transfer a bit.*

[18] *The 1000BASE-T encoding uses four pairs to transmit, and therefore could be called PAM5x5x5x5, a little wordy. It is better known as 4D-PAM5. Some people refer to 1000BASE-T's encoding as enhanced TX/T2 because it uses the PAM5 encoding from T2, plus the clock frequency and symbol rate of TX to transmit 1000Mbps. (The 10X-performance improvement is derived from the 5X-clock frequency improvement, multiplied by double the number of pairs used.)*

[19] *8B/10B encoding used by 1000BASE-X has the same efficiency as 4B/5B.*

[20] *If 100BASE-T would have used Manchester encoding, a 200MHz cable would have been required. MLT-3 reduces the bandwidth requirements so that 100MHz Category 5 can be used.*

Columns 7 through 11 deal with the physical layer properties of a particular encoding method:

- The PHY design engineer also chooses the Signal Conditioning/line encoding technology shown in Column 7. Of particular interest is 100BASE-TX, which uses MLT-3.

- Column 8 refers to a variable that depends on the clock frequency. This variable is key for determining the bandwidth requirements of the cable to be used. If the cable bandwidth is equal to or greater than this "zero of frequency spectrum" number, the signal can be easily transmitted across a particular cable.

- The Nyquist minimum frequency number refers to the minimum cable bandwith that is required to transmit the signal. Note that this is a theoretical minimum and in practice is almost impossible to achieve (column 9).

- The last two columns show you what cable the PHY design engineers have chosen (columns 10 and 11). Note how PHY design engineers have always chosen a cable that provides a bandwidth somewhere greater than Nyquist's number yet smaller than the "zero of frequency spectrum" number.

Figure 6.2 shows the different Ethernet encoding schemes used. The data line shows the raw unencoded data. The transmitter generates the clock signal, which provides timing information. The receiver requires a clock signal as well, and either the clock is sent on a separate line, or the transmitted data embeds the clock information. As a separate clock uses up another cabling pair, Ethernet uses self-clocking encoding methods. Over the years as Ethernet transmission speeds have increased significantly, IEEE engineers have resorted to more and more complex encoding schemes to allow Ethernet to be transmitted over the limited-bandwidth UTP cabling that is so pervasive today. Because Fiber optic cabling has so much more bandwidth, data transmitted over fiber is typically transmitted raw without any encoding.

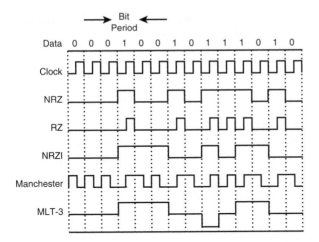

FIGURE 6.2 *A digital data stream and a number of different line encoding schemes.*

The analog signal present on the actual wire is a function of the block and subsequent line encoding. The frequency spectrum of the analog signal is important for determining the cabling requirements to transmit a particular signal. The cable acts like a filter: all signals that are injected into the cable but are at a frequency that are substantially beyond the rated bandwidth are effectively filtered out. The amount of energy that the entire frequency spectrum contains is called *power spectral density*. The cable used needs a bandwidth that permits a sufficient amount of the PSD to still be transmitted. Figure 6.3 shows the power spectral density of 10BASE-T, 100BASE-TX, and 1000BASE-T Ethernet. Notice how the PSD for each Ethernet version has been designed to decline rapidly at the bandwidth limits of the associated UTP cable.

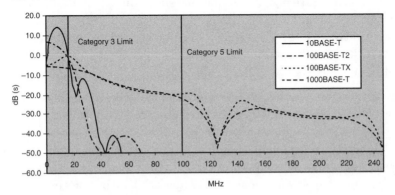

FIGURE 6.3 *Power Spectral Density (PSD) is a measurement of how much energy is contained within a signal at a given frequency. Shown are the PSD for 10Mbps, 100Mbps, and 1000Mbps Ethernet. The dashed lines show the bandwidth limits of the respective Category 3 or 5 cable. Simulation data is courtesy of Level One Communications, Inc.*

The IEEE has attempted to make both 100BASE-T and Gigabit Ethernet run on existing cabling as much as possible, so we will start off by describing today's existing cabling standards first.

Cabling Standards

We need to examine two perspectives with respect to Ethernet cabling: the guidelines used by cable installation companies, which are not Ethernet-specific but apply to voice and data cabling in general, and the Ethernet-specific IEEE-developed physical layer standards. Sometimes these two requirements come in conflict with each other. In this case, the more stringent requirement is typically chosen because, ultimately, your Ethernet cabling installation will need to satisfy both requirements.

Some Cabling Standards History

In the first few chapters of this book, we focused our discussion on data networking standards, the primary standards authority being the IEEE, which has been setting networking standards for almost two decades. Internationally accepted building cabling standards, on the other hand, are a much more recent phenomenon. Until the late 1980s, voice and data cabling were kept completely separate. The telecommunications industry chose cheap, easy to install (but low bandwidth!), twisted pair cabling, whereas the data communications companies or standards bodies (IEEE/Ethernet, IBM, and so on) elected higher quality coaxial or screened twisted pair cable for data transmission. Historically, two companies set the de facto standard for voice cabling. AT&T's Premises Distribution System (PDS) was the de facto standard in North America for voice and data premises cabling. On the data side, IBM had its own data cabling system, but this was only successful within IBM's customer base. Other customers chose Ethernet, and coaxial cable became popular for data transmission. Ethernet, of course, does not constitute an entire cabling system as such; it merely specified the type and length of cable on which Ethernet should run.

In the late 1980s, coax-based Ethernet adapted to the prevailing telecommunications (that is, voice) UTP-based star-configuration AT&T cabling system. Technically, UTP cabling was a step backward from the coaxial cable upon which Ethernet had grown up. The thick or thin coaxial cabling that Ethernet originally used can easily support several hundred MHz transmission rates at 100m, or alternatively much longer cable runs at 100MHz. Category 5 UTP, on the other hand, has a rated bandwidth of only 100MHz at 100m. Most industry experts and users, however, found the star-based UTP system to be much more manageable, reliable, and cost-effective than the Ethernet coax bus topology.

The adoption of the AT&T cabling standard was a breakthrough for Ethernet. It marked a change in the cabling industry, too. Prior to 10BASE-T, LAN cabling was either installed by the computer supplier (IBM, for example) or used a different cabling, such as coaxial cable. After 10BASE-T came along, data and voice cabling systems started merging. Today, many cabling systems in use carry both voice and data.

In the late 1980s, the key voice and computer industry associations met to start defining open, interoperable standards for both voice and data. In 1991, the Electronics Industry Association (EIA), in conjunction with the Telecommunications Industry Association (TIA), started publishing a series of cabling specifications. These are now known as the TIA/EIA premises cabling standards.

Many of the current TIA/EIATIA/EIA standards are based on the original AT&T and IEEE 10BASE-T and 10BASE-F specs, so there is a great deal of overlap. For example, AT&T specified either UTP or fiber optic cabling but no coaxial cabling. This concept was incorporated into the TIA/EIA standards. The TIA/EIA tries to make its standards network-independent. The focus is not on supporting a networking technology but rather meeting certain performance requirements.

In 1995, the IEEE again chose to use the existing TIA/EIA 568-A specifications as a basis for the new IEEE 802.3u Fast Ethernet standard for both UTP and fiber. For Gigabit Ethernet/IEEE 802.3z, the IEEE tried to go the same way, but it was forced to include a non-TIA/EIA cable in its standard (twinax). The IEEE/IEEE 802.3ab standard also managed to utilize the current Category 5 cabling for the 1000BASE-T, an incredible engineering feat that nobody thought possible when Category 5 was first conceived.

> **Note**
>
> *The TIA/EIA 568-A standard was published in 1995. A new version, called TIA/EIA 568-B, is in the works. In the meantime, the TIA/EIA uses both addendumns and technical service bulletins (TSBs) to keep the standard up to date. Addendums are additions to the specification, typically involving new installations. TSBs are more of an "FYI" nature and are not official specifications, but the industry has tended to treat them as such.*

TIA/EIA, ISO/IEC, and DIN

The TIA/EIA's focus is North America, but in some parts of the world the ISO/IEC 11801 standards are more commonly accepted. (Typically, the ISO/IEC standards accept more variations of cabling because of the need to address individual country preferences, such as 120ohm or shielded cables.)

ISO and IEC have, at times, based their work on the German DIN norm, in addition to the TIA/EIA. On occasion, this has led to different standards being developed by ISO/IEC and the TIA/EIA. Worldwide, the TIA/EIA standards are far more accepted than ISO/IEC because North America is the largest market for cabling and PDS equipment, most cabling and PDS vendors are headquartered in North America, and all the major LAN equipment vendors are based in the United States. It also appears that the TIA/EIA sometimes lags market reality: Products and de facto standards have emerged long before the TIA/EIA officially standardizes it. We will only focus on TIA/EIA standards in this chapter and not the ISO/IEC standards because this would make this chapter a entirely separate book.

The TIA/EIA 568 Specifications

The TIA/EIA 568 standard was first published in 1991 and has been evolving ever since. Organizationally, the EIA and TIA are similar to the IEEE in that they publish open standards that are based on the work of many different people and companies. The TIA/EIA 568 standard defines numerous aspects of premises cabling systems. In this context, *cabling* is, of course, a fancier word for *wiring*, and we use them interchangeably. The word *systems* is important: The TIA/EIA standards consider the entire cabling infrastructure as a complete entity, not just the wiring. Connectors, patch panels, and even installation rules and certification are part of the TIA/EIA domain. The latest version of the TIA/EIA standard is 568-A. It was published in 1995 and contains Category 5 and multimode fiber enhancements to the original 1991 standard. The focus of the TIA/EIA has been UTP cabling, but fiber standards are becoming increasingly important. The following sections look at some elements of the TIA/EIA 568 standard in more detail.

Elements of a Cabling System

A cabling system consists of many different elements. Individual components compose the entire system or channel:

- Wall plates (the data or information outlet close to the node)
- Station cables (the cable that runs from node to wall plate)
- Category 5-capable RJ-45 connectors everywhere
- The actual horizontal Category 5 cabling connection nodes
- Wiring closet patch panels

People often mistakenly think that the system performance is a function of cable quality alone, which is not the case. Consider what happened a few years ago when Category 5 was just introduced. People bought cheaper connectors, which turned out to be a huge problem because these cheaper connectors actually failed to meet the official system specifications.

The focus of this chapter is, however, cables because these days the other system or channel components have drastically improved in quality. At the end of the chapter, we will come back to touch on the quality issues surrounding connectors, patch panels, and other cross-connect devices.

Categories, Classes, Levels, and Types

The ISO/IEC uses the term *class*, whereas the TIA/EIA uses the term *category*. Classes are defined by letters, such as D, E, and F. The TIA/EIA equivalents are Enhanced Category 5, 6, and 7. The TIA/EIA wording can sometimes be a bit confusing because Category applies to both the individual components (for example, Category 5 cable) as well as the overall channel (for example, the overall channel meets Category 5 standards).

Anixter currently uses the term *level* as a performance indicator for its cabling. Anixter claims that it introduced Level 1, 2, and 3 cables, and later Levels 4 and 5, which the TIA/EIA incorporated in turn as Categories 1 through 5. Anixter is currently promoting Levels 6 and 7 components due to the absence of official TIA/EIA standards that go beyond the current Category 5.

IBM's cabling system uses the term *cable type* to describe the performance level of a particular cable.

UTP Cable Categories

The TIA/EIA standard describes five different UTP cable categories:

- Category 1 typically uses 22 or 24 American Wire Gauge (AWG) solid wire and can have a wide range of impedances. It is used for telephone connections and is not recommended for data transmissions.

- Category 2, like Category 1, is loosely defined and also uses 22 or 24 AWG solid wire without a specific impedance range. It is often used for PBX and alarm systems, as well as AppleTalk or IBM 3270 data transmissions. ISDN and T1/E1 data transmissions can utilize Category 2 cabling. It is tested to a maximum bandwidth of 1MHz.

- Category 3, also known as *voice grade cabling*, specifies 24 AWG solid wire. Category 3 has a typical impedance of 100ohm and is tested to 16MHz, making it suitable for 10BASE-T and 4Mbps Token Ring installations, although it is technically capable of running 16Mbps Token Ring as well. Most of the voice cabling in existing buildings is Category 3. A lot of the installed data wiring is also still Category 3.

- Category 4 is identical to Category 3, except that it has been tested at 20MHz, allowing it to run 16Mbps Token Ring with a better safety margin. Category 4 never took off because Category 5 superseded it shortly after introduction. Category 4 also provided no real advantage compared to Category 3 (merely 4MHz or 25% increased bandwidth) and was focused on a single, decreasing market share technology: 16Mbps Token-Ring.

- Category 5 is often called *data grade*. It has a bandwidth of 100MHz, allowing it to run high-speed protocols, such as 100Mbps Ethernet and FDDI. Category 5 also uses 22 or 24 AWG unshielded twisted-pair wire with impedance of 100ohm. Category 5 has been available for several years, and today is the de facto standard for new data and most voice installations.

Although Category 5 was the state-of-the-art UTP cable five years ago, this is no longer the case. Cabling and PDS vendors have been developing better quality cable during the past five years. They are now trying to jump on the Gigabit Ethernet bandwagon by marketing a number of higher quality UTP cabling options that are rated beyond 100MHz. This section separates the facts from some of the current vendor marketing hype.

Two major issues accompany these higher performance cabling offerings. First, any cabling that exceeds current Category 5 specifications could be a solution looking for a problem. The success of newer, higher speed UTP cabling choices that go beyond 100MHz is questionable because the IEEE 802.3ab 1000BASE-T working group is confident that Gigabit Ethernet will run over existing Category 5 UTP, with some additional tests. (We use future tense because, at the time of writing this book, no 1000BASE-T products are shipping.) This would make all the current higher speed UTP offerings an overkill until we move to LAN technologies that exceed Gigabit Ethernet speeds!

Second, the TIA/EIA is lagging market offerings in its effort to develop standards for higher speed horizontal cabling. Virtually all cabling vendors are shipping some higher speed cabling, but no standards are in place yet by which to measure or compare the faster cables. Some vendors, such as Anixter, decided to develop their own standards, instead of waiting for something official from the TIA/EIA. Some vendors pretend that standards do already exist, whereas there are only proposals at this point.

Here is an overview of the latest cabling developments:

- *TIA/EIA 568-A TSB-95 for 1000BASE-T/Category 5*—Gigabit Ethernet over UTP will stress current Category 5 cabling very close to its limit. Three additional tests that were not part of the original TIA/EIA 568-A standard, or the corresponding TSB-67 cable testing bulletin will be required to make sure your existing Category 5 installation can run 1000BASE-T reliably. The TIA/EIA is publishing TSB number 95 called "Additional Transmission Performance Guidelines for 100ohm 4-Pair Category 5 Cabling."

  This TSB-95 specifies three additional tests for equal level far-end crosstalk (ELFEXT), return loss, and skew. (We discuss these variables in detail later on in this chapter.) In essence, this TSB does not constitute a performance improvement over the current Category 5 specification but will instead clarify the parameters of crosstalk and return loss and skew because they were not defined in the current 568-A standard. Category 5 cable and connectors manufactured in the last three years shouldn't have a problem meeting these specs, but your cabling manufacturer will not guarantee this because these new parameters were not requirements at the time of manufacture. Recertification of installed Category 5 cabling will be required to ensure proper 1000BASE-T operation.

- *Category 5E*—Also known as 350Mhz, enhanced Category 5, Level 5, or Category 5+. All the major cabling companies have started promoting higher performance UTP cabling that goes beyond the current TIA/EIA Category 5 standard. Anixter, for example, is promoting a new cable that meets its own Level 5 definition, whereas Lucent and AMP are both selling Enhanced Category 5 products. Some analysts and journalists, confused by all this terminology, just refer to all these products collectively as Category 5+. What confusion!

  All these cables have one thing in common: their particular performance exceeds the current TIA/EIA 568-A Category 5 standard. The TIA/EIA is officially called "Additional Transmission Performance Guidelines for 4-Pair 100 ohm Enhanced Category 5 Cabling." It will be published as Addendum 5 to the TIA/EIA 568-A standard-5, or TIA/EIA 568-A-5. Addendum 5 may likely become part of a major rewrite of TIA/EIA 568-A standard, to be called TIA/EIA 568-B. Category 5E will still be rated up to 100MHz, but the Addendum will modestly improve the performance of Category 5 cabling in the areas of NEXT, ELFEXT, and return loss. The Addendum will also specify power-sum performance for both NEXT and ELFEXT to ensure that it exceeds the requirements for 4-pair transmissions, such as 1000BASE-T.

Traditionally, new generations of cable have offered significant performance increases. This is clearly not the case with Category 5E. Category 5E's improved performance will allow you to run Gigabit Ethernet with a higher noise margin as compared with installed, older Category 5, but offers no real advantages beyond that. A lot of the existing Category 5 and all "enhanced" Category 5 products being sold today will meet the new Addendum 5 specifications, so we just expect most cabling companies to rename their existing product Cat5E. Don't be misled by the 350Mhz misnomer: it merely means that the cable has been tested to 350MHz. This does not mean it delivers 350MHz of bandwidth! We expect a final draft of the Addendum or the new TIA/EIA-568-B standard to be distributed in late 1998 or early 1999.

At this point, the TIA/EIA is also looking at two copper cabling standards that offer more than 100MHZ of bandwidth. These are called Category 6 and 7. At the time of this writing, a draft specification is available for Category 6, but Category 7 specifications are still the subject of much debate.

- *Category 6*—The new Category 6 cabling standard will offer cabling users 200MHz bandwidth, as opposed to 100MHz for the current Category 5 or Enhanced Category 5. Category 6 hardware would look and feel like existing Category 5 hardware: the cable would be about the same diameter and stiffness, and a higher performance design RJ-45 connector is being envisioned.

- *Category 7*—The proposed higher performance Category 7 copper cabling would be specified to 600MHz. Unfortunately, we can only achieve this performance by interpair shielding. This will make a four pair cable at least 50% more bulky and much stiffer than Category 5 cable, resulting in a high level of difficulty in installation. Newer, larger, and more complex connector designs, which take longer to install, will also be required because of the need to terminate multiple shields. Lucent, one of the largest cabling manufacturers, estimates that Category 7 copper cabling will be more expensive than optical fiber installations.

Many vendors are shipping prestandard Category 5E, as well as Category 6. (Prestandard Category 7 products is shipping in small quantities, primarily in

Europe where shielded cables are sometimes required or preferred.) At the time of writing, the IEEE 802.3ab engineers will apparently be able to make 1000BASE-T run on existing Category 5. We called around to price the pre-standard Category 5E products, and it looks like the price premium is only about 10%. This price gap is bound to close even further over time. So you might as well go for enhanced Category 5, especially because it will allow a larger margin of error in the installation work, for example in accommodating less-than-perfect installations. (See the following section on installation.) We expect that classic Category 5 will be phased out during 1999 and be replaced by Category 5E.

Category 6 is a different story. What applications will Category 6 support? Let's not forget that we are talking about *desktop* cabling here. Most desktops today are still running at 10Mbps, some at 100Mbps, and a small number are con-nected via dedicated 100Mbps. Yet Category 5E will offer the capability to deploy shared or switched 1000Mbps all the way to the desktop, which would represent a tenfold or even hundredfold speed increase from today. Thus, Category 6 cabling effectively caters to network technologies that exceed Gigabit Ethernet speeds to the desktop. Even we bandwidth promoters have a hard time seeing that on our radar screen.

Then we face the question of standards compliance. If you buy prestandard Category 6 today, will it conform to tomorrow's Category 6 standard?

Finally, we have the issue of cost. Category 6 cabling is more than twice the price of Category 5, but overall, labor is the most expensive part of the installa-tion, as Table 6.2 illustrates. A complete Category 6 installation is only 40% more expensive than Category 5, so one could be tempted. If your vendor will guarantee that its cable will meet the future standard, you might as well future-proof your cabling installation for the next 15 years with Category 6. If cabling vendors bring down the price of Category 6 sufficiently, you could leapfrog Category 5E very quickly, just like Category 5 replaced Category 4 in a very short timeframe.

TABLE 6.2 A COMPARISON OF COSTS FOR 50M[1] SEGMENTS OF CATEGORY 5, CATEGORY 5E, AND CATEGORY 6 CABLE

Line Item	Category 5	Category 5E	Category 6[2]
Cable material[3]	$27	$36	$56
Outlet material[3]	$5	$5	$6
Closet material[3]	$5	$5	$6
Total material[3]	$36	$45	$72

continues

Table 6.2   Continued

Line Item	Category 5	Category 5E	Category 6[2]
Labor4	$81	$81	$81
Subtotal	**$117**	**$126**	**$153**
Patch cords[5]	$6	$12	$22
Grand total	**$123**	**$138**	**$175**

Source: AMP, Inc., June 1998.
[1] *The maximum distance for a horizontal run is 100m. The average horizontal run, however, is only around 50m.*
[2] *No Category 6 standard exists yet. The quote is based on the 200MHz cable that AMP currently sells.*
[3] *The cost estimate is for plenum cable, outlet and required jacks and connectors, patch panels, and required wiring closet connectors.*
[4] *Installation is one lump sum for cable pulling, cable termination, and cable testing. Note that labor depends very much on location. We have heard, for example, that the labor costs in New York City amount to over $300 per node! Needless to say, we are moving to New York City to get into the cabling business.*
[5] *While all offices or cubicles may be wired, not all outlets are connected to a hub. Therefore, the system integrator, not the cabling vendor, often supplies patch cords.*

Table 6.3 summarizes the different existing and proposed TIA/EIA cabling categories.

Table 6.3   The Evolution of TIA/EIA Cabling Categories

Cabling Category	Network Application Primarily Designed to Support	Rated Frequency (=Bandwidth)	Year of Standard
Category 1	Voice only	voice	1950s
Category 2	Voice or low-speed data. Used for PBX, or IBM 3270, ISDN, and T1/E1 data	1MHz	1960s
Category 3	Voice, 10BASE-T	16MHz	1991
Category 4	16Mbps Token-Ring	20MHz	1993
Category 5	CDDI, 100BASE-TX, ATM 155	100MHz	1994
Category 5 (1000BASE-T TSB-95)	1000BASE-T (better characterization of ELFEXT, delay skew, return loss)	100MHz	Early 1999
Category 5E (568-A-5)	1000BASE-T	100MHz	Late 1998
Category 6	None proposed at this time	200MHz	Late 1999
Category 7	None proposed at this time	600MHz	September 2000

UTP Connectors

The TIA/EIA568-A standard specifies the RJ-45 connector for UTP wiring.
There are two termination (or "pin-out") options: the T568A connector and the
T568B, which is the same as the AT&T 258A RJ-45 connection method. The only
difference between the two is that pairs 2 and 3 are reversed. It doesn't matter
which one you choose, as long as you use the same termination method on
both ends. Figure 6.4 shows the T568A, and Figure 6.5 shows the T568B connection. Both the T568A and T568B pin outs are acceptable RJ-45 connections.

Figure 6.6 illustrates the older IEEE 10BASE-T connector. Note that both
100BASE-T4 and 1000BASE-T require all four pairs. Note also that 1000BASE-T
requires good quality connectors.

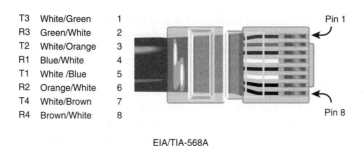

T3	White/Green	1
R3	Green/White	2
T2	White/Orange	3
R1	Blue/White	4
T1	White /Blue	5
R2	Orange/White	6
T4	White/Brown	7
R4	Brown/White	8

EIA/TIA-568A

FIGURE 6.4 *The T568A pin out is one of two acceptable RJ-45 connections.*

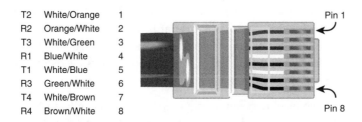

T2	White/Orange	1
R2	Orange/White	2
T3	White/Green	3
R1	Blue/White	4
T1	White/Blue	5
R3	Green/White	6
T4	White/Brown	7
R4	Brown/White	8

AT&T 258A and EIA/TIA-568B

FIGURE 6.5 *The TIA/EIA T568B specification is identical to the AT&T 258A specification and is shown. Most vendors now supply one product that is color-coded for both
options to allow for easy installation of either configuration.*

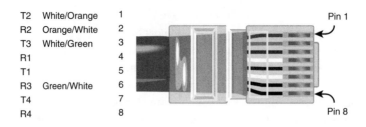

T2	White/Orange	1
R2	Orange/White	2
T3	White/Green	3
R1		4
T1		5
R3	Green/White	6
T4		7
R4		8

Pin 1

Pin 8

IEEE 10BASE-T

FIGURE 6.6 *The older IEEE 10BASE-T connector only terminates conductors 1, 2, 3, and 6. (Both 100BASE-TX and 1000BASE-T require all eight conductors to be terminated.)*

Note

The A in the T568A connector should not be confused with the TIA/EIA 568-A standard. There is no hyphen between 568 and the letter A in the T568A connector designation. This will become even more confusing when the TIA/EIA publishes the TIA/EIA-568-B revision of the whole standard!

Ethernet MDI/MDI-X and Crossover Cables

The Ethernet AUI, MII signal, or GMII is a digital signal that connects the MAC to the PHY. Once a PHY has encoded the signal for transmission, it is referred to as the Ethernet MDI. The MDI RJ-45 connector on a NIC uses this standard connection method. The NIC RJ-45 then connects to a straight-through cable, which is terminated at the repeater RJ-45 port. (A straight-through cable connects all the same Pin numbers on both ends: for example, Pin 1 is connected to Pin 1.) The NIC transmit signal, however, needs to connect to the repeater receive port, and vice versa. In order to accommodate this reversal, repeaters and workgroup switches use the MDI-X standard, short for MDI with crossover. In essence, the MDI-X port implies that the device has internally swapped transmit and receive around. In general, one always needs to connect an MDI port to an MDI-X port so that RX and TX always match up.

If you now want to connect two similar devices (for example, NIC to NIC) or cascade different repeaters or switches (for example, MDI to MDI or MDI-X to MDI-X), you have two choices:

- Many Ethernet repeaters and switches feature a single port that is called *MDI/MDI-X*. You can utilize this special port to cascade different repeaters with a straight-through cable. Just select the "opposite" of what's connected at the other end. Figure 6.7 shows the MDI/MDI-X button found on many repeaters.

- If your repeater doesn't have this button or if you are trying to connect two NICs directly, you need a special crossover cable. For 10BASE-T, this crossover cable internally connects the transmit and receive on the ends. For 10BASE-T, this means connecting Pins 1 and 2 on one end to Pins 3 and 6 on the other, and vice versa. Table 6.4 shows the connection diagram for a crossover 10BASE-T cable.

TABLE 6.4 CROSSOVER CABLE CONNECTION DIAGRAM

One End	The Other End
Pin 1 white/orange	Pin 1 white/green
Pin 2 orange/white	Pin 2 green/white
Pin 3 white/green	Pin 3 white/orange
Pin 6 green/white	Pin 6 orange/white

FIGURE 6.7 *The MDI/MDI-X button, found on many repeaters, reverses the TX and RX pairs on a particular RJ-45 connector in order to connect to a different repeater.*

Note that most switches are utilizing the MDI connection. That's because a switch is intended to connect to a repeater, which in turn utilizes the MDI-X convention. The workgroup device can then connect to the desktop or server NIC that in turn uses the MDI connection again. It's simple to remember: opposites connect with a straight cable. Equals connect with a crossover cable or an MDI/MDI-X port.

Fiber Optics

Fiber optic cabling has been around for many decades. Fiber optics offers huge bandwidth capabilities and other benefits, such as electrical noise immunity. Yet fiber hasn't taken over the world yet. In this section, we will examine the basic properties of fiber optic cabling and TIA/EIA fiber standards, and we'll voice our opinion in the "fiber versus UTP to the desktop" debate.

The first proponents of fiber cabling for LAN or data transmission were IBM and ANSI FDDI engineers. (Fiber has been in use in the telecommunications industry a long time.) IBM's cabling system includes a Type 5 cable, which is a 100micrometer ([ic:mu]m) diameter fiber cable, but this cable never became very popular. The ANSI FDDI specification accommodates different fiber cables, among them the IBM Type 5 cable as well as other multimode and single-mode fiber cables.

In the early 1990s, the TIA/EIA also started working on fiber standards. Today, the TIA/EIA 568-A standard mandates fiber for vertical backbones and makes fiber optional for horizontal runs.

Fiber Optic Cabling Basics

Fiber cabling is described through various parameters: the quality (single-mode fiber, abbreviated SMF; multimode fiber, abbreviated MMF; or graded MMF), the actual fiber diameter in micrometer (μm), the outside cladding diameter (also measured in μm), and the wavelength of the optical light transmission circuitry (measured in nanometers, or nm):

- *Types of fiber optic cable*—Two basic types of materials are used for fiber: glass and plastic. Glass is higher quality and is used for longer distance voice and data transmission. Plastic is cheaper but lower in quality and is used for very short-distance transmission (typically less than 50m). Glass fiber is used to manufacture multimode fiber (MMF) and single-mode fiber (SMF), the ultimate in high-bandwidth transmission media. Single-mode fiber is capable of transmission rates of several gigabits per second. For example, at 100m, single-mode fiber has a bandwidth of over 300GHz, well beyond the capability of all semiconductor electronics available today. At GHz speeds, single-mode fiber can still support distances of 60km to 80km! That's why fiber cabling has become the media of choice for long-distance data and voice transmission. Multimode fiber cable, on the other hand, can only carry the signals for a few kilometers due to higher attenuation. Single-mode fiber transmits the light in a straight line, whereas multimode bounces the light back and forth along the cable walls. Graded MMF uses slightly different material to create a hybrid of the two.

  Figure 6.8 illustrates the different transmission characteristics of MMF and SMF.

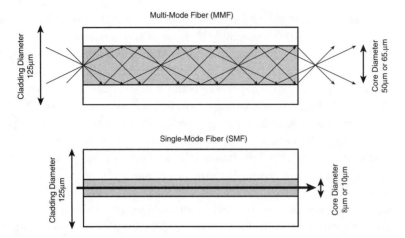

FIGURE 6.8 *In SMF, the light travels in a straight line down the fiber. With MMF, the light bounces back and forth down the fiber.*

- *Sizes of fiber optic cable*—The TIA/EIA specifiess multimode fiber cabling with a diameter of 62.5/125µm as its standard. In this case, the actual fiber core has a diameter of 62.5µm, whereas the outside cladding has a diameter of 125µm, hence the designation 62.5/125µm. Another version of MMF fiber making a comeback is the 50/125µm fiber. This type of fiber was included in the Gigabit Ethernet standard because of its performance advantages in supporting short wavelength lasers (VCSELs) described later. In addition, cabling giant AMP recently started advocating it again due to some cost and performance advantages over the more prevalent 62.5/125µm fiber.

SMF typically has a much smaller inside diameter, 8µ to 10µm, but the same 125µm outside measurement. The big difference between MMF and SMF is the attenuation, or signal loss incurred over a given distance. For example, MMF operating at 850µm has an attenuation of 3.75dB/km. SMF, on the other hand, has an attenuation of 0.5dB/km at 1310µm, a fraction of the attenuation of MMF. In practice, that means higher bandwidth and longer cable runs for SMF. MMF fiber cable jacket is typically beige or orange, whereas the SMF cable jacket is typically yellow. From an optical perspective, SMF fiber has superior properties. The big difference is in the price of the LEDs or lasers that connect to the fiber cabling. Moneywise, SMF fiber cable is less expensive than MMF, but SMF connectors are significantly higher than MMF connectors. Therefore, MMF cabling systems are less expensive than SMF cabling systems in premises cabling networks given the short distances but high level of connectivity.

- *Light sources of fiber optic cable*—You choose the wavelength of light to be transmitted over fiber optic cable in order to take advantage of variations in attenuation (or signal loss) in a cable. At different wavelengths, you'll find "dips" in attenuation over the cable. Different light sources take advantage of those dips to achieve better transmission characteristics. Two different light source categories have emerged over the past 20 years: short wavelength and long wavelength. Short-wavelength light has a wavelength that ranges between 770nm and 910nm. 10BASE-F popularized short-wavelength light transmission. FDDI uses long-wavelength light, which has a wavelength rating of 1270nm to 1355nm. The bandwidth of a cable typically increases with increasing wavelength: longer wavelength equals more bandwidth or cable length. The telecommunications industry uses a third wavelength, 1500nm light, for extremely long SMF runs, but the local area networking industry does not. The local area networking industry focus is local (that is, shorter distances), whereas the focus of the telecommunications industry has been worldwide, requiring long-distance transmission capabilities.

There are essentially two types of light source. Low-cost LEDs are typically used in conjunction with MMF cable and slower transfer speeds (10 or 100Mbps) operating at 850nm (10Mbps) or 1300nm (100Mbps). A more focused laser light source is required for longer distance SMF. SMF lasers are significantly more expensive than LEDs; therefore, most installed fiber hardware utilized LED transceivers in conjunction with MMF cabling. Two recent developments have changed that. CD players use a laser with a similar frequency to that of short-wavelength fiber LEDs. This has driven down the cost of short-wavelength lasers significantly (long-wavelength lasers are still very expensive). Second, only lasers can support Gigabit Ethernet data rates. Thus, lower costs plus market requirements have made short wavelength lasers in particular very popular. This has led to the development and introduction of Vertical Cavity Surface Emitting Lasers (VCSELs), which are easy to manufacture and test and are specifically designed for use with multimode fiber.

To summarize, the key differences between long-wavelength and short-wavelength lasers are performance and price. Short-wavelength lasers are relatively inexpensive but require a shorter transmission distance. Long-wavelength lasers cost significantly more but allow for more distance. Table 6.5 shows the key facts of both short- and long-wavelength lasers.

TABLE 6.5   FIBER OPTIC WAVELENGTHS FOR MMF AND SMF

Source	Possible Wavelength	IEEE 802 Nominal Wavelength	Type of Fiber-Optic Cable Used	Typical Transducer
Long-wavelength light	1270nm–1355nm	1300nm	SMF preferred, MMF possible	Laser
Short-wavelength light	770nm–860nm	850nm	MMF only	VCSELs or Laser

Optical Fiber Connectors

Some FDDI installations still use the MIC connectors shown in Figure 6.9, but this connector has become obsolete. The most common fiber connector installed today is the ST connector, shown in Figure 6.10. The newer SC connector, shown in Figure 6.11, was originally developed by the Japanese telephone company, NTT, and was found to be easier to install and use than the ST connector. Therefore, both the TIA/EIA and the IEEE have chosen the 568SC, as it is officially called, or just duplex-SC connector as the standard fiber connector. Due to the large installed base of ST connectors, however, the ST connector has been grandfathered for continued use in both current and future updates of existing optical fiber networks. The ST connector still represents more than 50% of all new connectors used, but the SC is becoming more prevalent every day. Many LAN hardware equipment vendors offer Fast Ethernet products with a choice of either the SC or ST connector, but with the advent of Gigabit Ethernet, the SC seems set to take over.

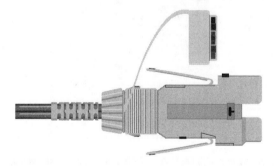

FIGURE 6.9   *The MIC connector was the FDDI standard connector.*

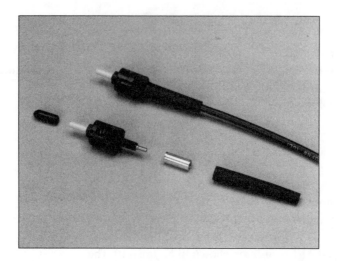

FIGURE 6.10 *10BASE-F and 100BASE-FX popularized the ST connector. Courtesy AMP, Inc.*

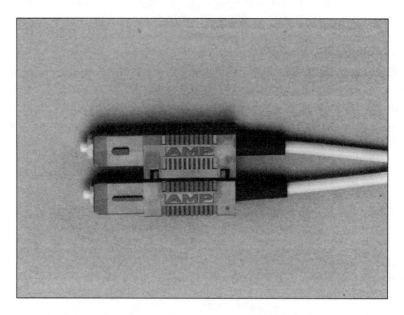

FIGURE 6.11 *The SC connector is the new TIA/EIA and Gigabit Ethernet standard. Courtesy AMP, Inc.*

Table 6.6 compares different key features of the major fiber optic LAN standards.

Cable Lengths

The TIA/EIA standard differentiates between backbone, or vertical, cable, and horizontal, or node, cabling. The backbone cabling links different wiring closets in a building, whereas the horizontal cabling connects different nodes on a floor to the wiring closet on that particular floor. Figure 6.12 illustrates backbone and horizontal cabling.

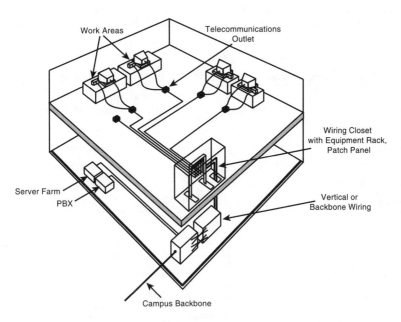

FIGURE 6.12   *The TIA/EIA model differentiates between backbone/vertical and horizontal/node cabling.*

For horizontal connections, the TIA/EIA 568-A standard segment length is limited to a maximum of 100m, the breakdown of which is shown in Table 6.7 and illustrated in Figure 6.13.

TABLE 6.6 SUMMARY OF DIFFERENT FIBER OPTIC LAN STANDARDS

LAN Standard	10BASE-F	FDDI
Cabling	MMF	MMF
Light frequency	800nm–910nm	800nm–910nm
Length	2000m[2]	2000m[3]
Connector	ST	Duplex MIC

1Some 100BASE-FX equipment supports SMF as well. Then some external SMF transceivers also allow you to run 100BASE-FX over SMF.

2Data shown is for 10BASE-FB or FL. 10BASE-FP has a maximum length of only 500m.

3There is actually a third version of FDDI: the low-cost fiber version uses lower performance transmitters and the

TABLE 6.7 TIA/EIA HORIZONTAL LINK SEGMENT LENGTH (FOR UTP AND FIBER)

Source	Destination	Maximum Length	Name of Connection
Network node	Wall plate	L1	Equipment cord
Wall outlet	Cross connect	90m	Horizontal wiring
Cross connect	Cross connect	L2	Cross-connect cable
Cross connect	Network hub	L3	Equipment cord
Total segment length		100m	Segment or link

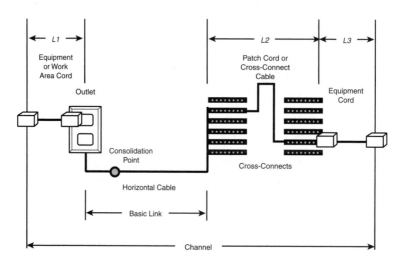

FIGURE 6.13 *The 100m TIA/EIA channel length is broken down into various different sections. The basic link, or the actual cable, constitutes only 90m.*

FDDI	100BASE-FX	1000BASE-X	
SMF	MMF[1]	MMF	SMF
1310nm	800nm–910nm	770nm–860nm	1270nm–1355nm
60km	320m–2km[4]	220m–5000m	5000m
Duplex MIC	Both SC and ST	SC	SC

SC connector. The low-cost fiber (LCF) MMF version of FDDI is rated at only 500m.

[4]Distance varies, depending on whether the connection is shared or switched, half-duplex, or full-duplex.

[5]Again, the actual distance varies, depending on whether SMF or MMF is used. The maximum distance for 1000BASE-LX running on SMF is 5000m.

For 10Mbps Ethernet transmission over UTP cabling, the 100m horizontal limitation is conservative. For example, a distance of close to 1km is possible with 10Mbps Ethernet and Category 5 cable. To cap fiber desktop or server links at 100m seemed a little ridiculous, so the TIA/EIA recently introduced a new fiber optic specification. The TSB-72 rule increases the distance from a central point (a collapsed backbone, for example) to the node to 300m. A cross-connect is not permitted. This configuration is also called a *home run* configuration and is broken down in Table 6.8 and illustrated in Figure 6.14.

TABLE 6.8 NEW TIA/EIA FIBER OPTIC HOMERUN LINK LENGTH (TSB-72, NO CROSS-CONNECT)

Source	Destination	Maximum Length	Name of Connection
Network node	Network hub	300m	Combination of horizontal/vertical wiring

In addition, the EIA specifies different backbone or vertical cable lengths. For MMF fiber, the limit is 2km; for SMF it is 3km. Table 6.9 shows the backbone specifications.

TABLE 6.9 TIA/EIA BACKBONE OR CROSS-CONNECT SEGMENT LENGTHS (FOR UTP AND FIBER)

Cable	Frequency	Source	Destination	Length
SMF	Not specified	Cross-connect	Cross-connect	3000m
MMF	Not specified	Cross-connect	Cross-connect	2000m

In most cases, the TIA/EIA specifications are more stringent than the IEEE-imposed limitations, which we will discuss in the next section.

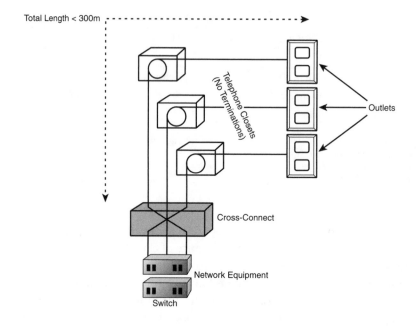

Total Length < 300m

Telephone Closets
(No Terminations)

Outlets

Cross-Connect

Network Equipment

Switch

FIGURE 6.14 *The TIA/EIA TSB-72 specification allows for a single 300m fiber home run connection from desktop hub.*

IEEE802.3/Ethernet Cabling Standards

We won't bore you with the technical details of yellow coax, thin coax, or 10BASE-T/ Category 3 UTP cabling, but we will briefly discuss the cabling requirements for Fast and Gigabit Ethernet in the next section.

Fast Ethernet Physical Layers

The IEEE 802.3u specification contains three new physical layers for 100Mbps Ethernet: 100BASE-TX, which requires two pairs of Category 5 UTP or Type 1 STP cabling; 100BASE-FX, which uses two strands or one pair of fiber; and 100BASE-T4, which requires four pairs of Category 3 or better cabling. Then comes the IEEE 802.3y 100BASE-T2 PHY standard, which was completed about a year after the original Fast Ethernet standard. 100BASE-T2 is virtually unknown and uses only two pairs of Category 3 cable. 100BASE-TX and 100BASE-FX are the most popular 100BASE-T physical layers and were based on the FDDI/CDDI physical layer, using the 4B/5B encoding method.

100BASE-TX is the de facto standard for high-speed horizontal connections, whereas 100BASE-FX is becoming more and more popular for vertical/ backbone connections. 100BASE-T4 is rarely used, while we know of no 100BASE-T2 products that are shipping.

The following sections provide an overview of the different 100BASE-T physical layers. We already covered some of this material in Chapter 3, so if you
read that chapter well, you might want to skip or just skim this next section
on PHYs.

100BASE-TX: Fast Ethernet for Category 5 UTP

100BASE-TX is based on the ANSI-developed copper FDDI Twised-Pair
Physical Medium Dependent (TP-PMD) sublayer technology, also known as
CDDI. Its features are as follows:

- *Segment length*—100BASE-TX has numerous similarities to 10BASE-T. It
  utilizes two pairs of unshielded twisted pair cable with a maximum segment length of 100m. This complies with the TIA/EIA 568 UTP wiring
  standard that has become commonly accepted for office LANs. As in
  10BASE-T, one pair of wiring is used to transmit data, the second to
  receive data.

- *Cable type*—The electrical signaling frequency for 10BASE-T is 20MHz,
  allowing transmission over Category 3 wire. 100BASE-TX, on the other
  hand, requires a much better cable quality due to its higher frequency.
  100BASE-TX uses a 125 MHz signal, but MLT-3 coding reduces the signaling frequency significantly. This makes transmission over Category 5
  cabling possible.

- *Connectors*—Category 5-capable eight-pin RJ-45 connectors are required.
  The same RJ-45 connector can be used for 100BASE-TX as well as
  10BASE-T. The very same conductors are also used, making 100BASE-TX
  backward compatible with 10BASE-T. Figure 6.15 shows the 100BASE-TX
  connection diagram.

  The original IEEE specification included IBM Type 1 STP wiring and
  DB-9 connectors, which were popular with Token Ring installations, but
  very few vendors or customers ever took advantage of this option.

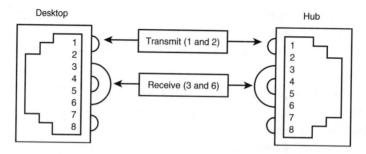

FIGURE 6.15 *100BASE-TX, 10BASE-T, and 100BASE-T2 all make use of the same conductors, making it possible to use the same cable for either technology (assuming the cable and connectors are of the right quality).*

100BASE-FX: Fast Ethernet for Fiber Optic Cabling

100BASE-FX (like 100BASE-TX) borrows its physical layer from the ANSI X3T9.5 FDDI PMD standard. The following are the features of 100BASE-FX technology:

- *Segment length*—The maximum segment length for fiber optic connections varies. For two switches or a switch-adapter connection using multimode fiber, 412m is allowed. This number can be increased to 2,000m if the link is full-duplex. (The IEEE did not specify SMF as part of the 802.3u standard, but numerous vendors are selling SMF-based equipment with distances ranging from 10 to 20km). 100BASE-FX repeater diameters can be up to 320m large. Table 6.10 illustrates the maximum link lengths for different fiber cabling installations.

TABLE 6.10 FIBER OPTIC LINK SEGMENT DISTANCE LIMITATIONS

Connection Type	Distance Limitation	Fiber Type
Full-duplex	10–20km[1]	SMF
Full-duplex	2,000m	MMF
Half-duplex	412m[3]	MMF
Half-duplex[2]	Maximum network	MMF, diameter 320m

[1]This is not in the official IEEE standard. Check with hub and cabling manufacturers for exact distance specification. Some vendors are specifying up to 20km.

[2]Maximum distances for connections involving repeaters depend on the type and number of repeaters. The 320m specification is the maximum network diameter of the repeated segment for one Class II repeater. This includes the repeater-node segment, as well. For a Class I repeater or two Class II repeaters, the network diameter must be reduced substantially. Please refer to the repeater section in Chapter 3 for details on network diameters.

[3]Many manufacturers make it easy and specify a round 400m.

- *Cable type*—100BASE-FX utilizes two strands of the multimode (62.5/125μm) fiber cabling made popular by FDDI. You can also run it on single-mode fiber cabling for even longer distances.

- *Connectors*—100BASE-FX specifies three different connectors: SC, MIC, and ST. The ST connector still appears to be the most popular at this time because both 10BASE-F and FDDI used it extensively. The IEEE and the TIA/EIA officially recommend the low-cost SC connector, which is gaining in popularity.

100BASE-FX is suitable for high-speed backbones, extended distance connections, or environments subject to electrical interference.

100BASE-T4: Fast Ethernet for Four-Pair Category 3 UTP

T4 was the only really new physical layer that was developed as part of the original IEEE 802.3u Fast Ethernet standard.

Why Did 100BASE-T4 Flop?

100BASE-T4 was supposed to cater to the huge installed base of Category 3 voice-grade wiring but has been a market flop. Here is why. In early 1995, the IEEE approved 100BASE-T4 as part of the original IEEE 802.3 Fast Ethernet standard, but it took another year before T4 products actually started appearing. That's because the T4 standard was a completely new development. The 100BASE-FX and 100BASE-TX physical layers, on the other hand, were based on the existing FDDI/CDDI work. As a result, FX and TX products started shipping well *before* the actual standard was officially ratified because existing FDDI/CDDI semiconductor and magnetics components were available to build TX or FX NICs, hubs, and switches. The bottom line was that while T4 transceiver were still being designed, 100BASE-TX was already building up market share. In addition, many people concerned with more bandwidth started recabling with Category 5, enabling them to use TX equipment. By 1996, the installed base of Category 5 had already grown to 50% of all installations worldwide. By 1998, less than 5% of 100BASE-T shipments were T4, over 95% being TX and FX. So if you have Category 3 cabling and are thinking about running Fast Ethernet on it, we would recommend you recable or utilize the existing cable to run switched 10Mbps because we are concerned about the long-term viability of T4.

The following are the features of 100BASE-T4 technology:

- *T4 segment length*—The maximum segment length for 100BASE-T4 is 100m. This complies with the TIA/EIA 568-A wiring standard.

- *T4 cable type*—100BASE-T4 utilizes all four pairs of unshielded twisted-pair Category 3 cable.

- *T4 connectors*—The same eight-pin RJ-45 connector used for 10BASE-T is also used for 100BASE-T4. (All eight wires need to be terminated!) Unlike 10BASE-T and 100BASE-TX, no separate, dedicated transmit and receive pairs are present, so full-duplex operation is not possible.

- *T4 Encoding*—100BASE-T4 uses an encoding scheme called 8B/6T, which encodes eight bits into six tri-level codes. 8B/6T is more efficient than the 10BASE-T Manchester encoding or the 4B/5B that 100BASE-TX uses. Because the signal frequency is only 25MHz, Category 3 wiring can be used. Three of the four pairs transmit data at one time, while the fourth pair is used for collision detection.

100BASE-T2: Fast Ethernet for Two-Pair Category 3 UTP

Most of you have probably never heard of 100BASE-T2, never mind seen any T2 products for sale. That's because T2 products never made it off the drawing board. We wanted to discuss it for completeness and also because the innovative DSP technology developed for T2 has found its way to the marketplace in the new 802.3ab Gigabit Ethernet standard.

100BASE-T4 was targeted at the installed base of Category 3 cabling. Yet 100BASE-T4 has two significant shortcomings. First, numerous 10BASE-T installations only have two pairs of Category 3 cable present, usable or terminated, making upgrading to 100BASE-T4 possible only with wiring work. The second issue with 100BASE-T4 is that it cannot do full-duplex because no dedicated transmit or receive channels exist. (100BASE-T4 uses two cable pairs in a bidirectional manner.) 100BASE-T2 was designed to address both these issues. Due to advances in digital signal processing (DSP) and integrated circuit chip technology, it has become possible to transfer 100Mbps over only two pairs of Category 3 UTP. The IEEE 802.3y/100BASE-T2 standard for two-pair Category 3 transmission was completed in 1997, about two years after the original Fast Ethernet standard was approved. If 100BASE-T2 standard and products had been part of the original 802.3u Fast Ethernet specification in 1995, T2 could have become a popular Fast Ethernet PHY. T2 was even later to market than T4, however, missing the market window by an extra two years. In this industry, two years is an eternity, so we will probably never see any T2 products. The following are the features of 100BASE-T2 technology:

- *T2 segment length*—Like all 100BASE-T UTP standards, the maximum segment length for 100BASE-T2 is 100m.

- *Cable type*—Like 10BASE-T, 100BASE-T2 requires only two pairs of Category 3 or better cable.

- *T2 connectors*—10BASE-T uses an eight-pin RJ-45 connector; it transmits on pins 1 and 2 and receives on pins 3 and 6. Because 100BASE-T2 uses the same connector and an identical pinout, it is 100% backward compatible with 10BASE-T.

- *T2 encoding*—100BASE-T2 manages to squeeze 100Mbps over two pairs of Category 3 cables. Two tricks were used to accomplish this: Like 100BASE-TX, 100BASE-T2 uses multilevel signal encoding. 100BASE-TX uses MLT-3, but in order to accommodate the inferior Category 3 cable quality, 100BASE-T2 uses a more complicated five-level encoding scheme called *PAM5*. (PAM5 is also known as *PAM5x5*.) PAM5 essentially transmits different voltages at different phases (+5V, +2.5V, 0V, -2.5V, -5V) to produce 25 different combinations of signals; hence the PAM5x5 designator. The second trick is that 100BASE-T2 uses simultaneous bidirectional transmission over both pairs, also known as dual-duplex technology.

Gigabit Ethernet Physical Layers

Next, we will look at the four different Gigabit Ethernet physical layers. The IEEE 802.3z or 1000BASE-X standard includes the Gigabit Ethernet MAC, as well as three physical layers that use the 8B/10B encoding originally developed by IBM for the ANSI X3T9.3 Fibre Channel technology. Essentially, the IEEE engineers bolted the existing Fibre Channel PHYs to the Ethernet MAC running at 1GHz. (The original Fibre Channel PHY ran at 1Mbaud, which equates to a data rate of 8/10 = 800Mbps. The IEEE therefore increased the Fibre Channel speed to 1,250Mbps in order to obtain a data throughput of 1000Mbps.) 1000BASE-X comprises two fiber physical layer standards, 1000BASE-LX and 1000BASE-SX, as well as one copper PHY, 1000BASE-CX.

The two fiber Gigabit Ethernet standards are all-encompassing. The IEEE made the fiber standard very broad, allowing Gigabit Ethernet to run on basically most installed fiber installations. Included in the specification are two different types of MMF fiber cabling, one type of SMF cabling, and the two different types of light sources available (short and long wavelength). This allows for many different permutations (confusing at times) but makes Gigabit Ethernet one of the most versatile backbone LAN standards because it caters to a wide range of cost and distance fiber options. The copper-based PHY was also inherited from the Fibre Channel standard and was included to enable cost-effective and quick cross-connects.

1000BASE-LX:Ethernet for Vertical or Campus Backbones

1000BASE-LX is targeted at longer backbone and vertical connections. (The *L* stands for *long wavelength*; you can remember it because it also means *longer* runs.) 1000BASE-LX borrows its physical layer from the ANSI Fibre Channel standard and uses 1300nm long-wavelength lasers (which are expensive). LX can use either SMF or MMF with conditioned launch patch cords. For SMF, the IEEE has specified *a* segment length of 5000m. For MMF, the distance is 550m (full-duplex connections). To this day, FDDI remains a popular interbuilding or campus backbone technology. The combination of a 5km-distance specification in combination with a 10X-speed improvement should make Gigabit Ethernet very attractive as a campus backbone technology.

1000BASE-SX: Gigabit Ethernet for Horizontal Fiber

1000BASE-SX is targeted at cost-sensitive, shorter backbone, or horizontal connections. (The *S* stands for *short wavelength*, which is easily remembered again because it implies *shorter* fiber runs.) 1000BASE-SX uses the same physical layer as LX, but uses the cheaper, lower performance 850nm short-wavelength optical diodes. 1000BASE-SX uses only MMF. The distance supported varies from 220m to 550m, depending on the type of fiber cable used (see Table 6.11).

The IEEE specifies the SC connector for both 1000BASE-SX and 1000BASE-LX. Table 6.11 summarizes the different 1000BASE-SX and 1000BASE-LX distance combinations.

The IEEE distance limitations for Gigabit Ethernet are extremely conservative. The Gigabit Ethernet Alliance boasts on its own Web page (www.gigabit-ethernet.org/) that it was able to demonstrate 1000BASE-SX running over 380m at a recent tradeshow. (The specification says 220m.) Mier Communications in New Jersey tested eight different 1000BASE-SX switches over a 1km 62.5um MMF fiber run. All of them ran flawlessly. Many 1000BASE-LX vendors guarantee their products for much longer distances: 10km seems to be the official number. Cisco, for example, ships a product called 1000BASE-LH (*LH* as in long-haul), which supports distances of 10km. The caveat dictates that a vendor will require its equipment to be present at both ends of the wire. Some vendors, such as Extreme, have started shipping fiber extenders, allowing for distances of up to 80km!

Differential Mode Delay: A Special Case of Gigabit Ethernet Transmission over MM Fiber

The IEEE Gigabit standards include both SMF and MMF fibers. Historically, multimode fiber has only been tested for use with light emitting diode (LED) sources. Due to the high data rate of Gigabit Ethernet, lasers and not LEDs are required for transmission. When the IEEE was testing 1000BASE-X equipment using lasers and MMF, this phenomenon called Differential Mode Delay (DMD) was observed. DMD limits the maximum transmission distance significantly.

A laser light source connected to an MM fiber will send off multiple light rays (henceforth, we'll use the term *multimode*). In a single-mode fiber, on the other hand, only one single ray of light is generated. In MMF, these different rays can possibly interfere with each other, creating "jitter" that can limit the maximum possible distance of Gigabit Ethernet over MM fiber. Figure 6.16 shows how two bits transmitted over MMF can interfere with each other, given enough time and distance.

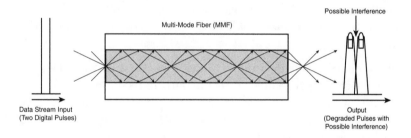

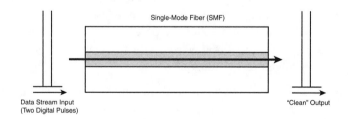

FIGURE 6.16   *Laser light on MMF operating at high speeds can cause jitter and interference. This is called differential mode delay (DMD).*

TABLE 6.11   1000BASE-SX AND 1000BASE-LX MAXIMUM LENGTH VARIES DEPENDING
ON TYPE AND QUALITY OF FIBER CABLING USED

Gigabit Ethernet Standard	Wavelength	Fiber Type	Fiber Size (μm)
1000BASE-SX	850	MMF	50/125mm[1]
			62.5/125mm[2]
1000BASE-LX	1300	MMF	50/125mm
			62.5/125μm
		SMF	10/125mm

1 *All distances are for full-duplex. We don't know of a single vendor building half-duplex 1000BASE-X equipment. For the record, half-duplex distances are 316m for all 1000BASE-LX connections and between 220m to 316m for 1000BASE-SX.*
2*The maximum length depends on the type of 50μm fiber used. The 400MHz×km stuff can only accommodate 500m, but the 500MHz×km fiber is specified at 550m.*

The solution is to spread the laser light out evenly over the MM fiber so that the laser light looks more like an LED light source. This is called a *conditioned launch*.

How does conditioned launch work in practice? DMD affects all MM fiber; therefore, the conditioned launch is required for all 1000BASE-SX and 1000BASE-LX when used in conjunction with MMF. (SX operates only over MMF, 1000BASE-LX can use both MMF and SMF.) For 1000BASE-SX, the IEEE requires that the conditioned launch be done inside the 1000BASE-SX transceiver, so there is nothing extra to worry about. 1000BASE-LX can operate over both SMF and MMF, so the internal launch conditioning wouldn't work. The IEEE, therefore, has specified a removable conditioned launch device for 1000BASE-LX operation over MMF. This is typically a short SMF jumper cable, also called offset patch cord, that is attached to the transmission (TX) side of the MMF fiber switch. Figure 6.17 illustrates this.

MMF and 1000BASE-LX are not your typical combination. MMF is used primarily for shorter runs (internal building backbones), whereas SMF is used for interbuilding, campus backbones, or extended distances. Normally, you wouldn't buy an expensive 1000BASE-LX switch and operate it over the inferior cable. The only time you would go for this combination is if you already had 62.5/125μm MMF installed, didn't want to install new SMF, and needed more than 220m distance (but less than the 550m allowed). We haven't yet found a single vendor that actually sells these conditioned launch patch cords.

Bandwidth	Attenuation	Maximum Distance [1]
400MHz×km	3.25	500m
500MHz×km	3.43	550m
160MHz×km	2.33	220m
200MHz×km	2.53	275m
400 or 500MHz×km	2.32	550m
500MHz×km	2.32	550m
Huge/infinite[4]	4.5	5000m[3]

[3]*Again, the maximum length depends on the type of 62.5μm fiber used. The 160MHz×km stuff can only accommodate 220m, but the 200MHz×km fiber is specified at 275m.*
[4]*SMF has a modal bandwidth that exceeds the capabilities of today's electronics components. For practical purposes, it cannot be measured and is therefore infinite.*

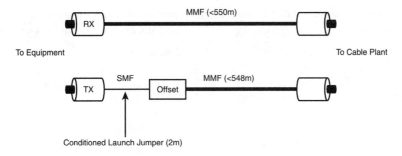

FIGURE 6.17 *The combination of 1000BASE-LX and MMF is rare. Note that a conditioned launch jumper cable is required when running 1000BASE-LX equipment over MMF.*

For further information, please go to the Gigabit Ethernet Alliance Web page (www.gigabit-ethernet.org/), which has an interesting white paper discussing DMD in all its detail.

1000BASE-CX: Gigabit Ethernet for Copper-Twinax Cabling

The 100BASE-CX physical layer was designed for short interconnects of hubs, switches, or routers in the wiring closet. (You can remember what the *C* stands for by thinking of cross-connect, interconnect, or copper.) Copper was the preferred media because it's easier and quicker to assemble copper jumper cables than fiber. The 150ohm balanced shielded cabling, known as Twinax, was chosen as a cable. (Twinax is similar to IBM's original Token Ring cabling.) Twinax is not an EIA-sanctioned cable, but as 1000BASE-CX is intended for wiring-closet only connections, this is a moot point. The maximum cable length is 25m (for half- or full-duplex). Two connectors are specified for 1000BASE-CX. Because the physical layer for all 1000BASE-X was derived from the Fibre Channel standard, it made sense to use the same connector: the high-speed serial data connector (HSSDC), commonly known as Fibre Channel Style 2 connector. The IEEE also specified the nine-pin D-subminiature connector, which is also used for Token-Ring and the STP version of 100BASE-TX.

1000BASE-X switches have been shipping for quite some time. At the time of writing this book, no 1000BASE-X switches are utilizing the CX PHY for interconnecting different switches. Many Gigabit products are chassis-based, where the switch-switch connection is made through a common backplane. Stackable hub vendors are recommending that you connect via one of the regular fiber ports. Unfortunately, 1000BASE-CX could end up being another one of those DOA (dead-on-arrival) technologies.

Table 6.12 summarizes the three 1000BASE-X physical layers.

TABLE 6.12 A COMPARISON OF GIGABIT ETHERNET PHYSICAL LAYER IMPLEMENTATIONS

Parameter	1000BASE-SX	1000BASE-LX	1000BASE-CX
Number of pairs required	2 strands	2 strands	2
Cable category required	50μm or 62.5 μm MMF or SMF	50μm or 62.5 μm MMF or 8μm to 10μm SMF	Twinax
Cable length	220m–550m (MMF)	5000m (SMF) or 550m (MMF)	25m
Encoding	8B/10B	8B/10B	8B/10B
Connector specified	SC	SC	HSSC or DB-9
Proven	√	√	√
Full-duplex capable	√	√	√
Broad product	√√	√	To be determined support

1000BASE-T: Gigabit Ethernet for Four-Pair Category 5 UTP

The IEEE 802.3ab committee is working on a new standard that defines Gigabit Ethernet transmission over four-pair Category 5 cable. 1000BASE-T, as the standard is known, is an incredible engineering feat. When 100MHz Category 5 cabling was first conceived, the maximum data rate was considered to be around 100Mbps. The IEEE engineers have managed to squeeze *ten times that* out of Category 5 cabling. It's worth spending some time discussing how they did this.

The following are the features of 1000BASE-T technology:

- *1000BASE-T cabling*—1000BASE-T uses all four pairs of Category 5 cabling. You can still use a regular Category 5 RJ-45 connector. The connection diagram is the same as the current EIA 568A connector shown previously in Figure 6.5.

  1000BASE-T uses simultaneous transmission and reception on all four pairs. All other physical layers in use today either transmit or receive, but never both. (100BASE-T2 pioneered this concept, called dual-duplex, but no 100BASE-T2 products ever made it to market.) Figure 6.18 contrasts 100BASE-TX and 1000BASE-T. 100BASE-TX uses one pair for transmission and one separate pair for reception. 1000BASE-T simultaneously transmits and receives on all four pairs.

- *1000BASE-T encoding*—To make better use of the available bandwidth, 1000BASE-T uses the same encoding scheme that was developed for 100BASE-T2: PAM5. 1000BASE-T operates at the same frequency as 100BASE-TX: 125 Mbaud, which is five times that of 100BASE-T2. Because 1000BASE-T is essentially a combination of 100BASE-TX and 100BASE-T2, this encoding scheme is also called *enhanced TX/T2*.

  As you can see in Table 6.13, 1000BASE-T has a half-duplex data rate of 1000Mbps. This was made possible by doubling the number of transmission pairs compared to 100BASE-T2 (four instead of two, a twofold increase) and operating at 125MHz clock frequency, as compared to 25MHz for 100BASE-T2 (a fivefold increase). This yields an improvement of 2×5 = 10.

TABLE 6.13 1000BASE-T COMPARED WITH 100BASE-T2

PHY	Number of Pairs	Encoding	Clock Frequency (and Symbol Rate)	Data Rate
1000BASE-T	4	PAM 5	125 MHz	1000Mbps
100BASE-T2	2	PAM 5	25 MHz	100Mbps

1000BASE-T operates at the same symbol rate as 100BASE-TX: 125Mbaud. Therefore, it also has a frequency spectrum very similar to that of 100BASE-TX. This lets designers use the existing 100BASE-TX magnetic components to build 1000BASE-T products. We could see auto-selectable, affordable 100/1000BASE-T switches and hubs at some point in the future, just like the 10/100 devices that are around today.

1000BASE-T combines many existing technological features. The combination of simultaneous transmission and reception on all four pairs, the complex PAM5 encoding, and the high symbol rate of 125MHz, however, require highly sophisticated DSP technology to make it actually work. The PHY transceiver chip at both ends of the cable will actually be a complex digital signal processor. It will contain more than 200,000 transistors, about the same processing power as an Intel 486 microprocessor!

- *Category 5*—The DSP circuitry in the transmitters and receivers will be able to compensate for some of the deficiencies of UTP cabling. The result is that 1000BASE-T will not need better attenuation or better crosstalk (near-end crosstalk, or NEXT) than existing Category 5 cabling. Category 5 cabling will be sufficient for 1000BASE-T with the warning that three new cable parameters will be measured that are not currently prescribed for Category 5 cabling systems. These parameters are ELFEXT, delay skew, and return loss. Figure 6.19 shows the block diagram of a single 1000BASE-T receiver. Note that every 1000BASE-T PHY chip contains four such receivers, one for each cable pair, plus four transmitters. Only sophisticated DSP technology can accomplish this.

The 1000BASE-T standard was completed in June 1999, at which point products were also expected to start shipping.

As Table 6.14 shows, 100BASE-TX is the de facto Fast Ethernet PHY standard for horizontal cabling. Very few T4 products are available. 100BASE-T2 forms the basis for the new 1000BASE-T standard.

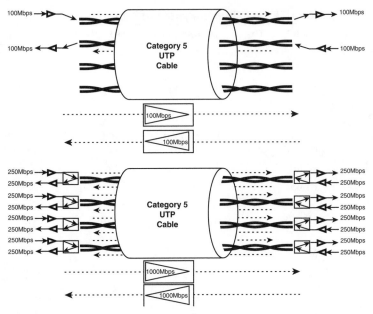

FIGURE 6.18 *100BASE-TX uses one pair to transmit and one pair to receive data. 1000BASE-T uses simultaneous transmission and reception on all four pairs.*

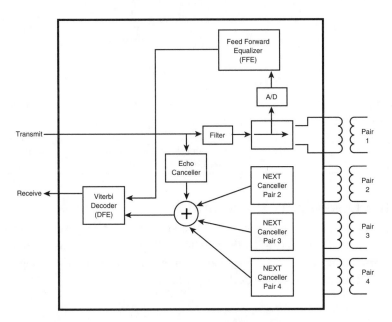

FIGURE 6.19 *1000BASE-T uses modern DSP technology to make transmission over Category 5 cable possible. Shown is a single receiver. Each 1000BASE-T PHY contains four of these receivers and four transmitters!*

Table 6.14 The different UTP-based Fast Ethernet physical layers

Parameter	100BASE-TX	100BASE-T4	100BASE-T2	1000BASE-T
Number of pairs required	2	4	2	4
Number of transmission reception pairs	1/1	3/3	2/2	4/4
Cable category specified	Category 5 or STP Type 1	Category 3 or better	Category 3 or better	Category 5 or better
Cable length	100m	100m	100m	100m
Connector specified	RJ-45	RJ-45	RJ-45	RJ-45
Data encoding scheme	4B/5B	8B/6T	PAM5x5	4D-PAM5
Line encoding scheme	MLT-3	None	None	Trellis forward error correction
Proven	√	√	Only Prototypes were built; never reached production stage	Not yet
Full-duplex capable	√	No	√	√
Broad product support	√	Some NICs and work-group repeaters available	Stillborn child; no products ever made it	To be determined, but success looks likely

Fiber to the Desktop: Is It a Reality?

Your cabling plant is a long-term capital investment and is supposed to last sevral years. So is fiber to the desktop (FTTD) the way to go? If you want to make sure your entire installation is state-of-the-art a few years from now, you will need to weigh the pros and cons of UTP versus fiber to the desktop carefully.

Fiber is, of course, the TIA/EIA standard for backbone cabling, and we strongly encourage you to use fiber in these applications, so that part is a no-brainer. The big question is what kind of cabling to install for horizontal runs and to the desktop. A lot of different opinions are out there, and we wanted to present you with an unbiased summary of the pros and cons of both fiber and UTP. In the following sections, we examine these issues one at a time.

Bandwidth

Fiber is, of course, capable of transmission rates exceeding several Gigabits per second. At 100m, single-mode fiber has a bandwidth of over 300GHz, well beyond the capability of all semiconductor electronics available today. One Gigabit per second is probably as far as Enhanced Category 5 can be stretched. So fiber wins this one.

Length

Fiber is of course capable of distances exceeding several kilometers. At speeds of 1GHz, single-mode fiber can still support distances of up to 80km! The best copper can do is a few hundred meters. But please remember that we are talking about *horizontal or desktop* cabling here. So cable length is unfortunately a moot point in this argument, as the *average* horizontal run out there is only 50m. The TIA/EIA also spells out limits for both copper and fiber runs, and its 100m for UTP and up to 300m for the new home run fiber configuration. Ignoring the 50m average length requirement that copper clearly exceeds, fiber wins this one.

Cabling Cost

Fiber optic cabling used to be expensive to buy and install, but over the past few years, the cost of fiber has declined to the point where it is becoming a very attractive option. Our analysis shows that fiber is only $60, or 40% more expensive than UTP, but there is one other very important consideration. During installation, at least two cables of Category 5 UTP are typically installed: one cable for data and the second cable for the good old telephone! (Sometimes a third, spare cable is installed, to be used as a modem or fax line.) No telephone extension runs on fiber, so everyone needs at least a single UTP cable connection in their offices or cubicles. Thus, with the incremental cost of wiring, an extra data UTP cable is much smaller than one thinks. We compared the cost of installing fiber to that of installing UTP; our results are shown in Table 6.15. UTP wins this one.

TABLE 6.15 A COMPARISON OF COSTS FOR 50M[1] SEGMENTS OF CATEGORY 5, CATEGORY 5E, 62.5, AND 50μM FIBER

Line Item	Category 5E	62.5μm	50μm
Cable material[1]	$36	$45	$39
Outlet material[2]	$5	$22	$22
Closet material[2]	$5	$13	$13
Total material[2]	$45	$80	$75
Labor[3]	$81	$81	$81
Subtotal	**$126**	**$161**	**$156**
Patch cords[4]	$12	$37	$37
Grand total	**$138**	**$198**	**$192**

Source: AMP, Inc. June 1998.

[1]*The maximum distance for a horizontal run is 100m. The average horizontal run, however, is only around 50m. A 100m run would narrow the difference between UTP and fiber. The 50μm fiber cable is about the same price as Category 5E cable, and that Category 6 cable is the most expensive option!*

[2]*The cost estimate is for plenum cable, outlet and required jacks/connectors, patch panels, and required wiring closet connectors.*

[3]*Installation is one lump sum for cable pulling, cable termination, and cable testing. Installation cost is similar for UTP and fiber these days. Labor depends very much on location. We have heard, for example, that the labor costs in New York City amount to over $300 per node! Needless to say, we are moving to New York City to get into the cabling business.*

[4]*While all offices or cubicles may be wired, not all outlets are connected to a hub. Therefore, the system integrator, not the cabling vendor, often supplies patch cords.*

Hardware Availability and Pricing

Backbone fiber switches are readily available; unfortunately, most workgroup components are UTP-based.

When we went shopping for an FX workgroup hub or switch, we couldn't even find one. Connecting workstations to a 100Mbps fiber backbone switch is a bit of an overkill. With NICs, we fared a little better, but not by much. Fiber-based NICs are few and far between (only recently did 3Com start making one!), whereas literally hundreds of 10/100 TX NIC manufacturers are out there. A fiber NIC will also cost you four times what a UTP NIC costs.

The bottom line is that a fiber connection will cost you serious money. Table 6.16 shows that fiber will cost you approximately four times the price per port of UTP equivalents. As a result, fiber to the desktop will be very difficult to implement and will cost significantly more. UTP wins this one hands down.

TABLE 6.16 A COMPARISON OF INSTALLATION COSTS FOR 50M SEGMENTS OF CATEGORY 5E AND FIBER CABLING

Line Item	Category 5E	50μm Fiber
Subtotal cabling cost (from Table 6.15)	$138	$192
100Mbps NIC	$90[1]	260[2]
NIC installation cost	$50	$50
Hub	$75[4]	$500[3]
Hub installation cost	$30	$30
Subtotal hardware[5]	$245	$840
Total for cabling plus hardware	$383	$1,032

[1]*We have taken suggested retail prices from market leaders 3Com and Intel and subtracted 10%. No-name brand 10/100 NICs are available for less than half this amount.*
[2]*Not too many FX NIC manufacturers are out there. 3Com only recently introduced a 100BASE-FX NIC with a suggested retail price of $299. Due to lack of competition, this price will stay quite high. We have again subtracted 10% from SRP for our analysis.*
[3]*We could not find a 100BASE-FX repeater or workgroup switch for love or money. The price we used in the end is for a 100BASE-TX switch with an added fiber module. We took the average price per port. We figured this was fair because you reap more performance from this kind of switch, but you also don't get charged the full price. A fiber module alone runs upward of $500/port.*
[4]*100BASE-TX workgroup hubs, on the other hand, are dropping in price daily. We even saw no-name brand hubs for less than $50 per port.*
[5]*Here's an interesting sidenote: the price of the 100BASE-T connection has dropped from $1,000 in 1995, the year of our first edition, to this year's $510. That's a decline of 20% per annum! Fiber pricing, on the other hand, has hardly changed in the last three years.*

EMI Immunity

One of the benefits of fiber is that it uses light, not electrical signals, for transmission. This makes fiber immune to electrical interference caused by heavy electrical equipment, such as motors, or strong radio transmission areas. In places where EMI noise is a problem, fiber is the only choice. Office workgroups however, are not exactly places where you would find these conditions, so electrical noise is not an issue for most workgroup installations. Fiber wins.

Wiring Closet Considerations and the Connector Choice

One of the biggest benefits of UTP is the compactness of equipment in general and the RJ-45 connector in particular. This sounds like a small deal, but consider the following: in workgroup wiring closets and patch panels, space is at a premium and the RJ-45 connector gives UTP a big advantage. The SC connector, being much larger, means that both patch panels and networking hubs can accommodate about half the port density of UTP equipment. This means "fiber closets" will require about four times the rack space of UTP equipment, which is a huge real-estate cost.

The SC connector, the current standard, has several other drawbacks, too. It takes longer to install than a RJ-45 and is more expensive. The TIA/EIA has recognized this problem and has embarked on finding a more modern connector. An TIA/EIA working group was chartered with the job of finding a next-generation connector. The contenders were the MT-RJ from AMP, Hewlett-Packard, Siecor, USConec, Fujikura, and numerous other connectors from a variety of vendors. At a TIA meeting in early 1998, the AMP MT-RJ connector barely missed the two-thirds vote required for official approval. The different vendors couldn't agree to back a competitor's product, and so now different connectors will compete in the marketplace. It's unlikely that a clear winner will emerge any time soon. The result of this fragmentation among vendors is that the SC connector will remain the de facto standard for quite some time, and fiber in general will be at a disadvantage for many years to come. UTP wins this one.

Future-Proofing

Fiber-to-the-desktop advocates have been talking about UTP running out of bandwidth "very soon." The only problem is that tomorrow never arrives. Let's not forget that we are talking about *desktop* cabling here. Most desktops today (including ours) are still running at 10Mbps, some are running at 100Mbps, and a small number are connected via dedicated (switched) 100Mbps. Yet UTP offers the capability to deploy shared or switched 1000Mbps all the way to the desktop, which would represent a tenfold or even hundred-fold speed increase. That's two orders of magnitude faster! We think that provides enough future-proofing for a few years. True, fiber can accommodate speeds far in excess of that, but when will you ever need that kind of bandwidth to the desktop? Even we bandwidth promoters have a hard time seeing Gigabit desktops on our radar screen, but fiber does officially win this one, too.

FTTD Conclusions

As recently as three years ago, 100MHz and 100Mbps were considered the practical limits of UTP. With the advent of superior DSP technologies, multi-pair and dual-duplex transmission, engineers have managed to push the limit for Category 5 to 1000Mbps. Category 6 will go even beyond that. It will be a long time before we will run Gigabit to the desktop, so UTP still leaves a lot of headroom. The big issues with fiber then seem to be hardware availability, cost, and the connector wars. The connector issue, in particular, illustrates the importance of standards. Without a low-cost, smaller, and easy-to-use connector, fiber will not make it to the desktop in the foreseeable future. For the time being, we recommend fiber for vertical backbones, but we also recommend that you stick with UTP for desktop connections.

The gray area consists of horizontal and shorter vertical backbones, base-ment/server farms, and power users. The answer could be to install both fiber and Category 6 cabling. That way you can future-proof your cabling plant. You can utilize UTP for the time being, and switch to fiber at some point in the future. If you don't terminate the fiber strands right now (who knows what connector will be used 10 years from now?), the cost will be within limits, at around 20%. That's because you will have to pay the overall installation labor anyway, and the cost of the cabling only will be small compared to the overall installation cost.

Running Fast or Gigabit Ethernet on Your Existing UTP Cable Plant

The next section contains some practical tips for you to consider when wiring a building for the first time and some discussion on running 100BASE-T or 1000BASE-T over your existing cabling plant.

Category 3 or 4 Cabling

Category 5 wiring has been available for about seven years, but it has only been used in significant volumes since about 1993. As a result, a fair amount of Category 3 and 4 wiring is still in use today. If your cabling system is more than five years old, your cabling is likely Category 3 or 4. In this case, you could use 100BASE-T4 products. (Note that 100BASE-T4 requires all four pairs of UTP wire, whereas both 10BASE-T and Token Ring only required two pairs.) As discussed previously, we do not recommend that you use 100BASE-T4 because we doubt that it will be around for the long term.

Your only choice then is to run switched 10BASE-T across your Category 3 or 4 cable, something that requires only a change of the hub to a switch. The PDS specifications from AT&T and the EIA have always required the presence (not use) of four pairs of cable for data and a separate telephone or modem line, but 10BASE-T uses only two pairs, so you should have two extra pairs available on your data cabling. You could run an additional 10BASE-T connection on these two pairs, and therefore double your capacity to 20Mbps. Please refer to Part IV of this book for more deployment details. Some installations may have used the two spare lines for a phone or modem connection, so make sure that the two spares are indeed available. One or both of the spare pairs may also be damaged.

Your other alternative is, of course, to recable with Category 5 or fiber. This will be expensive but is the only way to go for the long term. We recommend Category 5E right now. Recabling with Category 6 is still questionable because there is no standard yet, and the price for Category 6 is still a little too high. Therefore, start budgeting for new cable as soon as you have finished reading this.

IBM Type 1 Cabling

IBM has its own cabling system, which actually specifies many different types of cables, of which five are shielded twisted pair, one is fiber, and one is UTP cable. The only part of IBM's cabling system still in existence today is the legacy cabling used primarily in association with Token Ring networks. For Token Ring LANs, IBM specified wire Type 1 and data connector Type 1.

Type 1 wire has two shielded twisted pairs of 22 AWG solid wire, with an impedance of 150ohm. Each pair is shielded, and the entire cable is shielded again, providing 100MHz bandwidth capability. IBM also specified a Type 1 data connector and a DB-9 network adapter connector. Originally, Type 1 STP was the only cabling type capable of running 4Mbps and 16Mbps Token Ring, so the installed base of Type 1 cabling is still of some significance.

Token Ring was then changed to allow for Category 4 UTP cabling and RJ-45 connectors. Category 5 quickly superceded Category 4, so there is little Category 4 cabling in actual use today.

In 1992, when the original Fast Ethernet/IEEE 802.3u specifications were first drawn up, the IEEE decided to include support for IBM Type 1 wiring and the DB-9 connector in its 100BASE-TX specification. For a while, some Fast Ethernet NICs were available with DB-9 connectors to cater to the installed base of Token-Ring cabling, but these have subsequently disappeared.

If your cable plant still uses IBM Type 1 shielded twisted pair, you can convert to 100BASE-TX with some work. You can reterminate older installations and replace the DB-9 connector with a RJ-45. Most Token Ring installations that are less than five years old already use UTP and probably have Category 5 wiring and RJ-45 connectors installed. Be careful though: some may have Category 4 wiring/connectors, in which case you are out of luck.

Category 5 Cabling

Category 5 cabling has been the de facto standard for new installations for several years, but not all of these installations actually meet the system specifications.

We mentioned before that a network system is always as strong as its weakest link. The same concept applies to wiring, especially to Category 5 or better cabling plant installations. When you are installing or using Category 5, 5E, or

6 cable, you need to make sure that your entire cabling system is truly Category 5-, 5E-, or 6-capable. As mentioned before, a cabling system consists of many different elements, including wall plates, wiring closet patch panels or cross-connect devices, and, of course, connectors.

Often, people make the mistake of purchasing cheaper connectors, or wiring closet components. Also, early so-called Category 5-capable components were actually not meeting the official specs. If you installed Category 5 wiring system between 1993 and 1995, you should test your cabling system before running 100Mbps on it!

Cross-Connect Devices

The wiring closet is the center of the network, and the importance of quality work in the wiring closet is often overlooked. Figure 6.20 shows a typical wiring closet layout.

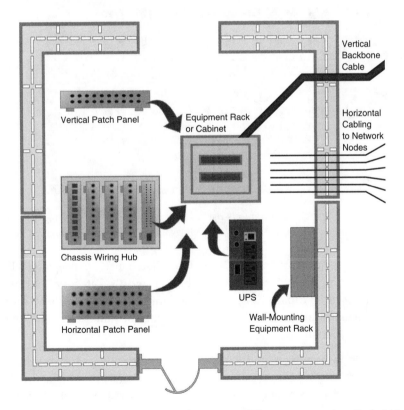

FIGURE 6.20 *A wiring closet includes many different components, all of which need to be Category 5-capable.*

You need wiring closet cross-connect devices to expand or reconfigure your network. Punch-down blocks were first used in the telephone industry to facilitate changing user connections and have been used for data connections over the last few years. Older punch-down blocks are not Category 5-capable, but the newer 110-style products are. (The older type was known as the 66-style punch-down block. The new one is called the 110-style and is manufactured by Lucent, Siemens, and others.) Over the last few years, many customers have installed a new type of cross-connect device called the *patch panel*, which is easily reconfigurable because the connection is made via a patch cable that uses RJ-45 connectors. You can mount these devices in distribution cabinets or racks, and the newer types of patch panels are Category 5 quality (see Figure 6.21).

FIGURE 6.21   *A patch panel connects the hub with the network node cabling. Category 5 or better patch cables terminated with RJ-45 connectors are used to cross-connect.*

Frequently, 25-pair bundle cabling is used for interconnects between panels and networking hubs. Early 25-pair bundle cable was mostly Category 3, so be careful here. Category 5-capable, 25-pair bundles only became available a year or two after regular Category 5 cable started shipping, so make sure you don't have Category 3 bundles.

Patch panels are extremely useful for upgrading or reconfiguring your network from 10 to 100Mbps, or for upgrading or reconfiguring a shared to a switched connection, or for accommodating user moves. Many patch panels switch both voice and data these days.

Possible Category 5/1000BASE-T Problem Areas

1000BASE-T will require a relatively high-quality Category 5 cabling system. Not all Category 5 installations out there will be capable of running Gigabit Ethernet.

At the time of writing, 1000BASE-T products are at least a year away. Some potential problem areas have been identified, and we will briefly discuss them here.

The biggest potential problem will be with poor quality connecting hardware that does not meet Category 5 standards. You could encounter problems, especially if these substandard components are in the middle of the channel. A typical patch panel installation will have either 3 or 4 RJ-45 connectors. (Two for the equipment cord and one or two from the hub to the patch panel.) You should be OK with three connectors. If you have four RJ-45 connectors total, make sure to test your cabling. (Both TIA and the IEEE recommend field retesting using a Level II-E instrument to ensure proper operation of 1000BASE-T.) Long cable runs near the 100m limit leave little margin for error. If in doubt, don't take 1000BASE-T to the specified limit of 100m.

At one point a few years ago, composite materials were used for constructing cable. These composite materials introduce a larger than acceptable delay skew.

Definitions of Some Important Cabling Test Variables

Consider this section background material or a tutorial in case you really want to understand cabling. Here we discuss the most important variables in cabling today and what they mean.

dB (Decibel)

Most, if not all, cabling variables are measured in a unit called the decibel (dB). The decibel is a measurement of relative voltage levels or power. Decibels are measured on a logarithmic scale. For example, the attenuation or loss of signal on a cable can be calculated as

$$Loss = \frac{Voltage\ out}{Voltage\ in}$$

$$\text{Attenuation} = 10 \times \log \frac{\text{Voltage out}}{\text{Voltage in}}$$

In dB, the attenuation would be

An attenuation of –3dB means that half the voltage was present at the receiving end:

```
(10 × log 2.5V/5V = -3dB)
```

We can also measure power in decibels, in which case the unit is db (W). A loss of 6dB (W) means half the power is present at the receiving end.

The nice thing about measuring things in decibels is that they can be added up to provide the total loss. For example, take a Category 5 channel, consisting of a patch cord, a cable, various connectors, a cross-connect, and so on. If the loss of each element is known in decibels, you only need to add up all the losses to determine the overall impact to the signal at the receiving end. If you were to attempt this same calculation in volts, it would be more complicated.

Attenuation

Another word for *attenuation* is *signal loss*. Cable resistance, inductance, and capacitance reduce the signal strength of a transmission from one end of the cable to the other. For UTP cable transmission to meet EMI emission standards, the original transmitted signal is relatively weak to start. Attenuation decreases with increasing frequencies and longer cable lengths. If the attenuation of the signal is too large (that is, the signal becomes very weak), the receiving end will not be able to distinguish a signal from noise, and data errors will occur. Attenuation is measured in decibels.

NEXT, FEXT, Power Sum Measurements, and ELFEXT

NEXT (near-end crosstalk) is the coupling of signals from one twisted pair to another twisted pair. It is undesirable because it represents unwanted spillover from one pair to the other. The term *near-end* means that the coupling takes place (and is measured) on the end of the cable where the transmission originates. NEXT increases with increasing frequencies and longer cable lengths. If NEXT becomes too large, data transmissions can be corrupted. The UTP cable itself causes some near-end crosstalk, but male and female RJ-45 connectors, patch panels, and wall plates can also contribute a significant amount of NEXT. Major contributors to NEXT are Category 3 or first-generation Category 5 connectors, crossed or split pairs, untwisted cables or patch panels, and cables that are damaged by being pulled so tightly that the pairs change position inside the jack. The larger the number in dB, the worse the spillover or noise is.

FEXT (far-end crosstalk) is similar to NEXT, except that it occurs at the far end, instead of the receiving end. It is measured at the far end of the link. NEXT and FEXT are always measured from one cable pair to another. Figure 6.22 illustrates NEXT and FEXT.

Things become even more complicated with four-pair operation like 100BASE-T4 and 1000BASE-T. In that case, three pairs always have an effect on the fourth pair that is being measured. You can calculate this effect by adding the effects of the three different crosstalk numbers together. Engineers have given this variable the name *power-sum*. In the case of 1000BASE-T, we have two power sum variables: PSNEXT and PSFEXT. Figure 6.23 shows PSNEXT and PSFEXT.

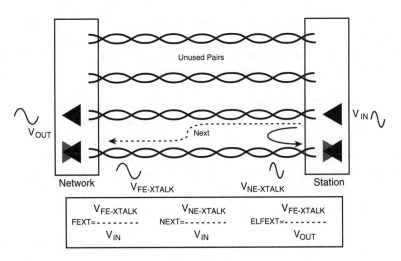

FIGURE 6.22 *NEXT is part of the existing TIA/EIA 568-A standard. FEXT is similar, only measured at the far or receiving end of the wire.*

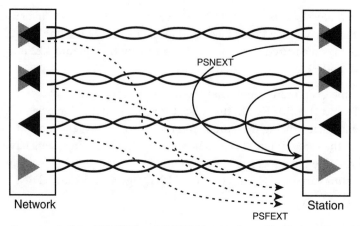

Network   Station
                                     PSFEXT

FIGURE 6.23 *PSNEXT and PSFEXT are only applicable to cables with more than two pairs. To date, most Ethernet versions have used two pairs, so PSNEXT and PSFEXT have not received a lot of attention to date. With the introduction of 1000BASE-T that's all about to change because 1000BASE-T utilizes four pairs simultaneously.*

The new 1000BASE-T standard pushes Category 5 cable performance to the limit. Therefore, two new variables have been specified: ELFEXT and PSELFEXT. The *EL* stands for "equal level," which means that FEXT is measured relative to the received signal, as opposed to the transmitted signal. (This means FEXT is measured relative to VOUT in Figure 6.22.) All of the variables discussed previously are measured in dB. You can simply calculate ELFEXT and PSELFEXT by subtracting the attenuation from FEXT:

```
ELFEXT = FEXT–Attenuation
```

```
PSELFEXT = PSFEXT–Attenuation
```

Return Loss

A signal transmitted via UTP will encounter various obstacles, such as connectors, in its path. These obstacles are an indication of an impedance mismatch and reflect part of the signal back to the source. Return loss is the power of all the reflected waves added up and compared to the original signal strength. Return loss is sometimes called *echo*. Return loss measurements are also a new requirement for 1000BASE-T.

Propagation Delay

A signal travelling over a copper cable has a certain velocity. It is typically a%age of the speed of light—yes, electrons travel at a velocity that approaches the speed of light, which is 300 million meters per second—and depends on the dielectric constant (K) of the insulating material. The nominal velocity is just the velocity as a%age of the speed of light:

```
Nominal Velocity = (1/square root K) × 100%
```

The TIA/EIA recently published an addendum (568A-1) that specifies that the nominal velocity of any pair should be no less than 61.1% of the speed of light, measured at 10MHz. TIA/EIA 568-A Addendum 1 also describes a maximum propagation delay of 545ns over 100m at 10MHz. In other words, the time to transmit a signal down a single pair of 100m cables at 10MHz cannot exceed 545ns. The most common insulating material is FEP fluorinated ethylene propylene, commonly known as Teflon. Teflon-based cable has a velocity of approximately 70% of the speed of light and a propagation delay of less than 450ns, well below the TIA/EIA specified limit of 545ns.

Delay Skew

When data is transmitted over four pairs at the same time, the different signals must be recombined in a synchronized fashion. This means that the different signals transmitted over individual pairs must arrive within a specified time to be successfully matched or recombined into a single 1000Mbps data stream for Gigabit Ethernet. While nominal velocity and propagation delay of individual pairs is important, it is the difference between the fastest and the slowest pair that is really critical. This difference is known as delay skew, and its measurement is also required for 1000BASE-T. TIA/EIA 568-A Addendum 1 specifies a delay skew of 50ns for Category 5 cabling at 10MHz. Figure 6.24 illustrates delay skew over four pairs of UTP.

Attenuation to Crosstalk Ratio

Attenuation to Crosstalk Ratio (ACR) is a computed signal-to-noise ratio for cabling and is a simple, single indicator of cable performance at a specific frequency. ACR is calculated by dividing attenuation by crosstalk. It basically allows you to compare different cable parameters by looking at one number only, similar to price-performance. Attenuation decreases as the frequency increases: the signal strength weakens. Crosstalk and external noise will increase as the frequency increases. If the ACR is greater than 0, the signal is greater than the noise, and the transmission can be decoded. At some point, the noise becomes larger than the signal, and the receiver will be unable to decipher the data transmitted from the noise.

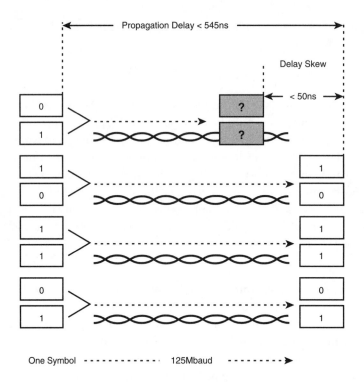

FIGURE 6.24 *Delay skew is important when transmitting on multiple pairs simultaneously. A 1000BASE-T symbol is split up over multiple pairs, and the receiver needs to receive the different bits at the same time in order to decode the transmission.*

TABLE 6.17 EXISTING AND NEW TIA/EIA 1000BASE-T MEASUREMENTS

Standard Name	Category 5 for 1000BASE-T	Propagation Delay and Delay Skew Addendum
TIA Standard	Existing TIA 568-A TSB-67	TIA-568-A Addendum 1
Rated Frequency	100MHz	
Attenuation at 100MHz	<22dB	
NEXT at 100MHz	27.1dB	
PS-NEXT at 100MHz		
Prop. Delay at 10MHz		<545ns
Delay Skew at 10MHz		<50ns
Return Loss at 100MHz		
ELFEXT at 100MHz		
PS-ELFEXT at 100MHz		

Because both attenuation and crosstalk are measured on the logarithmic scale in decibels, you need only to subtract attenuation from crosstalk to get the resulting ACR. A negative ACR (measured in dB) means that the receiver can no longer decod the signal.

Table 6.17 summarizes the variables we just discussed for the existing Category 5 and proposed Category 5E, 6 and 7 cabling standards.

Test Equipment

This section discusses the use and features of hand-held cable testers. Since UTP arrived a few years ago, hand-held cable testers have become part and parcel of every LAN administrator's tool kit. These cable testers are used for two things: to test and certify cabling installations and to troubleshoot wiring problems.

Many different cable testers have emerged over the last few years:

- Some test UTP cabling only, such as the Microtest Pentascanner.

- Other devices test fiber optic cabling only, such as the Microtest CertiFiber or the Fotec FOtest'R DCT Duplex Cable Tester.

- Most cabling testers offer the capability to test both UTP and fiber. The base unit is typically for UTP, and fiber can be tested via a special adapter Examples of this kind of tester are the Wirescope 155 from Scope Communications or the Fluke DSP-100 CableMeter.

Additional Category 5 Tests for 1000Base-T	Category 5E	Category 6 Proposal	Category 7 Proposal
TIA-568-A TSB-95 for 1000BASE-T	TIA-568-A Addendum 5	TBD	TBD
100MHz	100MHz	250MHz	600MHz
	30dB		
	27.1dB		
	8dB	10dB	
17dB	17.4dB		
14.4dB	14.4dB		

Before we discuss UTP cable testers in more detail, we need to introduce two key TIA/EIA concepts. The TIA/EIA standard defines two different types of test configurations, channel and basic link. The basic link includes only the actual horizontal cabling and is also known as the contractors link. The channel or users link defines the entire network connection from network node to hub and includes the actual cable as well as equipment and patch cables, connectors, cross-connects, and so on. Neither link includes the RJ-45 connectors that connect to the NIC or to the hub. The channel test is more comprehensive than the basic link test.

UTP Testers

UTP hand-held testers are quite an engineering feat. Although they look like Nintendo Gameboys, they are rather impressive measurement devices. All of them offer the same basic testing functionality plus features to spare. A typical test consists of plugging one end of the cable to be tested into the tester and the other end into some sort of loopback or injector module. Pressing a single button will then begin an autotest that will analyze the cable link completely. First, the tester will check the wiring map, looking for wiring faults such as discontinuities and miswired, split, reversed, open, or shorted pairs. Then a complete cable link analysis follows that includes the cable's electrical properties such as attenuation, internally generated noise (NEXT), external noise, length, resistance, and characteristic impedance. All of this happens in a matter of seconds. The tests can be run individually as well, and the results can be displayed, printed, archived, or transmitted to a PC via a serial link.

1000BASE-T Cable Testers

TSB-67 specifies that four variables be tested for certification: attenuation and NEXT as well as wiremap and length. The new 1000BASE-T/Cat5 TSB-95 and the Cat5E Addendum both specify three additional parameters: ELFEXT, return loss, and delay skew. A new accuracy level for certification is also specified, called Level II-E. Unfortunately, cable test manufacturers currently face a dilemma, called a "moving target." The 1000BASE-T/Category 5 TSB-95 and the Category 5E Addendum should be complete by the end of 1998. Finally, there is Category 6, which may be finalized before the end of 1999.

The cable tester manufacturers' dilemma is that most testers sold today cannot test for the three new parameters required. Whereas most testers are software upgradable, some hardware modification will be needed to test ELFEXT, return loss, and skew. Then there is the issue of a moving target. A test manufacturer could bring out a new version that tests in accordance with the new TSB, but what about Category 5E, and Category 6? Should the manufacturer hold off until these new standards are finalized before releasing a new tester?

The Scope Wirescope 155 is unique in that it is the only tester available today capable of testing the three new TSB variables. The Wirescope 155, shown in Figure 6.25, has been around for many years, but it has the built-in hardware to test for ELFEXT, return loss, and skew. A software upgrade does the rest: it allows users to load the new TSB and Category 5E requirements. As the name implies, the Wirescope 155 only tests up to 155MHz, so it will not be able to test Category 6 cabling.

FIGURE 6.25 *The Scope Wirescope 155 is the only existing tester that can test the three new 1000BASE-T variables ELFEXT, return loss, and skew by means of a software upgrade.*

The Omniscanner from Microtest promises to be the first of a slew of new 200MHz and beyond cable testers. All of them will test ELFEXT, return loss, and skew. All of them will claim to test cable for Gigabit Ethernet TSB, as well as the Category 5E and Category 6 standards. Yet these standards are far from final. It's a good thing that reprogrammable flash memory exists because all of these standards will require a software upgrade at some point in the future. The Omniscanner from Microtest is shown in Figure 6.26.

FIGURE 6.26   *The Microtest Omniscanner is the first of a new generation of cable testers that claim to be able to test Category 6 cabling (which is still a moving target).*

Fiber Optic Cable Testers

In general, fiber testers are much simpler than UTP testers. Crosstalk and noise exist only in the copper world, so fiber testers need to measure only two things: continuity and attenuation loss. Many different companies provide hand-held testers, which consist of two pieces of equipment. A fiber test light source connected to one end of the fiber sends a test signal that is then measured by a fiber optic power meter connected to the other end of the fiber cable. In this way, continuity and attenuation loss can be measured in a matter of seconds.

Many UTP testers can be turned into a fiber optic tester by means of a special attachment. So if you already own a UTP tester, you can merely buy an attachment and turn your existing tester into a fiber optic tester. Figure 6.27 shows the Scope Fiber SmartProbe that transforms the WirScope 155 into a MMF or SMF tester.

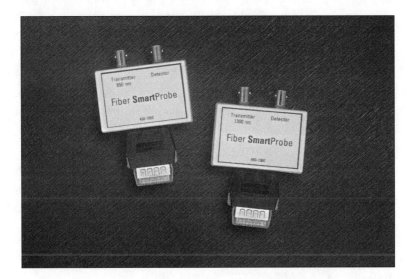

FIGURE 6.27   *The Scope SmartProbe turns the Wirescope 155 into a fiber optic tester.*

Most of the problems in fiber networks involve faulty connections. Connectors, in particular, require careful assembly and testing, but modern technology and suitably trained installers can now install a fiber connector in a matter of minutes. Troubleshooting can be relatively easy and can be done by injecting a bright visible light into the fiber and then finding the fault through visual inspection. This only works if the cable jacket is damaged.

If you cannot visually inspect the fiber, you may require a more expensive optical time domain reflectometer (OTDR). Reflectometers are expensive, so we suggest that you hire a professional company if you need to do this kind of troubleshooting.

Most fiber optic cable testers require a simple software upgrade in order to test for 1000BASE-SX or 1000BASE-LX.

Some General Tips for Dealing with Cabling Suppliers

The following are some things to keep in mind as you deal with cabling suppliers:

- *The importance of professional work*—People often take shortcuts when installing cabling, assuming that merely installing the right cable will be sufficient. Unfortunately, this is not the case, and shoddy work during the installation process can affect the overall quality of your cabling plant. For example, Category 5 cable needs to have the proper twisting retained right up to the RJ-45 connector (up to 13mm from the actual RJ-45 connector). Bending or pulling Category 5 UTP wire too much will change the carefully controlled twists and affect its performance.

  Fiber connectors are difficult to install without proper training and equipment. You should hire only reputable, quality contractors to install all your cabling for you, so hire only contractors that have received the proper training for doing optical fiber or Category 5 installations.

- *RFP*—In the United States, contractor companies install premises cabling. When working with contractors, deal with them the same way as you would with an electrical contractor putting AC wiring in your office or home. Detail your requirements in a request for proposal (RFP), and send it out to various contractors. Ask for feedback by a certain date. See who comes back with the best proposal. Look at price, schedule, quality, and warranty. Look for improvement suggestions.

- *Training*—Ask your cabling supplier if they are up to speed on the latest developments in cabling, testers, and certification. Have they read this book? Seriously, are they familiar with all the issues surrounding the 1000BASE-T TSB, Category 5E, and Category 6? Cabling is not as simple as it used to be. Make sure your contractor employs a properly trained staff. Make sure your contractor has copies of all the TIA/EIA standards and relevant drafts. (They have to be bought from Global Engineering.) Make sure your contractor *knows and understands* these standards.

- *References*—Ask for references of customer sites that are similar in size to yours. Contact these references and ask for feedback on your potential contractor, including what kind of after-sales service they received.

- *Negotiation*—Cabling suppliers work like general contractors. Things are often negotiable. Don't go for the lowest price, though. Keep in mind the saying "You get what you pay for"! Going for the lowest priced bidder could mean the lowest quality, too, and that's definitely not in your interest. Contractors will try to save a few cents by purchasing a cheaper RJ-45 connector: a simple shortcut like that could ruin your entire installation.

- *Documentation*—Make sure that your cabling plant is properly labeled and documented. Neatness is important. As we said in the beginning, more than half of all network troubles are cabling related, and proper documentation will make troubleshooting much easier later.

- *Warranty*—Most cabling equipment vendors now offer performance warranties of 15 to 20 years. See what kind of warranty your installation company provides. Ensure that the warranty is based on measurable performance parameters.

- *Cable plant certification*—Certification means comparing your cabling plant's performance to a predetermined set of values. Certification is important so that you know that your installer has done a quality job. In the old days of Category 3 cabling, certification of a cabling plant was not a big issue because a correctly wired installation was very forgiving and likely to pass all certification tests, the requirements being relatively easy. With Category 5, Category 5E, and Category 6 installations, all that has changed. Quality of installation, cross-connect equipment, connectors, and so forth now can make or break a good UTP installation. To address this need for certification, the TIA/EIA started publishing standards for certification testing. The first document, the TIA/EIA 568 TSB-67 Link Performance Test Standard, was adopted in September 1995. It defines a complete standard for test equipment, test methods, and guidelines for interpreting the results. TSB-67 specifies exact NEXT, attenuation, and other values that will form the pass/fail limits. Running 1000BASE-T on existing Cat5 also requires recertification with a Level II-E tester. Make sure your contractor is familiar with TSB-67, as well as the new 1000BASE-T/Category 5 TSB.

Summary

For further reading, or surfing, please refer to Scope Communications' standards page at www.scope.com/standards/. We found it to be the most informative online source of cabling information out there by far.

This chapter discussed the different cabling requirements for Fast and Gigabit Ethernet. Category 5 is the de facto standard for 100BASE-TX. With recent advances in DSP technology, Category 5 will also support 1000BASE-T. 100BASE-FX can run on multimode or single-mode optical fiber for longer distances.

For new desktop and server connections, we advise that you install Category 5E or Category 6 cabling and use 100BASE-TX. For vertical backbone connections within buildings, we recommend that you install multimode fiber, combined with 100BASE-FX or 1000BASE-SX. For campus backbones, 1000BASE-LX and single-mode fiber is ideal.

A reputable, well-trained contractor that can certify your wiring plant is important. Don't take shortcuts when installing new cable or equipment. Make sure your cabling plant will outlast your networking hardware!

Connectors and cross-connects are the weakest link. Whereas today's state-of-the-art UTP cable is capable of 350Mhz, connectors have a hard time going beyond 200Mhz. Then there are testers: the best one you can buy today is 160MHz!

A final word of caution: Cabling is a long-term investment. Cabling also accounts for many network problems. So make sure you don't underestimate the importance of quality cabling and workmanship.

CHAPTER 7

Bandwidth: How Much Is Enough?

"Ten years ago, we installed our first PC LAN. We decided to go for 10Mbps Ethernet, although the StarLAN and ArcNET sales people told us we would never need more than 1 or 2Mbps. Over the years we kept adding more users, servers, and laser printers, and as a result, network traffic grew. Fortunately, our Ethernet network had plenty of capacity left, so bandwidth never became an issue. Then, about seven years ago, everyone wanted email, and network traffic started growing more rapidly. Bandwidth became a problem, so we bought a bridge and segmented it into two smaller LANs, and that took care of it. Then, five years ago, we purchased our first application server and had to do something more significant: We bought a switch. Then came the Internet. Everyone seems to be permanently browsing the Net, downloading huge files, sending and receiving dozens of emails, or just surfing. Therefore we have a bandwidth problem again. I have decided to do something about it and upgrade my network."

This story probably sounds familiar to many of you. The focus of this chapter is networking bandwidth, *or the lack thereof*. Remember the days when we thought that 64K of RAM or a 10MB hard disk was a lot? Remember the days when nobody would ever need the power of a 386? If nothing else, two things are certain in the personal computer industry. First, you can never have enough RAM, CPU MIPS, hard-disk space, or bandwidth. Second, the stuff you buy today will automatically become obsolete a few years from now, or maybe sooner. Remember that when planning your network for future growth.

Before you spend piles of money on new networking hardware, you need to figure out whether it's really the hardware that's not keeping up or whether other bottlenecks are slowing down your network. The first objective of this chapter is to help you understand the bandwidth capability of your existing network: in other words, to help you find out if your network is really overloaded, and if so, by how much.

What is really driving this need for more speed on our networks? Some may say that the answer will be found on our desks. Ethernet can no longer keep up with clients and servers that now regularly feature Pentium II microprocessors with more than 200MIPS of computing power, 32MB or 64MB of RAM, and hard disks that exceed 2GB. The increased computing power available today is not just creating the demand for ultra-fast networks. Today's high-performance personal computers will only affect your network if they are actually *using* the network. In this chapter, we will examine some of the trends in networked computing and see how these trends are using up bandwidth at a rapid pace. We will discuss the familiar reasons behind the ever-increasing levels of network traffic: more users, larger files, and so on. We will also talk about the new types of networked applications, such as client/server, multimedia, the Internet, and the intranet, and how they use ever more bandwidth. Finally, this chapter will provide some guidelines on how to manage your network's growth over the next few years to accommodate these emerging applications.

Are All of Today's Ethernets Overcrowded?

A lot of the current hype surrounding high-speed networking equipment is being generated by a self-serving hardware industry trying to enlarge the market for its own products. The industry as a whole is trying to convince you, the potential buyer of networking equipment, that your LAN is running out of bandwidth fast. The motivation is clear: Vendors want to sell you newer, faster, more expensive, and more profitable (for them) equipment. How overloaded are today's networks? Is 10Mbps Ethernet really at the end of its life? Do you need to upgrade desktop connections to 100Mbps and install Gigabit server connections and backbones? Do you need Layer 3 switches?

Do all of today's Ethernet networks resemble Silicon Valley freeways? They probably do not. Literally millions of different Ethernet networks are out there, and most of them are doing fine as they are. Most of these networks feature one or two dozen users and single-digit network utilization figures. Networks with a small number of nodes are unlikely to saturate a 10Mbps Ethernet network any time soon. Larger enterprise networks featuring hundreds of nodes are starting to experience gridlock during peak hours. Furthermore, some smaller networks running network-intensive applications are also pushing Ethernet to its limits. That's why concepts like segmentation, backbones, and server farms have all become very popular for improving LAN performance.

Has the Network Infrastructure Become the Weakest Link?

When we speak of a network, we need to be more precise because today's network is a complex assembly of many different building blocks that interact with each other. Often we refer to the *network*, but we are actually talking about the complete networked system that consists of NICs, hubs, and physical cabling, as well as clients, file/print servers, application servers, network operating systems, applications, and other components. The *network* is just the network hardware, the plumbing, and a component of the overall system.

Your system is only as fast as the slowest link. The bad news is that there are often multiple slowest links. To improve the overall *system* performance, it may not be enough to just upgrade one part of it. At least one critical path item is always slowing the entire system down, but replacing only this one critical component may immediately reveal another performance-limiting piece that was invisible before.

The reality of today's client/server system is that you are probably currently using or buying some system elements that can outperform your network hardware infrastructure. For example, when you buy a Pentium Xeon processor-based server and install Microsoft Windows NT, you automatically have a server that delivers orders of magnitude more I/O performance than a 386-based NetWare 3.11 server did a few years ago. Today's desktop machines are also significantly more powerful than their counterparts from just a few years ago.

It makes sense, then, to take a good look at your 10Mbps LAN infrastructure to determine whether it is still capable of providing your system with adequate performance or whether your network has or will become the next critical path item. One word of caution: Don't just automatically assume that your networking hardware has become the bottleneck. In many cases, the LAN transmission speed is not the culprit. Installation errors, specification violations, less-than-perfect configurations, poor node performance, poor placement of firewalls, and overloaded file servers account for most of the bottlenecks in today's networks. The bottom line is that you shouldn't just look at upgrading your physical hardware infrastructure alone.

How to Tell if Your Network Is Overloaded

You have two ways to tell if your network is running out of steam: through your unhappy customers and through measurement of utilization and throughput. This section will help you figure out whether your network is indeed overloaded. Part IV tells you what to do about it.

The Customer Way: Unhappy Users

One way to tell whether your network is overloaded is to listen to your customers, the network users, who will be calling you and complaining about the sluggishness of the network. Unfortunately, this is also the reactive way because your customers are unlikely to notice that your network is overloaded until it is too late. If you are a network manager, it will be painfully obvious when your network has become overloaded. Ethernet and your network operating system will still make sure the data is delivered, but it could be a very frustrating experience. Your users will be calling you frequently to complain about sluggishness in loading networked applications. In the old days of Windows and NetWare 3.1, the infamous `Network Error` message indicated a disconnected or timed out server connection. These days the `operation timed out` browser message has become more common (see Figure 7.1). Look for signs of trouble especially during rush hour on the network, which is typically between the hours of 8 and 10 a.m., when everyone arrives at work and simultaneously logs on to the network. Obviously, you don't ever want to reach this stage; at this point, your patient, the severely overloaded network, will be so sick that lengthy and unpleasant treatment may be necessary to effect a cure.

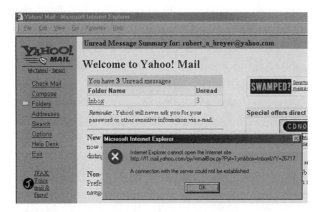

Figure 7.1   *This message typically indicates a very slow Internet or intranet connection, which is a sign of a busy network.*

The Technical Way: Measuring Utilization and Throughput

The second way to tell if your network is overloaded is the proactive way: Measure what's going on in your network. You should perform a regular checkup on your network even when it is working fine because, as the doctor says, prevention is better than cure.

This section will first discuss the capacity limits of Ethernet networks. The performance limitations of Ethernet are a subject of intense debate, and many legends abound. For example, one popular myth is that the maximum throughput of a large shared Ethernet network is 37%. The truth is that the throughput capability of Ethernet depends on numerous variables that are almost impossible to predict or assume. This chapter will provide some background to Ethernet and discuss the bandwidth capabilities of shared and Switched Ethernet. We will show that under certain conditions a shared Ethernet network can reach up to 80% utilization, whereas a Switched Ethernet connection can run at close to 100% utilization.

We will then discuss ways of measuring your LAN's actual data throughput in order to determine whether your network is indeed overloaded.

The Bandwidth Limits of Ethernet

Before discussing how to analyze your network bandwidth utilization, we need to recap the basics of Ethernet transmission theory. (We discuss the CSMA/CD protocol in detail in Chapter 3, "Ethernet, Fast Ethernet, and Gigabit Ethernet Standards.") Shared Ethernet networks use the CSMA/CD protocol, which has certain characteristics that make it unsuitable for high network utilization. A station wanting to transmit must ensure that no other nodes are currently using the shared-media wire, so a station listens to the cable first to make sure it is free. If the channel is free, the station will start transmitting. A collision may occur if two or more listening stations simultaneously determine that the wire is free and begin transmitting at almost the same time. This event would lead to a collision and would corrupt the data.

Definitions and Terminology

Before we tell you what the capacity limits of an Ethernet network are, we need to define and explain some terms that describe LAN traffic. This list is not complete: It includes only the most commonly used terms that are relevant to our discussion:

- *Capacity* is the practical maximum data carrying capability. *Utilization*, on the other hand, is defined as how much of the capacity is used at any particular point in time. Utilization could also be called *load*.

- *Wire speed* is measured in Mbps. Wire speed defines the actual speed of the data transmission over the cable once a transmission has started, not the actual capacity or throughput that the LAN is capable of (bits on the wire). StarLAN wire speed is 1Mbps, Ethernet 10Mbps, Fast Ethernet 100Mbps, and Gigabit Ethernet 1000Mbps.

On the following pages, we discuss Ethernet networks and their real-world throughput capability, and we will try to use percentages wherever possible. That way we can examine the properties of Ethernet in general, as opposed to a wire-speed–specific version. Keep in mind that the percentage would have to be multiplied by a factor of 10Mbps, 100Mbps, or 1000Mbps in order to obtain actual data rates in Mbps.

Note that the 10Mbps, 100Mbps, and 1000Mbps Ethernet versions operate in exactly the same way. The only difference is the absolute wire speed. All other concepts and properties are the same, except that absolute numbers (that is, Mbps) are 10 or 100 times as large. For example, Fast Ethernet still saturates at the same percentage point as regular Ethernet, but the throughput in Mbps is 10 times as large.

- *Overhead* is the portion of a transmission that does not represent actual data. Every Ethernet frame includes data, as well as a source and destination addresses, a type/length field, error checking, and maybe a pad. In addition, a preamble precedes every frame and is separated from the next one by the minimum interframe gap (IFG). The preamble, address, length of the field, and IFG comprise a significant amount of the total Ethernet frame length. We have lumped these bits and the IFG together and called them *overhead* because these bits do not represent actual data transmission. For the maximum frame of 1518 bytes, this overhead comprises 38 bytes and therefore takes up 2.5% of the total transmission time. This gives Ethernet a best-case efficiency of 97.5%. For a frame size of 500 bytes, overhead increases to 7.4%, reducing the efficiency to 92.6%. Table 7.1 illustrates how Ethernet efficiency varies as a function of frame size. Actual frame sizes vary depending on application and network software that you run, but the average is around 1000 bytes.

TABLE 7.1   THEORETICAL ETHERNET EFFICIENCY FOR DIFFERENT FRAME SIZES (EXCLUDES COLLISIONS)

Frame Size	Data Size	Overhead	Maximum Efficiency
1518 bytes[1] (maximum)	1492 bytes	2.5%[2]	97.5%
1000 bytes	974 bytes	3.8%	96.2%
500 bytes	474 bytes	7.4%	92.6%
64 bytes (minimum)	38 bytes (no pad)	50.0%	50.0%
64 bytes (minimum)	1 byte (plus 27 bytes pad)	98.7%	1.3%

1   *With the 802.1Q VLAN tagging standard, the Ethernet frame size has been increased by 4 bytes to accommodate the VLAN tagging/prioritization field. This means the maximum frame size is now 1522 bytes. Because most frames travelling the world's Ethernets are still of the 1518-byte variety, we have used the old numbers in our analysis.*

2   *Preamble, DA, SA, T/L field, and CRC add up to 26 bytes. The IFG is 96 bit times, or 12 bytes, so the total overhead is 38 bytes, or 2.5%.*

- *Collisions* are frames where transmission was not successful. In a lightly loaded network, collisions are infrequent and the network is being used only occasionally. As the network load increases, the idle time approaches zero, utilization increases, and so does the number of collisions. Collisions are measured in percentages.

- *Utilization* refers to the percentage of time that the wire is occupied. This includes both successful and unsuccessful frame transmissions (that is, collisions and errors). One could call this "wire occupied." The idle time plus utilization equals 100%.

- *Actual data throughput* is the amount of usable data delivered to the higher level Layer 3 software. Actual throughput can be calculated by taking the net utilization (that is, utilization minus collisions), multiplied by the efficiency from Table 7.1, multiplied by the wire speed. For example, consider a heavily loaded network, with 50% utilization and 3% collisions. If the traffic consisted of 1000 byte frames, the actual data throughput rate would be (50%-3%) × 96.2% × 10Mbps = 4.52Mbps.

- *Peak utilization* is the maximum utilization that has occurred within a given time period. Utilization peaks typically occur around 9 a.m., when everyone logs into the network, or around noon, when many people send another print job off before going to lunch. Be sure to measure peak utilization at various times during the day.

- *Frame rate* is the number of frames sent per second. This depends, of course, on frame size. For 1000 byte frames and 50% utilization, the frame rate for 100Mbps Ethernet is

$$\frac{50\% \times 1000Mbps}{(1000\ bytes \times 8)} = \text{Approximately 62,500 frames per second}$$

This calculation ignores IFG, which would reduce the frame rate by a few percentage points.

Some people (including authors) confuse packets and frames. Frames are associated with Ethernet and Layer 2; the Layer 3 protocol software, such as IP or IPX, generates packets. Packet size can vary, typically in multiples of 4KB.

Packets travel in frames: a frame encapsulates a packet. If the packet is larger than the maximum frame size, a packet is split up over multiple frames. Be careful about confusing frame and packet rates.

- *Packet rate* depends on the average packet size and the frame rate. IP packet size can vary from 4KB to 65KB, so packet rates are much smaller than frame rates.

- *Response time* is the transmission delay measured from the time the transmitter attempts the first transmission to the time the frame is successfully received. A fixed and small response time is essential for good quality of service (QoS). QoS is required for applications such as audio or video.

- *Saturation* describes the point at which an Ethernet network has reached its capacity limits. As described previously, Ethernet has a built-in overload mechanism. If nodes require more throughput than Ethernet is capable of carrying, a particular node will not receive access to the channel (carrier sense). A node will always receive access at some point, but the question is when. Saturation causes excessive delays or possible transmission errors due to timeouts. Ultimately, saturation results in an unsatisfactory response time.

- *Traffic flow* describes the typical composition of network traffic. Ethernet frames can vary in size from 64 to 1518 bytes. Most protocols in use today, such as IPX, TCP/IP, NetBIOS, and NetBEUI, create traffic that is called *bimodal*, which means that the frame distribution shows the predominance of two frame sizes. IP traffic for example consists of about 50% long frames of 1000 bytes, and another 50% will be acknowledgments of 100 bytes or less being returned. Figure 7.2 illustrates the frame size distribution in a multiprotocol network.

Typical Internet access, for example, follows this 50/50 rule relatively well. Internet access consists of large frames (less than 1KB) being downloaded from a Web server to a node, combined with small (typically around 64 bytes) acknowledgement frames being sent back. The resulting traffic, when measured in bytes, consists of about 90% receives and 10% transmits. Figure 7.3 illustrates the lopsided nature of IP traffic flow.

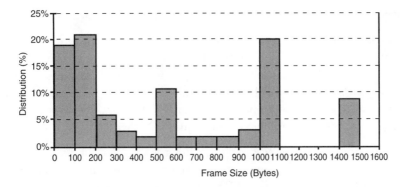

FIGURE 7.2 *Typical frame size distribution in real-world networks. Almost 50% of frames are more than 300 bytes. Also note the peaks at 1000 and 1500 bytes. (Data from tests performed at AMD, Sun Microsystems, and 3Com for 802.3z tests.)*

FIGURE 7.3 *The Windows 98 dial-up connection window shows the lopsided nature of Internet traffic, with 90% receives and 10% transmits or acknowledgements.*

What Exactly *Is* the Capacity of Ethernet?

The subject of Ethernet throughput is still a matter of great controversy, despite the fact that Ethernet is 25 years old. LAN traffic tends to come in bursts, and this tends to influence the perceived capacity substantially, so different people see different sides of the same technology. Let's look at the capacity of shared, Switched, and full-duplex Switched Ethernet. Note that the only difference between a shared and a switched (half-duplex) connection is the number of users on the network: A switched connection is limited to only two nodes!

Shared Ethernet Capacity

Ethernet's throughput capability depends on several different variables, so this question has no simple answer. The most important variable is the user, and the user's particular traffic pattern. Shared Ethernet is built on the premise that network traffic occurs in bursts. Different users will require network access at very different times and will transmit for different lengths. In this way, the capacity can be used to its fullest for the brief point in time that a particular user accesses the network. We'll find the random nature of bursts in typical network access very difficult to include, so we will assume a somewhat random, predictable traffic pattern from all users.

The maximum throughput then depends on essentially two variables:

- *Number of users*—The more users you have on a LAN, the more contention the channel will have and the more collisions occur. The maximum throughput is reached with just two nodes on a LAN, also known
  as a *switched connection*. This assumes that both nodes are capable of generating the maximum frame rate. The lowest throughput will be reached
  with the maximum number of users: 1024 for Ethernet.

- *Frame size*—As discussed previously, Ethernet throughput declines for
  smaller frames. This is intuitive because larger frames are more efficient.
  Larger frames provide the added benefit of providing less of an opportunity for channel contention and therefore collisions.

Figure 7.4 illustrates the relationship between the number of nodes, frame size,
and throughput.

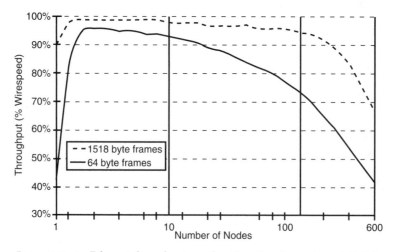

F IGURE 7.4 *Ethernet throughput as a function of node numbers plotted for minimum
and maximum frame size.*

Bob Metcalfe, the original inventor of Ethernet, and David Boggs calculated the
capacity of Ethernet as a function of frame length. They calculated the worst-case
capacity of Ethernet to be 37% for minimum frames and maximum number of
nodes: 64 bytes per 1024 nodes. With a maximum frame length of 1518 bytes,
Metcalfe and Boggs calculated that this would increase to 93%. Practical tests
have confirmed these calculations. Unfortunately, some people have taken the 64
bytes per 1024 nodes number, *the absolute worst-case capacity*, to be the *maximum*
throughput for Ethernet in all situations. As discussed, most Ethernet traffic is

bimodal, so an average frame size of around 1000 bytes is probably more realistic than 64 bytes! Most networks also don't have 1024 nodes on them, so in reality Ethernet has a capacity that far exceeds the 37%. Some real-world networks have seen utilizations of over 90%, which may sound very surprising.

The fact that Ethernet utilization can reach over 90% may surprise you. Most people will not run an Ethernet network at this kind of utilization because users will encounter unacceptable delays. Some users may find fixed delays, also known as *latency* or *response time*, acceptable, but variable delays, also known as *jitter*, are more problematic. For example, if one file transfer takes fractions of a second whereas a later, similar transfer takes several seconds, users will complain ("Why is the LAN so slow this afternoon?"). Protocol stacks also expect acknowledgment frames within a certain time window. If the acknowledgment frame does not arrive within that time, the protocol will assume the frame was discarded and will attempt a retransmission. Certain newer applications, such as audio or video, are unsuitable for transmission over a network with variable delays.

The key to determining the maximum utilization for an Ethernet network is then to establish the level of delay and jitter you are willing to tolerate. Figure 7.5 illustrates this point.

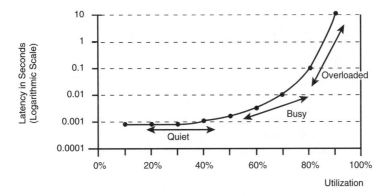

FIGURE 7.5 *A 10Mbps Ethernet response time measured as a function of utilization. Notice the three distinct operating regions. We recommend that you stay below 30% average utilization.*

Ethernet has essentially three distinct operating regions:

- *Light load (0%–50% utilization)*—When the network is running at less than 50%, the network is relatively quiet, with few collisions (less than 10%). The network is very responsive, and latencies are negligibly small, of the order of 0.001 to 0.01 second. In this mode, Ethernet provides the capability to carry audio and video traffic because jitter is not noticeable. We recommend that your average utilization stay well below this 50% line. If you find that your average utilization is approaching 30%, you should think about upgrading because an average of 30% probably corresponds to peaks of 50% or higher. An average of 30% also leaves you some headroom and therefore time to plan your upgrade properly.

- *Moderate to heavy load (50%–80% utilization)*—In this level of utilization, the network is starting to show measurable delays, ranging from 0.01 to 0.1 second. This is still acceptable for regular file transfers or accessing an application database, but jitter is becoming an issue. It is acceptable for short bursts of traffic to push the network into this level of utilization, but you shouldn't operate a network in this mode permanently.

- *Saturation (80% and higher)*—Here, the network is showing large delays, sometimes exceeding a second. The network is very busy, and the situation worsens by what is known as the *capture effect*: Some nodes are transmitting long streams of frames, whereas others are waiting seconds. This is the no-go zone for Ethernet: You'd better do something fast. When Ethernet is saturated, it is also known as *congested* or *overloaded*.

Switched Ethernet Capacity

A half-duplex Switched Ethernet connection is still a shared-media network. This means that all of the previous discussion still applies. The benefit of a switched connection is that only two nodes compete for the channel, and therefore collisions can still occur, although they are much less frequent. Accordingly, a switched connection can reliably and permanently operate at utilization levels of over 80%. Of course, the middle-of-the-road situation occurs in which a LAN consists of just a handful of users. In this case, the average utilization should be less than 90% but can still be higher than the 50% limit recommended for large LANs. From Figure 7.4, we can determine the maximum throughput by reading off the value for two nodes. For 1000 byte frames, the throughput can reach 90% of wire speed!

Full-Duplex Switched Ethernet Capacity

Full-duplex (FDX) Ethernet provides performance capabilities that exceed those of Switched Ethernet. FDX Ethernet requires a switched two-node connection. FDX Ethernet turns off the CSMA/CD MAC instead of continuously sending Ethernet frames down a transmit and receive channel. The channel has no contention, and consequently collisions cannot take place. Under ideal circumstances, full-duplex can sustain utilization rates of close to 100% on each channel. We recommend a maximum utilization rate of 95%. Adding up transmit and receive utilization then gives FDX Ethernet a limit of 190%.

In practice, the bimodal traffic flow discussed previously means that clients and servers are unlikely to exceed utilization rates of more than 130%. Full-duplex switch-switch connections, however, can reach the theoretical maximum utilization.

Improving the Ethernet MAC

Over the years, several attempts have been made to improve the Ethernet CSMA/CD MAC or increase frame size to improve the utilization level. Some of the proposed MAC changes were minor, and some proposals went as far as changing the access method altogether and doing away with collisions completely. The Gigabit Ethernet MAC also includes some very subtle changes that make the MAC just slightly different from the 10 and 100Mbps Ethernet variants. With the approval of 802.3z standard the IEEE for the first time officially modified the 25-year-old CSMA/CD Ethernet MAC algorithm. Let's look at the Gigabit Ethernet MAC in a bit more detail, as well as three other Ethernet improvements that haven't been successful.

100VG-AnyLAN

From 1991 to 1994, Hewlett-Packard developed the new 100VG-AnyLAN 100Mbps shared-media technology. The 100VG incorporated a new MAC called *demand priority*, which allowed time-critical applications to transmit ahead of other noncritical frames. 100VG uses a shared-media token-passing bus architecture without collisions to achieve very high throughput rates in heavily loaded shared-media networks. For backward compatibility, 100VG could use either Ethernet or Token Ring frame formats. Hewlett-Packard positioned 100VG as technically superior to 100BASE-T, whose supporters chose to maintain the existing CSMA/CD MAC. In the end, the IEEE decided that the CSMA/CD MAC would be maintained for the 100Mbps version of Ethernet. The IEEE did standardize 100VG as a new technology under the 802.12 umbrella. We also discuss 100VG in more detail in Chapters 1 and 2.

BLAM/IEEE 802.3w

Ethernet uses the Binary Exponential Backoff (BEB) algorithm to deal with overloading on the network. When a station senses a collision, it waits for a certain backoff time before it retries. If a collision occurs again, the backoff time is doubled from the previous attempt. If a condition of overloading occurs, the BEB ensures that different nodes wait longer and longer before being able to transmit their data. This causes the short-term load to adjust to a level that the network can support, providing for an overload control mechanism.

An individual node will attempt a retransmission up to 16 times. If transmission is still unsuccessful at that point, the backoff timer expires and the transmission is aborted. The frame is lost, and an error occurs. (The protocol stack will always ensure retransmission.)

The BEB mechanism does not treat all nodes equally. Assume that a node has been attempting to transmit for some time but has been unsuccessful. Its BEB counter has been escalated to ten, which is a significant lapse of time. If a new node now tries to attempt a transmission, its counter is still set to zero. This means the newer node may complete a transmission before the node that has been waiting. If a network is very busy, a node that has been waiting for some time may then suddenly gain access to the network and be allowed to send a series of frames in a row. This is known as the *channel capture effect* because it allows a node to capture the channel for quite some time, which is an undesirable condition especially in busy networks.

In 1995, the IEEE started the 802.3w working group to investigate an improved CSMA/CD backoff algorithm. The binary logarithmic arbitration (BLAM) was supposed to improve the existing CSMA/CD BEB algorithm. This would improve the maximum utilization levels that shared Ethernet can operate (discussed in more detail later). The BEB algorithm would also fix the Ethernet channel capture effect, which can allocate bandwidth in a preferential and unfair manner to certain nodes.

Unfortunately, BLAM was too little, too late. While the IEEE 802.3w engineers were investigating BLAM, other IEEE groups were already working on full-duplex and Gigabit Ethernet. Full-duplex Ethernet, in effect, turns off the Ethernet MAC, so BLAM is not applicable. The 802.3w efforts were abandoned in 1997.

802.3z/Gigabit Ethernet

With Gigabit Ethernet, the familiar CSMA/CD MAC has been modified for the first time. The IEEE 802.3z specification defines both half- and full-duplex operation. Half-duplex Gigabit Ethernet specifies a minimum slot time of 512 bytes, as opposed to 64 bytes for 10 and 100Mbps Ethernet. When frames of less than 512 bytes are transmitted, the CSMA/CD MAC adds carrier extension (CE) bits to meet the minimum slot time requirement. This makes Gigabit Ethernet very inefficient for small frames because large amounts of useless carrier extension bits are transmitted.

For example, let's assume that we wanted to transmit only 64 byte minimum size frames. The carrier extension would add 438 bytes of carrier extension to meet the spec of a 512 byte slot time. To calculate the overall efficiency, we still need to add the IFG overhead of 12 bytes: $64/(512+12) = 12\%$ efficiency, or 122 Mbps. This is only marginally better than 100BASE-T!

Small frames are quite common, so this inefficiency for small frame sizes needed to be addressed. The IEEE 802.3z Gigabit MAC also includes a feature called *burst mode*. In this case, a station may continuously transmit multiple smaller frames, up to a maximum of 8,192 bytes of data. The interframe intervals will also be filled with carrier extension so that the wire never appears free to any other stations during the burst cycle. Note that all these modifications apply to half-duplex shared operation only. So far, no half-duplex 802.3z equipment is available. Please refer to Chapter 3 for further details on the modified Gigabit Ethernet MAC.

Jumbo Frames

Another proposal is called *jumbo frames*, as in very large frames. Jumbo frames are not a CSMA/CD modification; in fact, they only work in a full-duplex environment. Jumbo frames are, however, one of those attempts to touch the "Holy Grail" of Ethernet, namely frame size and the CSMA/CD MAC.

Jumbo frames would increase the maximum frame size from the current 1,518 bytes to 9,000 bytes. As the overhead is fixed per frame, increasing the frame size will make Ethernet more efficient. For 1,518 byte frames, the overhead and IFG account for about 2.5% efficiency loss. Increasing the frame size to 9,000 bytes would increase the efficiency to over 99%. The second, and more important, reason some people are advocating jumbo frames is to improve server performance. Every individual frame transmitted requires the server CPU (or desktop for that matter) to perform some data processing. Once the frame transmission is underway, the server CPU can leave the task unattended. Increasing the frame size reduces the number of CPU interrupts and therefore improves the computers' utilization and throughput. Preliminary tests show that today's servers are not capable of completely filling a Gigabit Ethernet pipe. With 100% CPU utilization, servers at this point are only capable of delivering a maximum data rate of around 400Mbps. Increasing the frame size by a factor of 5 reduces the number of CPU interrupts considerably, and therefore allows servers to get closer to the 1Gbps mark. (1Gbps still can't be accomplished today due to other performance limitations, primarily the PCI bus.)

Ethernet Capacity Recap

We have no single rule of thumb as to what utilization a shared Ethernet network can accommodate because utilization is a function of numerous variables. In real networks with bimodal frame data flow, an average utilization of 50% and a peak utilization of 80% are good guidelines to determine the limits of your Ethernet LAN.

Delay or response time increases exponentially with the number of nodes. Consequently, we recommend that you stay below 200 users for a shared LAN segment. Collisions are a normal part of the control mechanism of Ethernet. Collisions of up to 20% are quite acceptable.

Switched Ethernet connections have two major advantages in that the available bandwidth does not have to be time-shared with numerous other stations. The connection can also operate at up to 90% utilization, if required. Full-duplex Ethernet provides even more performance by allowing for simultaneous transmission and reception. Under ideal circumstances, 95% utilization on each cable pair can be achieved, which increases the theoretical utilization limit to 190%. Table 7.2 summarizes the real-world throughput capabilities of 10Mbps, 100Mbps shared, Switched, and Switched FDX Ethernet.

TABLE 7.2   A RULE-OF-THUMB GUIDELINE FOR ETHERNET UTILIZATION LIMITS

Connection Type	Wire Speed	Average Utilization Limit
Shared Ethernet	10Mbps	30%
Shared Ethernet used for multimedia traffic	10Mbps	20%
Switched Ethernet	10Mbps	85%
Switched FDX Ethernet	10Mbps	190%
Shared Fast Ethernet	100Mbps	30%
Shared Fast Ethernet used for multimedia traffic	100Mbps	20%
Switched Fast Ethernet	100Mbps	85%
Switched FDX Fast Ethernet	100Mbps	190%
Shared FDX Gigabit Ethernet[1]	1000Mbps	60%
Switched FDX Gigabit Ethernet	1000Mbps	190%

[1] *At the time of writing this book, all Gigabit Ethernet products shipping were full-duplex. No products or even plans exist for half-duplex repeaters. A few vendors are, however, shipping a new kind of device called a full-duplex repeater or buffered distributor. This device doesn't share the bandwidth but essentially acts like a switch that operates permanently in broadcast mode. The utilization limits for FDX repeaters lie somewhere in between those of classic repeaters and switches and depend to a large degree on the internal buffering capabilities of the particular FDX repeater. To play it safe, we recommend the same utilization rates as for regular half-duplex repeaters, times a factor of two for FDX operation.*

Tools to Measure Loading

The nice thing about a shared-media network is that all the traffic is transmitted to all points on the network simultaneously. That means you can "tune in" or listen for traffic at any point on the LAN and find out what the utilization is like. For switched or segmented networks, the procedure becomes much more cumbersome. You may have to measure each segment or connection physically in order to get an accurate reading of the traffic on that segment. (Remote monitoring probes now allow you to measure utilization in different segments from one physical point. We discuss these in more detail in Chapter 11, "Managing Switched and Fast Ethernet Networks.")

Raw Data Throughput Limit	Peak Utilization Limit	Peak Data Throughput Limit
3.0Mbps	80%	8Mbps
2.0Mbps	50%	5Mbps
8.5Mbps	90%	9Mbps
19Mbps	190%	19Mbps
30Mbps	80%	80Mbps
20Mbps	50%	50Mbps
85Mbps	90%	90Mbps
190Mbps	190%	190Mbps
600Mbps	120%	1600Mbps
1900Mbps	190%	1900Mbps

Many kinds of tools are available for analyzing the loading of Ethernet networks. We mention a variety of products here that allow you to measure utilization levels in the hope that you will have at least one of them around to do the job. The most common tools available for network analysis are software-based traffic analyzers. Protocol analyzers will also do the job because they all include some traffic monitoring tools. Hardware-assisted protocol analyzers, the ultimate in networking tools, also allow you to measure traffic levels, although they are a complete overkill for the task of measuring network utilization. Last, a new breed of hand-held diagnostic tools may be the best choice for measuring utilization.

Traffic Monitoring Tools and Protocol Analyzers

You can buy a traffic monitoring software package for relatively little money. These applications measure the essential variables, such as packet sends and receives, network utilization, protocol distribution, and bandwidth utilization. For monitoring traffic levels in switched networks, some provide RMON support. Trending and charting capabilities are nice extras.

Protocol analyzers also allow you to figure out exactly where specific frames of data are coming from and going. Protocol analyzers are very sophisticated tools, primarily used for troubleshooting networks. (See Chapter 12, "Troubleshooting," for more details.) You can, however, use them to measure network utilization as well. Most protocol analysis packages sold offer both protocol analysis as well as traffic monitoring capabilities. For our purpose here, you really only need the traffic monitoring part, but for troubleshooting your network, the protocol analysis features will come in very useful, so protocol analyzers do deserve a closer look.

Many of today's desktop management suites also contain some protocol and traffic analysis tools. For example, Intel's LANDesk Management Suite, Novell's ManageWise, and Tivoli's TMS all contain some tools that allow you to monitor traffic levels. Figure 7.6 shows Intel's LANDesk Traffic Analyst, which is part of LANDesk Management Suite. The really useful network analyzers, however, are sold as separate applications. Many packages can do this job for you. We recommend that you look at specialized products from companies like Triticom or Network Instruments. Figure 7.7 shows Triticom's LANDecoder32 package in action.

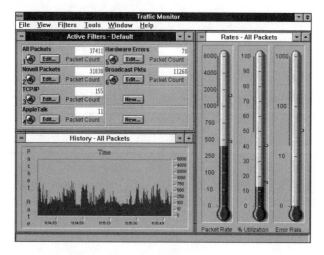

FIGURE 7.6 *Many desktop and network management packages, such as Intel's LANDesk Management Suite, feature built-in traffic monitoring capabilities.*

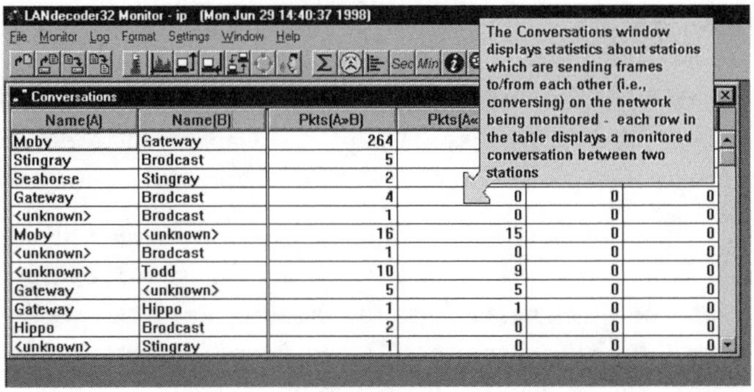

FIGURE 7.7 *A dedicated LAN analysis/protocol analyzer software package should be part of your toolkit.*

Hardware-Assisted Protocol Analyzers

Hardware-assisted protocol analyzers are expert tools used for analyzing and troubleshooting networks. Hardware-assisted protocol analyzers typically run on a PC and include a special network interface card. Probably the best-known protocol analyzer is the Sniffer, made by Network Associates (previously known as Network General).

The Sniffer protocol analyzer does exactly what its name implies: It analyzes data down to the protocol level, looking "inside" the actual data frame to capture information such as protocol type (IP, IPX, and so on). For larger switched or routed environments, Network Associates also makes a version of the Sniffer called Distributed Sniffer that lets you monitor remote sites either in-band with the aid of RMON or through an out-of-band telephone link.

Network Management Software

If you are running a network management application, you may already have the right tool to measure your networks' loading. Most manageable hubs collect statistics that include some traffic data. You can usually view this data from any SNMP network management platform, such as CiscoWorks, or Bay Networks Optivity. With switches, you'll have a little more difficulty monitoring traffic levels, but most switches these days also provide this capability. In this case, the management software allows you to look at the traffic of each switched port. The SNMP remote monitoring function, called RMON, often achieves this. We cover network management in more detail in Chapter 11.

Handheld Diagnostic Tools

To date, two very different kinds of portable testers have been available: protocol analyzers that run on a PC and small, hand-held cable testers. Some of the newer hand-held cable testers that we discuss in Chapter 6, "Cabling and More on Physical Layers," now incorporate some network utilization functions as well.

Recently, a new category of hand-held diagnostic tool has emerged that can test a variety of Layer 2 and 3 network functions. These new testers are primarily targeted at portable and quick network troubleshooting. Examples are the Compas from Microtest, the FrameScope 802 from Scope Communications, and the Fluke LANMeter. These new Ethernet "handymen" include a variety of features, such as cable testing, protocol and frame analysis, server monitoring and diagnostics, and general traffic measurements. We are interested in the last function. You can use these diagnostic tools to measure utilization and collision rates. Whereas these tools do not provide the level of functionality that a dedicated protocol or cable tester does, they are very useful portable tools. Table 7.3 summarizes the various functions these different hand-held devices perform. Figure 7.8 shows the focus areas of these different tools.

TABLE 7.3 SUMMARY OF THE DIFFERENT TOOLS PROVIDING INFORMATION ON TRAFFIC LEVELS

Tool	Example	Focus Area (OSI Layer)
Traffic monitoring software	Triticom EtherVision	L2 Traffic
Protocol analysis software	Triticom LANDecoder32	L3 packets plus L2 frames
Desktop management suites	Novell ManageWise 2.6	Managing clients and servers From L2 frames to L8 apps
Network management software	Bay Networks Optivity	SNMP hub, switch, router management
Hardware-assisted Protocol analyzers	Network Associates Sniffer	Detailed protocol analysis and troubleshooting
Handheld diagnostics tools	Scope Communications FrameScope 802	Portable cable and network diagnosis

[1] *In this table, use the following key:*
$ A few hundred dollars
$$ Around a thousand dollars
$$$ A few thousand dollars
$$$$ Tens of thousands of dollars

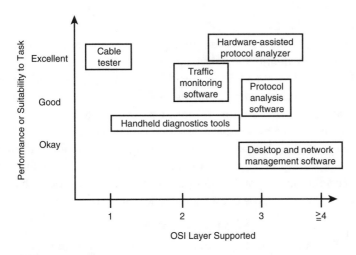

FIGURE 7.8 *A plethora of network tools are available, from handheld cable testers to enterprise management platforms. You can typically find the differences among all these products in the coverage area as well as the price.*

OSI Layer Supported	Price	Portability	More Info From
2, 3	$[1]	Any desktop notebook PC	www.triticom.com/
3, 2	$$	Any desktop notebook PC	www.triticom.com/ www.network instruments.com/
2-8	"free" — bundled	Any desktop notebook PC	www.novell.com/ www.intel.com/
3	$$$$	UNIX-based management console	hub or switch vendor
3 and 2	$$$	Any desktop PC plus special NIC	www.nai.com/ www.wg.com/
1, 2, 3	$$	Handheld	Www.scope.com/ www.fluke.com/ www.microtest.com/

Upgrading Your Network

You need to look at several areas in order to fix the bottlenecks in your network. First of all, you need to identify the individual nodes that are in need of more bandwidth. These nodes could be responsible for generating the high utilization rates on a shared or switched LAN. Examples are servers or power users generating a lot of traffic. You will also need to look at complete segments because congestion could be caused by the sheer mass of individual nodes all contributing to the problem. Lastly, an interconnect or backbone section could be the bottleneck. As we don't know what your network looks like, this section will only discuss some general concepts of discovering where in your network the bottlenecks are. You will have to figure out which upgrade steps to pursue.

Which Nodes Are Generating the Most Traffic?

In a truly switched environment, only one station exists on a segment, and that one node generates all the utilization or traffic. In a fully or partially shared network, you have a little more difficulty determining exactly where your bottlenecks are occurring because multiple nodes share the same wire.

TABLE 7.4 RECORDING INDIVIDUAL NODE TRAFFIC PATTERNS

Connection Name	Type of Connection	Client/Server Source Address
Client 1	Shared 10Mbps	00AAXXXX
Client 2	Shared 10Mbps	0020XXXX
Client 3	Shared 10Mbps	00EAXXXX
Client 4	Shared 10Mbps	0020XXXX
Client 5	Shared 10Mbps	00EAXXXX
Switch Uplink	Shared 10Mbps	N/A[1]
Server	Switched 10Mbps	00AAXXXX
Router	Switched 10Mbps	N/A[2]
Backbone	Switched 10Mbps	N/A[2]

[1] *In a shared network, the utilization is the same for all nodes. By looking at the Ethernet source address, you can determine the traffic being generated by individual nodes.*

[2] *Switches and routers also have their own MAC addresses but don't generate any data of their own, so looking at their MAC address is of no use to us.*

Most of the tools discussed previously can help you to figure out which nodes are creating the traffic. If you are dealing with a shared segment, you will need to look at the individual source addresses to determine the culprits. The good news is that most protocol analyzers display and group traffic for you in terms of source and destination address, quickly allowing you to figure out which individual nodes are creating the most traffic. Gathering this information will be most useful when you move on to Part IV, which discusses the upgrade options. Your network could, for example, look like the one shown in Figure 7.9. The network shown is in some trouble. The repeated segment is completely overloaded, and only through the use of a protocol analyzer can you determine that two power users cause the high utilization rate. Use Table 7.4 as an example of how to record individual traffic patterns.

Collision Domain Name	Traffic Generated	Segment Utilization[1]	Type of Station
Shared Workgroup 1 (switch port 1)	0.5Mbps	70%	Normal user
	0.5Mbps	70%	Normal user
	1Mbps	70%	Normal user
	5Mbps	70%	Power user
	5Mbps	70%	Power user
Switch port 1	3Mbps	70%	Switch uplink
Switch port 2	5Mbps	50%	Server
Switch port 3	1Mbps	10%	Router/WAN
Switch port 4	2Mbps	20%	Backbone

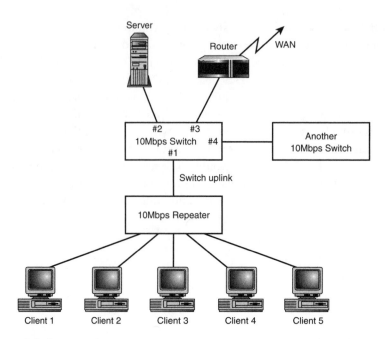

FIGURE 7.9   *Analyzing the different segments in a network in order to determine actual and planned utilization levels.*

What to Do When Your Network Is Overloaded

You'll find detailed how-to information in Part IV, but the following list will provide you with some early ideas on what to do.

TABLE 7.5   UPGRADE ANALYSIS

Connection Name	Type of Connection	Collision Domain Name
Client 1	Shared 10Mbps	Shared Workgroup 1 (switch port 1)
Client 2	Shared 10Mbps	
Client 3	Shared 10Mbps	
Client 4	Shared 10Mbps	
Client 5	Shared 10Mbps	
Switch Uplink	Shared 10Mbps	
Server	Switched 10Mbps	Switch port 2
Router	Switched 10Mbps	Switch port 3
Backbone	Switched 10Mbps	Switch port 4

- Note average and peak utilization rates for different segments over at least a 24-hour period.

- Decide on target utilization rates. Switched connections can operate at much higher utilization rates than shared ones. Decide whether any nodes, such as power users or servers, should have priority access.

- For some nodes, it may be beneficial to understand the destination address of the traffic. For example, it is not clear from Figure 7.9 whether the two power users are sharing files in a peer-to-peer fashion or whether they are both accessing the server a lot.

- If you decide that a connection or segment needs upgrading, think about any upstream repercussions. Let's look at our network shown in Figure 7.9 to see an example of this. Providing each client with a switched 10Mbps connection will probably result in the 10Mbps switch uplink becoming a bottleneck.

- Provide for some future traffic growth. For example, you may want to provide the engineering segment with a little more bandwidth because you expect the company to hire additional engineers over the next year. You may also want to provide the advertising department with a lower peak rate because of the large desktop publishing files the group transfers across the network.

Use Table 7.5 to note the data and guide you in your analysis.

Traffic Generated	Average Utilization	Target Utilization	Conclusion/ Upgrade Candidate?
0.5Mbps	70%	20%	Connection okay/No
0.5Mbps	70%	20%	Connection okay/No
1Mbps	70%	20%	Connection okay/No
5Mbps	70%	20%	Close to limit/Next quarter
5Mbps	70%	20%	Close to limit/Next quarter
3Mbps	70%	20%	Big bottleneck; connection saturated/ASAP
5Mbps	50%	40%	Close to limit/Soon
1Mbps	10%	20%	Connection okay/No
2Mbps	20%	40%	Connection okay/No

How to Upgrade Your Network

Part IV discusses a series of upgrade steps that will provide you incremental bandwidth for an overloaded network. After performing an upgrade, you will need to measure your utilization rate again and compare it with your targets. If the rates are still too high, you haven't done enough. If the rate has dropped below your target rate, you have excess capacity, which is perfectly acceptable. This means that you have room to enlarge in the future. Don't go overboard, however: there is no point in giving your average user a switched 100Mbps connection when he or she only generates 0.5 Mbps of data today.

The difficult part of any upgrade is what we call the *ripple effect*. For example, if you upgrade a shared workgroup with a switch, you will probably fix the problem for that workgroup, but you might at the same time cause another section of the network to become overloaded. In effect, removing a bottleneck in one area will only expose another one somewhere else.

You have three ways of performing an upgrade:

- You may need to base some of your upgrade work on trial ñand error, which is rather cumbersome. You can upgrade one section, measure loads again, and see if you need to perform an upgrade further upstream somewhere.

- Alternatively, if you know the traffic being generated by individual clients and servers, you can use a calculator and a diagram of your network to plot overall traffic flow patterns and possible bottlenecks. You could plot all clients and servers, hubs, switches, and routers on your network. You would need to know how much of a client's traffic is going to a server, or to the router. Then, add up all the individual traffic flows for the nodes at key hub, switch, or router points to determine theoretical utilization rates.

- Some sophisticated network modeling packages are now available that will, in essence, automate the task described in the previous option. One such application is NetSys, sold by Cisco. If you are building or upgrading a large network, this approach deserves a closer look.

Some of the software analyzers discussed previously also let you artificially generate traffic to expose hidden bottlenecks. This allows you to simulate future traffic growth, or different configurations, without physically changing things yet.

Why Today's Networks Are Running Out of Bandwidth

Ethernet, as we know it, is 25 years old. When Bob Metcalfe developed Ethernet at Xerox PARC in the early 1970s, it ran at 2.94Mbps. Later, the speed increased to 10Mbps, which seemed much faster than any computer network at the time could require. Metcalfe's intention was to create a technology that would last about 30 years: ten years to standardize and bring products to market, followed by ten years of growth, and then ten years of decline and obsolescence.

That model has worked relatively well, and now, 25 years after its invention, shared Ethernet is running out of steam. What Metcalfe did not envision in his 30-year plan were life extending technologies, such as Switched, Fast, and Gigabit Ethernet, which will give Ethernet at least another ten years of existence. Let's look at the theory and practical reasons for why today's 10Mbps Ethernet networks are running out of bandwidth.

Moore's Law

In the early 1970s Ethernet networks were primarily used to connect minicomputers, where one MIPS represented a lot of computing power. 10Mbps Ethernet was more than adequate to connect these types of computing devices. The PC revolution, driven by the microprocessor, also started during this time when Intel invented the first microprocessor, the 4004, in 1971. Almost ten years later, the IBM PC AT, powered by an Intel 80286 microprocessor, surpassed the 1-MIPS barrier. At about this time, Gordon Moore, cofounder and chairman of Intel, observed an empirical law describing semiconductor design and manufacturing capabilities. Moore's Law states the number of transistors that can be integrated into a semiconductor chip doubles every 24 months. For 25 years, this rule has been accurate. As a result, today's personal computers based on the Intel Pentium II processor feature more than 300 MIPS of processing power, a phenomenal threehundredfold increase from the 286 of 17 years ago. During those two decades, the speed of a desktop connection has remained unchanged at 10Mbps.

We would like to quote two examples of how personal computer throughput has advanced over the last 10 years. In 1988, Boggs, one of the inventors of Ethernet, published a major study on the capacity of Ethernet. The Titan PC that Boggs was using 10 years ago couldn't saturate a 10Mbps Ethernet connection. Also in 1988, another researcher, Van Jacobean, published test results featuring Sun workstations transmitting at 9.2Mbps. Many people considered these numbers phenomenal at the time, and some even viewed them with disbelief. Today, an entry-level Pentium II- based PC, featuring a PCI bus, can saturate a 100Mbps Ethernet connection. Figure 7.10 graphs the exponential growth of PC MIPS and Ethernet bandwidth.

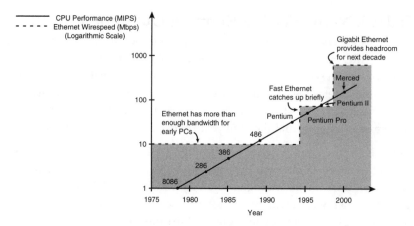

Figure 7.10 *Ethernet remained a 10Mbps technology for almost 25 years, whereas PC performance grew steadily during that same timeframe.*

Practical Reasons Why You Are Running Out of Bandwidth

Many factors explain today's alarming rate of bandwidth consumption. We have divided these "bandwidth consumers" into three categories:

- More of the same: just more of the same predictable growth in users, servers, and client-server applications

- The Internet and its radically different traffic flow

- New applications and the convergence of voice and data networks

Let's look at these in a bit more detail.

"More of the Same"

First, we will examine the impact that more users and more servers have on your network:

- *More users*—Corporate networks have been hit with a double whammy of growth over the last few years. First, personal computer sales have been booming, with year-to-year growth exceeding 20% for the last decade. As a result, around 100 million personal computers will be sold worldwide in 1998, up from just 20 million as recently as eight years ago. Most of these 100 million computers will end up being networked, either via an Ethernet connection in an office or via a modem in the home. Many new

PCs ship with a 10/100 Ethernet connection or a 56.6 analog modem bundled or built: an indication of how pervasive networking has become. More Ethernet nodes add directly to the traffic on your LAN, but all those home PCs also do so, although indirectly. That's because all those home PCs dial into some LAN network somewhere to access Internet servers, and this traffic ultimately gets added to your LAN traffic load somewhere.

Note

By the end of 1998, around 100 million PCs will have been sold, bringing the installed base to more than 250 million. Intel has predicted that the world will have a billion connected PCs in the next decade.

Every new white-collar employee automatically receives a PC these days. Soon after the PC arrives, it is connected to a LAN. Bingo: more traffic on your LAN! Look for the number of PCs in your company to continue increasing at about 20% per year, and look for the percentage of PCs that are connected to reach 95% by the end of the decade.

- *More file, print, and application servers*—Of course, all those new users mean more traffic, so you will need more servers and printers to service the growing client base. As we know, file, print, and email servers are just the beginning. Networked fax servers, centrally accessible CD-ROM drives, and other application servers will continue growing. These types of servers often transfer large files across the network, not just ASCII text any more. For example, an incoming fax being sent across the LAN can often be a few hundred kilobytes in size, which is two orders of magnitude larger than a regular email message.

- *More branch offices*—Only recently has networking infiltrated branch offices as well. Today, most branch offices only use their LANs to share printers and files, so their traffic doesn't affect your main office LAN traffic. As the push toward enterprisewide connectivity continues, these remote offices are being connected via a router/WAN to the main corporate network. Look for the routed traffic from these remote sites to start loading up your main network, too. The bottom line will be more nodes and more traffic. Here, email and database access will primarily drive applications.

- *Client/server computing*—Client-server computing, for years a buzzword, has finally arrived. Servers are replacing many mainframes and minicomputers, and while this doesn't necessarily add up to more traffic, the applications residing on these servers work very differently. Take, for example, SAP AG's R/3 business application program for client-server environments. The architecture of R/3 by definition consumes lots of bandwidth. SAP runs on a large central server, coupled to many smaller front-end servers, that in turn communicate with the desktops. Data is continuously sent back and forth among all components. R/3 is only one of a kind: Numerous other client-server applications are being sold today from companies like Peoplesoft, Baan, and AG Edwards.

- *More electronic mail*—A *killer app* is an application that every user needs or wants. The first killer apps were the word processor and the spreadsheet. For example, 20 years ago many people bought an Apple II to run the original spreadsheet called VisiCalc. Later on, many companies bought PCs to replace their typewriters with WordPerfect. Today, every PC features a word processor and a spreadsheet. Electronic mail is the latest such latest killer app. Electronic mail is also the first networked killer app: after all, there is no point in sending emails to yourself. More and more PC users are adopting email. To compound the email traffic growth, we are no longer just sending 3K ASCII files, but we are instead transmitting 3K ASCII text files with 3MB PowerPoint attachments. This represents a thousandfold file size increase!

- *More databases*—Server-based relational databases have become extremely popular among business today. Databases have become significantly larger and powerful. In addition, the front-ends available are more user-friendly, and therefore many more people now have access to some networked database somewhere. These relational databases consume large amounts of LAN bandwidth because lots of data is being transferred back and forth.

- *Niche applications everywhere*—For most desktop applications, 10Mbps Ethernet is enough. Several leading-edge applications in use, however, already have pushed 10Mbps Ethernet LANs to the limit. For example, design artists using their Macintosh computers for desktop publishing or prepress work need more than 10Mbps throughput rates if they hope to finish their work without too much delay. Engineers running computer-aided simulations on their workstations already run them at night when the network is empty. Stock traders doing time-critical financial analyses have already replaced their Ethernet equipment with higher speed networking hardware. While these applications aren't "killer apps," there are certainly so many different niche apps that your company is bound to have one or more of them running somewhere on your LAN.

- *More groupware*—PC LAN-based email as an application has been in existence for many years. Some newer applications, such as Microsoft Exchange, Outlook, and Lotus Notes, represent an interesting mix of email, scheduling software, and distributed databases. These types of applications are known as groupware and often involve a central database server and networked client platforms that communicate frequently with the central server to exchange all sorts of individual or group data.

- *More data to back up*—As the network becomes a much larger and more important company asset, it makes good business sense to protect and insure that asset. Today's network backup and storage products provide the programmability and flexibility to do this at night, but at a speed of 10 Mbps, you will soon run out of nighttime hours to do a backup job. For example, a server with 10 Gigabytes of data takes about six hours to back it up, assuming there's no other load on the network. If you have the network available from 7 p.m. to 7 a.m. for backup purposes, you can back up two servers in that time. That's it. It's easy to see how you can run out of backup time. You will soon discover that 10Mbps Ethernet just can't cope anymore. For example, your servers may be larger than 10 Gigabytes, other traffic may be on the LAN at night, you may have more than two servers, or you may choose to back up clients as well.

The Internet

Some analysts have called the Internet the most significant invention of the Twentieth Century. Only time will tell whether that will be true. We do know that in as little as five years, the Internet has become the most successful PC killer app ever. The Internet is really a conglomeration of applications including email, Web browsing, ftp file downloads, newsgroups, IRC chat rooms, online shopping, data warehousing, WAN connectivity, and a host of other applications. So how does the Internet add traffic to your self-contained LAN? Internet traffic will affect your LAN traffic in different areas. Your employees are accessing the Internet from *within* your network. The traffic goes from your LAN, to your WAN connection, and then onto the Internet. Your network users will use the LAN as a local, fast, and secure Internet, called an *intranet*. If your company puts up an FTP or WWW server of its own, remote Internet users may have to access your WWW server across the LAN.

We wanted to cover three elements of the Internet that affect your LAN traffic. First, the Internet is creating unprecedented amounts of raw traffic. Second, Internet data traffic flows are very different from LAN traffic patterns to which we have become accustomed, causing server and backbone bottlenecks. The

Internet has also made desktop PC-based multimedia a reality. Let's look at these three elements in a bit more detail:

- *More traffic*—The Internet, originally a worldwide WAN, is used to living on data rates measured in Kilobytes per second. Most home Internet users are still living with a 28.8 or 33.6 Kbps connection, and today's Internet infrastructure still caters to these slow users. Office-based Ethernet desktops connected to the Net are running at 10,000Kbps, so the desktop connection is never a problem.

  Routers, backbones, and servers are feeling the cumulative impact, though. Within a corporate LAN, many users are accessing the World Wide Web simultaneously, and given enough users, multiple smaller data streams do add up relatively quickly. These days, many Ethernet LANs are connected to the Internet via powerful 1.544 Mbps T1 links. This 1.544 Mbps already represents about 20% of the real-world capacity of a shared Ethernet LAN, which can put many a shared network over the top.

  Then there is the local intranet traffic. WAN router connections are not constraining this internal traffic, which has become a significant source of traffic volume. Employees now post huge files, such as photos or presentations, on their personal Web pages that fellow employees download. This increase in traffic tends to overload the backbone and uplink connections.

  Of course, a company's own public Web server presence will cause a lot of traffic, depending on the number of external connections and number of servers connected to the Web. For traffic and security reasons, this traffic is typically confined to a specific area of the network.

  Most companies still use private WAN connections to link different sites in a secure and reliable manner. A new development called *virtual private networks* (*VPNs*) allows you to use the Internet as a secure wide area networking connection. VPNs encrypt the data for secure transmission via the Internet and take advantage of the Internet as a lower cost alternative to a leased line. A VPN itself doesn't add any more traffic to your LAN than a leased line. VPNs do make WAN access cheaper and therefore more popular, causing more LAN traffic.

- *Very different traffic flows*—The Internet has turned existing traffic flows upside down. In the old "NetWare 3.11 file-and-print world," about 80% of traffic remained local within the workgroup. For example, the print job would be sent to a printer just down the hall, or the file to be shared with a coworker would reside on the server around the corner. The remaining balance of 20% traffic was email destined for a "remote" location, a file access to a server residing in a different department, or some kind of WAN access. With the Internet, this 80/20 rule has been turned upside down into a 20/80 rule. These days, 80% of traffic seems to be destined for a remote location. For example, users now access servers or personal Web pages in different workgroups far more frequently than those in their department. The WAN connection is permanently being upgraded to keep up with demand for remote access. Again, this change in traffic patterns can be accommodated with 10Mbps connections, but servers are feeling the burden of additional users. Backbones and uplinks in particular are straining under this increase in traffic because they were most likely designed to carry only 20%, not 80% of your traffic. Figure 7.11 illustrates this phenomenon.

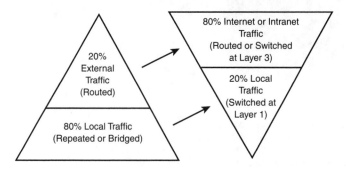

FIGURE 7.11   *The Internet has changed the rules of LAN traffic distribution, turning the 80/20 rule upside down. This has a huge impact of the network design.*

- *Multimedia—Multimedia* describes the content and the type of data that is being transferred across the network, rather than the use to which the data is put. Multimedia uses a lot of bandwidth. To many people, the phrase "a picture is worth a thousand words" captures the essence of multimedia very well. "Multimedia takes up 1000 times the bandwidth" is what it should mean to you as a LAN manager.

  For years, multimedia was one of the computer industry's buzzwords that never materialized. In the last three years, browser plug-ins from companies like RealAudio, ShockWave, Microsoft, and Netscape have brought multimedia to everyone's PC. Today, many Web pages feature photos and some kind of animation, and many browsers let you download audio and video clips, listen to speeches or concerts online, sample music CDs, and so on. Of course, these multimedia downloads generate a significant amount of traffic. (Most of them don't run well unless you have a 56.6 Kbps modem connection or better.) Figure 7.12 shows the MSNBC Web page, a joint Microsoft/NBC project that features many video and audio clips. Also, new applications, such as Pointcast (shown in Figure 7.13), download large amounts of data to your browser. Again, the individual data streams are not very significant, but multiplied by a few hundred certainly become significant.

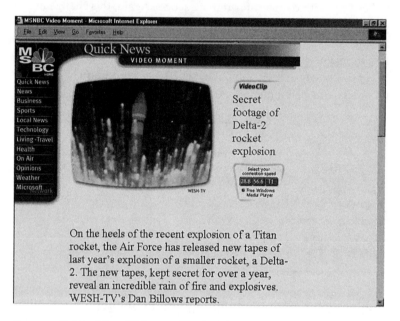

FIGURE 7.12 *Many Web pages like CNN's and MSNBC's now feature audio and video streams.*

Internet traffic growth volume is forecasted to double each year. Right now, individual modem speed and corporate WAN access speeds are a problem. Both issues are being worked on. ISDN and 56.6K modems offer data rates significantly higher than today's 33.6 connections. New technologies, such as Asynchronous Digital Subscriber Line (ADSL) and cable modems, will provide Internet access at speed of 1Mbps and beyond. For WAN access, companies can now buy more bandwidth at significantly lower prices. These factors mean that the bandwidth crunch being created by the Internet on your WAN will only get worse. Make sure that your backbone and server connections, in particular, are ready for a lot more traffic growth.

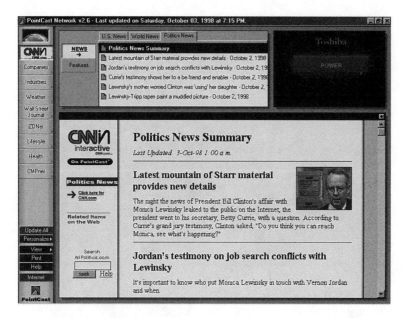

FIGURE 7.13 *Pointcast is a newscast application that downloads news from the Web automatically at a predetermined time. When it first came out, the automatically scheduled morning update overwhelmed many networks.*

New Applications

The possible applications of computers and networks seem to be endless. Many novel applications may or may not become your next killer app. Most, if not all of them, will involve some element of voice, video, file sharing, or animation. Let's look at some of the new applications that combine voice and video:

- *Videoconferencing*—For years videoconferencing has been discussed as the natural evolution of email and the telephone (as well as airline travel). Figure 7.14 shows a PC equipped with videoconferencing hardware and software. Video conferencing hasn't taken off in the last few years as forecasted because, among other reasons, the hardware has been expensive, has not been very user-friendly, and has required expensive and hard-to-get ISDN lines. (Group- or room-based videoconferencing has become very popular, but this kind of equipment is typically connected via dedicated ISDN lines and not the mainstream data network.) Internet voice or video calls seem to be becoming more popular by the day, especially when vendors like Microsoft integrate NetMeeting into their browsers.

FIGURE 7.14 *Videoconferencing hasn't become the next killer app yet, but if or when it does, it will consume large amounts of bandwidth.*

- *The networked computer model*—A few years ago, companies like Oracle, Sun, and IBM began promoting a new architectural computing model based on the network computer (NC). The NC architecture consists of a large server, surrounded by very thin clients. Originally, the NC didn't have a hard disk, it didn't have an Intel microprocessor, and it didn't run a Microsoft operating system. (In the NC world, this kind of device is known as a *fat client*.) The NC relies on a fast network connection and a powerful server to run all its server-based applications. The NC was positioned to be the ultimate in client-server computing, offering significantly lower total cost of ownership than the fat clients, as well as significantly lower purchase costs. So far, the NC hasn't made an impact, failing to deliver on most scores. In addition, for a LAN manager worried about bandwidth, the NC is a nightmare. Whereas the fat client model only transfers user files or contents back and forth, the NC transfers entire operating systems and applications back and forth. That's several Megabytes every time an application launches, which is too much for most LAN managers. The biggest drawback of the NC is that it doesn't run all of today's existing applications.

- *The convergence of voice and data networks*—Today, most people in the developed world have a telephone, and more than a billion phone numbers are in operation. By comparison, only about 200 million Ethernet nodes are installed. Yet voice traffic is going digital, so what could be a better transmission medium for digital voice than Ethernet? A lot of development is underway in this area.

Voice over IP and *IP telephony* describe the integration of voice traffic with today's private IP networks. Many hardware vendors (ranging from networking giant Cisco to startups such as Intelliswitch, Selsius, or WebSonic) are already selling equipment that integrates voice capability with IP. Voice over IP is an evolving technology. We see three main focus areas right now:

- Many large companies have large countrywide or global networks that consist of many fixed-cost leased lines. Today's voice over IP hardware typically uses the existing IP-based LAN/WAN infrastructure to carry some amount of internal voice traffic, as opposed to the PBX. Voice over IP sometimes uses the ITU H.323 standard for audioconferencing and videoconferencing to transmit voice over IP data networks.

- Internet-based long-distance calls are where companies are trying to take advantage of the low cost of Internet connectivity. International calls, being particularly expensive, are a focus area for Internet-based telephony.

- Some companies are looking at seamless integration of IP-based telephony with the public switched telephone network (PSTN). The IP fabric can route internal calls through the internal LAN/WAN infrastructure, whereas external calls are switched to the PSTN.

Figure 7.15 illustrates these three different examples of IP telephony.

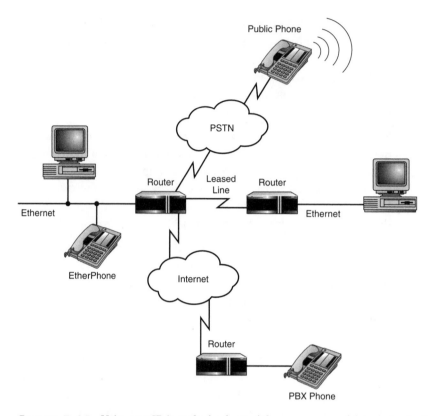

FIGURE 7.15 *Voice over IP is at the forefront of the convergence of data and voice technologies. The diagram shows three different examples of IP telephony: leased line, Internet, and seamless PSTN calling.*

Ultimately, the question of voice and data converging on Ethernet is a question that the entire voice and data networking industry is struggling to answer. It pits the new kids on the block like Cisco and 3Com against the established players like AT&T (now Lucent), Nortel, Siemens, and Alcatel. Will this be a convergence or a collision? Will Ethernet be able to provide the reliability, scalability, and resiliency to become your next-generation digital dial tone?

Gigabit Ethernet to the Desktop

Now that we have examined existing and new bandwidth consumers, we'll examine the topic of Gigabit Ethernet to the desktop. Let's talk about servers first and desktops second.

Should new servers be connected at 1000Mbps? Not quite yet. Tests done by Intel, numerous technical publications, and independent labs all confirm that today's servers are hard-pressed to deliver more than a few hundred megabits per second throughput. Therefore, right now it is cheaper and easier to install additional Fast Ethernet NICs if you really have a server than can deliver more than 200-Mbps FDX throughput. Of course, that's today. Next-generation servers will be able to deliver Gigabit data rates. By then, dual-speed 100/1000 NICs seem inevitable. We would recommend these upcoming 100/1000 NICs for your next-generation high-end servers. For the time being, stick with one, two, or more 100Mbps NICs for your server.

So when do you start planning for Gigabit Ethernet to the desktop? Not for a long, long time. Here is why: Today, we don't see any *mainstream* applications on our radar screen that will require more than dedicated 10Mbps connectivity. Yes, some *power* users already require a 100Mbps switched connection, but we are talking about mainstream desktops here. For those, 10Mbps Ethernet is sufficient to support today's and tomorrow's application requirements. Standardizing on 10/100 Ethernet NICs provides you with the ability to upgrade at any time.

Summary

This chapter discussed the maximum throughput capabilities of Ethernet, which is between 37% and 95% of its wire speed, depending on frame size and the type of connection. It discussed various methods to measure the utilization of your network so that you can be prepared to implement suitable upgrade options that we cover in the second half of this book.

This chapter examines why some of today's networks are running out of bandwidth and what the reasons are behind this trend. Your network traffic will continue growing, as the Internet and newer client/server applications will continue requiring more bandwidth.

We have some simple recommendations that you should keep in mind at all times when thinking about bandwidth:

- *Plan for lots of future growth*—It is part of your job as a network manager or IT professional to think long-term as well as short-term. Make sure that you buy new equipment that allows for lots of future traffic growth. Don't waste your time and the company's money on upgrades that only give you a year before you face the same network congestion problems.

- *Buy scalable products and technologies*—Remember to buy products or technologies with which you can grow. Buying things that are close to the end of their lifecycle means that you will need to change products or technologies soon, which is always a painful experience.

- *Be proactive, not reactive*—Don't let your network become overloaded. Measure your network utilization regularly and take the appropriate steps before you run out of bandwidth. Once your network is approaching saturation, you will be in a firefighting mode that will make your life and the life of your network users a misery.

- *Test new applications extensively*—Many of the new applications, such as videoconferencing and distributed or client-server databases, will consume a lot of your bandwidth. It will be difficult to tell exactly what the impact on your network will be without appropriate testing. We recommend that you run a "beta program" for new applications to study the compatibility of these new applications with existing applications, the impact that these new applications have on your utilization, and the satisfaction of your users with the new applications.

- *Buy products that are backward-compatible*—Don't trade the promise of terabytes of bandwidth for a completely new technology that will be difficult to integrate into your existing network.

- *Stay up-to-speed with the latest in technical developments*—Many good technical publications are available on the Web. Join a user group, and browse some of the news forums on the Net. Please refer to Appendix C, "Useful Web Links," for some listings.

CHAPTER 8

Network Components

Now that you have determined that your network could benefit from Switched, Fast, and Gigabit Ethernet, how do you go about implementing the correct solution? Before that can happen, you must first understand the basic building blocks of a Switched, Fast, and Gigabit Ethernet network and how they fit together to connect your local area network. Many of these building blocks may be familiar to you, so this chapter focuses on specific issues with different network devices as they pertain to Switched and Fast Ethernet. This chapter also discusses why some network device features might be more desirable than others in certain situations. If you want to know the theoretical performance of a crossbar matrix switch architecture, you have come to the wrong place. If you want to know how to actually use that switch in your network, however, the next few chapters can be of great help.

As in any hierarchical communications scheme, several distinct components make up most of today's Ethernet networks. Network administrators use these components to effectively deploy local area networking to their customers. These components fall into three broad categories: *end-station components*, *workgroup components*, and *backbone components*. Each group has its own distinct set of features and functions that make it critical to LAN operations. This chapter attempts to break down each category into its fundamental defining properties, organizing each by its feature set and performance characteristics.

An *end-station component*, also called a *network interface card* (NIC), is broadly defined as the *node*, or *client/server* piece of the network. Figure 8.1 shows a stylized version of a NIC. Every client, workstation, and server system must have a NIC, or NIC-equivalent, to connect to the network. Because of this,

NICs are crucial to LAN deployment, as illustrated by the 46 million NICs sold worldwide in 1997 (39 million of them Ethernet). Many view the NIC as the least important piece of the network puzzle; however, a good network administrator will weigh the NIC purchasing decision just as heavily as a workgroup or backbone decision. This chapter considers various trade-offs in the evaluation of desktop, server, and mobile NICs, and how the correct choice of a 10/100Mbps or Gigabit Ethernet NIC can make deployment easier.

FIGURE 8.1   *A network interface card.*

This chapter also introduces the workgroup device. A workgroup device is commonly thought of as a central point where several users tap into the network. Some examples of workgroup devices are standalone repeaters, stackable hubs, workgroup switches, and desktop switches. Throughout the rest of this book, we refer to these components by the symbols shown in Figure 8.2. This chapter explains how correct workgroup device selection can greatly increase network performance and decrease installation cost.

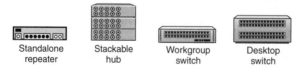

| Standalone repeater | Stackable hub | Workgroup switch | Desktop switch |

FIGURE 8.2   *Workgroup devices include standalone repeaters, stackable hubs, workgroup switches, and desktop switches.*

Backbone network components are typically used to connect several workgroup devices in the network architecture. Backbone components break down larger networks into manageable subnetworks and route traffic from one place to the next. Examples of backbone devices include bridges, routers, backbone switches, Layer 3 switches, and Gigabit Ethernet switches. Figure 8.3 shows the network symbols that represent these components. Backbone devices are expensive and their proper selection and placement is very important to overall network performance. The performance trade-offs and other relevant features of backbone devices are discussed later in this chapter. For the purposes of this book, we have included WAN access devices with backbone network components. The discussion on WAN access is limited to its impact on the Switched, Fast, or Gigabit Ethernet LAN.

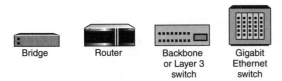

| Bridge | Router | Backbone or Layer 3 switch | Gigabit Ethernet switch |

FIGURE 8.3 *Backbone components include bridges, routers, backbone switches, Layer 3 switches, and Gigabit Ethernet switches.*

NICs

Many different NICs exist, each suited for a particular type of installation or application. Consequently, when you are looking at a NIC, you must consider several factors. With the availability of affordable 10/100 Fast Ethernet NICs, network professionals have to make conscious choices about the NICs installed in their networks. To make a well-informed decision, they have to consider not only wire speed, but bus type, performance, driver support, technical support, drivers, and compatibility; PC and workstation connectivity; and the differences between server, mobile, and desktop NICs.

Desktop NICs

Desktops, or clients, are often lower-performance systems and predominantly run Microsoft Windows (Windows 3.1, Windows for Workgroups 3.11, Windows 95, and Windows 98 operating systems; NetWare 3.x, 4.x, and 5.x; UNIX; and Windows NT 3.51 and 4 are common on servers). Client trends showed that 1996 and 1997 were years of transition from single-tasking operating systems, such as DOS and Windows 3.1, to multitasking operating systems, such as Windows 95 and UNIX (in fact, Apple Macintoshes have been shipping with multitasking operating systems for years). This type of OS will require a much different NIC from that of a DOS system because the NIC driver will have to be cognizant of how it uses the host CPU. This is referred to as *client CPU utilization* and has proven to be one of the differentiating factors in an otherwise commodity desktop NIC market. More and more desktop applications are requiring efficient use of the desktop CPU. The concept of intranets (internal corporate Web servers), for instance, may require each desktop PC to serve as both a desktop and a mini-Web server. This would require a client NIC that uses the CPU very efficiently.

Wire Speed

A NIC's wire speed indicates how fast the physical signaling can take place—for instance, 10Mbps, 100Mbps, or 1Gbps. Nobody wants to make the mistake of buying something today that can't grow to meet the needs of an expanding network infrastructure. This is evidenced by the 15 million 10/100Mbps NICs shipped worldwide in 1997. By the same token, no one wants to pay for something he doesn't need and will never use. A good compromise for these two seemingly opposed criteria is a 10/100Mbps NIC. Intel's EtherExpress PRO/100+ LAN Adapter is a good example of a 10/100Mbps NIC and is shown in Figure 8.4.

FIGURE 8.4   *Intel's EtherExpress PRO/100+ NIC runs at either 10 or 100Mbps.*

The following are factors to keep in mind when selecting a desktop NIC:

- *Media types*—After making the decision to purchase 10/100, the next choice is between 100BASE-TX or 100BASE-T4. Desktop NICs must be chosen based on the type of wiring found in that workgroup. Some workgroups have only Category 3 UTP and require 10BASE-T or 100BASE-T4 clients. Some have Category 5 UTP and can support 100BASE-TX. Because 100BASE-T4 never really gained critical mass in the marketplace, we recommend that 100BASE-TX be used whenever possible.

- *Full-duplex and flow control*—As discussed in Chapter 4, "Layer 2 Ethernet Switching," desktop NICs can support both full-duplex and half-duplex operation. Full-duplex does not typically enhance client performance more than 10% at 10Mbps or 100Mbps data rates, so it should not be considered as a criterion when buying the client NIC. You won't pay extra for 10Mbps or 100Mbps full-duplex support on a client NIC. If a NIC does support full-duplex, make sure it supports the 802.3x full-duplex flow-control specification.

- *Auto-negotiation*—Another factor in selecting client NICs is IEEE 802.3 Auto-Negotiation support. An auto-negotiating client NIC automatically determines the transmission scheme (100BASE-TX, 10BASE-T, full-duplex, and so on) with the far end of the wire, thereby making desktop connections automatic and painless. Auto-negotiation is a standard feature on most Fast Ethernet NICs that ship today.

Desktop Bus Type

When looking at the installed base of 10Mbps Ethernet NICs in 1995, the predominant bus architecture was the Industry Standard Architecture (ISA). When considering the ISA bus as a vehicle for delivering 10Mbps dedicated bandwidth (in the case of 10Mbps switching) or 100Mbps bandwidth, however, there were definite performance issues:

- The ISA bus is only 16 bits wide.

- The ISA bus runs at a clock rate of only 8MHz.

- The ISA bus doesn't allow burst data transfers.

- Most ISA bus adapters are I/O mapped, causing data transfers to be slower.

These factors produce a theoretical ISA bus bandwidth of 5.33MBps, or 42.67Mbps. A more realistic ISA bus bandwidth is determined by actual measurements of many different NICs in various ISA systems. The real-world ISA bus bandwidth available to the NIC is only about one-fourth of the theoretical amount, or 11Mbps—barely enough to fill a 10Mbps pipe, and definitely not enough for multiple 10Mbps or 100Mbps NICs.

In desktop systems built after 1995, however, the Peripheral Component Interconnect (PCI) bus started to become predominant. Extended Industry Standard Architecture (EISA), Micro Channel Architecture (MCA), S-Bus (Sparc Workstations), and NuBus (Apple Macintosh) systems were also shipping but were becoming smaller in numbers. In 1997, all Pentium processor class or higher systems had PCI slots.

PCI delivers a theoretical bandwidth of 132MBps and true plug-and-play features, much like Sun's S-Bus. Today, high-speed buses, such as PCI and S-Bus, are the logical slot for high-performance network adapters. Table 8.1 compares ISA, EISA, MCA, PCI, NuBus, S-Bus, and PCMCIA (PC Memory Card Interface Adapter) bus architectures. Note that the PCI bus is high performance, processor independent, and widely supported by computer manufacturers. Even Apple and Sun, two of the biggest non–PC-compatible computer manufacturers, have adopted the PCI bus.

TABLE 8.1 A COMPARISON OF BUS TYPES

Feature	ISA	PCMCIA	EISA
Supported architecture	PC	PC (Mobile)	PC
Bus speed (MHz)	8	8	8
Theoretical bus bandwidth (MBps)	5.33	5.33	32
Practical bus bandwidth for a NIC (MBps)[2]	1.4	1.4	8
Bus width (bits)	16	16	32
Burst mode data transfer?	No	No	Yes
Processor independent?	Yes	Yes	Yes
Widely accepted by major computer manufacturers?	Yes	Yes (in laptops)	Yes
Setup utilities	Manual or plug-and-play[3] BIOS	Card & socket services	EISA Config. Utility

[1] PCI and CardBus are inherently scalable beyond 33MHz. Work is currently underway to scale to PCI bus to 50 and 66MHz speeds.

[2] Includes measurements in buses with multiple adapters, such as SCSI, IDE, and VGA.

[3] Plug-and-play BIOS refers to the ISA plug-and-play specification.

Although PCI has become dominant, many systems still ship with both PCI and ISA buses. That said, performance isn't the only reason to move your desktops and servers away from the ISA architecture. ISA has also been traditionally difficult to configure with multiple adapters. In the PC world, true auto-configuration comes with a migration to PCI.

10/100Mbps NICs provide an affordable upgrade path from 10Mbps only, but how much should you be willing to pay for that upgradability? Currently, 10/100 PCI NICs cost about 10% more than 10-only NICs. This price difference is so small that you should start planning *when* to purchase 10/100Mbps client NICs instead of evaluating whether you should.

If you are not already doing so, look for PCI in your desktop systems and select PCI 10/100 LAN adapters to connect those systems. What do you do with all those old ISA systems? Continue to use them as an important part of your client base, but network them with 10Mbps switches as discussed in Chapter 9, "Deployment."

MCA	NuBus	S-Bus	Card Bus	PCI
PC	Apple	Sun	Mobile PC	All
8	8	33	33	16–33[1]
40	5.33	132	132	132
10	1.4	30–100	30–60	30–100
32	16	32	32	32–64
Yes	Yes	Yes	Yes	Yes
Yes	No	No	Yes	Yes
No	No	No	Yes	Yes
POR Register Conf Utility	True plug-n-play	True plug-n-play	True plug-n-play BIOS	True plug-n-play BIOS

Work is currently under way to extend PCI from a 32-bit data path to 64 bit in high-end workstations. The operating speed of PCI, currently 33MHz, is also being pushed to 50MHz and even 66MHz in some prototype workstations. So PCI in the desktop has a lot of headroom left.

Even so, far be it from the computer industry to sit still. In 1997, Compaq and Intel announced the Dual Independent Bus (DIB) architecture, which is even higher performance than PCI and allows for hot-plug capability in the desktop.

LAN on Motherboard

LAN on motherboard (LOM) is defined as a desktop, workstation, or server that has networking silicon right on the motherboard, obviating the need for an add-in NIC. Apple and Sun pioneered this concept, which was later implemented by Compaq, IBM, Hewlett-Packard, Siemens-Nixdorf, and other PC vendors. Traditionally, the LOM idea wasn't popular in the volume PC desktop market, mostly because there were too many different networking options to justify locking in one design. Now that 10/100 Ethernet has been integrated into a single chip (Intel's 82559), however, more PC vendors may start shipping products with this silicon on the motherboard. LOM may end up saving you a lot of money; therefore, depending on your network architecture and budget, you may want to consider LOM in your purchasing decision.

Network Interface Card Drivers

A *driver* is the piece of software that allows the desktop operating system to interface with the NIC hardware. Therefore a NIC has one driver for each kind of operating system. Common names for NIC drivers are NDIS (for Microsoft) and ODI (for Novell). Since the advent of Windows 95, it is common for a particular NIC driver to come included on the Windows 95 CD-ROM, thereby making it extremely easy to install the NIC.

The following are key issues when you are considering NIC drivers:

- *Driver support*—Brand-name NIC vendors typically develop much of their driver suite internally. This is important because if a driver wasn't developed in-house, it is possible that the vendor will not be able to support it very well. Many vendors strike a successful compromise with the network operating system (NOS) vendors, enlisting them to write a driver for that particular NOS. Although support for this kind of driver won't be the same as for one developed by the NIC vendor itself, it is still better than a complete third-party driver. As a hypothetical example, if 3Com and a third-tier NIC vendor both ask IBM to develop OS/2 drivers, it is likely that IBM will focus its efforts on 3Com. When using a non–brand-name NIC vendor, ask where the driver was developed. If you cannot get this information, ask where the customer support for that driver will come from.

Another point to consider when questioning driver support is hardware and software compatibility. Any brand-name vendor should be able to provide a list of OS versions tested. Likewise, any vendor that cannot produce a list of PC systems tested compatible with the NIC should be scrutinized.

- *Driver certification*—Most NIC vendors typically don't ship a NIC unless it has passed all major certifications. These include certification tests with NOS vendors, such as Novell, Microsoft, SCO, and IBM. Some NIC vendors sometimes bypass this expensive and time-consuming task. Without a certified NIC and driver, you have no way of confirming that the NIC vendor has tested the NIC and driver in a variety of configurations. Other tests that major NIC vendors perform are FCC emissions testing and environmental testing (temperature and mechanical stress tests).

- *Technical support and warranty*—A thorough review of a NIC vendor's technical support model should be as critical a factor in your NIC purchase decision as price or performance. If problems arise, you will be spending time with technical support long after the salespeople have disappeared.

As far as product quality goes, you must consider several key factors when selecting a NIC. NICs by vendors such as 3Com, Intel, and SMC all support lifetime warranties as well as 90-day money-back guarantees. Reliability is also a concern for mission-critical client/sever applications. NIC reliability is sometimes measured in *mean time between failures* (MTBF). Although this usually doesn't give you much information, you should be suspicious of any value below 180,000 hours. This indicates that a failure may occur, on average, every 180,000 hours, or 20 years. Most brand-name NIC vendors meet this level of reliability.

Setup Wizards

In the majority of cases, NIC installation at the desktop goes smoothly, but sometimes it is very helpful to have a setup wizard. A setup wizard is a program that will help in cases where system conflicts occur or when you have problems getting connected to the network. Intel's EtherExpress PRO/100+ LAN Adapter Setup software is particularly good in this regard and can even run cross-network diagnostics in case the server is not responding.

Desktop NIC Management

Simple Network Management Protocol (SNMP) is a well-defined network management protocol that garners information from various SNMP agents. An SNMP agent can reside internally in a hub or router, or even as a software liaison to a NIC. An SNMP management console can be configured to specifically ask all SNMP agents on the network for statistical information. Although this proves useful for network traffic management, it doesn't do much for desktop and server management. This is because the variables that SNMP was designed to collect do not reflect the relevant variables in a desktop PC.

This fallacy of SNMP is why the Desktop Management Task Force (DMTF) was formed and the Desktop Management Interface (DMI) specification developed. DMI requires all DMI-compliant NICs to keep information about network traffic and the system in a particular way. Network management software packages can then query NICs from multiple vendors to obtain information needed to effectively manage the traffic *and* the nodes on the network.

As DMI was evolving toward its current 2.0 specification, another interesting development was taking place in the computer industry. Network managers were finally convincing the computer and networking industry that the $2,000 spent on the PC purchase was really only a fraction of the cost of actually owning that PC. The Gartner Group captured this concept, referred to as *total cost of ownership* (TCO), very well. Gartner did extensive studies and showed that the up-front PC capital expenditures were only 20% of the total cost of that PC over its lifetime. Labor, upkeep, software upgrades, and end-user support amounted to the other 80%. In response to this, Intel, Microsoft, Compaq, and other industry leaders announced the Wired for Management (WfM) specification. If you are serious about keeping support costs down for your PC infrastructure, you should only buy desktops compliant with the WfM specification.

The first version of the specification was WfM 1.1a. To be 1.1a-compliant, a system had to be easily manageable. This basically meant that it would have the following characteristics:

- Comply with the DMI 2.0 specification

- Keep basic resources (BIOS ID, keyboard type, processor type, and so on)

- Keep system resources (IRQ, I/O, and so on)

- Keep memory information (type, size, and so on)

- Keep information on the NIC installed

- Allow remote boot capabilities

- Allow basic power management that supports the Advanced Configuration Power Interface (ACPI) standard

- Allow the system to respond to Wake-on-LAN requests

Most of the information in the preceding list is kept in a Management Information Format (MIF) on the desktop system, which can then be accessed by DMI 2.0 management consoles anywhere on the network. Of particular interest to this book is the Wake-on-LAN feature. This allows a "magic" packet to be sent by a management console to a desktop. If that desktop is in a low-power state, the NIC will recognize the special packet and wake up the desktop system. The desktop can then be checked for inventory or software upgrades can be made. Note that this can be done regardless of whether the desktop PC is actually turned on or whether the end user is in the office.

Note

The WfM standard refers to the software and hardware support needed on the desktop. The DMI standard refers to the management software interface.

Version 2.0 of the Wired-for-Management specification is currently under way. It will include several enhancements, including Alert-on-LAN capabilities. IBM and Intel co-developed this capability, which allows systems to alert a management console of certain events. Examples of alerts are POST failure, no operating system response, opening of the desktop chassis, or the addition of new hardware. More information on WfM, Wake-on-LAN, and Alert-on-LAN is available at www.intel.com/network.

Desktop NIC Performance

The performance of a desktop NIC is measured in a slightly different way from that of a server NIC. Throughput is the primary measurement used, but client CPU utilization is also important. Imagine throughput as how long you have to wait to download a large file from the server. Client CPU utilization will come into play if you are multitasking (that is, downloading email, sending print jobs, running Internet software, and so on). Therefore, throughput should be the primary measurement used to evaluate a desktop NIC, with CPU utilization being a close second.

Test Benchmarks

Where server benchmarks use multiple clients to maximize the traffic on the server NIC, client benchmarks use a one client/one server test setup. Maximum client performance is measured by using an ultra-fast server, attaching the one client to be measured, and running benchmark tests. In the client test, the server should remain constant and the client test conditions varied. Variable test parameters, in client NIC tests include file size, test duration, and NOS-specific parameters, such as packet burst size.

One fallacy of client testing is the concept of *matched-pair* testing. Some vendors claim higher performance with the same card in the server and the client, but a matched-pair test does not represent real life. The best test methodology is to put a high-performance server NIC in place and keep it constant for all client NICs tested. Table 8.2 examines the three top test suites, looking specifically at client performance aspects.

TABLE 8.2 THREE POPULAR CLIENT NIC PERFORMANCE TESTS

Test	How It Works	What It Measures	Drawbacks?
Perform3 (Novell Labs)	Copies variable file sizes from client cache memory to server.	Isolates the client NIC. Shows peak throughput from the client. Results are readily quantifiable.	Doesn't involve other server components such as the hard drive. Doesn't model real-life traffic very well. Doesn't measure client CPU utilization.
NetBench 4.0 (Ziff-Davis Labs)	Copies variable file sizes from client cache memory to server. Also performs read/write tests.	Isolates the client NIC. Shows peak throughput from the client. Results are readily quantifiable. Other options allow for hard disk interaction. ServerBench focuses on server performance.	Only some options allow for modeling of real-life traffic. Doesn't measure client CPU utilization.
NSTL (McGraw Hill Labs)	Simulates repetition of several accesses from multiple clients. Simulates random-length accesses.	Represents real-world performance, but doesn't indicate how good the client NIC is.	Doesn't isolate the NIC very well. Results are only as good as the slowest test component. Doesn't measure client CPU utilization.

Note

These tests are best referenced by their WWW addresses, which you can find in Appendix C, "Useful Web Links."

Newer desktop operating systems, such as Windows 95 and Windows NT, use network caching to improve network performance. Network caching occurs when a file is copied from the server to the client once, and thereafter only copied from the client cache memory. When testing a desktop NIC, make sure to have network caching disabled or you will only test the local desktop's memory-copy bandwidth, not the network performance. A good way to watch for this is to monitor the network utilization throughout the test; if it falls off after the first few seconds, you will know that network caching is occurring.

You may have noticed that none of these tests measures client CPU utilization very well. The best way to measure an adapter's client CPU utilization is to use software packages like those found in Windows NT or Norton Utilities. They give a relative indication of how each NIC uses the client CPU. In this measurement, a Fast Ethernet client NIC should not consume more than 50% of the client CPU when transferring data across the network. A 10Mbps Ethernet NIC shouldn't use more than 10%.

Buffering

Buffering also plays an important role in client performance because client systems may not always be able to handle the incoming data stream. Client NIC buffering will help, especially at 100Mbps wire speeds, by storing incoming data temporarily while a slower I/O bus can read it from the card. In a bus master client NIC, buffering is usually of the FIFO (first-in, first-out) SRAM type and 3KB is considered large. In a buffered slave client NIC, buffering is usually external DRAM and sizes can vary from 4KB to 32KB (more on masters and slaves later). Because every network is different, no one buffer size is best for a client NIC. A simple way to determine whether a particular client NIC does not have enough buffering is to look at how many overruns (loss of data due to the NIC buffers being full) occur on the client in a performance test. If more than a few occur, the client NIC buffer size is not adequate.

Mobile NICs

A LAN administrator also has to plan for users who frequently travel away from the office. Typically, these people require laptop computers. Laptops on desktops are becoming increasingly common, and connecting laptops to the LAN is somewhat of a challenge. One option is to invest in docking stations, which provide a special connector in the back of the laptop. The second option is to rely on NIC vendors to develop PCMCIA and CardBus LAN adapters that work in your laptop systems.

Mobile NIC Bus Types

The PCMCIA bus has come a long way in compatibility and availability, but PCMCIA, like ISA, is not fast enough to support high-speed LAN connections. Don't look to implement Fast Ethernet in laptops until CardBus sockets are available. Xircom, a well-known PCMCIA adapter vendor, has shipped a PCMCIA Fast Ethernet adapter as well as a CardBus version (shown in Figure 8.5).

CardBus Ethernet II 10/100

CreditCard Ethernet 10/100

FIGURE 8.5 *PCMCIA and CardBus 10/100 network interface cards from Xircom.*

If your strategy involves using add-in adapters, ask your laptop vendor about its support for the new CardBus specification. CardBus defines a higher-speed PCMCIA bus that is 32 bits wide and operates at 33MHz, much like the PCI bus. Most laptop vendors, Toshiba, IBM, and Compaq in particular, have adopted CardBus quickly.

Wire Speed

The same arguments for 10/100 exist on laptops. 10/100 capability in the network adapter gives the laptop a level of flexibility. Consider the traveler who goes from one office to the next. If the company is in a state of transition from 10Mbps to 100Mbps Ethernet, most travelers are likely to need both types of connectivity.

One of the drawbacks of running 100BASE-TX on laptops is that it draws a lot of power compared to 10BASE-T. Remember that 100BASE-TX is required to send an active idle signal at all times and this can drain laptop battery power. Some CardBus and PCMCIA 10/100 adapters offer power-management features that help alleviate this problem.

Combo Cards

Most PCMCIA and CardBus vendors offer NIC/modem combination, or combo, cards. These are especially useful because most laptops have only two slots.

Software Support

Software support for laptop NICs becomes very important because the inter-face between laptop hardware and software is buried with the operating sys-tem. For this reason, it is always a good idea to buy a mobile NIC that has its driver included in your mobile operating system. If you are using Windows 95, Windows 98, or Windows NT, check whether the NIC driver is listed in the supported hardware list.

Manageability

WfM applies to mobile systems as well. The upcoming WfM 2.0 specification will include several laptop extensions to the standard, not the least of which is advanced power-management capabilities. Because power usage is more important for battery-driven laptops, support for ACPI has to be implemented in conjunction with Wake-on-LAN capabilities. Because both standards are part of the WfM standard, make WfM-compliance a must for your laptop purchases.

LAN on Notebook Motherboard

Several laptop vendors, including Toshiba and Dell, have elected to design the network connection right in the laptop itself. This allows connectivity to the network without the need for an add-in adapter. If you go with this strategy, make sure the LAN on motherboard solution you choose works in the neces-sary environments. Some laptops may need an additional PCMCIA or CardBus NIC for dialup access anyway, so a combination LAN/modem card might be just what the doctor ordered.

Server NICs

A *server* is broadly defined as a specific kind of system built to be powerful, upgradable, and reliable. These qualities are also important in a good server NIC. One server may support hundreds of clients, which can put enormous stress on the server NIC. Unlike a desktop computer running Windows 95, where the CPU spends most of its time idle, the server is constantly working, trying to use every ounce of CPU power available. How hard a server CPU works is referred to as its *CPU utilization*. Imagine a server that spends 60% of its time providing data to a server NIC. That server only has 40% of its cycles left to perform other activities. In some Fast Ethernet adapters, the NIC can take up to 50% of the server CPU resources. Add a Gigabit Ethernet server NIC, and this number immediately pegs to 100%.

This is why the CPU utilization of a server NIC is very important. The less time the server CPU has to spend providing for the NIC, the more time it has to run applications, perform file transfers, and run NOS software. Servers also typically support more expansion slots than do desktops, which allows a wider variety of configurations, including additional hard drives and network adapters. In addition, many high-end servers offer fault-tolerant features, such as redundant power supplies and hot-swappable hard drives.

Server NIC Bus Types

With Fast Ethernet now widely installed in servers, many network managers have their sights set on Gigabit Ethernet. We discuss later why an investment in a high-speed expansion bus will help prepare your server for Gigabit Ethernet networking.

As discussed previously, ISA servers just won't support Fast Ethernet data rates. EISA, the historical server expansion bus of choice, supports Fast Ethernet data rates, but does not do so efficiently, both in terms of CPU utilization and price. EISA does not even come close to supporting Gbps data rates. PCI offers higher bandwidth and a path to the future through bus-width extensions and higher-frequency data transfers. When considering upgrades to current EISA servers, choose 10/100 NICs that offer lower CPU utilization, even at the expense of throughput. When considering new PC server purchases, you can choose from any number of PCI server NICs.

Most new servers support a 32-bit PCI bus running at 33MHz. This provides a total bus bandwidth of just over 1Gbps. Therefore, it is not very promising for a network manager looking to install a Gigabit server adapter. Fortunately, the PCI bus has been extended to 64-bit data paths and work is being done to increase its operating frequency to 66MHz. The combination of these two efforts effectively quadruples the available bandwidth of PCI to just over 4Gbps.

In addition, servers that support the PCI hot-swap feature allow you to add or remove peripherals while the server is powered on. This is obviously beneficial because many mission-critical servers have to be in operation 24 hours a day. Compaq has led the charge in this area of server development.

Wire Speed: 10, 100, or 1000?

Fast Ethernet, and specifically 10/100 NICs, started finding their way into servers as early as 1994. This means that some of those servers are ready for replacement today, and many network managers are considering Gigabit Ethernet NICs for the replacement systems.

Whereas Fast Ethernet server NICs ran at 10 or 100Mbps speeds and supported UTP and fiber, many early Gigabit NICs will run only at 1000Mbps and support fiber only. Because the NIC can't revert back to 100Mbps operation, the network manager should only selectively install Gigabit Ethernet NICs. It might be wise to keep the 10/100Mbps NIC in the server as a backup until the Gigabit Ethernet NIC is operational. It is important to make sure a Gigabit switch can be connected on the far end of the fiber connection. As in desktop NICs, server NICs should support IEEE Auto-Negotiation and full-duplex flow-control standards. (Gigabit Ethernet hasn't yet been added to the auto-negotiation standard at the time of this book's publication.)

Gigabit server NICs support 1000BASE-SX or 1000BASE-LX, which gives them an effective range of 260 meters and 550 meters, respectively, over 62.5μm multimode fiber. (See Chapter 3, "Ethernet, Fast Ethernet, and Gigabit Ethernet Standards," for a refresher on supported Gigabit Ethernet distances.)

Full-Duplex

In servers, full-duplex may give a NIC an extra 5% to 25% performance increase, but this increase is highly dependent on what the server and application are doing. Many protocols, such as IP and IPX, aren't structured to take advantage of full-duplex. Also, full-duplex NICs require full-duplex switched ports on the far end of the connection. When it comes to Gigabit Ethernet server NICs, however, full-duplex support is a must-have. This is due to the extra fiber distances allowed at full-duplex and not to the potential performance increase.

Multiport NICs

Some PCI servers are shipping with only two or three PCI expansion slots. In a modern 100Mbps network, where many servers have more than one NIC, this can be a restriction. Some NIC vendors, such as IBM and Adaptec, have recognized this fact and have designed multiport server NICs. These NICs provide two or more network connections on a single card and are useful in specific applications where server slots are at a premium.

Multi-NIC Servers

Many network managers add more than one NIC to a server. Historically, this was done to improve the performance of the network through segmentation. Say one server was connected to 40 clients with a 10Mbps shared hub. Adding an extra NIC to the server allows the network to be split, or segmented, into two 20-node segments. Each segment gets 10Mbps, so the effective bandwidth of the network is increased to 20Mbps.

Today, with low-cost workgroup switches and Fast and Gigabit Ethernet server NICs, the need to add multiple NICs to a server should not be as great. However, network managers continue to set up servers this way. Let's look at some of the reasons for this:

- *Redundancy/failover*—Having two NICs in a server allows the network manager to connect each to a different point on the network. This provides some amount of redundancy to that server connection. If one of the server NICs should fail, or if one of the cables should be accidentally cut, the server can still communicate with the network.

- *Port aggregation*—Several port-aggregation schemes are in use today, but most are proprietary. The IEEE802.3ad standard is concerned with standardizing port aggregation. Port aggregation allows multiple switch ports or server NICs to share the load of a given connection. This can be from server NIC-to-switch or from switch-to-switch. Port aggregation can be used at 10Mbps, 100Mbps, or even Gbps speeds because it is independent of the media type used. One type of port aggregation, Cisco's EtherChannel, works with two or four separate connections and in half- or full-duplex mode. With four full-duplex connections, EtherChannel provides 800Mbps of bandwidth between two devices.

  Some server NICs also provide load balancing, which provides a way for servers to parcel out traffic among several aggregated connections. Without load balancing, a server with two aggregated Fast Ethernet connections would use 100% of one connection and 10% of the other to transmit 110Mbps of data. With load balancing, each connection transmits at 55Mbps.

  Both sides of the connection must support the same port aggregation scheme (that is, server NIC-to-switch, or switch-to-switch) for the scheme to work. Intel, Cisco, Bay Networks, and several other networking companies have pledged their support for the upcoming IEEE802.3ab standard.

- *Fiber support*—Gigabit Ethernet runs only over fiber today, with support for copper in the works. Gbps uses the same kinds of fiber as 100BASE-FX, which should allow for an easy transition between the two. Table 8.3 is a quick recap of what kinds of fiber each standard supports.

TABLE 8.3 FIBER TYPES AND DISTANCES SUPPORTED BY THE 802.3Z GIGABIT ETHERNET STANDARD

Gigabit Ethernet Standard	Fiber Type	Fiber Size (μM)	Maximum Distance
1000BASE-SX	Multimode	50/125	500 meters
	Multimode	62.5/125	220 meters
1000BASE-LX	Multimode	50/125	550 meters
	Multimode	62.5/125	550 meters
	Single-mode	10	5 kilometers

Architecture

The architecture of a server NIC has a lot to do with its overall performance in the system. Master/slave operation, buffering, and CPU intelligence have the largest impact:

- *Master/slave*—Bus-mastering NICs access host memory directly and do not rely on the CPU to directly transfer data to them. Therefore, in servers, bus-mastering NICs are ideal because of the low CPU overhead required to operate them. Bus-mastering NICs typically have fast internal FIFO memory, with sizes ranging from a few bytes to 3KB or 4KB. Buffered slave NICs rely on the CPU to copy data to and from buffers on the NIC itself. Any server NIC based on a slave architecture is bound to show higher (worse) server CPU utilization.

- *Buffering*—At Fast Ethernet speeds, server NIC buffering is less critical than client NIC buffering because servers typically have high-speed expansion buses and subsystems capable of supporting Fast Ethernet throughput rates. When using a Fast Ethernet bus-mastering NIC in a PCI server, 1.5KB/1.5KB of transmit/receive FIFO should be adequate. If the NIC is slated for an older EISA system, more FIFO will help performance. Buffering at Gigabit speeds is discussed later in the chapter.

- *Intelligent NICs*—Intelligent server NICs are defined as having a local CPU on the NIC itself. The Intel EtherExpress PRO/100 Intelligent Web Server Adapter has an Intel i960 processor on the NIC itself, for example. The advantage of an intelligent NIC is that it can relieve the host CPU of many networking tasks, allowing it to focus on running applications and NOS software. Intelligent NICs are typically very expensive and should only be considered for a specific server application where they provide a real benefit. Some examples are application servers and servers with intensive I/O demands. Fast Ethernet intelligent NICs will also be popular in servers where the host CPU would otherwise be spending 100% of its time providing data for the 100Mbps wire.

- *Intelligent I/O*—Intelligent I/O (I_2O), refers to a server with a separate CPU dedicated to the processing of I/O, thus relieving the host CPU of that function. The dedicated I_2O CPU can reside on the server motherboard, or on a NIC or hard disk add-in card. Some intelligent server NICs support I_2O features.

  I_2O is beneficial in servers where the I/O demands are extremely high, such as transaction servers, or high-end database servers. I_2O also has the capability to transfer data between peripherals without interrupting the host CPU. This is referred to as peer-to-peer transfer and allows, for instance, files to be sent directly from the hard disk to the LAN controller without first passing through the host CPU or main memory.

The memory and processing requirements to meet the I_2O specification are expensive, but the benefits can be great, especially in lowering the CPU utilization of the server. Still, the prudent move is to evaluate I_2O on a server NIC first before deploying it in production servers. You can obtain more information about the I_2O specification from the Intel Web site at www.intel.com.

The Impact of Gigabit NICs on Servers

Gigabit Ethernet server adapters are just starting to become available at the time of this book's publication. NICs from Alteon, 3Com, Intel, and several smaller startup companies have all been announced and/or started shipping. Figure 8.6 shows Alteon's ACEnic Gigabit Ethernet adapter.

FIGURE 8.6   Alteon's Gigabit Ethernet NIC.

In general, Gigabit Ethernet NICs are hard on today's servers in that they can provide a bigger pipe than today's servers can fill. This will be rectified over time as server system technology steadily improves to match the speed of a

Gigabit connection. And when that happens, there will be a new push to fill a full-duplex Gigabit pipe, or who knows, maybe even 10Gbps!

Throughput and CPU Utilization

The latest data out of Intel labs is that a Gigabit server adapter can send about 670Mbps of data at close to 100% CPU utilization. This translates to a 6.7 Performance/Efficiency Index. Not bad for a first try. The performance battles between Gigabit NIC vendors have only just begun. Engineers are, at this very moment, trying to increase Gbps NIC throughput and reduce CPU utilization. Unfortunately, most of the improvements will have to take place in the server rather than on the Gigabit NIC.

Server Subsystems

Most new servers support a 32-bit PCI bus running at 33MHz. This provides a total bus bandwidth of just over 1Gbps. Not very promising for a network manager looking to install a Gigabit server adapter. Fortunately, the PCI bus has been extended to 64-bit data paths and work is being done to increase its operating frequency to 66MHz. The combination of these two efforts effectively quadruples the available bandwidth of PCI to just more than 4Gbps. Figure 8.7 shows this.

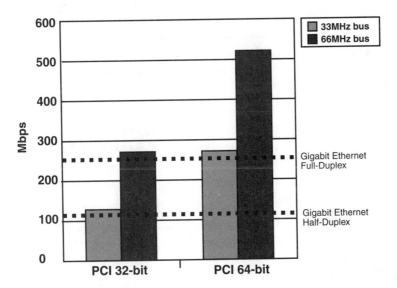

FIGURE 8.7   *Theoretical bandwidth of the PCI bus.*

The first recommendation for the Gigabit-inclined network manager is to buy servers with 64-bit PCI slots, and use 64-bit Gbps server NICs in those slots.

The second recommendation is to buy servers that have high-speed (50MHz or 66MHz) PCI buses.

Although the PCI bus can be extended in this fashion, it too will eventually need to be replaced by a higher-speed bus architecture. Let's hope it is backward compatible to PCI.

Servers running at Gigabit speeds will be CPU constrained for some time. This means that the server CPU is constantly busy just dealing with data going in and out at Gbps data rates. Therefore, servers planned for Gigabit deployment should be stocked with as much processing power (MIPS) as possible. Four 450MHz Pentium II processors would be a good starting point for a Gigabit server running Windows NT.

Hard Disks and Memory

The access time of even the fastest SCSI II hard disk is measured in milliseconds, whereas a bit of data goes out on a Gigabit connection in one *nanosecond*. Therefore, every time the server hard disk is involved in a transaction, it effectively halts the Gigabit network connection. Hard disk performance will increase steadily, but the only way around this today is to stock up on server memory.

In a Gigabit server, the more memory the better. This includes main memory, L1 cache, and L2 cache. The idea is to get as much network data cached in main memory as possible so the server doesn't have to access the hard disk as often. This is likely the best thing you can do to improve a Gbps server's effective network transfer rate.

In addition to the amount of memory, the type of memory used is important. Faster memory keeps throughput rates up and CPU utilization down. The fastest memory available today seems to be EDODRAM (extended data out DRAM) and can transfer about 100MBps. In addition, the main system bus, which connects the chipset to the memory subsystem, will be increased to 100MHz in the near future.

In the future, such memory types as SDRAM and Direct RDRAM may increase memory bandwidth to 500MBps and 3GBps, respectively.

Server NIC Management

Managing server NIC status is already a fine art, and is embedded into such well-known products as Novell ManageWise, Intel LANDesk Management Suite, CA Unicenter, and Compaq NetSight Manager. When trying to manage Gigabit server NICs, however, you may encounter unique problems. The main problem is that the speed of the Gbps server NIC is so great that today's management software cannot keep up with it. You might have to settle for a macro-view of your server, because packet-by-packet analysis just isn't feasible at Gbps speeds.

Performance

The performance of a server NIC is measured in a slightly different way from the performance of a desktop NIC. Whereas client benchmarks use a one client/one server test setup, server benchmarks use multiple clients to maximize the traffic on the server NIC. In a server test, the clients should remain constant while the server parameters are varied. Variable test parameters in server NIC tests include file size, test duration, and NOS-specific parameters such as packet burst size, and the number of clients involved in the test and the type of workgroup device used to connect them.

Understanding how to properly measure performance is a critical portion of the server NIC evaluation process. Certain types of tests give different information about the server NIC. Novell's Perform3 test determines the absolute maximum throughput a NIC can achieve and at what CPU utilization, for example, but it does not give a very accurate view of real-world server NIC performance. Ziff-Davis NetBench 4.0 and NSTL's test suites offer a much better evaluation of real-world performance because they incorporate other aspects of the server, including hard disk speed, file transfer overhead, variable file sizes, and bursty (erratic) client traffic.

NSTL tests show that even the fastest server with the fastest Fast Ethernet NIC only transfer files as quickly as its hard disk allows. Perform3 operates out of cacheable main memory and does not use the hard disk, so hard-disk performance does not affect test results. In all three examples, test setups should use multiple clients (six or more) and one server to properly test the server NIC.

Interpreting the Performance Measurements

You should really look for three things when testing a server NIC in a given system: throughput, CPU utilization, and response time. Combining the first two gives what is called the Performance/Efficiency (P/E) Index. The P/E Index is determined by dividing the total throughput of the server NIC by the CPU utilization required to generate that throughput. Therefore, a server NIC that transfers data at 90Mbps at a CPU utilization of 30% has a CPU utilization of 3.0. A 10Mbps NIC that transfers data at 9Mbps and 3% CPU utilization also has a P/E Index of 3.0; this doesn't mean these two performance levels are equal, however. It is important to realize that the P/E Index is only useful in comparing two like adapters (that is, two Fast Ethernet adapters or two Gigabit

Ethernet adapters). If server NIC A transfers at 90Mbps and 45% CPU utilization, whereas server NIC B transfers at 60Mbps and 30% CPU utilization, both have a P/E Index of 2.0; therefore, you will have to consider what's more important in that server, throughput or CPU utilization.

Let's look at these individual performance metrics in a little more detail:

- *Throughput*—Throughput measures the number of bits per second the server NIC can transfer. The most popular application to measure this is still Novell's Perform3 software, although a newer version is used now to run under Windows NT. Ethernet and Fast Ethernet server NICs should generate at least 9Mbps and 85Mbps of throughput respectively in a Perform3 test.

- *CPU utilization*—CPU utilization is measured with the MONITOR.NLM under Novell NetWare and with System Administrator under Windows NT. A Fast Ethernet NIC running under NetWare usually utilizes fewer CPU resources than the same NIC running under Windows NT. The average CPU utilization over the entire test period is used to calculate the result.

- *Response time*—Response time is typically measured by starting a file transfer application, or database search from a set of clients, and measuring how long it takes to complete the task. This test measures the entire desktop, network, and server as one system, but doesn't give you a specific server NIC measurement. ServerBench from Ziff-Davis Labs is a good tool for measuring response time.

Multi-NIC Testing

Having multiple NICs in a server doesn't affect the test setup at all; it merely changes the data set. If there are four NICs in a server, measure the throughput of all four NICs combined and divide it by the server CPU utilization to arrive at the P/E Index. Note that more than one Fast Ethernet NIC will tend to create high CPU utilization rates.

Types of Servers

Many types of servers require server NICs. Super servers (from Sequent and NetFrame, for example) running enterprise applications will probably be the first to incorporate Gigabit Ethernet NICs. But other applications, such as the following servers, may also need more than a single Fast Ethernet NIC to keep up with network demand:

- *Application servers*—Application servers, such as most Windows NT systems, are primarily for providing network applications to a multitude of clients. Because these servers are processing applications as well as sending data, they are susceptible to high CPU utilization rates. Lower CPU utilization is more important than throughput, so Intelligent server NICs should be considered for application servers.

- *File/print servers*—File and print servers are still the workhorses of today's networks, and Novell NetWare is still the most popular file server operating system. Throughput is essential for a file server because requests for data are received erratically. Consider multiple Fast Ethernet or Gigabit Ethernet NICs for these servers.

- *Database servers*—Database servers receive requests to process changes and run searches all day long. The incoming data stream is typically smaller than a file server, and the server processing power is often the bottleneck. Therefore, a good database server NIC is one that uses very few CPU cycles.

- *Multimedia servers*—Multimedia servers are in the business of providing steady traffic flows to multiple end stations. Whereas file servers operate on bursty, two-way traffic, multimedia servers typically have constant transmit rates and receive very little data. The most important aspect of a multimedia server is that the bandwidth required for the multimedia service is secured throughout the network. Protocols such as Reservation Protocol (RSVP) and Subnet Bandwidth Management (SBM) are useful in this endeavor. When deciding which kind of server NIC to install in a multimedia server, it is a good idea to choose one that has a high P/E Index.

- *Web servers*—Web servers are special in one regard: They almost exclusively use IP. If you are trying to convert your network to IP, you will be encouraged to hear that NIC vendors are trying to do the same for their server NIC offerings. One such improvement is performing the IP checksum in hardware. The benefit of this is that the server CPU does not have to perform this function resulting in lower server CPU utilization. Both Intel and 3Com offer this feature in select versions of their NICs.

  Often, Web servers also have built-in firewall software, which prevents access to certain parts of the network that might lay behind the firewall. A server running firewall software is in even greater need of CPU cycles.

NIC Wrap-Up

Desktop, mobile, and server NICs each have their individual intricacies and require a different mindset when evaluating. Desktop NICs need high throughput and low cost, whereas server NICs need a good balance of throughput and CPU utilization. Table 8.4 summarizes some of the interesting points to consider when choosing these end-station components. (Note that the prices listed in Table 8.4, like all prices of software- and hardware-related products, are outdated almost as soon as they are recorded; these prices should be used as a general guide only.)

Workgroup Components

A workgroup device, as it is aptly named, is the central connection point for most users of the network. In other words, workgroup devices allow multiple clients and local servers to connect to the network in one central location. Workgroup devices typically haunt the wiring closet, an area on a floor, or a location that is nearby. Workgroup devices fall into four broad categories:

- Standalone repeaters

- Stackable hubs

- Workgroup switches

- Desktop switches

Buying criteria for workgroup devices often include price per port, ease of installation, ease of management, scalability, port density, and upgradability.

TABLE 8.4 CONSIDERATIONS FOR DESKTOP, MOBILE, AND SERVER NICS

Server, Mobile, or Desktop NIC	Type of NIC	Bus Considerations
Desktop PC	10/100Mbps NIC or LOM	PCI
Mobile PC	10/100Mbps or combo	CardBus, PCMCIA
Standard file or print server	Basic server NIC	PCI
WWW-server or application server	Intelligent NIC	PCI
High-end server	Gigabit Ethernet NIC	PCI (consider 64-bit bus and 50-66MHz bus speed)

Standalone Repeaters

A *repeater*, also known as a *hub* or *concentrator* (see Figure 8.8), is a device that was first introduced into LANs via Thin Ethernet. Network architects needed a way to extend the reach of Thin Ethernet past a single cable. To do this, they first employed simple, two-port repeaters to receive weak signals in one port, regenerate them internally, and send them out the other port. When 10BASE-T came along, repeaters changed slightly to accommodate the new signaling scheme, but retained their basic purpose of regenerating signals.

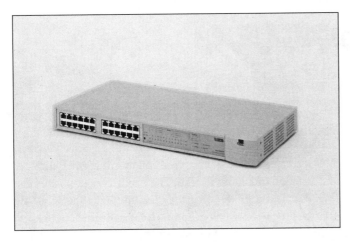

FIGURE 8.8 *A 10/100 standalone hub: the Dual Speed 500 Series Hub from 3Com.*

Management Features	Performance Features	Price Trends
WfM 1.1a	Throughput	$50–$75
WfM 1.1a	Throughput	$150–$200
WfM 1.1a	P/E Index (emphasis on throughput)	$100–$200
WfM1.1a	P/E Index (emphasis on CPU utilization)	$250–$400
WfM1.1a	P/E Index (balance throughput and CPU utilization)	$600–$1200

Figure 8.9 shows a basic repeater receiving an Ethernet frame on port A. It locks on to the incoming signal and recreates the data stream, passing it to the other seven ports. All other connected nodes, B for example, will see this frame and will defer their own transmission according to the rules of CSMA/CD. In this way, the total bandwidth of the wire, either 10 or 100Mbps, is shared between all ports on the repeater. This is how the term *shared network* came to be associated with repeaters.

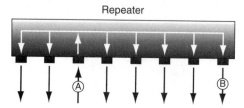

Repeater

FIGURE 8.9   *A repeater works by forwarding an incoming packet to all ports on the repeater.*

Repeaters are known as passive, or shared, components of the network because they do not logically act on incoming frames. Their only function is to regenerate weak incoming signals, thus extending the diameter of the network. In this way, repeaters are invisible to network events such as collisions, merely propagating them. Hence, a repeater cannot extend the collision domain of a network. Standalone repeaters are limited in their capability to extend network diameters, but their low cost makes them an excellent choice for small workgroups.

The following sections describe the features of standalone repeaters.

Performance

Standalone repeaters give good performance based on the amount of traffic and collisions propagated through them. Standalone and stackable repeaters are good for bursty, workgroup traffic where one node may have a short burst of activity, followed closely by another node. If too many nodes are put on the same repeater, or segment, collisions will start to occur. Too many collisions will invariably choke a shared-media network. Repeater performance is typically measured in esoteric terms of throughput latency, jitter tolerance, and packet-forwarding rates. In reality, most standalone repeaters, either 10Mbps or 100Mbps, display similar performance.

10/100 Capability

Traditionally, all standalone repeaters operated at 10Mbps speeds. Recently, however, many vendors have developed models that run at 10 or 100Mbps.

These hybrid devices are especially useful in small workgroups where some users have older Ethernet workstations and some have been upgraded to Fast Ethernet. Although these devices typically work with UTP connections only, they are still extremely versatile and inexpensive. Standalone hubs of this type are available from 3Com, Bay Networks, Intel, Accton, Dlink, and a host of other networking vendors. The operation of these types of hubs is more fully described later in this chapter.

Class I and Class II

One difference among Fast Ethernet repeaters involves their designs. Some Fast Ethernet repeaters are Class I, meaning that they fully decode incoming analog data into digital form before passing it to other ports. Class I Fast Ethernet repeaters may have all 100BASE-T4 ports, all 100BASE-TX ports, or some combination of the two. This last version is referred to as a translational repeater. Class II repeaters take the analog input signal from one port and forward it directly to all other ports. Class II Fast Ethernet repeaters are typically restricted to ports of only one type (either 100BASE-TX or 100BASE-T4). Class II repeaters exhibit lower port latencies than Class I repeaters because there is less overhead in forwarding a packet from one port to the next. Figure 8.10 illustrates the architectural differences between Class I and Class II Fast Ethernet repeaters.

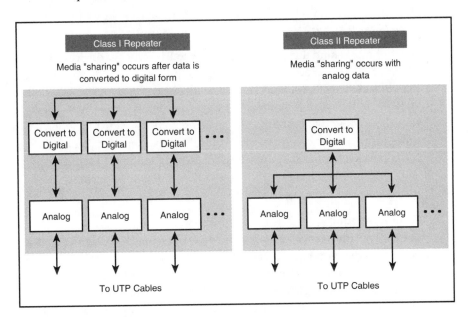

FIGURE 8.10 *Class I and Class II repeaters differ in the way they forward incoming data to other ports.*

When a signal is sent down UTP wiring, it suffers losses for many different reasons. A signal that initially started out as a perfect square wave, 5 volts peak-to-peak, loses amplitude and becomes somewhat spread out after traveling 100 meters of wire.

A repeater recognizes the weak incoming signal, re-creates it in its original form, and retransmits it to all other ports. In this way, repeaters are useful in overcoming the limitations imposed by the 100-meter distance restrictions of UTP cable. Because a repeater is a shared-media device and propagates all traffic, including collisions, however, it merely extends the collision domain of a network (remember that the collision domain is determined by the round-trip propagation delay of a packet, not the attenuation of the signal). A more powerful device, such as a bridge, router, or switch, is needed to extend the actual network diameter.

In 10BASE-T, standalone repeaters can be cascaded together with standard 100-meter UTP connections as long as the collision domain is not overrun. This could result in a network up to four repeaters deep. In 100BASE-T, however, the speed of the network signal has been increased by a factor of 10, so the collision domain must be shrunk by the same factor. As you remember from Chapter 3, this corresponds to a maximum of *two* Class II Fast Ethernet standalone repeaters cascaded together. If you skip ahead to Chapter 9, you will see that Figure 9.1 shows the different network diameters allowed under the Class I and Class II specifications.

Because most standalone repeaters have 8 to 24 ports per device, a Fast Ethernet network made up of standalone repeaters would have a limited number of users. This fact should emphasize the importance of stackable hubs and switches to the wide deployment of Fast Ethernet. Because the 802.3u specification allows only two Fast Ethernet repeaters to be cascaded together, it is much more critical that each repeater provides the maximum number of ports possible (as stackable hubs do). Switches can be used to interconnect groups of stackable hubs in such a way that the collision domain is never overrun. This is explained more fully in Chapter 9.

Troubleshooting

Another positive aspect of standalone repeaters (as opposed to all repeaters in general) is that you have the ability to *sniff*, or listen to, the network from any port. Because repeaters merely propagate signals to all existing ports, a signal that exists on port A also exists on port B or C. Network analyzers and sniffers, made popular by Hewlett-Packard and Network Associates, are designed to plug in to an empty repeater port and give a complete view of the network traffic at any given instant. With switches, however, this is not so easily done. This is one reason why many LAN administrators stick with their shared-media LANs—they are just easier to fix when problems arise. The same rules apply for Fast Ethernet repeaters. Several 100BASE-TX sniffers are on the market today, including the Expert Sniffer from Network Associates.

Stackable Hubs

A stackable hub can be thought of as a repeater with an expansion option. A stackable hub consists of several independent units, each with a given number of ports. Each unit acts as a standalone repeater in its own right, but also has an external connection for adding additional units exactly like itself. Because stackable hubs are shared-media devices, the effective bandwidth for a stack of hubs is always the same, no matter how many ports are in the stack. The more ports that are added, the less average bandwidth available to any given port. Figure 8.11 shows an example of a stackable hub stacked six units high.

FIGURE 8.11 *Intel's Express 200 Series of stackable hubs. The Express 220T supports 10 and 100Mbps operation on each port.*

The stackable hub's upgradability and inexpensive cost per port combine to make it the fastest growing segment of the entire hub market. Stackable hubs allow LAN administrators to purchase a single management unit to manage the whole stack, and thereby distribute the management costs over many ports. Stackable hubs are also extremely useful in connecting many nodes on a Fast Ethernet network due to the associated network diameter restrictions.

How Stackability Works

Stackable hubs are analogous to multiple standalone repeaters linked together with a high-speed stacking bus, yet sharing the same collision domain. This makes them look to the rest of the network like essentially one large repeater. Stackable hubs are currently quite popular in 10BASE-T, 100BASE-T, and newer 10/100 versions.

Stackable hubs are popular because they offer multiple connections at a low cost per port, they are manageable and easy to upgrade, and they fit well within the typical hierarchical network structure of large LANs. Figure 8.12 shows the architecture of a stackable hub.

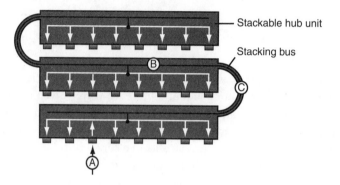

FIGURE 8.12 *In a stackable hub architecture, incoming packets are forwarded through the stacking bus to other hub units.*

Consider a situation where, at port A, an incoming frame enters the bottom unit of the stack. As in a regular standalone repeater, the frame is forwarded to all ports in that unit, but is also forwarded to the stacking bus , where it is forwarded to the next unit in the stack . The process repeats until all units in the stack are forwarding the same frame. This is how a set of stackable units can share the same collision domain, and thus act like one large, expandable repeater.

Port Density

Although stackable hubs are built for upgradability, they are not infinitely upgradable. There are limits to the number of units that can be added; this is often referred to as the *stacking height*. The stacking height has to do with how the hub propagates the signal across its stacking bus, and because these stacking buses are usually proprietary to the hub vendor, stacking height can vary. Most 10BASE-T and 100BASE-T stackable hubs can be stacked about eight units high and expanded to 120+ ports.

10/100 Autosensing Hubs

Fast Ethernet stackable hubs are currently widely available in many shapes and sizes, but a few features will separate a good Fast Ethernet stackable hub from an average one. One of these features is 10/100 autosensing capability on each and every port. This is accomplished by designing two stackable hubs in one box. The architecture of these devices consists of connecting every port on the device to both a 10 and 100Mbps repeater core. Because the ports can autonegotiate network speeds on their own, they can decide with which repeater core to connect (refer to auto-negotiation discussion in end-station component section). Essential in this design is an internal 10/100 bridge connection, which allows the 10Mbps and 100Mbps ports to remain connected. Figure 8.13 shows how a physical 10/100 per port stack resembles a virtual 10Mbps hub, 100Mbps hub, and 10/100 bridge.

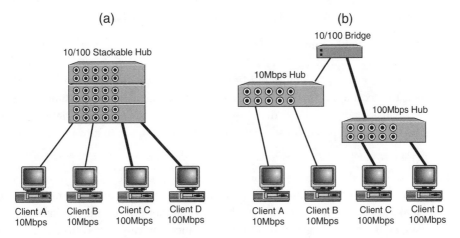

FIGURE 8.13 *(a) The actual connection of four clients. Clients A and B are connected at 10Mbps. Clients C and D are connected at 100Mbps. (b) The virtual representation of this scenario. Both descriptions are identical in terms of network characteristics, but the one shown in (a) is inherently more flexible.*

If you are in the market to connect a lot of users to the network and you are in the middle of a 10Mbps to 100Mbps transition, the 10/100 autosensing stackable hub is the device of choice. Because it is by far the most flexible design, and the cost is similar to 10-only versions, this will be the future direction of all stackable hubs.

Multisegment Stackable Hubs

Some vendors have designed stackable hubs that offer multisegment capability. This means that the stack of hubs can physically isolate any number of ports to a certain segment. Some designs, such as 3Com's SuperStack II PS50 stackable hub, allow ports to be mapped in to one of many segments. The designs either use internal bridging to connect all the segments or offer separate modules for this purpose. The obvious advantage of this design is that the available bandwidth of the workgroup is proportional to the number of segments offered. With the 3Com design, servers could be connected to their own segments while clients share a segment.

Be careful when considering these products, however, because they are still quite expensive. It is important to realize that when you extend the multisegment concept to each and every port, you have a switch. It is the author's opinion that if you want performance at each and every port, you should buy a switch. If you want inexpensive bandwidth for connecting a multitude of clients, buy a stackable hub. Multisegment stackable hubs are stuck in between, offering neither the performance of a true switch, nor the low cost of a stackable hub.

Other Stackable Hub Features

Some stackable hubs offer additional features, such as redundant power supplies and hot upgradability (adding units without turning off power to the stack). Redundant power supplies are a plus because if any one unit in the stack has a power failure, the others can compensate. Hot upgradability is useful because the stack doesn't have to be powered down to add more units.

Uplinks

Stackable hubs offer all sorts of media uplinks, but here is what you should look for. First, make sure the uplinks are switched, not shared. In other words, make sure the uplink doesn't just become another port on the stackable hub segment. This will seriously limit the distance you can extend from the workgroup. A shared 100BASE-FX uplink will only extend 160m from the stackable hub, for instance, whereas a switched, full-duplex 100BASE-FX uplink can stretch up to 2km.

Many vendors offer ATM and Gigabit uplinks for their stackable hub lines, but this is overkill. If you are sharing 100Mbps of bandwidth in the workgroup, (which in most of today's workgroups is more than enough) why would you need more than the 200Mbps of uplink capacity offered by full-duplex Fast Ethernet?

Management

Because standalone repeaters are used primarily in smaller workgroups, management may not be an essential feature. When it comes to stackable hubs, however, depending on the application, management options such as SNMP may be beneficial. Some stackable hubs allow for a management module, which can be added at any time. Therefore, if management is important in your workgroups, it is recommended you buy either managed hubs or unmanaged hubs with a management upgrade path.

Most stackable hubs offer a configurable management module capable of managing the entire stack. Therefore, it is only essential to purchase this management module for one unit in any given stack. The best approach to stackable hub management is to buy the management module and associated software up front, and thereby make it easier to add units to the stack later on. If you have ever tried to add management to an existing network, you know the effort involved. A few extra dollars up front will prevent headaches down the road. Also, considering the fact that stackable hubs are shared-media devices, a multitude of PC-based shared LAN management software packages can be used to manage the traffic on the stack.

SNMPv2 is essential to manage a stack of hubs. RMON is offered on some models, but as you will read in Chapter 11, "Managing Switched, Fast, and Gigabit Ethernet Networks," RMON would be overkill for most shared workgroups. Because RMON Group I is relatively inexpensive to add to SNMP, many vendors will include it in the price of the management module. Don't get stuck paying for more than SNMP and RMON Group I in stackable hubs. A good way to avoid this is to compare the price of the vendor's SNMP-only management offering to the SNMP and RMON offering. Many times, they will only promote the latter.

Gigabit Buffered Repeaters

Recently, the IEEE, spurred by a few vendors such as Packet Engines, developed the full-duplex buffered Gigabit repeater specification. The idea is that a Gigabit Ethernet shared-media device would be a lot cheaper to build than a Gigabit Ethernet switch.

A Gigabit buffered repeater relies on the concept of granting access to the Gbps shared media instead of using collisions to resolve congestion. Although nothing is technically wrong with this approach, and it will work with most vendors' upcoming Gigabit Ethernet server NICs, the design has limited appeal. You can pick up the Gigabit buffered repeaters for around $500 to $1000 per port, as opposed to Gigabit switches in the $1500 to $2000 range; the scalability of such a device is questionable, however.

It is a good idea to use Gigabit buffered repeaters to evaluate Gbps, or to connect future Gigabit server farms. When it comes to making a strategic decision about putting Gigabit Ethernet in your backbone, however, spend the extra money and get a Gigabit switch.

Workgroup Switches

Kalpana (bought by Cisco in 1994) made LAN switching a household concept, although all it really did was redesign and remarket a multiport Ethernet bridge. Not to take anything away from the brilliant EtherSwitch product, but the concept of switching is nothing new. The concept of marketing multiport bridges as "switches" is what is new. It also helped that Kalpana could drastically cost-reduce the switch by integrating the bridging function into silicon ASICs.

Switches can be generally classified into three categories. Workgroup, or seg-ment, switches are used to congregate many shared segments, servers, and high-performance desktops and are discussed in detail in this section. The Bay Networks 450T, shown in figure 8.14, is a good example of a workgroup switch. (Bay Networks was recently acquired by Nortel.) Desktop switches are a special breed of workgroup switch and are specifically designed to connect directly to nodes. Backbone switches are high-end devices used to congregate many sub-LANs. Backbone switches, including the Layer 3 variety, are dis-cussed later in the chapter.

FIGURE 8.14   *The Bay Networks 450T: a 10/100 workgroup switch.*

How Switches Work

In general, a switch is defined as a network component that receives incoming packets, stores them temporarily, and sends them back out on another port. Because a switch buffers incoming frames, it can be used like a bridge or router to extend the collision domain of a network indefinitely. Switches are crucial to Fast Ethernet deployment because of their capability to increase network diameter.

A switch's total potential for incoming bandwidth is determined by adding the bandwidth available to each port. For instance, a 16-port 100Mbps Fast Ethernet switch gives an aggregate throughput of 1.6Gbps (if you consider half-duplex incoming and outgoing traffic and no other architectural limita-tions), whereas a 16-port 100-Mbps repeater still only gives 100Mbps of throughput. However, a switch can be limited by its architecture. A switch with five 100Mbps ports, but only 300Mbps of backplane capacity, for example, can really only support three of these ports at full wire speed.

A switch can be receiving frames on any number of ports while at the same time forwarding frames to many other ports. Figure 8.15 shows this: Incoming frames on ports A, B, and C are sent simultaneously to ports D, E, and F. Although the collisions found in a repeater are avoided in a switch, contention can still occur when two incoming ports want to forward data to the same outgoing port. In this scenario, a switch would probably buffer one of the incoming frames.

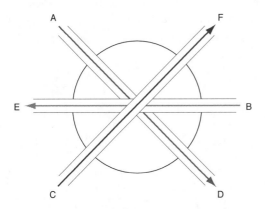

FIGURE 8.15 *How a switch works: Multiple data streams can pass through a switch without affecting each other.*

Switches can be very useful in constructing large, robust LANs because they provide one of the lowest prices per megabit of bandwidth of any network component available today. Ethernet and Fast Ethernet switches are also especially useful when sending steady-stream traffic, such as video, over the LAN because they provide dedicated bandwidth to each and every port. In a switched architecture, traffic levels depend not only on the number of users on the network, but also on the network architecture, buffering, and switch forwarding rates.

Another thing to consider with a switch is that the familiar carrier sense multiple access/collision detect (CSMA/CD) medium access scheme no longer applies. With a dedicated connection for each port, there is no contention for the wire, and therefore limited collisions.

A switched connection in half-duplex mode is not totally collision-free, however, because the switch port and the end node can still collide with each other. A full-duplex switched port is completely collision-free.

Packet Forwarding

Standalone bridges were historically popular because they could filter and forward packets, separating network traffic and increasing performance. In today's networks, switches have taken on the role of bridges.

Switches are basically invisible to all network software because they perform their functions at Layer 2, the MAC layer. A switch looks at a network address, analyzes it, compares it to an internal list of addresses, and sends the packet to one port. When a switch first powers up, it doesn't know anything about the network around it; as it starts receiving packets, however, it can develop a list of which addresses are coming from which port. Figure 8.16 shows three switch ports at three distinct points in time.

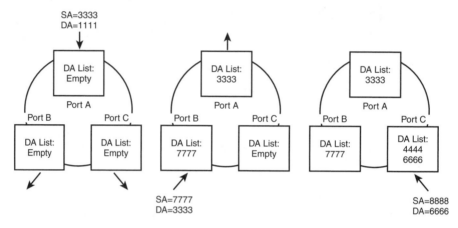

FIGURE 8.16 *How a switch forwards packets: The left part of the figure shows the switch after initial powerup, the middle shows forwarding a packet through the switch, and the right part of the figure shows a switch not forwarding a packet.*

The left part of Figure 8.16 shows a packet coming in on port A, with a destination address (DA) of 00AA00001111 and a source address (SA) of 00AA00003333. The switch has just been powered up, so it doesn't know where this packet is supposed to go and it has no choice but to forward it to all ports, hoping the right party eventually receives it. The switch also remembers that it received a packet on port A from SA=00AA00003333.

In the middle of Figure 8.16, the switch receives a packet on port B with a DA of 00AA00003333. It remembers that this address lies beyond port A, so it forwards the packet only to port A. Now, assume in the right part of Figure 8.16 that the switch has received traffic from many different nodes and the structure of its address table is as shown. A packet comes in on port C with a DA of 00AA00006666. Because the switch sees that the address lies beyond port C, it assumes the packet is already on the right segment and does not forward the packet to ports A or B.

Wire Speed

When considering wire speed of a switched connection, the following items should be considered:

- *10-only versus 10/100 in the workgroup*—Even today, most switches support 10Mbps operation only on most ports. This may be fine for a workgroup where you will never upgrade the connections (hubs, desktops, and servers) to 10/100. But if you have plans to upgrade the connections to 100Mbps in the future, install a 10/100 per port workgroup switch. The difference in price is two to three times that of a 10Mbps-only switch, but well worth it in terms of flexibility and performance.

- *Full-duplex and flow control*—Although it is not incredibly important to have end stations on full-duplex connections, network managers should still look for switches that support full-duplex and the IEEE 802.3x full-duplex flow-control standard. As you may recall from Chapter 3, flow control on a full-duplex connection consists of special start and stop packets. The case where too many requests are congesting one port on a switch is called *oversubscription* and can drag network performance down. This is crucial in workgroups where local clients are accessing local servers. Because many clients could potentially be asking for the server simultaneously, the server will need a way to let them know when it is busy. This is accomplished either by faking a collision in half-duplex mode, or sending a stop flow-control packet in full-duplex mode. This temporarily disables the sending station long enough for the switch to clear out its backlog of packets.

- *Port aggregation*—The more mathematically minded network managers may be asking this: "If 100Mbps is the maximum speed on a switch, how do I connect two 100Mbps switches together?" The answer to this question is twofold. Either some sort of port aggregation is used, or a higher-speed technology, such as Gigabit Ethernet or ATM, is employed. Port aggregation is important because most locations initially won't be able to use ATM or Gigabit Ethernet due to cost or product availability issues.

  As discussed in the section "Server NICs," port aggregation allows multiple switch ports to share the load of a given connection and can be used at 10Mbps, 100Mbps, or even Gbps speeds. In its best configuration (four full-duplex connections), one flavor of port aggregation, EtherChannel, provides 800Mbps of bandwidth between two devices. Figure 8.17 shows this.

As described in the section "Server NICs," both sides of the connection must support the same port aggregation technique for the scheme to work. Aggregating fast Ethernet ports in this way is a great step toward an eventual deployment of Gigabit Ethernet. The IEEE is working on an industrywide standard for port aggregation called 802.3ab.

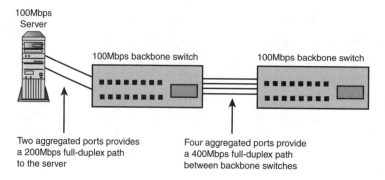

100Mbps Server

100Mbps backbone switch

100Mbps backbone switch

Two aggregated ports provides a 200Mbps full-duplex path to the server

Four aggregated ports provide a 400Mbps full-duplex path between backbone switches

FIGURE 8.17   *Two 100Mbps switches are connected together with four EtherChannel connections, providing 800Mbps of bandwidth (400Mbps in each direction). A server is connected with two server NICs in a similar fashion.*

Uplinks

Workgroup switches support a variety of uplink technologies. Here are a few to look for:

- *100BASE-FX*—It is essential that workgroup switches support 100BASE-FX full-duplex uplinks to overcome the 100m distance limitations imposed by UTP. 100BASE-FX uplinks allow fast Ethernet switches to be used in campus networks where distances routinely are in the 2km range.

- *Gigabit Ethernet*—Gigabit Ethernet uplinks are new to the world of work-group switching. 3Com, Cabletron, Cisco, Bay Networks, Intel, and several other networking companies have already announced Gbps modules for their switches. As the Gigabit Ethernet standard is completed, it is likely that these modules will be IEEE802.3z compliant. The network manager will have the choice of multimode or single-mode flavors of Gigabit Ethernet. Gigabit uplink modules should support full-duplex operation.

- *ATM*—ATM uplinks are important for Ethernet workgroup switches that may be connected to an ATM backbone. Because the ATM standard is still in flux, there is a chance that all 155Mbps ATM modules will not work together. Ask to see compatibility testing results if you are not sure about the interoperability of your ATM modules.

Switch Architecture and Performance

Four basic components fundamentally affect a switch's performance: backplane capacity, port speed and type, buffer size, and packet-forwarding mechanisms (including address lookup). Figure 8.18 highlights these areas. Although other things do affect switch performance—things like internal switching architecture, core bus architecture—they don't affect network design as much as the other four and, therefore, aren't discussed in detail here.

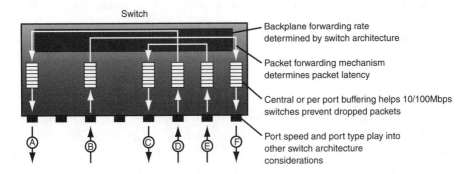

FIGURE 8.18 *Basic switch architecture.*

Backplane Capacity and Forwarding Rate

A switch's *backplane architecture* defines how packets are forwarded from one port to the other through the internal electronics of the switch. Backplane architecture is important to switch designers, but not so much to network designers. The *backplane capacity* of a switch is important to network designers because it determines the actual forwarding rate of the switch, depending on traffic patterns. A switch with very little buffering can achieve its maximum forwarding rate, for instance, only if all ports are the same speed and the traffic is equally loaded between the ports.

In most cases, a switch is limited by its backplane capacity. A 10-port 100Mbps switch with only 500Mbps of backplane capacity cannot service all 10 ports at full wire speed. Full-duplex support can further compound problems when a switch's backplane capacity is the architectural bottleneck. Even in worst-case traffic scenarios, however, switches will not see a condition where every port is receiving data at full wire speed. Because backplane capacity is expensive, the best thing to do is model your current and future traffic levels and buy a switch whose backplane capacity can handle those levels. A switch connecting four servers and 20 clients at 100Mbps may need 100Mbps full-duplex for each server, for example, but only 50Mbps for each client on average. A switch with backplane capacity of $200 \times 2 + 50 \times 20 = 1.4$Gbps would work fine in this instance. As silicon integration goes up, the cost of backplane capacity will go down. Today, 10Mbps switches, for the most part, have more than enough backplane capacity. 100Mbps switches are just getting there, and Gbps switches will be limited by their backplane capacity for some time.

Port Speed and Type

Although FDDI and Token Ring switching products are still shipping, most workgroup switches installed today are 10BASE-T or 100BASE-T. Switches with 10/100Mbps Ethernet ports allow for a seamless migration from existing 10Mbps Ethernet networks to 100Mbps Fast Ethernet networks. In addition to being 10 or 100Mbps, switch ports can also be 100BASE-TX or 100BASE-FX, and half- or full-duplex, depending on the switch design.

Buffering Scheme and Size

Buffering can play a large role in 10/100 switching, especially with Novell's Windows client software and other sliding-windows protocols. Sliding windows works with protocol stacks such as IPX and IP, allowing for many back-to-back packets on the wire. Consider a switch with port A connected to a 100Mbps server and port B to a 10-Mbps client, for instance. With some of today's network protocols, up to 16 frames can be sent back-to-back from the server to the client, which amounts to roughly 24KB of data. Each 1.5KB frame takes 122 microseconds to transfer at 100Mbps and 1220 microseconds to transfer at 10Mbps, which means that 10 frames can be received on port A before one is completely sent out on port B.

In the case of 16 back-to-back 100Mbps frames, port A will be deluged with 24KB of incoming data before port B can send out even one 10Mbps packet. If the switch 's buffer size is not 24KB or greater, the incoming data will overrun the buffer and be lost.

A logical deduction of this scenario is that larger buffers mean better performance. This assumption is basically true, but large buffers are inherently expensive. Therefore, many switch vendors have opted for a congestion-control mechanism to prevent an overrun case of this type. The congestion-control concept involves sending a "fake" collision back to the high-speed port, forcing it to back off. In our example, port B would recognize when its buffer is almost full and send a jam pattern back to the transmitting node.

The transmitting node interprets this jam pattern as a collision, so it enters the standard backoff state. The switch can keep the transmitting node in this state until it has emptied its internal buffers. This type of congestion control is specific to half-duplex switch ports and is implemented as a feature in most switches.

Because of the obvious advantages of switch buffering, switch vendors have
created designs with a large pool of shared memory. This pool, often 1MB or
more in size, can be doled out to the ports that need it most. Look for shared
buffering when shopping for workgroup switches.

Switch Buffering

There are two schools of thought on
switch design when it comes to buffering: shared buffering and dedicated
buffering per port. Shared buffering
may be slightly slower, but it is much
more flexible. Shared buffering uses
one big pool of memory for all switch
ports. This means that if one of the
switch ports happens to be overloaded

with incoming traffic, it can support
that configuration. Dedicated buffers
per port allow room for only so many
incoming frames per port. Therefore in
the preceding scenario, some ports
may not be using all their addressing
space, while others are overrun with
data. Always go for shared buffering if
possible.

Forwarding Mechanisms

The forwarding mechanism in a switch may be store-and-forward, cut-through,
or modified cut-through. Workgroup switches, such as the Cisco Catalyst 1900
switch, are configurable on a port-by-port basis. Other switches, such as Intel's
510T switch, automatically determine the best forwarding method for each port
and configure the port accordingly. In a workgroup switch, packet-forwarding
mechanisms will make a tradeoff between packet latency and error-checking
robustness. Let's look at the three types of switch-forwarding mechanisms
more closely:

- *Store-and-forward switches* completely store the incoming frame in internal
  buffers before sending it out on another port. In this case, the switch
  latency is equal to an entire packet, which could turn into a performance
  issue if enough of these switches are cascaded in series. However, store-
  and-forward switches provide excellent packet error-checking in the form
  of Cyclical Redundancy Check (CRC) checks, runt packet filters, and collision filters. A store-and-forward switch may be a good investment for
  critical points in the network, but not necessarily everywhere.

- *Cut-through switches* examine a packet only up to the destination MAC
  address, much like a bridge. This allows the packet to be forwarded
  almost immediately, resulting in very low switch latencies. The drawback
  to cut-through switching is that runt packets, collision packets, and packets with CRC errors will also be forwarded. In fact, any packet arriving
  with a valid destination address will be forwarded. Proponents of

cut-through switching point out that end nodes are, by default, set up to do this level of error checking so that a switch doesn't have to. This tends to be truer in workgroups than on the backbone; therefore, if your workgroups do not encounter many errors, a cut-through switch may be a good choice.

- *Modified cut-through switches* attempt to offer the best of both worlds by holding an incoming Ethernet packet until the first 64 bytes have been received. If a collision or runt packet occurs, it is very likely that it will occur in the first 64 bytes of a frame, so a tradeoff between switch latency and error checking is achieved. Modified cut-through switches act like store-and-forward switches for short frames, however, which are typically control frames, and like cut-through switches for large frames, which are usually made up of data. This is a shortcoming of modified cut-through switches because control frames require low-switch latencies and data frames require good error checking. This may be a moot point in many networks, however, because CRC errors are usually measured in parts per billion (a few errors in a billion packets).

The type of forwarding mechanism you use should depend on your network criteria. If your network needs speed and low latency, cut-through switches are the best choice. If your network needs efficiency and stability, store-and-forward switching is the way to go. To get a better understanding of the three types of packet forwarding, consider Figure 8.19. The point at which a frame is forwarded is shown for each type of forwarding mechanism.

The longer a switch has to wait to forward a packet, the more latency is introduced into the packet transmission delay. If a packet has to flow through several store-and-forward switches, the latency will be especially long. Long latency is not a particular problem when sending data across the network; but when sending voice or multimedia traffic, it could introduce ugly delays and cause the video and voice applications to appear jerky and clipped. This is why a switch that can automatically determine which forwarding method is best for each port is a good solution.

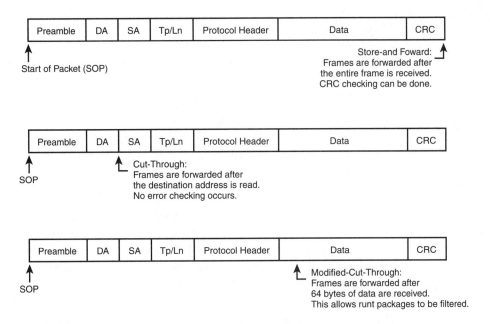

FIGURE 8.19 *Three types of packet forwarding mechanisms; the best switches will automatically determine the best forwarding method.*

MAC Address Lookup and Size

One of the ways a workgroup switch can be differentiated is in the extent of MAC address filtering that occurs within the switch. This section deals with the options that some switches offer for filtering addresses at Layer 2, or MAC address, level. We look briefly at content-addressable memory (CAM) size, multicast filtering, and address pruning:

- *CAM size*—CAM refers to a specific type of memory that allows switches to look up a particular address extremely quickly. Instead of describing how CAMs work here, we will just say that they are very expensive and, therefore, most switch vendors make a size-versus-cost tradeoff when designing switches.

The general rule of thumb that seems to work for both workgroup and backbone switches is to calculate the absolute maximum number of different MAC addresses you expect the switch to receive and multiply by four. Therefore if you have 1000 nodes on your campus network, buy a switch that supports at least 4000 MAC addresses.

- *Multicast support*—Some switches support extra filtering for multicast packets. Although this seems like a nice feature, most network managers use it only for specific multimedia applications. If you think you need it, it is not hard to find. Try a small networking company called Network Peripherals, Inc.

- *Address pruning*—Most network managers want to install workgroup switches once and not worry about them again. For this reason, switches must perform maintenance tasks on their internal forwarding tables. In the example in Figure 8.16, it is easy to see how a switch's address tables could be filled after only a short time on the network if the total number of connected nodes is greater than the size of the internal address table. This is why switches delete addresses they haven't seen in a while in a process called *address pruning*. Pruning also occurs when the address tables are full and a new address comes in. A switch will then drop the oldest address from its table. It is amazing what kind of problems this causes in certain networks and is why the authors highly recommend paying extra for a large amount of address capacity in workgroup and backbone switches.

Scalability

Scaling workgroup switches has been hotly debated within the networking industry for the past few years. You can basically do this in two ways. The first is to cascade switches together using port aggregation techniques. The second is to use a newer approach, called a stackable switch backplane. We talk more about how to use these two methods in your network in Chapter 9; the following is a brief introduction to the concepts, however:

- *Cascading workgroup switches*—Traditionally, the only way to connect multiple switches together in the wiring closet was to cascade them with high-speed ports. This is very inexpensive and supported by almost every switch vendor. For an idea of what this looks like with two Fast Ethernet switches, consult Figure 8.17. Note that this uses four ports on each Fast Ethernet switch and the interswitch bandwidth is limited by the number of connections between switches.

- *Stackable switch backplane*—In recent months, switch vendors have introduced switches that have a special connection that allows them to be effectively stacked together. The difference between this and the cascading method is the stacking interface is specially designed to allow the stacked switches to appear as one big switch. This means two things: The interswitch performance is not typically limited as in the cascading method, and switch ports are not wasted connecting the two switches together. Examples of stackable switches today are 3Com's SuperStack II 3300, Bay Networks 450T (Bay Networks was acquired recently by Nortel), and Intel's Express 510T switch. These switches are worth a look, although the extra gear required to stack them adds quite a bit to the overall acquisition cost.

Virtual LANs and Tagging

Virtual LAN (VLAN) support in a workgroup switch may or may not be required, depending on what's planned for the workgroup connections. You have already seen that the IEEE is working on the 802.1p standard for prioritizing packet flow, and the 802.1Q standard for VLAN tagging. Now the question becomes, "Do you really need VLANs in your workgroup switch?"

In a nutshell, VLANs allow switched networks to properly filter broadcast and multicast packets. This may sound like a simple way of describing VLANs—a complex technology—but it is basically true. If the MAC (or Layer 2) address and IP (or Layer 3) of a destination are already known, you don't need much more information to successfully get the packet to that destination. The only time you run into trouble is when you don't have that information, as is the case with broadcast and multicast packets. Because most network protocols use broadcast packets extensively to discover information about the network, it is a good idea to direct this traffic only where it needs to go. The options for doing this today are good-old routing (or Layer 3 switching, as we will soon discuss) or VLANs. Of the two, routing is much more stable and interoperable.

VLANs do have benefits besides performance. Many network managers use VLANs to ease the administration overhead of moving PCs and servers. VLANs also allow a broadcast domain to be defined by the type of user rather than their physical location. This is helpful, for instance, when users take their laptops into conference rooms and expect to connect to the same network services they receive in their office.

VLANs can be grouped by port, MAC address, protocol type, IP subnet, IP multicast domain, or 802.1Q VLAN packet tag. Because the IEEE 802.1p and

802.1Q standards are just now nearing completion, it will be difficult to design a multivendor VLAN architecture across your network. For this reason, it is strongly suggested that VLANs be used only within a given switch or in a single-vendor switched network.

Workgroup Switch Management

Switch management is a dilemma facing many switch vendors and LAN administrators today. With a shared-media network, the management is straightforward because all ports on a segment see all the traffic on that segment. Because switches actually filter traffic, they must have some other means of collecting vital network management statistics. So far, three methods have been developed for doing this. One method incorporates management into the backplane architecture of the switch. Statistics are collected on each packet that is forwarded on the switch backplane and are stored in a management unit with its own unique Ethernet address. This management unit may be polled from any station on the LAN. The only problem with this method is that each switch vendor has implemented its own scheme for doing this; so compatibility is at a minimum, usually limited to SNMP statistics. The second method is called *port aliasing*, and it allows the switch to "mirror" any given port to a dedicated management port. The management port is fed into a specific management terminal or a network analyzer. The sniffer can look at overall switch statistics and individual port information. Once again, no specific standard exists for this type of switch management.

The third method is remote monitoring, or RMON, which actually works in conjunction with SNMP. Almost all switch vendors have incorporated the new RMON Management Interface Base (MIB), which allows SNMP-based port-by-port management of a switch. Chapter 11 delves into more detail on RMON and the management problems associated with switching. For the purposes of this chapter, look for workgroup switches that support RMON Groups 1, 2, 3, and 9.

Desktop Switches

A desktop switch differs from a workgroup switch in several ways. First, a desktop switch is designed to be connected *only* to end stations, which means it can be designed much more inexpensively than a workgroup switch. Second, a desktop switch doesn't support the same higher-end features of a workgroup switch, such as large MAC address lookup tables and large backplane capacities. Third, a desktop switch is usually only 50% to 75% of the cost of an average workgroup switch. A good example of a desktop switch is the 3Com SuperStack II Desktop 1000. Table 8.5 compares a typical desktop switch to a workgroup switch.

TABLE 8.5 A COMPARISON OF A DESKTOP SWITCH TO A WORKGROUP SWITCH

Switch Feature	Desktop Switch	Workgroup Switch
Backplane performance	Full wire speed, but not on all ports simultaneously	Full wire speed on all ports simultaneously
Port density	High	Low-Medium
MAC addresses supported	One per port up to 1KB per switch	4KB to 32KB per switch
Management	SNMP, RMON Groups 1, 2, 3, and 9	SNMP, RMON Groups 1–9
Scalability	No scalability	Often allows switches to be connected together with a special high-performance connection
Modularity	Possible uplink port	Many uplink ports supporting a variety of modules
Price	Sub $100/port	Usually much more than $100/port

It is common for desktop switches to support many 10Mbps-only connections with a few high-speed fast Ethernet uplinks. These switches rarely support full-duplex, and have backplane capacities that don't allow for full wire-speed data transfer on all ports. In most, the number of MAC addresses supported is one to four per port. VLAN and management support is uncommon.

Although these desktop switches are well designed to connect clients in a workgroup environment and cost quite a bit less than their workgroup cousins, most network managers stay away from them. It is often the case that network managers have to move switches around after they are installed; and if you buy a specialty switch that can be used only to connect desktops, you may find yourself stuck in a proprietary solution down the road.

Backbone Components

A network can have anywhere from zero to several hundred backbone devices. The components themselves fall into three broad categories: bridges, routers, and backbone switches. Their function is to provide fast, robust, and efficient connections for a variety of different subnetworks. This function typically requires very fast silicon and/or microprocessors and is available only at a high price: It is not uncommon for a high-end router to cost tens of thousands of dollars. Although the backbone function may seem to be required only in large, multi-node networks, routers are also quite common in smaller networks. A branch office with 20 users, a few servers, and a connection to headquarters through a WAN can employ an access router to route traffic from the branch office LAN to the WAN, for example. This can hardly be considered a backbone application, but routers are nonetheless grouped in this category.

When describing backbone components, it is common to start with the most basic of these devices: bridges.

Bridges

A bridge is the evolutionary predecessor to the switch. Bridges are fast becoming extinct in the wake of high-performance switches, but it is still good form to understand basic bridging. Every Ethernet packet has a field defined as the *destination address*, which tells the packet for which node it is ultimately destined. A bridge can look at an incoming Ethernet packet and analyze the destination address encapsulated in its header. This is why a bridge is referred to as a Layer 2 device. From this information, the bridge can check its "memory" of past frames and determine whether to forward the packet to another port or do nothing. In this way, bridges can isolate network traffic between network segments. Figure 8.20 shows the general structure of an Ethernet or Fast Ethernet frame and the location of the destination address.

8 Bytes	6 Bytes	6 Bytes	2 Bytes	about 30 Bytes	about 1500 Bytes	4 Bytes
Preamble	Destination Address	Source Address	Length	Protocol Header	Data	CRC

Bridge analyze
destination address

F IGURE 8.20 *A bridge looks for the destination address of an Ethernet frame.*

The 802.1d Spanning Tree

Bridging is important in that it introduces the concept of a *spanning tree*. It basically consists of two ideas: loop prevention and redundant link configuration. Loop prevention is needed because a series of bridges or switches could be set up in such a way that a packet could be transmitted from one switch to the other, with the last switch forwarding the frame back to the first in an infinitely repeating cycle. Spanning tree identifies this situation and prevents it by shutting down one of the connections. Because spanning tree manages loop connections, it can therefore turn a loop connection back on if packets are not getting through the network. In this way, it provides redundant link configuration. The IEEE formalized the spanning-tree mechanism in the 802.1d specification. All bridges and most modern switches support 802.1d.

Routers

A router can perform all the functions of a bridge and more, which allows it to be used in many different applications (see Figure 8.21). A router differs from a bridge in its capability to examine the protocol header of a packet. The protocol header is part of the Layer 3 information embedded in a packet. This allows the router to break LANs into subnetworks based on IP or IPX network number (that is, network number) *and* destination address. This basic feature allows a router to be used for three distinct purposes:

- Improved network segmentation

- Routing between dissimilar LANs

- Routing to a WAN

The sections that follow discuss these applications in more detail.

Some of the leading routers today are the Cisco 7500, the Bay Networks ASN400 (Bay Networks was acquired recently by Nortel), and 3Com's NetBuilder III. Most router vendors provide chassis-based routing systems that allow Fast Ethernet modules to be added after the initial purchase. Fast Ethernet modules for these product lines provide the same type of service as their Ethernet counterparts except, of course, at 10 times the speed. Because routers are commonly found at critical junctures of the network, their modules are usually hot swappable and highly manageable. A router chassis will typically provide other features, such as redundant power supplies and dedicated management modules.

FIGURE 8.21 *The Cisco Catalyst 5000 system features slots that can be filled with RSMs (routing switch modules).*

Routing Protocols

IP and IPX have already been mentioned as two of the most popular routing protocols. Routing protocols, such as DECnet and AppleTalk, are some of the lesser-known routing protocols still used in many networks. These protocols refer to the way the Layer 3 addressing is configured and managed on a network.

Another flavor of routing protocol is those that routers use to talk to each other and communicate the routing address information they know. This is critical in large networks, such as the Internet, where the number of addresses is large and widespread. Originally, Cisco used such protocols as the Border Gateway Protocol (BGP) to do this, but customers forced the industry to standardize on the more widely accepted RIP, RIP2, and, later, OSPF. These *inter-router protocols* are distinct from Layer 3 protocols, such as IP and IPX, and are still in widespread use today. For more information on BGP, consult the IETF RFC 1774.

The Protocol Header

According to the Ethernet specification, the Layer 3 protocol header is merely part of the data field. A bridge understands the Layer 2 Ethernet details only (that is, the MAC addresses); a router, on the other hand, can look at the network field, interpret it as a frame originated by a certain protocol stack, and act on it accordingly (see Figure 8.22). Bridges automatically learn how to forward packets, whereas routers must be configured for this task. A router that understands the IPX protocol stack can tell the difference between a packet originated on IPX network 01 and IPX network 02, for example but only if it knows to look for this. In this way, a router can route not only between network segments, but also across different types of networks.

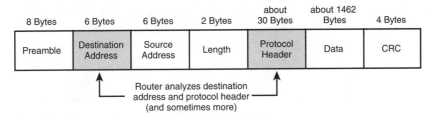

F IGURE 8.22 *A router examines the entire Ethernet frame, including the protocol header and data fields.*

The Routing Model

Another way to look at routing is to imagine a switched and routed network as the United States. A switch would act like the local post office of a given town. The local office knows where every house in that town is and who lives there and keeps the information in its list of addresses. The local post office is in one zip code and can only deal with mail that has that zip code. After a letter with a different zip code shows up, the local office has to forward it to the regional office (router). The regional office checks the known list of zip codes, but this office keeps only a few of the close-by zip codes on the list. If the letter's addressee is in an unknown zip code, the regional office must use RIP to query its immediate neighbors about the unknown code. Because every regional office knows who its neighbors are, this request will eventually find it is way to someone who knows where that zip code is and the RIP message will be answered.

It sounds complicated, but the scheme is optimized for the local postal worker because he or she only has to make the extra effort when a letter goes far away from his or her location, which is the exception rather than the rule.

Applications in Backbones

Routers are also good at specific backbone tasks—for example, segmenting large networks, handling multiple protocols, and accessing the wide area network. Let's look at each of these in more detail:

- *Better network segmentation*—Routers have traditionally been used to segment networks into subnetworks. This allows the routers to filter broadcast frames and keep them isolated to a smaller number of network devices, and thus improve performance on the other subnets.

  Subnetting is commonly used to describe breaking up TCP/IP networks into smaller subnetworks, although other Layer 3 protocols can also be subnetted. TCP/IP addresses use different formats, but let's assume that a router breaks a network into three subnets: 206.203.170.XXX, 206.203.175.XXX, and 206.203.176.XXX, where XXX represents the address space of a subnetwork, which is typically made up of many nodes, each with a unique IP address. If a packet has an IP address of 206.203.175.322, it will find its way through the routed network to the second subnet of the three. The real performance benefit occurs when broadcast packets are generated on one of the subnets—176.XXX, for instance. They won't be forwarded to the other two subnets.

- *Handling multiple protocols*—Another beneficial feature of a router is its built-in capability to communicate between dissimilar packet-based networks. Routers are commonly employed to allow Token Ring and Ethernet users to communicate. A router takes an incoming frame and stores it in memory. After the frame is stored, the router software strips off the data and protocol header fields, reforms a new frame based on the type used by the destination network, and sends the frame out on the correct port. In this application, routers are not invisible to the network like bridges, but must be directly addressed at specific destination addresses. Therefore, if an Ethernet user wants to send information to a user on a Token Ring network, the information will first be addressed to the router, which interconnects the two LANs. Figure 8.23 shows an example of a router in this application.

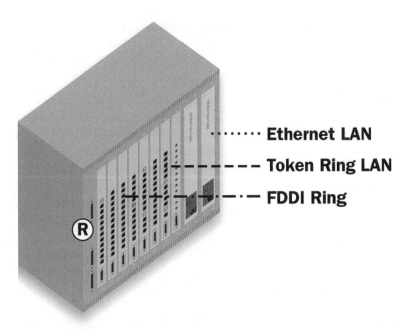

Ethernet LAN

Token Ring LAN

FDDI Ring

FIGURE 8.23 *Routers are often used to route between dissimilar LANs.*

- *WAN connectivity*—Routers also play an important role in WAN connectivity. WANs are typically much lower-speed (T1, T3) connections than LANs because the cost of WAN bandwidth is much higher. Because routers provide the highest level of packet screening, both at the destination address and IP level, they make good gates for outgoing traffic. WAN routers may also work with incoming and outgoing data at the application level, performing such functions as compression or encryption. Sometimes routers in this configuration are referred to as *gateways*. The branch office discussed previously is a good example of this type of router application. When users in a sales office send information to each other, the LAN-to-WAN router does not forward this information to the WAN. When those same users want to access information at company headquarters, however, the router allows LAN-to-WAN access. These branch-office and small-office routers are nowhere near as complex or expensive as traditional segmentation routers.

- *RSVP*—RSVP refers to a technology originally developed by Cisco, Microsoft, and Intel. It is now being standardized as RFC 2205. RSVP allows routers (and other Layer 3 devices) to reserve bandwidth across a switched network, and thus allows time-sensitive transfers, like voice and video, to run uninterrupted across the network. Proponents of running voice over IP should look for RSVP features in their routers. We discuss RSVP in more detail in Chapter 9.

Performance

Routers typically are measured by the number of packets they can examine and forward in a given amount of time. This usually is represented in packets per second (pps). It is important to know the size of packet being used in the measurement because a 64-byte packet takes a shorter time to transmit than a 1500-byte packet. A steady stream of 64-byte packets is harder on a router, however, because the router has less time to analyze one packet before the next one comes in. Therefore, routers typically are measured on 64-byte packets and 1500-byte packets. A 100Mbps switch usually can pass packets at wire speed or 144,000 pps (64-byte size).

Management

Routers also can be managed via SNMP, but this provides only basic information. Because of their high level of complexity, routers usually have proprietary management capabilities built in to the routing devices themselves. A high-end router will typically come complete with MIBs and associated software. Endless training classes and handbooks are dedicated to the fine art of managing routers, so we will leave that discussion for another book. Cisco Systems has several high-quality books on router programming (www.cisco.com).

PC-Based Routing

A less-expensive way to achieve routing is through PC- or workstation-based software products, such as Novell's MultiProtocol Router (MPR), or by using Novell NetWare's standard routing services to route within IPX. This will cost you far less than any of the dedicated routers discussed previously, but network architects tend to shy away from software-based routing because of its unreliability and low performance. As an example of the performance limitations of PC-based routing, most MPR servers cannot route frames at full Fast Ethernet wire speed without the help of an intelligent server card. This is a perfectly adequate solution for a small branch-office environment, however, where cost may be the predominant decision factor.

Backbone Switches

The concept of switching was introduced and defined in the "Workgroup Switches" section earlier in this chapter. Backbone switches, shown in Figure 8.24, are similar to workgroup switches in many ways; however, there are a few notable differences.

Backbone switches typically provide many more high-speed ports than do workgroup switches. Backbone switches come in Fast Ethernet and Gigabit Ethernet flavors and often employ full-duplex connections and port-aggregation mechanisms to improve bandwidth between switches. Some backbone switches also provide extra network management features, such as VLANs and advanced packet filtering. Backbone switches today are starting to support Layer 3 switching, which allows them to be used in network segmentation applications, formerly the exclusive home of traditional routers. In general, a backbone switch is much more expensive and provides much higher performance than its workgroup cousin.

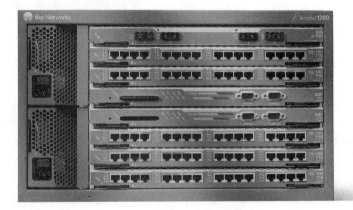

FIGURE 8.24 *The Bay Networks Accelar backbone switch.*

Layer 3 Switches

Don't let the hype about Layer 3 switching confuse you. Layer 3 switches are only beneficial when they are used as fast routing engines in the place of segmentation routers. A networking analyst at Dataquest had it right when he said "the traditional big box routers connecting various backbone segments will have to be replaced by a new generation of Layer 3 switches." In Chapter 5, we discussed the connection between Layer 3 switching and routing. The following are some of the things you should look for in a Layer 3 switch:

- *Protocol support*—Because Layer 3 switches are typically optimized for IP, as networks become more IP-centric, Layer 3 switches will become more popular. Some Layer 3 switches support IPX and a precious few support other protocols.

  In addition to Layer 3 protocols, you need to check which kind of inter-router protocols are supported in the Layer 3 switch. Most support RIP/RIP2 and some support OSPF.

- *Layer 3 switching performance*—Originally the forwarding rate of Layer 3 switches, of which the Bay Networks Accelar was the first, was measured in Kpps; but as silicon technology has increased, Layer 3 switches are approaching the million pps benchmark. As Backbone Layer 3 switches move into the Gigabit Ethernet segment, this mark will move even higher. As with routers, check to see what the 64-byte packet-forwarding rate is as well as the 1500-byte forwarding rate. Table 8.6 lists forwarding rates for a few of the Layer 3 switches, as well as traditional routers, shipping at the time of this book's publication.

TABLE 8.6 LAYER 3 SWITCH AND TRADITIONAL ROUTER PACKET FORWARDING RATES

Router or Layer 3 Switch	Product Type	Packet Forwarding Rate (pps)
Cisco 5000	Traditional switch/router	500Kbps
Cisco 7000	Traditional router	1Mbps
Intel 550T	Layer 3 switch	750Kbps

- *Comparison of types of Layer 3 switching*—Layer 3 switching comes in basically two flavors: Fast packet-by-packet routing, and flow-based routing. Examples of the former are the Bay Networks Accelar routing switch and Intel's Express 550 Routing Switch. Examples of the latter are 3Com's CoreBuilder 5000 switch and Cabletron's SmartSwitch 6000.

The best way to describe why there are two different kinds of Layer 3 switches is to look back at history. Originally, Cisco was the predominant router vendor and promoted BGP. Later, as more vendors got into the routing industry, the older and more standardized RIP (and later RIP2 and OSPF) were adopted. Routing was still slow, but at least multiple-vendor routed networks were being implemented. In response to routing's slow performance, companies such as Ipsilon (now owned by Nokia), 3Com (with its FastIP technology), and Cabletron (with its SecureFast technology) used packet tagging to establish routes through switched networks. This was extremely fast, but none of the implementations worked together—a big step forward in performance, but a bigger step back in terms of interoperability. An example of this type of switch is Cascade's IP Navigator.

Finally, with the advent of high-performance application-specific integrated circuits (ASICs), routing functionality was integrated directly into silicon. This silicon used RIP and OSPF, but routed packets at near switching speeds. This combination of interoperability and performance will inevitably make the other kinds of Layer 3 switching obsolete. Examples of this type of switch family are the Bay Networks (now Nortel) Accelar switch, Extreme's Summit switch, and Intel's 550 switch.

VLAN Support in Backbone Switches

Whereas VLAN support in a workgroup switch is optional, VLAN support in a backbone switch is required, if only as an enabling technology. As you may recall, VLANs can be grouped by port, MAC address, protocol type, IP subnet, or IP multicast domain. And because the IEEE 802.1p and 802.1Q standards aren't complete yet, multivendor switched networks with VLANs are still in the future. Regardless of what you hear, relying on a single vendor for your entire network is never a great strategy. You also have to look at what benefits VLANs bring to your network. In most cases, the benefit will be nothing more than advanced packet filtering, where broadcast packets are filtered between subnetworks. (In this implementation, VLANs are merely an enabling technology for Layer 3 switching.) If your network is not a switched network, from server to desktop, VLANs will not provide any functionality beyond what you would expect from a simple router.

Most backbone switches support a vast array of VLANs. If you are interested in implementing VLANs in your network, Chapter 11 goes into more detail on the subject.

Gigabit Ethernet Backbone Switches

As Fast Ethernet hubs and switches find their way to the desktop and workgroup, backbones will start to feel the strain. Gigabit Ethernet backbone switches certainly complement Fast Ethernet switching to the desktop. Most Gigabit switches today support full-duplex ports, port aggregation, and some even support Layer 3 switching capabilities. Gigabit startups like Prominet (acquired by Lucent), Foundry, and Extreme have been successful in getting press attention, but networking heavyweights like 3Com and Cisco have also entered the Gigabit race.

Although Gigabit switches are virtually identical to Fast Ethernet backbone switches (except in wire speed of course), there are a few exceptions.

First, the backplane capacity of a Gigabit switch will rarely be large enough to support all ports running at full-duplex wire speed. An eight-port Gigabit switch would require a 16Gbps backplane! This is not a big worry, however, because few servers or workgroups will deliver a Gbps worth of bandwidth.

Second, RMON management in a Gigabit Ethernet backbone switch will be implemented in a sampling fashion. RMON is designed to analyze each and every packet, and, at Gbps speeds, a management module would require three or four 400MHz Pentium II processors just to keep up!

Third, Layer 3 support in a Gbps backbone switch is just as essential as in the Fast Ethernet flavor. Layer 3 forwarding rates in Gbps switches will not be 10 times those of Fast Ethernet switches, however. Processing and ASIC power is just not adequate to keep up with Gbps routing. In the extreme case of back-to-back 64-byte packets, a Layer 3 Gbps switch would have to analyze and route a packet every 600 *nanoseconds*! Luckily, this is a situation that will not arise in a normal network.

Port Aggregation

Backbone switches are put under enormous traffic loads, which can lead to all sorts of bottlenecks between switches. If each switch port is a dedicated 100Mbps connection and the switch-to-switch connection is also 100Mbps, traffic forwarded from switch to switch may encounter extra delays. One way to overcome this effect is to provide full-duplex connections between switches. Another way is to support port aggregation.

In fact, switch-to-switch aggregated connections are the only place full-duplex really lives up to its bandwidth-doubling potential. As backbone traffic typically flows both in and out of the switch in equal measure, full-duplex is a true bandwidth enhancement.

Port aggregation support should be considered a must for both Fast Ethernet and Gigabit Ethernet backbone switches. In the future, look for switches that will support the merging IEEE 802.3a port aggregation standard.

Switch Performance Evaluations

A small company called NetCom happened to develop the right piece of equipment at the right time. The SmartBits network tester was developed to perform a series of high-speed data transmission tests over Ethernet networks and can be scaled to Gigabit Ethernet speeds. Every networking R&D lab had to have a few. The SmartBits analyzer is used in almost every modern-day switch test suite. Next we talk about two of these suites:

- *Harvard/Bradner testing*—Scott Bradner, who has been working in the Harvard Network Device Test Lab for the past few years, was instrumental in developing a suite of tests that measure the peak performance of a switch. The Harvard/Bradner test suite is synonymous with switch testing. These tests will give you a good idea of how big a network load is required to "break" a switch. Harvard/Bradner test results for the past two years can be found at www.ndtl.harvard.edu.

- *The Tolly Group testing*—The Tolly Group has developed a switch test suite that tests not only the Layer 2 forwarding qualities of a switch, but also the Layer 3 capabilities. Its suite includes the following:

  - Layer 3 forwarding rates at 64-byte and 1500-byte packet sizes

  - Backbone performance of the switch backplane

  - Minimum and maximum latency through the switch

  - Flow-control characteristics and congestion behavior—are frames dropped or stopped?

  - Maximum Layer 2 forwarding rate

  - Broadcast frame forwarding rate

  - Illegal frame filtering

  - MAC address handling

For more information on this test suite, consult www.tolly.com.

Scalability

Scaling an enterprise network is a tall order, as most network managers know. When it comes to scaling performance and port density on a large scale, it is still tough to beat a chassis-hub solution. A chassis hub generally refers to a chassis-based box that can accept modules based on repeaters, bridges, routers, or switches (see Figure 8.25).

A chassis hub is just a collection of the other components in this chapter. A chassis hub can be thought of as a "hub of hubs" in that it primarily provides a socket for individual modules. When a customer buys a chassis hub from a vendor, he or she is buying into a specific architecture and is expecting to purchase additional modules for that hub over time. Therefore, chassis hubs like the Bay Networks Series 5500 have become popular for their expandability and upgradability. Chassis hubs, like routers, usually have optional high-end features, such as uninterruptible power supplies, diagnostic ports, fault tolerance, and hardware and software tools for advanced hub management. Let's look at a few more reasons why chassis hubs are still popular in backbone applications:

FIGURE 8.25 *A Bay Networks Series 5000 chassis hub.*

- *A wide assortment of networking modules*—Chassis hubs are sometimes thought of as a convenient place to collect individual networking modules, providing a common power supply and chassis. Chassis hubs do not necessarily interconnect all the modules plugged into them, but chassis hubs do offer the promise of upgradability with the simple addition of a new module. Chassis hubs commonly support Token Ring, FDDI, 10BASE-T, Thin Ethernet, ATM, and Fast Ethernet. Most high-end chassis hubs also offer switching, bridging, or routing through a high-speed backplane.

A chassis hub should offer some type of backplane interconnectivity between modules. If it doesn't, external routing or bridging may be necessary, which can complicate network designs. Make sure the chassis hub supports various modules that perform Switched and Shared Ethernet and Fast Ethernet as well as Gigabit Ethernet. Also, a chassis hub should support internal routing or Layer 3 switching.

- *Cost and extra features*—Chassis hubs usually cost much more per port than do stackable hubs, and they often don't offer much better performance. The real benefit of installing a chassis hub comes from the extra features that usually accompany them. These include hot-swappable, redundant power supplies, hot-swappable modules, advanced network management modules, and a chassis designed specifically for rack mounting. If these features match your requirements, chassis hubs may be the best type of device for your backbone

Summary

Network components come in three distinct types: end-station components, workgroup components, and backbone components. Table 8.7 highlights some of the examples and features of each.

TABLE 8.7 A SUMMARY OF NETWORK COMPONENTS

Type of Component	Examples	Basic Features to Consider
End station components (NICs)	Server NICs, client NICs, mobile NICs	Wire speed: 10 or 10/100 Bus type: PCI, CardBus Brand name: 3Com, Intel Performance: throughput, CPU utilization, P/E Index, intelligent NICs, Gigabit Ethernet NIC/server integration Management: WfM1.1a

continues

TABLE 8.7 CONTINUED

Type of Component	Examples	Basic Features to Consider
Workgroup hubs	Standalone repeaters, stackable hubs, workgroup switches, chassis hubs	Port density (number of users supported) Performance or bandwidth Upgradability: Scalable stacking bus for switching Network diameter allowed Management: SNMP, RMON Switch forwarding mechanism Switch backplane architecture Gigabit Ethernet uplink support
Interconnect components	Bridges, routers, backbone switches Layer 3 switches Gigabit Ethernet switches	LAN segmentation Advanced packet filtering Packet error detection Routing between dissimilar LANs Routing from LAN to WAN Full-duplex switching Management: RMON Groups 1–9 Layer 3 support and packet-forwarding rate

Now, with a thorough understanding of the basic network components, you are ready to tackle the job of deploying Switched, Fast, and Gigabit Ethernet (see Table 8.8). Chapter 9 discusses the issues involved with implementing these components in the most important network of all: yours.

TABLE 8.8 A COMPARISON OF WORKGROUP HUBS

Feature	Standalone Repeater	Stackable Hub	Workgroup Switching Hub	Chassis Hub
Port density	Low	High	High	High
Is performance scalable?	No	No	Yes	Yes
Manageable?	Somewhat	Yes	Yes	Yes
Cost per port	Low	Low	High	High
Allows for 10BASE-T and 100BASE-T	No	Some	Yes	Yes
Allows large network diameters	No	No	Yes	Yes

PART IV

Deploying, Managing, and Troubleshooting

CHAPTER **9**

Deployment

In general, sources of information (servers), requesters of that information (clients), and communication paths for that information (the network) can represent an entire network. In network design, it is critical to understand the effects of server placement on various groups of clients. For instance, an Internet gateway shared by all clients on a network should be located at a central point. This is often the network backbone. A local mail, print, or file server that primarily services a set number of clients should be located in the workgroup. By locating the server close to the people who use it, you reduce network traffic on the other parts of the network. This concept is crucial to understand before embarking on a full-scale upgrade of your network.

Understanding the location of the sources and sinks of the network data will help you determine what kind of Switched, Fast, or Gigabit Ethernet network you need. This chapter focuses on seamlessly migrating your existing clients, servers, and 10Mbps shared Ethernet networks to incorporate Switched Ethernet, Fast Ethernet, Gigabit Ethernet, and even Layer 3 switching.

Switching and Ethernet go hand in hand because each needs the other for widespread deployment. Switched Ethernet is usually not of great benefit without a high-speed link, or fat pipe, to collect the various 10Mbps data streams. Fast and Gigabit Ethernet need switching to overcome basic diameter restrictions that would otherwise prevent them from being installed in all but the smallest of networks.

Switching and Fast Ethernet also combine well because switching is often thought of as a tops-down technology, required in high-end solutions. Fast

Ethernet, on the other hand, is thought of as a bottoms-up technology: a logical extension to the 10Mbps desktop of today. (A tops-down technology is one that is implemented first in the backbone, whereas a bottoms-up technology finds its way first into desktops and workgroups. Gigabit Ethernet is another top-down technology.) When used together properly, Switched, Fast, and Gigabit Ethernet products can increase performance in the desktop, the server, the backbone, and the network as a whole.

This chapter begins with the basic rules of deployment and installation for switched and shared 10BASE-T and 100BASE-T, as well as fiber rules for Gigabit Ethernet. We make many references to Part II, so we assume that you have a good understanding of the relevant standards and cable types. After discussing the general rules, we'll categorize the actual deployment of Switched, Fast, and Gigabit Ethernet into six steps. Each step has a specific role in the overall conversion from shared 10BASE-T to Switched 10BASE-T, 100BASE-T, and 1000BASE-SX/LX. Table 9.1 outlines these six steps.

Depending on how large or overloaded your network is, you may only want to implement some of the steps. For instance, if you implement 10Mbps switches, as discussed in step 1 and you find network performance acceptable, you may not need to proceed through the following steps. The steps are structured in such a way that you can implement them slowly, even over the course of a few years. In fact, implementing these steps slowly is often the best course of action when balancing network performance with risk mitigation. Note that as you implement the steps, network performance goes up, but the risk rises as well. It should be noted that even though adding Gigabit Ethernet in the backbone is a high risk, it is still a lower risk than converting the backbone to a more complex technology, such as ATM.

Table 9.1 Six steps to deploying Switched, Fast, and Gigabit Ethernet

Step	Phase of Deployment	Performance Impact	Risk Relative to That of Step 1	Cost Relative to That of Step 1
1	Add 10Mbp switches to your current network	Minimal	None	None
2	Deploy Fast Ethernet for the first time (10/100Mbps NICs into new clients and servers)	Minimal	Minimal	Minimal
3	Convert workgroups to Fast Ethernet	High/ minimal[1]	Medium	Medium

Step	Phase of Deployment	Performance Impact	Risk Relative to That of Step 1	Cost Relative to That of Step 1
4	Deploy Switched and Fast Ethernet in the backbone	High	Medium	High
5	Implementing Layer 3 Switching, VLANs, and Fast Ethernet routing in the backbone	Medium	High	High
6	Adding Gigabit Ethernet switching to the backbone	Very high	High	High

[1]*High when accessing resources local to that workgroup. Minimal impact accessing centralized resources.*

The term relative risk is used. The risk outline in Table 9.1 is relative to that of implementing step 1. As you can see from the table, adding a Gigabit backbone switch is a high risk compared to adding a 10Mbps workgroup switch.

We'll break these steps down into deployment examples later in the chapter. (Many of the deployment options reference Chapter 8, "Network Components," where we more fully explain each network component and its associated features.) We then discuss specific deployment examples from actual networks in Chapter 10, "Deployment Examples."

This chapter begins by covering the general rules of 10BASE-T and 100BASE-T.

General Rules of 10BASE-T and 100BASE-T

The basic rules of deployment for Switched, Fast, and Gigabit Ethernet depend upon the choice of cabling. Category 5 unshielded twisted pair and multi-mode fiber are common choices for today's networks. Although less common, single-mode fiber and inherited Category 3 UTP can enhance or reduce your ability to deploy Switched and Fast Ethernet network components. When it comes to Gigabit Ethernet, fiber is really the only reliable option today; although Gigabit Ethernet over Category 5 UTP may be just around the corner.

The 100m and 5m Rules

As we saw in Chapter 6, the EIA/TIA 568 cabling standard recommends 100m from hub to desktop in all UTP cabling infrastructures. This specification is mirrored in the international standard ISO 88023 (see www.eia.org for more details). The 100m is further broken down into the following distances:

- 5m from hub to patch panel

- 90m from patch panel to office punch-down block

- 5m from punch-down block to desktop connection

Most UTP installations conform to this 100m rule, as it is commonly called, which makes 100BASE-T very easy to install.

Cable installers also recommend that hub-to-hub UTP connections be made with 5m or less of cable (the 5m rule). Short cables in a noisy wiring closet translate to less induced noise on the wire and less crosstalk in large multiple-cable bundles. Short cables however, may restrict hub location in large wiring closets, so this guideline is often overlooked. In 10BASE-T networks, this rarely causes a problem, but when installing Fast Ethernet shared workgroups, the 5m rule should be strictly followed. We'll explain the reasons for this later in the chapter.

10BASE-T Shared Network Rules

10BASE-T requires that all collisions be resolved within 512 bit times (also called one slot time). In a 10BASE-T shared network, each component, including the cabling, adds transmission delays, which account for a shrinkage in the total network diameter. Today's technology allows for a worst-case 10BASE-T UTP network with roughly four repeater hops and three populated segments. Why only four hops? In order to lock on to an incoming signal, each repeater eats up bits of the signal. This can be accounted for as a loss of bit budget or network diameter. Each cabling segment and repeater represents a certain transmission delay, and the total round-trip delay cannot exceed one slot time, or 512 microseconds.

With current repeater technology, this results in 10BASE-T networks of no more than four repeater hops. So even though Ethernet's collision domain is specified at 2500m, in 10BASE-T form it rarely exceeds 500m. The 10BASE-F (Ethernet over fiber) allows for much larger shared 10Mbps networks due to the extended transmission length of fiber, but 10BASE-F is typically implemented as a switched connection.

10BASE-T Switched Network Rules

The 10BASE-T switched networks are no different from 10BASE-T shared networks, except that a new network diameter calculation begins at each switch port. Because switches provide dedicated connections, fewer collisions occur, and no real collision domain exists to restrict diameter. The 10BASE-T switches are only limited by the same EIA/TIA 568 rules that govern current installations: the 100m hub-to-node and 5m hub-to-hub rules. Therefore, a 10Mbps switched network will work in any existing EIA/TIA 568 compatible UTP cabling infrastructure with no network diameter constraints. Refer to Chapter 6 for more information on cabling standards.

100BASE-T Shared Network Rules

As discussed in Chapter 3, "Ethernet, Fast Ethernet, and Gigabit Ethernet Standards," shared 100BASE-TX and 100BASE-T4 networks require a much smaller collision domain: only 205m. This allows for a 100Mbps shared network of two repeaters with 100m cabling to each node and 5m cabling between repeaters. As you can see, purely shared Fast Ethernet networks require exact compliance to EIA/TIA UTP cabling specifications. If a network diameter greater than 205m is required, you must use switches, bridges, or routers somewhere.

Class I 100BASE-T repeaters and stackable hubs are further limited to only one repeater hop because they incur the additional delay of converting incoming analog data to the digital MII interface. The 100BASE-TX-to-100BASE-T4 translational repeaters are Class I by definition. Most Fast Ethernet stackable hubs are Class I.

Class II 100BASE-T repeater ports are usually all of one type (either TX or T4) and therefore allow two repeater hops. Figure 9.1 shows maximum shared network diameters for Class I and Class II stackable hubs.

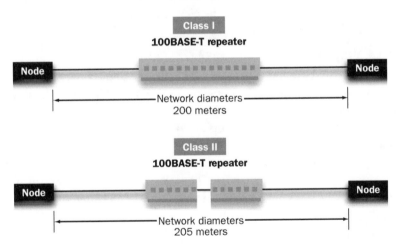

FIGURE 9.1 *Class I and Class II shared media network diameters are limited to 200m and 205m, respectively.*

In general, 100BASE-TX is less fussy about shared network restrictions than 100BASE-T4 because its bit budget has more flexibility. Some 100BASE-T4 components, however, allow for extended cable lengths over 100m or more repeater hops due to innovative designs. You should do a bit-budget analysis on any 100BASE-T installation that exceeds the IEEE 802.3u specification: more than two repeater hops or greater than 205m in network diameter (refer to Chapter 3 for details). 100BASE-T4 is also lower frequency than TX and therefore less susceptible to noise and crosstalk. 100BASE-T4 never really caught on in mainstream networks and therefore is only marginally supported by major networking vendors today. In general, you should avoid installing 100BASE-T4 in a network unless you absolutely cannot upgrade the Category 3 UTP cabling infrastructure.

100BASE-T Switched Network Rules

The restrictions of shared 100BASE-T networks further reinforce the importance of switching in Fast Ethernet deployment. Rarely do 100BASE-T workgroups have more than one repeater hop between the end-station and a Fast Ethernet switch. In other words, shared 100BASE-T networks are most likely deployed in workgroups via stackable hubs connected to switches. This means that in a properly constructed shared/switched 100BASE-T network, the 100BASE-T network diameter of 205m will never come into play. Switching is imperative to the successful deployment of Fast Ethernet. In fact, the bulk of this chapter is dedicated to explaining how switched and shared 10Mbps, 100Mbps, and 1000Mbps media can be blended together to form small and large LANs.

100BASE-FX Fiber Network Rules

Another necessity of today's LANs is the fiber optic connection. Fiber optic cabling rarely connects desktops but is commonly found in switch-to-server, switch-to-switch, and backbone applications (see Table 9.2). Due to its capability to carry signals for distances of up to 2km, fiber allows multiple campuses to connect to the same backbone. Currently, you'll commonly find FDDI running on multimode fiber optic cabling, which is why 100BASE-FX is designed for the same type of multimode fiber. The 100BASE-FX specification, also categorized under IEEE 802.3u, allows for many levels of extended distances, depending on the type of connection.

TABLE 9.2 TYPES OF 100BASE-FX FIBER CONNECTION

Type of 100BASE-FX Connection	Description of Rules
Shared-to-shared	In a true 100BASE-FX fiber repeater setting, the maximum distance from hub to node is 160m in accordance with the 100BASE-T bit budget. For this reason, 100BASE-FX repeaters will be in limited use.
Shared-to-switched	If one side of the connection is to a 100BASE-FX fiber switch, the same 100BASE-FX repeater mentioned above will be able to send signals over 210m of fiber. Again, this will limit the practical use of the properties of 100BASE-FX.

Type of 100BASE-FX Connection	Description of Rules
Switch-to-switch	A 100BASE-FX switched port connected to another 100BASE-FX switched port can transmit over 412m of fiber optic cable. This will be the entry point for most 100BASE-FX backbone products.
Switch-to-switch full-duplex	The 100BASE-FX specification calls for a special full-duplex switch-to-switch connection that allows for 2km of fiber cabling between switches. This allows 100BASE-FX to be run anywhere FDDI is used today. This represents the bulk of the 100BASE-FX switch market.

100BASE-FX is mainly used to extend networks to multiple floors or buildings. 100BASE-FX deployment beyond this function is a rarity.

Gigabit Ethernet Network Rules

Gigabit Ethernet also relies on fiber optic cabling. You can connect Gigabit Ethernet over single-mode fiber or one of two types of multiple-mode fiber. The main requirement for Gigabit links is a switched, full-duplex connection on each end of the fiber. Although Gigabit Ethernet can be deployed in a buffered-repeater design, most network managers opt to skip the shared approach and go directly for Switched Gigabit. We'll discuss the reasons for this later. For now, consult Table 9.3 for network diameters associated with Gigabit Ethernet.

TABLE 9.3 NETWORK RESTRICTIONS FOR **10BASE-T, 100BASE-T,** AND **1000BASE-SX/LX**

Technology	Network Diameter Shared Medium	Network Diameter Switched Medium	Switch-to-Switch Cable-Length Switched Medium
10BASE-T	About 400m	Unlimited	100m
100BASE-TX/ 100BASE-T4	205m	Unlimited	100m
100BASE-FX	320m	Unlimited	400m
100BASE-FX Full-Duplex	N/A	Unlimited	2000m
1000BASE-SX	Only possible with a buffered repeater	Unlimited	260m multimode fiber
1000BASE-LX	Only possible with a buffered repeater	Unlimited	550m multimode fiber, 3km single-mode fiber

The IEEE 802.3ab subcommittee is also looking at Gigabit Ethernet over UTP. This will likely result in a Gigabit Ethernet–over copper IEEE specification sometime in mid-1999. Several vendors have made a solid commitment to to bring out Gigabit Ethernet copper products, but those products are still forthcoming. The risk-conscious network manager should avoid Gigabit Ethernet over UTP until the standard has been fully ratified. Don't take this to mean that you should avoid Gigabit Ethernet over UTP cabling; just make sure your vendor adheres to the eventual IEEE standard.

The Golden Rules of Switched, Fast, and Gigabit Ethernet

The same specifications, the EIA/TIA 568 and the ISO 88023 standards, govern the general rules of both 10BASE-T and 100BASE-T deployment. Each specification outlines basic guidelines on how UTP and fiber-based network technologies should be deployed. In general, we can summarize the guidelines for Switched and Fast Ethernet deployment in five golden rules:

- Use 100m maximum UTP connection from desktop to hub.

- Stack Fast Ethernet hubs; don't cascade them.

- Use 100m maximum UTP connection from Fast Ethernet hub to Fast Ethernet switch.

- Use 160m maximum fiber connection from Fast Ethernet hub to Fast Ethernet switch.

- Use 2km maximum full-duplex fiber connection from Fast Ethernet switch to Fast Ethernet switch.

In addition, three new rules generally govern Gigabit network infrastructures. They may not give you all the flexibility that Gigabit Ethernet allows, but by following them, you'll be sure to stay within specification. These rules are as follows:

- *Multiple-mode SX*—Use 260m maximum multiple-mode, full-duplex fiber connection from 1000BASE-SX Gigabit Ethernet switch to GE switch or server NIC.

- *Multiple-mode LX*—Use 550m maximum multiple-mode, full-duplex fiber connection from 1000BASE-LX Gigabit Ethernet switch to GE switch or server NIC.

- *Single-mode LX*—Use 3km maximum single-mode, full-duplex fiber connection from 1000BASE-LX Gigabit Ethernet switch to GE switch or server NIC.

> **Note**
>
> *By using a 50μm core multiple-mode fiber optic cable, you can extend Gigabit Ethernet connections over longer distances. See Chapter 6 for details.*

An understanding of the general rules for switched and shared 10BASE-T, 100BASE-T, and 1000BASE-LX/SX deployment is essential before discussing how to implement them in a production network. The rest of the chapter is dedicated to the six steps of deploying Switched, Fast, and Gigabit Ethernet.

Deployment Step 1: Adding 10Mbps Switches

The first step toward upgrading your network involves determining where to implement 10Mbps switches. This section focuses on implementing 10Mbps switches in two applications: workgroups and switches of hubs. (Note that step 1 deals with 10Mbps-only switches. We discuss 10Mbps switches with 100Mbps uplinks in step 2.)

In the workgroup, you can effectively implement a 10Mbps switch in two ways:

- *Standard workgroup*—A workgroup switch is used as a replacement for 10Mbps repeaters in workgroups with clients and local servers.

- *Switch of hubs*—A workgroup switch is configured to provide 10Mbps of dedicated bandwidth to individual stackable hub units. In this configuration, a 10Mbps switch may look like a small, switched backbone.

We explore these two deployment options, plus some of their derivatives, more thoroughly in the pages to follow. Because this is the first step in an overall deployment of Switched and Fast Ethernet, the performance gained will be moderate, but the timing of the implementation can be immediate.

When buying 10Mbps switches for any kind of deployment, always look for products that can be upgraded later with 100BASE-TX or 100BASE-FX uplinks. You can usually accomplish this with upgrade slots. An upgrade slot, as described in Chapter 8, allows for the addition of newer technology into the switch, long after the original purchase. Not only does this allow a 10Mbps switch to connect to a 100Mbps backbone, but it is typically flexible enough to allow other types of modules (ATM, Layer 3 routing, and so on). A 10Mbps switch without 100BASE-T uplink capability is pointless and not a good investment.

The obvious benefit of deploying a 10Mbps switch is that you don't have to replace the 10BASE-T NICs already installed in desktops and servers. For this reason, we can consider 10Mbps switching a drop-in replacement. 10BASE-T, in both switched and shared form, runs equally well over Category 3 and Category 5 UTP cabling. For this reason, many companies with suspect cabling, or no re-cabling budget are opting for 10Mbps switching as their core network architecture.

We have already heard that ISA-based desktops and PCMCIA-based laptops will not gain much from the addition of a 10/100Mbps NIC. Therefore, any new systems based on these buses may be configured with a classic 10Mbps NIC. These types of systems will get more than enough network bandwidth from a 10Mbps switched connection. Also, if the system has particularly slow subsystems, like a slow server hard disk, you may determine that a 100Mbps connection is not needed. For instance, a server with a higher speed bus, like an EISA bus, but with a slower processor (Intel 80486 or lower) may not be a good candidate for a 100Mbps connection. The flexibility gained from a 10/100 solution is sometimes worth the cost, though. For instance, if you use 10/100 PCMCIA cards, you may never reach 100Mbps data rates, but you won't worry about finding the right speed hub port to connect to.

Standard Workgroup Deployment

Many clients, a few local servers, and a 10Mbps repeater compose the typical workgroup of today. By adding a 10Mbps switch, you can convert a shared workgroup to a higher speed switched workgroup. Consider the diagrams in Figure 9.2, where a workgroup has four clients and two servers connected through a 10Mbps repeater. All nodes share the repeater's 10Mbps of bandwidth. By replacing the repeater with a 10Mbps switch, you can increase the available bandwidth of the workgroup by several fold. In the switched example, each client has a dedicated 10Mbps connection, and each server has a dedicated, full-duplex 10Mbps connections. Each server can provide up to 20Mbps of data so that the new workgroup bandwidth is 40Mbps, or four times the original. In addition, the concept of simultaneous server access now becomes a reality with switches. One client can be accessing one local server while another is accessing a different local server. This type of switch deployment works well in small networks or isolated workgroups where most of the traffic stays local.

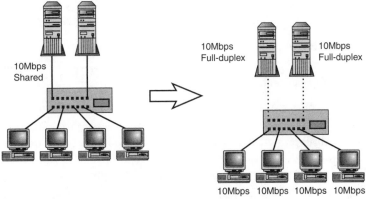

FIGURE 9.2 *10Mbps switches in a standard workgroup.*

When does it make sense to install a 10Mbps switch in this configuration? A few key indicators will give you a good idea of whether 10Mbps switching will help. These include counting the number of local servers in the workgroup and examining the amount of traffic that stays locally within the workgroup. Table 9.4 explains how these indicators determine whether 10Mbps switching is needed. If a workgroup exhibits one or more of these characteristics, treat it as a candidate for a 10Mbps switch upgrade.

TABLE 9.4 DETERMINING THE NEED FOR 10MBPS SWITCHING IN A STANDARD WORKGROUP

Workgroup Characteristic	Description
Multiple local servers in the workgroup	If the workgroup has only one server, the cost of a 10Mbps switch may not be worth the small performance gain. In cases where only one server is present in the workgroup, other features such as multiple server NICs, port aggregation, and full-duplex are needed to increase performance.
Primarily local traffic	At least 80% of the activity is between the clients and local servers.
Large amount of traffic	The 10Mbps shared workgroup is at least 30% utilized (that is, more than 3Mbps is utilized).

Once the need for a 10Mbps switch has been determined, the next question is what type of switch to deploy. Some key switch features to look for in a standard workgroup deployment are full-duplex support, port aggregation, cost per port, and slots for add-in uplink modules. This type of workgroup switching solution allows network administrators to make the most out of what equipment they already have. No new NICs are required for the clients and a 10Mbps switch is a quick replacement for a 10Mbps repeater.

Using a Switch of Hubs

A 10Mbps switch also improves performance in larger networks based on a number of 10Mbps stackable hubs.

Many large networks are configured with stackable hubs, which are typically used when connecting a large number of users in a workgroup. In this case, you can use a 10Mbps switch as a switch of hubs (as shown in Figure 9.3) to improve the performance of a 10Mbps stack. Instead of sharing a stacking bus, each unit of the stack is provided with 10Mbps of dedicated bandwidth from the switch. Once again, you can accomplish this with little impact on the network infrastructure. In fact, you can often physically place a 10Mbps switch right on top of the existing stack.

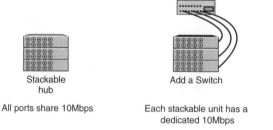

Stackable hub

All ports share 10Mbps

Add a Switch

Each stackable unit has a dedicated 10Mbps

FIGURE 9.3 *Upgrading a 10Mbps stackable hub with a 10Mbps switch. This is often referred to as a "switch of hubs" configuration.*

The performance gained is typically proportional to the number of switching ports used. In Figure 9.3, there is a three-fold performance gain (30Mbps versus 10Mbps). The main things to look for when using a switch in a switch of hubs configuration are port densities (are there enough switched ports for each stackable unit?) and the implications for network management. Because the management module in the main stackable unit can no longer "see" all network traffic (the switch blocks it), an alternative type of management must be used. For more on the management of switches in this configuration, see Chapter 11, "Managing Switched, Fast, and Gigabit Ethernet Networks."

Aggregating Ports

Many networks are constructed entirely of 10Mbps repeaters. In this case, all end nodes share the bandwidth available on the medium. When advanced network components such as bridges, routers, or switches are deployed, traffic can begin to be filtered and divided, thus increasing network performance. Networks with bridging, routing, or switching isolate sub-LANs because they can filter unwanted traffic. In this respect, a 10Mbps switched backbone can be extremely useful in improving the overall performance of a 10Mbps shared network. The deployment of a switch in such a network is analogous to the switch-of-hubs concept used for stackable hubs. Each independent 10Mbps repeater is connected to a dedicated 10Mbps pipe, as shown in Figure 9.4.

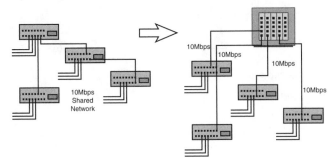

FIGURE 9.4 *Upgrading a 10Mbps shared network with a 10Mbps switched backbone. Total network bandwidth has increased by a factor of four.*

The theoretical network performance of the example in Figure 9.4 has increased from 10Mbps to 40Mbps by adding a single switch. This is very similar to adding four bridges to the network to isolate traffic between segments. In addition, you can cascade 10Mbps switches together with aggregated 10Mbps switched, full-duplex connections to improve throughput between switches. Port aggregation techniques such as EtherChannel or the upcoming IEEE 802.3ad standard are useful for this purpose. This type of deployment is really the beginning of a distributed backbone built from 10Mbps switches. This architecture is scalable as long as additional switch-to-switch connections are available and the port aggregation technique is similar throughout the network. An example of this is shown in Figure 9.5, where a new switch is connected via two 10Mbps, full-duplex switched connections. The interswitch bandwidth is therefore 40Mbps: 20Mbps in each direction.

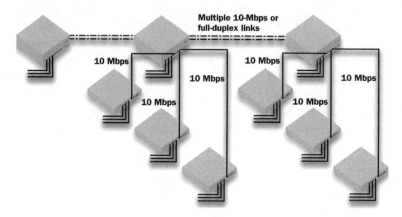

FIGURE 9.5 *10Mbps switches can be configured for multiple backbone connections. These connections may also be full-duplex.*

Server Farms: A Practical Application of 10Mbps Full-Duplex Ethernet Switching and Port Aggregation

A *server farm* is a collection of servers that reside on the backbone of a network. Servers in server farms are usually high-end systems that service a great number of users. Most servers in server farms are accessed indiscriminately by a large number of users, so the traffic patterns are fairly constant, as opposed to those of servers in the local workgroup. Data tends to come in regularly from all sorts of sources. Installing a 10Mbps switch in a server farm is yet another way to improve network performance with 10Mbps switching. Adding a 10Mbps switch in a server farm provides each server with dedicated bandwidth. The switched

architecture also allows for aggregated connections to the backbone in order to handle the increased traffic flow from the server farm.

A typical 10Mbps shared server farm is upgraded by adding a 10Mbps switch. The connection to each server is scalable by connecting additional 10Mbps dedicated lines to the server farm switch. The trick of scaling the connection is to weigh the amount of traffic typically generated by the switched server farm with the number of backbone connections. For instance, if the server farm typically generates an average load of 20Mbps with peaks of

continues

continued

30Mbps, you should use three aggregated 10Mbps backbone connections. In the case of multiple backbone connections, the switch must incorporate some sort of traffic balancing, similar to the load balancing of the workgroup scenario, to allow for the most efficient use of the switched ports. The IEEE 802.3ad port aggregation standard is taking these features into consideration.

Because the data stream contains traffic from many different nodes, the possibility of corrupted packets is higher than normal. Therefore, store-and-forward switches with some measure of error-checking and packet filtering is preferred in server farm applications. Error-checking reduces the amount of work the server NIC and network operating system have to do to filter unwanted packets. A 10Mbps switch might be a good short-term solution for a server farm, but as you'll see later in step 4, a 100Mbps switch is the solution of choice. Whenever possible, try to deploy 100Mbps switched connections to individual servers in server farms.

Managing Switches

Managing 10Mbps switches, or any switch for that matter, is a subject that has already spawned several books. Chapter 11 deals with this issue in more detail, but in this section, we'll focus on what to look for in step 1 of your deployment process. First, only select switches that support SNMP and RMON management. Because this is typically built into the switching silicon, it should be included in the base price of the switch. You'll learn more about this later, but suffice it to say that RMON Groups 1, 2, 3, and 9 are important for 10Mbps workgroup switches. Other important features to look for are support for your software management application (including Hewlett-Packard's OpenView and Bay Network's Optivity) and support for WWW-based configuration and management. Many switches will include an embedded WWW-server that will allow you to access the switch directly from your favorite browser.

Knowing When to Upgrade

Although you have many ways to improve network performance with 10Mbps switches, definite trade-offs are associated with deploying this technology. For example, many network management issues associated with switching must be addressed. Also, depending on how your networking traffic grows, 10Mbps switches may only support your network for a short time before high bandwidth devices are required. New, high-performance servers may quickly swamp a 10Mbps switch with data. Even with these potential drawbacks, however, the advantages of 10Mbps switches are numerous. You can attain increases in performance with little or no impact on the current network architecture (for instance, NICs rarely need to be replaced when 10Mbps switches are deployed). Also, 10Mbps switching is relatively inexpensive compared with other switching alternatives, such as switched Fast Ethernet, Gigabit Ethernet, and ATM.

In general, 10Mbps switches enhance network performance in two types of applications, which are summarized in Table 9.5.

TABLE 9.5 A SUMMARY OF 10MBPS WORKGROUP SWITCH DEPLOYMENT EXAMPLES

10Mbps Workgroup Switch Installation Type	Description	Deployment Issue
Standard workgroup	Provides dedicated pipe(s) to local clients and servers in any given workgroup.	Helps when most traffic is local. Workgroups with multiple local servers benefit the most. Full-duplex NICs and switch ports give added benefit. Load balancing software/hardware is sometimes needed.
Switch of hubs	Provides dedicated pipe to individual repeaters or stackable hub units.	Improves performance in almost all cases. Switch can be physically stacked with rest of stackable units. May affect stackable hub management strategy. Allows server farms to be deployed. Aggregating switch-to-switch connections starts a distributed backbone.

Deployment Step 2: Adding Fast Ethernet NICs

The second step in deploying Switched and Fast Ethernet is putting the first Fast Ethernet network components in place. The natural entry point for Fast

Ethernet in most networks is at the desktop and server. This is primarily because almost all NICs are 10/100Mbps, which means that they can operate at either 10Mbps or 100Mbps. A 10/100Mbps NIC installed today will typically run at 10Mbps for some time before a Fast Ethernet hub or switch is purchased. This section describes how to prepare new desktops and servers with 10/100Mbps NICs and how to plan your network architecture to accommodate a mixture of 10Mbps and 100Mbps workgroups.

Figure 9.6 is International Data Corporation's view of the 10/100Mbps NIC, hub, and switch markets. It is easy to see the causal relationship the 10/100Mbps NIC market has on the 10/100 Switch and Hub market. 10/100Mbps NICs were deployed into existing 10Mbps networks in order to future-proof new PCs. This, in turn, drove demand for 10/100Mbps hubs to connect those desktops and for 10/100Mbps switches to connect those hubs. Now, the prevalence of 10/100Mbps switching is causing demand for Layer 3 switching and Gigabit Ethernet in the backbone.

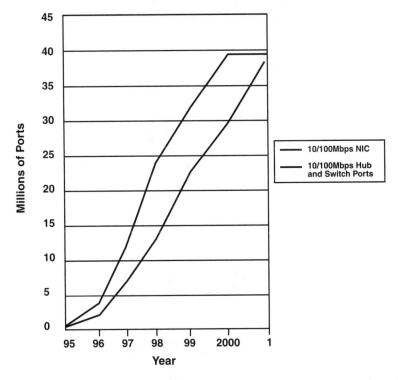

FIGURE 9.6 *IDC's predictions of the 10/100Mbps NIC, Hub, and Switch markets. Note how the 10/100Mbps NIC market leads the hub and switch market by approximately two years.*

10/100Mbps Future Proofing

A wide assortment of desktops and servers are connected to 10Mbps Ethernet ports today. With such a variety, it is practically impossible for new 10/100Mbps cards to fit into every existing system. That is why a practical plan for deployment of Fast Ethernet begins with installing desktop and server 10/100Mbps NICs in newly purchased or newly installed systems. As discussed in Chapter 6, older systems based on the ISA or PCMCIA bus are not ideal for Fast Ethernet upgrades; thus, older desktops and laptops should retain their 10Mbps-only NICs until they are retired from service. The next section (step 3) will discuss how to connect these systems to your new Fast Ethernet network.

Consider the simple network shown on the left side of Figure 9.7. In its current state, each existing desktop and server is connected by a 10Mbps NIC. The network hubs are 10Mbps repeaters. Now, two new servers and four new clients are to be added to this network to connect new employees to the LAN. These systems are enabled with 10/100Mbps-Mbps NICs and connected to the existing 10Mbps network, as shown on the right side of Figure 9.7. Note that these systems have been future-proofed in that they are 100Mbps-ready yet are running at 10Mbps today.

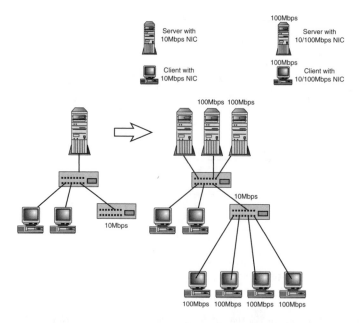

Figure 9.7   *A 10Mbps shared network before (left) and after (right) adding new systems with 10/100Mbps NICs. All clients and servers in this example are running at 10Mbps even though some have 10/10 NICs installed. This provides a network that is primed for a fast Ethernet upgrade.*

By adding 10/100Mbps NICs now, you are preventing an expensive and time-consuming future NIC upgrade. (Most network servers are so critical that they can't afford to be powered down. Desktops are usually too numerous to allow for a mass replacement of NICs once they are installed.) Lack of proper cabling to support 100BASE-T should not be a deterrent to installing 10/100Mbps NICs in new systems. Who knows where they may be moved to in the future. You can always upgrade cabling when the budget allows, and you don't want to have to upgrade all your desktops as well. Now that 10/100Mbps NICs are virtually the same price as 10-only NICs, 10/100Mbps should be the rule in all new systems.

Using 100BASE-TX Versus 100BASE-T4

The type of 10/100Mbps NIC to install depends primarily on the type of cabling used for the particular LAN. With Category 3 UTP, 100BASE-T4 is the only Fast Ethernet option. With Category 5 UTP, either 100BASE-TX or 100BASE-T4 deployment is possible. The best guideline to follow when choosing between TX and T4 is to determine which supports the majority of your cabling. Most network managers, however, are upgrading their cabling to Category 5 when they are upgrading their infrastructure. Combine this with the lack of 100BASE-T4 product availability, and it's no surprise that 100BASE-TX is the solution of choice in today's Fast Ethernet networks. In our opinion, you should avoid 100BASE-T4 whenever possible.

If you don't know what category your cabling is in or how many pairs are available, consult your cable contractor or try one of the many portable cable testers discussed in Chapter 6. Table 9.6 outlines the various TX and T4 options dictated by your cabling infrastructure. Pay special attention to Category 3 cabling with only two pairs available. Neither TX or T4 can run on this cabling so your best upgrade option is Switched 10Mbps Ethernet.

TABLE 9.6 CABLING OPTIONS

Cable Type	Connector Type	Number of Pairs Available for LAN	100BASE-T Signaling Scheme to Deploy
Category 3 or 4 UTP (voice grade)	RJ45	2	100BASE-T not deployable. Use Switched 10.
Category 3 or 4 UTP (voice grade)	RJ45	4	100BASE-T4
Category 5 UTP (data grade)	RJ45	2	100BASE-TX

continues

Table 9.6 Continued

Cable Type	Connector Type	Number of Pairs Available for LAN	100BASE-T Signaling Scheme to Deploy
Category 5 UTP (data grade)	RJ45	4	100BASE-T4 or 100BASE-TX
Type 1 STP	DB9	2	100BASE-TX
Coaxial Cable	BNC	N/A	100BASE-T not deployable

Upgrading Servers to Fast Ethernet

Servers have a special place in most networks as they hold the data and information to which most people want access. This often makes them vulnerable to overloading, especially in a 10Mbps shared environment. Therefore, the first place to look when adding 10/100Mbps NICs is in your servers. Once you have installed the 10/100Mbps NICs, upgrading the line speed to 100Mbps is basically automatic. In addition to adding the basic 10/100Mbps capability to servers, step 2 includes some other considerations about which type of NIC to use.

Specialty NICs include intelligent NICs and multiport NICs. Intelligent NICs have an intelligent processor or subsystem that relieves the host CPU of many of its tasks. Intelligent NICs should be considered mainly in four situations:

- Multiple-segment Fast Ethernet servers

- Application servers where CPU power is at a premium

- PC-based routers such as Novell's Multi Protocol Router (MPR) software

- Server Fault Tolerant (SFT) III-compliant links, such as Novell's Mirrored Server Link (MSL)

Because the on-board CPU does much of the network processing, intelligent NICs usually result in great throughput at a low CPU utilization. Intel's EtherExpress PRO/100 Intelligent Web Server Adapter, shown in Figure 9.8, is one such NIC. Because of their added cost, however, intelligent NICs are not very beneficial outside these four niche areas.

FIGURE 9.8 *Intel's EtherExpress Intelligent Web Server Adapter.*

Multiport NICs combine several NICs into one by providing up to four UTP ports on one card. Multiport NICs are useful in systems where expansion slots are scarce. Many PCI systems have only two or three PCI slots available for expansion cards. As server PCI slots start becoming more plentiful, multiport NICs will slowly become less popular.

Multiport NICs, or even multiple single-port NICs, can be aggregated to provide more bandwidth in and out of the server. As we've discussed, schemes like EtherChannel and 802.3ad port aggregation work well in these scenarios. Using one of these schemes, a server can have up to four Fast Ethernet NICs installed, delivering up to 800Mbps of data (400Mbps each way).

The Patch Panel Approach

Many large companies have network closets that house the connection from each office to a particular hub. This is typically accomplished with a patch panel (this concept is explored in Chapter 6). A patch panel allows maximum configurability of the network. For instance, the network administrator can rearchitect the network layout from the closet by switching the connections on the patch panel. A patch panel approach is very effective for converting from 10Mbps to 100Mbps. Suppose a network has several users with 10/100Mbps NICs operating at 10Mbps. If those systems are known, a quick restructuring of the patch panel wiring will condense these users onto one hub (later, we'll discuss how to automate this process with virtual LANs). When any given 10Mbps hub has all 10/100Mbps-enabled end stations attached, it is a prime candidate for step 3, adding a Fast Ethernet hub.

Deployment Step 3: Converting Workgroups to Fast Ethernet

The next logical step after installing 10/100Mbps NICs is to find a way to convert them from 10Mbps operation to 100Mbps operation. You can best do this by first converting workgroups from 10Mbps to 100Mbps. You can do this by using 10/100Mbps switches or 100Mbps repeaters, depending on the situation. In some cases, you will need to make trade-offs to merge the new Fast Ethernet LAN with the existing 10Mbps environment.

Four main types of workgroups are eligible for conversion to Fast Ethernet. Each requires a slightly different approach to achieve the best performance gain:

- *Existing workgroup*—10Mbps-only NICs; clients only (no local servers).

- *Existing workgroup with local servers 10Mbps-only NICs*—many clients and some local servers.

- *Newer workgroup 10/100Mbps NICs*—clients and/or local servers.

- *Newer power workgroup 10/100Mbps NICs*—clients and/or local servers.

If implemented correctly, each Fast Ethernet upgrade provides increased performance with minimal interruption to the network.

Existing Workgroups with no Local Servers

Replacing every NIC in your network is a seemingly insurmountable task. Therefore, the best Fast Ethernet workgroup solution for existing networks is one that allows you to leverage the installed base of 10BASE-T NICs. Most existing workgroups can achieve a significant benefit from the addition of a 10Mbps switch with 100Mbps uplinks. For existing workgroups consisting entirely of clients, a switch with many 10Mbps ports and a few 100Mbps ports is desirable (for connections to other workgroups and the backbone). Consider the leftmost workgroup in Figure 9.9, which contains only 10Mbps clients and a 10Mbps repeater.

In step 1, we saw how a 10Mbps switch could be deployed in this situation to enhance workgroup performance. A 10Mbps switch with 100Mbps uplinks can enhance performance even more and without the inconvenience of multiple full-duplex uplinks to the backbone. Figure 9.9 shows how a standard 10Mbps shared workgroup can be upgraded with a 10Mbps switch plus 100Mbps uplinks.

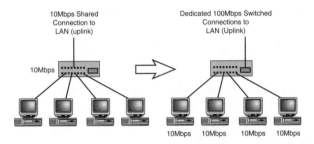

FIGURE 9.9 *Upgrading an existing workgroup to Fast Ethernet without replacing the 10Mbps NICs in the desktops.*

Now what do you do with the newly acquired 100Mbps uplink? Because Fast Ethernet won't be deployed in your backbone until step 4, you may have to live with a 10Mbps uplink for a little while. Performance won't approach 10 times current levels until the Fast Ethernet backbone connection is completed. A good way to approach this problem is by investing in a 10Mbps switch with an upgradable option for Fast Ethernet. One such switch is the Cisco Catalyst 2800, which can be bought as a 10Mbps-only switch with space for two Fast Ethernet modules. You can purchase the Fast Ethernet modules when the rest of your Fast Ethernet network—specifically, the backbone—is in place. Figure 9.10 shows this type of switch deployment.

Note

For an interesting practical example, have a look at www.cisco.com/partner/786/4.html. *This shows how the Hard Rock Cafe in Cleveland, Ohio, has implemented step 3.*

Note that this 10Mbps switch upgrade applies to existing workgroups that already have 10Mbps NICs installed, upgrading existing systems with 10/100Mbps NICs would not make sense. A workgroup with mostly ISA-based clients is a classic example of where to deploy 10Mbps switches and 100Mbps uplinks in this manner. Another good example is a workgroup with Category 3 UTP cabling.

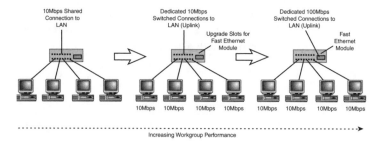

FIGURE 9.10 *Leveraging 10Mbps switches in a workgroup. On the left is the original 10Mbps shared workgroup. First it is upgraded with a 10Mbps switch (center). Finally, a Fast Ethernet uplink modules is added to the switch (right).*

Existing Workgroups with Local Servers

A slight variation on the previous scenario includes the addition of local servers in the workgroup. In some workgroups with local servers, the majority of the traffic (more than 80%) may be between those servers and clients in the workgroup. This is often referred to as a standalone or isolated workgroup. 10Mbps switches with more 100Mbps ports are preferable in these situations. Each local server can be connected to a 100Mbps pipe, and each client gets its own dedicated 10Mbps pipe. This is also referred to as personal Ethernet because each user has his or her own dedicated Ethernet line. Figure 9.11 shows this. Be careful when assessing the characteristics of a standalone workgroup. If many of the users are accessing the Internet through a centralized gateway, it is unlikely that 80% of the network traffic is local to that workgroup. Use a network analyzer or an RMON probe (discussed in Chapter 12, "Troubleshooting") if you are unsure.

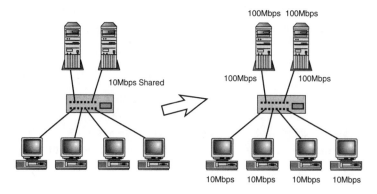

FIGURE 9.11 *A 10/100Mbps Mbps switch upgrade in a workgroup with local servers. Clients get dedicated 10Mbps. Servers get dedicated 100Mbps.*

Two types of 10/100Mbps switches are available to deploy in an isolated work-group. The first and most obvious type is a switch with many 10Mbps ports and more than a few 100Mbps ports. A good example is the Bay Networks 350T, which has a total of 16 ports that can be configured for 10Mbps or 100Mbps. This type of switch will give excellent performance and configuring capability, but the expense may be a little high for broad workgroup deploy-ment. Another way to achieve similar workgroup performance is to use an architecture like that of the Cisco Catalyst 2820. The Catalyst 2820 has 24 switched 10Mbps ports and upgrade slots for one or more switched 100Mbps ports or eight 100Mbps shared ports. This allows several servers to share the same 100Mbps bandwidth and still provides each client with 10Mbps of band-width. The single switched 100Mbps port connects the workgroup to the LAN backbone. This architecture, diagrammed in Figure 9.12, is less expensive than switching 10/100Mbps on a per-port basis.

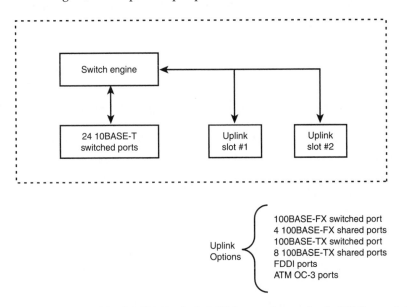

FIGURE 9.12 *Cisco's 2820 FastSwitch ES is a good example of a 10Mbps switch archi-tecture with several uplink options.*

For the 10/100Mbps switch to be of any use in this type of environment, the servers must be outfitted with 10/100Mbps-Mbps NICs. This means that the servers must be capable of supporting 100Mbps data rates. If the local servers are ISA based, a 10/100Mbps-Mbps switch may not dramatically increase per-formance. A 10Mbps switch may be more appropriate. If the local servers do have high-speed bus types, such as PCI, EISA, or S-Bus, and 100Mbps-capable NICs, the performance increase can be much greater.

New Workgroups with no Local Servers

Up to this point, we have discussed upgrading existing workgroups where the clients are restricted to 10Mbps NICs. Next, we will discuss how to implement Fast Ethernet in new workgroups. (The term new workgroup implies that the systems in that workgroup were recently added to the network.) In step 2, we discussed how to make sure each new system is installed with a 10/100Mbps NIC. The combination of many new systems being added to the network and the inclusion of 10/100Mbps NICs makes upgrading to Fast Ethernet very easy and inexpensive. The most cost-effective way to upgrade this kind of workgroup is with a 100Mbps standalone or stackable hub. The users will instantly jump from sharing 10Mbps to sharing 100 Mbps, which provides a tenfold performance improvement. The following sections describe how you can do this.

Small Workgroups

A small workgroup can be classified as 20 users or fewer. Depending on how you plan to enlarge that small workgroup, you may elect to connect it with a 100Mbps standalone repeater or a 100Mbps stackable hub. As described in Chapter 8, "Network Components," the standalone repeater will be less expensive in the short term, but the stackable hub offers greater flexibility for future growth. Let's look at an example of how a new workgroup is installed using a 10/100Mbps-Mbps standalone repeater. In this example, a new group of users will be added to a small network. We have already seen how existing systems can be connected using a 10-Mbps switch. Now those same systems can be connected using a 10/100Mbps-Mbps repeater. Part A of Figure 9.13 shows a small network with just a few 10Mbps repeaters, clients, and servers. Part B shows the new network after the addition of new users.

The newer clients share 100Mbps of bandwidth and the existing clients get 10Mbps dedicated connections. The 100Mbps capable servers have dedicated 100 Mbps connections. The number of users on the network has doubled, the available bandwidth has gone from 10Mbps to 100 Mbps, and no desktops were opened unnecessarily. The fact that the standalone repeater can operate each port at 10Mbps or 100Mbps makes it very flexible for this type of deployment. No matter what speed a client is running, it can be connected to the repeater. The cost of adding the 10/100 repeater is low, therefore providing cost-effective migration from 10Mbps to 100Mbps for this small workgroup.

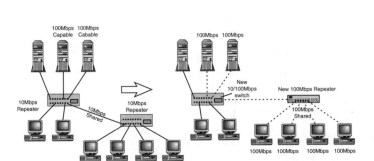

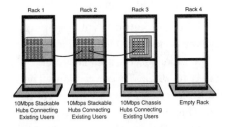

FIGURE 9.13 *Network before (a) and after (b) adding a new Fast Ethernet workgroup. Older clients with 10Mbps NICs are connected to a 10/100Mbps workgroup switch. New clients with 10/100Mbps NICs are connected to a 10/100Mbps repeater. Newer servers have dedicated 100Mbps connections.*

Large Workgroups

When deploying new users in a large network, 10/100Mbps stackable hubs or chassis hubs are the right choice. Large networks are typically upgraded from the network closet, where new users are connected through patch panels to rack-mounted stackable hubs or chassis hubs. Figure 9.14 shows a typical large 10Mbps Ethernet installation of several racks of stackable hubs and a chassis hub.

FIGURE 9.14 *A typical large 10Mbps wiring closet installation including stackable hubs and chassis hubs.*

You can add new users to this network by installing 10/100Mbps-Mbps stackable hubs and connecting the new users to them. You can connect the new users to the existing 10Mbps network via a 10/100Mbps switch module in the chassis. You could also connect additional new Fast Ethernet users via one of the ports on the 10/100Mbps stackable hub because they all run at 10 or 100Mbps speeds. Figure 9.15 shows the upgraded network. In this example, a 10/100Mbps switching module, like the Bay Networks System 5500, connects the 10Mbps and

100Mbps networks. You could also bridge 10 and 100Mbps by adding a 10/100Mbps Mbps-switching module to one of the stackable hubs. In either case, some of the network users are running at 100Mbps and some at 10Mbps.

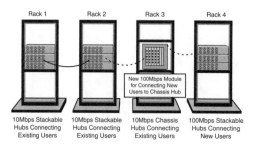

FIGURE 9.15 *Adding new Fast Ethernet users to a large 10Mbps wiring closet.*

New Power Workgroups with Local Servers

A small but growing percentage of new workgroups fall into the classification of power workgroups. This classification indicates that the workgroup puts so much local traffic on the network that even a 100Mbps repeater cannot handle the workload. A good way to recognize a power workgroup is to measure the amount of data that workgroup transmits on the wire, also called the workgroup network utilization. If the workgroup network utilization is above 30% of the total wire bandwidth available and over 80% of that traffic is local (meaning it is destined for another station or server within that workgroup), it may qualify as a power workgroup. Some examples of power workgroups are CAD workstation clusters, groups of multimedia systems, and desktop publishing centers.

You can connect clients and servers in power workgroups with per-port 10/100Mbps switches, such as the Bay Networks 28200. Each client in the workgroup is given a dedicated 100Mbps pipe. Servers are also given 100Mbps connections, or in some cases, aggregated 100BASE-TX connections. The connection to the backbone can also be multiple, aggregated 100Mbps connections, or a single Gigabit Ethernet connection. Therefore, look for 10/100Mbps switches that support Gbps Ethernet unlinks. Figure 9.16 shows a Fast Ethernet power workgroup deployed with a 100Mbps switch.

The Low-Cost 10Mbps/100Mbps Desktop Switch Factor

The rapid decrease in the cost of 10/100Mbps per-port switches has made 100Mbps switching to the desktop worth considering. Today for less than $150 per port—this price will have undoubtedly changed even before this book goes to print—you can purchase a 24-port 10/100Mbps switch from such big names as 3Com, Cisco, Intel, Bay Networks, and Hewlett-Packard. Although this price is far from the $30 to $50 per port cost of today's 10Mbps stackable hub, it is close enough to draw attention. At some point, the network architects will have to ask themselves if their network is ready for 100Mbps desktop switching.

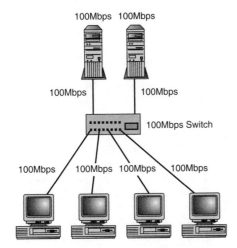

FIGURE 9.16 *A power workgroup connected via a Fast Ethernet switch. Each client and server gets 100Mbps of dedicated bandwidth. Half- or full-duplex modes can be supported.*

Deciding Between 10Mbps Switches and 100 Hubs

You may be thinking, "But I don't have any power workgroups on my network. My network utilization is about 30% and I only need a small performance boost." In this case, now may not be the time for Fast Ethernet deployment in your network. Step 1 (10Mbps switching) may be the answer to your current LAN bandwidth needs. In step 3, 100Mbps workgroups are advocated. Which gives better performance in a given situation? Vicious industry discussions have centered around which is better, shared 100Mbps or dedicated 10 Mbps. The simple answer is that both solutions measure about the same in terms of performance. 10Mbps switches offer a collision-free environment, whereas 100Mbps hubs,

although collision-prone, offer 100Mbps transfer rates all the way to the desktop. In the end, both solutions are good for about 95% of today's workgroups.

Our advice is this: If at all possible, run a desktop at 100Mbps. If this means 100Mbps stackable hubs are your choice, fine. If this means your budget allows for 10Mbps/100Mbps switched connections to the desktop (power workgroup), even better. New PCs will eventually outgrow 10Mbps-only switched connections.

Still, it helps to know when Fast Ethernet to the desktop is really necessary. Here are a few hints on how to determine whether 10Mbps switching

continues

continued

is enough power for a given work-group.

If the following are true, 10Mbps switching may be the final step need-ed in your high-speed deploment strategy:

- The total number of users in a given workgroup is under 40.

- The workgroup's primary network usage is basic file transfers and network printing.

- The current network utilization in the workgroup is under 30% (less than 3Mbps).

- End users do not complain about network performance or response time.

Also, as discussed previously, your desktop PC architecture or cabling infrastructure may dictate that 10Mbps switching is the highest performance solution available.

No matter what you deploy, though, always be on the lookout for increasing network traffic and plan your 10Mbps architecture in such a way that you can easily migrate to Fast Ethernet (step 3 and beyond) if the need arises. This includes deploying Fast Ethernet-ready 10Mbps switches and 10Mbps/100Mbps NICs in all new desktops and servers.

Luckily (or unluckily depending on your risk-taking tendencies), it will take some time for the industry to drive the price down. This is your chance to start evaluating 10/100Mbps desktop switches and start determining how you will connect 10/100Mbps switched workgroups with Gigabit Ethernet backbones (step 6). Worried? Well, read on.

Future Workgroup Considerations

As workgroups grow, changes will have to be made to the architecture of those workgroups. Most importantly, the location and type of local server should be considered. This will determine how much network traffic stays local to the workgroup and how much leaves the workgroup, destined for the backbone or WAN. Consider the following issues when planning future workgroup deployment:

- *Multimedia support*—Multimedia traffic differs from regular network traf-fic in that it is constant and not bursty in nature. A television-quality, full-screen MPEG video will consume 1.5 to 3.0Mbps of network bandwidth. If four or five such transmissions are occurring simultaneously in a work-group, you can easily see how 10Mbps won't be able to handle the load. Transferring voice and data together also causes problems because long latencies on voice packets can break up a live discussion. In the future, switches will support features such as RSVP bandwidth reservation protocol, 802.1p frame prioritization, and virtual LANs (VLANs) to overcome these issues, but this is still a few years away. In the meantime, use the best weapon you have to approach these applications: bandwidth. You'd be surprised what 100Mbps of dedicated bandwidth to a desktop will allow you to do.

- *Layer 3 filtering in the workgroup*—Layer 3 support is recommended primarily in the backbone in this book, but in the future, Layer 3 capabilities could be driven down into the workgroup. In theory, the earlier a packet is identified and filtered, the better it can traverse the network. Today, Layer 3 capabilities in a workgroup switch will significantly add to the cost. In the future, this capability may become standard.

- *Gigabit Ethernet and ATM support*—Many 10 or 100Mbps Ethernet switches already support Gigabit Ethernet and 155Mbps ATM uplinks. This is important if Gigabit Ethernet or ATM are being considered for the backbone. You should remember, however, that by mixing ATM and Ethernet, ATM becomes nothing more than a fat pipe. The QoS features inherent in ATM must be implemented with RSVP and 802.1Q/p tagging in an Ethernet workgroup. Therefore, consider ATM very carefully before combining it with an existing Ethernet network. You're better off using Gigabit Ethernet to uplink a 100Mbps workgroup switch.

Workgroup Options

The flexibility of switches that automatically configure to 10Mbps or 100Mbps on a per-port basis will help in the deployment of high bandwidth to your existing client and server base. These switches are jacks-of-all-trades because they can provide 100Mbps dedicated connections for backbones, repeaters, servers, and power users or 10Mbps dedicated connections for older clients and 10Mbps repeaters. Also, as described in Chapter 11, standard SNMP applications should be able to manage workgroup switches.

As an alternative to switches, 100Mbps stackable hubs are a cost-effective way to deploy Fast Ethernet to users with new systems and 10/100Mbps NICs. Table 9.7 illustrates the types of workgroups and the appropriate Fast Ethernet workgroup solution.

TABLE 9.7 WORKGROUP SWITCH DEPLOYMENT RECOMMENDATIONS FOR FOUR BASIC TYPES OF WORKGROUPS

Workgroup Type	Defining Characteristics	Recommended Fast Ethernet Upgrade Path (and Examples)
Existing workgroup	All nodes are clients	10Mbps workgroup switch with 100Mbps uplinks
Existing workgroup with local servers	Clients are legacy systems with 10Mbps-only NICs (usually ISA)	10/100Mbps workgroup switch
	Some local servers may be in the workgroup	
New workgroup	Mostly client nodes	10/100Mbps standalone repeater for small workgroups
	Local servers may be attached to the workgroup	10/100Mbps stackable hub for large workgroups
	Clients are new systems with 10/100Mbps NICs	10/100Mbps workgroup switches for large workgroups when budget allows
	Servers are new systems with 10/100Mbps NICs	
New power workgroup	Clients and servers are new high-end systems or workstations	10/100Mbps Workgroup Switch
	Clients and servers have 10/100Mbps NICs	
	Workgroup traffic level is above 30%	
	Most traffic is local (more than 80%)	

Deployment Step 4: Switched and Fast Ethernet in the Backbone

The next step after implementing Fast Ethernet in the workgroup is either to create a new backbone or convert your existing backbone to Fast Ethernet. First, we will discuss what defines a backbone and what types of backbones exist. Then we will discuss how to deploy Switched and Fast Ethernet in those backbones. If you have implemented the previous steps correctly, the backbone conversion should be straightforward. Also, by upgrading the backbone, your entire local area network will have increased performance instead of just the workgroup. Later, in step 6, we'll examine where Gigabit Ethernet fits in these backbones.

You can upgrade many different backbone implementations to Fast Ethernet from 10Mbps Ethernet. Two of the more common types are distributed backbones and collapsed backbones.

A distributed backbone is one that couples major sub-LANs via a chaining technique. A *sub-LAN* is defined as a floor, site, or other physical collection of workgroups. For instance, in a 10-story building, the LAN may incorporate all ten floors, plus the basement where the servers are kept. Each floor of the building is a sub-LAN, and each sub-LAN consists of several workgroups. As usual, the workgroups are concentrations of clients and local servers. Figure 9.17 shows a diagram of a distributed backbone. Distributed backbones include FDDI rings, Token Rings, and some switched Ethernet backbones.

Collapsed backbones are typically deployed when delays through the various switches or routers in a distributed backbone become too great. This occurs by deploying one high-end router in the basement and connecting each major sub-LAN to it directly. In a collapsed backbone, a packet from one sub-LAN must go through only the high-end router to reach any other sub-LAN. Collapsed backbones are also employed with FDDI Rings, Token Rings, 10Mbps switches, and high-end routers. A collapsed backbone is also shown in Figure 9.17.

The Location of Servers in a Backbone

Before we delve into the intricacies of distributed and collapsed backbones, we must spend a moment discussing server location. As discussed in the last chapter, servers represent information and clients represent users who create or use that information. Servers are located everywhere: in the workgroup (local), on the backbone, or across the wide area network. Because servers are included in almost every network transaction, you should understand how server location affects network traffic before embarking on a full-scale backbone upgrade.

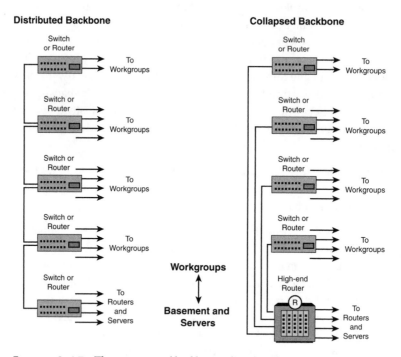

FIGURE 9.17   *The two types of backbones: distributed and collapsed.*

Consider Figure 9.18. Server A is a local file server. It contains spreadsheets, text documents, and other files that are of interest mainly to the local workgroup. Server B is actually a print server. Print servers, like Intel's NetPort, allow clients to print to many different printers. The clients in the workgroup will access server A and server B in almost a random fashion, causing the network traffic to burst from near zero to near 100 percent for short periods of time. This traffic, however, will not leave the workgroup.

Server C is an email server located on the network backbone. Access to the email server is typically periodic, with heavy access early in the morning and around lunchtime. Clients who access the email server do so across the backbone, so this traffic is not considered local. Server D is an Internet server that allows access to the Internet and WWW. Clients accessing this server will be asking it to be an Internet proxy. In other words, to keep the LAN secure, this special server will make requests of the Internet on a client's behalf. Traffic to and from the Internet server is typically bursty, or irregular, and can vary greatly in volume.

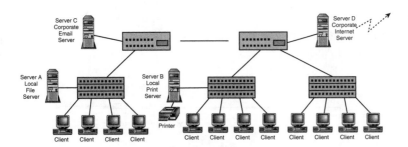

FIGURE 9.18 *Location of server resources drives the flow of network traffic.*

When traffic from all four servers is mixed, one can start to understand the traffic patterns that occur on today's networks. If servers A and B are used more often than C and D, the 80/20 rule applies, and the backbone only needs to support 20% of the traffic generated by each workgroup. If email and Internet access dominate the use of this network, the backbone must handle up to 100% of traffic generated by each workgroup. These two scenarios are completely different and require varying degrees of backbone power.

We intended this exercise to show what server placement can do to network traffic, but it illustrates another point as well. Unless you can accurately determine the location and type of your *future servers*, you can't really predict the requirements of your *future network*. For this reason we recommend overdesign of your network backbone to handle the possibility of most workgroup traffic propagating to the backbone. It may be overkill for today, but it will make your network more than ready for tomorrow.

Distributed Backbones

The distributed backbone deployment of today can incorporate a wide variety of solutions. On the performance scale, it can range anywhere from 10BASE-T to 1000BASE-T. In a distributed backbone, a high-end router is not necessary because each individual sub-LAN is connected via a particular switch or router. Therefore, the cost of a distributed backbone is usually lower than that of a collapsed backbone. The performance of a distributed backbone may be worse, however, due to high transmission latencies. In the example from Figure 9.17, a packet originating from the basement must pass through four backbone switches before reaching a destination on the top floor. In an application where latency matters, such as video-conferencing, this large latency can ruin performance.

This section will focus on how to upgrade an existing 10Mbps distributed backbone to Fast Ethernet and how to prepare for future backbone additions. Figure 9.19 shows how a 10Mbps distributed backbone would progress through steps 1, 2, 3, and finally step 4 of this chapter. By implementing Fast Ethernet in the backbone, step 4 marks the deployment of Fast Ethernet throughout the LAN.

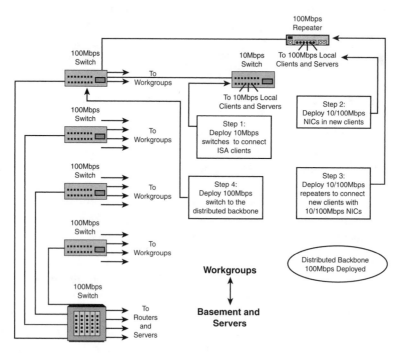

FIGURE 9.19 *Distributed backbone after Fast Ethernet deployment. Note that each step of Switched and Fast Ethernet deployment is shown.*

To complete the transition to Fast Ethernet, 100BASE-T switches have been added to the backbone in Figure 9.19. This nullifies any 100BASE-T network diameter constraints because switches don't suffer from collision domain restrictions. Therefore, a 100BASE-T distributed backbone of any size can be built with 100BASE-T switches. 100BASE-T switches enabled with a port aggregation scheme can provide up to 400Mbps dedicated bandwidth in and out of each backbone switch. The performance improvement over 10Mbps shared can therefore be anywhere from 10 to about 100 times, depending on the loading of the backbone.

The Bay Networks 450T 100BASE-TX switch provides this type of functionality. Each of the 24 ports on the 450T will auto-configure for 100BASE-TX or 10BASE-T operation. In the example from Figure 9.19, one workgroup hub is a 10/100Mbps stackable hub and should be connected at 100Mbps on the backbone switch. The other is a 10Mbps switch and should be connected to a 10Mbps port on the backbone switch (or a 10/100Mbps switch could be used in its place). The Bay 450T also provides modules for Gigabit Ethernet ports for connecting backbone switches. This feature alone can provide a tenfold bandwidth improvement in the backbone.

In this example, UTP wiring is used because the switch-to-switch connections of a multistory building will unlikely be greater than 100m. This doesn't hold true for a physically spread-out distributed backbone. Consider a multiple-building site where each building is 500m from the next. To connect these buildings to the same 100BASE-T backbone, 100BASE-FX fiber connections must be made. 100BASE-FX can transmit over 2km of multiple-mode fiber.

A drawback to deploying a 100BASE-T distributed backbone is the long latencies encountered in hopping from switch to switch. In cases where you'd like to deploy real-time LAN products, such as video conferencing, a 100BASE-T collapsed backbone may be the better choice. The advantage of a distributed backbone, however, is that you don't need a central, high-end router or switch in the basement.

Collapsed Backbones

A collapsed backbone is not much different from a distributed backbone. In fact, the sub-LANs and workgroups are structured the same in either case. The major difference is the types of switches or routers installed in the backbone and the way they are connected. For instance, there is no such thing as a shared-media collapsed backbone. Collapsed backbones are switched or routed by definition.

The issues with deploying Fast Ethernet into a collapsed backbone are of two varieties. First, determine what kind of router you have in your basement. Can you simply upgrade it with a Fast Ethernet module or will you need to purchase a whole new chassis-based router? Second, determine how your various sub-LANs are connected to the router and with what media type. It is highly possible that you can install Fast Ethernet in your collapsed backbone with no rewiring at all.

When upgrading a collapsed backbone to Fast Ethernet, you must replace the basement router and some sub-LAN switches together. Not all sub-LANs need to be upgraded to Fast Ethernet at the same time, however. As soon as the new Fast Ethernet-enabled router is in place, you can replace each sub-LAN switch as the need arises. Figure 9.20 shows a typical 10Mbps collapsed backbone. Figure 9.21 indicates how you can convert part of the backbone to Fast Ethernet by adding one module to the basement router and one 100Mbps switch to the sub-LAN.

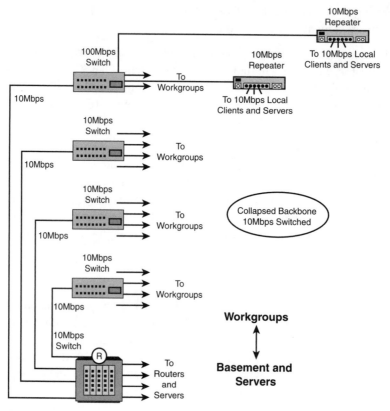

FIGURE 9.20 *A typical 10Mbps collapsed backbone. The high-end chassis router in the basement has many 10Mbps modules.*

By upgrading the basement router with Fast Ethernet modules, you can deploy 100Mbps collapsed backbones one step at a time. Of course, it is critical that the router support Fast Ethernet modules. Three such routers are the Cisco 7500 router, the Bay Networks Backbone Node router, and the 3Com NetBuilder II or CoreBuilder router. If you cannot upgrade the router at the center of your collapsed backbone to Fast Ethernet, you will either have to purchase a new router (very costly) or only deploy Fast Ethernet in the workgroup. Whether you use a new router module or a brand-new router, look for it to support fast and efficient routing between Ethernet and Fast Ethernet segments. In general, whatever features you look for in an Ethernet router, look for those in a Fast Ethernet router as well.

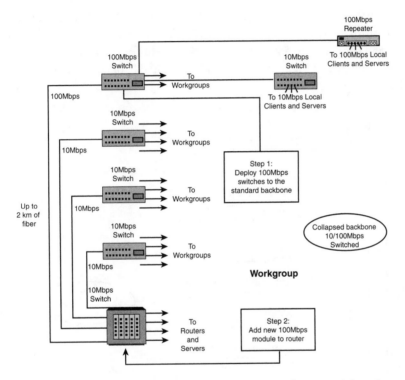

FIGURE 9.21 *The backbone after adding a new Fast Ethernet module to the router and a new Fast Ethernet switch in one sub-LAN. One sub-LAN at a time can be upgraded to Fast Ethernet in a collapsed backbone.*

Collapsed backbones are currently preferred over distributed backbones because of their performance benefits and lower packet latencies. However, a collapsed backbone has typically required a sophisticated piece of routing equipment, such as the Cisco 7500, which may be more expensive (we'll discuss how to get around this in step 5). Another problem that often arises with collapsed backbones is that, because of large physical distances between sub-LANs, the sub-LAN connections commonly require cable lengths greater than 100m. You cannot use UTP in these situations. FDDI has been a common solution until now, but 100BASE-FX provides a more cost-effective alternative.

For instance, if the example in Figure 9.22 requires a sub-LAN to be connected more than 100m away, you can insert a 100BASE-FX module in the basement router and connect it to a 2km fiber run. Be sure to consider that the sub-LAN switch (at the top of Figure 9.22) must also be capable of connecting to 100BASE-FX.

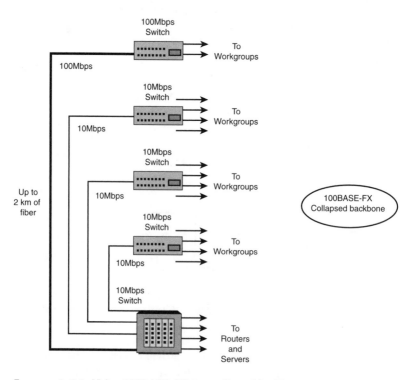

FIGURE 9.22 *Using 100BASE-FX in a collapsed backbone.*

Port Aggregation and Gigabit Ethernet Uplinks

We don't add Gigabit Ethernet to the backbone until step 6, but it's important to be prepared for it by using 100Mbps backbone switches with slots for Gbps Ethernet uplinks. The previously cited examples use Cisco's Fast EtherChannel port aggregation scheme to interconnect switches. This provides an economical way of increasing bandwidth between switches up to 400Mbps in each direction (in and out of the switch). Gigabit Ethernet provides a true high-speed uplink, however, which is capable of aggregating traffic from a 100Mbps backbone switch. In this step, when Fast Ethernet is the interswitch connection of choice, use a port aggregation scheme like Fast EtherChannel to connect switches.

Server Farms

Recall from step 2 that *server farms* are classically defined as a cluster of servers that are connected directly to the backbone. Server farms can also be of many shapes and sizes, some of the more popular versions being file servers, Internet servers, and application servers. File server farms are typically accessed randomly and provide file sharing and directory services to anyone on the LAN. File servers are subject to high-bandwidth spikes and bursty traffic, but their overall average utilization usually remains low. Internet servers are also accessed randomly, but they perform additional duties such as caching Internet data and protecting the LAN from Internet viruses and eavesdroppers. Application server farms are under more constant bandwidth demand because they are providing email, database, and multimedia services. The average traffic generated by application server farms is typically large.

File servers require high-speed disk subsystems, but little else. For instance, a Pentium processor-based file server will likely perform much like a Pentium II processor-based file server if similar hard drive subsystems are used in each. File servers also tend to be used randomly, with high bursts of network utilization when users open or close a file. For this reason, file server farms show large network utilization spikes but remain low in average bandwidth. As we have already seen, repeaters provide an excellent solution for this type of network. The trick is to determine how to distribute the shared bandwidth between servers. Consider the following, where 16 file servers are part of a server farm on a 10Mbps backbone. By measuring the amount of traffic generated by each server, one can determine how to upgrade it. Assume the servers put the following loads on the 10Mbps repeater to which they are connected:

File Server	Load
1	1.0Mbps
2	0.2Mbps
3	0.2Mbps
4	0.4Mbps
5	1.6Mbps

continues

File Server	Load
6	0.4Mbps
7	0.2Mbps
8	0.2Mbps
9	1.0Mbps
10	0.4Mbps
11	0.2Mbps
12	0.4Mbps
13	0.2Mbps
14	0.2Mbps
15	0.2Mbps
16	0.2Mbps
Total	**7.0Mbps**

When upgrading this particular file server farm to Fast Ethernet, you have the opportunity to optimize its configuration. First, replace the 10Mbps NICs in each server with 10/100Mbps NICs (if you haven't already done so as a result of step 2). Next, consider that the best way to segment these file servers is to put the few high traffic servers together, separating them from the others. Each group is connected with a 100Mbps repeater and attached to the network via a 100Mbps switched connection. This results in two server farms: one with servers 1, 5, and 9 and the other with the rest of the servers. Each server farm shares 100Mbps of bandwidth through a Fast Ethernet repeater. An even better solution would be to provide individual 100Mbps switched ports to servers 1, 5, and 9.

Internet and intranet servers are typically placed centrally and often connected to the backbone. (When an internet server serves information to internal users only, it is sometimes referred to as an *intranet server*.) These servers have almost single-handedly reversed the 80/20 rule that was common in most work-groups. That is, before the Internet, 80% of workgroup traffic stayed local to that workgroup. Now that so many corporate employees are accessing the Internet, a large portion of the network traffic they create is destined to or from the Internet. This makes Internet servers a constant source of action on a busy network and often causes their location to be on the high-speed backbone, rather than the local workgroup.

Application servers are also implemented as server farms. In this case, the bandwidth demands are usually too high and constant to use a repeater. A

100Mbps backbone switch may be the best solution for an application server farm. The deployment is very similar to that of the file server farm, except each server gets its own dedicated 100Mbps link. This way, when multiple users are accessing a database on an application server, it can respond without regard for bandwidth constraints from other servers. This type of server farm deployment also allows for multiple servers to be accessed simultaneously. Unlike file servers, an application server's performance gets much better as the quality of the NICs, processors, expansion bus speeds, and amount of system memory improves. Pentium processors, the PCI bus, and intelligent Fast Ethernet NICs may be worthwhile investments for application servers.

In addition, application servers (and to some extent file servers) are often critical parts of the network. If users cannot gain access to the information on these servers, productivity will drop, and users will become frustrated. For this reason, it is a good idea to consider redundancy when designing server farms. One of the best ways to provide redundancy is to populate each server with at least two NICs, connecting each of them to a separate 100Mbps switch. In this way, if the NIC, cable, or even the switch goes down, the server will remain connected to the network.

Managing Backbone Switches

Backbone switches are more instrumental to network uptime than workgroup devices. Therefore, you should pay more attention to managing these backbone switches. In a workgroup switch, RMON Groups 1, 2, 3, and 9 are recommended. In a backbone switch, all nine groups of RMON should be supported. Because this is an expensive option, look for switch vendors to provide add-in modules that support varying degrees of RMON support or look for roving RMON support (RMON groups 1 through 9 supported on all ports, but not all ports simultaneously). RMON2 support can also be beneficial where the benefits outweigh the costs of the RMON2 hardware and software. Chapter 11 goes into a more detailed discussion of switch management with RMON and RMON2.

Backbone Options

Deployment of a switched Fast Ethernet backbone will allow your entire LAN to communicate at 100Mbps. By deploying Fast Ethernet in the backbone, the lion's share of the upgrade from 10BASE-T to 100BASE-T will be complete. Access to both local and backbone servers will be at 100Mbps, and the performance gain should be evident in higher network traffic, faster network response time, and lower overall network utilization. Table 9.8 summarizes the important points of backbone deployment in each of these key areas.

TABLE 9.8 BACKBONE DEPLOYMENT ISSUES

Type of Backbone	Fast Ethernet Upgrade	Issues
Distributed backbone	Multiple 100BASE-T switches	A 100BASE-T switch is needed for each sub-LAN (floor, site, and so on) to be upgraded
		Distributed backbone can not be implemented a piece at a time
		Packet latencies may be high
		Use 100BASE-FX for multiple building backbones
		Less expensive than upgrading a collapsed backbone
Collapsed backbone	Multiple 100BASE-T switches and a 100BASE-T router module for basement router	A 100BASE-T switch is needed for each sub-LAN (floor, site, and so on) to be upgraded
		A 100BASE-T router module is needed for basement router
		If basement router does not support a 100BASE-T module, a new router may have to be considered
		Collapsed backbone can be implemented a piece at a time
		Packet latencies should be low
		Use 100BASE-FX for multiple building backbones
		More expensive than upgrading a distributed backbone
Backbone Server Farm	100BASE-T repeater or 100BASE-T switch	Upgrade all servers to 10Mbps/100Mbps NICs
		Connect server directly to 100Mbps switched port whenever possible
		When using repeaters, use one for high-usage file servers and another for the rest of the file servers

Deployment Step 5: Routers, Layer 3 Switching, and VLANs in the Backbone

With 100BASE-T implemented in the backbone, the foundation for high-speed local area networking has been laid. So far, the discussion has been concerned with increasing the network bandwidth, but we haven't tackled the issue of network traffic flow. Leaving the network in this state is like adding larger pipes to an outdated water system but not replacing the old valves and filters. The "valves" of a LAN are the routers, Layer 3 switches and VLANs in the network. Routers include WAN (T1, T3, ISDN) and LAN (Token Ring, FDDI) varieties, Layer 3 switches are simplified routers embedded in switches, and VLANs represent ways of segmenting a network based on certain properties. In this section, we'll discuss the routers and Layer 3 switches in the backbone and glance at various VLAN implementations.

Fast Ethernet Routers

In Chapter 8, we discussed three areas where routers are useful: LAN segmentation, connecting disparate LANs, and connecting to the WAN. In this section, we'll examine how each of these applications changes when upgrading to Switched and Fast Ethernet.

Fast Ethernet Segmentation Routing

If your current network is based on a collapsed backbone and a chassis-based router is its center, upgrading to Fast Ethernet is much like what we discussed in Chapter 8. In this application, routers filter broadcast traffic, keeping it only on the subnet where it originated.

A new Fast Ethernet routing module, such as the Cisco Route Switch Processor for the Series 7500 router, would do the trick nicely in this situation.

Of course, now that Layer 3 switches are available, there are sometimes less expensive ways to do this. For now, use Table 9.9 to determine whether you need a new Fast Ethernet routing module or whether you should consider Layer 3 switches.

TABLE 9.9 WHEN TO USE ROUTERS VERSUS LAYER 3 SWITCHES IN THE BACKBONE

Criterion	Use Fast Ethernet Routing Module	Use Layer 3 Switches
Protocol support	IP, IPX, DecNet, and so on	IP-only (some IPX)
Router connects to	Ethernet, Token Ring, FDDI, ATM, or other technology	Ethernet only

continues

TABLE 9.9 CONTINUED

Criterion	Use Fast Ethernet Routing Module	Use Layer 3 Switches
Router connects to WAN	Chassis-based router also has WAN routing modules	WAN connectivity is through a separate device, such as a standalone router

We discuss the use of Layer 3 switches as segmentation routers more in the following sections.

Standalone Routers

When connecting to the WAN, standalone routers are often used. This is because chassis-based WAN connectivity is usually very expensive. In contrast, standalone routers cost less but are less flexible. Even so, some standalone routers can be upgraded in performance via Fast Ethernet router modules, but only if they have slots for new modules. A good example of this kind of router is the 3Com NetBuilder III. Figure 9.23 shows the basement of a large networked site. The collapsed backbone router sits in the basement receiving many packets of data and concentrating on forwarding them. This router does not have time to filter and route packets to the WAN, so a standalone router is used for WAN access. Many networks use separate standalone routers in this configuration.

FIGURE 9.23 *Standalone routers may need to be replaced with Fast Ethernet versions because they are not inherently upgrade capable.*

Another way to upgrade this network is with new, low-cost, Fast Ethernet access routers. Intel's Express 8100 Access Router has a 10/100Mbps connection built right into the box. Sometimes a new standalone router will also come with other new features like RSVP bandwidth reservation, support for Internet virtual private networking, and encryption software. If WAN access is the primary need, standalone routers are often the best way to connect the WAN to your Fast Ethernet LAN.

PC-Based Routing

An even more cost-effective approach to LAN segmentation or WAN connectivity is PC-based routing. Many networks employ software or PC-based routing because it usually costs less than upgrading the modules in existing routers or adding standalone routers. In addition, you can specify Fast Ethernet and other network types by the type of NIC used, allowing an infinite number of configurations. Figure 9.24 shows an example of a software-based router.

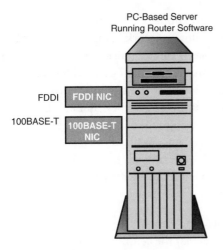

FIGURE 9.24 *Fast Ethernet PC-based routing (FDDI to Fast Ethernet). PC-based routing offers an economical alternative to expensive chassis-based routers, but the performance often leaves a lot to be desired.*

PC routing is limited to the performance of the PC on which it runs. As discussed in Chapter 8, quite a bit of PC horsepower is required to handle multiple Fast Ethernet connections. Therefore, PC-based routing should be limited only to networks where budget restrictions are the most stringent.

Layer 3 Switches in the Backbone

If your network doesn't have a backbone already, you should seriously consider Layer 3 backbone switches. Table 9.9 discusses the criteria for when Layer 3 switches can be considered. Basically, you should use them in networks where:

- Layer 3 protocols are converging to IP (and possibly IPX).

- Connectivity to FDDI, Token Ring, and other non-Ethernet technologies is not required.

- Connectivity to the WAN is done through a separate device.

- RIP, RIP2, and OSPF are the routing protocols used on the network. Most Layer 3 switches don't support other protocols, such as BGP, IGRP, EIGRP, and the like.

As the bottom line, if your network is consolidating around IP and Ethernet, Layer 3 switching is for you.

Where to Put Layer 3 Switches in the Backbone

Layer 3 switching is usually designed into a network in one of two configurations: *centralized* or *distributed*. Alert readers might notice that this is another way of saying *collapsed* or *distributed*, but the terminology used here insinuates different properties about the architectures. Distributed Layer 3 switching, unlike a distributed backbone, requires upgrades on all major sub-LANs (*subnets* if you're using TCP/IP or *floors* using the example from step 4). Centralized Layer 3 switching can be implemented a sub-LAN at a time, but it requires a central Layer 3 switch. Because centralized Layer 3 switching is more flexible, it is usually the preferred choice in existing networks.

Centralized Layer 3 Switching

A centralized Layer 3 switched architecture closely resembles a routed backbone from step 4. The only difference is that the central device is a Layer 3 switch and not a high-end router. Remember that a Layer 3 switch, when using a RIP or OSPF-based routing scheme, acts much like a router.

Adding a new Layer 3 chassis switch to the network is fine when a brand new network is being designed, but you're never quite so lucky. In most cases, a central router already exists in the collapsed backbone. Are we advocating throwing away this costly item and replacing it with a Layer 3 switch? Absolutely not (well, maybe if your network supplier has a liberal return policy). Instead, you can easily add Layer 3 switches to existing routed backbones, leveraging the existing router(s). Figure 9.25 shows how a Fast Ethernet Layer 3 switch is used to add two new IP subnets to an existing collapsed backbone.

In this example, the network is using only the TCP/IP protocol, and because the Layer 3 switch supports this protocol, it acts like another router. The Layer 3 switch communicates with the existing router via RIP, RIP2, or OSPF protocols, transferring the necessary routing tables. In this way, the Layer 3 switch resembles the routing modules in the existing router.

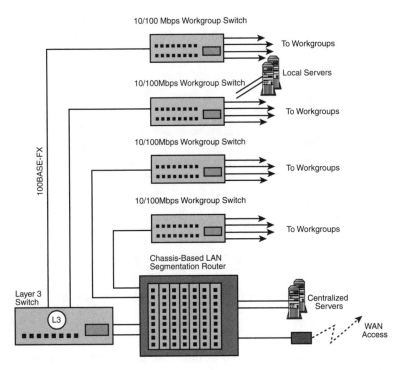

FIGURE 9.25 *The addition of a Layer 3 backbone switch to a routed, collapsed backbone.*

In the centralized scheme, you may want to consider adding Layer 3 capability to certain switches on each floor. For instance, on the third floor, the local servers may create a lot of broadcast traffic that doesn't need to be propagated beyond that floor. In this case, a Layer 3 switch in the third floor wiring closet will help alleviate the routing requirements of the central Layer 3 switch.

Be careful to consider all aspects of compatibility between your existing router and the new Layer 3 switch before connecting them. The following are some of the questions you should ask yourself before upgrading your network in this way:

- Does the Layer 3 switch support all required protocols (IP, IPX, and so on)?

- Does the Layer 3 switch support the required inter-router protocols (RIP, RIP2, OSPF, and so on)?

- Is port aggregation supported (Fast EtherChannel or 802.3ad)?

- Does the switch support enough ports? If not, can the port density be upgraded?

- Does the switch support fiber? Pay attention to the fiber connectors supported (see Chapter 6). You don't want to end up with a switch with SC connectors and a fiber run with ST connectors.

- Does the switch support uplink modules (ATM, Gigabit Ethernet, and so on)? Do those modules support Layer 3 switching?

Also, note that most router vendors provide Fast Ethernet Layer 3 switches on chassis modules. These modules are less expensive than full-fledged router modules but are often more expensive than buying separate Layer 3 switches. Consider all your options before selecting a solution.

Distributed Layer 3 Switching

Distributed Layer 3 switching is less flexible than the centralized model because it requires that all sub-LANs have a Layer 3 switch, which are interconnected by a high-speed, Layer 2 switch. While you are scratching your head, let us explain.

If you look at the example of a distributed Layer 3 switched architecture in Figure 9.26, the first thing you notice is that each floor has a Layer 3 switch in its wiring closet. The logic to this goes as follows. Because an end-station (either client or server) originates all the data on the network, that data will have to pass through a Layer 3 switch before it reaches the backbone. If each of the floors is equipped with a Layer 3 switch, the switch on each floor will perform all broadcast traffic filtering (and other routing functions). Thus, a broadcast packet originated by a client on the second floor will never propagate to the backbone, and therefore, to any other floor.

This is a more efficient way to filter the traffic because the central backbone switch does not deal with routed packets. If a packet needs to be routed from one floor to another, it is sent through the backbone switch, which forwards it according to Layer 2 (MAC address) information only. The Layer 3 switches on each floor need to update each other's routing tables (via RIP2 or OSPF), and these updates will also be sent across the backbone. Data traffic is reduced on the backbone, but additional router overhead traffic is increased, so it is hard to determine the net effect of the distributed architecture on any given network. It really depends, as in the centralized case, on the amount of data that needs to be routed.

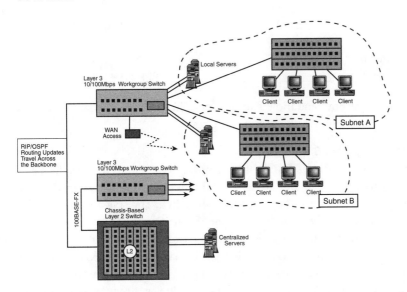

FIGURE 9.26 *Distributed Layer 3 switching in the workgroup. This architecture takes advantage of an existing Layer 2 switch in the core of the network.*

If you are going to deploy Layer 3 switches in each sub-LAN (or on each floor), you should also deploy a central switch with Layer 3 capabilities. This will cost more, but it gives you added flexibility in how you roll out future workgroups. A central Layer 3 switch signifies a centralized architecture, so our recommendation is this: if you have determined that you need Layer 3 switching, deploy a centralized Layer 3 switching architecture.

Performance and Cost Analysis

Distributed and centralized Layer 3 switched solutions cost approximately the same. With the centralized solution, the cost may be more in the central switch, whereas the distributed solution requires more, lower cost Layer 3 switches for each sub-LAN. Table 9.10 highlights the pros and cons of each architecture.

TABLE 9.10 A COMPARISON OF LAYER 3 SWITCH ARCHITECTURES

Issue	Centralized	Distributed
Layer 3 forwarding	Done in the core of the backbone and/or in the wiring closet	Done in the wiring closet
Backbone traffic	Higher than Distributed	Lower than Centralized
Requirements in workgroup	None	Layer 3 switching supported

Again, our recommendation is to use centralized Layer 3 switches and to use them in conjunction with your existing routers.

Configuring Layer 3 Switches

In the preceding discussion, Fast Ethernet was the inferred technology for the Layer 3 switches used, but Layer 3 capabilities can also be designed into a 10Mbps switch or into a Gigabit Ethernet switch. The speed of the central Layer 3 switch depends on the amount of traffic expected on the backbone. In a centralized architecture, because broadcast traffic is forwarded to the backbone, the central switch needs to be higher performance than the connected workgroup switches. If the workgroup switch is Fast Ethernet, the backbone switch should be Gigabit Ethernet, or at least multiple Fast EtherChannel aggregated 100Mbps connections. We'll discuss this more in Step 6.

Subnets

One of the primary benefits of a Layer 3 switch is its capability to filter broadcast traffic. This depends on how the subnets (sub-LANs, in some of our examples) are configured. *Subnets* refer to groups of IP addresses, which are often clustered according to physical location. A Layer 3 switch is most efficient when it is configured to map each port to an existing subnet, thus resembling a router. Figure 9.27 shows an example of this.

This configuration can be either manual or automatic, depending on the design of the switch. Switches that automatically determine the IP subnet on each port usually do so by monitoring the IP addresses and requests that are generated by the workgroup connected to that port. This is a clever system, but it can be easily corrupted by changing desktops or a faulty NIC. You're usually much safer directly assigning the subnet structure for the network and configure the Layer 3 switch to mirror that structure.

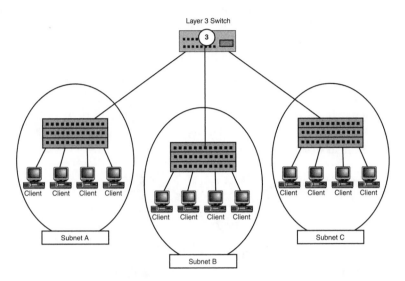

FIGURE 9.27 *Configuring a Layer 3 switch to match physical IP subnets.*

VLANs

Chapter 11 discusses VLANs in more detail, so this section is restricted to how you can use virtual LANs to aid in the deployment of Switched and Fast Ethernet. Virtual LANs are an important tool that, if used properly, can maximize the performance and minimize the maintenance of your network. VLAN implementations vary quite dramatically from vendor to vendor, but generally fall into five categories: port-based, protocol-based, MAC-based, IP multicast-based, or tagged.

Port-Based VLANs

Port-based VLANs were the earliest instantiation of the technology. They basically allow certain ports on a switch to be isolated from other ports on the switch. The two VLANs can be connected via an internal router (Layer 3 switch) or an external router. Some switches even support an interswitch communication scheme that allows ports on switch A to be on the same VLAN as ports on switch B. These interswitch communications are, however, proprietary and limited to single-vendor implementations.

Port-based VLANs can be helpful in isolating workgroups that use non-routable protocols, such as NetBEUI, from the rest of the network.

Protocol-Based VLANs

VLAN identification by protocol is perhaps the best way to use VLANs in an existing routed network. Switches that identify Layer 3 information, such as protocol type or IP address, can then assign that frame to a given VLAN. If an existing interswitch VLAN communication scheme exists, this VLAN identification can be transmitted to other switches on the network.

Most Layer 3 switches actually use protocol-based VLANs to segment traffic internal to the switch and then use RIP2 or OSPF to communicate the information to other switches. In this way, the switch is completely compatible with existing routers but still uses VLANs to segment traffic within the switch. Figure 9.28 illustrates this concept.

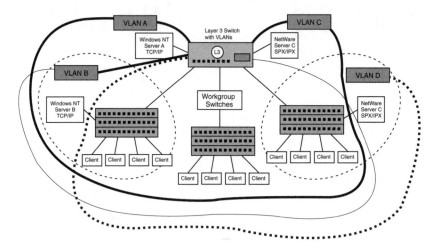

FIGURE 9.28 *Using VLANs to map servers and clients through a switched network. VLANs A and C span all clients but serve different protocols. VLANs B and D are workgroup specific.*

MAC Address-Based VLANs

A list of MAC addresses can be assigned to a particular VLAN, which means that a given end-station, no matter where it is on a network, can be assigned to a particular VLAN. This type of scheme works well in networks where users take their laptops with them to empty cubicles or conference rooms. Because the laptop has a given MAC address, the network can identify it no matter where it is attached.

The downside to MAC-based VLANs is that they need constant maintenance and monitoring. A laptop may contain a PCMCIA card with one MAC address and a docking station with another. Also, PCMCIA cards with new MAC addresses are installed all the time. Additionally, security is poor with the MAC-based method, as most NICs allow a software version of the MAC address to be used.

IP Multicast Address-Based VLANs

VLANs can also be identified with an IP multicast address. An IP multicast address is a proxy address for a larger group of IP addresses. If a frame needs to go to this group of IP addresses, it is sent first to the proxy IP address and then forwarded to the whole group. Membership in the group is voluntary, meaning that each desktop can determine whether its IP address should be included in the group. This kind of VLAN identification is useful in networks where video or audio data is being broadcast on the network and only a select few users are allowed to view or listen to the information.

802.1Q Tagged VLANs

The preceding VLAN implementations are nice, but if you want to implement VLANs in your production network, you might as well start getting used to the concept of a tagged frame (discussed in Chapters 3 and 8). The IEEE 802.1Q tagged VLAN standard is where most of the industry is headed, and where you should be as well. A tagged frame has a field called the *VLAN ID,* which indicates to which VLAN the frame belongs. All switches in the network would know this VLAN ID because switches are responsible for communicating VLAN membership amongst themselves.

What identifies which VLAN ID belongs in each frame? In theory, the end-station will identify the VLAN ID when the frame is originally created. If a frame comes into a switch with no VLAN ID, a switch can opt to insert a VLAN ID and forward the frame. Figure 9.29 shows the results of a forwarded frame depending on the final destination.

Should I Use VLANs in Step 5?

Through 1998, VLANs were still not standardized among major switch vendors and, therefore, were still proprietary. The 802.1Q standard will likely change this dramatically and become the de facto VLAN standard in 1999. Therefore, if you are considering VLANs, you should be considering 802.1Q support in your network components.

Although VLANs show a lot of promise, you can most likely meet the performance and segmentation needs of your network with simple Layer 3 switch deployment. Layer 3 switch deployment leverages existing routers and uses standard routing protocols. VLAN deployment means a new set of management tools and a proprietary interswitch communications scheme. With this in mind, you're best off using VLANs only in a limited fashion in workgroups where you can justify the need. Table 9.11 highlights some common examples of logical VLAN uses.

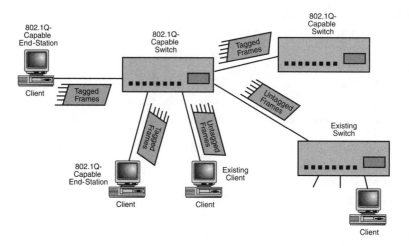

FIGURE 9.29 *802.1Q tagging and how tags are forwarded through a switched network.*

TABLE 9.11 PRACTICAL VLAN USES

VLAN Type	Complexity	Example of When to Use
Port-based	Low	All stations on port 10 are in VLAN 2.
MAC-based	High	Station 00-00-81-01-01-01 is in VLAN 3.
Layer 3 address	Med	IP subnet traffic 256.256.127.100 is on VLAN 1.
Protocol-sensitive	Low	IPX traffic on port 10 is in VLAN 4.
IP Multicast-based	High	IP Multicast address X is associated with VLAN Y.
Tagged	High	Standards-based 802.1Q/p tagged or proprietary tagging scheme.

> **Note**
>
> *3Com has a great white paper on its Web site (www.3com.com) that gives more detail on VLANs.*

Deployment Step 6: Gigabit Backbone Switches

Of all the recent developments in local area networking, Gigabit Ethernet has to be one of the most compelling. Not only does Gigabit Ethernet address the bandwidth requirements of today's backbones, but it has also shifted the bottleneck from the network to the server for the first time in nearly a decade.

This section identifies where Gigabit Ethernet should be deployed in your Ethernet network.

Connecting Multiple Workgroups

The obvious place where Gigabit Ethernet is needed first is the backbone switch. In step 4, we identified how to connect a collapsed backbone using aggregated Fast Ethernet switches. In step 6, we'll replace the central switch or router with a Gigabit Ethernet backbone switch.

Figure 9.30 shows the configuration of a Gigabit Ethernet collapsed backbone. The Fast Ethernet switches on each floor need to be upgraded with a Gigabit Ethernet uplink module in order to be connected to the central switch.

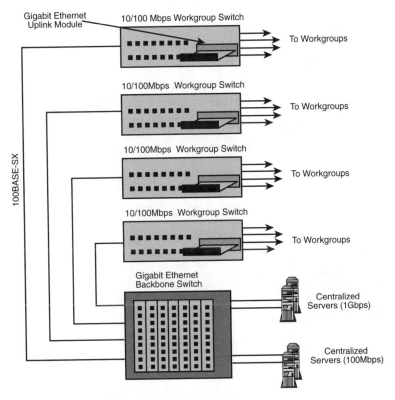

FIGURE 9.30 *Building a Gigabit Ethernet Backbone.*

In the previous section, we discussed the benefits of centralized Layer 3 switching, so the Gigabit Ethernet switch deployed should also be capable of Layer 3 switching. The packet per second routing performance of this switch should depend upon the model for backbone traffic in your network.

Because 1000BASE-LX Gigabit Ethernet over multiple-mode fiber is limited to 500m, you may need 100BASE-SX single-mode Gigabit Ethernet for especially long links. A 100BASE-LX Gigabit Ethernet switch with the capability to add a few 1000BASE-SX connections is the proper solution for this example.

This model for Gigabit Ethernet deployment allows for each desktop to connect at 100Mbps switched speeds.

Scaling Gigabit Ethernet Switches

What happens if more than one Gigabit Ethernet switch is needed in the backbone? There are really two options for this scenario. The first is to install a chassis-based solution with a multiple-Gbps backplane. A good example of this is the Extreme Networks Black Diamond 6800 Switch. Gigabit Ethernet modules can be added as the network grows, allowing for a flexible deployment. Of course, 48 ports of Gigabit Ethernet and 64Gbps of bandwidth doesn't come cheap: Extreme costs about $2,750 MSRP per Gigabit Ethernet port at the time of this book's publication.

The second option is to buy a fixed-configuration Gigabit Ethernet switch. A fixed-configuration switch will come with, say, eight ports. In order to enlarge this network beyond eight ports, an additional Gigabit Ethernet switch is needed. How would you connect these two switches? Our familiar port aggregation schemes (EtherChannel or 802.1ad) scale to Gbps speeds, allowing you to trunk up to four Gigabit Ethernet ports together. Figure 9.31 illustrates the Gigabit port aggregation scheme, creating a 12 port Gigabit Ethernet switched backbone. Because the interswitch connection is full-duplex, the transfer rate is 4Gbps to 2Gbps each way.

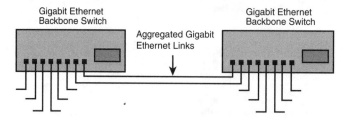

FIGURE 9.31 *Connecting two Gigabit Ethernet backbone Switches with port aggregation. The configuration shown here provides 4Gbps of bandwidth between the two switches: two in each direction.*

Connecting Gigabit Ethernet Switches to Gigabit Ethernet Servers

Another key aspect of Gigabit Ethernet deployment is how to connect backbone servers to the Gigabit Ethernet backbone switch. As shown in Figure 9.32, you can do this in one of three ways.

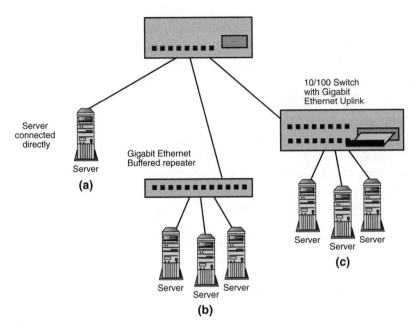

FIGURE 9.32 *Three different ways to connect servers to a Gigabit Ethernet backbone switch: (a) directly to a switched port, (b) through a Gigabit Ethernet buffered repeater, and (c) through a 10Mbps/100Mbps switch with a Gigabit Ethernet uplink.*

You should consider only the highest performance servers for a direct connection to a Gigabit Ethernet backbone switch. As discussed in Chapter 8, very few servers will be able to fill a Gigabit Ethernet pipe, so a direct connection may not be the most efficient method. Servers of the future, however, will be able to communicate at these speeds, so one should plan for a certain amount of direct Gigabit Ethernet server connections. This is shown in Figure 9.32 (a).

You can still connect servers via Gigabit Ethernet, but you can aggregate them to form Gigabit Ethernet server farms. A Gigabit Ethernet buffered repeater is used for this purpose. Because most servers can transfer data faster than 100Mbps but slower than 1Gbps, sharing a Gbps of bandwidth seems like an efficient option. A Gigabit Ethernet buffered repeater, used in this fashion, will be a good stopgap solution for a Gigabit Ethernet server farm. This is shown in Figure 9.32 (b).

The most common backbone connection will still be Fast Ethernet. Gigabit Ethernet switches will connect to these servers via a Fast Ethernet switch and a Gigabit Ethernet uplink module. This is shown in Figure 9.32 (c).

Summary

Table 9.12 outlines the six steps to Switched, Fast, and Gigabit Ethernet deployment. The right column provides examples of an actual company's history of moving through these steps. There were no shortcuts and no dramatic fix-all-your-problems revolutions.

The six-step deployment plan has built the company a network that has grown with its needs, been utterly upgrade capable, and still has plenty of room for future growth. And by the way, in June 1994, most of the company was FDDI and Token Ring. Today, it is mostly Ethernet.

TABLE 9.12 THE SIX STEPS TO DEPLOYING SWITCHED, FAST, AND GIGABIT ETHERNET AND HOW THEY MAP TO A LARGE COMPANY'S ACTUAL DEPLOYMENT

Step	Description	Timeline	Justification
1	Adding 10Mbps Switching	June 1994	Power workgroups in Engineering Department required more bandwidth.
2	Adding 10/100Mbps	June 1995	New PCs cost $2,000 each NICs, with $30 extra per PC for 10/100Mbps future-proofing was approved.
3	Converting Workgroups to Fast Ethernet	Feb 1996	New workgroups created from new PCs with 10Mbps/100Mbps NICs required hubs. After pricing a few 10Mbps hubs, MIS realized that 100Mbps hubs were not much more expensive.
4	Upgrading the backbone to Switched and Fast Ethernet	March 1997	This was the hardest step to get approved. When the Cabletron chassis-based FDDI router was overloading about every week, budget was approved for a new core device. A chassis switch with 100BASE- FX routing modules was approved and each department put up the funds for a new 10/100Mbps workgroup switch and FX uplink module.

Step	Description	Timeline	Justification
5	Adding Layer 3 switches and VLANs	March 1998	A cost comparison between 100BASE-FX routing modules and fixed configuration 100BASE-FX Layer 3 switches showed that Layer 3 switching was about 25% less expensive.
6	Adding Gigabit Ethernet switching to the backbone	TBD	Traffic on the 100BASE-FX backbone hasn't yet reached alarming levels, but the increase due to the Internet/intranet is causing backbone traffic to rise every month. Currently considering Gigabit Ethernet as a future-proofing option.

Many LANs may differ from the examples discussed in this chapter; therefore, you should think of this six-step plan as a guide rather than a strict set of instructions. The steps are outlined in such a way that you can plan their execution over a long period of time, with steady performance gains. This will result in an interesting phenomenon: the more users that are added to the network, the more Fast and Gigabit Ethernet will be deployed. The performance of the newer users will be dramatically better than the existing users will remember. When the existing users are upgraded with 10/100Mbps switches, they too will enjoy the increased performance of Switched and Fast Ethernet. Gigabit Ethernet and Layer 3 switching complete the picture.

In Chapter 10, we apply the lessons of this chapter to some specific deployment examples, including building brand new 100Mbps networks, attaching Fast Ethernet networks to FDDI, and using a real Gigabit Ethernet backbone.

Deployment Examples

In Chapter 9, "Deployment," a six-step deployment plan outlines some guidelines for migrating from 10Mbps shared Ethernet to Switched and Fast Ethernet. This chapter takes those basic principles one step further, giving practical examples. Each example described is a case study of a real network.

We will discuss the following specific examples:

- *Deploying Switched and Fast Ethernet in a new network*—This example describes how you can build a new network using state-of-the-art switching and Fast Ethernet products. Deployment examples cover client, server, workgroup, and backbone issues.

- *Adding Layer 3 switching capability to the backbone*—Using the previous example, this section shows how Layer 3 switching is practically configured, as well as how to mix in the use of virtual LANs.

- *Deploying Switched and Fast Ethernet in a LAN with an existing FDDI backbone*—This example describes how to convert or add on to an existing FDDI backbone. We discuss issues such as adding Fast Ethernet workgroups to an FDDI backbone and expanding an FDDI backbone with 100BASE-FX.

- *Deploying a Gigabit Ethernet switched backbone*—This example gives a real-life deployment scenario for a Gigabit Ethernet backbone. We discuss deploying switched 100Mbps to the desktop along with aggregated Gigabit Ethernet backbone connections.

- *Deploying a 10Mbps switch as a switch of hubs*—In some smaller networks, 10Mbps switching may be more than enough bandwidth. This example shows one of these networks and how to leverage existing 10Mbps hubs.

- *Deploying Fast Ethernet in a branch office*—This example shows a branch office with a classic small LAN. The issues for this type of Ethernet installation include cost of equipment and routing to the WAN.

In general, this chapter applies what we've discussed in the previous chapters to real-world deployment examples. Although every network is different, you should find some similarities between your LAN and one of the instances discussed in this chapter. These examples should help crystallize the concepts and principles discussed up to this point.

Example 1: Deploying Switched and Fast Ethernet in a New Network

Rarely do you have the pleasure of building a new network from the ground up with few constraints on the type of network used. Even when this does happen, the budgetary considerations of a new network sometimes prove to be a bit stifling. 100BASE-T addresses this problem by combining good price performance with a scalable, high-speed networking technology. This example highlights the issues involved with building a brand new 100BASE-T network, including how to deal with the individual nodes, workgroup hubs, and backbone switches.

In order to work through this example, we must make some assumptions. First, the new network will be installed in a building with four floors and a basement. Each floor is a square with 120-meter-long walls. Each floor will have roughly 200 offices per floor, and a CAD/CAM workstation cluster will reside on the top floor. Most of the servers and other critical network components will be placed in the basement of the building. High-performance Pentium II processor PCI-bus PCs will be purchased for the top three floors, but the bottom floor will be using existing Intel 80486 ISA-bus PCs. You only predict 150 users on the first floor, however. Each floor has two wiring closets, located directly opposite each other. Because plans call for future growth and the ability to upgrade, four pairs of Category 5 UTP cabling have been run to each office and 62.5/125μ two-strand fiber-optic cabling through the backbone. This building is shown in Figure 10.1.

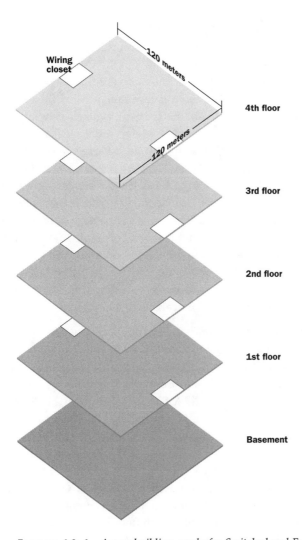

FIGURE 10.1 *A new building, ready for Switched and Fast Ethernet.*

The Backbone Solution: A 100BASE-FX Switched Backbone

After measuring the building for your formidable task, you discover that a 100BASE-T shared network won't be able to cover the entire area of the building. Not only is the building four stories tall, but each floor is 120 by 120 meters. The long distances involved also make a pure UTP installation messy because UTP must strictly follow the 100-meter rule. The only way to ensure less than 100-meter UTP drops to each office would be to situate the wiring closet for each floor in the center of the building. This is not practical because the wiring closets are already on the sides of the building.

With these facts in mind, a good solution for the backbone is switched 100BASE-FX. With switched 100BASE-FX, you can connect to any other FX switch over fiber runs of up to 2km. Fiber is desired in the vertical runs because it offers more potential for future technologies (such as Gigabit Ethernet), it is less susceptible to noise, and it is recommended by the EIA/TIA standard for this type of application. Also, this network can be easily upgraded in the future because a 100BASE-FX backbone switch is highly scalable. Therefore, you decide to install a high-end 100BASE-FX backbone switch in the basement and develop a collapsed backbone. The switch should be modular in nature with several slots for 100BASE-FX modules. If your budget allows, you may decide to deploy a 100BASE-FX router (like the Cisco 7500) or a 100BASE-FX Layer 3 switch (like the Intel Express 550F) instead of a normal backbone switch. (We'll discuss this in more detail in the second example in this chapter.) For the purposes of this example, we'll choose the Cisco Catalyst 5000 with Switched 10/100 Base TX FE (Fast Ethernet) modules for the backbone switch. The 5000 provides 1.2Gbps of backplane capacity, so it should be able to support eight Fast Ethernet connections and is scalable to many more.

In addition, the Catalyst 5000 can be configured to support between 16,000 and 64,000 MAC addresses, which allows it to handle the large number of clients in this particular network. What does the Catalyst 5000 connect to in each floor's wiring closets? In the wiring closets, the most important features are the following: connectivity to multiple 100BASE-FX fiber ports and scalable 100BASE-TX switching capacity. These are important because they allow you to scale the performance of a floor as the bandwidth demands increase. In each wiring closet, place a 100BASE-TX switch such as the Bay 450T. The Bay 450T has 24 10/100BASE-TX switched ports, and two slots that are upgradable to 100BASE-FX. This will come in handy later when you deploy 100BASE-TX to the workgroups on each floor. When installing the fiber cabling, it is highly recommended to install multiple fiber runs to each floor because this will allow you to scale the bandwidth to any floor without reinstalling more fiber later. In this example, four fiber runs are made to each closet, for a total of eight to each floor. Figure 10.2 shows this.

Also, the connection to a WAN link is done through the basement chassis hub via a T1 (or another type of WAN connection) module. All access to the Internet and other regional offices will be made through this type of basement router.

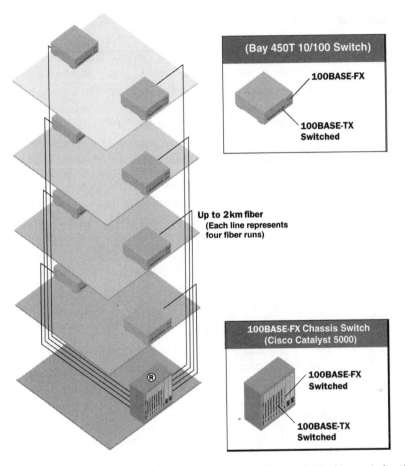

FIGURE 10.2 *Deployment of a new 100BASE-FX switched backbone. A chassis-based switch is installed in the basement and is connected to the wiring closets via 100BASE-FX fiber cabling.*

The Workgroup Solution: A Combination of Switched and Fast Ethernet

Now that your 100BASE-FX switched backbone is in place, you can address the deployment of 100BASE-T to the workgroups. The top three floors will all have new PCI-based PCs, so each of these can be outfitted with a 10/100 NIC. The first floor is using legacy ISA-based PCs, so they have to be installed with existing legacy 10Mbps ISA NICs. For this building, you have chosen 100BASE-TX for the 100Mbps option on your PCI NICs and 10BASE-T as the option for your 10Mbps-only NICs.

Top Floors: 10/100BASE-TX Stackable Hubs

Because many connections will be on each of the top three floors, you elect to deploy 10/100BASE-TX stackable hubs, such as the Intel 220T 10/100 Stackable Hub. Each of the stackable hubs is connected to one of the 100Mbps switched ports of the 100BASE-TX switch installed in the wiring closet. In turn, each one of the stackable hub ports is connected to a Category 5 UTP wiring segment that runs from the individual offices on the floor. By using stackable hubs that are capable of 10 or 100Mbps per port, you can automatically connect to both new Fast Ethernet nodes and existing 10Mbps nodes.

It is also important to recognize a potential cabling problem here. If UTP cabling is only allowed to run parallel to one of the walls, some of the offices will be out of range of the 100m UTP limit. What is needed in this example is a little foresight in planning the UTP cable runs. In addition to the normal cable trays in Figure 10.3 (a), this building should be enhanced with diagonal cabling trays. With this design, you can reach all points on a floor with less than 100 meters of UTP cable. This is shown in Figure 10.3 (b).

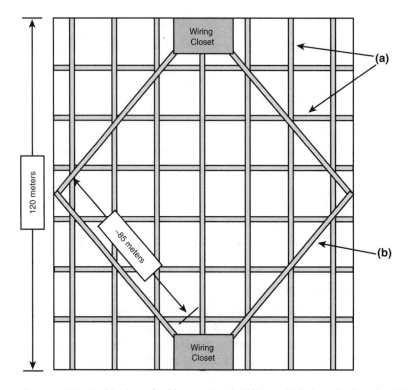

FIGURE 10.3 *(a) Normal cable runs in a building, which doesn't allow for 100 meters UTP, and (b) special diagonal cable runs that allow 100 meters UTP cabling.*

You might want to expand this network in the future (increasing the number of PCs per office, for example), so make sure you have room to grow. For this reason, you should buy 10/100BASE-TX stackable hubs that can be stacked at least six units high. Start by installing only two units per stack, which leaves room for the workgroups to expand beyond their current size. Each stackable unit has 24 10/100BASE-TX ports, so each stack of two units can service 48 users. Therefore, six stacks (three per wiring closet) of 48 ports each will service 200-plus users on each floor with ports to spare.

Each floor has two wiring closets per floor, so you can connect half of each floor to the stackable hubs in one closet and the other half to the other closet. Each workgroup of 48 users shares 100Mbps of bandwidth, and each workgroup is allowed a 100Mbps dedicated port into the 100BASE-TX switch in the wiring closet. Therefore, you should place three sets of stackable hubs in each wiring closet. There are also some local servers for each workgroup. Connect these directly to a Fast Ethernet port on the Bay 450T workgroup switch. Figure 10.4 shows the 100BASE-TX stackable hub deployment.

Luckily, you have spent some time reviewing the traffic in similar networks throughout your company. You know from network management software traces that different users and applications create different kinds of traffic patterns. By studying the trend analyses and prospective user profiles of the new network, you discover that in any given workgroup, about 50% of workgroup traffic stays local: that is, it never gets forwarded to the backbone. Therefore, you deduce that the 100BASE-FX backbone link to the wiring closet needs to support a worst-case 50Mbps of data from each 48 user workgroup in that wiring closet (average workgroups generate much less, but you want to plan for a worst case scenario). Because there are three workgroups (stacks of hubs) per closet on floors 2, 3, and 4, the backbone connection needs to support a maximum of 150Mbps. Two aggregated, full-duplex, switched backbone connections that are provided by the 100BASE-FX switch will support this rate. If more workgroups are added or the existing workgroups are segmented so that there is more than 150Mbps of demand for the 100BASE-FX backbone connection, an additional switched 100BASE-FX connection may be needed for that particular wiring closet. This is easily accommodated by connecting one of the extra fiber runs (remember we installed four) from the basement to an FX port in the wiring closet. The cost of running additional fiber at the time of initial installation is far less than doing it later.

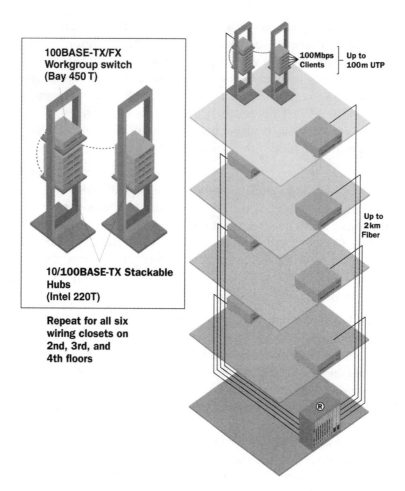

FIGURE 10.4 *Deployment of new 100BASE-TX workgroups. 100Mbps switches are connected to 10/100 stackable hubs in the wiring closet. This is ideal for clients with either 10 or 100Mbps NICs.*

First Floor: 10Mbps Switches

The workgroup situation on the first floor is very different. Because the bulk of the systems are ISA-based PCs, the majority of the connections will be 10BASE-T (ISA doesn't support 100-Mbps data rates very well). As we saw in Chapter 9, 10Mbps switches work well in workgroups with legacy 10BASE-T clients. The network installation, however, shouldn't preclude the possibility of adding newer PCI-based systems equipped with 10/100-Mbps NICs. The workgroup strategy for the first floor also has to account for local servers, which should already have 10/100-Mbps NICs installed.

10Mbps workgroup switches best handle this type of installation. Each workgroup switch has two or more 100Mbps switched ports and multiple 10Mbps ports. A good example of this type of switch is the Cisco Catalyst 2820. The Catalyst 2820 may be equipped with modules that have up to nine 100Mbps ports and 24 10Mbps ports. Every client is connected to a 10Mbps dedicated port on the 10/100 switch. Because each switch has 24 10Mbps ports, a total of eight switches are needed to connect the 150 clients on the first floor (four switches in each wiring closet). One of the 100Mbps uplink ports on the 2820 is connected to the previously deployed 100Mbps switch in the wiring closet. Figure 10.5 shows the first-floor installation.

There is one potential problem with this first-floor deployment scenario, however. Each workgroup switch collects data from 24 10Mbps clients. In this scenario, a workgroup switch could easily be forwarding 100Mbps of data at any given time. Because there are a total of eight workgroup switches, each providing 100Mbps of bandwidth, there is the potential for 800Mbps of traffic to be forwarded to the backbone. The 100BASE-FX backbone provides only one 100Mbps link, so it may become *oversubscribed*. Oversubscription occurs in switched environments when the sum of all data rates on the low-speed ports exceeds the data rate of the high speed port. Of course, not all traffic will be forwarded to the backbone, but if we assume half of the traffic is forwarded, as on the other floors, oversubscription could still occur. In order to prevent oversubscription, one of two things must be done. Either more switched fiber backbone connections must be run to the first floor, or the 100Mbps switch on the first floor must be equipped with a congestion control feature. As discussed in Chapter 4, "Layer 2 Ethernet Switching," a switch can use 802.3X full-duplex congestion control to tell its connections that it is in a state of oversubscription. The Bay 450T is a good example of a switch with this capability. In this example, congestion control will allow only 100Mbps of combined traffic to flow from the eight workgroups to the 100BASE-FX backbone connection. Because it is highly unlikely that all switches will be fully subscribed at 100Mbps at any given instant, congestion control provides a solid solution without the cost of additional switch backbone connections.

Local servers and clients with new systems can still connect at 100Mbps through one of the 100Mbps uplink ports on the Catalyst 2820 workgroup switch. Each new system deployed on the first floor should include a 10/100 NIC, so it can eventually be connected to a 100Mbps port. Another option for the new systems on the first floor is to connect them via 10/100 stackable hubs similar to the other floors.

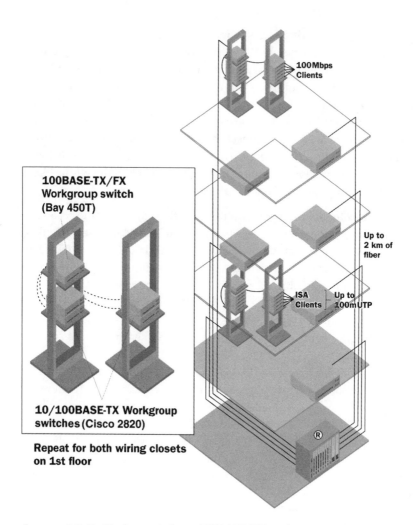

FIGURE 10.5 *Deployment of new 100BASE-TX workgroups with 10Mbps ISA clients. 10Mbps switches with 100Mbps uplinks connect these clients to the 100Mbps network.*

Cost Analysis

The cost of deploying Fast Ethernet in this new network example will be higher than the cost of deploying a similar 10BASE-T solution. The performance gained, however, is roughly ten times that of 10BASE-T. The cost of deployment for 100BASE-T has dropped and will continue to drop, quickly. As volumes and silicon integration go up, network vendors will be able to sell 100BASE-T at costs close to 10BASE-T. In fact, in the time since we published the first edition of this book, the price for 100BASE-T network equipment has literally fallen to within 10% of similar 10BASE-T equipment. For any new network, cost is easily determined by analyzing the cost of the network equipment in each case combined with the cost for installing and maintaining that equipment. Because installation and maintenance of a 100BASE-T network is basically identical to that of a 10BASE-T network, one should look closely at the initial purchase price. Below is a cost worksheet that compares the cost of deploying 10BASE-T and 100BASE-T. This worksheet can be used as a starting point to determine how much Switched and Fast Ethernet will cost. In Table 10.1, the equipment from this example is used. To analyze the cost of your new network, create a similar table and plug in the associated equipment costs.

TABLE 10.1 A SAMPLE COST WORKSHEET FOR JUSTIFYING 100BASE-T DEPLOYMENT

Network Equipment	100BASE-T Equipment	Equipment Example	100BASE-T Cost	10BASE-T Equipment	10BASE-T Cost
Backbone switch	100BASE-FX chassis-based backbone switch or router	Cisco 5000 24+ 100FX ports		10BASE-T backbone switch	
	8 100BASE-TX backbone switches with 100BASE-FX port	Bay Networks 450T 24 ports		8 10BASE-T backbone switch (nonmodular)	
Workgroup switch (2nd–4th floors)	6 100BASE-TX stackable hubs (6 units each)	Intel 220T 10/100 Stackable Hub 24 ports		6 10BASE-T stackable hubs (6 units each)	
Workgroup switch (1st floor)	8 10/100 switches	Cisco Catalyst 2820 24 ports		8 10BASE-T repeaters	
Workgroup NICs (2nd–4th floors)	600 10/100BASE-TX PCI NICs	Intel Corp. EtherExpress PRO/100+		600 10BASE-T PCI NICs	
Workgroup NICs (1st floor)	150 10BASE-T ISA NICs	Intel Corp. EtherExpress PRO/10+		150 10BASE-T ISA NICs	
Total					

Example 2: Adding Layer 3 Switching Capability to the Backbone

In this example, we'll look at adding Layer 3 switching to the network from example 1. Two factors are driving the need for Layer 3 in this case. First, the Catalyst 5000 routing module in the basement is becoming more and more saturated with routing tasks. This is because each floor has been segmented into one or more IP subnets. Second, a few existing NetWare servers are using IPX, and we want to isolate the IPX traffic only to those workgroups that require access. This will be accomplished by using protocol-based VLANs.

Adding Layer 3 switching capability is relatively straightforward in this case. First, the basement switch is upgraded with 100BASE-FX modules that support IP Layer 3 routing capability. Second, the wiring closet switches are upgraded to support Layer 3. These switches can be upgraded one by one, as the need to filter Layer 3 traffic becomes greater for that particular workgroup. In this example, shown in Figure 10.6, the Intel Express 550T has been used in the wiring closet. The Intel 550T has been used in place of the Bay Networks 450T because of its support for IP- and IPX-based Layer 3 switching.

Routing capability in the workgroup will prevent broadcast traffic reaching the backbone from that workgroup. In this example, the Catalyst 5000 in the basement is freed up to handle the switching of data packets instead of determining where a certain packet should go.

This design also requires that the IPX traffic from the NetWare server be isolated from the clients that don't need to access the NetWare servers. We do this by configuring the switches to support protocol-based VLANs. As discussed in Chapter 4, this will be a manual process because most switches don't support a standards-based way of automatically supporting protocol-based VLANs. In the future, this may be accomplished with switches and NICs that support the emerging 802.1Q VLAN tagging standard.

The Catalyst 5000 and the Express 550F each have to be set up to separate IPX traffic into a different VLAN. Broadcast traffic generated by the NetWare servers will only be forwarded to ports on this VLAN. This means that each switch must be set up in advance with the ports that are connected to clients and servers that might send IPX traffic. In this example, no one on the first, second, or third floors needs access to the NetWare servers in the basement, so IPX broadcast traffic will never reach those floors. The top floor, will, however, forward IPX broadcast traffic to the predesignated switch ports. This is not the only way to use VLANs in this scenario, but it achieves the design goal of separating the IPX traffic from the bulk of the network. If more flexibility is needed, the IPX traffic could be limited to three or four select VLANs instead of just one. Figure 10.7 shows this.

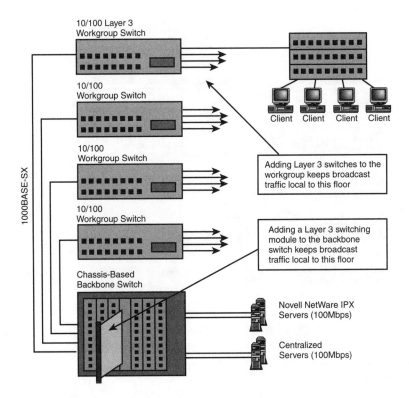

FIGURE 10.6 *Adding Layer 3 switching support to both the backbone switch and the workgroup switches. Broadcast traffic is contained in the workgroup and prevented from entering the backbone.*

Overall, VLAN segmentation can be beneficial, if not a little cumbersome. In this example, it is worth the effort because the number of clients that need access to the NetWare server is small, and they are isolated to one physical floor.

In this example, we have continued to use aggregated 100BASE-FX as the backbone technology of choice, however, the same model applies when Gigabit Ethernet is introduced. Instead of a 100BASE-FX Layer 3 switch module for the

Catalyst 5000, we could have selected a Gigabit Ethernet Layer 3 switch module. Gigabit Ethernet modules would also be needed in the workgroup switches (Intel 550Ts in this example). We'll discuss this more in example 4 of this chapter.

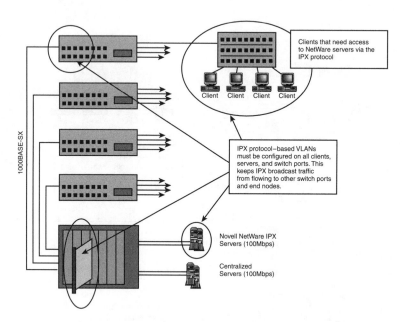

FIGURE 10.7   *IPX traffic generated by NetWare servers and clients is limited, by design, to a specific, predefined VLAN. Although this improves network performance, it requires some manual configuration of each switch involved.*

Example 3: Deploying Switched and Fast Ethernet in a LAN with an Existing FDDI Backbone

Many networks today feature an FDDI backbone ring. FDDI provides a high-speed, robust, semi–fault-tolerant technology that is ideal for backbones. FDDI, however, is considered expensive and difficult to maintain and manage. 100BASE-FX, on the other hand, is not designed with built-in fault-tolerant hardware; however, many 100BASE-FX switch and router products provide this function with port aggregation schemes, load balancing, and specialized software. 100BASE-FX and 100BASE-TX are less expensive than FDDI and provide the same effective data rate: 100Mbps. In addition, 100BASE-FX allows for full-duplex connections of up to 200Mbps data rates. In most cases, it is unwise to replace existing FDDI backbones with 100BASE-T. 100BASE-T, however, can be used as an inexpensive extension to an existing FDDI ring.

This example examines the issues involved in adding 100BASE-T to a network that already has an FDDI backbone. 100BASE-FX can extend the fiber backbone, and 100BASE-TX can distribute data from the FDDI ring down to the workgroups. We will first look at using 100BASE-T to improve the throughput of an FDDI ring to the workgroups.

Adding 100BASE-T Workgroups to an FDDI Ring

In this example, assume that an FDDI backbone exists with 10BASE-T-to-FDDI routers (or advanced bridges) providing the connection from the FDDI ring to the workgroups. Figure 10.8 shows that each workgroup shares 10Mbps of bandwidth provided by an FDDI-to-10-Mbps Ethernet switch, such as the Cisco Catalyst 5000.

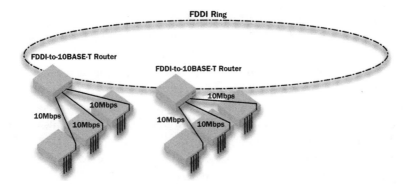

FIGURE 10.8   *A 10BASE-T network with an FDDI backbone. 10BASE-T workgroups access the FDDI ring via routers.*

When adding new workgroups to this network, 100BASE-T should be considered. Assume this particular network uses Category 5 UTP cabling for each workgroup. In this case, 100BASE-TX is the logical selection for 100Mbps connectivity to the desktop. In Figure 10.9, some new desktops have been connected to a 100BASE-TX stackable hub. This workgroup now needs to be connected into the FDDI backbone. Several products that perform this type of connection are available.

One type of product is a standalone FDDI-to-100BASE-TX switch or router, available from Bay Networks, Cisco, Cabletron, 3Com, and many other vendors. Because this is a multiport device, its addition allows multiple 100BASE-TX workgroups to be connected to the FDDI backbone. As in example 1, intelligent logic within the switch or router may use 802.3X congestion control mechanisms to prevent the 100BASE-TX workgroups from oversubscribing the FDDI ring with too much traffic.

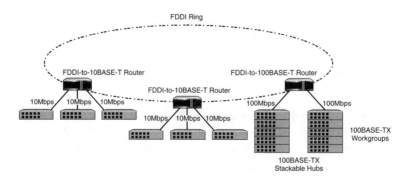

FIGURE 10.9 *Adding 100BASE-TX workgroups to an FDDI backbone. 100BASE-TX is routed to FDDI much like 10BASE-T.*

Extending an FDDI Ring with 100BASE-FX

Another way to add 100BASE-T to an FDDI ring is to consider extending the fiber backbone. In the previous example, the network utilized a distributed FDDI ring, which, in turn, had many FDDI-to-10BASE-T connections. A simple way to extend the backbone to 100BASE-FX or 100BASE-TX is to add an FDDI-to-100BASE-T router in a strategic location. By doing this, the backbone can be extended in a star configuration from the location of the router. If this router is modular in nature, the FDDI ring can be routed to 100BASE-FX, 100BASE-TX, or 10BASE-T via the addition of new router modules. In the example shown in Figure 10.10, the FDDI backbone has been extended to 100BASE-FX via a standalone router.

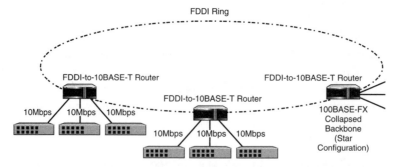

FIGURE 10.10 *Adding a 100BASE-FX to an FDDI backbone allows for the continued use of fiber in the backbone. 100BASE-FX expands on a star topology while FDDI is a ring topology.*

Proponents of FDDI often point to its fault-tolerant, dual-ring design, which helps prevent fiber faults from bringing down the backbone. 100BASE-FX can be set up similarly by using aggregated links. In this way, two switches can be connected with redundant 100BASE-FX links, thus providing similar robustness to the dual-ring architecture of FDDI. Also, there could be a tendency to oversubscribe the FDDI ring with several full-duplex 100BASE-FX ports. It is wise to consider the relocation of certain servers that may have resided on the FDDI ring. It might be more prudent to connect them directly to the 100BASE-FX switch.

Example 4: Deploying a Gigabit Ethernet Switched Backbone

In Chapter 9, we discussed how a Gigabit Ethernet backbone is built, so in this example, we'll focus on specific Gigabit Ethernet products available. This example assumes the same basic structure as the first two examples, but with a few notable differences. First, 100Mbps switching has been carried forward to the desktop. That is, many of the desktops are connected directly to a switched Fast Ethernet port. Second, a large amount of traffic is consistently present on the network. This comes from massive file transfers, high-access database servers, and multimedia applications. Last, network performance is paramount, but budgetary considerations still prevail. These three factors point squarely at Gigabit Ethernet.

Consider Figure 10.11. The Fast Ethernet desktop switch is a 3Com 3300, which provides 24 ports of dedicated Fast Ethernet connectivity and room for a Gigabit Ethernet uplink. Each floor in this example has between 30 and 40 clients, so two 3300s are required per floor. These switches are connected together via a special switching interface that allows two 24-port switches to act like one 48-port switch. This provides 100Mbps connectivity to the high-performance desktops.

Also in Figure 10.11, each stack of two switches is then connected to a Gigabit Ethernet switch. This is done via a Gigabit Ethernet uplink available from 3Com for the 3300. The Gigabit backbone switch used in this example is the Black Diamond 6800, from Extreme Networks. The 6800 offers up to 48 ports of Gigabit Ethernet with 64Gbps of backplane capacity. All four workgroups can be supported with a full gigabit of bandwidth if needed. A lower cost version of this switch could be Extreme's Summit1 switch, which comes configured with eight Gigabit Ethernet ports.

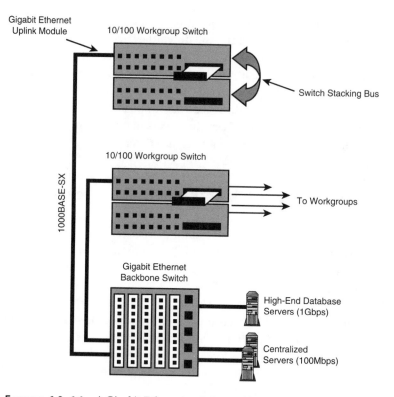

FIGURE 10.11 *A Gigabit Ethernet switch provides the backbone power for Fast Ethernet desktop switches. Two 24-port Fast Ethernet switches stacked together provide 100Mbps dedicated bandwidth to the desktop from a 48-port virtual switch.*

In addition, two very high-end database servers are connected directly to the Black Diamond 6800 Gigabit Ethernet switch. Both of these servers are equipped with an Intel PRO/1000 Gigabit Server adapter. These servers have large amounts of memory, have very fast multiprocessors, and support 64-bit PCI slots.

One could expect this network to outperform the networks deployed in examples 1 and 2 by a factor of 10. Not suprisingly, the actual performance increase will be on the order of 4 to 6 times. The operating system software on both the server and clients will likely limit the performance. The network in this example, however, is ready for faster, future generations of PC and server technology.

Example 5: Deploying a 10-Mbps Switch as a Switch of Hubs

In many cases, neither Gigabit nor fast Ethernet is required. A simple upgrade from 10Mbps hubs to 10Mbps switches might do the trick. In this example, we will examine a case where many clients and servers make up a 10Mbps shared network. The majority of the systems—roughly 50 users—are clients. The rest—about six systems—are servers. This particular network, shown in Figure 10.12, is experiencing average wire utilization above the 40% mark, but is nowhere near requiring 100Mbps of bandwidth. This has caused some concern and a small amount of funds have been budgeted to do something to reduce wire utilization and add bandwidth. An analysis of the network showed that most of the traffic was associated with two of the servers (A and B).

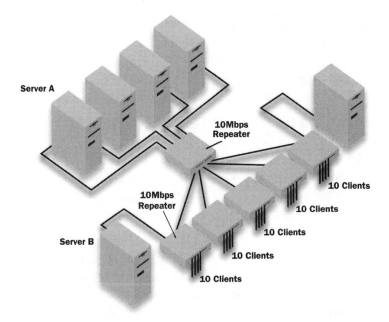

FIGURE 10.12   *A typical shared 10Mbps network.*

By applying the rules learned in step 1 of Chapter 9, it was determined that most of the traffic problems could be alleviated by adding a 10Mbps switch of hubs to this network. Each hub will now have its own dedicated segment with 10Mbps of bandwidth to share among all clients. The servers are also logically relocated on the network. The two busy servers are each given their own dedicated 10Mbps connection, and the other four servers share a 10Mbps connection. The newly configured network is shown in Figure 10.13.

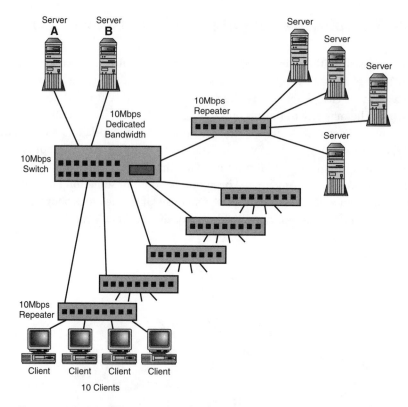

FIGURE 10.13 *The same network, after a 10Mbps switch of hubs has been added. The performance of the network has increased by a factor of 8.*

The new switch should have extra features, such as error-checking and advanced packet filtering, so collided frames and runt frames are not propagated throughout the network. This is a great example of using a well-placed 10Mbps switch to boost network performance without adding Fast Ethernet. Overall, each of the five workgroup segments shares its own 10Mbps of bandwidth, four servers share 10Mbps, and two other servers have a dedicated 10Mbps each. Thus, the total network bandwidth available increases by a factor of 8.

Of course, with the addition of switches come new challenges in network management and troubleshooting. These issues are addressed later in Chapter 11, "Managing Switched, Fast, and Gigabit Ethernet Networks."

Example 6: Deploying Fast Ethernet in a Branch Office

The last example addresses the concept of deploying Fast Ethernet in a branch office. The term *branch office* is often used interchangeably with *small network* or *isolated network* to refer to a network where the number of users is typically small and the amount of traffic is very localized. In addition, a branch office usually has a connection to a WAN link for sending and receiving information from a remote place, such as corporate headquarters. The WAN links are mostly used at certain points in the day, such as the close of business for a bank branch office. The following list points out some of the common traits of a branch office:

- There is a small number of users, typically fewer than 50.

- The physical network diameter is small.

- Replacement of network components requires a special visit to the site.

- The majority of daily traffic is localized.

- There are one or more WAN connections.

- WAN connection use is typically high during specific times and low at other times.

The branch office is a situation in which a shared Fast Ethernet solution excels. Because a branch office can be thought of as one large workgroup (although it is separated from the corporate backbone by the WAN link), the rules of workgroup deployment apply. Think back to example 1 where new workgroups were deployed using 10/100BASE-T stackable hubs. Stackable hub deployment applies in this example just as well. Consider the branch office shown in Figure 10.14. There are eight users, two local servers, and one router that provides a connection to the WAN.

In this particular example, assume that the branch office is an older building with a mixture of Category 3 and Category 5 UTP wiring. We don't know how much of each is installed, though. In this case, a 10/100 hub should be used throughout the network because of the uncertainty in cable quality. There are eight clients and two servers that have been equipped with either 10-only or 10/100-Mbps NICs. It's impossible to tell in advance without making a special trip to the office and examining each PC.

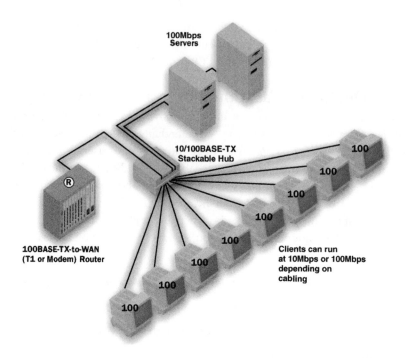

FIGURE 10.14 *A 100BASE-TX branch office. Branch offices usually have a small number of users and a need to access the WAN at regular times. 10/100 capability on the hub is especially important in a branch office because the client connectivity is much less regulated.*

Because it's impossible to make assumptions about how many nodes are 100Mbps-capable, a 10/100 repeater or stackable hub is recommended. In this example a 12-port Compaq Netelligent 2824 will do nicely. Nodes with 10Mbps NICs or connected via Category 3 cabling can operate at 10Mbps, whereas others can operate at 100Mbps.

We can use a simple standalone router to connect to the WAN. Typical WAN connections are T1- or modem-based and therefore much slower than even 10Mbps Ethernet. The routing capabilities of this device will prevent local traffic from being propagated on the WAN and wasting valuable WAN bandwidth. This is especially critical in this example, where the branch office is sharing 100Mbps of bandwidth and the WAN link is a 1.5Mbps T1 line (or worse yet, ISDN or simple dial-up modem access). Performance of the LAN/WAN router is not critical in this case, because the WAN links are slow compared to the LAN links.

In situations like this, we can also use PC-based routing. PC-based routers, which use software such as Novell's NetWare MPR (multiprotocol router), may provide the right level of performance at a low cost. In this example, however, we'll use a standalone WAN access router that supports 10/100 Ethernet connectivity: the Intel Express 8100 router.

In the Real World, Every Network Is Different

Examples allow us to gain insight into deployment issues, but in reality, every network is different. Although your entire network will not be exactly like one of the six cases discussed in this chapter, it is likely that parts of your network will be similar. These examples are designed to illustrate basic principles and highlight the deployment issues associated with Switched, Fast, and Gigabit Ethernet. The examples discussed in this chapter should not be used as strict rules, but rather as guidelines for your own Switched, Fast, and Gigabit Ethernet deployment strategies.

So far, we have looked at what defines Switched, Fast, and Gigabit Ethernet and how to deploy it in your network. In Chapters 11 and 12, we will discuss what to do with your Switched and Fast Ethernet network after it is installed: specifically, how to manage and troubleshoot a network that is both similar to and different from your 10Mbps Ethernet network of today.

CHAPTER 11

Managing Switched, Fast, and Gigabit Ethernet Networks

In earlier chapters, we touched on some of the issues encountered when managing Switched and Fast Ethernet networks. To do justice to this subject, it first must be broken down into its fundamental components: *network management*, *desktop management*, and *business management*. Combined, these components are often referred to as *enterprise management*. Network management takes into consideration the management of network devices, such as workgroup hubs and backbone devices (discussed in Chapter 8, "Network Components"). Desktop management considers the monitoring and controlling of both client and server nodes. Business management covers management of some of the financial risk and return-on-investment issues involved in managing an enterprise. Each of these three facets of management can be affected when you add Switched, Fast, or Gigabit Ethernet to your network.

This chapter discusses Ethernet network management in detail. In a completely shared Ethernet network, management is a relatively simple thing. Each and every node sees each and every packet on the wire. Due to the shared nature of the media, an event that happens in one part of the network is propagated to the rest of the network. When it comes to managing Fast Ethernet devices and desktops, the advantages and disadvantages of managing the classic 10Mbps Ethernet networks prevail. Within a shared environment, there is no difference between Fast and regular Ethernet when it comes to management. Because the frame format, data format, and network access rules have not changed for Fast

Ethernet, many of the network management applications do not need to change. If a problem occurs on the shared network, it can be easily isolated and remedied.

When Gigabit Ethernet is introduced to the network, the data rates on the wire (or fiber) are faster than management software can keep up with. For this reason, Gigabit Ethernet devices will need to be managed from a different perspective. The focus will be on trend analysis and sampling rather than measurement and monitoring of the raw data. Management software will have to become much smarter than it is today.

After you have decided to introduce switching into your network, you start introducing additional complexities into your managed environment. Managing a switched network raises many problems, including traffic-statistics gathering, protocol analysis, and event/alarm generation. With a dedicated connection to specific nodes, management applications have to rely on the switch itself to collect and forward all data relevant to the network traffic associated with those nodes. This was quite a problem in the early days of switching because each switch vendor implemented this function in a slightly different way. Today, however, the industry has centered around Simple Network Management Protocol (SNMP) and remote monitoring (RMON) as the switch management standards of choice.

This chapter discusses SNMP, RMON, RMON2, virtual LANs, and other tools that enable enterprise management of Switched, Fast, and Gigabit Ethernet environments. These standards and tools are used extensively in network management applications and have a large role to play in managing today's and tomorrow's networks. Finally, we give a short shopping list of what you need to look at when deploying management in a Switched Ethernet environment of any speed.

First, let's take a look at some network management basics.

Network Management

Network management is defined as the management of network devices, such as workgroup hubs, switches, routers, bridges, and so on, as well as the management of the wires interconnecting them. Figure 11.1 shows the network management model. The underlying base consists of the applications used to manage the network. These applications should have a consistent end-user interface and preferably a common data repository. It goes without saying that the user interface must be intuitive, user friendly, customizable, and consistent across all the applications. A common data repository is desirable to avoid duplication of data and to allow access to the stored information by all applications. In addition, network management applications should snap together seamlessly with desktop and business management applications.

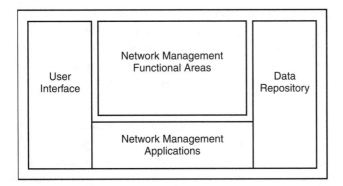

FIGURE 11.1 *A network management model.*

Different models in the industry describe the disciplines or functional areas for network management. Different people use different terms to describe these functional areas, but the theme is invariably similar. One framework depicted in management designs centers around the Open Systems Interconnection (OSI) FCAPS model of management functional areas (MFAs). Another is IBM's SystemView, on which IBM's system and network management applications are based.

Network management architectures have been in operation for a long time, especially in proprietary worlds, such as IBM's NetView for managing SNA, AT&T's Accumaster, and DEC's DMA. Although these systems eventually adopted open standards, they were never really designed to manage anything but the independent vendor's networking equipment.

The advent of SNMP allowed network managers to monitor and manage multi-vendor LAN and WAN components in a standard fashion. At this point, we will define SNMP and why it is so important. If you are already familiar with the SNMP standard, you might want to skip ahead to learn about how SNMP has evolved to include Switched, Fast, and Gigabit Ethernet network management.

SNMP

The first standard for network management evolved into a specification that became known as SNMP. It was based on the TCP/IP protocol stack and was given the Request For Comment (RFC) number 1098 by the Internet

Engineering Task Force (IETF). The workhorse of the SNMP specification is the Management Information Base (MIB). The MIB is a collection of information (or objects) about the managed device. Although the term *MIB* can be used to mean many different things, in this book, we use it to mean the actual data stored in an SNMP device or the description of that data. These MIB objects are standardized across a class of devices (that is, all routers support the same generic MIB), so a management station can retrieve all object information from various devices or cause an action to take place at an agent by manipulating these objects. You could even change the configuration settings of a device using this method.

By embedding SNMP within data communication devices, multivendor management systems, such as SunNet SNMP Manager and HP Openview, can manage these devices from a central site and view information graphically. The many SNMP management applications available today usually run on most of the current operating systems, such as UNIX (SCO, Linux, Solaris, and so forth), Windows 95, and Windows NT 4.0. Most high-end products are designed to cope with relatively large networks and thus run on powerful machines using the scalable UNIX operating system. Besides SunNet Manager, some of the most popular management systems are HP OpenView Network Node Manager, IBM NetView for AIX, Bay Networks Optivity, Cabletron Spectrum, and Solstice Enterprise Manager. Cisco's Internet Operating System (IOS) is also very popular, especially in the public carrier and Internet service provider community. Although IOS is technically much more than just management software, it does support several of the features you would commonly find in a management application.

The SNMP Operational Model

The SNMP operational model is based on four elements: the management station, the management agent, the network management protocol, and the Management Information Base. The *management station* serves as an interface tool to the managed elements of the network. The management station usually has a graphical user interface that is used to monitor and control the network via a network interface card (NIC).

The network management protocol used for intercommunication between the management station and the agents is actually called SNMP and has the following defined functions:

- Get enables the management station to retrieve the information on the management objects from the agent.

- Set allows the management station to set the values of the management objects at the agent.

- GetNext returns the next sequential information in the management object.

- Trap is an unsolicited message from the agent to the management station that notifies the management station of any important events.

Figure 11.2 illustrates these basic network management principles.

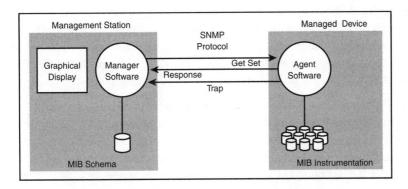

FIGURE 11.2 *Key elements in SNMP network management.*

A managed device has a management agent that responds to requests for information and requests for actions from the management station. This agent may also provide the management station with unsolicited information by means of a trap. Key network devices, such as hubs, routers, switches, and bridges, must therefore provide this management agent (often referred to as an SNMP agent or as being SNMP-capable) for them to be manageable via the SNMP management station. Sometimes this capability is built in to the device, but many times it is available as an upgrade module.

We mentioned earlier that there is a standard way of describing the objects contained in a MIB, but for a management station to understand and access objects on different devices, the representation of particular resources must be the same on each node. The structure of management information, which is specified in RFC 1155, defines the general framework within each MIB and can be defined generically and constructed to ensure consistency. (Examples of *generic MIBs* are MIB-II and the Ethernet-like MIB.) In addition, each enterprise can define its own private MIBs to provide more detailed information about its specific managed devices. The problem with a generic MIB is that the objects defined therein are sometimes not sufficient for detailed management of particular network devices. This is especially true with new Layer 3 switches—the private MIB is important with these devices because each vendor talks to its switch differently. This means each vendor must supply detailed information via the enterprise-specific private MIB. Management applications use private MIBs to provide detailed, expanded views of the devices, to map out topologies of networks on the management platforms, and to configure and control switched environments containing virtual LANs (VLANs) and segmentation. We discuss VLANs later in this chapter.

Drawbacks of SNMP

Although SNMP has greatly simplified the world of network management, it is a fairly old specification and does have drawbacks. These holes in SNMP are what prompted work on SNMP Version 2 and RMON. Some of the disadvantages of SNMP are discussed here:

- *SNMP overhead*—The premise of SNMP is that when the management station is initialized, it polls all the agents it knows about for key information, such as interface data or baseline performance statistics. It was originally thought this polling could perhaps take place once a day, and after the baseline had been established the management station would wait for an event to occur (trap) or only poll once in a while. This method is very economical because it saves the management station cycles by not having to poll, saves the agent cycles by not having to process requests, and conserves bandwidth, but it sacrifices reliability. It also sacrifices granularity because you only get a picture of the network every so often. There is clearly a tradeoff between SNMP overhead and network management reliability and accuracy.

- *SNMP is UDP based*—That is, the SNMP information is transmitted without a confirmation that it was received by the destination. This was done to keep SNMP traffic to a minimum, but again, it sacrifices reliability. Other management protocols (such as ICMP) get around this problem, but they aren't as well supported as SNMP.

- *Supporting new devices with SNMP*—Another problem arises when you need to add support for a new network device, such as a Fast Ethernet switch or hub. The remotely managed hub or switch will need to have an SNMP agent loaded to give it the capability to store all the information pertaining to its ports, slots, and interfaces in MIB objects. The management station also needs new software so that it can query the new device for its information. In an evolving network, it can be a challenge to keep up with all the new MIB requirements.

SNMP Version 2

SNMP Version 2 (SNMPv2) addresses some of the shortcomings of SNMP. We don't look at SNMPv2 in great detail, but here are a number of improvements over the original SNMP standards:

- *Enables secure communications*—Under SNMPv2, for example, a station entering a LAN or a network cannot get network information, such as traces, unless authorized. Another security feature disallows unauthorized management stations from retrieving management information.

- *Enables hierarchical management*—The manager-to-manager communications feature is lacking from the current SNMP standard. SNMPv2 defines a two-way, manager-to-manager conversation. This means that you can have distributed managers interacting, acting as backups, and sharing common management data.

- *Enables increased processing efficiency*—A bulk data retrieval function is part of the SNMPv2 specification. This allows data to be retrieved and processed far more efficiently than SNMP ever did.

- *Supports multiple network types*—SNMPv2 supports a single standardized specification for multiple network types, such as TCP/IP, IPX, AppleTalk, and OSI.

- *Enables more robust and intelligent reporting*—SNMP lacks any sophisticated error-handling functionality. SNMPv2 addresses this shortcoming by implementing meaningful error responses for Set and Get requests.

- *Enables more precise product definitions via improved structure of management information structures*—For instance, many well-known SNMP private MIB objects have now become public objects in SNMPv2.

SNMPv2 has been shipping in most products for some time now. In fact, SNMPv3 is now under serious discussion in the IETF. The main focus of SNMPv3 is to improve network security, both on the WAN and the LAN. SNMPv3, however, doesn't address all the shortcomings of SNMPv2, particularly in the area of switch management. For this task, a standard called Remote Monitoring (RMON) is required.

RMON

As mentioned earlier, basic SNMP capability alone does not really give us good information about the LAN as a whole, but rather information about devices on the LAN. Therefore, an essential extension to SNMP is RMON capability.

Because RMON is especially useful in monitoring and managing switched LANs, it is given extra attention in this chapter.

RMON was developed by the IETF and became a Proposed Standard in 1992 as RFC number 1271. The RMON specification was developed to provide traffic statistics and analysis on many network parameters for comprehensive network fault diagnosis, planning, and performance tuning. Ethernet was the initial focus and is described in the RFC 1271, but the remote monitoring functions were also extended to Token Ring in 1993 as RFC 1513.

RMON provides a standard set of MIBs that collect rich network statistical information not available through the basic SNMP MIBs. This information is basically everything you ever wanted to know about switches, so it is crucial in the management of switched networks. RMON allows proactive network diagnostics by utilization of its powerful Alarm group. The Alarm group enables thresholds to be set for critical network parameters to automatically deliver alerts to centrally located management consoles. This is especially critical when managing Gigabit Ethernet switches, because full-wire speed management at that speed is virtually impossible.

RMON is especially critical for managing switches from a remote location because a switch keeps a full MIB of information on a per-port basis, not a per-device basis. If you used regular SNMP to monitor a switch, port by port, it would result in a huge amount of SNMP traffic. With RMON support internal to the switch, this can be a quick and easy task. An RMON-enabled switch is responsible for collecting and acting on its own data as well as forwarding information to a central management station.

Functionally, the RMON management station and the RMON agent behave like the SNMP agents discussed earlier. The SNMP Set operation is used to issue RMON commands. Figure 11.3 shows the RMON operational model. Note that RMON fits into SNMP just like another MIB.

The RMON MIB

The RMON MIB is incorporated into the SNMP MIB-II, with a subtree identifier of 16. The RMON MIB consists of nine groups, summarized in Table 11.1; each group contains information pertinent to remotely managing a switched network.

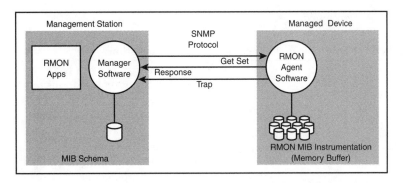

FIGURE 11.3 *The RMON model running on an SNMP framework.*

TABLE 11.1 **RMON MIB** GROUPS

Group Number	Group Name	Function	Description
1	Statistics	Measures utilization and error statistics for each monitored device.	Statistics characterize traffic load and error rates on local segments. Various error conditions, such as CRC alignment errors, collisions, and undersized and oversized packets are counted and kept for future reference. The major difference between this function and the MIB-II interface's group counters is that the RMON statistics counters provide information about traffic passing across the interface, as opposed to the traffic passing into the interface. This provides more meaningful statistics about the LAN segment than just looking at interface data.
2	History	Reports statistical samples within a given time period.	The History group provides historical views of the data from the Statistics group. From the management station the sampling scheme can be set to collect data. Some RMON agents automatically start the history collection when the agent is initialized. It is often convenient to have statistics already collected and to be able to retrieve

continues

Table 11.1   Continued

Group Number	Group Name	Function	Description
			data after an event has occurred, but the offset is that this function takes up memory on the probe, which might impair other functions.
3	Alarm	Compares the results from the History report to a known threshold and generates an event if the threshold is exceeded.	The Alarm group provides a facility for setting thresholds and sampling intervals for a remote monitor. For example, one could generate an alarm if more than n collisions occurred in a sampling interval of two minutes. The beauty of having such a function is that one can use this threshold alarm to trigger, for example, packet capture on the remote monitor.
4	Hosts	Measures statistics on each host on the network. A host is determined by a source address.	The Hosts group provides information about traffic to and from a specific network node residing on the same segment as the probe. The monitor automatically discovers new hosts on the segment by inspecting the source and destination MAC addresses in the packets. Statistics collected for each host include bytes sent to and from the host, errors from the host, packets in and out of the host, and broadcast and multicast packets sent by the host.
5	HostTopN	Keeps a record of each host with the highest counter in each of a group of statistics.	This group uses data collected from the Hosts group to generate a list of, for example, the 10 hosts that transmitted the most data. Such reports can be generated on each kind of statistical data described in the Hosts group.
6	Matrix	Measures statistics on packets that are	The Matrix group is used to collect information about traffic patterns between pairs of hosts

Group Number	Group Name	Function	Description
		transferred between two specific addresses.	on the same segment as the probe. This type of information typically would be used to determine what stations make the most use of a server. Note that both of these stations need to reside on the same segment, or switch, as the remote monitor.
7	Filter	Stores frames and data that pass a dynamic filter mechanism.	The Filter group contains templates that specify what packet types to capture and store. There are two kind of filters available: a data filter and a status filter. The data filter is used to compare a bit pattern that an incoming packet might contain, causing a match or a rejection. The status filter is used to screen packets on their status (such as CRC error). These filters can then be combined by using the logical AND and OR operators to form complex filters.
8	Packet Capture	Stores frames that pass a dynamic filter mechanism.	The Packet Capture group is used to create buffers where captured packets from the LAN segments are stored. Mechanisms exist to set controls, such as how much of a packet to capture, what to do when the buffer is full, and so on. Using this feature, a network manager can trace a remote segment or switch using RMON, upload the captured data to the management station, and analyze the packets captured.
9	Event	Controls the generation of events based on network information.	The Event group creates entries in the monitor log. An event may trigger a predefined action or cause an SNMP trap to be sent to a predefined destination.

RMON Advantages

The RMON MIB was designed to combine standard SNMP functionality with some of the following characteristics:

- *Effective operation*—RMON should be able to collect analysis, fault, and performance data continuously with minimal or no polling from the management station. This will ensure that even if the network management station loses communication to the remote monitor, all information will still be available at a later stage. The management station at a convenient time can then retrieve this data. This is especially critical to the management of switches, where large amounts of statistics must be kept on every port of the switch. Gathering all this data at once is much more efficient than gathering it a bit at a time.

- *Proactive management*—SNMP can be used to collect data from LAN devices (such as routers, hubs, and switches) to obtain statistical data, such as bytes passing through an interface, for trend analysis. This consumes a lot of bandwidth, however, because the agent device needs to be polled for each sample interval. A more efficient way of collecting such statistics is to use the remote monitor agent to store collected performance data, and retrieve this data periodically, say after-hours. This will allow the management station to obtain historical data without impacting the performance of WANs, and yet still allow it to create frequent trending reports. This is a crucial feature for switch management and is often the reason RMON groups 1, 2, 3, and 9 are specified for switch purchases.

- *Problem management*—Facilities for advanced problem determination are available using RMON. An example is the capability to start tracing the segment after a threshold level of errors has been reached.

- *Traffic analysis*—RMON is capable of analyzing and interpreting data collected on its subnet. The management station now only has to retrieve the analyzed data, so a significant savings of processing is realized. This is, once again, critical in switched networks because the management console would waste a huge amount of time just collecting the data from the switch, much less analyzing it.

- *Multiple managers*—Large corporations usually have a number of management stations, each distributed in major centers. It is possible to configure RMON to support multiple management stations.

A good example of a management application that makes heavy use of RMON is NetScout's NetScout Traffic Monitor (shown in Figure 11.4). In this example, Traffic Monitor is looking at packet distribution and utilization information provided by the RMON Statistics group embedded within a 24-port switch.

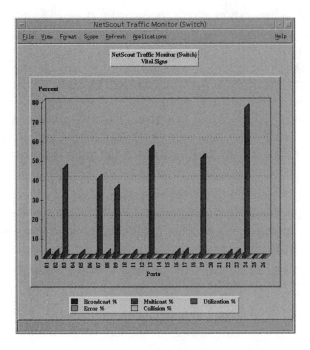

FIGURE 11.4 *NetScout Traffic Monitor, a good RMON-based management tool.*

RMON Shortcomings

It is clear that the RMON specification is very feature-rich. Is this then the solution that will allow us to manage Switched, Fast, and Gigabit Ethernet switched networks? Let's look at some of the problems that arise when using RMON.

Data Overload

Most monitoring analysis should be performed locally and selectively on the RMON agent within the switch. It would not make sense to monitor and capture every conceivable piece of information available. Further, RMON might not be able to cope with this load and might drop packets from capture and analysis, leading to inaccurate data. But worse, it could put stress on already overloaded subnetworks. Remember that the more functions you delegate to RMON, the more powerful the configuration of that device must be. This is a particular problem in Gigabit Ethernet switches, where the amount of data that can be stored far exceeds even the largest RMON switch agent's memory capacity. In a Gigabit Ethernet switch, emphasis needs to be placed on capturing and managing only the relevant information.

When RMON-enabled switches support only the Statistics group of RMON variables, for instance, network utilization and switch overhead is typically minimal. With the Hosts and Matrix groups, however, the overhead is much greater. Here the RMON probe or switch management software sends one packet per host on the segment. But if network managers know that they have a lot of hosts on the segments of interest, they can use the HostTopN group to limit the information sent to the most talkative hosts on these segments. In this case, the probe looks at all host data and sorts by the TopN factor. In the end, only the TopN number of packets are transmitted over the network. In accessing switches over WAN links, it may be especially important to limit the number of hosts reported in this way.

It goes without saying that you should try to keep the overhead at a minimum, but how does such a solution scale? Normally, RMON probes must send only small amounts of information in response to specific events that may indicate potential problems. Data-intensive applications, such as Matrix, Filter, and Capture, are required only when a problem must be diagnosed on a specific segment.

Note

Another creative way to circumvent the network overhead problems caused by RMON management is to create an independent network to carry the management information. This is referred to as out-of-band management because the management information is separated from the network data. Most RMON probes and Ethernet switches are configurable to send management information to a specified port. Each of these specified ports can be connected via an independent switched network and tied to a management console. The level of management traffic generated is therefore only limited by the bandwidth of the out-of-band network.

Memory Requirements

An RMON agent needs memory every time some operation is started by the management system. If you want to capture packets, a memory buffer needs to be allocated before this can be done. If you want to save multiple histories at different time intervals, multiple memory buffers need to be allocated. The RMON agent does all the memory allocation/de-allocation, but it is very important to be aware of the amount of memory available to the probe. When managing Gigabit Ethernet switches with RMON, memory can be consumed quickly. A common memory size for today's RMON probes is 32MB. A Gigabit

Ethernet link can fill 32MB of data in a quarter of a second! You can see the immediate importance of limiting exactly what information the RMON agent stores.

During the capture of RMON statistics, network managers can control overhead by insisting on a mechanism to specify the buffer size for captured packets or on a slice option that tells the switch to store only the relevant part of each packet captured. The larger the buffer (memory) on the probe, the more information the probe can collect, analyze, and work with before it loses this data. On most probes you can specify whether to use *circular buffering* (overwrite the oldest information) or *direct buffering* (drop packets when the buffer is full). It is up to you as the user, generally, to ensure the integrity of the data.

No Layer 3 Support

RMON is defined to manage Layer 2 information. It does not query Layer 3 information or statistics. There is no difference between an SPX/IPX and a TCP/IP frame to an RMON management agent. This is one of the areas being discussed in the RMON2 standard.

Table 11.2 highlights some other drawbacks of RMON.

TABLE 11.2 RMON LIMITATIONS AND SOLUTIONS

RMON Limitation	Solution
Layer 2 monitoring only	Vendor-specific Layer 3 solutions; RMON2 will extend to Layer 3.
Lack of integration with physical switch management	Integrated "probe-in-a-switch" solutions.
Can require significant network bandwidth	Vendor-specific optimized solutions; RMON2 and SNMPv2 provide increased efficiency. Alternatively, design an out-of-band management network.
Significant hardware architectural requirements	Optimized processing and frame handling architecture with adequate memory.
Mixed level of application and probe interoperability	Prior interoperability testing; vendor partnerships.
Detailed segment monitoring, but no enterprisewide view	Management applications that provide enterprisewide correlation.

Using RMON in Switched Networks

On shared segments, the traffic on a hub is echoed on all the ports. This means that there is no problem attaching an RMON probe to one of the ports: all data will be seen by this probe and analyzed. In a switch, however, there is only port-to-port traffic. When the client on switch port 1 talks to the server attached to port 3, for example, the probe connected to port 5 has no way of seeing this traffic unless some internal switch mechanism is put in place. This mechanism is often called *conversation steering* or *port mirroring* and is implemented by the switch itself. You can configure different criteria for data to be steered to a monitor port. The following are examples of how you could configure such echoing:

- Steer all traffic going to a specific port to the monitor port (mirroring).

- Steer all traffic between two ports to a monitor port.

- Steer all traffic between two MAC addresses to a monitor port.

- Steer all traffic between two VLANs to a monitor port.

Typically, the switch will support RMON monitoring internally, so you won't have to actually steer traffic to a given port. This concept is still used to determine exactly what RMON information the internal switch agent records, however. Most switches, especially the Gigabit Ethernet variety, don't have enough internal CPU power to process full wire-speed RMON so setting filters and data capture rules is an important part of switch management.

SNMP MIB-II Versus RMON MIB

To summarize the RMON functionality, let's look at a comparison of the RMON MIB versus the standard MIB-II, the repeater MIB, and the bridge MIB, shown in Table 11.3. This highlights the added value of RMON for switch management.

TABLE 11.3   **COMPARISON OF RMON, MIB II, REPEATER MIB, BRIDGE MIB, AND HOST MIB**

Feature	RMON	MIB II	Repeater MIB	Bridge MIB	Host MIB
Interface statistics		×			
IP, TCP, and UDP statistics		×			
Host job counts					×
Host file system information					×
Link testing			×	×	
Network traffic statistics	×		×	×	

Feature	RMON	MIB II	Repeater MIB	Bridge MIB	Host MIB
Host table of all addresses	×		×		
Host statistics	×		×		
Historical statistics	×			×	
Spanning tree performance				×	
Wide area link performance				×	
Thresholds for any nodes	×				
Configurable statistics	×				
Traffic matrix with all nodes	×				
Host top N studies	×				
Packet/protocol analysis	×				
Distributed logging	×				

RMON2

RMON seems to provide a powerful set of functions any network manager would welcome, so why is the current industry so focused on the RMON2 specification?

In the preceding section, we mentioned a number of shortcomings of the RMON implementations and saw that no monitoring facilities exist for Layers 3 through 7 on the OSI model, there are no enterprise views of network applications are possible, and there is an apparent inability to elegantly manage switched segments. As Layer 3 switches become more popular, it's clear that network management has to evolve to cover the upper layers of the OSI model. The RMON2 specification resolves some of these issues.

The RMON2 working group began its efforts in July 1994, and currently, RMON2 is standardized by the IETF. It is based on RMON and comes in two flavors:

- RMON2 Type A provides information up to Layer 3 in the OSI networking model.

- RMON2 Type B provides information for Layer 3 through Layer 7. RMON 2 also offers the following features beyond the functionality of standard RMON:

- RMON2 provides higher-layer information (in other words, not just MAC layer) for the Statistics, Hosts, Matrix, and HostTopN groups.

- Network layer addresses, such as IP addresses, can now be associated with MAC addresses, and duplicate IP addresses can be detected.

- There is a new user-defined History feature. Standard RMON had a static, predefined list of statistics the network manager could collect. Now there is the option to collect histories on any system counter.

- A more flexible and efficient filtering mechanism is implemented by RMON2.

- There is a common configuration method for all RMON probes.

- With RMON2 the network manager can isolate traffic by protocol and by application.

RMON2 also offers enhancements that make it better suited to enterprise management than basic RMON. Features such as protocol distribution, currently offered as vendor private extensions, have been incorporated into the new standard. But the chief addition has been higher-layer protocol support that provides for the monitoring of specific application types. This requires more bandwidth, so RMON2 also includes features, including time filtering and enhanced HostTopN filtering, to prevent excessive overhead.

Time filtering includes a mechanism to allow incremental data retrieval from RMON agents; when the management application requests information from probes, it will be able to access only data that has changed since the previous upload. A special Traffic Matrix group defined by the RMON2 MIB includes time stamps on conversation (application or session) entries, letting applications retrieve only the most recent conversation data at each interval. HostTopN filtering will provide a mechanism allowing management applications to retrieve only the most significant conversations at each interval.

Also, because RMON2 emphasizes end-to-end conversations—those at the network layer and above—it is no longer necessary to monitor every network segment. This is a boon for enterprise managers because they can concern themselves less with the network as a collection of physical LANs and more with the paths traffic uses to navigate the network. As for WAN links, RMON2 gives network managers the ability to monitor both sides of the link. But how high will the cost in bandwidth be? The answer depends on private extensions—the value vendors add to RMON2 to let their agents summarize and compress the data before sending it out over the WAN link. Look for products that offer flexibility in trading off WAN bandwidth versus remote manageability.

The Importance of RMON

So how important are SNMPv2, SNMPv3, RMON, and RMON2? In our view, SNMPv2 is essential in any switch. (SNMPv3 is still too new to be a hard requirement.) In addition, RMON groups 1, 2, 3, and 9 should be supported on workgroup and desktop switches. This is because these four groups are fairly inexpensive for the manufacturers to include and they provide good visibility into the switch. For more critical backbone or Layer 3 switches, all nine groups of RMON are essential. You will need this support for more robust statistics gathering and notification in case a problem arises. Because it is quite expensive to implement all nine RMON groups, a practical tradeoff is support for groups 1, 2, 3, and 9 on each and every port, and *roving* support for groups 5–8. Roving support means the switch will periodically sample each port for information, which cuts down on the cost of the switch management agent. RMON2 support is at your discretion as it too is an expensive add-on. A popular strategy is to buy switches that can be equipped with an RMON2 management module after the initial purchase. Currently Cisco, Bay Networks, Cabletron, and 3Com have products that can be purchased in this fashion.

Other Aspects of Network Management

Network management also incorporates other tools such as fault management, configuration management, and performance management. the following sections briefly discuss each of these topics.

Fault Management

Fault management is the detection, isolation, and correction of a problem to return to normal operation. A number of methods are used for fault detection. Many systems poll managed objects such as hubs, routers, and switches and search for error or threshold conditions. These thresholds need to be set by the operator and are modeled using baselined data. Baselined data represents the normal state of your network and can be obtained with the aid of trending software such as INS Enterprise Pro or Desktalk TrendSNMP. It is often difficult to decide how to determine the baselines, so we will discuss it later in this chapter.

When it comes to detecting faults, there are two well-known methods: polling and alerting. The polling method samples network devices for information at predefined intervals. This will give a good view of the network over time; however, the polling-based approach is only as reliable as the frequency of the poll. In addition, polling can potentially consume much of the available bandwidth of the network. The alerting method, on the other hand, creates an alert every time a certain network condition is met. A switch, for example, keeps information about its segment utilization internally. Rather than configuring the management station to poll for this data and then perform calculations to determine the health of that segment, it is more elegant to configure the switch to check for threshold conditions on its own segments. If conditions are in excess of the threshold, the switch's management agent sends an alert to the management station. The alerting approach is much more bandwidth friendly, but needs to be kept in check to avoid flooding the network management station with insignificant alarms.

Priorities of traps and events also need to be assigned, to assess the severity of a fault. An outage on a mail server, for example, would have a higher severity assigned than, say, an outage on a desktop PC. In addition, some faults might require the management station to page you 24 hours a day; others would only be logged in an event file. This brings up another good point. Make sure you keep accurate records of network events and the conditions that caused those events. A smart network manager will check to see whether a particular problem has occurred before spending resources on its resolution.

Configuration Management

Configuration management consists of two major elements. One is the tracking of the physical and logical configuration of your network, and the second pertains to the configuration and upgrading of network devices such as hubs, switches, and routers.

Configuration management of the physical and logical topology is probably the most important part of network management in that you cannot accurately manage a network unless you can manage the configuration of the network. This is often done with help from powerful network configuration tools such as Visio. Visio allows for both a physical and logical version of the network to be drawn, and keeps a history of adds, moves, and changes to the network. This history becomes especially important when making the transition from shared media to a switched environment. It may be advantageous to go back to a previous configuration should there be problems with the new one, so make sure to back up this precious data often. Changes, additions, and deletions from the network need to dynamically update the configuration application's database to ensure consistency between the mapping of the real network and what the application represents.

It is also useful to have an application that will automatically discover the configuration of the network in the first place. This has traditionally been a proprietary feature of each vendor's management software, but recent standards work shows the industry is converging in this area as well. In the Desktop Management Task Force (DMTF), the Common Information Model (CIM) and

Directory Enabled Networks (DEN) working groups are defining a standard way to attribute a managed object, such as a router, switch, hub, or NIC, to a particular database scheme. The database scheme, Microsoft's Active Directory for example, will use this information to map network objects, PCs, and servers into an overall configuration. The advantage of this method is the configuration will automatically be updated when a network device changes its location or configuration.

Device configuration also deserves some discussion. Today, most networking vendors include embedded Web browsers in their networking products. The configuration of the device is as simple as plugging it in to the network, starting up your favorite Web browser, and going to the device's IP address or URL. Typically, thanks to simple Web page instructions, configuration of the device is little more than answering a few questions. This configuration method has all but replaced Telnet as the device configuration method of choice. Most network management software packages also allow you to manage devices without this capability. Intel's Device View for Web software can access the device directly, or can use an NT Server as a proxy agent to manage a legacy device. The NT Server gets normal SNMP and RMON information from the legacy device and provides it in the familiar Web format. Think of the remote management possibilities. You can check up on critical network devices from home, and then jump right over to the NASDAQ home page!

Performance Management

Performance management is important for determining whether you need to upgrade an existing network to Switched or Fast Ethernet. (This is discussed in Chapter 7, "Bandwidth: How Much Is Enough?") Performance management, however, needs to be a continuous task. Performance management can also help identify areas where switching or Fast Ethernet technology is not being utilized to its full extent.

To determine the performance level of a switch, you can either configure the management station to poll for this data or set some thresholds in the switch and then perform calculations to compare the performance of that segment to some predetermined values. It is important to have some idea of what the baseline figures should be to make sensible decisions. Some applications, such as Bay Network's NetReporter, can be used to monitor segments for a period of time and then recommend threshold figures. Having said that, traffic patterns vary from segment to segment and are generally based on intimate knowledge of the network and your perception of how it should behave. Therefore, it is a good idea to sanity-check any automatic threshold settings. After the thresholds are set, a good tool for monitoring the performance of LAN segments is LANSummary, which is part of the Bay Networks Optivity package.

Desktop Management

With all the attention on lowering the total cost of ownership of a network, it's no wonder that desktop management tools have become popular in recent years. Applications such as Intel's LANDesk management suite and Computer Associate's UniCenter have successfully been deployed in hundreds of networks, helping managers keep track of their desktop PC assets. Fortunately for the network manager, this is done in a standard way, using the Desktop Management Interface (DMI) standard, which is now solidified in revision 2.0.

The Desktop Management Task Force (DMTF), which originally proposed the DMI, includes major networking vendors, such as Intel, Bay Networks, Novell, IBM, and Microsoft. The advantage of DMI is that its database, called the Management Information Format (MIF) file, is in an understandable language format. Because the MIF is written in an understandable language format, no codes or technical abbreviations confuse the manager. If a workstation's video display has changed from VGA to SVGA, the option will be presented in those terms.

In the past two years, the DMI standard has evolved into something called the Wired-for-Management (WfM, pronounced "woof-em") initiative. WfM describes key requirements for a desktop PC or server, which allows the PC or server to be managed in a standard, predefined way. Because of the industry concern over total cost of ownership, PC vendors such as Compaq, Hewlett-Packard, and IBM started shipping WfM 1.1-compliant desktops in 1997. In addition, network management applications started to build in support for managing WfM-enabled desktops and servers. In all, a WfM PC is a more manageable PC, not only because of its DMI compliance, but because it has the following attributes:

- Keeps basic resources (BIOS ID, keyboard type, processor type, and so on)

- Keeps system resources (IRQ, I/O, and so on)

- Keeps memory information (type, size, and so on)

- Keeps information on the NIC installed

- Allows for remote boot capabilities

- Allows for basic power management—Advanced Configuration and Power Management Interface (ACPI)

- Allows the system to respond to Wake-on-LAN requests

Wake-on-LAN features (described in Chapter 8) allow a *magic packet* to be sent by a management console to a desktop or server PC. If that desktop is in suspend mode or is powered off, the NIC recognizes the special packet and wakes up the desktop system. The desktop can then be checked for inventory or software upgrades can be made.

The upcoming WfM 2.0 standard will include Alert-on-LAN. Alert-on-LAN allows PCs and servers to initiate a conversation with the management console via a special alert packet. Examples of alert events are POST failure, no operating system response, opening of the desktop chassis, or the addition of new hardware.

With DMI and WfM as the basic framework for desktop management, important functions, such as asset and applications management, server monitor services management, and help desk services management, can be added to the network.

Asset and Applications Management

For the most part, managers responsible for asset and applications management are interested in the areas of software distribution, software license metering, and inventory. Asset management applications are needed in any area of the network where there are capital outlays (including the purchases of equipment and applications). Managers have an interest in making sure the capital expenditures are used efficiently and that they maximize return on investment. Reports are extremely important to people with these responsibilities.

MIS departments want to be able to manage desktop workstation software assets from a centralized location. To do that, they need to know what's on the network, how much of it is being used, and how to get more of it into place—all from a centralized location. Common uses include software license metering, software distribution, and inventory management. Examples of products include Network Associates Norton Tools and Intel's LANDesk Management Suite.

Server Monitor Services Management

To a large degree, the types of tools involved with technical infrastructure include SNMP management consoles and the software- and hardware-based protocol analyzers discussed earlier in this chapter. Another type of tool that belongs in the domain of the network administrator is the *critical node monitor*, or *server monitoring tool*. Server monitors, found in management applications such as HP's Openview Professional Suite, Microsoft's Systems Management Server (SMS), and Novell's NMS and GroupWise, often monitor both server software and hardware. Software and file information are monitored to ensure that proper service is provided to each user. Hardware is monitored to keep the server hard disk subsystem from getting too hot or becoming too fragmented. Compaq's Insight manager is a good example of a server monitoring product.

Help Desk Services Management

When a help desk engineer leaves his or her desk to go to an office, the time spent in transit is nonproductive. The goal of any desktop management system designed to assist the help desk engineer should be to allow him or her to resolve as many problems as possible without having to leave the center of responsibility.

According to one MIS help desk administrator, 60% of the calls that came in to the help desk were resolved using an advanced help desk system to remotely debug the problem. These are calls that would, in the past, have required help desk administrators to travel to the remote user's office.

Business Management

Business management is the application of the return-on-investment business model to network management. Network management does not only pertain to the physical and logical management of network devices, but needs to be perceived as part of every IT function. There are hidden elements in setting up an infrastructure to manage your environment. At the end of the day, what is the reason for creating an efficient and reliant enterprise management infrastructure? Is it not to increase the efficiency of the IT department and thus the profitability of the enterprise? Viewed in such light, a number of elements contribute to this goal.

Chargeback

Chargeback, a way to charge the end user for only the specific portion of the service that he or she uses, has long been and will continue to be used in the large mainframe environments. Chargeback on LANs presents new challenges in that so many services are provided. In many implementations, chargeback is accomplished on the individual server providing the service. Although chargeback is very difficult on broadcast-based networks such as Ethernet, it is realizable on networks that dynamically allocate bandwidth as the end users' needs dictate (ATM). The challenge here is the capability to have accurate accounting data available to bill the clients.

Cost Management

Cost management is an avenue by which the reliability, operability, and maintainability of managed objects are addressed. This one function enables upgrading of equipment, deletion of unused services, and tuning of the servers' functionality to the services provided. By continuously addressing the cost of maintenance, mean time between failure, and mean time to repair statistics, costs associated with maintaining the network as a system can be tuned. This area is an MFA that is driven by IT management to get the most performance from the money allocated.

Cost is a key factor in the management of networks today. Information from a recent Gartner Group study indicates that the cost of managing and supporting a networked PC is greater than the original cost of the PC, NIC, hub port, and associated network software combined. With the way hardware costs are dropping, it shouldn't be surprising that every study done in this area shows that hardware costs are lower than support costs. The cost of investing in network management applications is often justified when one or more of the following needs is a priority:

- *Tight control of corporate assets*—To provide payback for the distributed network devices the corporate management requires.

- *Control of complexity of the environment*—Increased complexity caused by the ever-changing topologies and the continued growth in network components, users, interfaces, and protocols is a common problem.

- *Improved network service for users*—In the form of access to more information or better, faster access to distributed resources.

- *100% uptime*—To serve applications that are becoming increasingly network centric with the advent of client-server topologies throughout organizations.

- *Cost control*—Through the use of trending and analysis tools to prevent over- or underspending.

Key Issues for Managing Switched Networks

So where does this leave the user who needs to convert from shared Ethernet to Switched, Fast, and Gigabit Ethernet environments while still keeping a grasp on network management? Customer configurations vary too much for most of the off-the-shelf applications to satisfy every management requirement. You almost always have to use a combination of management software and customized features.

The good news is that when it comes to managing Fast and Gigabit Ethernet devices and desktops, most of the management tools and models work very well. The bad news is that when you introduce switching into your network, new standards, tools, software applications, network hardware, and IT training must come together to give you the same management control you currently have on your shared Ethernet network. We already discussed one of these new standards, RMON, which is a basic requirement for switched networks.

Such structural differences pose some significant problems for managing the network. Management tools that were initially designed for shared-media networks have serious shortcomings in a switched network. For example, a tool that displays an Internet logical view of the network reveals only routers, router interconnections, and subnets (in IP networks). Typically, management software can only see the clients, servers, and hubs logically represented by their subnets. No physical representation of the actual network interconnectivity was possible. This is because there hasn't been a standardized way to automatically discover devices on a heterogeneous network.

Many other challenges are associated with managing a switched network, including traffic statistics gathering, protocol analysis, and event/alarm generation. RMON became the obvious solution because it was an SNMP-based way of monitoring switch information. The next step in managing switched networks is to raise the bar and take advantage of the switched nature of the new network. This has resulted in some exciting work in the area of VLANs.

VLANs

A VLAN is defined as a logical segment, not unlike a shared segment, except that a VLAN also has the following:

- *A single broadcast/multicast domain*—Broadcast packets generated within the VLAN do not propogate outside the VLAN.

- *No router hops*—A router or Layer 3 switch is required to route packets from one VLAN to another.

- *No bandwidth limitations*—A VLAN can include 10, 100, and 1000Mbps switched ports and devices.

- *No physical restrictions on where clients and servers must be on the network*—This means that a client in New York can theoretically be in the same IP subnet as a server in California.

A VLAN is basically a collection of network devices that share similar resources. The major benefit of a VLAN is that these resources do not have to be physically located next to each other in the network. The marketing department in building A and the marketing department in building B can share servers in building C, for example, yet still be on the same IP subnet. This is possible if, and only if, each device in the VLAN is connected to a switched port. There are a number of different types of VLANs, and each type may or may not be included in any given switch. Table 11.4 lists the most common types of VLANs.

TABLE 11.4   THE MOST COMMON TYPES OF VLANS

Type	Example
Port-based	All stations on port 10 are in VLAN 2.
MAC address–based	Station 00-00-81-01-01-01 is in VLAN 3.
Layer 3 address	IP subnet traffic 216.210.127.000 is in VLAN 1.
Protocol-sensitive	IPX traffic on port 10 is in VLAN 4.
IP multicast–based	IP Multicast address X is associated with VLAN Y.
Tagged	Standards-based 802.1Q/p tagged or proprietary tagging scheme.

How do these VLAN implementations help in the management of an enterprise network? We will look at each briefly.

Port-Based VLANs

When mapping a physical configuration to a virtual configuration using port-based VLANs, it is imperative that a master list of which port maps to which VLAN is kept. Many management tools allow this to be done in software as the VLANs are assigned. Because the assignment of ports to VLANs is manual, beware of losing the configuration because this will mean starting over from scratch.

Use port-based VLANs to isolate selected workgroups from the rest of the network. This requires that only a few VLAN-to-switch port configurations be done. Always use software to back up your port-based VLAN configuration in case the master configuration is lost or corrupted.

MAC Address–Based VLANs

In similar fashion to port-based VLANs, a list of MAC addresses can be assigned to a particular VLAN, which means that a given end station, no matter where it is on a network, will be a member of that VLAN. The management of MAC-based VLANs is also manual and requires a MAC address-to-VLAN configuration table. Use this management technique when your users connect laptops from anywhere in the building at any time.

Many software packages allow you to drag-and-drop clients, represented by MAC addresses, into various VLANs. Be careful with this approach because a client in one VLAN may not be able to access a server in another VLAN. Again, make sure the MAC-based VLAN configuration is always backed up in a safe place.

Layer 3 Address and Protocol-Based VLANs

This use of VLANs is very similar to subnetting within an IP network. A given protocol address range is assigned to a given VLAN. Any traffic with that address range (that is, within that subnet) is restricted to only the assigned VLAN. This type of VLAN management is suggested if your VLAN structure matches your physical IP subnet structure. Most Layer 3 switches use their internal routing engine to route between subnet-based VLANs. In this way, the Layer 3 switch is completely compatible with existing routers, but still uses VLANs to segment traffic within the switch.

In addition, a VLAN can be used to segment traffic by protocol *type* (IPX, IP, AppleTalk, and so on). This proves useful in limiting IPX traffic from NetWare servers and clients only to certain areas of the network, for instance. Again, a Layer 3 switch can use its internal routing engine to route between these proto-col-type VLANs.

In both scenarios, the Layer 3 switch can often automatically learn the VLAN configuration based on the network traffic it detects on the network. Because a Layer 3 switch understands the protocol header, it can determine which pack-ets belong to which subnets. This makes VLAN setup a breeze. Watch out for dynamic DHCP IP addressing, however. DHCP will change the IP addresses of your end stations on-the-fly, constantly messing up your VLAN configuration.

IP Multicast Address–Based VLANs

VLANs can also be identified with an IP multicast address. An IP multicast address is a proxy address for a larger group of IP addresses. If a frame needs to go to this group of IP addresses, it is sent first to the proxy IP address, and then forwarded to the whole group. Membership in the group is voluntary, meaning each desktop can determine whether its IP address should be included in the group. This kind of VLAN identification is useful in networks where video or audio data is being broadcast on the network and only a select few users are allowed to view or listen to the information.

802.1Q Tagged VLANs

If you're confused about which type of VLAN to implement in your network, you should look to the upcoming 802.1Q VLAN standard. In the 802.1Q standard, a special tag is added to an Ethernet packet. The tagged frame has a field called the VLAN ID that indicates to which VLAN the frame belongs. Figure 11.5 shows the VLAN ID.

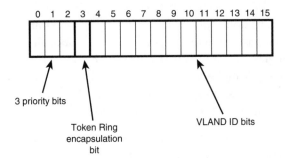

FIGURE 11.5 *The location and contents of the IEEE 802.1Q VLAN ID.*

The first three bits of the VLAN ID are actually priority bits. These bits allow each frame to have a priority between one and eight, depending on the importance of the payload in that frame. Microsoft's WinSock 2.0 specification, available in newer versions of Windows, allows applications to set a priority for certain tasks. This can be read by the protocol stack and translated into priority bits for the outgoing frames.

The next bit is the Token Ring encapsulation bit; it indicates that this frame is actually a Token Ring frame encapsulated in an Ethernet frame format.

The last 12 bits represent the VLAN ID, which assigns the frame to a particular VLAN on the network. All switches in the network would know this VLAN ID because switches are responsible for communicating VLAN membership among themselves. The interswitch VLAN communication is accomplished with the GVRP (Group VLAN Resolution Protocol), based on GARP (Group Address Resolution Protocol).

VLAN Membership

Who identifies what VLAN ID belongs in each frame? In theory, each end station identifies a VLAN ID when a frame is originally created. If a frame comes into a switch (ingress) with no VLAN ID, a switch can opt to insert a VLAN ID and forward the frame (egress). Ingress and egress rules are detailed in the 802.1Q/p standard and allow tag-aware switches to interoperate with existing tag-unaware switches.

Other work on protocols such as the VLAN Membership Resolution Protocol (VRMP) and Group VLAN Resolution Protocol (GVRP) are continuing with the purpose of predefining how VLAN IDs are set and communicated throughout the network. Expect these standards to settle out in early 1999.

Physical Versus Logical Mapping of VLANs

We mentioned earlier that it is important to have network topology views that display the physical and logical connections between hubs, frame switches, and ATM switches. This can be done only if your management application understands the VLAN relationships to the physical network, especially between different technologies. This means that your switches must be able to support and provide your application with this kind of information. The views and maps can potentially be used as a key enabler for system VLAN configuration, and are required for troubleshooting switched networks.

When looking at VLAN configuration tools, many vendors use a file-folder paradigm that allows users to drag and drop port-based VLANs. Bay Networks's LANArchitect, shown in Figure 11.6, is one such configuration tool.

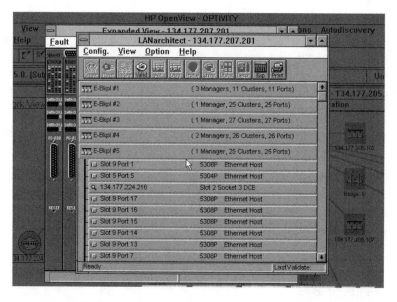

FIGURE 11.6 *Configuring VLANs with Bay Networks's LANArchitect.*

When you move into the protocol-sensitive VLAN configuration, however, more sophisticated applications are required. You cannot use the drag-and-drop technique that works for per-port–based VLANs. Unfortunately, most

management applications don't fully support this view of the network, but all
the major vendors are working feverishly to provide this functionality. An early
one is 3Com's Transcend VLAN Traffix Monitor.

VLAN Configuration

Other desirable features for a VLAN configuration tool would be

- Aliases

- Audit trails

- Risky-operation detection and warning

- Password protection

Traditionally, hubs have provided a device-level configuration system whereby
a user could attach a terminal to a configuration port at the hub and complete
the hub configuration. To be able to successfully configure a switch using this
method, the user would have to understand the network topology prior to configuration and manually configure all interconnect ports.

In large networks this is quite difficult, so a system-level tool (application) is
desirable. Such an application would present a higher-level view of the VLAN
spanning multiple devices and at the same time hide the complexity of the
underlying technologies. An automatic interconnect assignment would greatly
simplify the VLAN configuration.

Should You Use VLANs?

The 802.1Q/p standards are now completed, and networking vendors have
started to ship 802.1Q/p-capable devices. The question is do you really need
VLANs and how will they help in managing the network?

In a nutshell, VLANs allow switched networks to properly filter broadcast and
multicast packets. This may sound like an overly simple way of describing
VLANs, but it's basically true. Think about it—if the MAC (or Layer 2) address
and IP (or Layer 3) address of a destination are already known, you don't need
much more information to successfully get the packet to that destination. The
only time you run into trouble is when you don't have that information, as is
the case with broadcast and multicast packets. Because most network protocols
use broadcast packets extensively to discover information about the network, it
is a good idea to direct this traffic only where it needs to go. The options for
doing this today are good-old routing (or Layer 3 switching), VLANs, or both.
You can use routers or Layer 3 switches to route between physical subnets or
between logical VLANs. If you do employ VLANs, use them only where the

benefit, in terms of broadcast containment, is the greatest. Remember, you can implement port-based VLANs in one workgroup and protocol-based VLANs in another. As long as you use routers or Layer 3 switches to interconnect them, things will work just as if the VLANs were physical subnets. The obvious advantage is that VLANs do not have to be isolated to one physical location.

To summarize, VLANs are a way of partitioning *traffic flows* in a network such that each packet transmitted by an end station is assigned to a VLAN. An end station thus receives all the multicast and broadcast traffic on the VLANs to which it belongs, as well as all the unicast traffic addressed to it on that VLAN. Use VLANs in your network, only if you cannot use routers or Layer 3 switches and physical subnetting to solve the problems you have with broadcast and multicast traffic isolation. If Layer 3 switches or reconfiguring existing routers cannot keep the right traffic in the right place, VLAN management may be required.

Managing Service Levels

Another interesting aspect of switch management is providing different levels of service to various users. It's always smart to give the CEO the highest level of service from the network, but there are many other examples as well. Providing finance with the highest priority after the close of quarter, prioritizing time-sensitive voice information over data transfers, and prioritizing server backups when a fault has been discovered are just some of them.

Service levels come in two basic categories: class of service (CoS) and quality of service (QoS).

Class of Service

CoS provides a means to prioritize certain network tasks. There are many ways to do this, but the most fundamental involves the new 802.1Q standard. You will recall that there are three bits in the VLAN ID reserved to designate the priority of the packet. Applications can set priority when the frame is created and network devices can act on that priority.

A switch that supports 802.1Q will recognize the priority of the frame and process it before other packets of lesser priority. This is particularly useful when sending mission-critical information. It needs to go as fast as possible, without sacrificing a single packet. CoS allows data transfers to take a back seat to multimedia sessions. To use an analogy, CoS in the freeway system would allow a car to go to the front of the line in a traffic jam, with each car of lesser priority making way.

> ### Note
>
> *Actually, the 802.1Q priority bits were first developed in the IEEE 802.1p subcommittee. They were later moved into the 802.1Q standard when it became clear the 802.1p standard would be focused on multicast pruning and the 802.1Q standard was reserving room for the bits in the VLAN tag.*

Quality of Service

If CoS allows a car to go to the front of a traffic jam, QoS allows a car to have its own lane. QoS refers to the capability to reserve bandwidth through a network. In an ATM network, this capability is built in to the standard. In a Switched Ethernet network, this is only possible with a special Resource Reservation Protocol (RSVP).

RSVP allows a sending station to make a bandwidth reservation request of the eventual destination. The protocol works when the destination receives the request for a *path*, and responds asking for a *reservation*. The reservation request returns back to the sender, telling every network device along the way that bandwidth will need to be reserved. If bandwidth cannot be reserved by one of these devices, the reservation is flagged so the sending station will know the guaranteed bandwidth may not be available. If every device along the route can reserve bandwidth and has the extra bandwidth available, the RSVP protocol has successfully created a path of reserved bandwidth. This path (and the devices on the path) is polled every 30 seconds or so to make sure the path is still active and the bandwidth is still reserved.

This is very useful in sending voice or video over a Switched Ethernet network. The obvious drawback is that all the network devices in between must support RSVP. Because the installed base of switches, routers, and end stations don't support RSVP, its usefulness will depend on the adoption of RSVP-ready devices. Luckily, because RSVP is a Layer 3 protocol, RSVP-enabled products will fully interoperate with non–RSVP-enabled products. Therefore installing them in an existing network is fairly easy. Make sure the RSVP-enabled devices come with configuration software so the various resource levels can be set to match your network needs.

Cisco has a great strategy for QoS built in to their Internet Operating System (IOS). Figure 11.7 represents Cisco's view of how QoS should work. There are three levels of quality on the network: guaranteed, differentiated, and best effort. Guaranteed uses a protocol like RSVP to ensure the network application's bandwidth requirements are met. Differentiated services are those that get priority on the network, but don't necessarily have bandwidth dedicated to them all the time. Best-effort traffic basically gets to where it's going only after the other types of traffic are allowed to pass. Applications ask the network for a particular type of service. The network then grants these services based on a policy management scheme.

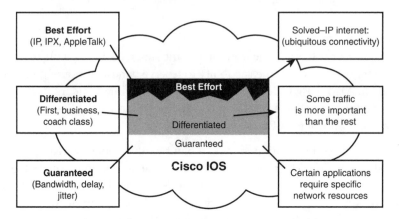

FIGURE 11.7 *Cisco's Internet Operating Software (IOS) view of quality of service.*

Policy-Based Management

Policy Based Management (PBM) is an interesting area of network management and particularly critical for switched networks. PBM involves the assignment of CoS and QoS levels to network traffic based on predetermined policies and guidelines. This central policy would then tell the end stations and network devices how to handle the network packets they encounter. A policy might dictate that Web traffic is best-effort between 8:00 a.m. and 5:00 p.m., for instance, or that Human Resources gets guaranteed bandwidth during the monthly employee database update. The policy manager would set the policies, which would then propagate to the desired parts of the network.

Standardization efforts in the IETF and DMTF are underway with the objective of defining technologies used by PBM. Only a few standards efforts actually define network policies, most just deal with the protocols, schemes, and architecture of a policy management solution. Common Information Model (CIM) and Directory Enabled Networks (DEN) are examples of these emerging standards.

Within the IETF, the RSVP and Differentiated services working groups are extending their standards to include the definition of the policy objects that can be controlled by compliant management applications. This would make the most common kinds of policies (time-based, location-based, password-based, and so on) easily implementable in most networks. Additionally the proposed

Common Open Policy Service (COPS) protocol standard is an extension to the RSVP working group and is defining a standard protocol for distributing policy information around the network.

QoS, CoS, and PBM Recommendations

Of all these interesting efforts, two standards, 802.1Q/p and RSVP, have the backing of the networking, PC, and software industry. Therefore, it's a good bet that they will be part of most network products and software. Note that 802.1Q/p and RSVP operate independently of each other, so you can evaluate their benefits one at a time. Your network management plans should include a trial for RSVP and 802.1Q/p if the budget allows. Select a workgroup that uses voice/video network applications and see how it works.

PBM is something that you should slowly embrace. Believe it or not, you probably already have some policies in effect on your network (blocks to certain Web sites?), so implementing an automatic policy management scheme shouldn't be philosophically difficult. Because the standards are so early in their development, however, you should proceed with caution. Evaluate PBM products fully, paying particular attention to the interoperability between the PBM software and your networking hardware.

Managing Switches at Gigabit Speeds

Switches that offer several ports of full-duplex, Gigabit Ethernet capacity have no chance of managing every packet that flows through the switch. Even though the standard protocols such as SNMP, RMON, and RMON2 don't fundamentally change for Gigabit Ethernet, the sheer capacity of data is enormous. Trying to analyze all the information is impossible, which makes the internal intelligence of the switch management unit much more important.

It is essential that a Gigabit switch support flexible, configurable management tools within the switch. Because you won't be able to analyze each packet of data, you will have to rely on the switch to tell you when problems have occurred. You must have a way of programming the switch to tell you what you want to hear. You may want to know when a certain level of traffic occurs on a given port, for instance. The Gigabit switch must have a configurable RMON Alarm group counter that can provide you with this information.

Table 11.5 indicates the implications of Gigabit speed switching on the various nine groups of RMON.

Table 11.5   RMON MIB groups

Number	RMON Group	Typical Use in a Gigabit Ethernet Switch
1	Statistics	The switch must have counters built into the actual switching silicon to get an accurate view of packet statistics and errors at Gigabit speeds.
2	History	Keeping a history of traffic at Gigabit speeds will require huge amounts of memory within the switch or RMON probe. Gigabit switches will have to know when to look for certain events and store histories only then. Alternatively, switches can sample the data at longer intervals.
3	Alarm	Alarms will be crucial to managing Gigabit Ethernet switches. Because you can't manage the information centrally, the switch will have to do the collection and analysis for you. Setting up the correct alarms and history baselines (sometimes manually) will be important in finding out when problems have occurred.
4	Hosts	Again, this will have to be built in to the switching silicon to operate at Gigabit speeds. It is likely that this will be implemented as a polling-only group in most Gigabit Ethernet switches.
5	HostTopN	Very expensive to do at Gigabit speeds.
6	Matrix	Even more expensive than group 5.
7	Filter	The Filter group may be used in conjunction with the History group to capture problem packets. Make sure the filters are flexible in your Gigabit Ethernet switch so that you can seek out problem packets if necessary.
8	Packet Capture	Similar to Filter group. Memory constraints will limit the number of packets that can be stored at Gbps speeds.
9	Event	Events are important in the same way as alarms. Events will provide notification of a problem in a Gigabit Ethernet switch versus the up-front analysis of data. Events can also be used to start and stop the filter or packet capture process.

By association, RMON2 is equally important in a Gigabit switch, but the processing power required to analyze frames at these speeds is not economically viable in today's switches. Therefore, RMON2 will be implemented using sampling techniques in Gigabit Ethernet switches. For example, the switch might pick one frame in ten and analyze it to the level of RMON2.

Planning for Future Needs

Another important question to ask is how large a switched network can you manage, monitor, and configure? Scaling management tools is a big issue in large enterprise networks and is definitely something you will need to ask your vendors about. Also, check where the applications are already installed, to what degree are they being used, by how many people, and on what platforms.

Even if you have today's management situation under control, you may find that large switched networks require customization to maximize performance and redundancy. The application will need sophisticated, graphics-oriented performance tools because it will be very difficult to detect certain problems using data collection methods and polling strategies. Logical views that graphically display spanning trees (active/standby links), for example, will be extremely valuable. With such information you can highlight a switch trunk port with intermittent errors that might cause frequent spanning tree reconfiguration. Also, you may find that misconfigured ports create suboptimal topologies.

Trend Analysis

When planning and designing your network, you will need to leverage collected information, and proactively use some trending tools to plan for the future. Trend analysis represents the change in traffic characteristics over time, often in the form of line graphs. They are historical in nature, covering a defined period with data points at regular intervals. Trend analyses provide a view of traffic fluctuations and therefore are useful to identify and understand regular, predictable changes in network utilization.

Additionally, it is useful if the applications have features to take collected trending information and simulate a move of clients or servers, showing what impact this would have on the network. This functionality provides you with a comprehensive planning and design tool. Information-gathering tasks you need to trend an Ethernet environment might include the following:

- Analyze top talkers within a VLAN.

- Analyze broadcast and multicast traffic in a VLAN.

- Collect historical inter- and intra-VLAN traffic data (bear in mind that traffic analysis between VLANs requires Layer 3 traffic matrices, an RMON2 function).

- Analyze top conversations between VLANs.

Using the simulation tools, you can enable what-if analysis on alternative configurations before any changes are made to the physical network, almost like a playback of real data from your network.

After you have analyzed this data, you may find that adding dedicated 100Mbps desktop switch ports can alleviate congestion within a VLAN without additional router segmentation, but often router segmentation will be required to reduce significant background traffic. The practical limit usually averages 50–500 users per VLAN, depending on the user configurations, applications, and traffic profiles. At the end of the day, you really want to move resources (servers, printers, and so on) to the VLAN where the users of those resources reside. This will maximize performance and minimize the use of routing in your network.

We mentioned in the section "Network Management" that it's important to dedicate resources and use them to develop VLAN operations, procedures, and management disciplines. Although it might seem that the switched LAN management issues are under control, you might still need to consider issues such as the following in the traditional, physical environment:

- How many moves, adds, or changes need to be made per week?

- Are the moves usually individual or in groups? Individual moves may be better suited for one-at-a-time configuration using GUI tools. Group moves may be better suited for batch processing, either overnight or on weekends. How often will physical wiring closet changes be required?

- What is the trade-off between prewiring ports and physical moves?

- How can changes be backed out of? How is the configuration data backed up?

New issues in virtual LAN administration for you to consider might include tracking of the following:

- Cubicle/office jack ID, wiring closet/cabinet ID, cable ID

- Device MAC and IP address

- Switch/slot/port ID

- VLAN ID (or IDs)

- Username, function, password, and department

To get assistance with these functions, look to applications that can map MAC addresses to IP addresses to switch slots/ports; such applications enable large enterprises to easily locate users and manage the switched environments. Ultimately, VLAN administration depends on the chosen VLAN model, the management application capabilities, and on your operation's requirements.

What to Look for in Switched Management Tools

So how do we apply the technologies and standards previously described? In this section, we try to provide you with a cookbook-type approach to management of newly deployed Switched Ethernet environments. We attempt to address the following hot issues pertaining to switched environments, and provide an additional checklist to help choose the right applications and infrastructure to manage your network. In other words, we try to provide a shopping list of features and functions for your switched network management. Although there is no all-encompassing list, the following items, together with the previous examples, provide you with a good start to creating the right environment.

Look for these switched management features:

- SNMPv2 support in all your critical devices.

- Support for all RFC 1271 RMON MIB groups.

- Adequate processing and memory, especially for Gigabit Ethernet switches (4–8MB dedicated to RMON management information is common).

- Port level RMON information, groups 1, 2, 3, and 9 for workgroup and desktop switches. Groups 1 through 9 inclusive for backbone and Layer 3 switches.

- Automatic correlation with switch port and network addresses (IP and MAC).

- Layer 3 traffic statistics and protocol-type distribution (IP, IPX, or other).

- RMON events that can be configured to trigger actions and alarms.

- Layer 3 address monitoring (IP and/or IPX depending on your network).

- Embedded Web servers for easy first-time configuration of the network device.

Look for applications that provide the following:

- Performance monitoring

- Baselining and trending

- Design and optimization

- Protocol interpretation and decoding

- Troubleshooting

- Event management

- Support for configurable alarms and thresholds within a Gigabit Ethernet switch

- Network configuration auto-discovery and logging of adds, moves, and changes to the network configuration

Possibly, you might also want to look at additional vendor criteria, such as the following:

- Commitment to support RMON2 (both in hardware as well as in applications)

- Interoperability testing with other major vendors (Bay Networks, Cisco, Cabletron, 3Com, Intel, Compaq, and so on)

- Integration with HP Openview, IBM NetView, and other open management platforms

- Devices that reduce management overhead traffic on the WAN

- Support for virtualization capabilities that enable RMON probe "roving," especially for RMON groups 5 through 8 and RMON2

- Strategy for providing monitoring and analysis in switched environments

- Integration strategy between Windows or UNIX-based management and Web-based management

The Future of Managing Switched Networks

Finally, we need to briefly look at the future. Where is network management going and which technologies will be used in the future?

Probably one of the most significant technologies that will influence switched network management in the short term will be RMON2. As discussions of

RMON2 show, enhancements should make the standard better suited to enterprise management. Embedded Web servers seem to be becoming commonplace in most Fast and Gigabit Ethernet switches. This makes configuration and monitoring of these devices very easy.

Also, the impact of managing much higher-speed data flows like those found in a Gigabit Ethernet switch is an interesting challenge. The monitor-every-bit-on-the-network approach isn't going to work anymore. Network managers will have to look at new tools that analyze trends and ask devices to send alarms when something is wrong. Management software aimed at managing higher-speed devices will have to be much smarter than today's relatively dumb shared-media approach to management.

Many excellent software products provide capabilities to manage not just hardware, but also services and applications. Policy-based management products are probably the most exciting of these. PBM management software will use embedded quality of service and class of service features found in newer switches to guarantee bandwidth to critical network applications. Standards such as IEEE 802.1Q/p and RSVP will be essential in creating a network infrastructure that can support and enforce these policies. The bottom line for you as a network manager is that applications and tools for managing Switched, Fast, and Gigabit Ethernet networks are here today, but the tools for really taking advantage of those switched networks are still on the horizon. Don't let that stop you from deploying switches today. Just go into it with both eyes open. Be ready to stretch a little to get the level of network management you have grown to expect.

CHAPTER 12

Troubleshooting

This chapter addresses the troubleshooting issues associated with upgrading your network to Switched, Fast, and Gigabit Ethernet. Quick and efficient troubleshooting may be a lifesaver, depending on the state of your network and the extent to which your customers depend on its services. When do you need to troubleshoot your network? The obvious answer is when problems occur, such as downed servers, lost connections, and increased traffic levels. The best troubleshooting, however, is done proactively and on a consistent and continuous basis. By the time users begin complaining about network problems, it may be too late to respond quickly and correct the situation. You can prevent, or at least predict, many of the problems in today's networks with a small amount of proactive troubleshooting.

This chapter focuses on how traffic analysis and troubleshooting methods change with the addition of Switched, Fast, and Gigabit Ethernet. The chapter does *not* cover other, more general topics, such as how to troubleshoot a faulty NIC, examine a NET.CFG file, optimize a NetWare server, set up an IP addressing scheme, or configure a router. These issues are thoroughly discussed in many other books and change only slightly when moving to Switched, Fast, or Gigabit Ethernet networks. A good example of a book of this type is *Managing Switched Local Area Networks, A Practical Guide*, by Darryl P. Black, or *Troubleshooting Local Area Networks*, by Othmar Kyas and Thomas Heim.

In contrast, this book delves into various hardware and software changes necessary to upgrade current diagnostic equipment to support switching, 100BASE-T, and 1000BASE-T. We also explore some common problems to expect when deploying Switched, Fast, and Gigabit Ethernet. We pay particular attention to analyzing Gigabit Ethernet networks, as the high transmission rate makes analysis of the raw data impractical.

Before addressing the troubleshooting methods applicable to all speeds of Ethernet networks, it is a good idea to cover the basics of troubleshooting today's 10BASE-T networks. Therefore, we start by classifying common troubleshooting products available today.

Dedicated Troubleshooting Products

Dedicated troubleshooting products consist of diagnostic equipment, such as LAN analyzers (LAN sniffers), traffic generators, cable testers, RMON probes, and other standalone devices. You can use these products to analyze anything from cable integrity to individual bits on the wire. Their common identifier is that they are used independently of the servers and clients on the network. For this reason, dedicated troubleshooting products offer superior performance but are often difficult to learn and use. Let's look at some of these types of products in more detail.

Handheld Cable Testers

One of the main considerations when deploying Fast Ethernet is cabling. For instance, if you deploy 100BASE-TX, only two pairs are needed; however, the entire cabling plant, including the patch panel, must be Category 5 certified. In addition, 1000BASE-T (Gigabit Ethernet over UTP copper cabling) will require four pairs. If you are trying to future-proof your cabling installation, this may be an issue. Thus, before deploying Fast Ethernet, you should determine whether you have Category 5 UTP wiring and/or four pairs available to the LAN. Several products assist in network cable studies. An example is the Microtest PentaScanner 350, which tests UTP cabling up to 100MHz. You can use this handheld device to help determine cable type, number of pairs available, and cable integrity. Also available from Microtest is the OmniScanner, which tests up to 300MHz. For more on cable testers, see Chapter 6.

Handheld Frame Analyzers

Handheld frame analyzers, like the FrameScope 802 shown in Figure 12.1, provide simple troubleshooting features similar to those of LAN analyzers. These devices often allow for link testing, traffic statistics gathering, and traffic utilization monitoring, and they even break down frames by protocol type (the FrameScope 802 supports more than 250 protocol types). Handheld frame analyzers are especially useful in switched networks where connecting a LAN analyzer to every switch is neither physically nor economically feasible.

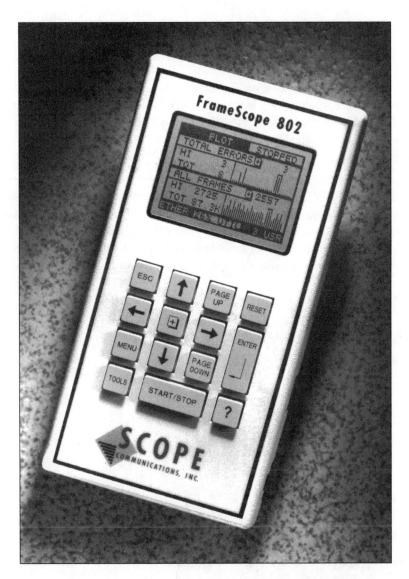

FIGURE 12.1 *The FrameScope 802 from Scope Communications provides many LAN Analyzer troubleshooting functions in a handheld device.*

The FrameScope 802 connects directly to UTP cabling, making it a very quick way to troubleshoot a large number of ports. One of the drawbacks of a hand-held device is that the data is usually a snapshot of the network: that is, the history or logging functions of these devices are typically poor. The LANMeter from Fluke solves this problem by logging data through a serial port interface.

Another drawback is that the user interface screens are typically small and monochrome, resulting in data that is hard to read and understand. Overall, however, the price makes these devices a must-have of any LAN manager.

Some companies are working on Gigabit Ethernet support for handheld frame analyzers. One such company is Finisar, which has announced the GT-Jammer Handheld Analyzer for Gigabit Ethernet. At the time of this book's publication, the GT-Jammer has not shipped, but you can check up on its progress at www.finisar.com.

PsiberNet also has a unique set of products for troubleshooting Ethernet networks. For 10BASE-T, it has an ingenious design that allows a view of network data without unplugging any cables. This device, the PsiberNet 10BT, clamps a passive amprobe around the UTP cable. The magnetic field generated by the electrical signal in the cable can actually be picked up by the PsiberNet 10BT and displayed as network utilization. Figure 12.2 shows the PsiberNet 10BT.

FIGURE 12.2 *The handheld frame analyzer PsiberNet 10BT.*

PsiberNet also has a version that supports 100BASE-TX, but this is an active device and requires the UTP cable to be unplugged. PsiberNet is currently working on a passive version for 100BASE-T as well.

LAN Analyzers

LAN analyzers, or *sniffers*, such as the Network Associates Distributed Sniffer System (Network Associates is the merged company made up of Network General and MacAffee Associates), can see all packets traversing a particular network segment when directly attached to that shared network. The Sniffer cannot only see all packets, but it can also break down and store each packet in its internal memory. The LAN administrator can later examine packet details, such as frame type, protocol type, CRC integrity, and source address. You can also use the sniffer to collect network statistics, such as number of collisions, number of runt packets on the network, and number of broadcast packets sent. You can achieve detailed packet analysis through the packet capture function. Special software, called *Expert Analysis*, aids in the interpretation of the captured packets. In addition, an analyzer is a good tool for determining how much traffic is coming from each node on the network. This last feature is one that makes a LAN analyzer an invaluable troubleshooting tool.

For today's networks, it's a good idea to buy a LAN analyzer that supports both 10BASE-T and 100BASE-TX. Network Associate's Network Analyzer Ethernet 10/100 model does this. In addition, you might want to consider an analyzer that supports other technologies found in your network (Token Ring, FDDI, and so on). You don't need to buy multiple analyzers when one can do the job. A few LAN Analyzers are available today that support Gigabit Ethernet, but we'll discuss these later in the chapter.

Traffic Generators

A *traffic generator* is a device that can generate a preprogrammed data pattern on the network. Traffic generators can be standalone devices, or you can integrate them into LAN analyzers like the Hewlett Packard's 3270 or NetCom's SmartBits 1000. A traffic generator may not seem like a useful tool for a LAN administrator who is constantly trying to reduce network load, but it can be helpful when modeling a future network. For instance, assume you are planning to add three more users to a six-user network and you want to examine how the added traffic will affect network performance. By properly modeling the amount of traffic generated, you can perform an experiment with very reliable results. Some traffic generators allow you to monitor and store all traffic from a specific node and then use that traffic pattern to simulate an actual client. This can give an accurate indication of how additional clients will affect the network. Figure 12.3 illustrates this.

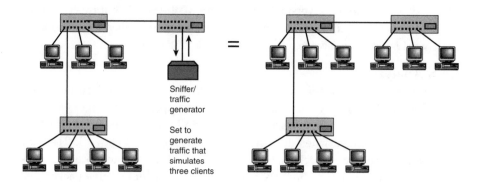

FIGURE 12.3 *Using a traffic generator to simulate additional users is useful in determining what effects future growth will have on your network.*

A traffic generator is also useful in simulating the addition of constant-stream services to your network. This includes real-time applications, such as video distribution and video conferencing. For instance, assume you know that a network video service, such as Precept's IP/TV (Precept has since been acquired by Cisco Systems), will add a constant 300Kbps of traffic to your network. You can use a traffic generator to model the impact of this application on your production network without actually purchasing the video product. This can help you determine whether these types of applications are deployable in your current LAN or whether you need to upgrade your LAN infrastructure. This will be especially useful in determining whether a particular shared infrastructure can handle an increased load. If not, that area could be a candidate for a switch upgrade.

Dedicated RMON Probes

One of the latest developments in LAN management and troubleshooting is the RMON probe. As you read in Chapter 11, "Managing Switched, Fast, and Gigabit Ethernet Networks," RMON is a standard that examines a network remotely and keeps track of information at a very detailed level. RMON probes monitor traffic on LANs that may not have a designated person monitoring them from a management console. RMON probes offer most of the features found in LAN analyzers, and they are remotely accessible. Thus, they are good tools for monitoring remote locations, such as branch offices. The big drawback to RMON probes is their exorbitant prices: They may cost up to $10,000.

Three of the largest RMON probe manufacturers, 3Com, Bay Networks, and NetScout, support dedicated RMON probes. 3Com sells the Transcend Enterprise Monitor with a 10/100 module, which can be managed by 3Com's Transcend Traffix Manager RMON management software. Similarly, Bay Networks sells the Optivity Series 2000 Fast Ethernet StackProbe, along with

Optivity TrafficMan. NetScout sells the NetScout Intelligent Probe as a hardware-based RMON probe solution. The NetScout Intelligent Probe has been especially successful, winning many awards, both for its feature set and for its support of RMON2. All three of these solutions offer a dedicated hardware RMON probe with a useful software management package. If you can't spare an extra $5000, RMON software packages, like Triticom's RMONster, are also available. These products will turn an ordinary PC into an RMON probe, but the performance (that is, data collection capability) does not nearly reach the level of the dedicated hardware-based RMON probes.

PC-Based Troubleshooting Products

You can also use software products to troubleshoot networks. These commonly are cheaper and easier to use than their hardware counterparts. Because they are typically used on a PC or workstation, they do not offer the same level of performance as a dedicated hardware product. With software diagnostic products, the amount of data that can be collected depends on the PC, the NIC, the drivers and network operating system, and the amount of memory available to collect incoming data. Software troubleshooting products include software sniffers and LAN management products.

Software-Based Sniffers

If you don't have a few thousand dollars to spend on a hardware-based LAN analyzer or if you want more functionality than a handheld frame tester provides, you may want to consider several software packages that can turn a PC into a respectable LAN analyzer. NetScout Manager Plus from NetScout and Novell's ManageWise (LANalyzer for Windows is integrated into ManageWise) are two examples of this kind of product. ManageWise runs as an application on a PC system with a NIC and NIC driver. Therefore, ManageWise doesn't care whether the network is 10BASE-T, 10BASE-5, or 100BASE-T. It collects statistics and data as fast as it can, regardless of the network type. Although this software runs very well at 10Mbps network speeds, you'll need a high performance PC to avoid dropped packets and missed frames at 100Mbps. Attempting to capture data at 1000Mbps is a waste of time on today's PCs. The software is just not built to handle data at those high speeds. Also, you'll need a network adapter that can run in *promiscuous mode*. This means the adapter will accept all packets on the wire, not just those sent to a certain MAC address. Although most vendors support this feature, you'll often find it difficult to discover how it is enabled. Both Intel and 3Com have sections on their technical support Web sites that tell how to do this.

ManageWise can provide a large assortment of basic diagnostic information for 100BASE-T networks, but a hardware product is required for individual frame capture and analysis. In general, a software-based analyzer can perform some functions well and some functions not so well. The functions a software (PC-based) analyzer can perform well include

- Looking at frame statistics (collision rate, runt packets, and so on)
- Counting the number of packets sent and measuring traffic levels
- Collecting time-average information

The functions a software (PC-based) analyzer cannot perform very well include

- Performing data integrity checking and CRC checking
- Analyzing the protocol header of a frame
- Reporting on packet filtering (how much traffic is being generated from each node address)

LAN Management Suites

The two previous examples are applications that are part of comprehensive LAN Management Suites, which is another category of software-based troubleshooting products. This category includes such packages as NetScout's NetScout Manager Plus, Intel's LANDesk Management Suite, Cabletron's Spectrum, Hewlett Packard's OpenView, and Novell's ManageWise. These products provide methods to obtain real-time graphical information on the traffic level and type of traffic on the network. The traffic analyzer in OpenView for NT allows users to monitor traffic levels and generate warnings when levels become too high. The troubleshooting tools in LAN management packages tend to be proactive in nature: They warn when network conditions look bad, but they rarely help the LAN administrator actually fix the problems. Usually more sophisticated equipment, such as a LAN analyzer, is needed for this.

LAN management suites often work in conjunction with network trending tools. Trending tools are helpful in identifying recurring trends in your network traffic. Two examples of these products are INS Enterprise Pro and Desktalk TrendSNMP. These products rely on the basic data gathering techniques of software-based LAN Analyzers, but they also apply intelligent software to the data in hopes of identifying trends and patterns in the network usage. This is helpful because it often points out problems before they happen.

Summary of Troubleshooting Product Categories

As we discussed, many types of diagnostic devices are available to help you troubleshoot your network. These devices can be placed into two categories: hardware devices and software devices. Table 12.1 recaps some of the basic features of each type of product.

TABLE 12.1 TROUBLESHOOTING PRODUCT CATEGORIES AND THEIR FUNCTIONS

Troubleshooting Device	Can Be Used For	Should Not Be Used For
Hardware Devices		
LAN analyzer/ sniffer	Detailed packet analysis Detailed packet filtering Traffic source analysis Traffic level monitoring Collision frequency CRC and data integrity checking	Small networks where the cost of the analyzer is prohibitive Networks where special training cannot be justified
Traffic generator	Modeling addition of new clients or server Modeling addition of new network services (such as video)	Modeling complex network scenarios (like the addition of new segments)
Cable tester	Testing UTP cable type (Category 3, 4, or 5) or coax Testing number of pairs (2 or 4) Testing cable length and integrity	Guaranteeing connectivity beyond the cable itself
Hardware and Some Software Devices		
RMON probes	Obtaining advanced statistical data about network traffic Detailed packet analysis Detailed packet filtering Traffic source analysis Traffic level monitoring	Small networks where cost is an issue Networks where management software cannot read RMON data
Software Devices		
Software analyzers	Traffic level monitoring Collision frequency	CRC, data integrity checking Detailed packet analysis Detailed packet filtering Traffic source analysis
Software network management suites	Traffic level monitoring Warning of problematic network conditions Combining network information with desktop and server information	Determining the cause and/or solution to network problems Managing a specific switch and its proprietary features
Trending tools	Analyzing data captured by LAN Analyzer or the management suite and suggesting positive and negative trends	

Troubleshooting Techniques in a Shared Environment

A typical network environment may include several segments of 10Mbps shared networks. Each of these segments shares 10Mbps of bandwidth between all clients and servers on the segment. Therefore, when a problem occurs on one node, it usually affects all other nodes on the segment, and, in some cases, all other nodes in the entire LAN. For instance, if one node on a shared LAN has a NIC that starts transmitting bad data on the wire, the other clients on that segment may not be able to send or receive data. Because you can see the problem anywhere on the segment, however, you can usually find, isolate, and remedy it. Troubleshooting on a shared network can be done with a wide variety of devices, but a hardware-based LAN analyzer can detect the most problems.

This section begins by discussing some basic shared network troubleshooting techniques, such as monitoring traffic levels and analyzing individual packets. The goal here is to provide a clear understanding of the common problems found on a shared network. The next section then applies these common problems to Switched, Fast, and Gigabit Ethernet networks, explaining how problem isolation is different in each environment.

Intermittent Connections

When connections are lost or become intermittent, we can usually trace the cause to a bad connection. This could occur where the cable meets the RJ-45 connector, where the cable meets the patch panel, or where the cable meets the end node. A thorough test with a handheld cable analyzer should isolate this problem quickly.

Traffic-Level Analysis

High or erratic traffic levels are one of the leading causes of poor network performance and productivity. Too many nodes on any shared network can cause a level of traffic that may hinder the productivity of some network components. Also, the addition of nodes that transmit large amounts of data at frequent intervals, like powerful workstations or data backup servers, can increase traffic and decrease the overall performance of the network. Luckily, you can easily identify and remedy this situation in a shared network. Traffic monitoring software and hardware can provide constant updates on the overall traffic level and what constitutes the traffic.

In Figure 12.4, a screen output of Intel's LANDesk Traffic Analyst shows how overall network traffic is monitored. The instantaneous traffic level is plotted as well as the average network traffic level. You can monitor other information, such as peak and low traffic levels as well as the times they occurred.

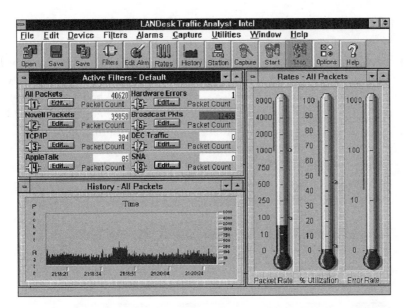

FIGURE 12.4 *This screen capture of LANDesk Traffic Analyst is an example of how network utilization and individual packet information can be kept over time.*

Traffic analysis provides basic information about the network and can be instrumental in identifying certain types of problems. Two common problems that cause high levels of traffic are newer, faster nodes and too many stations on the segment. We discuss both in the following sections.

Problem: Faster Nodes Dominate LAN Bandwidth

In the past, it was rare to find a server or client system that could continuously transmit packets at the maximum Ethernet rate because older cards could not sustain the minimum 9.6μs interframe spacing (IFS) of the IEEE 802.3 specification. This resulted in many nodes on the network vying for the wire at different points in time in a truly random fashion. This randomness on such old networks worked well for the CSMA/CD nature of the Ethernet specification because the specification was built around the low probability that two stations would get on the wire at the exact same instant.

With the advent of newer, faster systems and NICs, almost all nodes on the network can sustain the minimum 9.6μs IFS transfer rate. This causes a multitude of problems, the foremost being the *capture effect* (wire hogging) and increased secondary collisions (frames that collide more than once). These problems cause the network utilization to go up and the efficiency to drop. New schemes such as dynamic, adaptive IFS algorithms may help marginally, but even with them, the basic problem will still occur.

In order to find this type of problem, the traffic level can be monitored and compared to previous levels. Trend analysis tools, as discussed previously, can be particularly useful in this instance. A network characterized by a large number of high traffic peaks and a higher overall average traffic load is probably suffering from this problem. Consider Figure 12.5, which shows traffic levels after state-of-the-art NICs are added to a few nodes in the network. The additional peaks and higher average traffic level may indicate that some stations are hogging the wire for extended periods of time. Two potential solutions for this problem are to upgrade to a switched workgroup in the areas where these NICs are installed or to increase the bandwidth of the workgroup by deploying 100Mbps Fast Ethernet NICs and hubs.

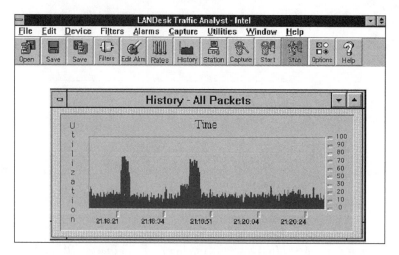

FIGURE 12.5 *Traffic levels with many fast nodes on the network. The two extended spikes in network utilization may indicate that the newer nodes are much faster than the rest of the nodes on the network and could be causing traffic problems.*

Problem: Too Many Nodes

The other problem that plagues shared networks is too many nodes on the network segment. When too many nodes are on a single 10Mbps shared network, the traffic reaches levels at which network efficiency decreases. The efficiency is measured by taking the total number of packets on the wire and determining how many of them are valid data packets and how many are collisions. The more traffic on the wire, the more likely any one packet is a collision. A shared Ethernet network that is over 50% loaded will suffer from poor efficiency. The bottom line is that even though the level of network traffic appears to be high, users will complain about long network response times. Most traffic analysts who can separate collisions from good packets can easily see this problem. No details of the packets need to be seen. Figure 12.6 shows what a network with too many nodes (and too many collisions) registers on a typical traffic analyst.

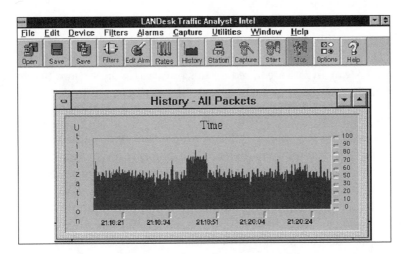

FIGURE 12.6 *The traffic level with too many nodes on the shared network. Note that the average utilization is around 50 percent, which results in a network with less than optimum performance.*

Sometimes, the problem may not be too many nodes, but increased activity from the nodes that are already on the network. This is typically caused by a new application that has been deployed on the network. For instance, desktop video conferencing can increase a client's traffic generation substantially. When several clients are using desktop video conferencing simultaneously, the average network utilization increases, and a pattern shown in Figure 12.6 can emerge.

In the past, this problem was remedied with Ethernet bridging or segmenting, which provided a short-term solution at best. Adding switches or higher bandwidth devices is the best way to avoid this problem in the long term. Limit the number of clients per segment to a number that matches their bandwidth requirements. If the bandwidth requirements have suddenly doubled, you'll probably need to halve the number of clients per segment. We discuss the deployment of switches in this manner in Chapter 9.

Individual Frame Analysis

Although monitoring overall traffic levels can give a good indication of when your network is overloaded, it may not tell when other problems occur. Traffic levels on the network may not be high, but the packets that are on the network could be problematic. Examples of these problems include the following:

- Imbalance in packet distribution

- Large number of broadcast packets

- Bad packets on the network

Sometimes, the only way to find the source of these problems is to analyze individual packet statistics and contents. Usually, a high-performance device such as a LAN analyzer is required for this purpose. In the sections that follow, we explain how to diagnose each of these three problems.

Problem: Improper Packet Distribution

Packet distribution statistics can tell you whether one or more nodes are dominating most of the network bandwidth. By monitoring the source address of each packet on a shared network, you can create a distribution pie chart showing who is using what portion of the network. Problems arise when an isolated client is using more than 5% of the available shared bandwidth for any extended period of time. This client is likely performing some LAN-intensive task, such as videoconferencing or database queries, which requires a lot of bandwidth. Clients like these, often referred to as *power users*, should be given a dedicated switched connection or should be congregated together on a faster 100BASE-T network. In a normal shared environment, you should expect servers to be responsible for the majority of the packets.

Problem: High Level of Broadcast Packets

A broadcast packet is designed to reach all nodes on the network. Because a broadcast packet's destination address is FFFFFFFFFFFF, each individual node knows it must receive the packet. A bridge or switch does not act like a firewall for broadcast packets (as a router does). Bridges and switches always forward broadcast packets, so they tend to flow freely throughout the network. Because these packets must flow to all nodes on the segment, the probability that they will collide is higher. When many broadcast packets are being transmitted simultaneously on a network, broadcast overload occurs and network performance can be affected. When many stations send broadcast frames at once, broadcast overload is likely. When this phenomenon happens because of a faulty network device or configuration, the effect is called a *broadcast storm*.

Broadcast overload is easy to detect by measuring how many broadcast frames are on the network at any given time. A packet distribution that shows a large number of broadcast frames concentrated in a small amount of time is likely broadcast overload. In general, if broadcast frames, as measured as a percentage of total frames, exceed 5% over an extended period of time, you have a broadcast overload problem. You'll usually find broadcast overload in networks with many NetWare servers (which send broadcast keep-alive packets every 30 to 60 seconds) or with NetBIOS/NetBEUI networks (NetBIOS/NetBEUI uses broadcasting extensively). In a NetWare environment, the keep-alive timers can be increased to 5 minutes (or more), thus reducing the overall number of broadcast packets. You can also remedy a broadcast overload problem by adding routers, adding switches with virtual LAN broadcast-filtering capabilities, or adding Layer 3 switches. The latter is preferred because it is the most long-term solution of the three. Refer to Chapters 8 and 9 for examples of how to add Layer 3 switching to a network.

Problem: Bad Packets

Errors in packets occur in various ways. Often packet errors are caused by subpar cabling infrastructure, bad NICs, faulty hubs or interconnect devices, or noise interference. Software analyzer products can usually detect packet errors, but to troubleshoot the *cause* of the error, more sophisticated hardware-based analyzers may be required. Figure 12.7 shows where each type of error occurs in an Ethernet frame.

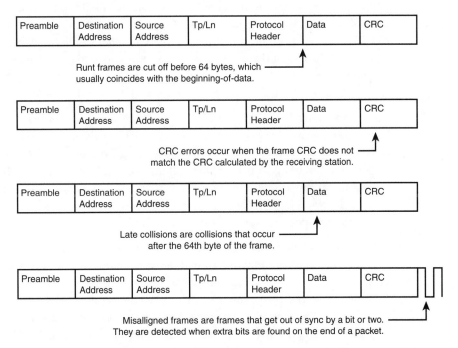

FIGURE 12.7 *Locations of common Ethernet packet errors, including runts, CRC errors, late collisions, and misaligned frames.*

The following are some of the most common errors found in today's Ethernet networks:

- *Runts (collisions)*—*Runt packets* are packets that are shorter than the minimum Ethernet frame length. This is currently defined as 64 bytes, including CRC, destination address, source address, type/length field, and data. If a frame is received with fewer than 64 bytes, one of two things has probably occurred: The frame has collided somewhere on the network, and the remaining portion of the frame is the collision jam signal; or the station that transmitted the frame encountered an underrun during the transmission process, and the transmitted frame was cut short. Regardless of the cause, a runt frame is useless and must be discarded. Usually, runt frames of the underrun variety must be dealt with at the source: the transmitting station.

- *CRC errors*—The Cyclical Redundancy Check (CRC) is a 4-byte field at the end of every frame that tells the receiving station the frame is valid. When the frame is transmitted, it is fed bit by bit through a linear feedback shift register in the transmitting station. The output of the register is a 4-byte value that is appended to the end of the frame. During reception, the receiving station then computes the CRC just as the transmitting station did. The receiving station compares the value it obtains with the value received at the end of the frame. If the two values are equal, no errors have occurred during transmission. When the values do not add up, the receiving station should report a CRC error and discard the frame.

  Most LAN analyzers can detect CRC errors. In any network, more than a dozen CRC errors a day should be cause for alarm. CRC errors usually indicate that a portion of the network is suffering from bad cabling, external noise, or excessive transmit jitter. All three conditions can be isolated by looking at the source address of the CRC-error frame and tracing the path of the frame back to its original point of transmission. It is likely that one of the components along that path is at fault.

- *Late collisions*—Late collisions are rarely seen in today's 10Mbps networks because they are a product of a shared network diameter that is too large. However, because the shared network diameter is much smaller in Fast Ethernet networks, people are more likely to connect networks that exceed the 205m network diameter rule. In networks such as these, late collisions may occur. If you are seeing late collisions on your network, recheck all the shared network diameters for compliance to the IEEE 802.3 specification (see Chapter 9).

- *Misalignment*—Misaligned frames are also very rare, but they can occur when network conditions deteriorate. A misaligned frame is one that somehow gets out of sync with the receiving station's receive clock recovery circuit. A misaligned frame is actually valid on the wire, but the receiving station sees it as a CRC error. Misalignment is reported if the frame ends with a CRC error and extra bits are also detected. These are called *dribble bits* and are shown at the end of the misaligned frame in Figure 12.6.

Troubleshooting in a shared environment requires an understanding of many problems and encompasses many techniques. Table 12.2 summarizes some of the problems discussed in this section.

TABLE 12.2 TROUBLESHOOTING TECHNIQUES FOR A SHARED NETWORK

Problem	Technique for Troubleshooting	Potential Solution
Overall Traffic-Level Analysis		
Too many with nodes	Look for sustained shared media traffic levels near 30%.	Segment existing network switches. Add more bandwidth to current network (Fast Ethernet, shared or switched).
Fast nodes Hogging bandwidth	Look for bandwidth spikes above 50%.	Add switching capabilities to current network. Add more bandwidth to current network (Fast Ethernet, shared, or switched).
Individual Packet Analysis		
Imbalanced packet distribution	Look for high percentages of packets from any given node address.	Segment with active nodes should be connected to a switched port or upgraded to Fast Ethernet.
Broadcast overload	Look for many broadcast packets in a concentrated amount of time.	Add Layer 3 switches as broadcast "firewalls." Add more bandwidth to current network. Add virtual LAN capabilities to network with switches. Tune to protocol or application so that it does not generate so many broadcast packets.

continues

TABLE 12.2 CONTINUED

Problem	Technique for Troubleshooting	Potential Solution
Individual Packet Analysis		
Runt frames	Count the number of runt frames reported by LAN analyzer.	Determine whether the frames are collisions or underruns. If collisions occur, try segmentation, adding switches, or adding more bandwidth. If underruns occur, trace node address of the generating station or switch.
CRC errors	Count the number of CRC errors reported by LAN analyzer.	Trace CRC errors back through network to original transmitting node. The problem may be anywhere along that path. The probable culprit is a bad NIC at the transmitting station.
Late collisions	Count the number of late collisions reported by LAN analyzer.	Network diameter is probably out of specification. Recheck cabling distances and repeater Hops, especially for Fast Ethernet.
Misaligned frames	Count the number of misaligned frames reported by LAN analyzer	Trace misaligned frames back through network to original transmitting node. The problem may be anywhere along that path.

Troubleshooting Switched Networks

In a switched network, the problems and solutions of a shared network don't always apply. Each node may have a dedicated switched port, so bad packets from that node don't affect the rest of the nodes on the network. This feature is somewhat offset by the fact that troubleshooting switched networks is more difficult and requires more specialized tools. No longer can a LAN analyzer see all packets and determine which node is the cause of the problem. For this reason, measuring overall traffic levels and studying individual frame statistics is not straightforward in a switched environment. Several switch vendors have proposed ways to remedy this problem with innovative techniques, such as internal RMON and RMON2 data collection and switch port aliasing. We will discuss these techniques and their effectiveness on traffic-based problems.

Traffic-Level Analysis in a Switched Network

Monitoring traffic levels in a switched environment is not straightforward. Remember the description of a switch? A packet is only forwarded to one port on the switch, so a LAN analyzer connected to one port of a switch will not, by definition, catch all packets flowing through the switch. Many switch vendors have attempted to solve the traffic-monitoring problem by designing statistic-collecting modules into the switch. These modules are either based on RMON statistics or a proprietary collection mechanism. For instance, the Bay Networks 28200 switch keeps RMON and SNMP statistics on each packet and can report overall switch traffic levels to any SNMP agent or Bay Networks Optivity management software. Intel does this in a similar way with the 500 series switches and Intel Device View software. Figure 12.8 shows an example of Intel Device View monitoring an Intel Express 550T switch.

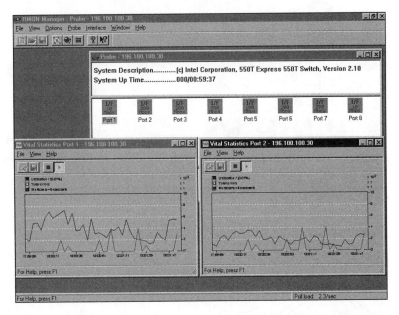

FIGURE 12.8 *Intel's Device View software, monitoring RMON statistics.*

You can diagnose traffic-level problems on a switch with the previously mentioned techniques. Unlike shared networks, however, switched networks do not suffer from throughput degradation due to faster nodes and too many nodes, so these may not cause problems on a switched network. In a workgroup switch, each new user receives a certain amount of dedicated bandwidth. As long as the high bandwidth connection to the switch can handle the traffic, no traffic-level problems should occur.

For instance, the switch in Figure 12.9 (a) has six clients connected to 10Mbps ports and a local server connected to a 100Mbps port. Odds are that the traffic-level in this switch will not be more than the switch can handle. Even if all clients are sending a maximum amount of data, only 60Mbps of the server link will be used. Now consider the same workgroup with double the number of clients, as shown in Figure 12.9 (b). In this case, the clients could possibly create enough traffic to cause an overall traffic level problem in the switch. The solution to this problem is to attach some of the clients to a repeater and connect the repeater to a switched port. If the sum of the total bandwidth of all the clients is not greater than the bandwidth of the server link, the clients will never overrun the server with too much traffic.

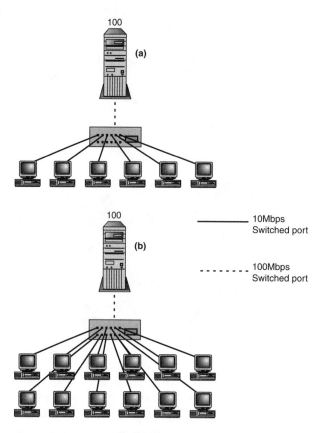

FIGURE 12.9   *A switch without the potential for a traffic problem; even if all six clients are transmitting at maximum rates, the 100Mbps server connection will not be overrun. A switch with the potential for a traffic level problem; with 12 clients, the server could receive 120Mbps of requests at the same time, resulting in an overrun situation.*

Sometimes, hardware in individual ports on a switch may fail. If this happens, the switch can suffer from increased traffic levels due to the faulty port. The switch's own internal management module, which periodically checks the integrity of each port, can usually detect this.

Individual Frame Analysis

Individual frame analysis on a switch also provides an interesting proposition. Packets are not forwarded to all ports on a switch, so there is no logical place to plug in a LAN analyzer and view all packets. Switch vendors have designed many ways to overcome this troubleshooting drawback. Two ways are port aliasing and adding a repeater to monitor a port.

Port Aliasing

Port aliasing, also called *port mirroring* or *port spanning*, is a mechanism by which a switch monitors all traffic flowing through a given port and mirrors it to a special alias port. This allows a LAN administrator to examine switch traffic one port at a time. If problematic packets are coming from a switch, they can usually be isolated in this fashion. Figure 12.10 shows how port aliasing works.

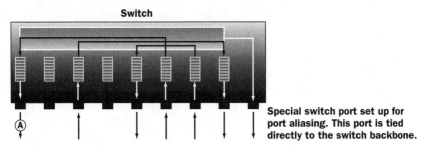

Switch

Ⓐ

Special switch port set up for port aliasing. This port is tied directly to the switch backbone.

FIGURE 12.10 *In port aliasing on a switch, the alias port can be set to mirror the traffic on any given port of the switch.*

Port aliasing is useful for isolating some of the packet errors mentioned previously in this chapter. The following is a brief description of how each type of error manifests itself in a switched environment and how a typical switch deals with the problem:

- *Imbalanced packet distribution*—A few nodes accounting for most of the traffic on a switch will not cause as big a problem as in a shared environment. Because the switch, and not the shared media, is the arbitrator between ports, it can intelligently determine the relative priority of each port. Because of this feature of switches, bandwidth hogging is rarely a problem in switched networks.

- *Broadcast overload*—Switches that forward packets according to bridging schemes, like store-and-forward and cut-through, are especially susceptible to broadcast overload. Because broadcast packets are intended for everybody, they are forwarded to every port on a switch. In effect, broadcast packets make switches act like repeaters so that a broadcast overload will have the same effect on switches as it does on repeaters. Switches with virtual LAN capabilities can filter broadcast packets from some ports, but this will only address the symptom, not correct the cause. As in a shared network, the best way to remedy a broadcast overload situation in a switched network is to decrease the amount of broadcast packets on the network. This often means going to the source of the broadcast packets. As mentioned previously, modifying network operation system parameters, such as NetWare's keep-alive timer, can often remedy a broadcast overload problem.

- *Runt packets*—Because switches help nodes avoid collisions, a runt frame is usually not due to a collision. Frames that have underruns on the transmitting station, however, will still show up as runt packets at the switch. You can configure most switches to store-and-forward forwarding mode. Store-and-forward switching filters runt frames, thus preventing them from propagating through the switch to the rest of the network.

- *CRC errors*—Depending on the features of your switch, CRC errors may not be a problem. Some store-and-forward switches check the integrity of the CRC of every packet before forwarding it to a specific port. CRC-errored packets will never make it through the switch. If the switch does not do CRC checking, the packet will be forwarded as normal. A bad port on a switch could actually induce a CRC error. In this case, the end node or another switch will have to catch the error.

- *Late collisions*—Collisions in general are less frequent in switched networks. If they occur at all, it is because they are propagated to the switch from shared networks that connect to a switched port. Switches will typically handle late collisions like they handle regular collisions: by dropping the packet.

- *Misaligned frames*—To a switch, misaligned frames are seen as CRC errors. If the switch can filter CRC errors, it will filter misaligned frames as well.

Adding a Repeater

Even if a switch does not have advanced troubleshooting features, such as statistics-gathering modules and port aliasing, you can still use a few tricks to troubleshoot problematic switched networks. Adding a repeater is one such method. *Adding a repeater* refers to cascading a suspected problem node through a repeater into a switch, as shown in Figure 12.11. A port and a LAN analyzer are both connected to the repeater, and the repeater is, in turn, connected to the switch port. In this fashion, you can monitor any port on a switch for bad frames and other error conditions.

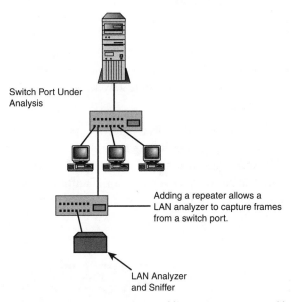

Switch Port Under
Analysis

Adding a repeater allows a
LAN analyzer to capture frames
from a switch port.

LAN Analyzer
and Sniffer

FIGURE 12.11 *Sometimes, adding a repeater to troubleshoot a switch is the only way to view the traffic going in and out of a switched port.*

> **Note**
>
> *Although adding a repeater is a cheap and simple way to troubleshoot a switched network, it does have its drawbacks. When you insert a repeater between the end node and the switched port, you are effectively changing the characteristics of the connection. For instance, collisions may now occur on the wire, whereas before they did not. If the switch-to-client connection was full-duplex before, it will become half-duplex after adding a repeater. These subtle changes in the connection could change the dynamics of the problem you are trying to troubleshoot.*

Troubleshooting Switch Configurations

When looking at switched networks, we've seen that it's necessary to rely on capabilities built into the switch itself. These include RMON management and port aliasing. However, other parameters that can be configured on a typical switch could cause problems, such as VLANs, port security, and MAC forwarding. These are discussed below.

VLANs

The promise of cross-vendor virtual-LAN interoperability lies with the emerging 802.1Q standard. Today's virtual LAN configuration, however, is often vendor-specific and requires manual setup of each switch in the network. Add to this that most of today's interswitch VLAN communication is also propri-etary, and you end up with a potential for problems. When troubleshooting a switch, confirm how the VLANs are configured. Are they port-based, MAC-based, or protocol-based? Do switches share VLANs; if so, how do they com-municate this information? Is a VLAN configuration preventing a client from accessing a server? The best way to determine whether your VLANs are the problem in a given switch is to see if the problem persists when the VLAN configuration is removed. Make sure that you can restore the original VLAN configuration after trying this experiment.

Consider Figure 12.12 (a), where a server has been placed on port-based VLAN A. The clients on VLAN B can no longer reach the server because all traffic is filtered between the two VLANs. If all clients need access to this server but you still want to segregate the traffic between VLAN A and B, Figure 12.12 b might provide a better solution. In this figure, all clients can access the server because the switch port it is connected to is *shared* between the two VLANs.

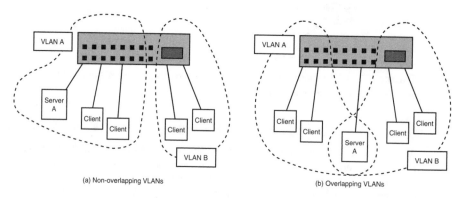

(a) Non-overlapping VLANs   (b) Overlapping VLANs

FIGURE 12.12   *A switch with two configured VLANs. VLAN A cannot see traffic from VLAN B, so server A is cut off from clients on VLAN B. The server is connected to a port that is shared between VLAN A and B, so all clients can see the server.*

Port Filtering and Security

Some switches offer packet filtering at the port level. This can be based on source MAC addresses or other packet parameters. When troubleshooting problems with packet flow through a switch, make sure these packet filters are set correctly. For instance, sometimes packets with a particular MAC address cannot get through a given switch. Try disabling any port filtering capabilities, and see whether the problem persists.

MAC Forwarding Tables

Other problems occur when a switch's MAC address tables become corrupted. This could occur because two NICs on the network have the same source address, causing the switch to become confused (just like if a friend called you from New York and then immediately called again from Paris). Also, sometimes the 802.1d spanning tree protocol will detect a loop in the switched network and shut down a particular connection. When this happens, the MAC forwarding tables need to be relearned. If connections are going down and coming up repeatedly, a switch may never forward packets quite right. Be sure to check the 802.1d counters in the switch when troubleshooting these kinds of problems. Pay particular attention to the number of times the spanning tree algorithm has run. A high number could indicate a defective link somewhere in the network.

Troubleshooting in a switched environment involves many new techniques to obtain the same level of information found in a shared environment. Two basic troubleshooting methods, monitoring traffic levels and analyzing individual packets, take on a new meaning in a switched environment. In a shared network, you accomplish this level of monitoring with a software or hardware LAN analyzer. In a switched network, LAN analyzers must be paired with features of the switch itself to obtain similar information. Table 12.3 briefly summarizes the techniques used to troubleshoot a switched network.

TABLE 12.3 TROUBLESHOOTING TECHNIQUES FOR A SWITCHED NETWORK

Method for Troubleshooting	Switch Features Necessary
Traffic-Level Analysis	
Monitoring switch statistics	Internal switch statistics-gathering module
Individual Frame Analysis	
Port aliasing	Special switch hardware that allows for port aliasing (some switches allow any port to be an alias)
Adding a repeater	No special switch feature required
Troubleshooting Switch Configurations	
VLAN configuration	VLANs by port, MAC, protocol, and so on; VLAN Management software from switch vendor
	Special switch software can be used to mirror all traffic from a given VLAN to a special alias port (Cisco does this in the Catalyst 5000 with their Enhanced SPAN feature)
Port filtering and security	Software from switch vendor
MAC forwarding tables	Software from switch vendor to examine internal MAC address tables
Any SNMP management software to examine 802.1d spanning tree counters

Troubleshooting Fast Ethernet Networks

Fast Ethernet networks may be shared or switched and may incorporate 10Mbps networks. This introduces some interesting challenges to the troubleshooting of a Fast Ethernet network. In general, however, you can diagnose Fast Ethernet network problems with the techniques discussed earlier in this chapter. The challenges involve enabling troubleshooting equipment for Fast Ethernet and preparing for any new problems Fast Ethernet may bring to your network. This section starts by briefly describing how to upgrade current software and hardware analyzer products to Fast Ethernet. It then finishes with a detailed look at some of the problems to expect after deploying Fast Ethernet in your network.

Changing Diagnostic Hardware

You can sometimes upgrade troubleshooting hardware products, such as LAN analyzers, handheld frame analyzers, and traffic generators, to include Fast Ethernet diagnosis capabilities. Devices that can be upgraded are often products that can already handle some form of high-speed module, like FDDI or CDDI. Modules that do not have a Fast Ethernet upgrade are probably built around an architecture that is too slow to analyze 100Mbps data rates. Most hardware-based products have an independent user interface that needs to be aware of the type and speed of the network it is monitoring. Therefore, sniffers and LAN analyzers will likely need a firmware upgrade when a new 100BASE-T module is added. The Network Associates Sniffer is a product with an upgrade module for 100BASE-TX, the Network Analyzer Ethernet 10/100. This particular product, shown in Figure 12.13, can also adapt to many high-speed technologies, such as Fast Ethernet, FDDI, and CDDI.

In general, diagnostic products support 100BASE-TX, 100BASE-FX, and even 100BASE-T4. If you have any thoughts of deploying more than one type of Fast Ethernet, be sure to determine whether the network troubleshooting device you are considering will support them.

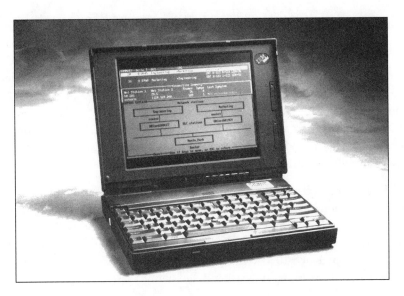

FIGURE 12.13 *The Network Associates Sniffer 10/100BASE-T Model.*

Changing Diagnostic Software

Most diagnostic software is PC-based and relies on a NIC and a promiscuous-mode device driver for its interface to the wire. For this reason, you can easily upgrade most software-based troubleshooting products to Fast Ethernet by simply adding a new NIC and driver. However, most PCs are not powerful enough to receive, store, *and* analyze incoming data at 100Mbps rates. Therefore, as in 10Mbps, software-based analyzers make better traffic-level analyzers than they do individual packet analyzers. You can also upgrade LAN management suites, such as Intel's LANDesk Management Suite, to Fast Ethernet. A simple NIC and driver replacement provides the path to 100Mbps. Because LANDesk Management Suite doesn't examine every packet at the byte level like a LAN analyzer would, its applications can keep up with the 100Mbps traffic at a macro level.

You have a few things to watch out for in any software-based LAN diagnostic package. First, be sure the program is not hard-coded for specific data rates, like 10Mbps for Ethernet or 16Mbps for Token Ring. Flexibility in the maximum data rate is needed for a smooth upgrade to Fast Ethernet. Second, determine which protocols are supported when you upgrade to Fast Ethernet. Although your 10Mbps software may support IPX, TCP/IP, NetBios, and DECNet, new modules may not support the same variety. Last, make sure that any software-based product you purchase can run at both 10 and 100Mbps speeds and will support 100BASE-TX and 100BASE-FX.

Potential Problems with Fast Ethernet

With the inclusion of Fast Ethernet in your network, you have some new problems to consider. In addition to the common problems of 10Mbps Ethernet, Fast Ethernet networks could encounter problems with network diameter, UTP cable type, mismatched 100BASE-T ports, and noisy environments. Each of these problems is discussed in further detail here:

- *The shared network diameter is too large*—As described previously, a shared Fast Ethernet network can have a diameter only up to 205 meters. If the correct network diameter is not used, such problems as late collisions and undetected dropped packets may occur. Network diameters usually become too large in one of two ways. Either the two-repeater rule or the 100m hub-to-node rule is not followed. Shared Fast Ethernet networks with diameters greater than 205 meters should be immediately enhanced with a Fast Ethernet switch (either Layer 2 or Layer 3) or router.

- *100BASE-TX is running on Category 3 UTP*—Another common problem occurs when a 100BASE-TX hub or node is connected using Category 3 UTP cabling, which will simply not work. Category 5, or data grade, UTP cable is required for 100BASE-TX. If this happens in your network, you will most likely encounter many CRC errors and lost packets. You may not even get a good link integrity indication. Switched or shared 10Mbps is the correct choice for the portion of your network that uses Category 3 UTP cable.

- *100BASE-T4 is running on UTP with only two pairs*—You'll rarely encounter this problem because 100BASE-T4 is not widely used. When 100BASE-T4 *is* used, however, four pairs of cable are required. If you have only two pairs of your Category 5 UTP cable dedicated for the LAN, 100BASE-TX should be used. If you have only two pairs of Category 3 available for LAN connections, you may need to rely on switched or shared 10BASE-T in those portions of your network.

- *100BASE-TX and 10BASE-T ports are mismatched*—10BASE-T uses a start/stop style of communication. This means that the voltage on the wire is zero when no transmission or reception is occurring. 100BASE-TX, however, uses a special data pattern, called the *TX Idle sequence*, to designate idle times on the wire. One of the drawbacks of this difference is that if a 100BASE-TX station is connected to a 10BASE-T 4 port, the TX Idle transmissions will jam the 10Mbps hub with what amounts to garbage packets. You may have problems of this type if you mistakenly connect 100BASE-TX NICs to 10BASE-T ports. Luckily, most connections on Fast Ethernet NICs, hubs, and switches are 10/100Mbps: They automatically detect the correct operating speed and are not susceptible to this problem.

- *Noisy environments*—In some noisy environments, such as 25-pair cabling bundles and wiring near fluorescent lighting, 100BASE-TX may not work reliably. For that matter, 10BASE-T may not work either. If you are encountering problems that are isolated to a specific cable segment, you should have the noise level checked on that segment. 100BASE-FX is not susceptible to electrical interference because it is based on optical transmission. This property makes 100BASE-FX the best choice in extremely noisy environments.

Troubleshooting Gigabit Ethernet Networks

Gigabit Ethernet networks are very similar to Fast Ethernet networks, and the tips of the previous section apply, except for one small problem: Gigabit Ethernet networks are just too fast to monitor fully. In fact, you'll often be relying on your Gigabit switch vendor's management tools to do your troubleshooting. Because Gigabit switches often lie at the heart of the network, this isn't a settling prospect.

Gigabit Ethernet Analyzers

Collecting Ethernet packets at Gigabit speeds requires a tremendous amount of hardware and processing power. The brute force method of collecting a huge amount of packets and sifting through them later is not possible at Gigabit speeds. Imagine a Gigabit Ethernet link transmitting at full wire speed. This translates to 125MB of data every *second*. Not many analyzers have the kind of memory capacity to store this amount of data. The best approach to troubleshooting Gigabit Ethernet is to use a hardware analyzer in conjunction with highly intelligent packet capturing software. Train the analyzer to look for the problem packets specifically instead of analyzing each and every packet.

An analogy would be a police force that wants to catch speeding cars. It can pull over every car and examine each to determine whether it has been going over the speed limit, or the police can use a filtering tool, a radar gun in this case, and pull over only the problem vehicles. The same method applies to analyzing Gigabit Ethernet networks. You will need an analyzer that is smart enough to focus on the problem packets and let the good packets go about their business.

Examples of early Gigabit Ethernet analyzers are Hewlett-Packard's LAN Internet Advisor, Network Associates' Gigabit Sniffer Pro, and Wandel & Goltermann's Domino Gigabit Analyzer.

Gigabit Ethernet analyzers vary in their specifications, but here are the key features to expect:

- First and foremost, the amount of memory determines how much data can be captured. Considering that most Gigabit Ethernet links are not fully utilized, a deeper memory buffer allows for a longer sampling time. Look for sizes of 64MB or more.

- Filtering packets is essential for a good Gigabit Ethernet analyzer. Because the internal memory buffer will fill up quickly, it's important to focus only on the frames that could be causing a problem. Look for analyzers that allow maximum flexibility of the filtering variables. W&G provides software called the "problem background interview," which helps you determine which filter variables to set.

- Protocol support is also crucial for capturing problematic packets. According to Othmar Kyas and Thomas Heim, 22% of network problems actually occur in Layer 3 or Layer 4 of the OSI model. This is probably a conservative figure because a faulty TCP/IP configuration can actually cause problems at Layer 2 as well. Look for IP, IPX, RIP, SAP, OSPF, and other relevant Layer 3 protocol support. Also look for Layer 4 support for filtering UDP, SNMP, RSVP, SPX, and TCP information.

- VLAN information should be easily decodable by the analyzer. Support for 802.1Q should be standard as well as support for interswitch VLAN schemes, such as GARP and GVRP.

- The capability of upgrade for the analyzer software is very important. Because many of the VLAN, Layer 3, and Layer 4 standards are evolving, the Gigabit Ethernet analyzer will likely need a few upgrades over its lifetime. Just saying that the device can be upgraded is not enough. You need to know exactly what can be upgraded and cannot. For instance, can you upgrade the number of segments supported? Can you upgrade the media type (100BASE-SX, 100BASE-LX, 1000BASE-CX, or the upcoming 1000BASE-T)? Your $30,000 investment should last you a few years at least.

The three vendors mentioned previously all have Gigabit Ethernet analyzer products on the market. Table 12.4 summarizes the key features of these products. (The prices given are current at the time of publication and will likely change.)

TABLE 12.4 COMPARING GIGABIT ETHERNET ANALYZERS

Vendor and Product	Memory Buffer Size	Number of Protocols Supported	Media Supported	Price
Hewlett-Packard LAN Internet Advisor	64MB (upgradable to 128MB)	200+	1000BASE-SX 1000BASE-LX	Around $50,000
Network Associates Gigabit Sniffer Pro	72MB	60+	1000BASE-SX 1000BASE-LX	Around $38,000
Wandel & Goltermann Domino Gigabit Analyzer	64MB	300+	1000BASE-SX 1000BASE-LX	Around $41,000

Gigabit Ethernet Internal Switch Management

The hardware analyzer is an important tool for troubleshooting Gigabit Ethernet networks, but management software for a Gigabit Ethernet switch is even more critical. In fact, you should consider the management software of a Gigabit Ethernet switch as much as the switch's backplane capacity or Layer 3 forwarding rate. This is because the best way to troubleshoot a Gigabit Ethernet switch is from the inside out. The serial data is converted to parallel data inside the Gigabit Ethernet switch. In this form, an internal processor can perform an analysis similar to a Gigabit Ethernet analyzer. Here are some key things to look for in a Gigabit Ethernet switch and associated management software:

- *Support for full SNMPv2 and RMON Bridge MIB*—RMON Groups 1 through 3 and 9 are essential. RMON Groups 4 through 8 and RMON2 are almost impossible at Gigabit speeds today. (See Chapter 11 for more information about RMON groups.)

- *The capability to focus all the management processing power in the switch onto a single port*—This will give you the ability to see as much data as possible when you've narrowed down problems to a single port. If the internal switch CPU is focused on a single port, it has a much better chance of capturing a specific event on that port.

- *The capability to support Gigabit RMON probes or analyzers*—This will require special software in the switch that will mirror data from one port to another. Gigabit analyzers are available from Hewlett-Packard, Network Associates, and Wandel & Goltermann. Other vendors, such as Finisar and NetCom, should be shipping similar products soon.

- *Any software that abstracts incoming information and notifies the user of common problems in the switch (for example, excessive MAC table updates, excessive broadcast traffic, saturation by a single port)*—This is perhaps the most important feature of a Gigabit Ethernet switch management hardware/software solution. Because you cannot capture a full Gigabit Ethernet data stream, you'll have to train the switch to look for specific situations in order to troubleshoot it effectively. These include the following:

  - Excessive broadcast traffic above a certain configurable percentage

  - Frames to or from a specific MAC address

  - Frames to or from a specific IP address (if the switch is Layer 3-capable)

  - Frames that are specifically RIP, RIP2, or OSPF updates

  - SNMP updates and control frames

  - Spanning Tree bridge protocol frames

  - Frames that meet certain RMON or RMON2 criteria

  - Frames that are certain lengths or are within a range of lengths

  - Frames with new MAC addresses, causing excessive MAC table updates

  - Frames that are part of a specific VLAN in the switch

  - 802.3X flow-control start/stop frames

  - Frames containing a specific data pattern

This is just a small sample of what you might want to capture in your Gigabit Ethernet switch. Remember, the best place to troubleshoot your Gigabit Ethernet network is within the Gigabit Ethernet switch, so pay close attention to what filtering hardware and software the vendor offers.

Don't let the small selection of Gigabit Ethernet troubleshooting products deter you from installing 1000BASE networking gear. Remember that two years ago, when the second edition of this book was being written, there was a distinct lack of 100BASE-T diagnostic equipment. In two short years, many quality products emerged on the market. There's no reason to believe Gigabit Ethernet will be any different.

Summary

Troubleshooting networks today can be a tricky business. With networks evolving toward switching and high-speed alternatives, such as Fast and Gigabit Ethernet, the chance for problems to arise becomes much greater. This chapter outlined some of the common problems associated with shared networks and Switched, Fast, and Gigabit Ethernet networks, as well as some of the products you can use to identify these problems. In addition, we discussed hardware and software products that you can use to aid in the isolation of these problems. When Gigabit Ethernet switches enter the picture, Gigabit Ethernet analyzers and internal switch hardware and software become extremely important troubleshooting tools.

Although troubleshooting Ethernet networks may seem complicated at first, once the proper infrastructure is in place, diagnosis and resolution of network problems is usually straightforward. Hopefully, this chapter provided some insight into how to prepare that infrastructure and how to approach common problems.

Epilogue

Fast-Track Future

Gigabit Ethernet roared onto the networking scene faster than any networking technology in memory. (In that respect, you can think of it as ISDN in reverse.) Before the Gigabit Ethernet standard was even ratified, in the summer of 1998, products had been shipping for a year. Even "prestandard" products were breaking all records in throughput tests.

In one early test of Yago/Cabletron Systems gear, conducted by The Tolly Group at Networld+Interop (Las Vegas, 1998), the multiport Gigabit Ethernet switch achieved a constant rate throughput of some 30 million packets per second. That's close to 2 billion packets through the system every minute! Just months later, wirespeed, full-duplex, multiport switches are almost commonplace. What will network managers do with all of that bandwidth?

A glib response would be to cite conventional wisdom that one can never have enough resources, that, once available, end users will find ways to consume it, or that what seems like huge overkill today will be laughably small a few years down the road. There is, of course, some truth to that last statement. Don't forget that when Microsoft chose 640KB as the memory limit for MS-DOS, it considered this so high as to be beyond practical limits.

To me, though, such a discussion misses the central point: Gigabit Ethernet has extended the life of Ethernet yet again, and it can probably push the technology even further than its current limits. In doing so, however, we risk extending the technology to the point where applications can't take advantage of it. Gigabit Ethernet already may exceed the practical limits of most normal applications to take advantage of its ample bandwidth.

Can Applications Respond to the Challenge?

We build fast networks, ultimately, to help applications deliver unprecedented throughput. An unstated but assumed premise is that applications are able to drive the newly found bandwidth. Unfortunately, that's rarely the case. In this day of high-density, wirespeed, Layer 3 switches, the application—not the underlying network—is usually the bottleneck.

For Ethernet to reach new heights, application vendors must take a serious look at rearchitecting and redeveloping key applications to take advantage of the high-bandwidth networks now being deployed.

Most of today's applications were designed and developed when 10Mbps Ethernet was the highest LAN bandwidth available—more than four years ago. This bandwidth usually had to be shared among 50 or more stations. Then, an application that consumed more than 1Mbps or 2Mbps in such a bandwidth-constrained environment would be exhibiting behavior that was not just anti-social, but downright destructive.

Applications were unintentionally self-limiting. Writing to high-level APIs, developers contributed to sluggish network throughput. Run-time configurations using default protocol settings typically resulted in traffic high in small frames and acknowledgment packets, both of which could throttle traffic flows. Still, these applications appeared relatively fast.

That all changed when Ethernet switching and Fast Ethernet arrived on the scene. No longer was a fraction of 10Mbps a reasonable cap on application bandwidth consumption. With the arrival of Gigabit speeds, the sky is the limit, but applications just can't keep up.

Here's a sample of what application developers need to address:

- *Application efficiency*—It's time to rewrite key routines in a lower level language, such as assembly rather than C++, to reduce the application cycles required to process data. Effective network utilization is often low simply because the network adapters are waiting for the application.

- *Protocol stack efficiency*—As noted earlier, simple tuning to optimize the frame and window size can improve network throughput dramatically. In the 16-bit world, several companies made a living providing compatible alternatives to Microsoft's protocol stacks. I find it astonishing that the third-party protocol stack has disappeared since the debut of Microsoft's 32-bit operating systems. I doubt Microsoft builds the highest performance TCP/IP stack possible.

- *Parallel multitasking*—For companies serious about building turbocharged, Giga-applications, radical application redesign will be necessary. A single data stream will never be able to use Gigabit-speed links effectively. Parallel multitasking (usually reserved for more exotic, scientific applications) may be required for more mundane tasks.

Unless application vendors take a serious look at rearchitecting applications for high-speed Ethernet networks, the gargantuan, billion-bits-per-second pipes supported by Gigabit Ethernet vendors serve only as the networking equivalent of water mains: capable of carrying the combined load needed to support hundreds of users, but offering no particular benefit to any single user. In effect, Gigabit Ethernet becomes relegated to a central office-type technology that improves the core of the network but offers little apparent benefit to applications at the network's edge.

How Far Can Ethernet Evolve?

The applications conundrum is one issue that may act as a governor on the burgeoning growth of Gigabit Ethernet and beyond, but it can be conquered. As we consider the two orders of magnitude velocity increase we've witnessed in just the past few years, we can't help but ask how far can Ethernet evolve? We've assumed that we can just ratchet up Ethernet without a serious look at the underlying architecture. In reality, Gigabit Ethernet is a 10Mbps architecture grafted upon a 1000Mbps physical layer. Such Frankenstein-like techniques may eventually mean the technology needs major reconstructive surgery. Just look at the evidence.

Cabling requirements have, naturally, become more stringent with each transmission speed increase. With Gigabit Ethernet, the IEEE 802.3 specification had to be tweaked a bit—with the addition of carrier extension—in order to support shared Gigabit Ethernet with any reasonable diameter. But the essence of Ethernet—the frame format and maximum frame size—has remained unscathed through it all.

To many observers, the artificial 1,500-byte cap on frame size is a major hindrance to high-performance networking, especially at Gigabit speeds.

If you are not aware of the frame size fracas, you're missing a good fight. Debating the benefits of large frame sizes for fast frame networks has garnered a lot of industry attention of late.

Frame size is an issue that not only pits Token Ring vendors against Ethernet vendors, but also Ethernet vendors against one another. Performance, efficiency, and backward compatibility are the main arguing points in the discussions to date.

I've already gone on record about the benefits of large frames with Token Ring. In early 1998, prominent Gigabit Ethernet vendors squared off on the subject. A point-counterpoint that appeared on the Network World Fusion Web site between Alteon Networks' Selina Lo and Packet Engines' Bernard Daines illustrates the divisive nature of the argument and that a plausible sounding argument can also be one that has no basis in fact.

Daines dismisses the performance benefits of jumbo frames, using a specious argument based on "header-to-data" efficiency. Comparing the header-to-data ratio of 1,538-byte frames to that of 9,038-byte frames, he calculates the efficiency of the former to be 97.5% compared with the latter's 99.6%.

He writes, "The difference in time required to send a 1547MB file is only 0.1 msec." To him, this is proof that performance benefits of large frames are close to nonexistent. Were his logic correct, his conclusion might be correct, but that is not the case. His premise is that, in both scenarios, the typical 1MB file is streaming across the net at wire speed, and therein lies the problem with his argument.

To assume wire speed as the starting point is to miss the point. It is the pursuit of wire-speed application throughput that causes us to consider large frame sizes. Just because frame generators can drive Gigabit Ethernet at wire speed doesn't mean real applications can (as I alluded to earlier). The entire purpose of expanding the frame size is to optimize applications so that they may come close to reaching wire speed.

Only with the reduced packet handling and the more efficient data pipe-lining made possible by jumbo frames can we approach this level of efficiency. The best way to view 1,500-byte versus 9,000-byte frames is to consider how many of each size frame it takes to fill a Gigabit Ethernet pipe. It takes more than 80,000 frames of the former but only about 14,000 frames of the latter. You can't get about the fact that this is a dramatic difference in workload and performance.

Consider also the ever shrinking ratio between the maximum frame size and the media speed. Taking Ethernet's speed up to the Fast Ethernet level without increasing the maximum frame size is equivalent to chopping the maximum size of a standard Ethernet frame to 150 bytes. Taking Ethernet to Gigabit speeds chops the relative maximum frame size to just 15 bytes. Thus, having a maximum frame size of 1,500 bytes in Gigabit Ethernet is equivalent to having a maximum frame size of 15 bytes in standard Ethernet. One can imagine how inefficient that would be and how taxing it would be on switches.

The capability of the original Ethernet architecture to remain effective at Gigabit and multi-Gigabit speeds is no red herring: It is the real issue. As of late 1998, the party line with many vendors seems to be that next generation, high-performance server adapters will offload much of the frame processing burden from the server CPU. This, they maintain, will eliminate the CPU processing burden. While it might very well reduce the CPU burden, it still does not eliminate the problem caused by the relatively puny 1,500-byte limitation.

The implications of making a major architectural change (like frame size) are significant, but vendors may eventually have to face the fact that original Ethernet may have evolved as far as it can possibly go.

Will Ethernet Fall into the ATM Trap?

As the evolution continues, one wonders whether Ethernet will fall into what I call "the ATM trap," where the focus is lost on pragmatic needs and the architectural complexity becomes overwhelming and, ultimately, counterproductive.

The area where this might happen is with quality of service (QoS). Although some vendors profess a "simple, but effective" prioritization scheme using the bits now defined by the IEEE 802.1p standard, others maintain that implementing that function alone buys very little.

These vendors talk of policy-based and directory-enabled networks but often respond to questions of detail with incredibly vague or esoteric answers. Whenever I hear answers that are too complex to make sense to knowledgeable network managers, I worry. ATM's immense complexity was supposed to deliver incredible benefits, benefits that most network managers decided they could do without.

History has shown us that simplicity usually wins over complexity. If some vendors are not careful, they may be setting themselves up for failure.

Evolution in Support of Revolution

Finally, it is ironic that the "most evolved" of all networking technologies will provide the communications base for self-proclaimed "revolutionary" systems that will appear in the not-too-distant future.

Distributed computing environments, such as Sun's JINI, IBM's T Space, and Lucent's Inferno, will undoubtedly communicate using Ethernet.

Environmental automation systems that today run over X-10 powerline connections or primitive serial connections will no doubt take advantage of business and even home-based Ethernet networks to communicate with system components.

Ethernet has unquestionably established itself as the unrivaled common transport for data networking and is probably the most profound change of the past 10 years. All of the other options for building connectivity—Token Ring, ATM LANE, FDDI, ARCnet, LocalTalk—are today considered also-rans. For now, Ethernet provides our data utility plug, the networking equivalent of the standard power outlet. In fact, one could say it is even more standard than power because the signaling and physical connection remain constant around the globe.

In closing, I'd like to thank the authors for inviting me to add a few closing thoughts to their expansive work. The views I express, of course, are my own.

—Kevin Tolly

Kevin Tolly is President and CEO of The Tolly Group, a strategic consulting, independent testing, and industry analysis organization. He is a leading industry consultant and is responsible for guiding the technology decisions of major vendor and end user organizations. Tolly writes regularly for *Business Communications Review, Network World, LAN Times, Communications Week,* and *Computerworld* on architectural and technology issues, and has been widely quoted in leading business publications such as *Business Week, Forbes, PC Week, Datamation,* and *VAR Business.*

Portions of Mr. Tolly's comments are © 1998, International Data Group.

PART V

Appendixes

APPENDIX A

Gigabit and Fast Ethernet Vendors

Vendor Name	Product Type	Phone Number[1]	WWW URL[1]
Accton Technology	NICs, Hubs, Switches	800-926-9288	www.accton.com
Adaptec[2]	NICs, Hubs	408-945-8600	www.adaptec.com
Advanced Micro Devices (AMD)	Silicon	408-732-2400	www.amd.com
Acacia Networks	Switches	888-4-ACACIA	www.acacianet.com
Alteon Networks	NICs, Switches	408-360-5500	www.alteon.com
Asante Technologies	NICs, Hubs	800-662-9686	www.asante.com
Ascend Communications[3]	WAN, Remote Access	510-769-6001	www.ascend.com
Bay Networks[4]	Hubs, Switches, WAN, Remote Access, Routers	800-822-9638	www.baynetworks.com
Broadcom	Silicon	310-443-4490	www.broadcom.com
Cabletron Systems[5]	Hubs, Switches, Routers, WAN Access	603-332-9400	www.cabletron.com
Cisco Systems[6]	Switches, Routers, WAN, WAN Access, Modeling and Management Software	800-818-9202	www.cisco.com
Compaq Computer Corp.[7]	NICs, Hubs, Switches	512-433-6756	www.compaq.com
D-Link Systems	NICs, Hubs, Switches	800-326-1688	www.dlink.com
Extreme Networks	Switches	408-342-0980	www.extremenetworks.com
Farallon Computing	NICs, Hubs	510-814-5000	www.farallon.com
Fluke Corporation	Test Equipment	206-347-6100	www.fluke.com
FORE Systems[8]	Switches	412-635-3300	www.foresystems.com www.berkeleynetworks.com
Fujitsu	Silicon	(81) 44-754-3234	www.fujitsu.com
G2 Networks	Silicon, NICs	408-399-3800	www.g2networks.com
Mitel Corporation[9]	Silicon	613-592-2122	www.mitel.com
Galileo Technology	Silicon	408-367-1400	www.galileot.com
GigaLabs, Inc.	Server networks	800-LAN8120	www.gigalabs.com
Hewlett Packard	Hubs, Switches, Test Equipment, Management Software	408-246-4300	www.hp.com

Vendor Name	Product Type	Phone Number[1]	WWW URL[1]
Intel Corporation[10]	Silicon, NICs, Hubs, Switches, Routers	800-538-3373	www.intel.com/network
IBM	NICs, Hubs, Switches, WAN Access	919-543-7698	www.ibm.com
Jato Technologies	Switches	512-342-0770	www.jago.com
LANart Corporation	Hubs, Switches	800-292-1994	www.lanart.com
LANOptics	Hubs	972-738-6900	www.lanoptics.com
LANQuest group	Network Testing	800-487-7779	www.lanquest.com
LSI Logic	Silicon	408-433-7387	www.lsilogic.com
Level One Communications	Silicon	916-854-2871	www.levelone.com
Lucent Technologies[11]	Switching, WAN Switching	888-584-6366	www.lucent.com
Madge[12]	Hubs, Switches	714-752-6638	www.madge.com
Micro Linear	Silicon	408-433-5200	www.microlinear.com
Microtest	Test Equipment	602-952-6400	www.microtest.com
MMC Networks	Silicon	408-653-1810	www.mmcnet.com
National Semiconductor	Silicon	800-272-9959	www.national.com
Nbase Communications	Switches	818-773-0900	www.nbase.com
NetCom Systems	Test Equipment	818-700-5100	www.netcomsystems.com
Network Associates[13]	Test Equipment, Network Management	415-473-2000	www.network-associates.com
Network Peripherals	Hubs, Switches	1-800-NPI-8855	www.npix.com
Newbridge Networks	Switches, WAN Switching	703-834-3600	www.newbridge.com
Nortel			www.nortel.com
Olicom	NICs	800-265-5266	www.olicom.com
Plaintree Systems	Switches	800-370-2724	www.plaintree.com
Packet Engines	Silicon, Switches	510-489-3162	www.packetengines.com
Psiber Data Systems	Test Equipment	619-670-7456	www.psiberdata.com
Quality Semiconductor	Silicon	408-450-8053	www.qualitysemi.com
SEEQ Technology	Silicon	510-226-7400	www.seeq.com
Scope Communications	Test Equipment	508-393-1236	www.scope.com
Sun Microsystems	NICs	800-821-4643	www.sun.com

Vendor Name	Product Type	Phone Number[1]	WWW URL[1]
Texas Instruments	Silicon	713-274-2000	www.ti.com
3Com Corp.[14]	Hubs, NICs, Switches, Routers, WAN Access	800-873-6381	www.3com.com
Triticom	Test and Analysis Software	612-937-0772	www.triticom.com
Xircom	Mobile NICs	800-438-4526	www.xircom.com
XLNT	Switches	800-956-8638	www.xlnt.com
XYLAN	Switches	818-880-3500	www.xylan.com
Yago Systems[15]	Switches	818-878-4714	www.yagosys.com

1 Phone numbers and URLs change often, so no guarantees are made to the accuracy of those found in this table.
2 Adaptec bought Cogent Technologies, a small, Washington-based networking company.
3 Ascend merged with Cascade Communications.
4 Nortel Communications acquired Bay Networks but will retain the Bay Networks name. Bay Networks was itself a merger of Wellfleet and SynOptics Communications.
5 Cabletron acquired NetVantage, a small switch startup, and part of SMCs switch product line.
6 Cisco Systems has made numerous acquisitions, among them Kalpana (Ethernet switching inventors), Crescendo Communications (FDDI/CDDI pioneers), Grand Junction Networks (Fast Ethernet founders), Granite Systems (early Gigabit Ethernet silicon company), and NetSys (management/modeling software).
7 Compaq bought NetWorth and Thomas Conrad a few years ago.
8 FOREe Systems, originally a devout ATM company, bought Alantec, an Ethernet switching company, and recently bought Berkeley Networks, another Ethernet switch vendor. Looks like reality is setting in.
9 Mitel bought GEC Plessey semiconductor (Fast and Gigabit Ethernet silicon).
10 Intel bought Case Technologies (a Danish switch and router company) and Dayna Communications (a Utah-based small business networking company).
11 Lucent bought Prominet, a Gigabit Ethernet switch startup.
12 Madge bought LANnet, an Israeli switch startup.
13 Network Associates is the merger of Network General (the "sniffer" company) and MacAffee Associates (known best for virus protection software).
14 3Com has also acquired a plethora of companies, the biggest of which was US Robotics in 1997.
15 Cabletron Systems very recently acquired Yago Systems.

APPENDIX B

Further Reading

3Com Corporation. White paper: *FastIP*. Santa Clara, California: 3Com Corporation. Available at www.3com.com.

3Com Corporation. 1994. White paper: *100Base-T Fast Ethernet, A High-Speed Technology for Accelerating 10BASE-T Networks*. Santa Clara, California: 3Com Corporation (September).

ATM under the gun. 1996. *Network World SA, 1-2* (August).

Alteon Networks. 1998. White paper: *Extended Frame Sizes for Next Generation Ethernets*. San Jose, California. Available at www.alteon.com.

———. 1998. White paper: *Next Generation Adapter Design and Optimization for Gigabit Ethernet*. San Jose, California. Available at www.alteon.com.

AMP, Inc. 1998. White paper: *Link and Channel Performance* (July). Available at www.scope.com.

Anixter Inc. 1996. *Structured Cabling. Typical TIA/EIA-568A Cabling System; Guide to TSB-67* (May). Available at www.anixter.com.

Bassett B., F. P. Henrich, D. Kuhl, and A. Shadman. 1990. Customer network management: A service provider's view. *IEEE Communications Magazine* (March) 31-34.

Bay Networks Press. 1995. *Bay Networks Guide to Understanding ATM* (345A-1104-BK, October). Santa Clara, California: Bay Networks Press.

Bay Networks. 1998. White paper: *Implementing the Routing Switch. How to Route at Switch Speeds and Switch Costs.* Santa Clara, California. Available at `www.baynetworks.com`.

Bell, J. 1990. How standard can network management be? *Telecommunications* (April): 33-37.

Ben-Artzi, A., A. Chandna, and U. Warrier. 1990. Network management of TCP/IP networks: Present and future. *IEEE Network Magazine* (July): 35-43.

Berkeley Networks. 1998. White paper: *The Integrated Network Services Switch: A New Architecture for Emerging Applications.*

Biagi, Susan. 1994. The myth of Category 5. *Stacks* (July): 18.

Black, Darryl P. 1998. *Managing Switched Local Area Networks. A Practical Guide.* Massachusetts: Addison Wesley Longman, Inc.

Boardman, B. and P. Morrissey. 1995. Probing the depths of RMON. *Network Computing* (February).

Boggs, David R., Jeffrey C. Mogul, and Christopher Kent. 1988. Measured capacity of an Ethernet: Myths and reality. *Digital WRL* (September). Palo Alto, California.

Branch, Richard, and National Semiconductor. 1995. ISO-Ethernet: Bridging the gap from WAN to LAN. *Network World, Data Communications* (July).

Bruno, Charles. 1996. Is Gigabit Ethernet for real? *Network World* (February 26).

Bruno, Charles. 1996. What's beyond Token Ring? *Network World* (June).

Buerger, Dave. 1996. And the winning Fast LAN of the future is Ethernet. *Network World* (May 13).

Buerger, Dave. 1997. Fiber is good for you. *Network World* (August 4).

Cabletron Systems. 1997. White paper: *IP Host Communication in Bridged, Routed and SecureFast Networks.*

Capacity planning: Product comparison: Tools reveal benefits and challenges of capacity planning to network managers. 1998. *LAN Times* (August 3).

Cisco Systems. 1996. White paper: *Extending Virtual LANs to the Server.* San Jose, California. (Also Portland, Oregon: Intel.) Available at `www.intel.com/network` or `www.cisco.com`.

Cisco Systems. 1997. White paper: *Fast EtherChannel.* San Jose, California. Available at `www.cisco.com`.

Clark, Elizabeth. 1998. Network cabling's new high-wire act. *Network Magazine* (March 17).

Clark, Elizabeth. 1998. Special report: Gigabit Ethernet: fast and faster. *Network Magazine* (September).

Costa, Janis Furtek. 1994. *Planning and Designing High-Speed Networks Using 100VG-AnyLAN*. New York: Hewlett-Packard Professional Books/Prentice Hall Professional Books.

Crane, Ron C. 1991. White paper: *The Case for High Speed CSMA/CD (Ethernet) Network Links to Desktop* (September 30).

Crane, Ron C. 1991. White paper: *Transmission System Issues for 100 Mb/s Ethernet (802.3)* (October 10).

Daly, Rob. 1997. Boost for a neglected standard. *PC Magazine Online* (November 10).

Davis, B. 1996. RMON market to continue exploding. *Communication Week* (April 8).

Derfler, Jr., Frank. 1991. *PC Magazine Guide to Connectivity*. Emeryville, California: Ziff-Davis Press.

Derfler, Jr., Frank. 1993. *Guide to Linking LANs*. Emeryville, California: Ziff-Davis Press.

Derfler, Jr., Frank, and Les Freed. 1993. *Get a Grip on Network Cabling*. Emeryville, California: Ziff-Davis Press.

Digital, Intel, Xerox (DIX). 1980. Blue book: *The Ethernet* (September 30).

Extreme Networks. 1998. White paper: *Network Design Guidelines*. Cupertino, California. Available at `www.extremenetworks.com`.

Farrow, R. 1993. Tutorial: Local protection for networked systems. *Unix World* (July): 64-72.

Fast Ethernet Alliance. 1994. White paper: *Introduction to 100BASE-T Fast Ethernet* (June).

Feldman, Robert. 1994. Proactive management tools. *LAN Times* (January).

Fogle, David. 1996. Lesson 90: Ethernet frame types. *Network Magazine Tutorial* (February).

Fore Systems. 1996. White paper: *LAN Emulation, Virtual LANs, and ATM Internetworks* (January).

Frymoyer, Edward M. and Hewlett-Packard. 1995. Fibre Channel fusion: Low latency, high speed. *Data Communications* (February).

Getting on the Fast Stack. 1998. *PC Magazine* (February 24).

Gigabit Ethernet Alliance. 1998. White paper: *Gigabit Ethernet 1000BASE-T*. Cupertino, California. Available at `www.gigabit-ethernet.org`.

Gigabit Ethernet Alliance. 1998. White paper: *Gigabit Ethernet: Accelerating the Standard for Speed*. Cupertino, California. Available at `www.gigabit-ethernet.org`.

Grand Junction Networks. 1994. White paper: *Fast Ethernet, An Evolutionary Alternative to High Speed Networking* (October).

Grand Junction Networks. 1994. White paper: *Switched Ethernet. An Evolutionary Alternative to High Speed Networking* (March).

Gunnerson, Gary. 1994. Switching hubs: Switching to the fast track. *PC Magazine* (October).

Hayes, James. 1994. *Fiber Optic Testing*. Boston: Fotec, Inc.

Hayes, S. 1993. Analyzing network performance management. *IEEE Communications Magazine* (May): 52-58.

Held, Gilbert. 1994. *Ethernet Networks, Design, Implementation, Operation, Management*. New York: Wiley.

Henderson, Tom. 1995. Protocol peacekeeping. *LAN Magazine* (May): 129-137.

Henderson, Tom. 1998. Gigabit Ethernet blueprint. *Network Magazine* (September).

Hewlett-Packard. 1994. Designing HP AdvanceStack Workgroup networks. Internal document P/N 5962-7968E (June).

Horwitt, Elizabeth. 1996. IP over ATM. *Network World* (July): 12-13.

IBM. 1998. White paper: *Migrating to High-Speed Token Ring*. (July 16) Armonk, New York. Available at `p8025.york.microvitec.co.uk/`.

IEEE 802 Tutorial Developments in Copper Cabling. 1998. Available at `grouper.ieee.org/groups/802/3/tutorial/july98/index.html`.

IEEE Draft Standard P802.1Q D11. 1998. Virtual Bridged Local Area Networks. (Standard expected to be complete by late 1998.)

IEEE Draft Standard P802.3ab D4. 1998. Physical Layer Parameters and Specifications for 1000 Mb/s Operation over 4 pair of Category 5 Balanced Copper Cabling, Type 1000BASE-T. (Standard expected to be complete by late 1998.)

IEEE Standard 802.3x. 1997. Specification for 802.3X Full Duplex Operation.

IEEE Standard 802.3z. 1998. Media Access Control (MAC) Parameters, Physical Layer, Repeater and Management Parameters for 1000 Mb/s operation.

IEEE Standard P802.1p. 1998. Supplement to Media Access Control (MAC) Bridges: Traffic Class Expediting and Dynamic Multicast Filtering. Incorporated in new edition of IEEE Std 802.1D-1998.

IEEE Standards Department. 1995. 802.3u Supplement to 1993 version of ANSI/IEEE Std. 802.3. Piscataway, New Jersey: IEEE publications (May).

IEEE Standards Department. 1995. Draft Supplement 802.3u/100BASE-T to 1993 version of ANSI/IEEE Standard 802.3. Version 4. Piscataway, New Jersey: IEEE publications (January).

IEEE Standards Department. 1995. Draft Supplement to 1993 Version of ANSI/IEEE Std 802.3. Document #P802.3u/D4-D5 (January 11).

IEEE Standards Department. 1996. 802.3v (100BASE-T2) Draft Supplement to 1993 version of ANSI/IEEE Std. 802.3. Piscataway, New Jersey: IEEE publications (March).

IEEE Standards Department. 1996. 802.3x (Full-Duplex/Flow Control) Draft Supplement to 1993 version of ANSI/IEEE Std. 802.3. Piscataway, New Jersey: IEEE publications (January).

Intel Corporation. 1998. White paper: *Layer 3 Switching and High Speed Routing.*

Introduction to Gigabit Ethernet. 1998. *The Gigabit Ethernet Conference* (July 1-2). Various industry speakers and presentations. London: IBC UK Conferences Ltd.

Janah, Monua. 1996. High-speed networks—ATM in for a LAN slide? Fibre Channel, IP Switching fight for space at the desktop. *Information Week* (April 15).

Jander, M. 1992. SNMP: Coming soon to a network near you. *Data Communications* (November): 66-76.

Jander, Mary. 1998. Trading up to switches. Life on the street isn't easy, especially when it means building a hierarchical switched network. *Data Communications Magazine* (March).

Klessig, Bob. 1995. The status of ATM data networking interoperability specifications. *3TECH* (July). 3Com Corporation.

Klessig, Bob. 1996. Advancements in ATM. *3TECH* (May) vol. 7, no. 2. 3Com Corporation.

Klessig, Bob. 1996. ATM LAN emulation. *3TECH* (May). 3Com Corporation.

Kosiur, Dave. 1996. Advancements in ATM. *PC Week* (April 22).

Kyas, Othmar and Thomas Heim. 1995. *Troubleshooting Local Area Networks*. Reading, Massachusetts: Addison-Wesley Longman, Inc.

Laepple, Alfred, and Heinz-Gerd Hegering. 1993. *Ethernet: Building a Communications Infrastructure*. Wokingham, England: Addison-Wesley.

Larson, A. K. 1996. RMON comes up to speed. *Data Communications* (April).

Lawton, Stephen. 1998. It's the next generation of copper. *LAN Times* (February 2).

Leary, Mark. 1998. *The New LAN Backbone: A Technology Report*. Framingham, Massachusetts: International Data Corporation.

Leinwand, Allan and Karen Fang Conroy. 1996. *Network Management: A Practical Perspective*, 2nd edition.

Lewis, L. and G. Dreo. 1993. Extending trouble ticket systems to fault diagnostics. *IEEE Network Magazine* (November): 44-51.

Lippis, Nick. 1997. Routing switch revelations. *Data Communications Magazine* (December).

Lipschutz, Robert P. 1997. Mastering the plans: Network design tools. *PC Magazine* (December 16).

MacAskill, Skip. 1994. Full Duplex Ethernet holds its own in test. *Network World* (May 2).

Mace, Scott. 1997. ATM's shrinking role. *Byte Magazine* (October): 58-70.

Makris, Joanna. 1997. Premises Wiring. *Data Communications* (August 21).

McConnell Consulting, Inc. 1995. White paper: *RMON Methodology: Towards Successful Deployment*.

McDysan, D. and Spohn. 1994. *ATM Theory and Application.* McGraw-Hill.

McQuillan, J. 1996. Strategic overview of ATM-Year 96 ATM. Technology Transfer Institute (May 6).

Medford, C. 1996. Life in the fast lane—new net management tools help Fast Ethernet live up to its promise. *VARBusiness* (April): 45.

Metcalfe, Bob. 1993. Computer/network interface design: Lessons from Arpanet and Ethernet. *IEEE Journal on Selected Area in Communications* (February) vol. 11, no. 2: 173-179.

Michael, Wendy H., William J. Cronin, Jr., and Karl F. Pieper. 1992. *FDDI, An Introduction.* Newton Massachusetts: Digital Press/Butterworth Heinemann.

Mick, C., The Mick Group, et.al. 1998. IEEE. 802.3ab Tutorial Presentation (June).

Mier, E. and D. C. Meir. 1995. A handful of SNMP managers battle it out at the low-end. *Communications Week* (February).

Molle, Mart L. 1994. A new binary logarithmic arbitration method for Ethernet. CSRI, University of Toronto (April).

Morse, Steven. 1994. As seen on TV: NetWare-based video servers. *Network Computing* (December).

Nemzow, Martin A. W. 1992. *LAN Performance Optimization.* Windcrest-McGraw-Hill.

Nemzow, Martin A. W. 1993. *The Ethernet Management Guide,* 2nd ed. McGraw-Hill.

Nemzow, Martin A. W. 1993. *FDDI Networking, Planning, Installation, & Management.* McGraw-Hill.

Nolle, Thomas. "The great QoS debate: IP vs. ATM is only the tip of the iceberg." *Network World* (October): 50.

Olicom. White paper: *High-Speed Token Ring.* Denmark. Available at www. olicom.com or p8025.york.microvitec.co.uk/.

Packet Engines. 1998. White paper: *Gigabit Ethernet Networking with Full-Duplex Repeater Technology.* Spokane, Washington. Available at www.packetengines.com.

Packet Engines. 1998. White paper: *A Gigabit Ethernet White Paper: A Walk through the Evaluation Parameters of Gigabit Ethernet and ATM Networks.* Spokane, Washington. Available at www. packetengines.com.

Paone, Joe. 1998. A broad future for backbones: Careful design supplemented by added bandwidth can be the key to expanding campus networks. (August 3).

Parnell, Tere. 1995. Comparison: Switching hubs. *LAN Times* (February 13).

Passmore, David and John Freeman. 1996. White paper: *The Virtual LAN Technology Report*. Decisys, Inc. Available at www.3com.com.

Passmore, David and John Freeman. 1998. White paper: *The Virtual LAN Technology Report*. 3Com Corp.

Pearce S. 1993. RMON standards for network monitoring. *Telecommunications* (August): 71-78.

Perlman, Radia. 1992. *Interconnections: Bridges and Routers*. Addison-Wesley Professional Computing Series (May). Reading, Massachusetts: Addison-Wesley.

Presti, Ken. 1996. Gigabit Ethernet to threaten ATM. CRN SA (August): 47.

Price, Ted. 1995. ATM = After The Millennium. *BYTE Magazine* (June).

Proceedings from The Gigabit Ethernet Conference. 1998. Various industry speakers and presentations. IBC UK Conferences Ltd. London, UK (July 1-2).

Raynovich, R. Scott. 1995. Is the time right for fiber? *LAN Times* (April 10): 27-30.

Roberts, Erica. 1998. Easing into IP routing. *Data Communications Magazine* (January).

Roese, John T. 1998. *Switched LANs: Implementation, Operation, Maintenance*. McGraw-Hill Series on Computer Communications. New York: McGraw-Hill.

Rose, M. T. 1993. Challenges in network management. *IEEE Network Magazine* (November): 16-19.

Rose, Marshall T. 1994. *The Simple Book: An Introduction to Internet Management*, 2nd ed. Prentice Hall.

Ross, Floyd and James Hamstra. 1993. Forging FDDI. *IEEE Journal on Selected Area in Communications* (February): vol. 11, no. 2: 181-190.

Saunders, Stephen. 1994. Bad vibrations beset Category 5 UTP users. *Data Communications* (June): 49-53.

Saunders, Stephen. 1995. A quick read on LAN problems. Hot Products column, *Data Communications* (January).

Saunders, Stephen. 1998. *Gigabit Ethernet Handbook.* Reading, Massachusetts: Addison-Wesley Longman, Inc.

Saunders, Stephen. 1998. *Gigabit Ethernet Handbook.* New York: McGraw Hill.

Schulzrinne, Henning. 1995. ATM: Dangerous at any speed? Position paper abstract in *Gigabit Networking '95.*

Scope Communications, Inc. 1997. White paper: *Gigabit Ethernet Over Category 5. Part I and II.* Scope Communications, Inc. (October). Available at www.scope.com.

Scope Communications, Inc. 1998. White paper: *Certifying Fiber Optic Cabling for Gigabit Ethernet.* Scope Communications, Inc. (May 14). Available at www.scope.com.

Seifert, Rich. 1991. Ethernet: Ten years after. *BYTE Magazine* (January): 315-319.

Seifert, Rich. 1998. *Gigabit Ethernet: Technology and Applications for High-Speed LANs.* Reading, Massachusetts: Addison-Wesley Longman, Inc.

Semeria, Chuck. 1998. White paper: *Next Generation Routing for Enterprise Networks.* 3Com Corporation.

Shimmin, Bradley F. 1994. Comparing three methods of Ethernet switching. *LAN Times* (January 10).

Shipley, Buddy and William F. Lyons. 1992. *Ethernet Pocket Reference Guide.* Silver Springs, Maryland: Shipley Consulting International.

Shoch, John F., Yogen K. Dalal, David D. Redell, and Ronald C. Crane. 1982. The Evolution of Ethernet. *Computer.*

Shok, Glen. 1998. Gigabit Ethernet at the core. *LAN Times* (July).

Stallings, W. 1993. *SNMP, SNMPv2, and CMIP-The Practical Guide to Network Management Standards.* Reading, Massachusetts: Addison-Wesley.

Stallings, W. 1993. SNMP-Based network management: Where is it headed? *Telecommunications, International Edition* (June): 87-92.

Sterling, Jr., Donald J., 1996. *Premises Cabling.* Albany, New York: Delmar Publishers.

Tansey, Thomas. 1994. Virtual LANs no longer a fantasy. *LAN Times* (March 28).

Tolly Group. 1998. Test Report #8283: *3Com Corp Corebuilder 3500 Layer 3 Switch and Fast EtherLink XL10/100 Adapter with Dynamic Access Software.* End-to-end traffic prioritization with 802.1p. Available at www.tolly.com.

Tolly, Kevin. 1994. 100VGNowhereLAN. *Data Communications* (November): 37-38.

Tolly, Kevin. 1995. RMON: A ray of hope for Token Ring managers. *Data Communications* (October).

Tolly, Kevin. 1998. Frames reaffirmed at ATM's expense. *Network Magazine, Technology Report* (September). Available at www.networkmagazine.com.

Tolly, Kevin and David Newman. 1993. High-End Routers. *Data Communications* (January).

Tolmie, Don, Los Alamos National Laboratory, and Don Flanagan. 1995. HIPPI Networking Forum. HIPPI: It's not just for supercomputers anymore. *Data Communications* (May).

Trulove, James. 1997. *LAN Wiring: an Illustrated Guide to Networking*. New York: McGraw-Hill.

Wilson, T. 1996. Just managing—advice to users: There is no such thing as free remote monitoring. *Communications Week* (March 25).

Witt, Jeffrey G. 1998. Street-smart switches. *PC Magazine* (June).

Wittman, A. and B. Boardman. 1995. Enterprise management is just around the corner. *Network Computing* (October).

Yasin, R. 1996. RMON2 products will be ready to roll out by end of summer. *Communications Week* (April 22).

Zimmerman, Christine. 1998. Gigabit analyzers: Digging into data or missing in action? *Data Communications Magazine* (September).

APPENDIX C

Useful Web Links

These Web sites may come in handy if you're doing some of your own research.

Vendor and Organization Web Sites by Chapter

Chapter	Source Type	Summary
1	Individual	Bob Metcalfe's personal Web page
1	Vendor	Alohanet
1	Standards Authority	IEEE Bookstore
2	Industry Alliance	The ATM Forum
2	Industry Alliance	High-Speed Token Ring Alliance
2	Vendor	Olicom
2	Vendor	Madge
2	Vendor	IBM
2	Standards Authority	IEEE 802.5 home page
2	Industry Alliance	Welcome to HNF! The High-Performance mance Networking Forum
2	Industry Alliance	Fibre Channel Association
2	Standards Authority	NCITS (National Committee for Information Technology Standards)
2	Standards Authority	American National Standards Institute
2	Links	100VG-AnyLAN links
2	Individual	100VG-AnyLAN links
2	Industry Alliance	ANSI X3T12 (FDDI) Home Page
2	Individual	Dave Hawley's isoEthernet Page

Description	Address
Bob Metcalfe, inventor of Ethernet, is now a columnist for Infoworld and a senior big-wig with IDG. His weekly columns are always fun to read.	`www.idg.net/metcalfe/`
Ever wonder what Norman Abramson, the inventor of Alohanet in Hawaii, is up to? We found him, and he's not surfing...	`www.alohanet.com/info/manage.html`
Norman Abramson and Bob Metcalfe's original Alohanet/Ethernet papers are reprinted in a book that Norman edited. Not available online.	`www.ieee.org/ieeestore/` `commbk.html#pc2873`
ATM Forum works on defining new standards.	`www.atmforum.com`
100Mbps Token Ring.	`www.hstra.com`
Olicom is one of the proponents of Token Ring and HSTR.	`www.olicom.com`
Madge is one of the proponents of HSTR. Very anti-Ethernet.	`www.madge.com`
IBM is the main proponent of Token Ring and HSTR.	`www.ibm.com`
IEEE 802.5 high-speed Token Ring activities.	`p8025.york.microvitec.co.uk`
Vendor alliance to promote HIPPI and Gigabyte System Network.	`www.esscom.com/hnf`
Vendor alliance to promote Fibre Channel.	`www.fibrechannel.com`
FDDI, HIPPI, and Fibre Channel are all ANSI X3 standards. (NCITS was previously known as X3.)	`www.x3.org`
ANSI is an overarching standards authority. Eventually all IEEE, X3, EIA/TIA standards become part of ANSI.	`www.ansi.org`
University of NH IOL Tutorial on 100VG.	`www.iol.unh.edu/training/vganylan/`
Richard.	`www.io.com/~richardr/vg/`
FDDI home page. (Love the warning message!)	`Sholeh.nswc.navy.mil/x3t12/`
A trip down memory lane: isoEthernet page. Collecting lots of dust.	`members.aol.com/dhawley/` `isoenet.html`

Chapter	Source Type	Summary
2	Industry Alliance	Welcome to the Frame Relay Forum!
2	Vendor	Publisher O'Reilly & Associates
2	Vendor	Ascend
3, 4, 5	Standards Authority	IEEE 802 General Information Page
3, 4, 5	Standards Authority	IEEE page
3, 4, 5	Standards Authority	IEEE page
3, 4, 5	Standards Authority	IEEE page
3, 4, 5	Vendor	Cisco RFC page
3, 4, 5	Standards Authority	IEEE Computer Society
3, 4, 5	Individual	Charles Spurgeon's Ethernet Web Site
3, 4, 5	Individual	Gigabit and 100Mbps Ethernet Technology
3, 4, 5, 8	Individual	Michael A. Patton's list of Ethernet codes
3, 4, 5, 8	Individual	Don Provan explains Ethernet frame types
3, 4, 5	Individual	Small Office and Home Office Networking DIY Site
5, 8, 9, 10	Vendor/Lab	University of New Hampshire InterOperability Laboratory
3, 4, 5, 8, 9, 10	Industry Alliance	Gigabit EthernetAlliance
5, 8, 9	Vendor/Lab	The Tolly Group Online
8	Independent Lab	National Software Test Lab

Description	Address
Frame relay is becoming an alternative to ATM as a high-speed WAN pipe, with many advanced features.	/www.frforum.com/
Publisher O'Reilly & Associates has a great online dictionary to many networking terms.	www.ora.com/reference/ dictionary/terms/ S/Standards.htm
Ascend has a lot of Frame Relay info.	www.ascend.com/
IEEE page with some useful stuff: approved standards, drafts for sale, ftp directories, tutorials. Some specific links are listed below.	grouper.ieee.org/ groups/802/index.html
IEEE Draft Standards and Standards are available for purchase only.	standards.ieee.org/ catalog/drafts.html
IEEE FTP directory.	ftp://stdsbbs.ieee.org/ pub/802_main/
IEEE 802 Tutorial on Developments in Copper Cabling.	grouper.ieee.org/ groups/802/3/tutorial/ july98/index.htm
Sometimes you get lucky and find free copies of the IEEE draft standards on the Web. Cisco's RFC page is one such place (don't tell anyone).	www.cisco.com/public/rfc/IEEE802/
Interesting stuff on computers in general.	www.computer.org/
Useful Ethernet reference stuff and troubleshooting links.	www.host.ots.utexas.edu/ethernet/
Information on Ethernet NICs and chips, for serious programmers only.	cesdis.gsfc.nasa.gov/linux/misc/
Ethernet type fields, vendor identifiers, and multicast addresses.	www.cavebear.com/ CaveBear/Ethernet/
Ethernet frame types explained.	ftp://netlab1.usu.edu/ pub/mirror/misc/ethernet.txt
Useful home networking site.	www.digitalmx.com/wires
UNH tests a lot of equipment for interoperability. Nice links to a variety of networking tutorials.	www.iol.unh.edu
Vendor alliance to promote Gigabit Ethernet.	www.gigabit-ethernet.org
Independent hardware testing and industry analysis page. Great 802.1p and L3 switch test reports.	www.tolly.com
NSTL does independent testing of network components.	www.nstl.com

Chapter	Source Type	Summary
8	Independent Lab	LANQuest
6, 12	Test Equipment Vendor	Scope Communications
6, 12	Test Equipment Vendor	Fluke
6, 12	Test Equipment Vendor	Microtest
6, 12	Test Equipment Vendor	FOTEC
6	Publication	Cabling Installation & Maintenance
6	Publication	Cabling Business Magazine
6	Standard	Telecommunications Industries Alliance
6	Standard	Electronic Industries Alliance
6	Standard	Global Engineering Documents
6	Cabling Vendor	AMP
6	Cabling Vendor	Anixter
6	Cabling Vendor	ITT-Cannon
6, 8	Cabling Vendor	Lucent
6	Cabling Vendor	NordX
6	Cabling Vendor	Siemon
6, 8, 9, 10	Tutorial	Cabletron
7, 11	Vendor	Triticom

Description	Address
LANQuest does independent testing of network components.	`www.lanquest.com`
Excellent page for EIA/TIA cable standards.	`www.scope.com`
Largest manufacturer of cabling and handheld network testers.	`www.scope.com`
Cable plant testing and certification.	`www.microtest.com`
Fiber-optic test equipment vendor. Web site/vendor with a slightly different perspective.	`www.fotec.com`
Cabling installation and maintenance.	`www.cable-install.com570`
The Telecommunications Copper and Fiber Optics Cabling Magazine for Voice, Data, and Image Processing.	`www.cablingbusiness.com`
Official Web page of the TIA; basic information only.	`www.tiaonline.org`
Official Web page of the EIA; basic information only.	`www.eia.org`
Official supplier of IEEE and TIA/EIA standards documents. They cost money. This shows you where to buy them.	`global.ihs.com`
Cabling, connector, EIA/TIA standards information.	`www.amp.com`
Cabling, connector, EIA/TIA standards information.	`www.anixter.com`
Cabling, connector, EIA/TIA standards information.	`www.ittnss.com`
Cabling, connector, EIA/TIA standards information. Lucent also bought Prominet, a Gigabit Ethernet startup.	`www.lucent.com`
Cabling, connector, EIA/TIA standards information.	`www.nordx.com`
Cabling, connector, EIA/TIA standards information.	`www.siemon.com`
Basic cabling, connector, tutorial.	`www.cabletron.com/ support/techtips/tk0398-9.html`
Triticom makes a range of software-based network analyzers. Nice demos available to preview.	`www.triticom.com`

Chapter	Source Type	Summary
7, 11	Vendor	Network Associates
7, 11	Vendor	Wandel & Goltermann
7, 11	Vendor	H-P
7, 11	Vendor	Novell
7, 8, 9, 10	Vendor	Cisco Systems
7, 8, 9, 10	Vendor	Bay Networks
8, 9, 10	Vendor	Intel
8, 9, 10	Vendor	3Com
8, 9, 10	Vendor	Extreme
4, 8	Vendor	Alteon
Epilogue	Industry Alliance	Home Phoneline Networking Alliance (HomePNA)

Description	Address
Network Associates is the manufacturer of the SNIFFER range of L2/3 network analyzers (previously Network General).	www.nai.com
WG makes network analyzers.	www.wg.com
H-P makes network analyzers.	www.hewlett-packard.com
Novell sells many network management tools, some of which include traffic and network analysis.	www.novell.com
Cisco sells hubs, switches, and, of course, routers. Cisco also sells various network management software packages, as well as the NetSys modeling software.	www.cisco.com
Bay makes Optivity, a very popular management tool.	www.baynetworks.com
Intel makes a range of software-based network analyzers. Nice demos available to preview.	www.intel.com/network
3Com makes almost everything. NICs, Hubs, Switches, Routers, WAN Access.	www.3com.com
Extreme is one of the most successful Gigabit Ethernet startups, specializing in L3 Switches.	www.extremenetworks.com
Alteon makes Gigabit Ethernet NICs and is one of the key advocates of Jumbo frames.	www.alteon.com
The HomePNA is promoting Ethernet over Category 1 networks in the home.	www.homepna.org/

Interesting Publications

Title	Description	Address
PC Week	NetWeek section is useful.	www.zdnet.com/pcweek/
PC Magazine	Sometimes good, in-depth reviews of networking hardware and software.	www.zdnet.com/pcmag/
Byte Magazine	Good coverage of general computing stuff.	www.byte.com/
Infoworld	Typically editorial and news-centric. Good for ATM-vs-Ethernet debates, for instance.	www.Infoworld.com/
Network World	Stays mostly to the industry high road, with the occasional product comparison.	www.networkworld.com/
Computerworld	PC focused, but has a smart section on networking.	www.computerworld.com/
Data Communications	Probably the best place to go for head-to-head product comparisons.	www.data.com/
Network Magazine	Dedicated to networking news.	www.NetworkMagazine.com/
LAN Times	Specializes in feature articles on the benefits of technology.	www.LANTimes.com/

Newsgroups

Description	Address
General Ethernet	comp.dcom.lans.ethernet
Cabling discussion	comp.dcom.cabling
Focused mostly on software	comp.dcom.lans.misc
Network management	comp.dcom.net
Network management	comp.dcom.net-management

Index

Symbols

3bit field, 184
3Com Corporation, 556
  EtherLink, 9
  market share, 27, 29
  Optivity Series StackProbe, 516
  routers, 200
  standards, 8-11
  Transcend Enterprise Monitor, 516
  Web site, 200, 438, 574
5m network requirements, 386
10/100Mbps switches
  autosensing stackable hubs,
    348-349, 450-451
  cables, 450
  collision diameter, 120, 125
  cost, 410, 412
  error checking, 464
  Ethernet MAC, 92
  future trends, 400-401
  network requirements, 386
  packet filtering, 464

  repeaters, 120, 124-125
  shared network, 463
  standalone repeaters, 344
  switches, 411, 452-453
    adding, 391-392
    hubs, 398
    management, 397
    relative risk, 385
  wire speed, 355
  workgroups, 392-398, 407
10BASE-F, 98-100, 216, 356
10BASE-T, 94-97, 100, 216, 389
  10Mbps switches, 452-453
  cost, 454-455
  frame analyzers, 514
  IEEE standards, 15-16
  LAN analyzers, 515
  mismatched connections, 539
  noise level, 539
25-bundle cabling, 262
100BASE-FX, 216, 389
  backbones, 448, 460-461
  physical layer, 105, 242-243

R

W

X-Z

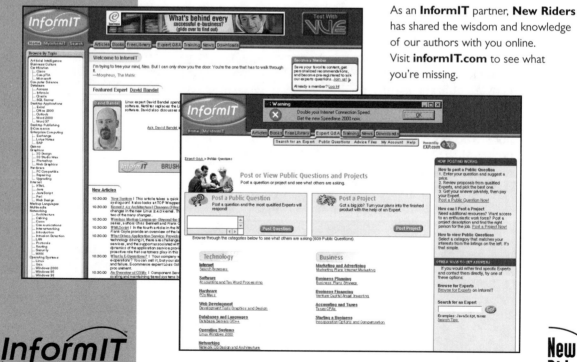